DEDICATION

To Charles C. Young, whose love, faith, and support gave life to this book.

DONA J. YOUNG

A teacher and facilitator for about thirty years, Dona has a passion for making learning exciting and relevant. For the past fifteen years, she has been facilitating writing programs at major corporations. Prior to that, Dona was the director of general education at Robert Morris College, Chicago and Springfield, Illinois. She was responsible for curriculum development, faculty training, and program management of general education studies.

Dona has been a speaker at conferences and conducted numerous training programs throughout the country. She holds a B.A. in Sociology (with minors in secondary education and business education) from Northern Illinois University, a Teacher Education Program certificate from the Chicago Institute for Psychoanalysis, and an M.A. in Curriculum and Instruction from The University of Chicago. Dona considers herself a lifelong learner, believing that who we become is a result of what we learn. Beyond that, her dog Reggie keeps her from taking work, or life, too seriously.

FOUN
BUSIN

Contributions by:

Monica Francois Marcel
Co-Founder, Language & Culture Worldwide

David L. Wondra
President, Wondra Group

McGraw-Hill Irwin

Boston   Burr Ridge, IL   Dubuque, IA   Madison, WI   New York   San Francisco   St. Louis
Bangkok   Bogotá   ~~Caracas   Kuala Lumpur~~   ~~Lond~~on   Madrid   Mexico City
Milan   Montreal   Sydney   Taipei   Toronto

FOUNDATIONS OF BUSINESS COMMUNICATION: AN INTEGRATIVE APPROACH

Published by McGraw-Hill/Irwin, a business unit of The McGraw-Hill Companies, Inc.,
1221 Avenue of the Americas, New York, NY, 10020. Copyright © 2006 by The
McGraw-Hill Companies, Inc. All rights reserved. No part of this publication may
be reproduced or distributed in any form or by any means, or stored in a database or retrieval
system, without the prior written consent of The McGraw-Hill Companies, Inc.,
including, but not limited to, in any network or other electronic storage or transmission,
or broadcast for distance learning.

Some ancillaries, including electronic and print components, may not be available to
customers outside the United States.

♻ This book is printed on acid-free paper.

1 2 3 4 5 6 7 8 9 0 QPD/QPD 0 9 8 7 6 5

ISBN   0-07-111682-6

www.mhhe.com

■ NOTE TO THE STUDENT

Welcome to the first edition of the *Foundations of Business Communication: An Integrative Approach*. This text will assist you in improving your communication skills regardless of your current skill level. Here are some major elements about the curriculum design of this text:

1. In the **Orientation and Assessment** section, you will measure your writing skills. The skill profile provides a realistic picture of your skills and your learning gaps.

2. **Chapter 1** reviews the writing process, surveying process tools to generate writing, such as mind maps and page maps. You may have learned some of these techniques in introductory writing classes such as composition. However, some of you have not learned writing as process, so a full survey of tools and techniques are there for you.

3. The text breaks writing into various skill sets entitled **Explore, Practice,** and **Apply.**

   a. **Explore activities** allow you to discover the relevance of new concepts.

   b. **Practice exercises** reinforce cohesive sets of principles through repetition.

   c. **Apply exercises** give you an opportunity to incorporate principles into your decision-making strategy as you produce quality writing.

4. **The Writer's Handbook** at the end of this text is both a learning tool and a useful reference section. **Parts 1 and 2** contain substantial materials to assist you with grammar and punctuation. **Parts 3 and 4** deal with formatting business messages and conducting research. **The Writer's Handbook** is designed as a step-by-step guide and tailored for you to use individually, as part of a team, or in whole-class instruction.

5. **At-a-Glance** sections of The Writer's Handbook are placed between chapters throughout the book so that you can have an abbreviated review of Handbook topics. For in-depth coverage of these topics, refer to the full **Writer's Handbook** chapters.

6. Margin features such as **Vocabulary Builders** and **Coaching Tips** will help you understand the differences between similar words (such as *affect* and *effect*) and offer you additional learning cues.

7. **Unit 1** of the text helps you learn how to *structure* your words effectively. You will learn to make editing decisions first at the sentence level and then at the paragraph level. After you have developed an editing strategy with sentences, you will learn to develop cohesive, coherent paragraphs. **Units 2** and **3** of the text relate to composing, editing, and revising business correspondence, reports, presentations, proposals, and research projects (including newsletters and Web sites), among other applications.

8. Some classes may begin with **Unit 2.** (If your class begins with Unit 2, you would still benefit from a quick survey of **Chapter 2: What is Good Business Writing?** and **Handbook At a Glance, Part 1: The Mechanics of Writing.**) You could then use **Unit 1** of the text as a reference, working through selected sections alone or with a partner.

9. Chapters include **End-of-Chapter** activities, one of which is a **process memo.** You can use a process memo to describe your writing strategy and how your skills change throughout the program. Process memos can also be attached to "re-dos" to describe corrections and changes (part of your goal is to become more conscious of the patterns of mistakes you make so that you can gain control of your writing). The process memo is an excellent learning tool. You may also find it a vital communication tool which enables you to personalize messages to your instructor.

One of the premises of this text is that you will feel more freedom to write by becoming competent with mechanics (grammar and punctuation) and then writing style (active voice, parallel structure, removing redundancy, and information flow). Then, after you are proficient with grammar, punctuation, and style, you will be ready to compose, edit, and revise effective business documents.

No one writes English perfectly, and no one speaks perfectly. Learn early on to use your mistakes as learning opportunities rather than moments of failure. In the first chapter, you may be asked to write about your past experiences with writing. Once you understand that writing is difficult for everyone at times, you may no longer feel isolated in your mistakes or fears about writing. So consider this: *the more you write, the stronger your skills will become.* Apply the principles you are learning, and your writing will become easier and more effective every day.

As noted above, you will have access to various types of resources and instructional assistance online, at the *Foundations of Business Communication: An Integrative Approach* Web site at www.mhhe.com/djyoung.

This textbook can be used in several ways. The next few pages will assist you and your instructor in designing a learning strategy tailored to your skill profile.

Thank you for giving this class your best and for using this text to its max. Set your goals high and chase your dreams passionately—you will achieve whatever you set your heart and mind toward achieving.

Dona Young

■ EXPLORE, PRACTICE, AND APPLY

Writing is a complex skill, and improving writing skills can be a complicated process. To simplify the process, this text breaks writing into smaller components, or skill sets. This approach teaches you to base your writing decisions on principles related to each skill set. You will start by exploring new ideas and practicing principles to learn them thoroughly; then you will gain experience by applying them in broader, more realistic contexts. To help you achieve proficiency, the text provides three types of exercises: **Explore, Practice,** and **Apply.**

- **Explore.** Exploration exercises engage your creativity so you discover more about new concepts and how to integrate them into your thinking and writing.

- **Practice.** Practice relates to repetition. With practice exercises, you achieve proficiency with specific skills or principles.

- **Apply.** Once you understand a principle, you apply it in new and broader contexts. Application exercises require you to make more complex decisions similar to what you will find on the job. With application exercises, you are often creating a product that can be evaluated.

Thus, exploration exercises introduce concepts, practice exercises develop skill in specific areas, and application exercises demonstrate what you have learned.

Throughout the text, you will be invited to supplement your learning by visiting the *Foundations of Business Communication: An Integrative Approach* Web site at www.mhhe.com/djyoung. At the *Foundations* Web site, you will explore new concepts, hone your skills, or be given direction to navigate the resources on the World Wide Web.

■ SKILL SETS

Writing is a decision-making process, and you will learn to make decisions from various skill sets as you solve writing problems. Here are the various skill sets and what you will learn:

- **Process:** How to push through writer's block using techniques to get your ideas on paper.

- **Planning:** How to develop your purpose, connect with your audience, and adjust your tone.

- **Mechanics:** How to use punctuation and grammar correctly.

- **Style:** How to write in a simple, clear, and concise manner.

- **Structure:** How to make sentences and paragraphs flow logically. How to connect with readers, get to the point, and identify next steps.

- **Critical Thinking:** How to analyze problems and solve them effectively.

- **Format:** How to structure e-mail, letters, memos, and various reports by developing a sense of visual layout for business documents.

■ DIAGNOSTIC APPROACH

This text includes pretests and learning inventories to help you identify your strengths and diagnose your learning gaps. With skill sets that can be measured objectively, you will assess your ability through pretests. With skill sets that cannot be measured objectively, you will inventory your understanding. As you make more effective writing decisions in each skill set, the overall quality of your writing will improve. (You can gauge your improvement through posttests at the end of each chapter, which provide a measuring stick for what you have learned.)

By the time you have worked through this text, you will understand what good writing is and how to produce it. Writing will no longer seem like a mysterious process, and you will make writing decisions confidently. You will also learn to analyze writing for its effectiveness. Thus, you will not only produce good writing but also successfully edit another's writing.

■ DESIGNING YOUR LEARNING STRATEGY

Here's how to design your learning strategy:

1. **Skill Profile.** Each pretest measures a different skill set relating to proofreading and editing.

   - **Skill Profile Part 1: Proofreading Skills**

     Pretest No. 1: Punctuation Skills (commas and semicolons)

     Pretest No. 2: Grammar Skills

     Pretest No. 3: Word Usage Skills

   - **Skill Profile Part 2: Editing Skills**

     Pretest No. 4: Editing Skills

     The Editing Inventory

2. Proofreading skills are the foundation for editing skills; hence, editing will make more sense after you have a solid foundation in proofreading. Take the time to become proficient with proofreading skills *before* you do serious work on your editing skills. (You will begin learning principles related to editing in **Chapter 2: What Is Good Business Writing?**)

3. When you have an accurate skill profile, set goals and develop a plan. You will find a place to record your objectives at the end of this section (page xii).

Pretest No. 1: Punctuation Skills

Insert commas and semicolons where needed in the following sentences.

1. If you are unable to attend the meeting find a replacement immediately.
2. Should Bob Jesse and Marlene discuss these issues with you?
3. As soon as we receive your application we will process your account.
4. Your new checks were shipped last month therefore, you should have received them.
5. Will you be attending the seminar in Dallas Texas later this year?
6. Fortunately my manager values my efforts and believes in my ability to do quality work.
7. Mr. Anderson when you have time please review this contract for me.
8. We received his portfolio on May 15 and we promptly developed a new strategy.
9. Ali brought her report to the meeting however it was not complete.
10. Ms. Suarez sent a letter to my supervisor the letter was very complimentary.
11. The merger however required that each corporation learn to trust the other.
12. Thank you Mrs. Dodd for supporting our quality assurance efforts.
13. I am not sure about the costs but I recommend we consider this proposal.
14. You must file your application by July 15 2003 to meet all requirements.

Pretest No. 2: Grammar Skills

Underline each error in the following sentences; write the correction in the space provided. If there is no error, just write OK.

1. The issue should remain between Jim and yourself.   1. _____
2. If you want the promotion, take their recommendations more serious.   2. _____
3. Your department did very good on last week's report.   3. _____
4. The funds in our department will be froze until next quarter.   4. _____
5. Thank you for inviting Charles and I to the discussion.   5. _____
6. The customer should of enclosed the check with the application. 6. _____
7. Her and her manager will achieve their goals by working together.   7. _____
8. They gave us the project at the most busiest time of the month. 8. _____
9. Mr. Brown asked you and I to design the workshop.   9. _____
10. My supervisor has spoke about that policy many times.   10. _____
11. Everyone in the marketing department felt badly about the problem.   11. _____
12. The new accounts should be divided between Bill and I.   12. _____
13. Seth is the person that made the referral.   13. _____
14. If you have more experience than myself, you should be the project director.   14. _____
15. If Tim was available, he would accept the challenge.   15. _____
16. The manager has not yet given the information to no one.   16. _____
17. When you need assistance, call Joe or myself.   17. _____
18. We would have been pleased if the pilot project had went better. 18. _____
19. Don't Ms. Becker need to approve the proposal before we accept it?   19. _____
20. Ed, along with his team, are going to the conference.   20. _____

Pretest No. 3: Word Usage Skills

Correct the following sentences for word usage.

1. The policy changes will effect every department in the company.
2. The total amount reflects your principle and interest.
3. He ensured his manager that the project would be completed by June.
4. The title of the report did not accurately reflect it's content.
5. Our assets may not be sufficient for the bank to loan us the capital we need.
6. The finance department has to many new policies to consider before the merger.
7. There interests are not being taken into consideration.
8. What references do you plan to site?
9. You can reach me this Wednesday some time in the afternoon.
10. We ensure the quality of all items we carry.

Pretest No. 4: Editing Skills

Edit and revise the following sentences for structure and style. (Sentences may be grammatically correct but still benefit from editing.)

1. Bob was the right person for the job because he is the most qualified.

_____

_____

2. There are many issues relating to current policies that our committee will resolve during the April meeting.

_____

_____

_____

3. The supervisor asks that every manager report their findings by the 15th of the month.

_____

_____

_____

4. If a student does not get a good education, they may not be successful in the business world.

_____

_____

_____

5. Improving writing skills promotes critical thinking, will enhance career opportunities, and develop confidence.

_____

_____

_____

6. Either the research will assist us in our decision making or it will not.

_____

_____

_____

7. Working right up to the deadline, Marie's presentation was finally completed.

_____

_____

_____

8. The contract was negotiated by the attorney and corporate representatives for hours.

_____

_____

_____

9. The applicant, although well prepared for the interview, failed to make her points clear.

_____

_____

_____

10. Concerned managers asked for changes in company policies, are appealing recent decisions, and will plan to schedule a meeting to discuss their recommendations.

_____

_____

_____

11. Management will take all applicants into consideration.

_____

_____

_____

12. Account managers purchased new software from a reliable source that cost only $2000.

   _____

   _____

13. It is Gerald's recommendation that the executive committee take into consideration the proposal.

   _____

   _____

14. Per our discussion, the corrected form is being sent to you by our customer service department.

   _____

   _____

15. We are discontinuing the contract due to the fact that your shipments are always late.

   _____

   _____

The Editing Inventory: A Self-Assessment

Based on the challenges you had on **Pretest No. 4: Editing Skills,** please rank your knowledge of the following editing topics. On a scale of 1 to 5, 1 means little or no competence and 5 means complete competence. Your self-assessment of these topics will help you develop learning objectives for Chapter 2. (If you don't know what the category means, rank it as a "1.")

1. Controlling Sentence Structure	1	2	3	4	5
2. Using the Active Voice	1	2	3	4	5
3. Using Real Subjects and Strong Verbs	1	2	3	4	5
4. Being Concise	1	2	3	4	5
5. Being Consistent with Point of View (pronouns)	1	2	3	4	5
6. Being Consistent with Verb Tense	1	2	3	4	5
7. Using Parallel Structure	1	2	3	4	5
8. Avoiding Misplaced Modifiers	1	2	3	4	5

The keys to the proofreading and editing pretests are located on the Web site.

■ TOTAL SKILL PROFILE

How did you score?

Part 1   **Posttest Scores**

Pretest No. 1: Punctuation Skills   _____ incorrect answers (20 possible)   _____

Pretest No. 2: Grammar Skills   _____ incorrect answers (20 possible)   _____

Pretest No. 3: Word Usage Skills   _____ incorrect answers (10 possible)   _____

Part 2

Pretest No. 4: Editing Skills   _____ corrected sentences (15 possible)

The Editing Inventory
(self-assessment)   _____ average from scale:

                                 1 = no competence; 5 = complete competence

Skill Profile for Pretest Nos. 1 and 2

How did you score? Each of the following pretests had 20 possible correct answers. Deduct 5 points for each error and then subtract your total from 100. How did you score? (Your score represents your percentage of accuracy.)

Punctuation Skills	_____ incorrect answers	_____ percentage correct
Grammar Skills	_____ incorrect answers	_____ percentage correct

Note:

For Pretest No. 1: Punctuation Skills: if you made 4 or more errors, work on **The Writer's Handbook, Part 1: The Mechanics of Writing.**

For Pretest No. 2: Grammar Skills: if you made 4 or more errors, work on **The Writer's Handbook, Part 2: Writing Essentials—Grammar for Writing.**

Your instructor will determine the learning strategy for your class. The following plans are recommended based on pretest performance:

Plan 1 *(Scores below 80 percent on Pretest Nos. 1 and 2)*

1. Chapter 1: Communication and the Writing Process
2. Handbook, P1: The Mechanics of Writing
3. Chapter 2: What Is Good Business Writing?
4. Handbook, P2: Writing Essentials—Grammar *for* Writing
5. Chapter 3: Developing and Revising Short Business Messages

Plan 2 *(Scores below 80 percent on Pretest No. 1 or Pretest No. 2)*

1. Chapter 1: Communication and the Writing Process
2. Handbook, P1 or 2: The Mechanics of Writing or Writing Essentials—Grammar *for* Writing
3. Chapter 2: What Is Good Business Writing?
4. Chapter 3: Developing and Revising Short Business Messages

Plan 3 *(Scores 80 percent or above on Pretest Nos. 1 and 2)*

1. Chapter 1: Communication and the Writing Process
2. Chapter 2: What Is Good Business Writing?
3. Chapter 3: Developing and Revising Short Business Messages

■ OBJECTIVES

Now that you have completed the assessment, you have a better understanding of your skill profile and what you need to do to improve your writing skills. Please take a few moments to write objectives. Your objectives should reflect what you would like to achieve from this text-book and your class.

1._____
2._____
3._____
4._____
5._____

ACKNOWLEDGMENTS

■ CONTRIBUTIONS

Linda Schreiber, whose vision and leadership inspired this project; James Riley, an insightful and relentless editor who guided me into becoming a writer; Tammy Higham, whose organizational skills helped keep us on track; Trisha Svehla, Managing the Mosaic, who shared her expertise on communication and diversity; Jane Curry and Diana Young, Curry-Young Associates, who contributed to persuasive writing; Dave Wondra, who helped me find my voice as well as my purpose; Monica Francois Marcel, who shared her knowledge on global communications with courage and grace; Gerry Nangle-Reece, who coached me out of stuckpoints; Dolores Lehr, who shared her expertise on PowerPoint and résumés; Scott Jones, a connoisseur of Web design; and Elizabeth Anderson and Philip E. Mikosz for creating integral support materials.

■ ACKNOWLEDGMENTS

Elaine C. Weytkow, a fellow business education teacher, as well as cousin and friend, who gave timely, insightful advice; Kathleen Sutterlin, whose passion spurred this project on from its inception; Denny Spisak, David Fosnaugh, and Jerry Hagan, who supported this project behind the scenes; Charles Yanulevich, whose integrity and strength were surpassed only by his love; Rose and Robert Lindsey, who pushed me to my best; Peggy Patlan, who provided research resources critical to the development of this text; and my associates at Bank One, LaSalle Bank, ABN Amro, the American Dental Association, and Blue Cross and Blue Shield Association who support writing instruction at the corporate level, where much of the original research was done.

■ SPECIAL PEOPLE WITH SPECIAL TALENT

An extraordinary appreciation goes to the folks who gave their best in shaping the design, layout, art, photos, and special features of this book: Christine Vaughan, Lead Project Manager; Keith McPherson, Director of Design; Artemio Ortiz, Designer; Betty Hadala, Media Project Manager; Damian Moshak, Media Producer; Pete Vanaria, Editorial Assistant; Sesha Bolisetty, Senior Production Supervisor; Jess Kosic, Senior Managing Editor; Jeremy Cheshareck, Senior Photo Research Coordinator; Anthony Crivaro, Illustrator; and Keari Bedford, Marketing Manager.

■ TEACHERS WHO MADE A DIFFERENCE

Fred E. Winger, whose passion for teaching and love for students remains unequalled; John Ginther and Ralph W. Tyler, great men who taught with humility; Doris and Floyd Crank, who made every student feel as if he or she mattered; Jack and Margie McCartan, who provided leadership that shaped my values for teaching and resources that led to my understanding; Janet Day, who set the right priorities for teaching; Lynn Schumacher, whose passion for job placement spilled over on everyone; Cynthia Reynolds, whose intense focus served as a model, and Janice Caudy and Vern Sims, two of the best English teachers I have ever known.

I would also like to thank the following instructors for reviewing the text:

Rosalyn R. Amaro, *Florida Community College at Jacksonville*

Andrea Parsons, *Aon Consulting/Cox College*

Rawda Awwad, *Pittsburgh Technical Institute*

Rebecca J. Timmons, *University of Arkansas at Fort Smith*

Yvonne Block, *College of Lake County*

Mary Bowers, *Northern Arizona University*

Don Cassiday, *North Park University*

Cathy Dees, *DeVry University*

Patrick Lee, *Hong Kong Polytechnic University*

David Swarts, *Clinton Community College*

Deborah Valentine, *Emory University*

Frederick J. DeCasperis, *Sienna College*

Diane Hartman, *Utah Valley State College*

Donna Mayes, *Blue Ridge Community College*

Vincent C. Trofi, *Providence College*

Duane Miller, *Utah Valley State College*

Graham N. Drake, *SUNY Geneseo*

Holly Littlefield, *University of Minnesota*

Larry R. Honl, *University of Wisconsin, Eau Claire*

Mrs. Jaunett S. Neighbors, *Central Virginia Community College*

Dana Loewy, *California State University, Fullerton*

Mary Jane Ryals, *Florida State University*

Raffaele DeVito, *Emporia State University*

Renee A. Rodriguez, *South Texas Vo-Tech*

Victoria M. Yann, *International Academy of Design and Technology, Pittsburgh*

FOUNDATIONS OF BUSINESS COMMUNICATION:

AN INTEGRATIVE APPROACH

emphasizes an approach that links creativity to skill development, leading to effective problem-solving skills. This text encourages students to explore concepts before they practice and apply their skills, a process that motivates them to become better business communicators.

OPENING MATERIAL

UNIT OPENERS

A *BusinessWeek* article with critical thinking questions bringing real-world communication samples and their impact in the business world.

CHAPTER-OPENING MATERIAL

Each chapter begins with a chapter outline, an introduction, chapter objectives, and a learning inventory to prepare students for the lessons.

MARGIN FEATURES

Coaching Tips, Communication Challenges, Vocabulary Builders, Internet Exercises, and **Learning and Working in Teams** are margin boxes in each chapter. **Coaching Tips** give additional advice on topics covered in the chapters—from recognizing verbs in Chapter Two to keeping your résumé updated in Chapter Nine. **Communication Challenges** offer additional information on practical uses of communication and ask students to answer questions or complete "challenges" based on that information. **The Vocabulary Builders** expand on terms used in the text and relate them to real-world use. **Internet Exercises** are provided to give students extra chapter-specific practice by leading them to the book's Web site. **Working and Learning in Teams** boxes provide information and advice on working in a team environment—something very real in the business world—and include team activities to reinforce that information.

THE WRITER'S HANDBOOK

Handbook chapters cover writing mechanics, recognizing the challenges many students have with basic content. The four handbook chapters appear at the end of the text; however, shorter versions, entitled "Handbook At a Glance," are integrated throughout the text.

HANDBOOKS AT A GLANCE

At-a-Glance sections allow for an abbreviated review of these topics for those students who require only a refresher. They contain pretests and posttests to help students determine their understanding of the material. If students need more help, they can go to the corresponding full handbook chapter.

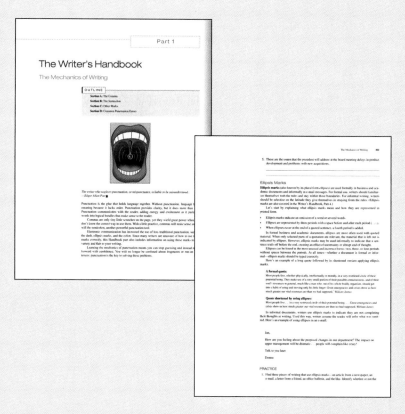

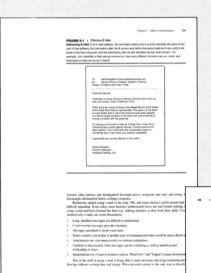

over the habit into a business environment. Consistently using fillers and tag-ons in the business world can affect the way more sophisticated speakers judge your talent.

✓ SECTION B: CONCEPT CHECK

1. Write a short paragraph that leads to a valid point but is filled with empty meta-discourse.
2. Revise the paragraph so that you get right to the point.
3. Identify common hedges, emphatics, fillers, and tag-ons.
4. Write a few sentences that contain unnecessary hedges, fillers, or tag-ons: you *might like just* work *kind of* hard on this one, but you will see results! Now, edit out the empty words so that each sentence states its point concisely.
5. Write a few sentences that include emphatics: *really, really try* to make your point! Now edit out the emphatics so that your message is clear.

■ SECTION C: REVISING

Revising deals with *substance* as well as *structure*. You are reshaping content on the basis of meaning, putting the most important information first. With paragraphs, you are moving the best-written and most comprehensive sentence to the topic-sentence position. On a larger scale, you are moving your most relevant information to the beginning, clearly stating your purpose up front.

Revising is a *re-visioning* process. According to writing instructor Cathy Dees, revising is "reseeing, rethinking, questioning, rewriting, and re-creating. Revising is recursive; it is a cycle."[3] Being a cyclical process, revising requires that you recycle your thinking; you must see your material with fresh eyes and an open mind and set new priorities to restructure the content.

Revising demands that you shed some of your original thinking; it also demands that you shed some well-constructed sentences and paragraphs that do not add value. Cutting is painful; you worked hard to sculpt ideas and shape paragraphs that you now discover do not add strength to your document.

Here are some factors in the revising process:

*   *Re-visioning:* Step back and evaluate your document and its purpose. Has your vision shifted? Does your thesis or purpose statement still capture the essence of your document? What are your main points? Can your reader readily identify your main

CONCEPT CHECKS

The **Concept Checks** at the end of each section provide a quick overview of the material just covered, to keep the learning process flowing.

SAMPLE DOCUMENTS

Throughout the text, sample letters, memos, and e-mails are provided with callouts to specific features to give examples of business documents.

EXPLORE, PRACTICE, APPLY

The **Explore, Practice, Apply** features are running themes that are mirrored in the text parts. The learning philosophy behind the text finds its origins in the pioneering philosophy of Alfred North Whitehead. The text applies Whitehead's rhythm of learning in a process that guides the reader through the stages of romance, precision, and generalization.

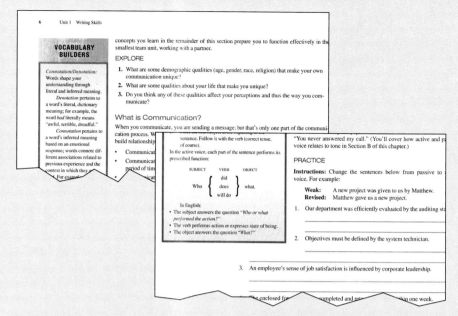

- **EXPLORE: Romance** ties fun and exploration to learning. Through freedom to discover, create, connect, and innovate, the learner finds relevance in the subject and becomes motivated.

- **PRACTICE: Precision** develops expertise through practice. Students internalize skills through repetition and feedback, leading to confidence, a sense of quality, and effective decisions.

- **APPLY: Generalization** applies skills and principles to problem solving. Critical and creative decision-making skills honed through practice are applied to solve real-world problems.

END-OF-CHAPTER ACTIVITIES

At the end of each chapter, the students will find several activities to reinforce the lesson, including a **Chapter Checklist**, a **Process Memo** serving as an important communication tool, an **All Pro Temps** activity (a running real-world application), a **Team Activity**, and a key to the **Learning Inventory** from the beginning of each chapter.

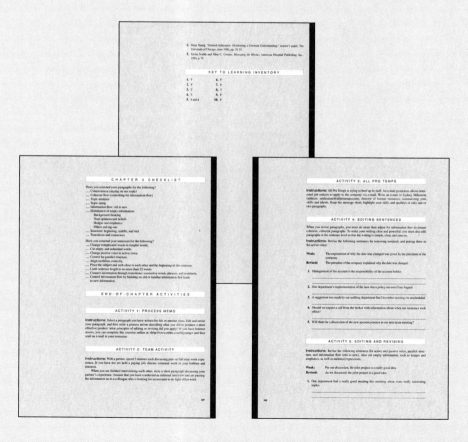

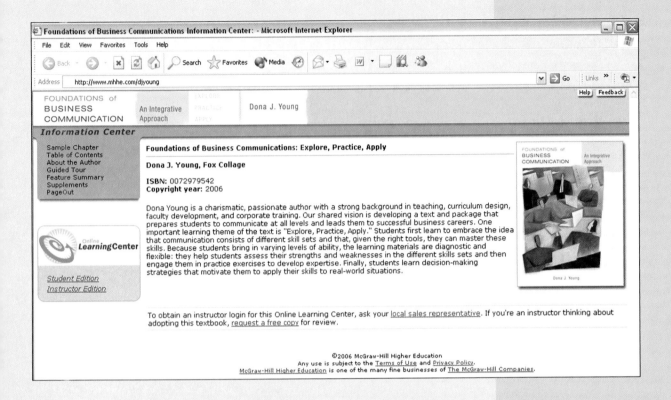

ONLINE LEARNING CENTER

Online Learning Center (OLC) is a Web site that follows the text chapter-by-chapter. OLC content is ancillary, supplementary, and relevant to the textbook. As students read the book, they can go online to take self-grading quizzes, review material, or work through interactive exercises. OLCs can be delivered multiple ways: professors and students can access them directly through the textbook Web site, through PageOut, or within a course management system (for example, WebCT, Blackboard, TopClass, or eCollege).

The Web site to accompany the text will also have templates of the Process Memos from the end-of-chapter material, as well as interactive chapter exercises, additional practice exercises, Internet-specific exercises, and additional study tools.

ANNOTATED INSTRUCTOR EDITION

The AIE offers instructional strategies that reinforce and enhance the core concepts presented in the student text. These include margin notes, an introduction to each chapter, and a special AIE feature on the Web site—a comprehensive variety of teaching support. Lecture Notes are also available on the Web site for the instructors.

IRCD

The IRCD is an electronic version of all the instructor material from the AIE. It will include materials such as PowerPoints, Lectures Notes, and additional instructor materials.

 # Primis Content Center

PRIMIS CUSTOM PUBLISHING OPTIONS

Through McGraw-Hill's custom publishing arm, Primis, instructors are able to customize the text in a number of ways. **McGraw-Hill/Primis Online**'s digital database offers you the flexibility to customize your course including material from the largest online collection of textbooks, readings, and cases. Visit the Web site for information (**www.mhhe.com/primis**).

MCGRAW-HILL'S KNOWLEDGE GATEWAY

The Complete Resource for Teaching Online Courses. McGraw-Hill/Irwin, in partnership with Eduprise, is proud to bring this unique service to instructors. This comprehensive Web site contains a wealth of information for any professor interested in teaching online. Level one is available to any instructor browsing our Web site. Level two is reserved for McGraw-Hill customers and contains access to free technical and instructional design assistance. For more details, visit **http://mhhe.eduprise.com/home.nsf**.

PAGEOUT

PageOut is McGraw-Hill's unique point-and-click course Web site tool, enabling you to create a full-featured, professional quality course Web site without knowing HTML coding. With PageOut, you can post your syllabus online, assign McGraw-Hill Online Learning Center or eBook content, add links to important off-site resources, and maintain student results in the online grade book. You can send class announcements, copy your course site to share with colleagues, and upload original files. PageOut is free for every McGraw-Hill/Irwin user and, if you're short on time, we even have a team ready to help you create your site!

POWERWEB

Harness the assets of the Web to keep your course current with PowerWeb! This online resource provides high-quality, peer-reviewed content including up-to-date articles from leading periodicals and journals, current news, weekly updates with assessment, interactive exercises, Web research guide, study tips, and much more! **http://www.dushkin.com/powerweb**.

BusinessWeek EDITION

Your students can subscribe to *BusinessWeek* for a specially priced rate of $8.25 in addition to the price of the text. Students will receive a passcode card shrink-wrapped with their new text. The card directs students to a Web site where they enter the code and then gain access to *BusinessWeek*'s registration page to enter address information and set up their print and online subscriptions. Passcode ISBN 0-07-251530-9.

Wall Street Journal EDITION

Your students can subscribe to *The Wall Street Journal* for a specially priced rate of $20 in addition to the price of the text. Students will receive a "How To Use the *WSJ*" handbook plus a passcode card shrink-wrapped with the text. The card directs students to a Web site where they enter the code and then gain access to the *WSJ* registration page to enter address information and set up their print and online subscriptions; they can also set up their subscription to *Dow Jones Interactive* online for the span of the 10-week period. Passcode ISBN 0-07-251950-9.

SUPPLEMENTS

CONTENTS

UNIT | TWO

PROFESSIONAL COMMUNICATION 115

Watch What You Put in That Office E-Mail 115

Writing Skills

BusinessWeek

Calm in a Cyclone: Profile of a Leader

The first woman to head the National Transportation Safety Board relies on her ability to stay focused and gather information.

Just eight weeks after two airplanes rammed into the World Trade Center towers, American Airlines flight 587 crashed in Queens, N.Y., and became the second-worst aviation disaster in U.S. history. The public, still traumatized by the events of September 11, was eager to know whether this was another terrorist act or a horrible accident.

The crash site, a neighborhood that is home to many New York police and firefighters, swarmed with recovery workers, political leaders, and shell-shocked residents. Into the chaos stepped a calm and reassuring presence—and I'm not talking about then–New York City Mayor Rudolph Giuliani. It was Marion Blakey, the first woman to head the National Transportation Safety Board (NTSB), the federal agency that investigates civil airplane crashes.

Moments after the crash, and throughout the next week, Blakey held frequent briefings on the progress of the investigation and reported as early as possible that there was no evidence of terrorism, putting many people's worst fears to rest. "There was a feeling of being in the vortex of a cyclone," recalls Blakey, 54.

I asked Blakey to explain what wisdom she has gained that might help others lead and maintain public confidence in times of turmoil. The key thing to remember, she says, is to avoid self-absorption. "You will need all of your attention and strength focused on the circumstances around you," she says. "Remember that this is not about you."

Once focused, it is essential to concentrate on the information others give you, as well as on your own observations. She has found that when she's truly tuned into others, "Many of the requests are more simple and straightforward than they first appear." Immediately after the crash, she was afraid family members would inundate her with as yet unanswerable questions about the cause. What they really wanted to know, however, were immediate concerns, such as when to expect recovery of their loved ones' remains.

Perhaps as a result of her communications background, Blakey sees the need to work hand-in-hand with the press. While many people want to explore circumstances thoroughly before deciding what to tell the media, "the public has a need to know, and you must stay ahead of their expectations and the story," says Blakey. To that end, she provides facts in a straightforward manner and acknowledges publicly what she knows and doesn't know.

In a crisis, leaders are often judged on how well they communicate. By that measure alone, Blakey already has proved herself an effective leader.

EXPLORE

1. Marion Blakey's advice for responding to a crisis situation is to "Remember that this is not about you." How can self-absorption weaken your response in any situation?

2. Think about all the ways you communicate with others around you. Do you approach written communications differently than oral communications? For example, do you go through a different process when turning in a paper than you do when giving a speech, even if it is intended for the same audience? Why?

Source: Toddi Gutner, April 1, 2002. For a complete transcript of the article and additional critical thinking questions, go to the *Foundations of Business Communication* Web site at <http://www.mhhe.com/djyoung>.

Communication and the Writing Process

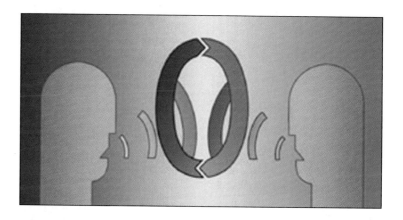

I know what I have given you. I do not know what you have received.—Antonio Porchia, writer (1886–1968) ■

Whether you are working toward an associate's or a master's degree, your communication skills will play a major role in determining your success in business. As an assistant, a manager, or even a corporate executive, you will use your skills every day to build effective business relationships. The business world demands good communication skills: this issue is not open for debate.

Communication is a broad topic that relates to developing relationships based on mutual benefit and built on trust and respect. Listening to client needs and adapting your service or product to them is integral to the process. Though this chapter only briefly introduces listening skills, they are reinforced throughout the text. Also briefly discussed here are global and team communications, with each of these topics being the theme for an entire chapter later in this text.

For now, your entrée into broad aspects of communication provides a context for building your career skills. The vast majority of jobs today require daily writing in the form of e-mail.

(At some companies, select meetings even include an online component.) Since writing skills take time and diligent effort to develop, the first unit of this book focuses on writing skills.

This chapter details composing: you learn prewriting and planning tools such as mind mapping, page mapping, concept webs, and forced writing. Then you examine purpose, tone, and audience. If you are unfamiliar with the *process* of writing, you may find that these composing tools liberate your writing. The remaining chapters in Unit 1 develop your editing and revising skills so that you can structure messages that are simple, clear, and concise.

Writing may or may not be one of your current strengths; you may even dread writing. Regardless of your past writing experiences, put aside any nagging feelings: *now is the time to turn writing into a career asset.*

This text guides you step-by-step as you achieve expert writing skills. You will explore new ideas, practice them until you reach a level of expertise, and then apply them to gain deeper levels of understanding. By the end of this class, you will be equipped to handle any business-writing task with confidence: you will not only improve your competence but also your opportunities. Here are two vital connections you will make by improving your writing:

1. *Your critical thinking skills will develop at a deeper level.* Writing enhances the ability to analyze and evaluate information. As you refine your writing, you will also improve your ability to plan, organize, and prioritize information for the reader (and yourself). You will use writing to reach insight into questions and solve problems. As you revise your writing, you also revise the way you define and solve a problem.

2. *You will build successful relationships with clients and business associates.* By connecting with others through writing, you will get more in tune with their needs and interests. Your writing becomes a tool for listening and responding to problems. You will become a more effective problem-solver.

You can take control of your writing and use it to build your communication skills. If you learn what you need now, you will be an asset to any organization—and your value will continue to increase as your skills grow.

OBJECTIVES

When you have completed Chapter 1, you will be able to:

- Understand how professional relationships build through the communication process.
- Shape a business document for purpose, audience, and tone.
- Demonstrate an effective writing strategy on familiar and unfamiliar topics.
- Describe the purpose and format of a process memo.
- Use prewriting techniques to overcome writer's block.
- Solve writing problems by applying mind mapping, page mapping, and focused writing.
- Apply the first steps of composing: prewriting and planning.
- Identify the parts of a memo.

Learning Inventory

Instructions: Before reviewing the content in this chapter, take a moment to read and answer the questions below. Evaluate each question on a scale of 1 to 5. When you have finished, turn to the end of this chapter (page 32) for the key to this inventory.

1 = Never   3 = Sometimes   5 = Always

1. Do you try to figure things out in your head before you put the words on the page?
2. Do you try to write your first draft so that it is good enough to turn in?
3. If your first draft isn't good, do you think there is something wrong with your skills?
4. Do you correct grammar, spelling, and word usage as you compose?
5. Do you lose your train of thought because you are correcting and revising as you are writing?

6. Do you avoid the task until the due date is in sight, and the adrenaline kicks in?

7. Are you critical of your writing and think everyone else writes better than you do?

8. Do you shut down and avoid the task completely?

9. Do you finish documents *without* connecting your purpose with your reader's needs?

10. Do you overlook controlling the tone of documents?

■ SECTION A: COMMUNICATION—AN OVERVIEW

This section gives a brief overview of the communication process. Writing is a critical piece of business communication, but people more frequently communicate through spoken (and unspoken) words, body language, and actions. In fact, nearly everything you do (or don't do) makes a statement.

In today's fast-paced, ever-changing business world, communication is a multidimensional skill. One moment you may be speaking with a peer who has a similar educational background and cultural experiences; the next moment you may be conveying information to someone from the other side of the world who just happens to be in the office next to yours.

Communication Variables and Diversity

What kinds of factors affect how you communicate? Right now, you may not feel unique; but in the world setting, you are unique—and so is everyone else. How you communicate relates to your individual profile: who you are (partly defined through demographics such as age, gender, race, religion) and what you have experienced (shaped through education, relationships, and life experiences). Thus, diversity is a major theme in developing communication skills, whether within a team or throughout a global setting.

For the sake of study, communication can be broken into some broad categories:

• *Intrapersonal* communication: making sense of your own experiences.

• *Interpersonal* communication: relating to other people on an individual basis.

• *Team* communication: understanding the dynamics of working in groups.

• *Global* communication: relating to people across cultural lines.

If you are in a meeting with people from all around the world, you have dynamics from each category going on at once. Everyone in the meeting will interpret words or actions in subtly different ways; you will be on guard to say the right thing at the right time. In contrast, when you are speaking with a person who has a background similar to yours, the dynamics are less complicated. You understand each other's slang and body language; at times, you can even convey meaning to each other without words.

Many issues in communication (or rather miscommunication) relate to diversity and people misunderstanding each other's meaning and intent. Here are some of the diverse qualities that influence perceptions and understanding:

• *Cultural differences* and *norms* affect global communications.

• *Gender differences* affect interpersonal and team communications.

• *Generational* or *age-related differences* affect interpersonal, team, and global communications.

• *Personality traits* reflect your intrapersonal style and affect interpersonal, team, and global communications.

• *Personal life experiences* filter your perceptions for all types of communication.

Some of these topics, such as team and global communications, have an entire chapter in this text devoted to them. Other topics, such as personality and gender differences, are developed more fully at our Web site.

Communication takes a lifetime to "master": the dynamics are complex. Before going into depth on any of these broad topics, you will explore concepts on a level that relates to your daily life with friends and family. By starting with concepts that you can apply immediately, you are developing the groundwork for understanding global and team communications. The

VOCABULARY BUILDERS

Connotation/Denotation:
Words shape your understanding through literal and inferred meaning.

Denotation pertains to a word's literal, dictionary meaning; for example, the word *bad* literally means "awful, terrible, dreadful."

Connotation pertains to a word's inferred meaning based on an emotional response; words connote different associations related to previous experience and the context in which they are used. For example, in some contexts, the word *bad* connotes "cool, good, current," as in, "That's a *bad* jacket you're wearing."

concepts you learn in the remainder of this section prepare you to function effectively in the smallest team unit, working with a partner.

EXPLORE

1. What are some demographic qualities (age, gender, race, religion) that make your own communication unique?

2. What are some qualities about your life that make you unique?

3. Do you think any of these qualities affect your perceptions and thus the way you communicate?

What is Communication?

When you communicate, you are sending a message; but that's only one part of the communication process. When you communicate, you are using your words and your listening skills to build relationships. Here are some key points about communication:

- Communication is about building relationships.

- Communication builds relationships through establishing trust, which develops over a period of time.

- Communication relates to the environment in which it occurs. The environment constantly changes; thus, communication changes or evolves over time.

Building relationships through communication also involves developing understanding. As you discuss an issue with one other person or an entire group, you are doing more than just expressing your view: you may also be constructing (or reconstructing) your perceptions as well as the perceptions of those with whom you are communicating. By affecting perceptions, communication helps people form their view of reality.

Sometimes, as you learn new information about an issue, your conclusions change. At other times, you may refuse to take in new (and valid) information, so your view remains unchanged. In other words, when you do not consider *valid* information that is *different* from your viewpoint, your mind is closed.

The process of communication is complex and involves more than words alone. Regardless of the information this text presents about communication, apply the suggestions and guidelines here in a flexible rather than an absolute, rigid way. Communication is an art (not a science), and guidelines are not equivalent to recipes or absolute formulas.

Thus, communication is a live process that changes based on the people and circumstances involved. Outcomes cannot always be planned or predicted, and it can take a lifetime to master the *art* of communication. With that said, let us examine the process and how to become more effective communicators.

The Communication Exchange

One way to explain communication is through the **telegraph model.** The telegraph model explains communication as consisting of a "sender" and a "receiver"—in other words, a **speaker** (sender) and a **listener** (receiver). This starts the discussion about communication by acknowledging that when two people are communicating, both are speakers *and* listeners. In order for communication to occur, they must hear and understand each other's point of view.

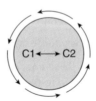

Understanding another's point of view does not necessarily mean that you agree with it. Many issues in communication relate to one person trying to change another person's point of view. Instead, think of communication as a process to clarify meaning. When people work toward understanding each other and their positions, communication flows more effectively. In addition, communication occurs in **cycles** until those involved reach an understanding and are ready to move on.

If you speak to someone and that person does not connect to your message through an appropriate response, you cannot assume that communication occurred. If you reflect on the role communication plays in your life, you may find that communication has the potential to bring incredible joy as well as immense frustration.

Communication and Relationships

A primary purpose of communication is to build relationships. This is especially true in professional situations. In your personal life, you may take relationships with family and friends for granted; that is, you have established patterns of relating. Some of those patterns are effective, others are not. You may not be aware of the extent to which your communication patterns affect your relationships; some relationships may even feel out of your control.

To be successful in the business world, you must remain aware of how your communication affects others and work toward constructing good, consistent relationships. You can make progress toward this end by using the following effectively:[1]

- Recognition
- Response
- Respect
- Responsibility

Practice the suggestions given in this section as you remember that communication is a *live* process that is *ever changing*. According to Vernon Howard, author of *Thinking on Paper,* short of telepathy, there is no way to ensure with 100 percent success that your message will be received as you intended.[2] Communication intertwines feelings, expectations, and behaviors of people who have diverse interests. Expect challenges in an ever-changing world that gives you many opportunities to show your best.

Recognition and Response   How do you feel when another person does not respond to what you are communicating? A normal reaction to not being recognized is to feel hurt or angry. Overlooking another's message can happen when people become so involved with their own lives that they become shortsighted. When communication breaks down at this basic level, other issues are going on that should alert those involved that there might be a problem.

Communication occurs in cycles, and an exact starting or ending point is difficult to identify because spoken words begin as thoughts. One way to ensure that you understand another's point of view is to make a validating comment that reflects what the other said. Here's a possible communication cycle between two coworkers:

DORIS: The monthly report is causing me problems.

TIM: So, you're having trouble with the monthly report. What's happening?

DORIS: Thanks for asking. The line managers are not sending me their numbers.

TIM: Not getting line numbers on time makes crunching final numbers impossible. Is there anything I can do to help?

Notice that Doris and Tim stay connected with the topic. In contrast, here's how a disconnected conversation might sound:

DORIS: The monthly report is causing me problems.

TIM: Yes, I'm having problems with my reports too.

DORIS: I just can't seem to get all the numbers I need.

TIM: We're not getting a lot of calls today—I think I'll go to lunch early.

To help ensure you stay connected with another communicator,

- First, recognize or acknowledge what the other person has said.
- Next, consider the message with an open mind.
- Finally, respond to the other person's communication.

Since communication occurs in cycles, this pattern continues until those involved feel a sense of completion. In other words, the intended message was heard, acknowledged, and responded to.

When someone leaves you a phone message or sends you an e-mail and you do not respond, expect that person to experience anything from irritation to hurt feelings. When someone asks you a question and you don't give an answer, realize that the person may feel incomplete about the communication. Responding to another's message is the most basic aspect of communication. When discussing *important* issues, you are more likely to remain clear about issues if you reflect (or validate) the speaker's points or feelings before you respond.

EXPLORE

Think of a time when you communicated to a person but received no response. How did it feel? What did you do next? Did you do something to try to get the person's attention or did you give up and walk away?

Respect   At work, you will communicate with a wide range of people, from the head of your organization to the intern in the accounting department. An important point to remember is that whenever you communicate, you are communicating to a human being who has feelings, interests, hopes, dreams, and a sense of honor. Start your career by realizing that *everyone* deserves respect, not just your peers and superiors.

Another important aspect of communication relates to realizing that other people are free to believe and act in whatever way they choose (within ethical and legal bounds, of course). In other words, you may or may not like another's behavior or point of view, but communication involves accepting others for who they are, not who you *want* them to be.

You are unique, and so is everyone else. You will be a more successful communicator if you respect differences. When one person tries to change another's point of view or dislikes someone for being different, it is an issue of control. Everyone falls into the control trap at one point or another. Remember, if you use your energy to try to control others, you are likely to frustrate yourself as much as you frustrate those around you.

Expect differences and keep your mind open. As human beings, we have far more in common with each other than we realize. Focus on similarities and use differences to gain deeper understanding of yourself and those with whom you interact.

Responsibility   Communication reaches a roadblock when mishaps occur but those involved do not take responsibility for their words or actions. By taking responsibility, you are pushing the communication process in a positive direction. By denying responsibility for the results of your words and actions, you are jeopardizing the communication process and your relationship with those involved.

Unfortunately, we live in a world in which we see established business, political, and even religious leaders commit crimes and then shirk responsibility. As a young person, you could see leaders commit transgressions and then interpret their lack of responsibility as permission for everyone to do the same. That is faulty logic. Although some people (even among the famous and powerful) do not take responsibility for their actions, one irresponsible action does not excuse another.

Everyone makes mistakes. When you take responsibility for the impact your words and actions have on others, you build relationships based on trust. Trust is precious, and its impact on your success cannot be underestimated. Once trust is lost, it is hard to regain.

Also realize that we live in a globally networked world; photos, videos, and the written word move around the world via the Internet without participants even knowing it. When it comes to taking responsibility, you will make life easier for yourself if you don't do anything you wouldn't mind seeing on your local 6 o'clock news. As a general rule for written communications, don't say anything about someone or write a message that you wouldn't say directly to that person's face.

Listening Skills

Listening is a major part of communication. Sometimes even as a person's words are coming out, the words are being judged and, at times, misconstrued. Many problems could be avoided if everyone listened with an open mind until there was understanding.

Listening is complicated partly because each of us perceives the world differently due to our "filters." A **filter** can be described as an expectation. Some filters come from culture, others from family and friends, and still others from a person's emotions and unique experiences. Other factors contributing to filters are age, gender, geography, economics, and personal interests.

Your filters function as screens through which you perceive others and the world around you. By becoming aware of your expectations and the way you filter information, you can become more receptive, objective, and accepting of others. (You will explore the concept of filters in more depth in Chapter 7, Global Communication and Technology.) Start now by identifying how your expectations affect how you think and feel about others; consider how your expectations affect how you listen and communicate. Explore how you can become more accepting of yourself and others so that you can listen with an open mind.

One approach to improving listening skills is to practice **active listening.** Active listening involves focusing on the meaning, intent, and feelings of the person who is speaking. Rather than let your mind drift toward your own interests or your response to the speaker, concentrate on understanding the speaker's message. At times, you can rephrase the main points to ensure that you are getting the real message.

The opposite of active listening is passive listening, or "verbal volleyball." One person makes a comment, and the other makes a comment, which does not directly connect in meaning. For example:

C1: I am upset about the new changes in policy.

C2: I'm not happy with the policy either.

C1: I don't know what feedback to give management so they reconsider the change.

C2: I'm glad you brought that up. I need to give one of my vendors feedback on a new product.

C1: The new policy makes me mad because it makes my reports too complicated.

C2: I'm going to call my vendor before I leave for the day. What is on your agenda?

Instead, active listening might resemble the following:

C1: I am upset about the new changes in policy.

C2: The changes upset me too. What is it about the new policy that bothers you?

C1: The new policy makes my monthly reports more complicated without adding value.

C2: In what way does it make your reports more complicated?

C1: Now marketing has to send me the same data that I already get from customer service.

C2: That sounds like a time waster. What can you do to streamline the process? Is there anything I can do to help you?

Notice how the statements and questions in the second conversation remained connected. There is a flow of ideas that develops toward a meaningful understanding between the two communicators.

Some listening techniques involve **mirroring** or paraphrasing what the speaker said to ensure the message was received clearly. For example:

C1: I'm upset about the grade I received on my last paper.

C2: You're feeling bad about your last paper—what about it makes you feel bad?

C1: I put a lot of work into it, but it still got a lousy grade.

C2: So you worked hard, but it didn't turn out the way you hoped.

C1: Yes. Even though I worked hard, I turned it in without finding some silly errors.

Mirroring can be an effective communication technique for understanding a situation more clearly or validating a person's experience. Oftentimes, receiving validation from a friend can lead to insight about how to solve a problem.

Effective listening does not necessarily mean that you agree with what someone is saying. Drop your expectations so that you can connect with others and deepen your understanding of them. Improve your listening skills, and you will improve your relationships.

The Smallest Team Unit: Working With a Partner

In the workplace, you work with partners often, and you will be asked to work in teams in exercises throughout this text. To remain efficient, here are some "ground rules" for working effectively in a small team:

1. *Share responsibility equally.* Spend equal time speaking and listening to each other. Make sure you allow enough time for both of you to express yourselves. (If an exercise consists of a numbered list of questions, take turns.)

2. *Coach each other effectively.* Support each other, but don't immediately give an answer or correction without giving adequate thinking time.

3. *Respect time frames.* Get right on task and stay on task the entire time. If you finish early, find more ways to relate your own experiences to the task at hand.

4. *Avoid bringing personal issues to a task.* Though your personal life may be filled with issues (good or bad), discuss them outside of class and not on task time.

5. *Start and end on time.* Keep momentum flowing; don't get stuck on one part only to leave other parts unfinished.

6. *Use honesty, directness, and objectivity.* Say what is on your mind but remain objective (not emotional).

By working effectively with one person, you are building a foundation for working effectively in larger groups. In fact, when you work on a larger team, make it your objective to communicate as you would with just one other person whom you respect.

Next, we'll examine the process of writing. Understanding the process of writing will help you push through all sorts of blocks on the way to developing better communication skills.

EXPLORE

With a partner, select a topic of mutual interest, and use active listening to discuss your topic for 3 minutes. Stay connected with the topic and mirror your partner's words or feelings. After the discussion, analyze the techniques you used and any insights you had about the communication process and listening.

 SECTION A: CONCEPT CHECK

1. What are some of the diverse qualities that influence perceptions and understanding in business communication?

2. What strategies can you employ to help ensure you stay connected with another communicator?

3. What is active listening?

■ SECTION B: THE WRITING PROCESS

Just as communication is a process, so is writing. If writing challenges you, it may be because you focus on the product—the outcome—rather than the process of writing. The writing process consists of three distinct phases or types of activities: composing, editing, and revising.

This chapter focuses on composing, giving you tools to get your words on the page. Chapter 2 develops editing principles, and Chapter 3 gives you strategies for revising. Your objective should be to separate and develop expertise in each phase (composing, editing, and revising) so that you gain control of your writing. Once you develop expert skills, you will no longer need to separate these activities as rigidly as you must learn to do now. By understanding the process and forcing yourself to compose and edit effectively, you will develop a strategy that produces good results consistently.[3]

Phases (*Not* Stages) of Writing

Writers often find themselves stuck because they "multitask": they work on different types of writing activities simultaneously. To make progress, consciously focus on only one phase of the writing process at a time: composing *or* editing *or* revising. You do not need to complete an entire paper before editing or revising, but try to complete one or two pages first. Here's how the various phases differ:

1. **Composing:** creating, inventing, discovering, and molding your topic.
    a. **Prewriting:** researching, reading, and discussing a topic to gain insight; taking notes and mapping; thinking reflectively about a topic.
    b. **Planning:** organizing and prioritizing key ideas; clarifying purpose and audience.
    c. **Drafting:** getting your ideas on the page in narrative form.
2. **Editing:** making stylistic changes so that writing is clear, concise, and reader-friendly; proofreading for correct grammar, punctuation, and word usage.
3. **Revising:** restructuring, rethinking, or reorganizing content so that your message is effective.

Keep in mind that these are not distinct "stages" that you need to do in a specific order. Thus, you will find yourself going back and forth from composing to editing or revising throughout the entire production of a document. (In fact, when people know their topic well, they can often start drafting without doing prewriting or planning activities.) The key is doing only one activity at a time.

Many people find writing difficult because they edit and revise *as* they compose. When you stop to correct grammar, punctuation, or spelling as you compose, your ideas may evaporate. If you start to revise before your ideas are mapped out, you may be wasting time and energy. After you learn specific editing skills, editing will become easier than composing. Allow yourself to make mistakes when you compose; force yourself to correct mechanics and reshape your ideas when you edit and revise. You will feel less stress, and your results will improve immediately and dramatically.

Before you learn to edit and revise, you must embrace the composing process. Composing entails ignoring expectations of the final product. To compose freely, you must *shut down your critic.* When you let critical voices shut you down, whether the criticism comes from yourself or another, you are facing **critic's block** (see Figure 1.1).

Critical Voices: Yours and Theirs

Your words will never string together perfectly; perfect writing does not exist. Start by recognizing the difference between your criticism of your writing (and yourself) and other people's criticism. Another person's criticism of your work *never* causes as much harm as your own. You can either dwell on what someone has said or learn from it and make a change; it's your choice.

Even important writers sometimes feel critical about their ability to write well. While in the midst of writing *Grapes of Wrath*, John Steinbeck wrote in his journal, *"I'm not a writer. I've been fooling myself and other people. I wish I were. My work is not good, I think—I'm desperately upset about it. Have no discipline any more. . . ."*[4]

Since *perfect* writing does not exist, do not worry about sounding perfect. Use each mistake as a doorway leading to growth. Turning criticism into feedback

---

COMMUNICATION CHALLENGES

Writer's Process When Dr. Maya Angelou got the call to write the poem for President Clinton's first inauguration in January 1993, she said the task scared her. One of the first things she did was check into a hotel and start writing. She kept all distractions away and wrote until she had drafted about 200 pages. That's when she focused on getting rid of the ideas that didn't work. Her editing and revising shaped into a final version entitled *On the Pulse of Morning*. The poem Dr. Angelou read was about 13 pages in length and captured the heart of our nation.[5]

Ask yourself: *How do I approach writing challenges? Do I need to sit in a certain chair, write at a certain time of the day, or have a room alone to myself? Are there certain conditions under which writing is easier for me?*

FIGURE 1.1 | Writing Blocks

Ask yourself: Which types of writing blocks do you have? What changes do you need to make to improve your progress in building writing skills?

Writing Blocks

Writer's Block: *If you avoid a writing task at all costs, you may lack confidence due to criticism you received in the past.* When you get a writing task, don't avoid it. Jump right into the task: read about your topic, discuss it (with a peer or an expert), or jot down the free flow of ideas that come to mind as you reflectively think about it. The only way to push through writer's block is to get your ideas on the page: the more you write, the more confident you will feel (and the better your skills will become).

Editor's Block, Type A: *When you edit as you compose, your ideas get jammed in your head and never reach the page.* Do not try to get a sentence exactly right as you put your words on the page; force yourself to shift into a composing mode. If you compose fast, furiously and fearlessly, your ideas will not evaporate before they reach the page. Then edit ruthlessly to achieve an effective product. The key is keeping the two processes—composing and editing—separate activities.

Editor's Block, Type B: *If you do not proofread or edit your work before it goes out, you may be unsure of your skills.* With practice, you will learn how to sculpt your words to achieve a nicely flowing product that is correct. The first step is having the discipline to read and reread your work, correcting what you can based on your current knowledge. Then build your skill by practicing principles that lead to good writing. Also, shift how you react to red marks on your papers: take the time to understand what feedback means so that you can stop repeating the same mistakes.

Critic's Block: *Every time you think of writing, you remember all your failures.* Stop imagining that everyone else is a better writer than you are: no one speaks or writes perfectly. Think of criticism as *feedback* that leads to growth. Turn off that strong, critical voice in your head which tells you that nothing you do is good enough. With practice, you will make progress. Keep your focus on feedback and progress, rather than feeling bad about not being perfect.

---

will make your writing stronger. Ask yourself: *What did I learn from this feedback, and how can I use it to improve? What changes can I make?*

EXPLORE

1. Have you received comments that at first seemed negative but which you then used positively? What did you learn? What changes did you make in your writing?

2. Are there comments that you still don't understand or that make you feel unsure about your writing?

3. Take a moment to analyze the strengths and weaknesses of your writing and set some goals for areas in which you would like to improve.

The First Steps of Composing

The first phase of the writing process consists of *prewriting* (to map your ideas) or *planning* (to define your purpose and adapt your message to your audience). Only after you know your topic well enough will you be successful with drafting.

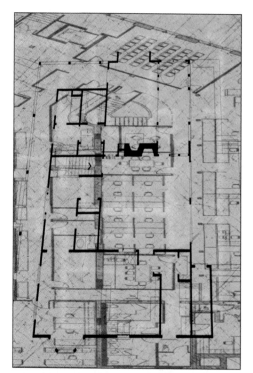

Develop a Blueprint: Much of what occurs in the business world is the result of careful planning. What can happen if a multilayered, complex project such as the construction of a building begins without adequate planning?

Prewriting activities assist in starting a paper, speech, or even an important conversation. Capturing your ideas on paper is important: with your thoughts sketched out, even in random order, you no longer face a blank page or empty screen. You are then free to probe the subject more deeply, which is critical with writing that involves research or with topics that need "to cook" before you are ready to write.

Prewriting helps you learn your content. You can then reshape your ideas for your audience and clarify your purpose. You may have devised prewriting techniques different from those presented in the following pages, and that is good. Do what works for you. There is no *one* right method: there are many right approaches.

Formal Outlines   At one time, a formal outline seemed to be the only option to start the writing process. Many people are intimidated by formal outlines because an outline is difficult to structure before becoming thoroughly familiar with the topic.

Today a formal outline is only one option among many, and it is used in a more flexible way. You can use the outline as a brainstorming tool (see Figure 1.2 below) before you start to write or as an organizing tool after you have a draft. (Most computer software programs offer a template for creating a formal outline.)

Start with your **central idea** (or thesis statement). Write a skeleton outline and then fill in your ideas. Be flexible with your outline until it is time to turn it in, at which time make sure it meets the standards of a formal outline. In terms of structure, each part of the outline should contain at least two or more points: that means for every "I," you should also have at least a "II"; for every "A," you should also have at least a "B"; and so on (see Figure 1.2).

Scratch Outlines   Rather than using a formal structure, roughly sketch your ideas on paper before you begin to write. Many people do this informally, thinking they are doing something wrong because they are not developing a formal outline. In

FIGURE 1.2 | Skeleton Outline

Building a skeleton outline around a central idea can be a first step in creating a formal outline.

Developing a Marketing Plan

I. Introductory paragraph

II. Body

    A. The Benefits of Product X

        1. Detailing the Need for the Service or Product

            a. Analyzing the Market

            b. Comparing the Competition

        2. Advertising Versus Marketing

            a. Developing a Brand

            b. Creating a Logo

    B. Development of Sales Materials

    C. Division of the Market into Territories

III. Concluding Paragraph or Section

    A. Summary of Main Points

    B. Recommendations

fact, if your topic is unfamiliar, scratch outlines can be superior to formal outlines; they are more flexible and more adaptable to change. (You can also think of a "scratch" outline as a "draft" outline: planning is a process. Your ideas will evolve as you learn more about your topic.) Let go of rigid structures so that your ideas can take shape as you gain insight.

Brainstorming Sessions

Brainstorming is an opportunity for writers to share thoughts and generate ideas without fear of criticism. Discuss your topic with a colleague and record the ideas that flow from your discussion. Do not judge or discard any idea presented during brainstorming—sort your ideas after the session is over.

Remember, you do not need to isolate yourself when you write; collaborating with your peers is good for team building. In the workplace, seeking input enhances cooperation and subdues competition.

Note Taking

Keep track of your ideas in a pocket-sized notebook; write your insights as they come to you, wherever you are—in a class or meeting, at the grocery store, on a walk with your dog. If you do not record your ideas as they come to you, you may lose important insights. Writing things down helps you to remember, even if you never read your notes.

Tools for Organizing and Prioritizing

Along with the traditional outlining methods described above, the following techniques do more than get your ideas on the page; they also help you organize and prioritize your ideas.

Mind Maps

Originally known as *clustering,* mind mapping is a freeform way to get your ideas on the page (see Figure 1.3). First, write your topic in the middle of a page and draw a circle around it. Next, cluster related ideas around it, branching off into any direction your ideas take you. Stay focused on your mind map for about 3 minutes.

Exploring ideas without traditional boundaries provides freedom and creative energy. A mind map also shows relationships that help you organize and prioritize your information; you get a bigger picture much faster. (Mind mapping can also be used before you make an important phone call or as a time management technique; start your day by mapping the various activities you need to accomplish.) Using Figure 1.3 as a sample, take 3 minutes to do your own mind map.

Information Wheels

This tool is similar to the mind map. Instead of drawing circles, however, use spokes for the information wheel (see Figure 1.4).

FIGURE 1.3 | Mind Map

Mind mapping as an organizational technique offers exploration without traditional boundaries. Creating a mind map will help you to better define your dream job.

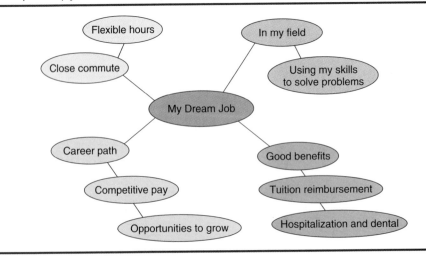

FIGURE 1.4 | Information Wheel

An information wheel is an alternative method of generating ideas.

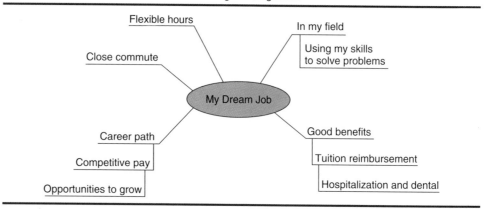

Page Maps Page mapping is different from mind mapping. With page mapping, you are already familiar enough with your topic to have an idea of the major sections your piece will contain. Turn each major point into a side heading (see Figure 1.5).

The page map may help keep you from being stuck because you already have a skeleton of your ideas mapped on the page. Taken from the outline on page 13, the side headings in Figure 1.5 are the skeleton of a page map.

Using a page map, you would start your paper with side headings to guide you. (If you preferred, you could put each heading on a separate page.) Start writing by filling in details that you already know about each subtopic. Complete the information that you know; do research and collect notes under the various headings; add and delete headings as your project evolves. Page maps are powerful tools that reinforce writing as a building process—you never feel as if you are starting from scratch!

Concept Webs With a mind map, you are starting with a topic that does not yet have clear parts. When you work with a project that has clear parts (such as a monthly report) start with a concept web and then fill in the information for each part (see Figure 1.6).

FIGURE 1.5 | Page Map: The Benefits of Product X

When page mapping, you can use the information from your skeleton outline as a starting point. Begin by filling in the details that you know about each subtopic.

Introduction (define the product)

Part 1: Analyzing the need

Market

Competition

Part 2: Marketing plan

Developing a brand

Creating a logo

Sales materials

Part 3: Distributing the product

Conclusion

FIGURE 1.6 | Concept Web

This concept web relates to parts of a monthly product development report. Are you responsible for any reports or papers that have consistent parts, for example, a monthly inventory report or minutes from a meeting?

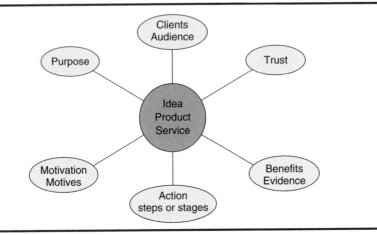

EXPLORE

1. Spend 3 minutes doing a mind map, information wheel, or page map to develop responses to the following:

   a. What are you looking for in your first job? What skills and ways of thinking do you have that will make you successful on the job? What kind of job will you seek in business? What are your career goals?

   b. Which composing tools (such as mind map, page map, or information wheel) did you use to get your ideas on the page? What insights did you have?

2. Review the Working and Learning in Teams sidebar on page 14. When you think of working on a team in the workplace, what perceptions come to mind? What strengths, weaknesses, abilities, or perspectives would you contribute to a team project?

Composing Tools: Freewriting, Focused Writing, and Forced Writing

Prewriting techniques such as mind mapping or page mapping can help jump-start any writing task. They energize the process and help you avoid the habit of procrastinating. These activities start you on the right track, but keep in mind a most important principle related to writing: *Do not edit as you compose.*

Composing allows you to write for yourself first so that you reach clarity in your thinking; you are *discovering* your topic. Later, you will revise your message to adapt it to your reader's needs.

The following sections describe three tools to encourage you to compose freely: freewriting, focused writing, and forced writing.

Freewriting   Freewriting involves putting whatever is on your mind on paper in a free form. You are free-associating, not screening your thoughts. Bounce around from one idea to another if that is what is going on in your head. If you do not know what to write about, say that on paper: "I don't know what I'm writing about." When you let go of your anxiety, ideas will start to jump onto the page.

Freewriting is similar to some types of journal writing. Write to release your feelings and to gain insight into unresolved issues. You do not need to go back and make sense of what you wrote; put your finished product through a paper shredder if you wish. There is an ancient saying, "If you hold it in, it will destroy you; if you let it out, it will free you." The value of freewriting comes from doing it; you need achieve no other goal.

On the job, there will be times when you receive a phone call or e-mail message that provokes your emotions. When that happens, freewriting can get you in touch with a professional response so that you do not need to answer on the basis of emotions. Within a short time, possibly as little as a minute or two, you will put the incident in perspective and regain your professional approach to solving problems.

EXPLORE

1. Spend 8 to 10 minutes freewriting. Allow your mind to jump from topic to topic, and do not worry about grammar, punctuation, or the "right word." Write whatever comes to mind and keep your pen moving the entire time.
2. Did you enjoy freewriting, or did it feel frustrating?

Focused Writing   **Focused writing** is more structured than freewriting: it involves only one topic, so do not jump from idea to idea. Choose your topic *before* you begin writing and focus only on that topic. Set a limit for yourself—for example, two to three pages or 10 to 20 minutes—and let the ideas flow. If you work much longer than 20 minutes or three pages, you may begin to avoid this activity. Keep it short and simple; do not set expectations. You are not trying to produce something you will use; you are simply getting your ideas on the page without losing your train of thought.

Focused writing is the perfect way to use 20 minutes attacking a writing assignment you want to avoid. Focused writing sets limits so that your writing anxiety will *not* go on forever: only 20 minutes or three pages. After that, you can walk away from the project, take a deep breath, and return again for a short period when ready. This activity helps you start a writing assignment sooner so that you do not wait until the last minute. The sooner you start to work, the further away the deadline will seem.

You may find that after you have gotten some ideas on the page, the assignment does not seem so intimidating. Your creative thinking skills will take over, and you will begin to solve the problems the assignment presents. A quote attributed to Leonardo da Vinci tells us that "inaction weakens the vigors of the mind . . . action strengthens the essence of creation." Get into action and you may be surprised how much progress you make.

EXPLORE

1. Select a familiar topic (one you would enjoy writing about).
2. Spend 8 to 10 minutes doing a focused writing. Stay on the topic and keep your pen moving; do not worry about grammar, punctuation, or the "right word."
3. Did you enjoy focused writing? How did it differ from freewriting?

Forced Writing   With **forced writing,** you are producing something you plan to use. You are staying focused on one topic and developing a usable draft. Write for a short time (about 10 or 20 minutes). After you finish writing, spend a few minutes correcting (editing) your draft. Thus, you begin with a topic, a time limit, and expectations. Set the clock, start writing, and see what you can achieve.

Forced writing is a great activity when you are up against a deadline or practicing to take an exam. Break the project into smaller tasks and then do a forced writing for each part. This short, intense process helps you gain value out of the 10 minutes before a class starts or at the end of the day. Forced writing takes discipline. The activity is short, but you will see results.

EXPLORE

1. Select a topic that you have to write about (or one on communication or listening).
2. Do a 3-minute mind map or information wheel.
3. Spend 8 to 10 minutes doing a forced writing. Stay on the topic and keep your pen moving. Use your mind map or information wheel to propel your writing if you are stuck.
4. When you are finished writing, read your paper and make corrections.

INTERNET EXERCISE 1.1

Rules of Conduct Throughout this textbook, you will be asked to log on to the *Foundations of Business Communication* Web site at <http://www.mhhe.com/djyoung> for added coverage of topics, additional exercises and activities, and other supplementary material. As a first step in using this text's online resources, you'll need to familiarize yourself with the rules of Internet use at your school, business, library, or home.

Once you have accessed this text's home page, select "Student Side" and then click on the Chapter 1 link to find instructions for getting started.

SECTION B: CONCEPT CHECK

1. What techniques did you learn or review to assist you with writing?
2. How do composing, editing, and revising differ?
3. What happens when a writer tries to edit and compose simultaneously? What is the solution?

■ **SECTION C: PURPOSE AND AUDIENCE**

Most of your writing will lead to answers. Answers are good, but you must be clear about the questions you are answering so you can prioritize information, screen for ideas that don't fit, and find gaps in your thinking.

The best way to do this is to clarify your purpose and analyze your audience. The best time to clarify purpose and audience varies because your thinking is evolving. However, your writing task won't be complete until you have examined both purpose and audience.

Purpose

Gertrude Stein, an early-twentieth-century writer, once said, "What is the question? If there is no question, then there is no answer."[6] Writing is a problem-solving activity: it is about questions *and* answers. On some level, all writing involves solving a problem, even though the problem may not always be obvious.

To understand purpose, we will first examine various types of writing. By understanding the context of your problem, you will solve the problem more effectively. The first concept to examine is the difference between academic writing and business writing.

Academic Versus Business Writing

You are probably more familiar with **academic writing** than business writing. Basic academic writing includes essays on various topics and creative writing in the form of short stories or poetry. Advanced academic writing includes research papers, summaries, and arguments in which you are dealing with facts in an objective way. With most academic writing, writers follow a standard format: start with a thesis statement or central idea, and then develop the introduction, body, and conclusion. Some academic writing involves inventing a story line, embellishing ideas to make points stand out, or using emotion to draw in the reader. These characteristics almost never occur in business writing.

Here's how **business writing** differs from academic writing:

1. **Context** defines the purpose of most business writing. Understanding the purpose involves analyzing the situation and then determining how to address it.
2. Business writing is direct and to the point; the writer stays within boundaries and conveys the message in a concise way. (In Albert Einstein's words, "Everything should be made as simple as possible, but not simpler.")
3. Most business writing has the underlying purpose of establishing or enhancing good relationships (regardless of whether the audience is internal to the organization or external).
4. When you structure information in a business document, the key components are to *connect* with the reader, *relate* the main points, and then *clarify* action the recipient and writer may take. These key components should occur whether the document is a business letter, a memo, or an e-mail.

Basic Business Documents

Let's review three basic types of business documents you will be expected to produce on a daily or weekly basis:

VOCABULARY BUILDERS

Intranet/Internet What's the difference between an intranet and the Internet? Let's start by taking the words apart.

- *Intra* is a prefix meaning "within" or "inside of."
- *Inter* is a prefix meaning "between" or "among."

An *intranet* is a computer network that functions *within* an organization or corporation. Only members can access information or communicate with each other on an intranet. The *Internet,* on the other hand, is open to everyone. The Internet is also referred to as the "World Wide Web," hence, the prefix *www* for Web addresses.

Many companies have their own intranet system but also have a connection to the Internet. Some companies do not give all employees access to the Internet. When you start working for a corporation, find out its policies for intranet and Internet use. *In your experience, how do employers feel about employees using company resources, such as computer networks and phones, for personal reasons?*

- **Memorandum:** Memorandums, or *memos,* are reserved for communicating with peers, subordinates, and supervisors within an organization; memos are not sent to external clients. You will study the memo in depth in Chapter 4, Section C. For now, familiarize yourself with the format shown in Figure 1.7.

- **E-mail:** Electronic mail has become the most widely used form of written communication and is used to communicate with colleagues in-house (on an intranet) or with associates outside of the company (on the Internet).

- **Business Letters:** Though used less frequently than in the past, business letters are most effective in communicating formally with outside clients.

Of course, there are many other types of business documents; for example, reports, proposals, minutes, and position statements. These documents along with e-mail, memos, and business letters, will be covered in depth beginning with Chapter 4 and in the Writer's Handbook, Part 3.

EXPLORE

Instructions: Examine whether a business letter, an e-mail, or a memorandum would be the best option in achieving the objective in the following tasks:

1. A coworker asks you to inform several departments about an upcoming meeting that everyone is expected to attend.

2. One of your clients asks for information about your company's customer service policy. The client believes your company made an error and that it was not handled appropriately.

3. An associate leaves you a message stating that she needs the names and phone numbers of 20 people in your department. She is out of town and will not return until next week.

FIGURE 1.7 | Business Memo

To communicate within your organization, write a memorandum. Memos contain a heading and a list of guide words to route the message, and this information can be displayed in many ways.

The body of the memo starts two or three lines below the heading. A full-blocked style (no indents, with a space between paragraphs) is efficient; however, you can adapt the style and format to reflect your needs. You can use the words "Interoffice Memorandum" or "Memorandum" rather than "Memo." The information following the guide words should align at least two spaces after the longest guide word (and the colons are optional). The writer of a memo usually does not sign his or her name to it. However, the writer may put reference initials at the top (next to the typed name) or at the end of the memo. Many companies design software for memos sent electronically.

Memo

To:	The name or names of those to whom you are sending the memo
From:	Your name
Date:	The current date
Subject:	A few words that reflect the purpose and content of the memo. "Subject:" can be replaced "Re:" (for "Regarding")
CC:	The names of those who will receive "courtesy copies"

Modes of Writing

Purpose also relates to the type of writing you are doing and the type of problem you are solving. For the sake of analysis, most writing falls into one or more of the following three categories: informative, expressive, or persuasive.[7]

- *Informative writing answers questions.* Informative writing summarizes facts, information, data, decisions, questions, actions, and so on. It provides details and instructions, passing information from one person to another. Informative writing conveys complex ideas in an objective way. Most business writing is informative.

- *Expressive writing conveys emotions.* Expressive writing is often creative writing and aims to reach the reader at a feeling or an emotional level. Forms of expressive writing include journals, memoirs, poems, songs, screenplays, novels, and short stories (fiction or nonfiction). Expressive writing can inform or persuade, and some business writing will reach the reader through emotion. However, for most business writing, be cautious if you find yourself expressing your emotions (especially if you are not objective about an issue).

- *Persuasive writing influences the reader or argues a position.* With persuasive writing, the writer attempts to bring the reader to agree with the writer's conclusion. Business writing that is persuasive usually relates to sales letters, position statements, and proposals. However, even in letters, memos, and e-mail, the writer often wants to sway the reader's point of view. Most advanced academic writing is persuasive and adheres to a traditional format (see Chapter 5, Persuasive Communication). Although some business writing persuades, it does so indirectly and does not follow a rigid format.

EXPLORE

Instructions: Analyze the following business problems and identify the degree to which the writing should be informative, expressive, or persuasive. What type of writing would dominate your response in each of the following business scenarios?

1. A client asks for information about the accounts your bank has for corporate clients.
2. Your manager wants you to fill her in on the status of a proposal you submitted.
3. One of your coworkers had a death in his family.
4. You receive an e-mail from a client who criticizes the way your company handled a serious problem.

The Journalist's Questions

When covering a story, a journalist focuses on basic questions such as *who, what, when, where, how,* and *why;* this ensures coverage from all angles.[8] These questions can be used in business writing to tease out the dynamics of a problem and develop potential solutions. They can be especially helpful on problems that are complex and controversial. Rather than relying on a superficial first response, use the journalist's questions to examine the problem before finalizing your answer.

- *Who?*   Who is involved or affected? What are their skills, attitudes, and beliefs?
- *What?*   What problems need to be resolved? What are the desired outcomes? What details are important or irrelevant? What does the client want?
- *When?*   When did the event happen? What is the timeline? Is the time frame relevant?
- *Where?*   Is a specific location involved? Is the location significant? What is unique about the location? Can another location be chosen?
- *How?*   How did the events occur or the situation evolve? Who did what?
- *Why?*   Why did this happen? Why is this important? Why is your solution the best?

In addition to using these questions to identify purpose, you may also adapt them to plan your task:

- *Who?*   Who is my reader? Am I writing to a coworker or client or perhaps a prospective client?
- *What?*   What outcomes can I expect? What does the reader (client) expect from me?
- *When?*   When is the task due? What is the client's time frame? What is my time frame?
- *How?*   How will I complete this task? How can others assist me?
- *Why?*   Why is this issue important?

Purpose Statements

For academic writing, a *thesis statement* defines purpose or expresses the central idea. The thesis statement typically occurs in the first paragraph, with the entire first paragraph developing the thesis.

For business documents, also present the purpose at the beginning and get right to the point. Shorter business documents (such as letters, memos, and e-mail) would *not* include an entire paragraph elaborating their purpose. In fact, for business documents, you would rarely elaborate on topics; you are more effective presenting your points with a minimum of explanation.

To know your point and get right to it, you can construct a **purpose statement.** Though a purpose statement does not necessarily appear in your document, it captures your mission in one sentence. You may choose not to take the time to write a purpose statement unless you are working on a large project or paper. However, some writers find that capturing the essence of short pieces through a purpose statement enhances their planning process. Here are some questions to get you started:

- What is the question?
- What are the key ideas?
- What is the main point for the reader to understand?
- What action should the reader take?

In a letter, avoid using the word *purpose* as you describe your purpose. An inexperienced writer might start with a statement such as the following:

> The purpose of this letter is to inform you that the application you returned to our office was incomplete and we need more information.

> The purpose of this paper is to examine various international issues that affect domestic trade.

A more experienced writer would state the mission in an indirect way:

> Recently you returned an incomplete application to our office. We need additional information from you.

> Various international issues affect domestic trade. Some of these issues are . . .

If you can't clearly articulate your purpose, assume that your reader won't understand it either. Knowing your purpose helps you identify which ideas are most important; once you know your purpose, it will shape your writing. Consider the two purpose statements above. In the first example, a simple purpose statement would specify the mission:

The client's application needs to be complete before we can process the account.

In the second example above, the purpose statement (or thesis) would present a broader picture of the topic:

By analyzing international issues related to domestic trade, we can develop policies that support our economy.

Purpose and Process

Once you understand your purpose, that purpose will drive the writing process. However, until you articulate your purpose clearly, you will not reach your audience. If your writing lacks a clear purpose, your reader may be confused. In other words, the piece may make total sense to you, the writer; however, your reader will struggle to find the meaning. Here are two mistakes writers often make:

- Trying to understand their purpose fully before they start writing.
- Thinking their response is complete without defining their purpose.

To avoid these common mistakes, start writing about what you know. To define your purpose or question, analyze your task and data with an open mind: *What is my question? What outcomes do I expect to achieve? What is the core or root problem? What is my point?* As your ideas take shape, you will gain deeper insight into your topic. Then, when you revise your draft, move the sentence that most clearly defines your purpose to the beginning. (Then cut all unnecessary information.) In this way, readers will understand your message with less effort.

For letters, reports, and even e-mail, state your purpose up front, not at the middle or end.

Audience: Your Reader and Client

When you compose, you are writing primarily for yourself. Your message is the most important element because you are learning about it as you are writing. However, when you edit and revise, you need to refocus. Your objective is to connect the message with readers' needs. To make objective editing decisions, you may need to detach yourself from the content so that you can focus on the needs and interests of your readers, your clients.

Here are some things to consider in defining your audience:

- Are you writing to a *specific person?*

    Do you know the person, or is this someone with whom you are unfamiliar?

    Is the person internal or external to your organization?

    Are you writing to a subordinate, peer, or supervisor?

- Are you writing to a *group of people?*

    Does the group know very little about your topic, or is the group specialized, knowing a great deal about your topic?

    Is the audience friendly or critical?

    Does the group interpret the problem differently than you do?

    Are emotions involved, or is everyone objective?

- Have you learned your purpose or question well enough to remove yourself from it?

    Are you able to see the purpose/problem objectively?

    Have you developed the purpose so that it is relevant to your readers' interests (rather than just your own)?

When you don't know your reader personally or he or she is an outside client, use a more formal tone. Tailor your writing to the background of your readers by leaving out

Process at Work: *Understanding your purpose will help you define the process by which you achieve your goal. Do you think your process can similarly help you understand your purpose?*

COMMUNICATION CHALLENGES

Client Relationships
Success in business depends on building good client relationships. At first, it seems obvious that clients are those outside of an organization who buy goods or services. But they are not your only clients. In business, all of your contacts are clients. Your coworkers are also your clients, deserving as much respect as customers and clients outside of the organization.

Ask yourself: *What reasons might I have for presenting myself differently to people in the workplace, depending on whether they are coworkers, clients, or vendors (the people who sell goods and services to the company)?*

information the reader already knows. If you are writing for an inexperienced audience, take a simpler approach by filling in gaps between ideas. Screen out thinking that does not directly relate to your purpose. For example, you usually do not need to tell your reader about your background thinking or how you arrived at your conclusions. Unless your background thinking is directly relevant, edit it out.

Writing to a peer or subordinate may seem easier than writing to your supervisor or manager. However, remain objective about your audience, and imagine that your reader wants to understand and appreciate your message: you write with more confidence to a friendly audience. Also, try to understand your reader's point of view even if you do not agree with it. If emotions are involved, focus on becoming objective and solving the problem.

EXPLORE

Instructions: In the message below, assume the writer is responding to a question asked about internship opportunities in his or her company, and answer these questions:

1. What information would be irrelevant to the reader?
2. Consider purpose and audience; how could you revise the message below to be more effective?

I have received your e-mail and reviewed the question you posed about interning opportunities in our company. In fact, I have asked several coworkers if they knew anything about training possibilities at our corporation. Most of them were unaware of anything that was available at the present time. However, a colleague of mine by the name of John Applegate suggested that you might be interested in our mentor's program. I wasn't even aware we had a mentor's program! I then did a little research and found out that our mentor's program offers interns from nearby colleges opportunities to get experience in their major fields. You can apply for this program through our human resources department. Let me know if you are interested, and I will have them send you the forms.

Thank you for your inquiry. I wish you success in your career choices and, if you choose, this mentoring program. I look forward to hearing from you soon.

 ## SECTION C: CONCEPT CHECK

1. Describe some qualities or characteristics of business writing.
2. Name the three categories of writing. Most business writing falls into which category? Which is the least likely category for business writing?
3. When you are planning your writing strategy, what are some questions you can ask to get a clearer sense of your purpose?

■ SECTION D: THE TONE OF BUSINESS DOCUMENTS

Whether you are speaking or writing, **tone** relates to *how* you convey your message. Your tone can either help build a relationship or tear it down. If you have strong feelings about your topic or the person to whom you are communicating, your tone will reflect your attitude (possibly without your even realizing it). By controlling the tone of your business documents, you also ensure clearer communications.

Affect/Effect Even the most articulate people find these words confusing. This simplified explanation advises you to substitute the meaning for the word as a self-check.

- *Affect* is usually a verb meaning "to influence."
- *Effect* is usually a noun meaning "result."
- *Effect* is occasionally used as a verb meaning "to cause or bring about."

To use these words correctly, substitute the word with the meaning.

- *Affect* as a verb:
  His decision will *affect* (influence) us.
  Will you be *affected* (influenced) by the change?
- *Effect* as a noun:
  The *effect* (result) is not yet known.
  Have they researched the *effects* (results) of the vaccine?
- *Effect* as a verb:
  It is imperative that we *effect* (cause or bring about) a new policy.
  We must *effect* (bring about) a solution to the shipping problem.

In this section, we will examine how each of the following influences tone:

- An objective response.
- The "you" point of view.
- A positive attitude.
- Gender-neutral language.
- Slanted language, slang, and jargon.
- A thinker or feeler approach.

An Objective Response

Everyone confronts controversial issues. When conflict arises, so do strong feelings. However, in a professional environment, expressing strong feelings in writing is rarely appropriate.

If you are responding to a message that has an emotional charge, your words will convey your feelings as well as your ideas. Even though you successfully address an issue on the intellectual side, you can create problems if you do not present your ideas objectively. In other words, you can win an argument but lose the relationship with your client.

When someone writes to you with emotion, try to understand what provoked the person's actions; take time to look beyond the obvious. If you respond with anger, expect that it will be expressed back to you or conveyed to someone in a position of higher responsibility. When you cannot present your ideas objectively, wait until you gain a clear perspective before you respond.

Here are a few other considerations:

- *Avoid being defensive.* Everyone makes mistakes, usually on a daily basis. The best way to correct a mistake is to take responsibility for your part; some situations will call for an apology. You do not become less of a person for admitting a mistake; some would argue your character becomes stronger.

- *Do not go on the offensive.* There will be times when you receive a message that strikes you the wrong way. When these situations happen, the best approach is to clarify the message. Though your first inclination may be to "fight back," stay calm and remain objective. Do not put anything in writing until you are objective.

The "You" Point of View

As you compose a message, you are writing for yourself because you are in the midst of understanding your purpose and the points you wish to make. You may find that many sentences are formed from the "I" point of view. In other words, you may write sentences such as the following:

I am writing you to ask if you would be able to attend a meeting on Friday.
I am happy to hear that you are doing well on your new job.
I have a few questions that I would like your feedback on.

When you write from the "I" point of view, you keep the focus on yourself. However, when you focus on your reader rather than yourself, you set a more effective, reader-friendly tone. For example,

Would you be able to attend a meeting on Friday?
Congratulations for doing so well on your new job.
Your feedback is valuable. Would you help me with a few questions?

Not all writing can be or should be written from the "you" point of view. At times, the "I" point of view is necessary and important. However, when you can use the "you" point of view, you set a tone that keeps the focus on the reader. When your words reach your audience directly, your readers feel respected and remain more involved. We will discuss the "you" attitude in more detail in Chapter 2.

A Positive Attitude

Everyone appreciates positive words; even subtle comments add energy. In writing, you help set a positive tone by describing situations in affirmative language. In other words, rather than saying what will go wrong if procedures are *not* followed, say what will go right if procedures are followed. Here are some examples:

Negative:	If you do not return this within 10 days, you will not receive a full refund.
Positive:	If you return this within 10 days, you will receive a full refund.
Negative:	If you do not respond by Friday, I will not be able to use your input.
Positive:	Only if you respond by Friday will I be able to use your input.
Negative:	By not going to the meeting, you will miss important information.
Positive:	By going to the meeting, you will learn valuable information.

Focus on what will go right if things are done according to plan rather than what will go wrong if things are not done accordingly. This simple shift sounds less threatening to the listener or the reader.

Gender-Neutral Language

Gender-neutral language relates to word choice. During the past two decades, English vocabulary has dropped many of its sexist references. Many professions that were once identified with one gender are now gender neutral. The change in language actually opens doors of opportunity because it opens people's minds to all possibilities.

At one time, a person's career choices seemed limited because of sexist references. For example, men were not as likely to be enthusiastic about becoming *beauticians,* and women did not feel compelled to become *firemen.* However, now that terms such as *stylist* and *firefighter* are commonly used, both men and women experience more career options. Your writing and even your speaking should reflect these changes. Here are a few examples. Can you think of others?

Sexist	**Gender Neutral**	**Sexist**	**Gender Neutral**
policeman	police officer	salesman	sales representative
waiter/waitress	food server	TV anchorman	news anchor
stewardess	flight attendant	mankind	humanity
mailman	postal worker	chairman	chair or chairperson

Slang, Slanted Language, and Jargon

Slang is commonly used on a daily basis by most people. Phrases such as "biting the bullet," "run it up the flagpole," and "carved in stone" are taken for granted by many American speakers. However, even these common **colloquial** or **idiomatic** terms should be avoided in business writing and speaking, especially in formal situations.

In addition, word choices can present a neutral picture or a slanted one. To control the tone of a written document, choose words that have a neutral tone rather than those that create negative overtones.

Slanted:	George deceived me about his ruthless behavior at the meeting.
Neutral:	George was not truthful about how he acted at the meeting.
Slanted:	Our congressional representative is notorious for voting to spend humongous amounts of money on undeserving projects.
Neutral:	Our congressional representative is known for voting to spend large amounts of money on controversial projects.

Readers prefer to make objective decisions. If you use slanted language, your reader may think you are trying to manipulate the information. In the end, you will lose credibility. Also, avoid sarcasm in business writing and limit the use of humor. You have no idea what your reader's mood will be when your message arrives. Always stay on the safe side and leave out anything that can be misinterpreted.

Jargon is in its own category. Jargon relates to using initials, abbreviations, technical, or occupational terminology as a sort of verbal shorthand. For example, *customer service representative* would be *CSR; New Accounts Department* would be *NAD.* While such abbreviations pose no problem for those familiar with them, they frustrate new employees or customers who must tediously labor to define the writer's message. Imagine you are at a new job and you find the following message in your mailbox. Would you have difficulty responding?

Keiller and Claire: DLK encoders are available as LK-to-Go files in a STG cell phone prototype/POC. Orton DLK Sec-Patch *is also slated* for the cell phone prototype. David Schreiber is working with Zana, Park, and Tobe to apply the TP document from the new RUP methodology to the CSB database. Any comments?

Avoid jargon as much as possible when you are working with the public, and use it sparingly with your coworkers. Take the time to spell out titles and departments. Your extra effort will save time and frustration for your reader.

EXPLORE

With a partner, compose a list of idiomatic expressions that you use regularly in your speech or writing. How might the terms you've listed be misinterpreted by the audience?

A Thinker or Feeler Approach

That people have different personalities from each other is no secret. One tool which determines personality tendencies is the Meyers-Briggs test, which is based on the psychology of Swiss psychiatrist Carl Jung.[9] The Meyers-Briggs test is used widely in business to identify personality tendencies that might affect how a person achieves a task.

Thinker or Feeler? Imagine a business situation in which one approach or the other would be more appropriate, for example, the birth of an important client's first child. What do you think the result would be if you chose the wrong approach in your message? When you are composing your message, do you need to consider whether the receiver is a Thinker or a Feeler?

One of the major categories on the Meyers-Briggs is the "thinking-feeling" category. Scoring high on either "thinking" or "feeling" will influence how a writer approaches a task. Thinkers tend to base their decisions on hard facts without considering emotional factors. Feelers, on the other hand, consider emotional factors a priority. Neither approach is right or wrong; however, a balanced approach is more effective.

Thinker approach: getting right to the point and making little or no effort to connect with the reader as one human to another.

Feeler approach: placing more emphasis on connecting with the reader than on the information being conveyed.

While thinkers take a straightforward approach, feelers have the urge to be social and friendly. Thinkers resist using fluff and niceties, but feelers search out ways to express things other than their direct message.

Thinker message: We need additional forms. Please send them immediately.

Feeler message: Hi Jorge,
Hope your day is going well. I just wanted you to know that we need more forms. If it isn't too much trouble, I'd appreciate if you could help me with this. Thank you so much.

Balanced message: Hi Jorge,
I need some additional forms. Please send them to me when you can. Thanks.

Of course, everyone exhibits characteristics of each type; personality type is a matter of degree. Whether you're a thinker or a feeler, the key is to find a balance between the two.

 SECTION D: CONCEPT CHECK

1. Why does a writer need to be concerned about tone? What are some elements that influence the tone of a document?

2. Do you consider yourself a thinker or a feeler? How does this affect your writing?

SUMMARY

Communication and writing are both processes. Though effective communication takes a lifetime to master, you can focus on active listening as a tool to help you understand others. Other aspects of communication that build relationships are showing respect for others and taking responsibility for your words and actions.

When it comes to completing a writing task, everyone's mind works differently. Some people need freedom to write; others thrive on structure. Some people prefer to examine purpose and audience as the first step; others find it important to clarify their thinking about a problem first. Practice both of these techniques to gain insight into what works best for you.

Give yourself authority to design your work with as much or as little structure as you need. You may want to do a mind map, construct a concept web, or develop a purpose statement and an outline first. If you prefer, do a page map and then a focused or forced writing. Remember, when you are stuck, *write to learn about your topic or question.* Writing will reveal answers even if they are not apparent when you start writing. All approaches—other than procrastination—will achieve results.

Process techniques will only go so far in helping you achieve success. If you want to improve your writing, you must apply what you are learning and write more. Your mission now is to practice composing techniques on topics that are familiar to you. You need to feel the freedom of getting your words on the page so that you can write with confidence. The more you write, the stronger your skills will become

CHAPTER 1 CHECKLIST

When communicating, consider the following:

Purpose and Audience:
___ Who?
___ What?
___ When?
___ Where?
___ Why?

Tone:
___ Are you being objective?
___ Are you using the "you" point of view?
___ Are you focusing on the positive (rather than the negative)?
___ Are you using gender-neutral language?
___ Are you avoiding slanted language, slang, and jargon?
___ Are you balancing your thinker or feeler approach?

Prewriting Toolkit:
    Mind map
    Page map
    Information wheel
    Concept web
    Scratch outline
    Formal outline
    Focused writing
    Forced writing

END-OF-CHAPTER ACTIVITIES

ACTIVITY 1: COMMUNICATION AND ACTIVE LISTENING

Part A

Instructions: With a partner, you will explore how your mood can affect your tone.

1. List three or four different moods that you will attempt to convey to your partner, such as happy, sad, angry, nervous, optimistic, pessimistic, or irritated.

2. Select a mood and say one of the following sentences to your partner:

   "I received the report that you sent me."

   "This afternoon I am presenting at the meeting."

3. Was your partner able to infer the mood you conveyed?

4. Repeat step 2 two or three times (use the same sentence for each mood you selected in step 1), and then change roles and sentences.

Part B

Instructions: With your partner, select a topic that you will discuss. Select something that you have in common, such as class schedules or plans for the weekend.

1. One of you will play the role of speaker, and the other will play the role of listener. As a speaker, talk to your partner about your topic. As a listener, be preoccupied and do not connect with your partner.
2. Discuss how each role—speaker and listener—felt.
3. Change roles and repeat the exercise.

ACTIVITY 2: FOCUSED WRITING

Instructions: Choose one of the following topics: purpose, tone, or audience.

1. Without referring to the text, complete a 3-minute mind map of what you have learned about your topic (purpose, tone, or audience).
2. Use the mind map as a guide for a 10-minute focused writing.
3. Review your topic. (Purpose, tone, and audience were presented in Sections B and C of this chapter.)
   a. What information have you left out?
   b. What new information have you added?

ACTIVITY 3: AUDIENCE

Instructions: List the audiences for whom you have written in the past year, both in and out of school (for example, a relative, a coworker, an instructor, or a customer service representative).

1. Select two of these audiences and explain how you wrote differently for each.
2. Explain why you chose the writing style you did for each particular audience.
3. How did you adapt your writing for each audience?

ACTIVITY 4: WRITING HISTORY

Background: Students using this text have a background in writing which has shaped their feelings about writing and their skills. Here are some things to consider about how you approach a writing task:

- Do you struggle with grammar, punctuation, and word usage when you write?
- Do you prefer to write an outline first, or do you avoid writing an outline?
- Do you jump right into a task, or do you put it off until the last minute?
- Do you edit as you compose? Do you allow time for editing between your first and final draft?
- Are mind maps and process tools helpful when you compose?
- How does criticism or feedback affect your writing or motivation to write?
- What are your personal challenges with writing? In what areas are you making progress?

Instructions: By understanding how you approach writing assignments and the experiences that have shaped your feelings toward writing, you will gain more control. Therefore, on the basis of your instructor's directions, write a short paper (one to two pages long) or a process memo (three to five good paragraphs) about your current writing skills. Describe how you approach a writing task as well as what causes you problems when you write. Select the title (or subject line) from those below, or create one of your own based on your writing experiences.

- Why I Don't Write.
- Why I Enjoy Writing.
- My Strengths and Weaknesses as a Writer.

ACTIVITY 5: THE PROCESS MEMO

Background: A *process memo* is a tool you can use to communicate with your instructor. (See the memo discussion on page 19.) In a process memo, you relate information about your learning process. For example, you could discuss the concepts and principles that are helping you make progress with your writing and the areas of writing that still cause you problems.

For your instructor, the process memo is a diagnostic as well as a communication tool. By knowing more about what gives you difficulty with writing, your instructor can assist you more effectively with your learning process. Thus, periodically, your instructor may ask you to compose a process memo about the concepts and principles you are learning or the areas that you find difficult. Likewise, when you are resubmitting a paper your instructor may ask you to attach a process memo to it in which you describe changes and corrections you made.

Here is an example of a process memo:

To:	Ms. Young
From:	Danuta Torres
Date:	October 5, 2004
Subject:	Writing Progress

So far, I have learned a lot about writing and its process. Mind mapping is very helpful in getting me started to write about a topic. Before I learned how to mind map, I would struggle with my topic and forget what I wanted to say before I could get words on the page. Freewriting sometimes helps me, too, but not as much as mind mapping.

I have also learned that I like to write more than I thought. I still struggle with punctuation and would like to learn more about the proper way to use commas.

Thank you for asking about my progress in this class.

Instructions: Following the steps below, write a process memo to your instructor about the concepts and principles in this chapter that will be useful and helpful in the workplace.

1. Take 3 minutes to do a mind map, and then take 8 to 10 minutes to do a focused writing.
2. Before giving the memo to your instructor, use the above model or the one in the chapter to format it correctly.

ACTIVITY 6: TEAM ACTIVITIES

1. **Situation:** Recently, you inherited two acres of avocado groves in California. In yesterday's mail you received a letter from the National Organization of Avocado Growers,

(NOAG), which you are now an official member of, seeking your input on an upcoming overseas marketing campaign.

Instructions: Working with a partner or partners, brainstorm a list of what you consider to be the most winning characteristics and uses of avocados and thus the ones that should be emphasized by NOAG in the campaign.

2. **Situation:** Rock the Vote, an organization dedicated to getting American youth involved in the political process, is conducting focus groups of students to measure interest and participation in the voting process.

Instructions: Working individually, use one of the prewriting techniques described in this chapter to outline your response to the following question: "Why did you vote in the last election?" (If you did not vote in the last election, explain the reason for that instead.) Then, working with a partner or partners, use your team's outlines to brainstorm a list of ideas that your team thinks would improve voter participation in the upcoming election. Remember, your partner(s) might have opinions that differ from your own. You are seeking understanding, not agreement.

3. **Instructions:** Do you suffer from any writing blocks? Describe to your partner or partners what gets in the way when you have a writing assignment. Then, using Figure 1.1 (page 12), diagnose the types of blocks your partner or partners are suffering from. Working with your partner(s), brainstorm a list of possible solutions to the blocks you are experiencing. Ask yourself: *What do you do that works well to help you achieve your goals?* Then, from your brainstorming notes, create an outline suggesting how each member of the group can overcome his or her individual blocks.

ACTIVITY 7: ALL PRO TEMPS

Situation: Temporary employment agencies offer good opportunities for beginners and seasoned workers. While you are working with this text, you will be doing some part-time work for All Pro Temps.

You have already been screened and approved by their human resources manager, Alice King, to work on some entry-level jobs. Ms. King has asked all new hires to write a memo to their placement manager, Bob Barton, telling him about current skills and work experience. He is also interested in the kinds of firms you would like to work for. All Pro Temps places temps in all fields, including law, manufacturing, finance, insurance, and medicine.

The more Mr. Barton knows about your skills, interests, and experience, the more effective he will be in placing you in temporary positions.

Instructions: On your computer, prepare a memo telling Mr. Barton about yourself and explaining why he should consider you for future positions. If you have question about formatting a memo, refer to Figure 1.7 on page 19.

REFERENCES

1. Ashley Bennington, Assoicate Professor, Texas A&M University, teaches "the four R's" of communication; ABC Conference, Cincinnati, Ohio, October 26, 2002.

2. V. A. Howard and J. H. Barton, *Thinking on Paper,* Quill/William Morrow, New York, 1986, p. 21.

3. Peter Elbow, *Writing with Power, Techniques for Mastering the Writing Process,* Oxford University Press, Inc., New York, 1981. Note: Peter Elbow is an exceptional source for learning about the process of writing in depth.

4. John Steinbeck quoted from Nancy Hathaway, "Unleash Your Creativity," *New Worman,* November 1991, p. 48.

5. Maya Angelou, *On the Pulse of Morning* (1993).

6. Gertrude Stein, last words, according to Elizabeth Sprigge, *Gertrude Stein, Her Life and Work,* 1957, p. 265.

7. Jim W. Corder and John J. Ruszkiewicz, *Handbook of Current English,* HarperCollins Publishers, New York, 1989, pp. 354–58.

8. Corder and Ruszkiewicz, pp. 385–87.

9. Carl Jung, Meyers-Briggs test; Katherine Briggs and her daughter Isabel Briggs Meyers built on the model developed by Carl Jung in his 1921 publication *Psychological Types,* expanding it and giving it a practical application. Where Jung described three personality preference scales and eight personality types, Briggs and Meyers determined that there were four personality preferences and sixteen personality types.

KEY FOR LEARNING INVENTORY

The best answer for all of the questions is 1 (never). If your score was above 10 you are not alone. The higher your score, the more changes you need to make in complete writing tasks. Repeat this process Inventory after you finish Chapter 1 to see if you lowered your score by applying the proven process tools described in the chapter.

10 = The ideal process skills; if you scored this high, you will one day write your own book.

11–20 = Stop editing as you compose as this will only give you a headache.

21–30 = Apply processing tools (such as mind mapping and focused writing), which you will learn in this chapter to help you get started with writing assignments sooner.

31–40 = Pay special attention to improving your punctuation and grammar skills which you will review in the Writer's Handbook chapters.

41–50 = Build your skills and change your attitude about your writing ability—you can improve!

Handbook at a Glance, Part 1:

The Mechanics of Writing

This section contains an *intense* review of commas and semicolons. For complete coverage of these topics, turn to the full chapter of **The Writer's Handbook, Part 1: The Mechanics of Writing,** which you will find in the last section of this text.

In this ***At a Glance,*** you will build an understanding of commas and semicolons in a short time (about two hours or less). In the process, you will also learn about the sentence core and the three types of conjunctions that signal comma use: coordinating, subordinating, and adverbial conjunctions. At first, these terms will seem difficult, but they are critical in learning how to use commas and semicolons correctly. Get a handle on these conjunctions quickly, and everything about punctuation will seem easier; the key is repetition—practice the terms until you know them without hesitation.

Do not underestimate the power of punctuation: once you understand commas and semicolons, you gain control of sentence structure and writing style. You can then eliminate fragments and run-ons from your writing, and your confidence with writing will soar. Because these exercises are intense and challenging, you can improve substantially regardless of how bad (or even how good) you think your current skills are. If possible, work with a partner or in a group of three on practice exercises. Now roll up your sleeves and go to work!

Pretest

Instructions: Insert commas and semicolons in the following sentences.

1. If you are unable to attend the meeting find a replacement immediately.

2. Should Bob Jesse and Marlene discuss these issues with you?

3. As soon as we receive your application we will process your account.

4. Your new checks were shipped last month therefore you should have received them by now.

5. Will you be attending the seminar in Dallas Texas on December 15 2006?

6. Fortunately my manager values my efforts and believes in my ability to do quality work.

7. Mr. Adams when you have time please review this contract for me.

8. We received his portfolio on May 15 and we promptly developed a new strategy.

9. Ali brought her report to the meeting however it was not complete.

10. Mr. Suarez sent a letter to my supervisor the letter was complimentary.

11. The merger however required that each corporation learn to trust the other.

12. Thank you Mrs. Donaldson for supporting our quality assurance efforts.

13. I am not sure about the costs but I recommend that we consider this proposal.

14. We received the contract yesterday however we have not yet reviewed it.

15. Mr. Wells will arrive on Wednesday November 18 as he stated in his letter.

After you complete the pretest, turn to the next page to complete the Learning Inventory.

Learning Inventory

1. Commas are placed in sentences on the basis of pauses.   T/F
2. A sentence has a _____ and a _____ and expresses a complete thought.
3. In English, the subject of a sentence generally precedes the verb.   T/F
4. If a subordinating conjunction such as *if, when,* or *although* is placed at the beginning of an independent clause, the clause will become dependent.   T/F
5. Conjunctions signal where to place commas in a sentence.   T/F
6. Place a comma in places where the reader should "take a breath."   T/F
7. One comma can be correctly placed between the subject and verb of the sentence.   T/F
8. A sentence is the same as a dependent clause.   T/F
9. The word "therefore" is an adverbial conjunction.   T/F
10. A subordinating conjunction such as "although" should always be followed immediately by a comma when it is the first word of a sentence.   T/F

The Plan

1. Take the **pretest.**

2. Answer the questions in the **Learning Inventory**.

3. Review the **Basic Comma Rules**.

4. Complete **Review Worksheet A: Commas**.

5. Go over the answers to **Review Worksheet A**

6. Review **Using the Semicolon**.

7. Complete **Review Worksheet B: Commas and Semicolons**

8. Go over the answers to **Review Worksheet B**

9. Take the **posttest.**

10. If the results indicate you need more practice, turn to **The Writer's Handbook, Part 1**.

COACHING TIPS

1. When identifying subjects and verbs, identify the verb first and then work backward in the sentence to identify the grammatical subject.
2. Remember to consider "you understood" or an "implied you" as the subject when the grammatical subject is not easily identified. You can represent *you understood* as follows: (you). Example: Please take a seat. (you)
3. The base form of a verb is known as an *infinitive*. Infinitives do not transfer action and do not function as the verb in the sentence.

Basic Comma Rules

1. When In Doubt, Leave It Out

If you don't know the reason why you are putting in a comma, don't use one.

"To pause" or "to take a breath" may have been your major reason for placing commas. It is a shock to many that neither pauses nor "breaths" determine comma placement. If your comma does not fulfill an established rule, don't put in a comma. To follow this guideline, you must learn all the basic comma rules and the requirements for using them.

2. The Cardinal Rule

Do not separate a subject and verb with only one comma.

Incorrect: <u>Mr Jones,</u> <u>asked</u> that the meeting begin on time.

Correct: <u>Mr. Jones</u> <u>asked</u> that the meeting begin on time.

When identifying subjects and verbs, identify the verb first and then work backward in the sentence to identify the grammatical subject. (In the examples that follow, (1) underline main verbs two times, and (2) underline simple subjects one time.)

3. Conjunction (CONJ)

Use a comma to separate independent clauses when they are joined by a coordinating conjunction (and, but, or, for, nor, so, yet).

<u>Mary</u> <u>would</u> like to go to the meeting, but <u>she</u> <u>has</u> a conflict.

What is an *independent clause*?_____

_____

4. Introductory (INTRO)

Place a comma after a word (an adverbial conjunction), phrase, or dependent clause that introduces a main clause.

What is a dependent clause? _____

In the sentences below, which clause is dependent? _____

Which word in the dependent clause keeps it from being an independent clause? _____

Furthermore, their discount reduced our cost.

After the meeting, George offered to chair the committee.

When your client arrived, you both began working on the project.

Furthermore is an **adverbial conjunction.** Can you think of a few more?

_____

After is a **subordinating conjunction.** Can you think of a few more?

_____

(See more examples of adverbial and subordinating conjunctions and learn more about how they function in the Coaching Tip on the next page.)

5. Nonessential Elements (NE)

Use commas to set off nonessential (nonrestrictive) elements.

A. Phyllis Smith, who ran for office last year, attended the meeting.

B. The woman who ran for office last year attended the meeting.

When nonessential information is removed, the sentence remains complete and clear in meaning. (Nonessential information often comes in the form of *who* or *which* clauses.) Do not use commas if the sentence must contain the information to be clear in meaning.

COACHING TIP

Comma Signals: The three types of conjunctions function as comma signals, indicating where to put a comma or semicolon.

A. COORDINATING CONJUNCTIONS connect independent clauses or items in a series. When needed, put a comma before a coordinating conjunction, not after. There are only 7 in total: *and, but, or, nor, for, so, yet.*

B. SUBORDINATING CONJUNCTIONS are words and phrases that introduce dependent clauses and phrases. Subordinating conjunctions show relationships. Here is a sampling: *as, after, since, unless, because, although, until, whereas, if, even though, while, as soon as, when, though, so that, before,* among others.

C. ADVERBIAL CONJUNCTIONS introduce and interrupt independent clauses. Adverbial conjunctions build bridges, helping the reader infer the writer's intent. Here is a sampling: *however, in addition, furthermore, consequently, therefore, thus, accordingly, in conclusion, in short, in summary, as usual, in general, usually, for example, unfortunately, of course,* among others.

For more information, see the Writer's Handbook, Part 1, or Chapter 2.

6. Direct Address (DA)

Use commas to set off the name or title of a person addressed directly.

    A. Our company, *Mrs. Roberts,* appreciates your business.

    B. *Mr. Adamlee,* our mission supports your cause.

    C. Please, *sir,* take a seat in front. (you)

When you cannot easily identify the grammatical subject, consider whether the sentence has an implied subject, such as "you understood" or "I understood." Represent an implied subject between parentheses. Example: Please <u>take</u> a seat. (<u>you</u>)

7. Independent Comment (IC)

Use commas to set off a word or phrase that interrupts an independent clause.

    Our team will, however, need more time to complete the report.

An independent comment often comes in the form of an adverbial conjunction such as *however* or *therefore.* (See Coaching Tip to the left.)

8. Appositive (AP)

Use commas to set off a word or phrase that describes or identifies a preceding noun or pronoun.

    A. Charles, my associate, will join us at 8 o'clock.

    B. The president, Mr. Sims, prefers that meetings begin on time.

9. Address/Date (AD)

Use commas to set off an address or a date.

    A. John listed January 5, 2000, as his start date.

    B. She has lived in Springfield, Illinois, for the past six years.

    C. Boston, Massachusetts, is a great city for a conference.

Notice that a comma is placed *before* and *after* the year and the state names.

10. Series (SER)

Use a comma to separate three or more items in a series.

    A. George would like potatoes, peas, and carrots for dinner.

    B. The estate was left to George, Alice, Bob, and Rose.

- For grammatical correctness, the comma before *and* in a series is optional; however, putting in the comma makes the meaning clearer.
- For legal documents, it is important that a comma be placed before "and" so that parties are recognized as separate entities.

Basic Semicolon Rules

1. No Conjunction (NC)

Use a semicolon to separate two independent clauses that are joined without a conjunction.

This rule is sometimes referred to as "semicolon in place of period."

> They invited me to join the board; I decided that I would.

- A general rule of thumb: You can use a semicolon where you could use a period. A semicolon is considered a "full stop."
- Semicolons are used when one or both sentences are short and both are closely related in meaning.
- Notice that sentences can be punctuated correctly in more than one way.

2. Transition (TRANS)

Place a semicolon before and a comma after an adverbial conjunction (such as however, therefore, consequently, *and* nevertheless) *when it acts as a transition between independent clauses.*

> Jane invited Tim to the meeting; however, he was not able to attend.

PUNCTUATION PRACTICE

REVIEW WORKSHEET A: COMMAS

Instructions: Correct the sentences below by applying the comma introductory (INTRO), comma appositive (AP), comma direct address (DA), and address and date (AD) rules. For each sentence, do the following: (1) Insert any missing commas. (2) Underline the verb in each clause twice and the subject once; if you cannot locate the subject, it may be "you understood." For "you understood" subjects, insert (you). (3) After each sentence, write the reason (*INTRO, AP,* or *DA*) for using each comma.

Example: As the <u>doctor</u> <u>ordered</u>, I <u>stayed</u> in bed all week. (INTRO)

1. Before he entered the building the young man checked the address.
2. If you would like the banking center to return your call leave your number and a time to reach you.
3. George can I count on your assistance?
4. Mr. Jones the building manager keeps all of the leases.   (This could also be a direct address: Mr. Jones the building manager keeps all of the leases.)
5. So that you are able to enjoy your dinner we will hold all calls and interruptions.
6. After the chairperson announced the changes the group was in chaos.
7. In general we do not include that information on our Web site.
8. Ms. Whitehead please summarize the information in an e-mail.
9. Even though you do not like the proposal it is our final offer.

10. Cathy when will you inform your manager?

11. Please speak to Louise my assistant if I am not in the office.

12. Although it is important to be on time it is also important to be prepared.

13. Until the president arrives we cannot begin the meeting.

14. She bought that in Grand Rapids Michigan last year sometime.

15. Mr. Jones asked if Josephine's start date was November 12 2000 or December 11 2000.

REVIEW WORKSHEET B: COMMAS AND SEMICOLONS

Instructions: Correct the sentences below by applying the comma conjunction (CONJ) and comma independent comment (IC) rules, as well as the semicolon no conjunction (NC) and semicolon transition (TRANS) rules. For each sentence, do the following: (1) Insert any missing commas and semicolons. (2) Underline the verb in each clause twice and the subject once; if you cannot locate the subject, it may be "you understood," so write in (you). (3) After each sentence, write the reason (*CONJ, IC, NC,* or *TRANS*) for using each comma and semicolon.

Example: <u>Ty</u> <u>went</u> to the meeting; however, <u>Marcia</u> <u>stayed</u> to meet with a client. (TRANS)

1. George wanted to go to the conference but he had a previous commitment.

2. He had told her about the meeting she refused to go.

3. We therefore are sending the material by Federal Express.

4. Mr. Sampson spoke of the economy in positive terms but there were skeptics in the audience.

5. We resolved the issue with the Turner Corporation this development was a great relief.

6. Alexander went to the library Martin preferred to go to the museum.

7. They told us the information too late so we were not able to attend.

8. The new printer does not work as effectively as the old one but it is ours now.

9. Mary wants to go to the seminar however her manager will not approve the expenses.

10. Susan did very well on the proposal unfortunately she was not in the meeting to receive feedback.

11. Mr. Anderson never arrives on time for example he arrived ten minutes late to our last meeting.

12. The contract states however that delays are not acceptable.

13. Please send the resolution to George Schmidt he expected it earlier this week.

14. We therefore look forward to seeing you on Friday please call if your schedule changes.

15. Bill is a good candidate for the job he received a recommendation from his manager.

Posttest

Instructions: Insert commas and semicolons in the following sentences and write the reason for using each after the sentence.

1. We received his letter from Bill Sable director of marketing explaining his objections.

2. Mr. Harris will be here on Tuesday September 18 as stated in the memo.

3. When you have finished Mr. Harkness please review this contract for me.

4. We received your application yesterday however we have not yet had a chance to review it.

5. Unfortunately my manager does not value my work as much as she should.

6. I am not sure about the benefits but I recommend we consider this plan.

7. Will you be attending the conference in Springfield Illinois on November 10 2007?

8. Thank you Ms. Vandergelt for your support of our quality assurance efforts.

9. Your order was shipped on Tuesday therefore you should have received it by now.

10. The proposal however required that each corporation learn to trust the other.

11. As soon as we receive these documents we will send you the verification.

12. Ms. Smith sent a letter to my supervisor the letter was very complimentary.

13. Would you like for Mark Jodie and Arlene to bring up these issues with you?

14. Della brought her calendar to the meeting but I forgot mine.

15. If you are unable to attend the conference inform your supervisor immediately.

Key for Learning Inventory

1. F	6. F
2. subject; verb	7. F
3. T	8. F
4. F	9. T
5. T	10. F

Tally Your Score

Deduct 4 points for each comma and then subtract total from 100.

Pretest Score _____   Posttest Score _____

No. Difference _____   Percentage Improvement* _____

*To tabulate percentage of improvement, divide the difference by the pretest score.

For example: If your pretest score was 60 and your posttest score was 80, the difference was 20. Divide 20 by 60 to get .33 or 33 percent improvement.

What Is Good Business Writing?

Less is more. —Robert Browning ■

Writing is a skill that evolves over a lifetime. Getting better is what counts; becoming perfect is not even possible. Thus, do not expect your first draft of anything to be a great piece of writing; that's what editing is for. With effective editing techniques, you can turn a mediocre draft into quality writing. In this chapter, you will learn to shape your writing so that it is reader-friendly and objective, two qualities of good writing.

When you start composing, just getting ideas on the page is a tremendous accomplishment. After the ideas are on the page, the process demands that you use critical thinking skills to make decisions. In Chapter 1, you learned about purpose, audience, and tone: (1) to analyze the problem to define the purpose; (2) to identify the reader's needs and interests so that you connect with your audience; and (3) to control your tone and make the reader's needs more important than your own. Now, in this chapter, you will learn about style and also more about tone: you will learn how to shape the tone of your writing through your writing style (or the way you structure sentences).

Our topic is business writing. That not only narrows the audience but also helps define their needs. In business, readers prefer writing that is **simple, clear, and concise.** Time is precious, and writing that is complicated or wordy loses the reader quickly. Readers want to get to the point and know the actions they must take to respond. In Section A, you will learn principles that relate to developing a style that is simple, clear, and concise. Then, in Section B, you will apply principles to control the tone of your writing so that you connect with your audience.

This chapter provides the foundation for an **editing strategy.** Once you can make clear editing decisions, you will manage the writing process effectively. For now, your goal is to understand the principles that lead to simple, clear, and concise writing.

O B J E C T I V E S

When you have completed Chapter 2, you will be able to:

• Manage aspects of style that lead to simple, clear, and concise writing.

• Revise sentences from passive to active voice.

• Develop an editing strategy to remove empty information, redundancy, and outdated expressions.

• Correct sentences for parallel structure and align modifiers with their subjects.

• Build transitions with adverbial and subordinating conjunctions.

• Apply principles of style to shape the tone of a business document.

Learning Inventory

1. Parallel structure relates to keeping similar parts of a sentence in the same grammatical form.	T/F
2. A grammatical subject is always the same as a real subject.	T/F
3. Formal, complicated writing makes readers think the writer is smart.	T/F
4. New information should always be presented at the beginning of a sentence.	T/F
5. A *nominal* is a misplaced modifier.	T/F
6. A sentence written in the passive voice always has a *real* subject.	T/F
7. Conjunctions build bridges in meaning for readers.	T/F
8. Parallel structure relates to being tactful.	T/F
9. The active voice is the best voice to use when someone makes a mistake.	T/F
10. In the active voice, the real subject and grammatical subject are the same.	T/F

■ SECTION A: A SIMPLE, CLEAR, AND CONCISE STYLE

The topics in this section deal with style. Before we start, think of **style** as *many individual writing decisions that add up to an overall effect.* Each writing decision—or aspect of style—produces a different result. The idea is to make decisions that simplify the message for your reader. Here are some topics that affect style:[1]

• Controlling sentence structure, length, and content.

• Using the active voice.

• Being concise.

• Building old to new information flow.

• Using parallel structure.

• Avoiding misplaced modifiers.

• Using conjunctions to show relationships.

• Bridging ideas effectively.

As you work on these concepts, you will be one step closer to developing a writing style that is simple, clear, and concise. However, please keep in mind that these are editing tools and that you must practice these principles a great deal before you build expertise. Let's get started.

Control Sentence Structure

The **subject** and **verb** are the core of a sentence. Readers or listeners must hear both the subject and the verb of a sentence before they begin to understand its meaning. Putting too many

A Clear Pathway: What are the benefits of keeping the structure of your business messages clear and simple? Are there any drawbacks?

words between the subject and the verb complicates the process. Thus, *keeping a subject close to its verb helps the reader understand the message more easily.* In each example below, the subject is underlined once and the verb is underlined twice.

Warren Buffet, one of the most successful businessmen in the world who is known for speaking his mind freely and honestly as he advises young entrepreneurs as well as government leaders, built his financial empire by identifying small, successful businesses and then acquiring them.

One of the world's most successful businessmen, Warren Buffet built his financial empire by identifying small, successful businesses and then acquiring them. He is also known for speaking his mind freely and honestly as he advises young entrepreneurs as well as government leaders.

Putting the subject and verb closer together makes the sentence easier to read. Breaking the longer sentence into two shorter sentences also makes it more manageable.

Control Sentence Length

Sentence length relates to the amount of information the average reader retains. Try to keep sentences between 10 and 22 words in length. Beyond 22 words, a reader may find it necessary to reread the beginning of the sentence to understand its meaning. For example:

Writing experts suggest keeping sentences to fewer than 22 words in length because readers may have difficulty retaining information in longer sentences and may need to read the beginning of a sentence over again if the meaning of the beginning becomes lost by the time the end is reached. (49 words)

COACHING TIP

Identifying Subjects and Verbs In statements, *the subject almost always precedes the verb.* A common practice has been to identify the subject first and then the verb. By reversing this process—finding the verb first and then the subject—you are more likely to be correct. Here is an efficient way to identify subjects and verbs:

1. *Identify the verb first.* Look for a word or words that express **action** (*identify, analyze, gain, precede*) or **state of being** (*is, are, was, were, seem, feel*). Underline the verb twice so that it stands out.
2. After you identify the verb, *work backward to identify the subject.* Underline the subject once. If you read the subject and verb out loud, they should make sense together (*you identify, you read, they should make*).

As you map out subjects and verbs, you are gaining a visual sense of sentence structure.

This is a bad sentence, but you get the idea. Sentences more than 22 words in length become unmanageable for the reader (as well as the writer). When you edit your writing, count the number of words in sentences that take up more than two full lines. For sentences that contain more than 22 words, either break the information into two shorter sentences or cut unnecessary information. By doing so, you improve both the quality and the readability of your writing.

Control Sentence Content

Each sentence should have only one controlling idea. When a sentence contains more than one controlling idea, the meaning is not clear.

> The president needs to examine policies about workers' compensation, and he is spending his time planning a new plant in Iowa.

What is this about? Where will it lead? These ideas appear disjointed, but each is given equal weight. You can correct this by showing how the ideas are related.

> Although the president needs to examine policies about workers' compensation, he is spending most of his time on the new plant in Iowa.

> Because the president is spending his time on the new plant in Iowa, he has not yet examined policies about workers' compensation.

Use the Active Voice

Experts agree that the **active voice** is easier to understand than the **passive voice.** The active voice is direct and uses fewer words. More important, with the active voice, the *subject, verb,* and *object* perform their prescribed grammatical functions. Here is an example:

Active:

Billy threw the ball.

The subject *(Billy)* is transferring action to the object through the verb *(threw). Billy* is the **grammatical subject** based on position: in English, the grammatical subject generally precedes the verb. *Billy* is also the **real subject.** The real subject is the "who" or "what" that performs the action of the verb.

Passive—Version 1:

The ball was thrown by Billy.

In passive voice, the subject is acted upon. In this example, the subject *(ball)* is not performing an action. Billy is still performing the action, but he is in the **object** position. Thus, the verb does not transfer action from the subject to the object. The grammatical subject *(ball)* is different from the real subject *(Billy).*

Passive—Version 2:

The ball was thrown.

In this passive construction, the grammatical subject is *ball,* and it performs no action. Because the real subject is not in the sentence, even this simple construction is somewhat abstract.

- In the active voice, the grammatical subject performs the action of the verb. *Thus, the grammatical subject and real subject are the same.* Active voice is clear, direct, and concise.

COACHING TIP

Clues to Recognizing Verbs
Verbs can express either *action* or *state of being.*

- The most common state-of-being verb is *be* and its various forms, including *am, is, are, was, were.* Whenever you see a form of *be,* tag it as a verb and possibly the word or words that follow it:

    Sue and George <u>are</u> in my department.
    The director <u>was going</u> to the theater.
    The actor <u>is walking</u> slowly.
    Bob <u>is being asked</u> to attend the meeting.

- One way to determine if a word is a verb is to put *will* in front of it: *will go, will see, will do, will buy, will communicate.*

- Another clue is the word *not.* A verb will either be on one side of *not* or be on both sides:

    I <u>will</u> not <u>go</u> to the meeting.
    He <u>was</u> not there.
    They <u>do</u> not <u>provide</u> that information.

- In the passive voice, the grammatical subject does not perform action. *The real subject is not the grammatical subject.* Thus, the passive verb *describes,* but it does not *act;* at times, the passive structure is abstract and wordy.

Even though the active voice is usually the preferred voice, passive voice is a grammatically correct construction. In fact, passive voice is more effective when you do not know who performed an action or do not want to call attention to that person. For example, it is more tactful to say "My phone call was not answered" than to say "You never answered my call." (You'll cover how active and passive voice relates to tone in Section B of this chapter.)

PRACTICE

Instructions: Change the sentences below from passive to active voice. For example:

> **Weak:**   A new project was given to us by Matthew.
> **Revised:**   Matthew gave us a new project.

1.   Our department was efficiently evaluated by the auditing staff.

   _____

   _____

2.   Objectives must be defined by the system technician.

   _____

3.   An employee's sense of job satisfaction is influenced by corporate leadership.

   _____

   _____

4.   The enclosed form should be completed and returned by you within one week.

   _____

   _____

5.   Any assistance that you need will be provided by our guest services department.

   _____

   _____

COACHING TIP

The Active Voice To change a sentence from passive to active voice, follow these steps:

1.   Identify the verb.
2.   Identify the real subject (not the grammatical subject). You can find the real subject by asking, "Who or what performed the action?"
3.   Place the real subject at the beginning of the sentence. Follow it with the verb (correct tense, of course).

In the active voice, each part of the sentence performs its prescribed function:

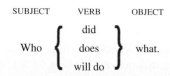

	SUBJECT	VERB	OBJECT
Who		did / does / will do	what.

In English:

- The subject answers the question *"Who or what performed the action?"*
- The verb performs action or expresses state of being.
- The object answers the question *"What?"*

Be Concise

Due to insecurity or the pure challenge of composing, writers often use too many words. At times, writers are afraid that short messages won't be considered important enough. At other times, a writer may not even understand the key points of a message until thoroughly developing the topic. Regardless of why too many words appear on the page, cut the message and get right to the point once you understand your key points and are ready to edit.

When you edit, remember: *Less is more.* Excessive words bog down the reader; the fewer words you use, the more your meaning or purpose will stand out.

> **Wordy:**   When you finally decide to sit down and start working on your paper, you should try to have all necessary resources organized and available so that you do not waste precious time looking for them.
>
> **Concise:**   When you start working on your paper, organize your resources so that you do not waste time.

COACHING TIP

Be Specific General language does not provide detail for your audience the way specific language does. For example, the word *airplane* is general, but the term *Boeing 727* is specific. The word *music* is general; the term *classical jazz* is specific. When you use specific terms, your reader gets a more vivid picture of what you are describing.

For example:

General: The Riley Company's proposal was well done.

Specific: The Riley Company's proposal was comprehensive, and its recommendations were reasonable.

General: The design for the new brochure is good.

Specific: The design for the new brochure is unique and uses graphics well.

Being concise also relates to eliminating *redundant phrases* and *outdated expressions.* Here are some examples:

Completely eliminate the problem.	*Eliminate* the problem.
That was a *terrible tragedy.*	That was a *tragedy.*
His book was *cheaper in cost.*	His book was *cheaper.*
Her suit is *red in color.*	Her suit is *red.*
As *per* your request . . .	As *you requested* . . .
Attached please find the requested form.	The form you requested *is attached.*
Thank you in advance for your assistance.	*Thank you* for assisting us.

PRACTICE

Instructions: Remove redundancy and outdated expressions from the sentences below (and change from passive to active, if needed). For example:

Poorly worded: As per the instructions, the proposal must be completed by Friday.

Revised: As instructed, we must complete the report by Friday.

1. Enclosed please find the papers that were requested by you.

   _____

2. As per our discussion, the new policy should be received by your office this week.

   _____

3. You can completely eliminate one step in the process by using a cover that is green in color.

   _____

4. I would like to thank you in advance for your consideration of my application.

   _____

5. Per your instructions, the application you requested from us has been enclosed.

   _____

Build Old to New Information Flow

When a sentence starts with a familiar idea as a lead-in to an unfamiliar idea, readers have an easier time making connections. While composing, you may find yourself putting down new ideas (the unfamiliar) and then linking them to your topic (the familiar). When editing, move the familiar idea to the beginning of the sentence and move the unfamiliar idea to the end.

For example, suppose you are sending a message about an upcoming meeting. As you compose, you may start with the new information:

Poorly worded: Branch office policies that differ from those of the main bank will be the topic of our next meeting.

When you edit, switch the order so that the sentence begins with the familiar (meeting):

Revised: At our next meeting, we will discuss branch office policies that differ from those of the main bank.

Beginning the sentence with the familiar concept (meeting) eases your readers into the unfamiliar information.

| **Poorly worded:** | New reporting procedures will be developed as a result of ongoing problems. |
| **Revised:** | Because of ongoing problems, we will develop new reporting procedures. |

PRACTICE

Instructions: In the sentences below, adjust the information flow so that "old topics" precede new information. For example:

| **Poorly worded:** | Getting work completed faster and more efficiently is what we need to do to keep their business. |
| **Revised:** | To keep their business, we need to complete work faster and more efficiently. |

1. There has been a major delay for traffic going west on Interstate 55 near County Line Road.

    _____

    _____

2. A change in consumer spending patterns is one reason the economy has shifted.

    _____

    _____

3. The applicant who graduated from Fox College has been hired as your new assistant.

    _____

    _____

4. The revised budget will be the topic of our next meeting.

    _____

    _____

5. Please consider the cost as well as the time required to make the revisions as you complete your report.

    _____

    _____

Road to Somewhere: *Parallel structure creates balance.* Why is balance important in business writing? Are there other reasons for using parallel structure?

Use Parallel Structure

Parallel structure relates to **syntax** and **clarity.** Parallel structure creates balance by presenting related words in the same grammatical form. Make sure that you present related nouns, verbs, phrases, and clauses in a consistent form. Here are some examples:

| **Incorrect:** | The team envisioned a successful future through *strong leadership, making decisions effectively,* and *new approaches being tried.* |
| **Corrected:** | The team envisioned a successful future through *strong leadership, effective decisions,* and *new approaches.* |

| **Incorrect:** | Bob's duties are *surveying* the employees, *to prepare* the agendas, and *chair* the meetings. |
| **Corrected:** | Bob's duties are *surveying* the employees, *preparing* the agenda, and *chairing* the meetings. |

| **Incorrect:** | The Baker project would have gone smoothly if *reports were prepared on time, we returned their calls,* and *would have included some sort of follow-up.* |
| **Corrected:** | The Baker project would have gone smoothly if *we had prepared reports on time, returned their calls,* and *included some follow-up.* |

Parallel structure adds flow through consistency in form. When checking for parallel structure, look for consistent verb tense, word endings, and voice (active or passive). Correcting for parallel structure comes while you are editing your work, not composing it. You will find more on parallel structure in this text in the Writer's Handbook, Part 2, "Writing Essentials—Grammar for Writing."

PRACTICE

Instructions: Correct the sentences below for parallel structure. For example:

Incorrect: Two new duties for the job are making cold calls and to call on clients.
Corrected: Two new duties for the job are making cold calls and calling on clients.

1. Mitzi is responsible for making cold calls, the ordering of supplies, and for following up with vendors.

     _____

     _____

2. The issues we need to discuss are accounts that are delinquent and the revised budget.

     _____

     _____

3. Complete the inventory, calls should be made to distributors, and the accounts tabulated.

     _____

     _____

4. Your new investment should perform well in these markets and a high dividend produced.

     _____

     _____

5. Their suggestions were to complete the application form, return it within 5 days, and then a call should be made to find out the results.

     _____

     _____

Avoid Misplaced Modifiers

Modifying words, or words that describe, take as their subject the noun closest to them. When modifiers are misplaced, the writer or speaker knows the intended meaning; however, the reader or listener can be confused, or even amused, by the incorrect placement. Here are two examples:

Incorrect: Mr. Jones is the person speaking to Susan with the gray mustache.
Corrected: Mr. Jones is the person with the gray mustache speaking to Susan.

Incorrect: Entering the conference room, John's briefcase opened and all his papers fell out.
Corrected: As John entered the conference room, his briefcase opened and all his papers fell out.

PRACTICE

Instructions: Realign the modifiers as needed in the sentences below. For example:

Incorrect: The client will meet you in the reception area for the new account.
Corrected: The client for the new account will meet you in the reception area.

1. He referred to the economics book located on the top shelf with the missing cover.

    _____

    _____

2. Resigning at the board meeting, everyone was surprised by the CEO's action.

    _____

    _____

3. The corporate headquarters were moved to a large skyscraper on the west end of town made with green marble.

    _____

    _____

4. A green delivery truck pulled into the lot with red fenders.

    _____

    _____

5. Looking scruffy and torn, my manager replaced our old office furniture.

    _____

    _____

Use Conjunctions to Show Relationships

Good writing follows a logical flow of thought. One way to achieve logic is to use connecting words that show relationships between ideas. That's where conjunctions play a major role. You can use these three types of conjunctions to make connections for readers:

*   Coordinating conjunctions
*   Subordinating conjunctions
*   Adverbial conjunctions

Since these conjunctions also play a major role in punctuation, learn how to recognize them and how they affect the structure of a sentence.

Coordinating conjunctions join items of equal grammatical structure: they connect items in a series or **independent clauses** (an independent clause is a unit of words that has a subject and verb and expresses a complete thought). There are only seven coordinating conjunctions, and you should know them. Some people remember them because together they spell the acronym *FANBOYS: For And Nor But Or Yet So.*

Subordinating conjunctions are words and phrases that introduce **dependent clauses** (a dependent clause is a unit of words that has a subject and verb but does not express a complete thought). Subordinating conjunctions show relationships between the ideas they connect; for example:

Weak:	Bob met with the office manager. They discussed ordering new laptops.
Revised:	*When* Bob met with the office manager, they discussed ordering new laptops.

Here are a few common subordinating conjunctions:

after	because	in order that	unless
although	before	no matter what, how, why	until
as	even though	since	whereas
as soon as	if	so that	while

COMMUNICATION CHALLENGES

Different Tongues In the broadest sense, English has two categories: standard and nonstandard.

*   **Standard American English** is the language of business; it is found in most books, classrooms, and professional forums. Standard American English is basically the same as **Edited American English.** The advantage of Edited American English is that it speaks to a broad audience.
*   **Nonstandard varieties** consist of language patterns that vary from the standard in grammar and word usage. Nonstandard varieties are dialects. This text uses the term **community dialect** to refer to all varieties of English other than the standard. Though every community dialect has a narrow audience, each builds a strong rapport among those who speak it.

    To some degree, everyone speaks a community dialect. We all have our own unique language pattern, speaking somewhat differently from our friends and family. These individual language patterns are known as **idiolects.** If you think about it, you might find that your language pattern is as unique as your fingerprint.

    Ask yourself: *Can I identify qualities of my own dialect or idiolect? What are they?*

**INTERNET
EXERCISE 2.1**

Language Patterns To learn
more about different dialects
spoken in the United States,
visit the *Foundations of
Business Communication*
Web site at <http://www.
mhhe.com/djyoung>.
    Once you have accessed
the Web site, select "Student
Activities"; then click on the
Chapter 2 link.

Although you do not need to memorize this list of subordinating conjunctions, you should do the following:

1. Know the term *subordinating conjunction*.
2. Understand the role subordinating conjunctions play in a sentence.
3. Be prepared to give a few examples.

You can tell if a word is a subordinating conjunction by placing it in front of a simple independent clause. If the independent clause no longer sounds complete, then the word is likely to be a subordinating conjunction. For example:

Bob went to the meeting. (independent clause)
Although Bob went to the meeting, (dependent clause)

Thus, adding a subordinating conjunction (such as *although*) makes an independent clause dependent; it becomes incomplete in meaning and needs an independent clause to complete it.

Although Bob went to the meeting, he did not share his ideas.

There are too many subordinating conjunctions to memorize. However, develop a system such as the one above so that you can recognize whether a word is functioning as a subordinating conjunction. (For a more thorough discussion of how conjunctions relate to punctuation, refer to the Writer's Handbook, Part 1, "The Mechanics of Writing.")

Bridge Ideas Effectively

Adverbial conjunctions build bridges between ideas and help the reader understand the writer's intention. Adverbial conjunctions are "transition words." Here are a few common adverbial conjunctions:

therefore	in summary	that is	consequently
however	as usual	in conclusion	nevertheless
for example	in addition	of course	on the contrary
fortunately	hence	otherwise	unfortunately
furthermore	in general	thus	otherwise

Here is an example of how adverbial conjunctions show relationships between ideas and provide a transition:

We submitted a good proposal. They rejected it. *(choppy, no bridge between the clauses)*

We submitted a good proposal; *however,* they rejected it. (*However* provides a transition between the two actions and shows the relationship between them.)

If you place an adverbial conjunction at the beginning of an independent clause, the clause will still be complete. For example:

George was offered the job of his choice.
Fortunately, George was offered the job of his choice.

When ideas are connected effectively, writing flows and readers are able to follow the line of thought. Both adverbial conjunctions and subordinating conjunctions bridge ideas and show relationships. They help the reader understand the writer's intent. When they are used at the beginning of a sentence, readers have a clue to the meaning of a sentence or paragraph *before* they read it. The list below shows common conjunctions and the clues they indicate:

however on the contrary although even though	The idea that follows will contrast with the one that came before it.
fortunately	Something good is about to happen.
unfortunately	Something not so good is about to happen.
thus therefore consequently as a result because	The writer is reaching a conclusion for the reader.
finally in summary in conclusion	You can relax; we've finally reached the end.

The editing principles discussed in this section assist a writer in making a document simple, clear, and concise and thus reader-friendly. Next, in Section B, you will see how to use these principles to affect the tone of a document, making it more or less formal.

PRACTICE

Instructions: Use adverbial, subordinating, or coordinating conjunctions to add transitions to the sentences below. (Experiment with different transitions to see how the meaning changes.) For example:

> **Weak:**   I knew about the position. I did not apply for it.
> **Revised:** I knew about the position; however, I did not apply for it.

1.   The audit was not complete. They had already made the announcement to shareholders.

_____

_____

2.   Lindel awarded the contract to our competitor. They will open bids on a new contract later today.

_____

_____

3.   Marjorie Lou's employer announced a cutback in staff. Human Resources said that her position was not among those cut.

_____

_____

4.   Lester insisted the software technician would know how to solve the problem. The technician said he could help us.

_____

_____

5. Conference calls should be scheduled at least two days in advance. The Boston office was not informed until the morning of the call.

_____

_____

 ## SECTION A: CONCEPT CHECK

1. List at least three principles that would be part of an editing strategy. Give an example of each.

2. What are the three types of conjunctions? Give examples of each. What role do they play in writing?

3. To remain reader-friendly, a sentence should contain a maximum of how many words?

4. What is the preferred voice for business writing, active or passive? Why?

■ SECTION B: TONE AND STYLE

This section shows how writing style (or the way you structure your sentences) affects the tone of your document.

By adjusting your writing style, you can make your message more inviting to the reader. For example, you connect with your audience by using a professional tone (rather than a formal tone) and by focusing on your reader. Here are the concepts you will cover in this section:

- Focusing on the "you" point of view.
- Turning nominals into active verbs.
- Using real subjects and strong verbs.
- Using voice to control level of formality.
- Choosing simple language.
- Writing in the affirmative.
- Using voice to control tone.

Focus on the "You" Point of View

Have you ever had a conversation with someone in which the person began every other sentence with the pronoun *I?* How did it make you feel?

When people start many or most of their sentences from the "I" viewpoint, this doesn't mean that they don't care about others. They simply may not have thought about the benefit of placing their focus on the listener or reader. Since much of your speaking and writing comes from a personal viewpoint, learn how to use pronoun point of view to connect with others.

The various subject pronoun viewpoints are listed below:

	Singular	**Plural**
First person	I	we
Second person	you	you
Third person	he, she, it	they

INTERNET EXERCISE 2.2

Customer Service
Technology has taken the "you" attitude to new levels. From car manufacturers to cell phone makers, many companies now offer customers the ability to "have it their way" in terms of customizing their order to meet their tastes. Similarly, Internet companies have been competing for online users by emphasizing customer support and personalized service.

For a closer look at the important role the "you" point of view plays on the Internet, visit the *Foundations of Business Communication* Web site at <http://www.mhhe.com/djyoung>. At the home page, select "Student Activities." Click on the Chapter 2 link to find activities and links.

The "you" viewpoint connects your readers to your message because it speaks directly to them, allowing an easier understanding of your message. By keeping the highlight on your readers and their needs, you may also become more client-oriented in your thinking.

As you compose, do not worry if you state things from the "I" point of view. When you edit, change appropriate sentences to the "you" point of view. Here are some examples:

"I" viewpoint:	I don't know anyone who is more efficient than you are.
"You" viewpoint:	You are one of the most efficient people I know.
"I" viewpoint:	I would like to invite you to our next meeting.
"You" viewpoint:	You are welcome to attend our next meeting.
"I" viewpoint:	I respect your opinions and hope you will continue to offer them.
"You" viewpoint:	Your opinions are always helpful; please continue to offer them.

At one time, business writers were discouraged from starting any sentences with *I*. As a result, writers overused the passive voice. Since active voice is usually more effective than passive, "I" once again became an appropriate viewpoint and is no longer a business-writing taboo. For example:

Passive voice:	The report was completed and sent to you last week.
Active voice / "I" viewpoint:	I completed the report and sent it to you last week.

Though sentences are more effective when they highlight the reader's position, the "you" viewpoint is not always possible. To be effective, use the "I" viewpoint, but don't overuse it.

In formal reports, neither the "I" nor the "you" viewpoint is stressed; writers often use the third person *(he, she, it, the company)* and first-person plural *(we, our company)*.

PRACTICE

Instructions: Adjust the tone of the sentences below to the "you" viewpoint. For example:

Weak: I am including you on the list of advisers.
Revised: You are being included on the list of advisers.

1.   I would like to inform you that your input made a difference in our decision.

   _____

2.   I have received your proposal within the deadline.

   _____

3.   Our company would like to inform you that your application can be resubmitted after 30 days.

   _____

4.   I am interested in learning more about the program that was designed by you.

   _____

5.   I would like to encourage you to consider applying for the job.

   _____

Turn Nominals Into Active Verbs

A **nominal** is a noun that originated as a verb. For example, the verb *appreciate* becomes *appreciation* in its nominalized form. Using a nominal often makes writing more complicated.

Nominalized: I want to express my *appreciation* for your help.
Active: I *appreciate* your help.

As in the example above, the nominal may displace an action verb, replacing it with a weak verb, such as *make, give,* or *have.* As a result, using nominals encourages complicated, passive writing.

Sometimes writers prefer to use nominals because they think using longer, more challenging words sounds smarter. However, as a writer, *your goal* is to make complex messages as *simple* as you can. Though there is no exact formula, most nominals are formed by adding *tion* or *ment* to the base of the verb. Here are a few examples:

Verb	Nominal	Verb	Nominal
transport	transportation	encourage	encouragement
develop	development	accomplish	accomplishment
dedicate	dedication	validate	validation
separate	separation	evaluate	evaluation

A few nominals form in other ways:

Verb	Nominal
analyze	analysis
criticize	criticism
believe	belief

At times, nominals are necessary; however, use them only when they improve the efficiency and quality of your writing. When nominals do not improve the writing, the reader has a more difficult time decoding the message.

Here is an example using *negotiate* and *negotiation:*

Nominal: The *negotiation* between the attorney and the client lasted for many hours.
Active: The attorney and client *negotiated* for many hours.

Below is an example using *discuss.* The first sentence uses *discussion,* which is the nominal form of *discuss.* In the second sentence, the nominal is removed; however, the sentence is still passive. In the third sentence, *discuss* is an active verb.

Nominal: The *discussion* about revised policies occurred at the board meeting in April.
Passive: At the April board meeting, the revised policies *were discussed.*
Active: The board of directors *discussed* the revised policies at their April meeting.

PRACTICE

Instructions: Underline the nominals in the sentences below. Rewrite the sentences by changing the nominal into the active form of the verb. Some sentences may also need to be changed from passive to active.

Poorly worded: The distribution of the list was made by Margaret.
Revised: Margaret distributed the list.

1. Management completed the implementation of the dress policy last August.

    _____

2. A suggestion was made by our auditing department that we use new forms.

    _____

3. Will there be a discussion of the new account at our next team meeting?

    _____

4. Our president made an announcement about the merger in the October meeting.

    _____

5. My boss gave a recommendation that I arrive at work on time.

    _____

Use Real Subjects and Strong Verbs

Since the subject and verb are critical elements, focus on using real subjects followed by strong verbs. (See Table 2.1 for examples of active verbs.) Here is how to keep your subjects real and verbs strong:

*   Use the active voice.
*   Avoid starting sentences with *it is* or *there are*. (These are called **expletive forms.**)
*   Use action verbs rather than state-of-being verbs *(is, are, seem)* and weak verbs (such as *make, give, take*).
*   Eliminate nominals when possible.

In each example below, the main subject is underlined once and the verb is underlined twice. Compare the subjects and verbs between the two groups:

There are many clients waiting in the lobby.	Many clients are waiting in the lobby.
It is well known that his preference is golf.	Everyone knows that he prefers golf.
He made everyone aware of the information.	He informed everyone.
We will take that into consideration.	We will consider that.
There are many policies that need to be changed.	Many policies need to be changed.
It is her belief that we should remodel the office.	She believes we should remodel the office.

PRACTICE

Instructions: Revise the sentences below so that they have real subjects followed by strong verbs. For example:

> **Weak:**   It is urgent for us to discuss why we are losing new clients.
> **Revised:**   We must discuss why we are losing new clients.

1. There are many issues for us to consider before we agree to the merger.

    _____

2. Mr. Johnston will take your proposal into consideration.

    _____

3. The accounting manager gave an indication that the date might change.

    _____

4. The report is a summarization of previous activity in the department.

    _____

5. There are new clients who must be contacted by us.

    _____

TABLE 2.1 | Active Verbs

accelerate	edit	interpret	produce
accept	empower	introduce	promote
adapt	encourage	invent	propose
aid	energize	inventory	provide
amplify	enhance	judge	rank
analyze	enlist	justify	rate
apply	establish	launch	rearrange
appraise	estimate	lead	recognize
arrange	evaluate	learn	reconcile
assemble	examine	listen	reconstruct
assist	expand	maintain	reinforce
awaken	explain	modify	relate
break down	extend	mold	reorganize
build	focus	monitor	report
challenge	formulate	motivate	restore
change	fortify	negotiate	review
choose	generalize	observe	revise
compile	generate	operate	rewrite
complete	guide	orchestrate	score
compose	heal	organize	seek
compute	help	orient	serve
construct	hypothesize	originate	simplify
consult	ignite	outline	solve
convert	illustrate	participate	stimulate
coordinate	implement	perform	summarize
counsel	incorporate	persuade	support
create	increase	pinpoint	synthesize
demonstrate	influence	plan	teach
describe	initiate	point out	train
design	inspect	predict	unify
develop	inspire	prepare	use
devise	install	present	widen
devote	institute	preserve	write
direct	instruct	process	

Use Voice to Control Level of Formality

Writing can range from being very informal and unstructured to being highly formal and complicated. Most writing falls between these two extremes.

The most informal style is the way people chat with their friends online. Most grammar and punctuation rules are thrown out; everything may be in lowercase; phrases take the place of sentences; and there may be no beginning or ending. If you write informally to your friends, be mindful that *all* other situations are more formal and require that you follow the rules of Edited American English (see the Communication Challenges sidebar on page 49).

Some of the topics covered in Section A of this chapter help determine tone, such as using the active or passive voice and choosing simple or complicated words. Here is a brief explanation of the active and passive voice:

- *Active voice:*   The subject performs the action of the verb. *Bob wrote the report.*
- *Passive voice:*   The subject does not perform the action of the verb. *The report was written by Bob.* (*Report* is the subject, and "report" is not performing the action of the verb.)

At times, the passive voice sounds more formal than the active voice. The passive voice can be abstract and indirect; it also encourages the use of complicated words such as nominals, which may give a pretentious effect. Other elements that affect the level of formality include the use of personal pronouns and contractions.

Business writing is neither highly formal nor highly informal: business writing falls in the category of "medium formality" and can be described as **professional**. In professional writing, use the active voice and choose simple words. In addition, use personal pronouns (such as *I, you, us,* and *we*) so that you may refer to your reader and yourself in a direct and personal way. At times, you can also use contractions, such as *can't* for *cannot* and *don't* for *do not*. In contrast, **highly formal** writing has the opposite characteristics, as the following comparison shows:

Professional	Highly formal
Active voice	Passive voice
Simple words	Complicated language
Personal pronouns (such as *I, you,* and *we*)	Nominals, abstract references
	No contractions
	Latin abbreviations

Here are examples of formal and professional writing:

Highly formal: The implication was that the issue will need to have been resolved prior to the conference that will be held in August.

Professional: We need to resolve the issue before the August conference.

PRACTICE

Instructions: Adjust the tone of the sentences below from highly formal to professional. For example:

Weak: The opening of the account in accordance with current procedures will have occurred prior to the beginning of business tomorrow.
Revised: We will open the account before tomorrow.

1. The incidence of tardiness among our employees has reached epidemic proportions.

2. Your advice has been taken into account, and I will make changes accordingly based on your recommendations.

3. There is an issue of insufficient funds relating to recent transactions in the Atlas account, and it may be necessary to involve security in an investigation of the account in question.

4. The letter would need to have been sent prior to the date on which they closed their account.

5. The deposit of funds into your account should have been made in advance to your writing checks for payment from the account.

Choose Simple Language

Whether you choose simple words or more complicated ones also affects the tone of your document. When possible, use a simple word instead of a complicated one. Here are a few examples:

We *utilize* the best methods.   We *use* the best methods.

Our manager is *cognizant of* the policy   Our manager *knows* the policy.

We *endeavor* to give the best service.

We *try* to give the best service.

Their decision is *contingent upon his reaction.*

Their decision *depends on how he reacts.*

Prior to their involvement, we made progress.

Before they became involved, we made progress.

PRACTICE

Instructions: Simplify the sentences below. For example:

Poorly worded: We will ascertain the cause of the problem and correct it immediately.
Revised: We will find out the cause of the problem and correct it immediately.

1.   The decision for the utilization of that product was made by our advertising department.

     _____

2.   Subsequent to their involvement, we made little progress.

     _____

3.   If the merger is contingent upon our utilization of their software, we should endeavor to make the change.

     _____

4.   Always endeavor to do your best, especially when you are cognizant of the challenges.

     _____

5.   If we are able to ascertain by whom the comment was made, we will follow up on the remark.

     _____

Write in the Affirmative

English is easier to understand when the "negative" is not used. Writing in the affirmative takes fewer words and keeps information clear and sometimes more positive. In the business world, keeping writing simple and positive is important. Here are some examples:

William *did not remember* the agenda.

William *forgot* the agenda.

It is obvious that he *will not be on time.*

He *will be late.*

She *does not have* the resources.

She *lacks* the resources.

The messages *are not the same.*

The messages are *different.*

In addition, writing in the affirmative helps focus the message on positive results. For example:

If you *do not contact* the clients today, you *will not meet* their deadline.
If you *contact* the clients today, you *will meet* their deadline.

Whenever you can, edit a sentence to state the same message without the word *not.* Your writing not only will be written in the affirmative but also may sound more positive.

PRACTICE

Instructions: Revise the sentences below so that they are written in the affirmative. For example:

Weak: The committee will not be able to consider your request.
Revised: The committee is unable to consider your request.

Weak: If you do not send your résumé by the deadline, you will not be considered.
Revised: If you send your résumé by the deadline, you will be considered.

1. Blanchard Corporation will not provide us information until we make our request in writing.

    _____

    _____

2. The auditor will not be able to give us the information until he updates his records.

    _____

    _____

3. Five participants did not remember to bring their information packets to the training.

    _____

    _____

4. The policies are not different even though they said that they would revise them.

    _____

    _____

5. If you do not return the signed form within 10 days, we cannot help you with your account.

    _____

    _____

Using Voice to Control Tone

Although the active voice is usually more effective than the passive voice, the active voice is not always more effective. Here is a summary of how active and passive voice affect the tone of a document:

Use the Active Voice:
*   When you want to connect directly to the reader.
*   When you know the real subject and want to get to the point efficiently.
*   When you want to set a professional tone.

Use the Passive Voice:
*   When you do not know who or what the real subject is.
*   When you want to be tactful about making your point without assigning responsibility to a specific person. With the passive voice, you can leave the real subject out of the sentence. For example, when someone has made an error, it is more effective to say "An error has been made" than to say "You have made an error." (Unless, of course, you want to ascribe responsibility for specific actions.)

PRACTICE

Instructions: Below are five sentences written in the passive voice. First, change the sentences to the active voice. Second, determine which sentences are actually more effective in the passive voice.

1. The check should have been deposited two days ago in order for you to have avoided an overdraft.

    _____

    _____

2. Your application was returned by our hiring manager because several questions were not answered.

    _____

    _____

3. Your explanation should have been given when the project was turned in.

_____

_____

4. A failing grade has been given in my class based on your incomplete assignments.

_____

_____

5. Your position in our department has been upgraded effective immediately.

_____

_____

 SECTION B: CONCEPT CHECK

1. Why is the "you" point of view important in business writing?
2. What is a nominal? Give three examples of nominals; then turn them into verbs.
3. What are the differences between the active voice and the passive voice?

SUMMARY

Section A covered aspects of style that make writing simple, clear, and concise and thus more readable. Section B continued the discussion of tone (which was begun in Chapter 1) by showing how style affects tone. By incorporating the principles of style into your editing strategy, you will achieve writing that not only is simple, clear, and concise but also connects with your readers.

As you complete the exercises in this book, your skills will improve. However, remember that *principles of style relate to editing, not composing.* Apply these principles when you edit, not when you compose, or you may lose your train of thought.

Writing, like every other skill, demands practice. The more you compose and edit, the better your skills will become. As you reshape your writing for your reader, you will expand your thinking, taking mediocre pieces and turning them into excellent final drafts.

CHAPTER 2 CHECKLIST

For style, have you incorporated the following principles?
___ Keep sentence length to 10 to 22 words.
___ Structure subjects and verbs close together.
___ Keep sentence content to one main idea.
___ Use the active voice when possible.
___ Use the passive voice when appropriate.
___ Turn nominals into active verbs.
___ Use real subjects and strong verbs.
___ Cut empty and redundant words and phrases.
___ Write in the affirmative.
___ Start with old information and lead to new information.
___ Use parallel structure.
___ Keep modifiers close to the word or words they modify.
___ Use conjunctions to show relationships.
___ Bridge ideas effectively.

For tone, have you considered the following?

___ Keep an appropriate level of formality.

___ Use the "you" viewpoint.

___ Balance the thinker or feeler approach.

___ Give an objective response.

___ Use a positive attitude.

___ Keep language gender-neutral.

___ Avoid slanted language, slang, and jargon.

END-OF-CHAPTER ACTIVITIES

ACTIVITY 1: PROCESS MEMO—WRITING ABOUT WRITING

Instructions: Write a process memo to your instructor. Summarize the concepts from this chapter that have made a difference in your writing. Identify key principles that you would like to continue practicing. Are you feeling more confident about your writing? Are your skills improving? What changes have you made in your writing so far? If you have Internet access, you can complete this assignment online at <http://www.mhhe.com/djyoung> and then e-mail it to your professor.

ACTIVITY 2: TEAM ACTIVITIES

Instructions: Working with a partner or partners, complete the following exercises:

1. **Active/Passive Voice:** With your partner, create a list of ten action verbs (such as *drive, develop, plan, call, finish,* and *create*). Write a sentence in the active voice for each word on the list. Your partner will then rewrite each sentence using the passive voice. Both sentences for each verb should have the same meaning. For the verb *call,* the active sentence might read *Bob called June last night;* the passive sentence would read *Last night June was called by Bob.*

2. **Coordinating, Subordinating, and Adverbial Conjunctions:**

    a. With a partner, try to list the seven coordinating conjunctions. Compare your lists. Who remembered all seven?

    b. List as many subordinating conjunctions as you can remember. Who had the longer list?

    c. List as many adverbial conjunctions as you can remember. Who had the most correct?

    d. Randomly select a conjunction and see if your partner can determine whether it is a coordinating, subordinating, or adverbial conjunction. Do several rounds until you each know your conjunctions well.

ACTIVITY 3: ALL PRO TEMPS

Instructions: Mr. Barton, the placement director at All Pro, has given you the following memo to edit so that he can determine if you are ready to be placed in a position that entails proofreading and editing skills.

Memo

To:	All Pro Temp Temporary Employees
From:	Bob Barton
Date:	August 5th
Subject:	Employees who arrive late to work are causing problems.

Our department has been in receipt of correspondence from various clients who hire are temps and are confused about our employee standards. To many of our employees are not showing up to work on time and this is obviously not a priority with which they are familiar.

Though you may be one of the culprits who consistently arrives too work late, you already no this is a problem. Any suggestions that may be given by yourself or your colleagues to help assist me in improving this serious problem would be appreciated. Also, this is to put those of you who arrive on time on notice that this behavior will not be tolerated should you start arriving late.

In fact, we are changing our policy so that any temporary worker who arrives late to work for any of our clients even one time will be put on probation. After the next tardy, the temporary employee will be suspended.

ACTIVITY 4: BEING CONCISE

Situation: When Angles and Saxons came together in Europe centuries ago, redundant phrases were necessary. Each group had its own expression; two words were needed so that everyone could understand the meaning. Although this habit has outlived its usefulness, the pattern of using redundant phrases lives on.

Instructions: Rewrite the following redundant phrases, leaving out the unnecessary words so that the meaning becomes clear. If it helps, add a word or place the redundant pair in a phrase. For example, *any and all situations* might become *all situations; a full and complete report* might become *a complete report.*

Paired Expressions:

any and all	hope and trust
at this day and time	problems and issues
basic and fundamental	questions and problems
each and every	separate and distinct
facts and figures	true and accurate
first and foremost	true and honest
full and complete	various and sundry
goals and objectives	ways and means

Modifiers:

completely eliminate	final completion
close proximity	final result
close together	following after
each individual	free gift
exactly alike	important essentials
final outcome	more perfect

most unique	precisely accurate
new breakthrough	totally accurate
one hundred percent complete	two equal halves
one hundred fifty percent better	true facts

Verb Add-Ons:

add together	grouped together
add up	plan ahead
cancel out	refer back to
combine together	repeat again
continue on	send out
continue to remain	start out
finish up	still continue

ACTIVITY 5: INFORMATION FLOW— PROOFREADING AND EDITING

Instructions: A software glitch jumbled the following travel advisory, which your company received via e-mail in the days following the 9/11 attacks on the World Trade Center. On a separate sheet of paper, reorganize the information presented so that it will be more helpful to travelers.

Airport Security Guidelines:

- Do not accept any item from a stranger or carry any package with unknown contents.

- Take only those items truly necessary for the trip. Once at the airport, be prepared to have your belongings searched by security personnel. Laptop computers and other electronic devices might require additional time to clear security.

- Be aware that there might be special parking and unloading restrictions. Some airports might have eliminated curbside check-in.

- Reconfirm your flight directly with the airline 24 to 48 hours prior to departure.

- After checking luggage, passengers should go directly to their gate.

- Make sure all luggage, both checked and carry-on, is tagged with the passenger's name. Identification should be placed on both the outside and the inside of each piece of luggage.

Back to Basics—Preparation Can Help Cut Down on Travel Delays:

- Never leave luggage unattended or under the watch of a stranger.

- Upon arrival at your destination, go immediately to the baggage-claim area to pick up your luggage. Have the claim stubs available.

- Arrive at the airport up to two hours before departure for domestic flights and up to three hours before departure for international flights. Carry at least one form of photo ID at all times. A second photo ID might be required at some airports.

- Travelers can help ease airport security delays by following these simple guidelines.

ACTIVITY 6: ACTIVE AND PASSIVE VOICE

Instructions: Change the sentences below from passive to active voice. For example:

Weak: The meeting was canceled by my manager.
Revised: My manager canceled the meeting.

1. The audit was performed by a certified accountant.

   _____

   _____

2. All agenda items for next month's meeting were selected by the Human Resources Department.

   _____

   _____

3. The report was written by George and was approved by the district manager.

   _____

   _____

4. A short surgical procedure will be performed by Dr. Miochi.

   _____

   _____

5. The top sales representative will be given an award by the president at the dinner this evening.

   _____

   _____

6. The truck was left running by the UPS driver.

   _____

   _____

7. Juanita's achievement will be recognized by her supervisor.

   _____

   _____

8. The credit department received calls from angry customers whose invoices were incorrect.

   _____

   _____

9. His letter of application was returned unopened from the human resources department.

   _____

   _____

10. The check was endorsed by Carl.

   _____

   _____

11. Your request may be approved by the manager later this week.

_____

_____

12. The invoice will be sent to you tomorrow by our accounting department.

_____

_____

13. You have been given an incomplete report by our auditing staff.

_____

_____

14. Your assistance will be appreciated by our entire committee.

_____

_____

15. You and your team were praised by the president at our annual meeting in Boston.

_____

_____

ACTIVITY 7: ELIMINATING REDUNDANCY AND OUTDATED EXPRESSIONS

Instructions: Edit the sentences below to remove empty information, redundancy, and outdated expressions. For example:

Poorly worded: Enclosed please find our latest report.
Revised: Our latest report is enclosed.

1. Attached please find the information you requested.

_____

_____

2. Per your request, we will ship the item by overnight express.

_____

_____

3. First and foremost, we hope and trust that our customer service department has completely eliminated all the problems and issues you are having with your account.

_____

_____

4. We are announcing a new breakthrough that makes our bicycle design even more perfect than it was before.

_____

_____

5. Each individual employee should identify basic and fundamental issues that affect the final outcome of this project.

   _____

   _____

6. Before you reorder, please review and examine all the items on your list so that you are absolutely certain that you have not ordered the same exact item more than once.

   _____

   _____

7. Before we send out surveys requesting their true and honest feedback, we are updating our customer service list so that it is current and up to date.

   _____

   _____

8. A free gift has been sent out to you because of your fast and prompt response to our survey.

   _____

   _____

9. Per our conversation, you and I will completely finish the preparations for the June conference by dividing the work into two equal halves between us.

   _____

   _____

10. The latest facts and figures provide a full and complete picture of our progress.

    _____

    _____

ACTIVITY 8: EDITING STRATEGY

Instructions: Edit the following short paragraph so that the message is simple, clear, and concise. Try to use active voice, cut excess words, and use simple words.

EVALUATION PROCESS

The topic that needs to be discussed at our next meeting is the process of evaluation that will be used by our department during the next year. For a long period of time, the issue was considered by many employees to be a very serious concern. To get ready and prepare for the meeting, current practices of evaluation need to be researched, analyzed, and examined so that we identify and utilize the best and most current procedures. If your input is to be included, suggestions and recommendations should be summarized and sent to my office no later than Wednesday of this week.

_____

_____

_____

_____

_____

_____

ACTIVITY 9: PARALLEL STRUCTURE

Instructions: The sentences below lack parallel structure. Make changes where appropriate. For example:

Incorrect: Writing is a good way to express creativity, develops your critical thinking, and will make you feel relief from stress.

Corrected: Writing is a good way to express creativity, develop critical thinking, and relieve stress.

1. Getting too many phone calls distracts me and are causing me to make mistakes.

   _____

   _____

2. Mathew's job duties are writing quarterly reports and to edit the company newsletter.

   _____

   _____

3. The director gave her employees two options: attending the meeting or to complete the report.

   _____

   _____

4. The applicants are similar in that both have good qualifications and their experience is extensive.

   _____

   _____

5. The director suggested that our committee focus on novel solutions, outside advice should be sought, and remaining open to our options.

   _____

   _____

6. Please suggest research studies that are informative, will be interesting, and provoke our thinking.

   _____

   _____

7. Weekly meetings help your staff to stay current with department goals, innovative solutions can be discussed, and they keep everyone updated.

   _____

   _____

8. John would neither apologize nor would he promise to change.

   _____

   _____

9. We discussed the project over lunch, and an agreement was made to go forward with it.

   _____

   _____

10. To improve how I manage my time, my supervisor advised me to structure my time, staying focused on one task at a time, and similar projects should be consolidated.

_____

_____

ACTIVITY 10: MISPLACED MODIFIERS

Instructions: In the following sentences, look for modifiers that should be placed closer to the word or words they modify.

Incorrect: They provided a memo to our team that explained the objectives of the meeting.

Corrected: They provided our team with a memo that explained the objectives of the meeting.

1. Lorraine suggested an idea to her department on improving customer relations.

_____

_____

2. The report said that we should fill the position with a computer technician who has a van in our Boston office.

_____

_____

3. At our company dinner, we awarded gift certificates for a local Italian restaurant worth $100.

_____

_____

4. Our department prefers to go to the conference in New Orleans on staff development.

_____

_____

5. My associate made a comment to our manager filled with emotion.

_____

_____

6. You can find many Web sites that list job openings with your major for college graduates.

_____

_____

7. The company bought a new computer for my assistant with five times the power.

_____

_____

8. A temporary worker chased Mr. Blake down the hallway with a message.

_____

_____

9. The report was on the vice president's desk about computer upgrades.

_____

_____

10. The controller purchased new computer chairs for our conference room without rollers.

_____

_____

ACTIVITY 11: TRANSITIONS AND BRIDGES

Instructions: In the sentences below, examine how adverbial and subordinating conjunctions show relationships and function as transitions between clauses. Circle each *adverbial conjunction (AC)* and *subordinating conjunction (SC)* and identify it. In each clause, underline each subject one time and underline each verb two times.

Example: (Before)(SC) <u>you</u> <u>order</u> office supplies, <u>Jen</u> <u>would like</u> to speak with you.

1. Although we lost the first contract, we won the next five.

_____

_____

2. I do not like the new report; however, I will analyze the data.

_____

_____

3. Even though June is the best time to hire new employees, we have good applicants all year.

_____

_____

4. We are offering you the position; therefore, you should request your college transcripts.

_____

_____

5. John's report included important information on the merger; unfortunately, he did not foresee the serious problems that would result.

_____

_____

6. Because my best friend is having a party on Friday, I cannot attend the team meeting.

_____

_____

7. If Mark had played basketball last year, he would have made first string this year.

_____

_____

8. Denise's assistant prepared the agenda; however, Denise did not bring it to the meeting.

_____

_____

9. Although Bob edited the magazine for hours, several errors remained when it went to print.

_____

_____

10. When our department lost its manager, I did not expect to be offered the position.

_____

_____

REFERENCES

1. Joseph M. Williams *Style: Toward Clarity and Grace,* The University of Chicago Press, 1990. The author attended Joseph Williams's class, Academic and Professional Writing, at The University of Chicago in 1988. This class had a profound affect on the author's insight into writing in a clear, concise manner. Some of the concepts discussed in this chapter, such as the active voice, old to new information flow, being concise, and end stress were originally learned in Academic and Professional Writing. Joseph M. Williams's book, *Style,* is a must-read for writers who want to learn more advanced concepts related to style, structure, and clarity.

KEY FOR LEARNING INVENTORY

1. T		6. F
2. F		7. T
3. F		8. F
4. F		9. F
5. F		10. T

Handbook at a Glance, Part 2:

Writing Essentials—Grammar for Writing

Many people find grammar tedious. In addition, experts argue that learning grammar principles does not improve writing skills. The experts are correct. Improving your grammar skills will not necessarily improve your *writing* skills, but it will improve your *editing* skills. Effective editing ensures that your documents are not only correct but also clear. Apply the language principles in this section as you edit, and you will end up with high-quality documents.

People often focus on their weaknesses, and only an error or two can deflate most egos. By improving your grammar *for* writing, you will edit with more expertise and speak with more confidence. Once you can analyze your mistakes and correct them, you won't worry as much about criticism. *In the end, it is your ideas that count.*

The Plan

1. Take the pretest.
2. Answer the questions in the Learning Inventory.
3. Review individual sections, and complete the review worksheets.
4. Take the posttest.
5. Compare your pretest and posttest results.
6. If the results indicate you need more practice, turn to the Writer's Handbook, Part 2.

Pretest

Instructions: Make corrections in the sentences contained in Parts A through D. In most cases, you can correct a sentence by changing a word or two. In Part C, you may need to rewrite a sentence to put it in correct form.

Part A

1. Mary says the meeting was cancelled due to logistics.

   _____

2. The accounting manager has receive the wrong report for the second time.

   _____

3. I bought that notebook because I need a new one.

   _____

4. The company has actually did five times the work we asked them to do.

   _____

5. That invoice has went to the wrong customer service agent several times.

   _____

Part B

1. Each flight attendant is responsible for their own cabin.

   _____

   _____

2. An employee can violate policy if you are not careful.

_____

_____

3. Issues relating to finances should be handled by you and I.

_____

_____

4. Between Jacob and yourself, who will be the team leader of the project?

_____

_____

5. A supervisor should include everyone in their staff meetings.

_____

_____

Part C

1. His instructions were to complete the reports, print them, and they should be filed in binders.

_____

2. James indicated that he would facilitate the meeting and be handling the follow-up.

_____

3. Fill out the employment forms and then they should be sent to my office.

_____

4. Joyce asked that I finish the report and then the project should be started.

_____

5. After you attend the seminar, the invoice should be sent to Human Resources.

_____

Part D

1. The owner's manual was not available at the service desk for my VCR.

_____

2. The delivery truck stopped short of hitting the dock with the dented fender.

_____

3. The estimate was sent to the Wilson Company for roofing damage.

_____

4. A letter was sent to the maintenance department complaining of poor repairs.

_____

5. Bill's memo was sent out on June 14 listing the seminars.

_____

Your Pretest Score

1. Tally your results. How many did you get wrong in each part?

A. Verbs	0	1	2	3	4	5
B. Pronouns	0	1	2	3	4	5
C. Parallel structure	0	1	2	3	4	5
D. Misplaced modifiers	0	1	2	3	4	5

2. Add the number of wrong answers in each part.

3. Multiply the total number of incorrect answers by 5 points.

4. Subtract the total number of points from 100.

For example: If you missed a total of six questions, multiply 6 × 5 to equal 30 points. Deduct 30 points from 100. Your pretest score is 70.

The baseline of good writing is correct writing. This at-a-glance section gives you a review of common grammar mistakes in writing that are related to the following:

- *Verbs:* using verbs correctly in past time; remaining consistent with tense.
- *Pronouns:* using case correctly; remaining consistent with point of view.
- *Parallel structure:* representing words, phrases, and clauses consistently.
- *Misplaced and dangling modifiers:* placing modifiers close to the words they modify.

Learning Inventory

1. Pronoun case relates to how pronouns *function* in a sentence, such as subjects or objects.   T/F
2. A common pronoun mistake is using the subject case *I* when the object *me* is needed.   T/F
3. Use a helper with the past tense form of a verb.   T/F
4. To form past time with all verbs, add *ed* to the base form of the verb.   T/F
5. Pronouns must agree in gender and number with their antecedents.   T/F
6. Keep verbs in a consistent tense within a sentence.   T/F
7. Parallel structure relates to consistency of form.   T/F
8. Placing modifiers close to the word or words they modify keeps meaning clear.   T/F
9. To be parallel in structure, a sentence should include active and passive voice.   T/F
10. When modifiers are misplaced, the literal meaning of a sentence can be funny.   T/F

Grammar Essentials

A. Verb Basics

Verbs in Past Time

A common type of mistake with verbs is using *verb parts* incorrectly. To avoid such mistakes, follow these guidelines.

- For regular verbs, add *ed* to indicate past time.
- Do *not* use a helper with the *past tense* form of a verb.
- Use a helper with the *past participle* form of the verb. Helper verbs include forms of *to be (is, are, was, were), have,* and *do.*

Examples of irregular verbs:

Base	Past Tense	Past Participle (With Helper)
go	went	*(has)* gone
do	did	*(have)* done
fly	flew	*(was)* flown
give	gave	*(is)* given
see	saw	*(have)* seen
write	wrote	*(was)* written

Incorrect:	I *had wrote* the e-mail before I received complete information.
Corrected:	I *had written* the e-mail before I received complete information.

PRACTICE

Instructions: Find and correct the errors related to verb use in the sentences below.

     Incorrect: The contractor would have saw the mistake if he had been looking.
     Corrected: The contractor would have seen the mistake if he had been looking.

1.   The project was complete before its due date.

     _____

2.   Accounting has wrote a new policy about issuing checks.

     _____

3.   I had spoke with Jill's references before we hired her.

     _____

4.   The budget has been froze for two quarters.

     _____

5.   Our sales manager have chosen the territories.

     _____

Using Consistent Verb Tense

Within a sentence, the verbs should remain in the same time (past, present, or future) unless the writer cues the reader otherwise. Speakers and writers often violate this principle.

     Incorrect: The work *was completed,* but I *am* not aware of the time you received it.
     Corrected: The work *was completed,* but I *was* not aware of the time you received it.

Note: After completing the Practice exercise, complete Review Worksheet A: Verbs on Page 79.

PRACTICE

Instructions: Find and correct the errors related to verb use in the sentences below.

     Incorrect: Patricia says that the project ended yesterday.
     Corrected: Patricia said that the project ended yesterday.

1.   My report was late because they give us too much information.

     _____

     _____

2.   The speaker directed the unprofessional comment at me, and I am unsettled by it.

     _____

     _____

3.   Since we did not give them updated information, their actions are justified.

     _____

     _____

4.   The board was unanimous in their decision that we are to continue the training.

     _____

     _____

5.   Ms. Franco's assistant was helpful, and I am very grateful.

     _____

     _____

B. Pronoun Basics

Pronouns are categorized by *case;* the four basic cases are *subjective, objective, possessive,* and *reflexive.* (See Table HG1.1.)

TABLE HG2.1 | Personal-Pronoun Cases

	Case			
	Subjective	Objective	Possessive	Reflexive
Singular:				
First person	I	me	my, mine	myself
Second person	you	you	your, yours	yourself
Third person	he, she, it	him, her, it	his, hers, its	himself, herself, itself
Plural:				
First person	we	us	our, ours	ourselves
Second person	you	you	your, yours	yourselves
Third person	they	them	their, theirs	themselves

- Pronoun case is determined by the pronoun's *function* in a sentence.
- Pronouns must *agree with their antecedents.*
- Pronouns must have a *consistent point of view* (or viewpoint).

Determining Pronoun Case

To determine pronoun case, identify the role the pronoun plays in the sentence. Ask yourself if the pronoun functions as a *subject* or an *object* in the sentence.

Incorrect:	The issue should be kept between you and *I.*
Corrected:	The issue should be kept between you and *me.* (object of the preposition *between*)

Incorrect:	The trainer asked Marc and *he* to do to the report.
Corrected:	The trainer asked Marc and *him* to do the report. (object of the verb *asked*)

Incorrect:	Feel free to call *myself* when you are in town.
Corrected:	Feel free to call *me* when you are in town. (object of the infinitive *to call*)

Incorrect:	*Her* and her manager agree on the strategy.
Corrected:	*She* and her manager agree on the strategy. (subject of the verb *agree*)

To determine whether you need a subject or an object, use the following rule of thumb: *If you could substitute* we, *use* I; *if you could substitute* us, *use* me.

PRACTICE

Instructions: In the sentences below, find and correct the errors related to pronoun use.

Incorrect:	Sharon Prieto informed Human Resources that a colleague and myself would go to the conference.
Corrected:	Sharon Prieto informed Human Resources that a colleague and I would go to the conference.

1. The project was assigned to Jackson and yourself.

_____

2. How can they split the work between you and I?

_____

3. Further along you can include Neil and he in the decision.

_____

4.   Debra said that she would consult with Michel and I.

_____

5.   Her and her manager asked Nick and I to lunch.

_____

Using a Consistent Point of View

Pronouns should agree with their antecedents and remain consistent in a point of view. In other words, make sure your pronouns agree in *number* and *gender;* and once you establish a point of view in a sentence (or paragraph), do not shift that point of view unnecessarily.

Incorrect:	When *a manager* gives instructions, *they* expect them to be carried out.
Corrected:	When *managers* give instructions, *they* expect them to be carried out.

Incorrect:	I informed *Sara* that *you* can't be too careful with the complaint responses.
Corrected:	I informed *Sara* that *she* can't be too careful with the complaint responses.

Note: After completing the Practice exercise, complete Review Worksheet B: Pronouns on page 80.

PRACTICE

Instructions: In the sentences below, find and correct the errors related to pronoun use.

Incorrect:	I like to crunch numbers because you see your results immediately.
Corrected:	I like to crunch numbers because I see my results immediately.

1.   A manager should give feedback to their employees on a regular basis.

_____

_____

2.   Jorene prefers to work in payroll because you have contact with all departments.

_____

_____

3.   Before a supervisor changes their employee's schedule, they should check with them.

_____

_____

4.   I am pleased with the new procedure because you can see results more quickly.

_____

_____

5.   An accountant should get their numbers from the correct source.

_____

_____

C. Parallel Structure

Present similar sentence elements in the same form for *words, phrases,* and *clauses.* Pay special attention to the following:

- Listing gerunds ("ing" form of verbs, *seeing*) and infinitives (base form of verbs, *to see*) inconsistently.
- Shifting unnecessarily from active to passive.

Incorrect:	Johnson said that he preferred *collecting* information and *to summarize* it.
Corrected:	Johnson said that he preferred *collecting* information and *summarizing* it.
Incorrect:	The instructions were *to develop* a policy and *staff should be informed.*
Corrected:	The instructions were *to develop* a policy and *inform the staff.*

Note: After completing the Practice exercise, complete Review Worksheet C: Parallel Structure on page 81.

PRACTICE

Instructions: In the sentences below, find and correct the errors related to parallel structure.

Incorrect:	Estimate the cost and then the information should be given to your client.
Corrected:	Estimate the cost and then give the information to your client.

1. Jamie's duties include answering phones, to file dockets, and greet clients.

   _____

   _____

2. When you have time, call the distributor and the delivery date should be confirmed.

   _____

   _____

3. At the meeting, we plan on discussing the survey and to make recommendations.

   _____

   _____

4. Open the file, make changes, and then the information should be saved.

   _____

   _____

5. Spend time checking the registration of participants, contact new registrants, and information packets should be sent.

   _____

   _____

D. Modifiers

To keep your meaning clear, place modifying words and phrases close to the word or words they modify. The incorrect placement of modifiers can cause two types of errors:

- *Misplaced modifiers* result when modifiers are placed away from the word or words they modify.
- *Dangling modifiers* result when the subject of the phrase does not immediately follow the modifying phrase.

Misplaced Modifiers

Correct misplaced modifiers by moving them next to the word or words they modify.

Incorrect:	The *computer* is on the other side of the room *with the missing keyboard.*
Corrected:	The *computer with the missing keyboard* is on the other side of the room.

PRACTICE

Instructions: In the sentences below, find and correct the errors related to misplaced modifiers. For example:

Incorrect: The article discussed a business losing clients because of rudeness in Rhode Island.

Corrected: The article discussed a business in Rhode Island losing clients because of rudeness.

1. Items returned by customers that are broken should go directly to customer service.

    _____

2. Your letter explaining the revised policy is welcome news about returned items.

    _____

3. The delivery courier left the package outside Jasmine's office full of supplies.

    _____

4. You will find the updated information at the front desk on the Gonzalez account.

    _____

5. Jacobsen's new assistant finished the report two days early on cattle numbers.

    _____

Dangling Modifiers

To correct a dangling modifier, place the modifier immediately next to its correct subject *or* turn the modifying phrase into a clause that contains a subject and its verb.

Incorrect: *Arriving late to work, John's meeting* was over.

Corrected: *Arriving late to work, John* missed his meeting.

Or: Because *John arrived* late to work, he missed his meeting.

Note: After completing the Practice exercise, complete Review Worksheet D: Misplaced and Dangling Modifiers on page 82.

PRACTICE

Instructions: In the sentences below, find and correct the errors related to dangling modifiers. You may need to reword the sentences to make them correct. For example:

Incorrect: Living in the city, Glen's office was close to his apartment.

Corrected: Glen lived in the city, and his office was close to his apartment.

1. Accidentally deleting his entire proposal, the only recourse George had was to rewrite it.

    _____

    _____

2. To assist new hires, an updated policy manual was prepared by Human Resources.

    _____

    _____

3. Missing information and a signature, we moved the application into the inactive file.

    _____

    _____

4. Getting the long-awaited promotion, John's goals were now completed.

    _____

    _____

5. For constantly losing new accounts, the director dismissed the two new sales
    representatives.

    _____

    _____

    _____

G R A M M A R   P R A C T I C E

REVIEW WORKSHEET A: VERBS

Instructions: Correct the verbs in the sentences below.

Incorrect: Jeffrey was the one who seen the mistake, but he didn't say anything
                    about it.

Corrected: Jeffrey was the one who saw the mistake, but he didn't say anything
                    about it.

1. The administrator had wrote a new policy for the car insurance.

    _____

2. Verna left the sales meeting because she is late for an appointment.

    _____

3. I would have saw you if you had arrived on time.

    _____

4. Their receptionist says that we should wait in the hallway because we were late.

    _____

5. The new budget will be froze until next quarter.

    _____

6. An hour's time was lost because we are in the wrong room.

    _____

7. Marshall said that the proposal will be complete before the deadline.

    _____

8. The office assistant might have went to the wrong office.

    _____

9. Dave said that he seen the report on the news.

    _____

10. Workshop materials were ordered late because we are not sure what to order.

    _____

11. Georgia saved the receipt even though she doesn't need it.

    _____

12. Jeremy has flew to Boston more times than he can remember.

_____

13. The subsidiary has accomplish all objectives that were wrote in the plan.

_____

REVIEW WORKSHEET B: PRONOUNS

Instructions: In the sentences below, make corrections for pronoun use.

Incorrect: A new hire should check with Human Resources for their employment packets.

Corrected: All new hires should check with Human Resources for their employment packets.

1. Mr. Kraft will know if the letter should be signed by myself or my assistant.

_____

_____

2. Inform the attorneys that the case between Jones Investment and I has been settled.

_____

_____

3. The check was endorsed by my partner and myself.

_____

_____

4. Between you and I, we have enough work to last the whole month.

_____

_____

5. The finance department should send the report to Ben and I before the end of the week.

_____

_____

6. A manager can give feedback regularly if they build it into their schedule.

_____

_____

7. I don't like to work on the accounting report because you never get numbers on time.

_____

_____

8. A customer always knows what they want in a product.

_____

_____

9. Since her and her manager agree, they will proceed with the project.

_____

_____

10. Contact she and her associate directly so that you get correct information.

_____

REVIEW WORKSHEET C: PARALLEL STRUCTURE

Instructions: Correct the sentences below for parallel structure.

Incorrect: As soon as Felicia finishes the report, it should be given to the administrator.

Corrected: As soon as Felicia finishes the report, she should give it to the administrator.

1. After you fill out the forms, they should be given to the receptionist.

   _____

   _____

2. Karl's favorite duties are recruiting new clients and to provide training seminars.

   _____

   _____

3. When you find out the correct address, the records should be updated.

   _____

   _____

4. If you work on the new software and are finding it easy, you can have more projects.

   _____

   _____

5. Our client wishes to return the item and getting a full refund for it.

   _____

   _____

6. You finished the table for the report, but the index was not finished.

   _____

   _____

7. List the missing items, and then the form should be given to Customer Service.

   _____

   _____

8. After completing the document, it should be filed with the clerk by you or your staff.

   _____

   _____

9. It was urgent that I return the phone call immediately, so it was returned.

   _____

   _____

10. After I check the responses, the mailing list will be updated.

    _____

    _____

REVIEW WORKSHEET D: MISPLACED
AND DANGLING MODIFIERS

Instructions: In the sentences below, place modifiers next to the word or words they modify.

Incorrect: Arriving late for the seminar, the door was locked and Janine could not enter.

Correct: Arriving late for the seminar, Janine could not enter because the door was locked.

1. Following the instructions, the message didn't make sense to me.

    _____

    _____

2. Before sending the application, all parts should be filled out by you.

    _____

    _____

3. To make a policy change, the details must be approved by Human Resources.

    _____

    _____

4. The package arrived safely at the front desk filled with new application forms.

    _____

    _____

5. When applying for a job, your first step is preparing your résumé.

    _____

    _____

6. To find the job right for you, networking is something you should consider.

    _____

    _____

7. The delivery truck is in the parking lot with Joe's materials for the seminar.

    _____

    _____

8. Walking into the conference room, the team leader's cell phone began to ring.

    _____

    _____

9. As low as $10, you can buy leather portfolios at the office supply shop located on the corner of State and Madison.

    _____

    _____

10. After completing the check request, Martha in accounting should be sent a copy.

    _____

    _____

Posttest

Instructions: Make corrections in the sentences contained in Parts A through D. In most cases, you can correct a sentence by changing a word or two. In Part C, you may need to rewrite a sentence to put it in correct form.

Part A

1. Miles has went to great lengths to ensure the project's success.

   _____

   _____

2. The conference have been held in Dallas every year for the past six years.

   _____

   _____

3. January was the worst month for returns, and Monday is the worst day.

   _____

   _____

4. We had a meeting last month, and not one of the supervisors mentions the inventory problem.

   _____

   _____

5. The policy was wrote before I became office manager.

   _____

   _____

Part B

1. Will Bob and him be able to start the meeting on time?

   _____

   _____

2. Her and her manager both think the requirement is fair.

   _____

   _____

3. A consumer must conserve their finances so that they don't go into debt.

   _____

   _____

4. If Mr. Jones agrees, give the report to Bill and I when it is finished.

   _____

   _____

5. Each participant should bring all their registration materials to the conference.

   _____

   _____

Part C

1. Go to the meeting, discuss the issues, and a report should be filed within two days.

_____

2. Once you find the answers, your client can be informed.

_____

3. Kim's job duties are to tabulate the types of inquiries and making follow-up calls.

_____

4. When Andersen calls you, the updated information can be given to him.

_____

5. The first applicant said that he liked working with customers and to inventory stock.

_____

Part D

1. Sue's desk is the one located near the window with all the papers piled on top.

_____

2. Will Vincent apply for the job next week in the Accounting Department?

_____

3. Finding out the information too late, applying for the job was not an option for Samuel.

_____

4. Missing the last train, Steve's only option was getting to work late.

_____

5. Place the completed form on my desk for budget requests.

_____

Your Posttest Score

1. Tally your results. How many did you get wrong for each category?

A. Verbs	0	1	2	3	4	5
B. Pronouns	0	1	2	3	4	5
C. Parallel structure	0	1	2	3	4	5
D. Misplaced modifiers	0	1	2	3	4	5

2. Add the number of wrong answers in each part, and multiply the total by 5 points.
3. Subtract the total number of points from 100.

Your Percentage of Improvement:

1. Subtract your pretest score from your posttest score.
2. Divide the difference by the pretest score.

   For example: If your pretest score is 60 and your posttest score is 80, the difference is 20. Divide 20 by 60 to get .33, or 33 percent improvement.

Pretest score	_____	Posttest score	_____
Difference	_____	Percentage improvement	_____

Key for Learning Inventory

1. T	6. T
2. T	7. T
3. F	8. T
4. F	9. F
5. T	10. T

Developing and Revising Short Business Messages

Everything should be made as simple as possible, but not simpler. —Albert Einstein ■

So far you have focused on editing sentences to achieve simple, clear, and concise writing. Now you will examine how to edit and revise short messages, focusing specifically on effective paragraphs. The paragraph is the basic unit of all business correspondence, including e-mail, letters, and memos. Once you feel confident composing and revising paragraphs, you will have control over every business and academic document you write.

With paragraphs, you will apply principles of information flow, going from old to new information. Controlling information flow ensures that your messages are *cohesive* and *coherent.* You achieve a cohesive, coherent paragraph by constructing a topic sentence that builds into a topic string. In this chapter, you will be introduced to the PEER model, a guide to structuring information as you compose or revise. In addition, you will review transitions as a means of connecting larger chunks of information.

In the next chapter, you will use all the principles you have learned to compose, edit, and revise e-mail, letters, and memos. Before you take that step you will gain practice in editing short messages so that they are cohesive, coherent, and reader-friendly.

OBJECTIVES

When you have completed Chapter 3, you will be able to:

- Develop cohesive and coherent paragraphs.
- Build effective paragraphs by using a topic sentence and a topic string.
- Eliminate empty information from sentences and paragraphs.
- Identify transitional elements and apply them to paragraphing decisions.
- Compose, edit, and revise paragraphs for effective information flow.
- Learn how to format e-mail.

Learning Inventory

1. Effective paragraphs are coherent, which means that sentences can be about different topics as long as each sentence makes sense.   T/F

2. Three types of information to control when you are writing are old, new, and empty.   T/F

3. A writer's background thinking is considered "empty information."   T/F

4. In business communication, share all the details of *how* you decided on a course of action.   T/F

5. Which two of the following choices characterize effective paragraphs?

   a. topical   c. edited and revised   e. PEER

   b. cohesive   d. coherent

6. When structuring a document, give substantial background information before stating the purpose.   T/F

7. Which of the following is true?

   a. A topic string leads to a topic sentence.

   b. A topic sentence develops into a topic string.

8. Conjunctions function as transitions between sentences and paragraphs.   T/F

9. Since most e-mail messages are short, writers should use abbreviations.   T/F

10. Hedges and emphatics provide transitions for readers.   T/F

■ SECTION A: DEVELOPING PARAGRAPHS

Business documents of all types depend on well-written paragraphs. Readers are confused when writers present ideas haphazardly, jumping from one idea to another without developing a line of thought. Thus, whether you are writing an e-mail, a letter, or a research paper, you need to make good paragraphing decisions.

Readers assimilate information in chunks, and they have difficulty reading one long narrative with no breaks. If you do not insert paragraph breaks naturally as you compose, put them in when you edit and revise. Read your writing out loud, or have someone read it to you. When you hear a new topic, start a new paragraph. Remember, just looking at one long paragraph that seems to go on forever puts dread in the heart of a reader.

Once you have enough experience writing, you will make paragraph breaks as a natural part of composing. When you edit, you will structure the content to make your paragraphs cohesive and coherent.

- **Cohesive paragraphs** present *one main idea* or topic. A cohesive paragraph demonstrates *connectedness* among ideas. Ideas are related; they adhere together for a common purpose. Adequate details support the main idea so that the reader understands the main point.

- **Coherent paragraphs** develop the main idea in a *logical way.* A coherent paragraph demonstrates a *logical flow of ideas.* The writer develops the topic in a consistent, rational way. Readers can make sense of the content because one idea leads to another.

Cohesive Paragraphs

Cohesive paragraphs develop one main idea, and this idea controls the content of the paragraph. The sentence that presents the main idea or topic in the most effective way is called the **topic sentence.** A topic sentence is a broad, general sentence that gives an overview of the paragraph. It presents the main or controlling idea, and the rest of the paragraph radiates from that idea. Though the topic sentence can be placed anywhere in the paragraph, it is most effective as the first or second sentence.

Each sentence in the paragraph should relate to the topic sentence, thereby developing a **topic string.** A topic string is a *series of sentences* that develop the specific idea captured by the topic sentence. Each sentence extends the readers' knowledge about the controlling idea, helping readers digest the topic before linking it to the next main idea.

By developing a topic string from a topic sentence, you are ensuring that your paragraph is cohesive. The topic sentence introduces the common thread, and the topic string pulls that common thread through every sentence in the paragraph.

Here is an example of a topic sentence followed by a topic string:

Listening is an important part of communicating. If you take the time to listen to them, most people will tell you about their lives. Senior citizens, for example, will tell you about the world and the problems they have. People will also reveal more about themselves if you ask them questions. Once you understand people through listening, you can become better friends, even if they think differently than you do.

What is the topic sentence in the paragraph above? Is it the first sentence or the second? The paragraph above is *cohesive* because the topic string develops only the aspect of listening that relates to the second sentence: *getting to know people by taking the time to listen.* However, the paragraph above was originally written as follows:

Listening is an important part of communicating. You can find out about a person just by listening to them. I find that most people will tell you just about anything if you have the time to listen to them. Senior citizens, for example, will tell you everything about the world and problems they have if you listen to them. Asking questions can also encourage the person to reveal more about themselves. One of the areas in retail sales is to find out what the person really wants, and then to sell it to them. If you show an interest and are genuine in your concern, you will make a sale. A good salesperson takes time with a customer and listens to their needs and concerns.

Though the entire paragraph above is about listening, it jumps to very different aspects of listening. For example, *getting to know someone* is a different aspect of listening than *making a retail sale.* Thus, staying on the same broad topic is not necessarily the same as developing that topic through a cohesive and logical flow of ideas. (The paragraph also contains several grammatical mistakes; can you find them?)

By focusing on the ideas related to sales, the writer developed a cohesive paragraph about that aspect of listening:

Listening is also involved in retail sales. A good salesperson takes time with customers and listens to their needs and concerns. As a salesperson, if you find out what a

COMMUNICATION CHALLENGES

Pop Quiz The job application for an entry-level position at a local advertising agency includes the following: Congratulations! You just won the grand prize at the National Business Leaders of America convention—a fully paid, one-year apprenticeship with a Fortune 100 company of your choice. Write a paragraph describing the position and company of your choice. Also describe what you want to learn during that year and how you will be different when your assignment is finished.

CHALLENGE

In a timed exercise, take 10 minutes to prepare the paragraph requested by the ad agency. Remember, you want to impress!

COACHING TIP

Consolidating Colors, Consolidating Ideas One way to rearrange a room so that it looks less cluttered is to group similarly colored items together. By consolidating similar colors, a room may appear more cohesive.

The same is true with writing. Readers are confused if writing pulls them in too many directions without bringing them to a point or conclusion. By consolidating similar ideas into paragraphs, the reader gains a deeper understanding more easily. The ideas pull together to demonstrate a point.

Thus, a cohesive paragraph develops the main point its topic sentence presents, leaving diverse ideas as the topics for new paragraphs. *Can you find a paragraph that you've written recently that jumps from idea to idea, lacking a cohesive structure?*

customer really wants, you can then sell it to the person. If you show a genuine interest in your customer by listening to the person's needs, you will make a sale.

Identify your topic sentence by selecting the sentence that best captures the broader, more general topic that the rest of the paragraph develops through specifics. Every sentence in the paragraph should develop some element of the topic sentence; every sentence should also directly relate to the other sentences in the paragraph. Otherwise, you need to start a new paragraph to develop the new topic.

Though a topic string ensures a cohesive paragraph, it does not ensure a coherent paragraph. Staying on the same topic is not the same as developing that topic through a logical flow of ideas. Let's examine how to develop paragraphs that are coherent as well as cohesive.

PRACTICE

Read the paragraph below about health and safety programs, and then answer these questions:

1. Which sentence is the topic sentence? (That is, which sentence best captures the topic in a broad, general way?)

2. Which sentences develop the topic string? (Which sentences directly support the topic sentence and remain related to each other?)

3. Which sentence or sentences should be removed so that the paragraph is cohesive? (Which sentences start to develop a different topic?)

By implementing health and safety programs for employees, a corporation can reap multiple rewards. Reduced absenteeism, increased productivity, and improved employee morale are often the results of a comprehensive health program. In addition, substantial savings in reduced insurance claims and premiums are another result of having a health program. Our corporation implemented a health and safety program and had good results. In addition, the families of the employees appreciated the program almost as much as our employees.

INTERNET EXERCISE 3.1

Proofreaders' Marks
Knowing how to use and read **proofreaders' marks** can simplify the editing process in a professional environment. A chart of the most frequently used marks appears on the inside back cover of this text. For additional coverage of proofreaders' marks, including practice exercises, log on to the *Foundations of Business Communication* Web site at <http://www.mhhe.com/djyoung>.

Once you have accessed the home page, select "Student Activities" and then click the Chapter 3 link to get started.

Coherent Paragraphs

In a coherent paragraph, one idea leads logically to the next idea as it extends the reader's knowledge. To achieve a coherent paragraph, aim for a logical flow of ideas: apply principles of information flow, developing ideas from the familiar (old) to the unfamiliar (new). (To review information flow, refer to Chapter 2.)

In each sentence, put old information first and follow it with new information. The old information relates to the main idea (topic) of the paragraph; the new information extends the reader's understanding of the topic. Creating an old to new information flow helps readers make connections; familiar ideas ease readers into the unfamiliar.

The paragraph about health and safety programs in the Practice above sounds choppy and incoherent because new information is presented first and then attached to old information. This cohesive paragraph can become coherent by adjusting the information flow:

- Move the topic *health and safety programs* (old information) to the beginning of each sentence.

- Move information about *rewards* (new information) to the end of each sentence.

The topic string then flows from the topic of "health and safety programs" (which is a constant topic) to new information or "rewards" (which varies or expands). In the examples that follow, old information is in bold and new information in italics.

Puzzling Over Pieces: In writing that is cohesive, separate pieces—thoughts, words, and sentences—stick together to form a picture that is both logical and consistent. What happens to the reader when the pieces of the message don't fit together?

Topic sentence:	**By implementing health and safety programs for employees,** *a corporation can reap multiple rewards.*
Second sentence:	
New to old:	*Reduced absenteeism, increased productivity, and improved employee morale are often the results* **of a comprehensive health program.**
Old to new:	**A comprehensive occupational health program** *reduces absenteeism, increases productivity, and improves employee morale.*
Third sentence:	
New to old:	In addition, *substantial savings in reduced insurance claims and premiums* are **another result of having a health program.**
Old to new:	In addition, **a health program results** *in substantial savings by reducing insurance claims and premiums.*

Now, here is the Practice paragraph revised to have *old to new information flow:*

> **By implementing health and safety programs for employees,** *a corporation can reap multiple rewards.* **A comprehensive occupational health program** *reduces absenteeism, increases productivity, and improves employee morale.* In addition, **a health program** *results in substantial savings by reducing insurance claims and premiums.*

You may have noticed that the topic "health and safety programs" has changed subtly in its form though not in its meaning. This variation in form adds creativity and keeps the writing from being monotonous.

Composing and Editing: The Process of Writing Paragraphs

When composing, do not concern yourself with writing cohesive, coherent paragraphs. Also, as you get your ideas on the page, don't be concerned about information flow; you may find yourself first capturing new information and then linking it to the old. You are still learning about your topic; organize and prioritize your ideas when you edit and revise.

When composing, you may write several sentences before writing your topic sentence, the sentence that best captures your topic. You will know your topic sentence partly because it

WORKING AND LEARNING IN TEAMS

One Step at a Time How do proofreading, editing, and revising differ?

- When you *proofread,* correct the grammar, punctuation, spelling, and word usage. Proofreading is part of the editing process, but it also stands on its own: proofreading is the final—and critical—step in producing any document.

- When you *edit,* improve the flow by changing the wording as well as cutting unnecessary words and phrases. Do not edit as you compose; edit your draft periodically as a break from composing.

- When you *revise,* change the way the ideas are presented on the page. Move sentences to make sure the major parts of the document do what they are supposed to do.

Intertwine revising and editing as your document grows. Then do one final revision check before you proofread for accuracy.

A word of caution: If someone asks you to proofread a document and instead you edit or revise it, you may be disappointed by the response you get. Many people do not like to have their work edited or revised.

TEAM EFFORT

With a partner, review the process memos you produced for Activity 6 in Chapter 1 and for Activity 1 in Chapter 2. Proofread each other's work, marking errors in grammar, punctuation, spelling, and word usage. After you are finished, return the memos and discuss with your partner anything that you wanted to revise but didn't because this is not an editing exercise.

crystallizes your insight and acts as an umbrella for the details of your topic. When you edit, tag your topic sentence and move it to the beginning of your paragraph. Then work through the paragraph sentence by sentence to adjust the information flow and create a topic string. You may need to cut some sentences and move others. *Cutting is the painful part of editing!*

Even though your objective is cohesive and coherent paragraphs, you cannot follow a recipe: A paragraph cannot be defined by a specific number of sentences or words and cannot be designed by a formula. Good paragraphs relate more to art than to science. Each paragraph is unique, and its development depends on its content and the meaning you create and convey.

PRACTICE

1. Follow these steps to revise the information flow in the paragraph below: (a) Identify the topic sentence and topic string. (b) If a sentence is not part of the topic string, remove it. (c) Adjust the information flow so that old information (or the main topic) introduces new information.

   Our corporation implemented a health and safety program and had good results. Employees were encouraged to take an active role to prevent disease in our new program. A health center was provided by this innovative program where employees could conveniently get daily aerobic exercise and weight training. Periodic tests to monitor blood pressure, cholesterol, and triglycerides were also provided as part of the package. Some employees did not set aside the time to participate in the program. Within one year, a significant percentage of employees had reduced risk factors for heart disease.

2. Write a two- or three-paragraph memo to your instructor about one of the following concepts:

   - *Editing sentences:* What principles can be applied to create simple, clear, and concise sentences?

   - *Today's news:* What interesting business developments have you recently read or heard about?

   - *Your objectives:* What are your career goals? What kind of job do you want to have two years from now?

   Compose freely until you get your main ideas on the page. Then look for the sentence that best captures the essence of your paragraph (your topic sentence). Move your topic sentence to the beginning of the paragraph, and edit each sentence so that it is simple, clear, and concise. Does each sentence relate to the topic sentence? If not, edit it out or use it to start a new paragraph.

 SECTION A: CONCEPT CHECK

1. When building a paragraph, where should you move the sentence that best captures the essence of your topic?

2. When evaluating the "flow" of your paragraph, should you arrange information from new to old or from old to new?

3. Two words that describe well-written paragraphs are *cohesive* and *coherent.* What does each quality entail?

■ SECTION B: ELIMINATING EMPTY INFORMATION

As previously discussed, information flow relates to old and new information, but there's another important element: **empty information.** Empty information consists of words, phrases, sentences, and maybe even paragraphs that add no value for your reader. Here is a summary of the three types of information to control when editing:

- *Old information:* information that is obvious or that the reader already knows.
- *New information:* information that you wish to convey to the reader.
- *Empty information:* information that adds nothing of value for your reader.

At first glance, empty information may seem like an irrelevant category. However, writers often include empty information on the way to discovering their message. While editing, a writer needs to identify key points and evaluate the message from the reader's point of view. Information that is insignificant to the reader should be cut.

Joseph Williams, author of *Style: Toward Clarity and Grace,* identifies various types of unnecessary information.[1] Williams uses the term **meta-discourse** for the language a writer uses to describe his or her own thinking process. A great deal of meta-discourse is empty information. Here are some types of meta-discourse to avoid:

- Background thinking
- Your opinions and beliefs
- Reader's perception
- Hedges and emphatics
- Fillers and tag-ons

Background Thinking

Background thinking can be defined as *how* you arrived at your conclusions. Explaining background thinking is different from explaining an issue or giving evidence to support a point. Here is an example:

Poorly worded:

After giving much thought to our discussion about product innovation, I realized I might find some answers by doing some informal research. I first called several of our colleagues, but none of them had heard of the product. Although I was discouraged, I continued to search. That's when I realized that I could go right to the source to find the information. I checked out our competitor's Web site and found out that they will be putting a similar product on the market this summer.

Revised:

After our discussion, I checked our competitor's Web site. They already have a product similar to the one that we discussed, and it will be on the market this summer.

Your Opinions and Beliefs

You do not need to tell how you feel about the points you make. When you can, delete phrases such as *I think, I feel,* and *I believe.* Sometimes these phrases make writers sound indecisive. Get right to the point.

Weak:	**Revised:**
I think that this is an issue worth pursuing.	This issue is worth pursuing.
I believe we ought to go ahead with the project.	We ought to go ahead with the project.
I feel that now is the time to address the issue.	The time to address the issue is now.

However, leaving out *I believe, I think,* and *I feel* will change the tone of your document. Some writers may choose to soften the tone by leaving them in. (In such situations, it is still a good idea to avoid overusing "I" statements.)

Also, at times you may use these phrases in conjunction with someone else's position. Rather than boldly telling someone what to do, you can soften the tone and sound less assuming by leaving in the "I" statements. For example:

I believe this issue is important to you.
I think you should go to the meeting.
I feel you should consider the proposal.

Otherwise, your comments might sound as if you are ordering someone to do something rather than offering your advice. For example, these revisions may sound too bold:

Go to the meeting.
Consider the proposal.

Reader's Perceptions

Do not tell your reader *how* to interpret your message; such comments may give the reader the impression that you are unsure of your message or that you lack confidence. Thus, remove phrases or sentences that tell your readers *how you think* they will react. For example:

Poorly worded:
I'm not sure if you will be interested in the information in this message, but I am sending it along just in case this could help you with the current project you are working on. I know you are under the wire to make progress with a project relating to our New York office. So, in case you don't already know this, I'd like to let you know that the New York office has a new district manager, and her name is Sylvia Reynolds.

Revised:
Good luck with your work on the New York project. Did you know our New York office has a new district manager? Her name is Sylvia Reynolds.

Poorly worded:
You may already be aware of the information I am sending in this message. If it is the case that you already know this, please forgive me for taking up your valuable time with another unnecessary message. I believe that by reviewing this, you will be more equipped to make a decision in regard to our sales staff and the use of rental vehicles. I have just discovered that our company can rent vehicles at a discount if we do so in minimum numbers of 25 rentals per month.

Revised:
Since you are working with the sales staff, you may be interested to know that we can rent vehicles at a discount if we rent at least 25 a month.

Hedges and Emphatics

Joseph Williams also encourages writers to use hedges and emphatics sparingly.[2] A **hedge** qualifies a statement; an **emphatic** "supposedly" places emphasis on the word it describes. Getting rid of hedges and emphatics will make your point stand out more. As Robert Browning said, *less is more*. Here are some common hedges *to avoid:*

kind of	may be	for all intents and purposes
sort of	perhaps	to a certain extent
rarely	rather	supposedly
hardly	in my opinion	usually
at times	more or less	often

tend	possibly	almost always
sometimes	probably	and so on
maybe	seemingly	

Weak:

For all intents and purposes, listening is an important part of communicating. Listening *may* help you connect with your audience by understanding *some of* their needs. By becoming a better listener, *to a certain extent* you become a better communicator, *at least in my opinion.*

Below are some common emphatics; *use them sparingly* or they will detract from the meaning.

very	certainly	totally
most	inevitably	it is quite clear that
many	as you can plainly see	as you may already know
often	as everyone is aware	undoubtedly
literally	as you know	first and foremost
virtually	always	and so on
usually	each and every time	

Weak:

As everyone knows, listening is a *really* important part of communicating. Listening *certainly* helps you connect with your audience by understanding *most, if not all, of* their needs. By becoming a better listener, you *literally* become a better communicator, *as you may already know.*

Without the hedges and emphatics, here is the short paragraph:

Revised:

Listening is an important part of communicating. Listening helps you connect with your audience by understanding their needs. By becoming a better listener, you become a better communicator.

Fillers and Tag-Ons

Fillers are empty words and add no value to your message. Two words that are often inserted as fillers in speech and writing are *just* and *like:*

| **Incorrect:** | She *like just* said that we could *like* go to the meeting. |
| **Correct:** | She said that we could go to the meeting. |

| **Incorrect:** | I *just like* went to the meeting before *like* I knew it was canceled. |
| **Correct:** | I went to the meeting before I knew it was canceled. |

In addition to fillers, pay attention to **tag-ons.** Sentences should not end in unnecessary prepositions; at times, speakers and writers place a preposition unnecessarily at the end of a sentence as a tag-on. Tag-ons are grammatically incorrect. The word *at* is a common tag-on:

| **Incorrect:** | Where do you work *at?* |
| **Correct:** | Where do you work? |

Incorrect:	Where did you go to school *at?*
Correct:	Where did you go to school?

Which unnecessary words do you repetitively put in your speech or writing? Have you ever used words such as *like, just,* or *totally* unnecessarily? Do you have a tendency to use these words when you are feeling confident, or are you more likely to use them when you are unsure of yourself? Is this use an unconscious habit?

Some people refer to such habits of speech as "Valley girl talk"; however, they are common in all parts of the country. In social situations, using fillers and tag-ons is acceptable. However, if you use these types of expressions in a social situation, you are likely to carry over the habit into a business environment. Consistently using fillers and tag-ons in the business world can affect the way more sophisticated speakers judge your talent.

SECTION B: CONCEPT CHECK

1. Write a short paragraph that leads to a valid point but is filled with empty meta-discourse.

2. Revise the paragraph so that you get right to the point.

3. Identify common hedges, emphatics, fillers, and tag-ons.

4. Write a few sentences that contain unnecessary hedges, fillers, or tag-ons: you *might like just* work *kind of* hard on this one, but you will see results! Now, edit out the empty words so that each sentence states its point concisely.

5. Write a few sentences that include emphatics: *really, really try* to make your point! Now edit out the emphatics so that your message is clear.

■ SECTION C: REVISING

Revising deals with *substance* as well as *structure*. You are reshaping content on the basis of meaning, putting the most important information first. With paragraphs, you are moving the best-written and most comprehensive sentence to the topic-sentence position. On a larger scale, you are moving your most relevant information to the beginning, clearly stating your purpose up front.

Revising is a *re-visioning* process. According to writing instructor Cathy Dees, revising is "reseeing, rethinking, questioning, rewriting, and re-creating. Revising is recursive; it is a cycle."[3] Being a cyclical process, revising requires that you recycle your thinking; you must see your material with fresh eyes and an open mind and set new priorities to restructure the content.

Revising demands that you shed some of your original thinking; it also demands that you shed some well-constructed sentences and paragraphs that do not add value. Cutting is painful; you worked hard to sculpt ideas and shape paragraphs that you now discover do not add strength to your document.

Here are some factors in the revising process:

- *Re-visioning:* Step back and evaluate your document and its purpose. Has your vision shifted? Does your thesis or purpose statement still capture the essence of your document? What are your main points? Can your reader readily identify your main points? Rethink your content on the basis of what you now understand.

- *Questioning:* Questions are the doorways to answers; continue to probe and explore your content. Are there gaps in your thinking? Have you developed your thinking beyond first responses or superficial ones? Are you overly attached to an answer that may not be complete? Are you trying to make answers fit where they don't? Change is inherent in the thinking process, and answers will change as your thinking evolves.

- *Identifying critical issues:* When your content is familiar, you are ready to prioritize key points. Have you presented critical information first? Do you need to reorganize information or eliminate empty information? What is relevant to your readers, and what adds clutter? Highlight the most important information by presenting it first.

- *Rewriting:* On the basis of a new perspective, you may need to rewrite parts of your document. First drafts are the most difficult because the content is unfamiliar. When the topic becomes familiar, ideas flow and writing becomes easier. Your deeper understanding will reflect your new vision.

Even successful writers sometimes take their own words too seriously, thinking there is one "right way" to state information. Most ideas can be stated in many different ways, each having a slightly different effect on the reader. It's a matter of syntax and choice.

An important skill in revising is presenting the same information in different ways and understanding how readers might be affected by the differences. Once you capture an idea in writing, you have completed the most difficult part of the process. Try not to become attached to a specific sentence.

To loosen up your revising skills, let's examine how to write the same information in different ways. The following six sentences all present the same information:

We would like to convey our appreciation for your assistance with the discrepancy in our account.

Thank you for helping us to correct the misinformation in our account.

We appreciate your help with the problem in our account.

Your help with our account was valuable, and we appreciate it.

The valuable assistance you gave us with our account is appreciated.

Please accept our appreciation for your assistance with the discrepancy in our account.

With which of the above sentences would you have started your letter? Why did you choose that sentence? Could you have stated the same information in a more effective way?

Here's another example:

The accumulation of funds in your checking account is not sufficient to cover recent activity such as checks and withdrawals.

Your checking account does not have sufficient funds.

You need to deposit funds into your checking account.

Your withdrawals have exceeded the amount of funds in your checking account.

Your checking account is overdrawn.

PRACTICE

Instructions: Revise each of the sentences below in three or four ways. Use principles you have learned to make changes; for example, change voice (active or passive), turn nominals into verbs or verbs into nominals, change the point of view, and add or eliminate redundancy. You may even add words to improve the tone (such as words of appreciation or apology) or turn one sentence into two sentences.

As you work through these sentences, analyze the changes you are making. Be creative; your goal is *variety,* not clarity.

1. An incorrect invoice was accidentally sent to you last week by our accounting department.

   _____

   _____

   _____

   _____

2.   Your position for a sales representative is of interest to me.

_____

_____

_____

_____

_____

_____

3.   George was not in attendance at the meeting.

_____

_____

_____

_____

4.   An omission was inadvertently made in your order, and the items in question are being sent to you immediately.

_____

_____

_____

_____

_____

_____

_____

Basic Structure: The Beginning, Middle, and End

All documents, even short ones, have a beginning, a middle, and an end. It might sound trite to discuss this topic; however, many writers think basic structure applies only to longer documents or formal ones.

- The *beginning* of any document should connect your purpose with your reader. With short, informal documents, the beginning sets the tone of the message. Thus, beginnings are important even with the shortest, simplest documents, such as e-mail. Of course, with formal documents, the introduction is critical and must be developed meticulously.

- The *middle* contains the body of evidence and examples that support your purpose, validating its relevance. If a bit of information does not support your purpose, cut it. Every time you give the reader excess or irrelevant information, it diminishes your purpose.

- The *ending* brings closure for the reader and indicates next steps, defining action for the reader and/or writer. For formal documents, the ending should tie back to the problem initially posed in the introduction. The conclusion may reveal new questions for readers to explore, opening the door for further discussion and research. For informal documents such as e-mail, you may bring closure in much simpler ways by ending with a short closing.

For writing an academic essay, some writing models recommend a specific number of paragraphs. For example, a five-paragraph essay would include one paragraph for an introduction, three for the body, and one for the conclusion. This model may be a good point of reference for academic writing; however, for business writing, no writing model provides such an absolute formula.

In business, all writing must be tailored for its purpose, which varies from piece to piece. The number of paragraphs will vary from document to document. Whether you are writing a business letter, an e-mail, a memo, a proposal, or a research paper, the purpose will determine its length and format.

FIGURE 3.1 | E-Mail Format

Electronic messaging is one of the most common forms of communication in business. Although memos are used only for internal clients, e-mail is sent to both internal and external clients. An e-mail is more casual than a business letter.

To: The name or names of those to whom you are sending the e-mail

Cc: The names of those who will receive courtesy copies

Subject: A few words that reflect the purpose and content of the e-mail

An e-mail is like a phone call in that you should respond within a day or two. Try to keep the body of an e-mail short, one screen if possible.

Use correct grammar and punctuation. Also, do not take unorthodox shortcuts: follow standard rules for capitalization, and do not abbreviate unnecessarily. Keep information short and to the point. Also, don't press the send button if you have any doubts about your message. If you feel unsure, either save your message as a draft or make a phone call.

Let's review the purpose of each part.

Introduction:

- States the purpose and provides an overview.
- Explains why the purpose is relevant.
- Connects the reader to the purpose.
- At times, poses questions.

Body:

- Breaks the topic into component parts.
- Covers all main points.
- Supports main points with evidence, examples, and details.
- Answers questions that may be posed in the introduction.

Conclusion:

- Summarizes and draws conclusions for readers.
- Clarifies and restates main points.
- Reinforces the introduction, solidly establishing the purpose.
- At times, reveals new questions and suggests additional research.

The introduction is usually the most difficult part of any document to write. A good beginning captures the essence of the entire document, but you may be unclear about your purpose when you begin to write. Once you have composed your document, your purpose should be clear and meaningful to you. Let's take a moment to examine how this relates to the process of writing.

Process and Structure

While you are composing, the easiest place to start writing is the part of your document that reflects your current understanding of the topic. Thus, you may wish to start writing the body of a document before writing the introduction. In the body, you are immersed in research, discovering the main points of your topic. As you develop the body of evidence and evaluate data, your thinking will evolve. The insights you gain will lead to the conclusion. After writing the conclusion, your purpose will be clear to you; you can now articulate it clearly to your audience.

When you finally have a deep understanding of why your topic is relevant, you may even feel intense about what you have learned. Translate this excitement to your introduction; this critical piece sets the stage for how the reader will perceive everything that follows. If you wrote your introduction first, go back and read it freshly now that the body and conclusion are completed. Does your introduction capture your vision?

We will now examine how to structure information through a model. Though writing shouldn't follow a recipe, a model can help you organize your ideas as you are composing and revising.

The PEER Model

You are familiar with peer editing, but now *peer* will be used to assist you in structuring information. Rather than relying on "introduction, body, and conclusion," the **PEER model** breaks down each part on the basis of purpose. Use this model during the composing or revising stage of writing for documents of any length.

If you loosely apply the PEER model as you compose, your content will be somewhat structured before you revise. The letters in *PEER* correspond to the four elements of the model:

P   What is your *purpose*? What *points* are you making, and why are they relevant?

E   What *evidence* demonstrates your main points? What are the facts and details?

E   What *explanation* do you need to make, or what *examples* do you need to provide so that the reader understands the evidence and its significance?

R   What are your *recommendations* for your reader? *Recap* the main points and draw conclusions for the reader.

By breaking down each part according to purpose, the PEER model can serve as a memory tool. Use it as a self-check to ensure that you have developed all relevant aspects of your documents. Here is how the paragraph on health and safety programs (see the Practice on page 92) breaks down:

Purpose:	By implementing health and safety programs for employees, a corporation can reap multiple rewards.
Evidence and examples:	The results of a comprehensive health program include reduced absenteeism, increased productivity, and improved employee morale. In addition, a health program results in substantial savings and reduced insurance premiums.
Recap:	Thus, consider adding a health and safety program to your existing employee benefit program.

When you are composing, use the PEER elements as *side headings,* or a page map, as you rough out your ideas. When you are revising, make sure you have developed each aspect of your topic, giving specific evidence and adequate examples.

EXPLORE

Instructions: Read an article in a recent publication and summarize it. Use the PEER model as a template to organize and prioritize your ideas as you read and compose.

 **SECTION C: CONCEPT CHECK**

1. What are some of the factors in the revising process?

2. What are the basic parts of a business message? What information is contained within these parts?

3. Describe the PEER model by identifying its elements.

■ SECTION D: USING TRANSITIONS AND CONNECTORS

Transitions are important because readers need to make connections to find meaning. Good writing makes those connections for the reader through transitional words, phrases, sentences, and even paragraphs. Transitions enable the reader's thinking to follow along with the writer's intention. At times, readers may argue with a narrative because the writer has not drawn a sufficient connection between ideas. When good transitions are missing, the reader may need to stop, question the meaning, and reread a section.

Think of transitions as connectors: they are the elements that bridge ideas between sentences and paragraphs. After a short review of transitional words, we will examine larger transitions, such as transitional phrases, sentences, and paragraphs.

Conjunctions as Connectors

The three types of conjunctions (adverbial, coordinating, and subordinating) function as transitions and connectors. Since these were covered in previous chapters, only a few points are included here on using conjunctions as transitional words and connectors.

* **Adverbial conjunctions** provide transitions between sentences and paragraphs. Each signals the meaning of the ideas that follow; here are some of the roles adverbial conjunctions play:

Contrasting:	however, nevertheless, conversely, on the other hand
Drawing attention:	indeed, accordingly, as usual, in any event
Adding information:	furthermore, in addition, also, what is more, moreover
Drawing a conclusion:	consequently, as a result, therefore, thus, of course, in general
Concluding:	in summary, in conclusion, finally
Illustrating:	for example, for instance
Showing reaction:	fortunately, unfortunately, regrettably
Summarizing:	in short, in summary

* **Subordinating conjunctions** define the relationship between ideas. The subordinating conjunction shows an inequality between ideas, highlighting one idea over another. Here are a few common subordinating conjunctions and their roles:

Contrasting:	even though, although, if, whereas, though
Indicating time:	after, before, while, as soon as, during, as, when, until
Drawing a conclusion:	whereas, since, because, unless, so that, in order that

* **Coordinating conjunctions** also provide transitions between ideas. These conjunctions can help smooth the flow of choppy writing. Each coordinating conjunction defines a different relationship between ideas; for example:

  And: similar to *as well as;* implies an addition.

  But: similar to *however;* implies a *contrast.*

  Yet: similar to *even though;* implies an exception.

* **Correlative conjunctions** are pairs of conjunctions that add power to the connection because they place emphasis on the comparing or contrasting aspect of it. Here are the common pairs:

either . . . or

neither . . . nor

both . . . and

not . . . but

not only . . . but also

When conjunctions come in pairs, the structure following the second part of the correlative must be parallel with the first part. Therefore, you must create parallel structure, or your writing will be *not only* grammatically incorrect *but also* choppy. For example:

Incorrect: We will *not only* service your account *but also* are providing monthly reports.

Incorrect: We *not only* will service your account *but also* provide monthly reports.

Corrected: We will *not only* service your account *but also* provide monthly reports.

Incorrect: The messenger *neither* brought the new product line *nor* the samples.

Corrected: The messenger *neither* brought the new product line *nor* brought the samples.

Corrected: The messenger brought *neither* the new product line *nor* the samples.

PRACTICE

1. Correct the following sentences for parallel structure.

   a. My manager said that our department will not only break sales records but also will surpass quality standards.

      _____

      _____

   b. Neither Margaret will go to the meeting nor George.

      _____

      _____

   c. Sam will either deliver the proposal on time or he will not.

      _____

      _____

2. Write three sentences demonstrating *incorrect use* of correlative conjunctions. Share them with a partner, who will correct the structure. Then reverse roles.

   a. _____

   b. _____

   c. _____

Transitions to Add Flow

You may already use transitional elements effectively but not be aware of it. The objective now is for you to use transitions consciously and purposefully. Without transitions, writing is choppy because no connections are drawn for the reader. Here is how choppy writing can get without transitions:

Weak:

We left for the off-site meeting at 11 o'clock. No one remembered to bring directions. Mark had been there before. He remembered how to find the correct location. The meeting had already started when we arrived. Not much had happened yet.

How boring and monotonous. Even without being aware of transitions, a novice writer puts them in. Once you become aware of the function of connectors, you can consciously control how you use them. With transitions, you can combine sentences to achieve rich ideas and maintain an effective flow. Here is the paragraph above with transitions added:

Revised:
We left for the off-site meeting at 11 o'clock, but no one remembered to bring directions. Fortunately, Mark had been there before, and he remembered how to find the correct location. The meeting had already started when we arrived, but not much had happened yet.

Here's another possible revision:

We left for the off-site meeting at 11 o'clock. However, no one remembered to bring directions. Because Mark had been there before, he remembered how to find the correct location. Even though the meeting had already started when we arrived, not much had happened yet.

Phrases as Transitions and Connectors

A *phrase* is a group of words without a subject and verb (whereas a *clause* has both a subject and a verb). Phrases can function as transitions for clauses. When a prepositional or verbal phrase (gerund, infinitive, participial) introduces a main clause, the phrase defines the context for the clause that follows it.

Prepositional Phrases   A *preposition* is a connective that shows a relationship between ideas. Here are some common prepositions: *to, from, by, with, between, before, after,* and *during,* among others. The following are examples of **prepositional phrases** used as introductory connectors:

> *During that time,* we welcomed their suggestions.
> *After the game,* Bill wanted to resume the meeting.
> *Between the two of them,* Martin always had more work.
> *From that time on,* they never asked us another question.

Of course, when a prepositional phrase is used as an introductory phrase, a complete sentence must follow.

PRACTICE

1. In the sentences below, use connectors to bridge ideas. Develop two or three different versions for each set.

    a. We will review the feedback. We will not immediately suggest changes.

        _____

        _____

        _____

    b. Our company has changed its mission. Our brochures need to be updated.

        _____

        _____

        _____

Building Bridges: *Transitions connect ideas between sentences and paragraphs, thereby making it easier for the reader to follow along. When the transition is not smooth, or simply is not there at all, what is the effect on the person who receives the message?*

c. The conference was canceled. Several members protested.

_____

_____

_____

2. Revise (or rewrite) the paragraph below by adding transitions and adjusting the information flow; you may change words as well as add or delete information.

The shipment of designer jeans had not arrived at our Pittsburgh outlet. Several customers called to complain that the jeans were not in stock. A national sales campaign had promoted the brand intensely. Sales were negatively affected. Customer relations were jeopardized. Customers could not purchase the jeans. The jeans were not in stock. TV and newspaper ads ran a promotional price. The ads promised an abundant supply of jeans were in stock.

_____

_____

_____

_____

_____

Gerund Phrases **Gerund phrases** often function as introductory connectors. (A _gerund_ is the "ing" form of a verb that is used as a noun.) Here are examples of gerund phrases that could be used as introductory phrases:

Walking into the meeting late, Jeff stumbled and dropped his papers.
Stopping to speak to employees, the president developed increased rapport.
Finding the key on the ground, the director immediately chastised the staff.
Listening with great intent, the instructor nodded compassionately.

When a gerund phrase begins a sentence, be careful to construct the sentence correctly. Not only must a subject and verb follow the phrase, but the subject of the sentence must also be the subject of the phrase.

PRACTICE

Instructions: The sentences below have introductory gerund phrases. To correct the errors, you will need to rewrite part of each sentence. Your goal is either to turn the phrase into a clause (with a subject and verb) or to make the subject of the phrase the subject of the independent clause. For example:

Incorrect: Arriving late to the interview, the résumé was not in Linda's briefcase.
Corrected: Arriving late to the interview, Linda could not find her résumé in her briefcase.

1. Running across the hallway, the copy paper fell from the assistant's hands.

_____

2. Waiting impatiently, the résumé of the applicant became crumpled.

_____

3. Causing a commotion in the hallway, the security guard asked the visitors to leave.

_____

4. Filling the cup to the brim, the hot coffee spilled on Allana's desk.

_____

5. Leaving his attaché case in the taxi, it was 10 o'clock before Mark reached his office.

_____

COACHING TIP

Ernest Hemingway's Quest Ernest Hemingway had an unusual quest: he had an obsession to write what he considered "one good sentence." Although the world of literature is graced by many of his eloquent pieces, he was never completely satisfied by the work he produced. In his quest to write one good sentence, he refined his writing and brought it to standards rarely reached.

Hemingway reminds us that writing is a skill that a person never completely masters.

Infinitive Phrases   **Infinitive phrases** can also be used to introduce clauses. (An *infinitive* is the base form of the verb plus the word *to*.) For example:

To go to the conference, he first had to complete his presentation.
To communicate effectively, a person must express feeling behind the words.
To show compassion, Jasmine sent her heartbroken colleague a bundle of roses.
To avoid a confrontation, Rodney called Alex before the meeting.

As with gerund phrases, when an infinitive phrase begins a sentence, place the subject of the phrase immediately after the phrase.

PRACTICE

Instructions: Find the errors in the sentences below and correct them. You may need to select a subject that is not in the sentence, such as "you understood." To determine the subject, identify who is the subject of the infinitive phrase; you may need to reword the entire sentence. For example:

Incorrect: To arrive on time, it was urgent that Jim leave immediately.
Corrected: To arrive on time, Jim needed to leave immediately.

1.   To fill out the application form, a pen was needed.

_____

2.   To succeed in life, your dreams should not be abandoned.

_____

3.   To find an answer, another book should be referenced.

_____

4.   To get the job, a good interview is a prerequisite.

_____

5.   To finish the assignment, the resource must be cited.

_____

INTERNET EXERCISE 3.2

Editing Tools Need more practice with editing and revising, or are you just looking for a little software support as a backup? To hone your skills as well as familiarize yourself with the benefits and drawbacks of spelling- and grammar-checking software, visit the *Foundations of Business Communication* Web site at <http://www.mhhe.com/djyoung>.

Once you have accessed the home page, select "Student Activities" and then click the Chapter 3 link to get started.

Transitional Sentences and Paragraphs

Transitional sentences and paragraphs relate to information flow; they connect old information to new information on a broad level. **Transitional sentences** provide logical connections between paragraphs. The transitional sentence glances forward and links the topic of one paragraph with the main idea of the next. Transitional sentences prepare the reader to understand the content of the next paragraph by "seeding" the purpose of that paragraph. By the time the reader reaches the new paragraph, key ideas are already familiar. Here are examples of transitional sentences:

In the next section, a detailed analysis will demonstrate the strengths and weaknesses of the model employed in our study.

Next we will show how communication relates to corporate success.

Although production waste relates to the economy, it also relates to the environment.

In addition to transitional sentences, transitional paragraphs play an important role for readers. **Transitional paragraphs** need to achieve two purposes:

*   Summarize the key ideas of the current section.
*   Indicate how the major theme of the document will be developed in the next section.

Here are some transitional paragraphs:

The educational reform process enabled the faculty to make effective curriculum changes. The new construct of general education reflected a common understanding of courses and adapted content to our unique educational environment. The evolving curriculum also brought us closer to achieving the aims and purposes of general education within our stated mission, which is discussed in the next section.[4]

This chapter discusses several of Deming's famous 14 points, known as the Deming Management Method, as they relate to workforce diversity and managing change. . . . The following sections discuss barriers that can limit an institution's performance: poorly implemented management systems, disrespectful and fearful work environments, interdepartmental antagonism, and weak leadership.[5]

 SECTION D: CONCEPT CHECK

Find transitional sentences and paragraphs in papers that you have written (for this class or other classes), textbooks, and newspapers. Then answer these questions:

1. Do some transitions seem awkward to you? Identify why that might be.
2. Are there cases where an abrupt transition is acceptable, even necessary?
3. How do the transitions in your papers compare with the textbook transitions?

SUMMARY

In this chapter, you learned more about editing and revising paragraphs. A paragraph is a group of sentences that develop a controlling idea (or specific line of thought) in a logical way. Two words that describe effective paragraphs are *cohesive* and *coherent*.

In cohesive paragraphs, each sentence contains a thread of a common element that holds them together. The common thread is introduced in the topic sentence and is developed through a topic string.

In coherent paragraphs, information flows logically. To adjust a paragraph for information flow, move your most effective sentence to the topic-sentence position at the beginning of the paragraph. Then make sure that each sentence starts with the familiar and extends the reader's knowledge to the unfamiliar. Sentences that contain only old information will not extend the reader's knowledge and should be revised or eliminated. Sentences that contain only new information will seem overwhelming to the reader; they should be edited so that the new information connects with familiar information.

You are now familiar with many principles that enable you to edit sentences and revise paragraphs effectively. In the next unit of this text, you will work on longer, complete documents such as letters, memos, and e-mail.

CHAPTER 3 CHECKLIST

Have you screened your paragraphs for the following?
___ Cohesiveness (staying on one topic)
___ Coherent flow (controlling for information flow)
___ Topic sentence
___ Topic string
___ Information flow: old to new
___ Elimination of empty information:
     Background thinking
     Your opinions and beliefs
     Hedges and emphatics
     Fillers and tag-ons
___ Structure: beginning, middle, and end
___ Transitions and connectors

Have you screened your sentences for the following?
___ Change complicated words to simpler words.
___ Cut empty and redundant words.
___ Change passive voice to active voice.
___ Correct for parallel structure.
___ Align modifiers correctly.
___ Place the subject and verb close to each other and the beginning of the sentence.
___ Limit sentence length to no more than 22 words.
___ Connect information through transitions: connective words, phrases, and sentences.
___ Control information flow by building on old or familiar information that leads to new information.

END-OF-CHAPTER ACTIVITIES

ACTIVITY 1: PROCESS MEMO

Instructions: Select a paragraph you have written for this or another class. Edit and revise your paragraph, and then write a process memo describing what you did to produce a more effective product: what principles of editing or revising did you apply? If you have Internet access, you can complete this exercise online at <http://www.mhhe.com/djyoung> and then send an e-mail to your instructor.

ACTIVITY 2: TEAM ACTIVITY

Instructions: With a partner, spend 3 minutes each discussing part- or full-time work experience. If you have not yet held a paying job, discuss volunteer work or your hobbies and interests.

    When you are finished interviewing each other, write a short paragraph discussing your partner's experience. Assume that you have conducted an informal interview and are passing the information on to a colleague who is looking for an assistant to do light office work.

ACTIVITY 3: ALL PRO TEMPS

Instructions: All Pro Temps is trying to beef up its staff. An e-mail promotion allows interested job seekers to apply to the company via e-mail. Write an e-mail to Sydney Milestone (address: smilestone@allprotemps.com), director of human resources, summarizing your skills and talents. Keep the message short; highlight your skills and qualities in only one or two paragraphs.

ACTIVITY 4: EDITING SENTENCES

When you revise paragraphs, you must do more than adjust for information flow to ensure cohesive, coherent paragraphs. To make your writing clear and powerful, you must also edit paragraphs at the sentence level so that the writing is simple, clear, and concise.

Instructions: Revise the following sentences by removing nominals and putting them in the active voice:

Weak: The explanation of why the date was changed was given by the president of the company.

Revised: The president of the company explained why the date was changed.

1. Management of the account is the responsibility of the account holder.

   _____

   _____

2. Our department's implementation of the new dress policy occurred last August.

   _____

3. A suggestion was made by our auditing department that December meetings be rescheduled.

   _____

4. Should we expect a call from the broker with information about when our insurance took effect?

   _____

5. Will there be a discussion of the new account process at our next team meeting?

   _____

ACTIVITY 5: EDITING AND REVISING

Instructions: Revise the following sentences for active and passive voice, parallel structure, and information flow (old to new). Also cut empty information, such as hedges and emphatics, as well as outdated expressions.

Weak: Per our discussion, the pilot project is a really good idea.

Revised: As we discussed, the pilot project is a good idea.

1. Our department had a really good meeting this morning about some really interesting topics.

   _____

   _____

2. Investment portfolios were discussed by Gerry at the meeting.

_____

_____

3. As per your recommendation, a follow-up call was made by myself to the human resources director.

_____

_____

4. At the Chicago Mercantile, where commodities are traded, investors make money and money is lost every day.

_____

_____

5. The implementation of new trading hours will occur at our branch offices next week.

_____

_____

6. Management training was one of the significant factors identified in the survey.

_____

_____

7. A survey was conducted by an organizational development specialist to gain an accurate view of our perceptions of ourselves.

_____

_____

8. My associate in finance is looking for someone to hire with experience in accounting and who has also done telemarketing.

_____

_____

9. The development of management skills in new hires is a key responsibility for the training department.

_____

_____

10. The expectation of our president is that we will make an acquisition of the Houston corporation by early fall.

_____

_____

ACTIVITY 6: TOPIC SENTENCES AND TOPIC STRINGS

Instructions: The paragraph below provides information about the Chicago Mercantile Exchange. From this information, write a topic sentence and develop a topic string. (You do not need to include all the information below in your paragraph.) Apply all the editing principles you have learned so far to write a cohesive, coherent paragraph (or two) that consists of three to five sentences.

The Chicago Mercantile Exchange (CME) is the largest futures exchange in the United States. Beef, dairy, hogs, and lumber are some of the commodities traded at the CME to this day. A futures exchange is a market where investors can protect against price changes in commodities and investments and even profit from those changes. Investors started trading in the fluctuating value of domestic and foreign currency in the 1970s. The CME was founded in 1898 as a not-for-profit corporation to protect investors from price changes in physical commodities. When it was first organized, most investors were farmers who wanted to protect themselves so that they would not lose their farms if the price of livestock dropped significantly before they could get them to market. Financial commodities, including equity indexes such as the S&P 500 and NASDAQ, are also traded at the CME.

_____

_____

_____

_____

_____

_____

_____

_____

_____

_____

ACTIVITY 7: ELIMINATING EMPTY INFORMATION

Instructions: In the paragraph below, cut empty and irrelevant background information. Your changes will assist the reader in getting right to the point. (Assume you are writing a short thank-you note to someone you interviewed about financial institutions.)

As per our discussion, I immediately began to research the Chicago Mercantile Exchange (also referred to as "the Merc"). Prior to our discussion, I didn't even know such financial exchanges even existed. I am very excited to learn more about the CME and even plan to visit it some day. You mentioned the Merc traded commodities other than beef and hogs but weren't sure what they were. Well, I was so motivated by our discussion that I visited its Web site and found out investors can also trade in T-bills as well as other equities. If you'd like to find out more about what the Merc is like today, you can visit its Web site at <http://www.cme.com>. Once again, thank you for telling me about the Chicago Mercantile Exchange and your part-time job as a runner when you were in college.

_____

_____

_____

_____

ACTIVITY 8: OLD TO NEW INFORMATION FLOW

Instructions: Revise the following paragraph by changing the information flow and adding transitions that relate to old information.

New members is something our investment club is seeking. We organized our investment club two years ago. We have been meeting once a month since then. Identifying stocks and bonds that we can agree to purchase is a goal for every meeting. We are waiving the initial orientation fee to generate interest in our club. Call me today if you are interested in joining our club and investing.

_____

_____

_____

_____

_____

ACTIVITY 9: EDITING REVIEW—WORDS AND SENTENCES

Instructions: Edit the following paragraphs.

1.

Qualities of an Effective Paragraph

A paragraph consists of a group of sentences that really only discuss one main topic. The presentation of the main topic is made in the topic sentence. The development of the topic occurs through a topic string. A paragraph is cohesive when it totally stays on the same topic. Old to new information flow is the deciding factor in making a paragraph more coherent. A specific number of sentences for a paragraph is not a requirement. There is no exact recipe in how a person should write a paragraph. Paragraphs are dependent on the content the writer is attempting to convey. A writer shouldn't jump from idea to idea when writing a paragraph. All of the sentences should absolutely support the topic sentence.

_____

_____

_____

_____

_____

_____

_____

_____

_____

2. You may include a list in your paragraph, if you choose.

Qualities of a Good Sentence

A sentence is a group of words that have a subject and a verb. It expresses a complete thought. The length of a sentence should be between 10 to 22 words. Only one main topic should be presented in a well written sentence. The active voice is often more effective than the passive voice. Avoid nominals by turning them into active verbs. You should try to keep the subject and verb close to each other. Maybe you should even try to keep the subject and verb close to the beginning of the sentence. The reader can become really confused if the subject and verb are way too far apart. Also remember to make an adjustment of the sentence for information flow. New information should occur subsequent to old information. That is some of the information about how to write an effective sentences, even though they will vary. And the bottom line is that sentences should be clear in meaning and correct.

_____
_____
_____
_____
_____
_____
_____
_____
_____
_____
_____

ACTIVITY 10: COMPOSING, EDITING, AND REVISING PARAGRAPHS

Instructions: Follow the steps outlined below:

1. Compose a paragraph about your perfect job.

2. Exchange your paragraph with a partner.

3. Edit your partner's paragraph, and explain why you made your selected changes.

4. What kinds of changes did your partner make with your paragraph?

REFERENCES

1. Joseph M. Williams, *Style: Toward Clarity and Grace,* The University of Chicago Press, 1990.

2. Ibid.

3. Cathy Dees, "Revision as Play: Crossing the Boundaries between Good and Better Business Prose," Association for Business Communication, 67th Annual Convention, Cincinnati, Ohio, October 25, 2002.

4. Dona Young, "General Education: Developing a Common Understanding," master's paper, The University of Chicago, June 1988, pp. 32-33.

5. Trisha Svehla and Glen C. Crosier, *Managing the Mosiac,* American Hospital Publishing, Inc., 1994, p. 75.

KEY TO LEARNING INVENTORY

1.	F	**6.**	F
2.	T	**7.**	b
3.	T	**8.**	T
4.	F	**9.**	F
5.	b and d	**10.**	F

Professional Communication

BusinessWeek | Watch What You Put in That Office E-Mail
As the dark side of messaging comes to light, here are some do's and don'ts to avoid landing in trouble.

Kellie Pelletier loathed many things about her boss in her former job as an associate at a division of the Smithsonian in Washington. The worst, though, was his habit of flaming Pelletier with e-mails jabbing her performance, which so exasperated her that she finally forwarded one to a friend, adding: "I hate him, I hate him, I hate him" in bold across the page. Then she got a sinking feeling. Was that "forward" she had pushed? Or "reply"? She found out soon enough—after her enraged boss hauled her into his manager's office. There, they were both called to task for their virtual gaffes.

Will we never learn? Seven years after it gained widespread acceptance in Corporate America, e-mail is encountering a backlash, fueled by a rash of research now emerging about its dark side: creating corporate embarrassment, undermining teamwork, draining employee energy, and breeding "toxic worry" by spreading miscommunication.

The criticism comes because so many of us are using e-mail improperly. Now it's blamed for fueling "conflict spirals" that escalate ill feeling at double the rate of face-to-face communiqués. Experts say this is due to the anonymous, remote nature of e-mail: It serves as a kind of psychological sandpaper that strips away the social veneer that keeps people in check. E-mail can also be a crutch for lame managers leery of confrontation.

While those may be the most egregious offenses, the subtler ones can also inflict damage. Perhaps the biggest mistake you can make, experts say, is replacing conversations with e-mail. One of e-mail's drawbacks is that it masquerades as communication when it is best used for informing, broadcasting, or scheduling. That's because real communication about job activities often depends upon real-time, face-to-face feedback, along with the vocal nuances that clarify intent. Interestingly, Siegel's research at large corporations has found that senior executives are the worst offenders in this regard. They often use e-mail to wield power—issuing orders, handing down edicts, and nitpicking workers' performance.

Experts advise people never to put anything sensitive or critical in an e-mail that touches on employees' self-esteem or job competence. Nor should you use it to give direction about a job activity or desired outcome if there is a risk of misinterpretation or political sensitivity. And when angry, remember: Keep your hands off your keyboard. E-mail's stripped-down, free-form nature sets off workers' hair-trigger responses and lends itself to venting rude behavior, much as road rage overtakes people in the bubble of their cars.

"People say things in e-mails they'd never say face to face," says Steven Currall, management professor at the Rice University Graduate School of Management in Houston.

You also don't want to make the common mistake of treating your account as if it were your personal mailbox. In other words, don't write anything to anyone unless you'd be happy having it blown up as an exhibit in court.

Source: Michelle Conlin, September 2002. For a full transcript of the article and additional questions, see the *Foundations of Business Communication* Web site at <http://www.mhhe.com/djyoung>.

EXPLORE

1. When a phone call would be the most effective way of communicating, why would you instead choose to send an e-mail? Does it save time?

2. Does the knowledge that your employer has a record of your time spent on the Internet affect what you put in your e-mail? Why or why not?

3. Are there times when you might want to have a record of all the e-mail you've sent while working at a particular company? What benefits can you see in having this kind of documentation? What drawbacks?

4. Consider your own experience with e-mail, memos, letters, or any other business correspondence. In terms of business communication, would you be comfortable "having it blown up as an exhibit in court"?

Office Communications

Words form the thread on which we string our experiences. —Aldous Huxley, novelist (1894–1963) ■

Only a few years ago, the daily life of a business professional was very different from what it is today. Executives had assistants who sometimes composed their letters or at least cleaned up the mechanical errors. Real people answered phones. Letters and memos followed a standard protocol, and everyone knew the rules.

Now a real person rarely answers the phone for someone else, and everyone entering the business world must write effectively. Communications have reached warp speed. The letter is no longer the most common form of business writing; e-mail is. With e-writing, most people expect a response the same day or the next; many responses occur within the same hour. Needless to say, professionals must make their own writing decisions quickly and effectively without assistance.

In this chapter, you will learn basic guidelines for structuring and formatting e-mail, business letters, memos and e-memos, and faxes. Since e-mail has replaced the business letter as the most common written communication tool, e-mail appears first in this chapter. Business professionals now use e-mail routinely to communicate with both internal and external clients, at times sending letters and other documents as attachments. In addition to learning guidelines for written correspondence, you will also examine the role of voice mail and learn how to prepare an effective voice mail message. Finally, you will evaluate which tools most effectively respond to specific business problems.

OBJECTIVES

When you have completed Chapter 4, you will be able to:

• Connect with your reader through the structure of e-mail and letters.

• Format and use e-mail, letters, memos, and faxes effectively.

• Apply the read/reflect/respond strategy to composing, editing, and revising messages.

• Shape correspondence into direct or indirect messages.

• Use the CTA format to structure business letters and the CAT format to structure e-mail messages.

• Plan effective voice mail messages.

Learning Inventory

1. In business, the letter is the most common type of written communication.   T/F
2. Professionals waste hours every day because they use e-mail ineffectively.   T/F
3. When a message contains bad news, the writer should get right to the point.   T/F
4. Which type of written communication includes next steps or action at the beginning of
   the message?

   a.   letters   c.   e-mail

   b.   memos   d.   faxes

5. Which three of the following are basic parts of a business letter?

   a.   dateline   d.   direct messages

   b.   typed signature   e.   salutation

   c.   next-day air

6. Give substantial information before stating the main point of an indirect letter.   T/F

7. For written documents, which of the following is true?

   a.   Use a direct approach to convey basic information.

   b.   Use an indirect approach to convey basic information.

8. Memos can be sent to internal and external clients.   T/F

9. E-mail can be sent to internal and external clients.   T/F

10. Which of the following communication options is most effective if you have an urgent message?

   a.   e-mail   c.   voice mail

   b.   fax   d.   business letter

■ SECTION A: E-MAIL

Though letters and memos are still critical business documents, the most common and demanding writing task today relates to *electronic messages,* or **e-mail.** When used effectively, e-mail enhances a busy professional's ability to communicate and solve problems. Information can be exchanged at a moment's notice.

However, just as e-mail can enhance getting a job done, e-mail also adds new challenges. When composing e-mail, writers must make effective decisions quickly. Decisions must also be objective: a business relationship can be severed with the push of a button. Communication mishaps usually relate to sending inappropriate or emotionally charged messages that express anger or frustration.

E-mail consumes a major portion of the average professional's time on the job, with many busy professionals wasting hours each day because they use e-mail inefficiently. First, many professionals are not confident about their writing skills and struggle to write effective messages.

FIGURE 4.1 | Effective E-Mail

Addressing E-Mail: *In an e-mail address, the information before the @ symbol identifies the name of the user of that address; the information after the @ symbol and before the period (referred to as a* dot*) is the name of the host computer; and the information after the dot identifies the top-level domain—for example,* .com *identifies a Web site as commercial.* How many different domains can you name, and what types of sites are found in them?

To: HereTodayGoneTomorrowInfo@netweb.com Cc: Carson D'Anca, President, Adulation Clothing Subject: Problems with Order 73126 Customer Service: Yesterday our store received a delivery of button-down shirts for men and women, Order 73126 from HTGT. There are a few items (6 pieces of the Abigail Blouse and 8 pieces of the Scale Shirt) that are questionable. The pattern on the fabric is much darker than it was in the showroom and looks splotchy. I've tried a couple of pieces on the store rack, and everybody is having a problem with the splotches. I'm hoping you'll be able to help us. Though Here Today Gone Tomorrow has a policy against refunds, a refund would be the ideal solution. If we could switch the questionable pieces for something else in your stock, that would be acceptable. I appreciate your prompt attention to this matter.   Elaine Gonzalez Inventory Manager Adulation Clothing, Ltd.

Second, when unclear and disorganized messages arrive, recipients take time and energy to disentangle information before crafting a response.

Businesses started using e-mail in the early '90s, and many business professionals had a difficult transition. Even today, most business professionals have not had formal training in using e-mail and have learned the hard way, making mistakes as they hone their skills. Used ineffectively, e-mail can create frustrations:

- Long, unedited messages are difficult to understand.

- Controversial messages provoke emotions.

- Messages unrelated to work waste time.

- Some e-mail is sent in lieu of another type of communication that would be more effective.

- Attachments are sent unnecessarily or without explanation.

- Untitled or inaccurately titled messages can be confusing as well as unethical and misleading at times.

- Inappropriate use of special features (such as "Read Now" and "Urgent") causes distraction.

Part of the skill in using e-mail is being able to make decisions that keep communication flowing without wasting time and energy. When personal contact is the only way to dissolve misunderstanding, don't rely on e-mail. When a phone call would be more efficient, do not spend a great deal of time drafting an e-mail. Also, if a communication problem exists, do not let yourself fall into an avoidance trap. Take the time to meet with a colleague for an informal, impromptu chat.

Some aspects of e-mail are not in your control. Namely, you cannot control the content or tone of someone else's message. Messages that do not meet your expectations may provoke your emotions and waste your energy: some messages sound too direct, while others ramble on without getting to the point; and there may even be the occasional message that sounds accusatory. Stay in control by focusing on the messages that you send and remaining objective about what others write.

Guidelines for E-Mail

In general, keep your e-mail messages to the length of one screen. If your message is much longer than one screen, consider using another method of communicating (such as a phone call). Though e-mail standards and protocol are still evolving, here are some basic guidelines:

1. Respond to e-mail within a day or two. (Use an "out-of-office" response when you are unavailable for more than one day.)

2. Use a salutation and a closing, even if the salutation consists of only the recipient's name and the closing consists of only your name.

3. Start the message with the most important information; clearly state the information you need from the reader at the *beginning* of the message (or even in the subject line).

4. Use bulleted or numbered lists so that items stand out.

5. Use conventional rules for punctuation and capitalization: do *not* write in all uppercase or lowercase. (All uppercase connotes "shouting" or "screaming"; all lowercase implies that you do not know how to make capitalization decisions.)

6. Avoid jargon, slang, and abbreviations.

7. Use an accurate and updated subject line so that your recipient can refer to your message and file it easily.

8. Avoid using "Read Now" and "Urgent" unless absolutely necessary.

9. Do not convey extremely sensitive or confidential information via e-mail; whenever possible, do not convey bad news.

10. Keep an open mind about messages you receive; if you infer there is a problem, you may actually create one.

11. Stay current about your company policy for e-mail use; even if personal messages are allowed, send them sparingly.

12. If you have doubts about whether you should send a message, do *not* send it; save it as a draft until you are sure. *When in doubt, leave it out.*

When *forwarding or replying to* messages, do the following:

1. Update the e-mail by changing the subject line to reflect the new content.

2. Delete the previous message if the recipient does not need to know the history.

3. Add a note at the beginning of forwarded messages explaining how the e-mail relates to the reader and specifying the action he or she should take.

4. Do not press "Reply All" unless everyone needs the information. Unnecessary replies to "all" create confusion and clutter.

5. Do not respond to controversial or emotional messages until you are clearheaded and objective.

6. Do not forward messages that you consider inappropriate. (Every year, many people lose their jobs as a result of forwarding inappropriate messages.)

With these guidelines in mind, compare Figure 4.1 and 4.2.

COACHING TIP

Making Copies Besides addressing an e-mail message to multiple recipients, you will often have to send copies to recipients who need to be informed but do not need to follow up or take action related to the message. Use the *cc* (*courtesy-copy*) function for such recipients.

If a recipient needs to take action, you may consider *forwarding* the message instead of sending a cc; include a note at the top of the message describing the action the recipient should take. Otherwise, the cc recipient may not read the message thoroughly to discover what is expected.

A *bcc* (*blind courtesy copy*) is very different from a cc. With cc's, everyone receiving the message is aware of all the cc recipients. However, with bcc's, the person to whom the message is addressed (as well as any cc recipients) is not aware that blind copies are being sent. Many people use the *bcc* function for mailing lists when they do not want recipients' addresses disclosed. Be cautious in sending blind copies for the purpose of documentation: a better solution may be to forward the message.

FIGURE 4.2 | Ineffective E-Mail

First Impressions: Is this reply an effective response to the e-mail in Figure 4.1? How do you think the message will be received by the customer?

To: Elaine Gonzalez, Adulation Clothing, Ltd.
Cc: Carson D'Anca, President, Here Today, Gone Tomorrow Clothing
Subject: Query on Order 73126

Dear Elaine:

Thank you for your continued interest in Here Today Gone Tomorrow clothing. We have had an 88 percent sell-through on the May product line, and with your help, we are hoping to do even better in June!

In regard to your query regarding the Abigail and Scale tops, for women and men respectively, please refer to the manufacturing label affixed to your delivery. "The fabric you have chosen is hand-dyed in India using an age-old process. Smudges, smears, and occasional spotting are a natural part of this process and enhance the natural beauty of the garment."

Before we discuss exchanging any pieces, it is our policy to urge store owners to put the goods on the sales floor for a four-week cycle to see how they perform. It really is a partnership we've entered into; we've done our part by producing garments as specified by you, and now it's up to you to do your part by putting them out on the floor and giving them a chance to sell.

As you have notified HTGT within the 7-day period indicated on your contract, I will keep the file for this invoice open an additional thirty days, at which point you can contact us for a follow-up. I'm sure you will be pleased with how the garments sell through.

Chloe Harris
Service Desk
Here Today Gone Tomorrow, Inc.

Companies can monitor employees' computer use without their knowledge. Businesses have the legal right to monitor their workers in this way; they own the equipment and are paying for their employees' time. As a result, every year companies terminate employees for using e-mail and the Internet inappropriately on the job.

Now let's examine other basic aspects of using e-mail. We will consider the following:

- *Purpose:* Compared to letters, memos, and voice mail, when is e-mail the best option?
- *Format:* What are the basic parts of an e-mail? What is the format?
- *Structure:* How should you structure the message so that it connects with the reader and conveys the purpose?

Purpose: Why Send an E-Mail?

When you are on the job, you will rarely stop to ask yourself if sending an e-mail is the best method to use. In most situations, the answer will be apparent. You will develop a *flow* with communication, and e-mail will be a natural part of that flow.

COMMUNICATION CHALLENGES

Instant Messaging The help-wanted ad asks that you apply by e-mail only—*no calls accepted.* However, there's a bug in the system somewhere: the employer e-mails you back that for some reason she isn't able to open either your e-mail or the résumé you attached.

She is able to read only the first snippet of your message, about six lines of type. You can't figure out the problem with the computer or fix it, but you'd like a shot at the job.

CHALLENGE:

Compose a brief e-mail that explains how you will get your résumé to the prospective employer.

COACHING TIP

CAT Strategy The structure of an e-mail is slightly different from the structure of a letter. With e-mail, put requested action toward the beginning of the message (sometimes readers don't read entire messages, especially long ones).

Try to keep most messages to about one screen or less in length. Ask only one or two questions in an e-mail; if you need to address multiple topics, consider presenting each main topic in a separate message. Messages that get to the point make it easier for readers to respond. Use the **CAT strategy:**

• **Connect:** Personalize the beginning so that the message reflects that you are a human being writing to another human being.

• **Act:** For longer messages, list the requested action at the beginning of the message. Readers sometimes glance at a message and then save it to read when they have more time. For time-sensitive messages, list the due date in the subject line of the message. (Or, better yet, make a phone call.)

• **Tell:** Use the remainder of the message to provide information.

Finally, sign off. You can use an informal closing or simply end with your name. If you are writing to an outside client, use an automatic sign-off that includes your mailing address and phone number.

E-mail is much less formal than a business letter, and it is often more appropriate than a phone call. Here are some reasons for using an e-mail rather than a phone call:

1. To send details in writing, making information easier for the recipient to access.
2. To send a message to multiple people at the same time.
3. To communicate at odd times of the day when a phone message or meeting is not feasible.
4. To save time; with e-mail there is much less "small talk."
5. To convey information when you do not need an immediate response.
6. To give short bits of information.

Do not rely on e-mail if your information has a critical time element. The recipient may not even read your message before the deadline. It is irresponsible to think that once you send information, the other person is now responsible to take action. When you need a fast response, call to say that you are sending an urgent message that needs an immediate response.

If you find yourself avoiding face-to-face communication with someone, your avoidance may indicate that a problem exists. Thus, an e-mail may not be your best option. The purpose of communication is to build relationships; don't hide behind e-mail. Phone the person or stop by for a brief visit, if possible.

When sending an e-mail, consider these questions:

• What time frame is involved? How soon do I need a response? If my e-mail is a reply to another person's message, how soon do I need to respond?

• Would a phone call be more or less effective?

• Do I need to meet with a colleague personally to discuss issues?

• Should I schedule a meeting to brainstorm options?

• Would a more formal communication, such as a letter, address the situation more effectively?

EXPLORE

Instructions: Analyze the e-mail messages below. What would you change about them? Recommend two or three changes for each message.

Message 1:

Kevin,

Due to an editorial deadline, I will not be able to attend Wednesday's Diversity Council meeting. Attached you will find two project plans that I have put together for the Diversity Fair and cookbook that the Communications Committee has been working on. We are waiting for the final approval from you to go ahead with these. I sent you a couple of updates via e-mail a few weeks ago, but you never responded.

Since I will not be able to attend the meeting on Wednesday, you should either take me off the agenda or assign my piece to someone else. Because these projects require a great deal of time and commitment, we need to begin action now if we are to go ahead with them. I would appreciate it if you would review these project plans by Friday and get back to me with any additions/corrections.

Thanks in advance.

Jeremy

Message 2:

Lorrine:

Your name was inadvertently omitted from the list of invitees for the Project Management Kickoff meeting. The meeting will be held from 2 p.m. until 3 p.m. tomorrow afternoon in Conference Room 1196. Bob Michaels is facilitating the meeting and would like you to present updated information related to your department. Will you please contact me with your availability?

Sorry for the late notice.

Darrin Parker

Message 3:

Vera and Rose,

Here is a brief (tentative) outline of what our plan is for the software training. Vera, this should be a recap of what you and I talked about earlier today. Rose, I know you are out of the office Thursday and Friday, but I wanted to make sure you're in the loop.

To simplify things on my end I would like to have you two be my DC point people. Vera for OPR, etc.; Rose for OPS. Also to simplify things, we'd like to just have one training location when we come to DC. Based on training rooms and available dates, it's my understanding that we can use the OPS training room for the entire time. I think it's just 1 Metro stop to get there. This would help us with only having to set up one training environment, and help the trainees by having a few time slots to choose from as opposed to 1 at each place.

We will help set up rooms for the 9th and 10th. I think they're already set up for the 17th through 20th. Vera and Rose will keep track of attendees on your end and make sure everyone is signing up. I can write the copy that you should send out in the meeting invites, follow-ups etc.

I need to solidify the plans and we need to talk more before setting anything in stone, but I wanted to make sure we are all on the same page.

Let's talk Monday morning at 10 a.m. Get back to me by noon today if you need to make a change.

Sophie

E-Mail Format and Structure

Although e-mail standards are still evolving, all business writing must follow standard rules for grammar, punctuation, and abbreviation. Though more casual than a business letter, e-mail is a business document that portrays an image of you and your company. Thus, do not be too casual with e-mail. (In other words, do not use abbreviations or other inappropriate short-cuts to save time.)

Start an e-mail with a **salutation.**

- Since e-mail is somewhat informal, the word *dear* does not need to be part of the salutation.

- In the United States (but not necessarily other parts of the world), most business professionals feel comfortable communicating on a first-name basis; if you are on a first-name basis, you can consider the recipient's name your salutation.

- If you choose to be somewhat formal, use *Dear* and follow the recipient's name with a colon (for example, "Dear Dominic:"). If you choose to be less formal, omit *Dear* and follow the recipient's name with a colon (for example, "Phillip:"). If you choose to be familiar, follow the recipient's name with a comma (for example, "Celina,").

- If you do not know the recipient and your e-mail is your first communication with that person, follow the most formal guideline: use the recipient's last name preceded by *dear* (for example, "Dear Mr. Stevens:").

The purpose of the first part of any business document is to connect with the reader. Using a salutation is the simplest way to connect. Many writers jump right into the message without addressing the recipient by name. This approach is not recommended, but it is acceptable when writers exchange several messages with each other on a daily basis.

E-mail is best when the message is short. Limit each message to one main issue. Start with the most important information and get right to the point (because the recipient may not read the entire message if it is unusually long). If you need the reader to take action, put the relevant information at the beginning of the message.

Figure 4.3 is an example of an e-mail that connects with the reader, gets right to the point, and puts the requested action at the beginning. The message also includes a brief explanation and has contact information in the automatic sign-off.

PRACTICE

Reflect/Respond/Revise—A Process Strategy: Time is critical when you are responding to e-mail. In the business world, you are expected to respond to many messages daily. This short **reflect/respond/revise** process strategy allots 12 minutes in total for you to reflect, respond, and revise a question that is somewhat familiar to you.

FIGURE 4.3 | E-Mail

An effective e-mail message is concise and informative. This e-mail includes a clear call to action while supplying the information necessary for the recipient to respond effectively.

To: Bob Andrews
Cc:
Subject: Inventory Query

Bob:

Thank you for assisting us with the invoice. Now I need your help with another matter. Could you please send me an updated inventory list by Wednesday afternoon?

We have promised our customer in New Castle that we would ship 10 chairs by the end of the week. Your updated inventory list will let me know if I need to contact another distibutor.

Regards,

Janet

Janet S. Sparacio
Distribution Manager
Alliance Health Systems
4453 Oak Cliff Boulevard
Arlington, TX 76016
972-555-8990

You will spend time planning, composing, and editing your message. The time frame may seem short, but the time is adequate for writing a brief and accurate message. Get used to moving from one phase of the writing process to the next; your confidence will grow as you get more practice.

Instructions: You applied for a part-time position at your local bank, and to your surprise Robert Diaz from Human Resources sent you an e-mail asking for more information. What kind of details would you give him about your experience that show you are responsible and motivated?

1. Take 3 minutes to reflect upon the question and map your response.

2. Take 6 minutes to compose a brief response.

3. Spend 3 minutes editing and revising your message.

 SECTION A: CONCEPT CHECK

1. What are some of the problems or frustrations associated with e-mail?

2. When would a phone call or personal visit be preferable to sending an e-mail?

3. Should all e-mail messages contain a salutation and complimentary closing?

4. List three or more e-mail guidelines that you will start using.

■ SECTION B: BUSINESS LETTERS

A **business letter** is a formal communication tool. Not so long ago, a business letter was the only communication option other than speaking to someone in person or on the phone. Today the business letter is used infrequently compared to e-mail and voice mail. However, the business letter is still important, and at times no substitute equals a business letter. In examining the business letter, we will discuss the following issues:

*   *Purpose:*   Compared with e-mail and voice mail, when is a letter the best option?

*   *Structure:*   How should you structure the message so that it connects with the reader and conveys the purpose?

*   *Basic format:*   What are the basic parts of any business letter, and how should you display them?

*   *Mailing options:* What options do you have for sending mail, and what factors should you consider in making a decision?

Purpose: Why Send a Letter?

Letters take time to write and can be expensive to mail if sent next-day air. When another form of communication would work just as well, you may be saving yourself time, energy, and money by using it. However, in some cases a letter would be more effective than an e-mail or a phone call. Use a letter for any of the following purposes:

*   Inform a reader of lengthy, detailed information.

*   Document information formally. (*Note:* E-mail also provides documentation.)

*   Communicate with individuals you do not know personally (when a voice mail or an e-mail would seem too personal).

*   Obtain documentation that a letter was received (via return receipt).

*   Convey sensitive information or bad news.

*   Communicate formally, as in a thank-you letter.

- Demonstrate appreciation and respect.
- Meet a client's expectations or requirements.
- Obtain signatures.

Can you think of other situations in which a business letter would be the most effective method of communicating?

FIGURE 4.4 | Letter

Business Query: Is the tone of this letter appropriate? What does this letter tell you about the sender?

Adulation Clothing, Ltd.
11135 Couer D'Alene Boulevard
Couer D'Alene, ID 80251
208-555-1234

August 7, 2006

Ms. Chloe Harris
Here Today Gone Tomorrow Clothing, Ltd.
6511 Hurston Street
Baleview, WI 56489

Dear Chloe:

It has been a month since we last exchanged communications. I last wrote you to discuss some challenges I foresaw in selling 6 pieces of the Abigail Blouse (Style J89) and 8 pieces in the Scale Shirt (Style J92) that were part of Adulation's June order from Here Today Gone Tomorrow (PO 73126). Please understand, for a small business like mine, every square inch of the place has to keep moving if I want to stay ahead.

As you suggested in response to my e-mail, I have had the pieces out on the floor in a prominent display position. And as I anticipated, while I did sell every other piece from the order, the blouses and the shirts remain.

Now that I have done my part in this partnership, I would like to know what you can do to help me with these tops. I sense you are fairly strict about your refund policy, and I would be satisfied with a credit against your line. When I'm in New York for the show next month, I'll place another order against it.

I really love your designs and enjoy having your label in the store. Let me know the best way to go about sending these back to you.

Sincerely,

Elaine Gonzalez
Adulation Clothing, Ltd.

Message Structure

The business letter is an excellent vehicle for building business relationships. Your letters represent you and your company and may be the only image your client has of your company. Although the content and purpose of letters vary, you can organize most letters successfully by applying the following **CTA format:**

- For an introduction, *connect* with the reader as one human being communicating to another. Don't be stiff and abstract. Be friendly, and connect your purpose to the reader's needs and interests.
- In the body, *tell* your reader details, explanations, and facts. Summarize and highlight information supporting your purpose.
- In the closing, state the *action* or next steps that you will take or that you request the reader to take. Express goodwill; invite the reader to contact you for more information.

In addition to using the basic structure of "connect, tell, and act," you also need to determine whether you will communicate information with a *direct approach* or an *indirect approach.* The direct approach is the most common way to convey information; use the indirect approach when your letter conveys news the recipient will not welcome or expect.

The Direct Message
Most letters take a **direct approach** to conveying information, putting the purpose and main point in the first paragraph. Once readers understand the purpose, they are able to use supporting information in the body to confirm and expand their understanding of the message.

The bulk of the letter is in the **body,** which can consist of one paragraph (or as many as it takes to convey your message). Give as many details as necessary, but do not stray from the principle *less is more.* If you include too many details, you make it harder for yourself and more complicated for your reader. (Screening out unnecessary details is a part of editing, not composing.)

The closing in a direct message is usually short; it states action or next steps that you intend to take or that you request your reader to take. The closing also expresses goodwill and opens the door for additional communication.

To simplify the structure, think of the direct message as a diamond, with the top representing a short introduction; the middle, the bulk of the information; and the bottom, a short closing. (See Figure 4.5.)

Here is an example of a direct message:

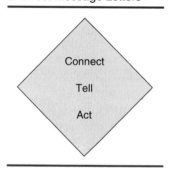

FIGURE 4.5 | Structure of Direct-Message Letters

Dear Ms. Matczak:

Your bank has provided valuable services to me over the years, but an error has been made on my account.

On October 12, I made a direct deposit to my checking account, No. 793 332, for $500. The deposit was made at your Main Street branch. However, the deposit was not posted on my October 30 statement. Enclosed is a copy of my receipt.

Thank you for assisting me with this. Please let me know if I need to take additional steps to reconcile this mistake; you can reach me at 555-9797.

Sincerely,

Bernard Olsen
Enclosure

Some experts say that it is redundant to close with a statement such as, "If you need additional information, please call me at 555-5567." However, reminding your readers—your clients—that they are welcome to interact with you helps build the business relationship. Thus, state your phone number in the closing, especially if you are writing to someone for the first time. Cater to your clientele; make it easy for them to communicate with you.

PRACTICE

Situation: You've become an avid fan of online auctions and have made a small profit buying and selling goods on auctionblock.com, a Web site where goods are sold either to the highest bidder or to the first buyer who meets the seller's automatic sale price (ASP). According to auctionblock.com guidelines, an auction closes when a buyer agrees to pay the ASP on a product. All sales are binding, and those who violate the rules are liable to be fined.

You recently listed a 1950 classic Schwinn two-seater bicycle in exceptionally good condition with an ASP of $2000. Days after posting the listing, David Walker—a fellow who lives in your neighborhood and who had on several earlier occasions noticed the Schwinn parked in your garage—stopped by unexpectedly and offered you $3000 for the vintage bike. You agreed to sell it to him, intending to immediately go online and remove the bike from auction. David was leaving town for a week and wouldn't be able to pay you until he returned, so there was time to take care of the details. You and David shook hands on the deal.

However, you didn't make it online until the following morning, at which time you discovered that your ASP had been accepted by a buyer during the night.

Instructions: Assume the situation unfolds as described below, and respond accordingly.

1. It would sure be nice to make that extra $1000. Write an e-mail to the buyer, Abbygail@mailpost.com, explaining that you had already sold the Schwinn before the closing bid was entered and that you wish to honor that sale. Remember to consider audience, purpose, and tone when you are developing your message.

2. The buyer doesn't agree with the argument you've presented. She wants the bike at the listed ASP price, and she doesn't want to barter over it. In addition, she's reminded you that all ASP bids are binding when entered at the Web site, regardless of what is happening offline. Compose a letter to the Web site's main office, Auction Block, Inc., 21203 Central Avenue, Toluca Lake, Tennessee 38233, explaining why you believe you should be able to accept the first offer that you received without having your auction profile negatively affected.

3. Auction Block has ruled that the first "sale" of the bicycle, to David Walker, was nullified by the second, legally binding sale made online. Auction Block contends that once the bike was listed at the auction site, its sale was no longer your sole decision. Regardless of your verbal agreement about the bicycle, you need to let Mr. Walker know that the deal with him has fallen through. You have his phone number, his address, and his e-mail address. What is the best way to communicate the outcome of the situation to Mr. Walker—by phone, in person, or by e-mail?

The Indirect Message   Some letters purposefully take an **indirect approach.** When conveying unexpected or bad news, first explain the rationale before stating your main point or decision. State the purpose in a general way, but give enough detail and explanation so that the rationale leading to the news makes sense to the reader (or as much sense as possible). In this way, the reader becomes more equipped to accept the news by understanding the logic behind it. The indirect approach is tactful and shows respect for the reader.

Your main point or bad news will appear in the body or possibly in the conclusion. As in a direct message, the closing paragraph of an indirect message lets the reader know that he or she may contact you or someone else for additional information.

Here is an example of an indirect message:

Dear Mr. Beery:

We appreciate your business and would like to keep you as a valued customer.

We have considered your request to change the lease agreement on your printer and copier by three months. For several years, our policy has been that the minimum time frame for leasing office equipment is one year. Part of the reason for the one-year time frame relates to lowering your costs and giving customers the option to buy equipment at a fraction of the retail price. Since you are a valued customer, we would be able to reduce your lease only if a charge is added to your final billing to reflect our increased costs. The fee would equal 25 percent of the cost for the unused time left on your contract.

Because of the fee, you may decide that it is more cost-effective to keep the equipment until your contract expires. Let me know if you need more information; I am here to assist you in any way that I can.

Sincerely,

Donald P. Macki

Using a direct approach, the above letter might read as follows:

Dear Mr. Beery:

We appreciate your business and would like to keep you as a valued customer.

In response to your request that we change your lease agreement, we must charge you a fee equal to 25 percent of cost for the unused time left on your contract. This fee reflects our increased costs and would be added to your final billing. For several years, our policy has been that the minimum time frame for leasing office equipment is one year. Part of the reason for the one-year time frame relates to lowering your costs and giving customers the option to buy equipment at a fraction of the retail price.

Because of the added fee, you may decide that it is more cost-effective to keep the equipment until your contract expires. Let me know if you need more information; I am here to assist you in any way that I can.

Sincerely,

Donald P. Macki

What response did you have to each letter? Was the tone of the second letter different from the tone presented in the first one?

Figure 4.6 compares the structures of an indirect message and a direct message. In a direct message, get right to the point; with an indirect message, state the purpose in a general

FIGURE 4.6 | Comparison of Indirect and Direct Messages

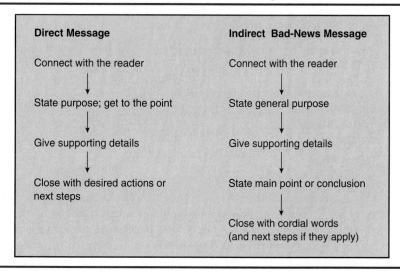

Mailbox Deliveries: *How do business letters differ from e-mail? When would a business letter be preferable to sending an e-mail?*

way, including details and explanations, before presenting the main point. In effect, with the indirect approach, you present information to soften the message for the reader before you get to the main point. Giving the reasoning first not only shows respect for the reader but also shows that you take the situation seriously.

EXPLORE

1. Does it make sense to give a rationale before presenting bad news? Why?

2. Think of situations in which you have had to say no to a friend's or relative's request. How would you draft a letter giving your answer?

3. Determine whether to use the indirect or direct approach in letters for the following situations:

    a. You are writing to let an applicant know that the job has been filled by someone else

    b. You are formally requesting a leave of absence because of a family member's illness.

    c. You are providing information about your availability to work part-time.

PRACTICE

Instructions: Use the reflect/respond/revise process strategy on the following:

1. Draft the body of a letter describing the differences between the direct and the indirect approaches to writing letters.

2. Draft a letter to a relative or friend that explains why you have made a decision different from the one he or she expected. (For example, have you decided on a different career path than your parents expected? Have you ever told a friend no?)

Note: Keep your drafts handy; you will use one of them later in this chapter.

Format: Business Letters

Business letters contain basic, standard parts. Not only do these parts appear in all business letters, but they always occur in the same order. Here are the standard parts of a business letter:

*   Date
*   Address
*   Salutation
*   Body
*   Closing
*   Writer's name
*   Title, when appropriate

In addition, some letters also contain the following:

*   Attention line
*   Subject line
*   Copy notations
*   Enclosure notations
*   Attachment notation
*   Postscript

Figure 4.8 shows an example of a business letter with each part labeled.

The formatting information in this section is a simplified guide to creating a balanced business letter. Although the guidelines are general, they will help you achieve a good-quality letter with the least amount of effort. (If you have studied formatting in detail in keyboarding or another class, apply the information you learned there.)

FIGURE 4.7 | Business Letter

Customer Service: Is this reply an effective response to the letter in Figure 4.4? What risk does Here Today Gone Tomorrow Clothing accept in adhering so tightly to company policy? What would be your response to this message?

Here Today Gone Tomorrow Clothing, Ltd.
6511 Hurston Street
Baleview, WI 56489

August 15, 2006

Elaine Gonzalez
Adulation Clothing, Ltd.
11135 Couer D'Alene Blvd.
Couer D'Alene, ID 80251

Dear Elaine:

Thank you for your follow-up message and for bringing me up to date on the salient facts of your story. A lot of merchandise flows through here; it's sometimes hard to track each item, each style, in every store.

First, I want to congratulate you on achieving an 83 percent sell-through on your June order: those numbers are a winner for any clothing line. One suggestion, particularly effective as summer's end draws near, might be marking the items down. At this point, with your terrific sell-through numbers, even if you had to sell these units at wholesale, your store has made a nice chunk of change for the month. Sometimes a good markdown is all you need to keep things moving.

Please consider that HTGT produces and ships 80,000 garments monthly. To expect us to take personal responsibility for the sell-through of each individual garment is not reasonable, when we have neither influence nor awareness of such factors as store location, store design, customer profile, etc. We do look to the bottom line, as this is business, and it would seem you have numbers that support your continued interest in our line.

I can make one offer to you. Although it is not traditionally our policy to allow customers to run credits, we do make exceptions once in a while. I will provide you with the information required to return the goods to our warehouse. The one caveat is that the credits cannot be applied against new orders, they can only be placed against re-orders or restock from inventory.

Sincerely,

Chloe Harris
Service Desk

COACHING TIP

Hard Copy Versus Soft Copy A **hard copy** is a printed paper copy. A **soft copy** is an electronic version. At one time, a hard copy with an authentic signature was the only type of document that was legally binding. Today, electronic copies can be legally binding.

When you are proofreading documents created on your computer, it's best to read the copy onscreen and also print a hard copy.

The most common letter format is the **block style,** which is the easiest to produce and remember (writers also have fewer opportunities to make mistakes). With the block style, *all lines start at the left margin.* Do not indent paragraphs: all parts (the date, salutation, body, close, and writer's name) are flush with the left margin, as shown in Figure 4.8. (For more detailed instructions for formatting business letters, see the Writer's Handbook, Part 3, "Formatting Standard Business Documents.")

Your completed letter should appear centered on the page with approximately equal top and bottom margins. Since most software programs provide 1-inch side margins, you do not need to adjust margins for medium or long letters. For a very *short* letter, make the following adjustments so that your letter looks balanced:

1. Start the date a line or two lower on the page.

FIGURE 4.8 | Standard Parts of a Business Letter

Readers are able to locate certain information—the writer's name, the subject, the date—with ease when writers use a standard business letter format; this allows readers to focus on the body of the message. Do you think the use of a standard business letter format simplifies the process of writing?

The Writing Institute
180 North Michigan Avenue
Chicago, Illinois 60611
312-555-1222

October 29, 2006	**Date**
Mr. Bob Allison Global Communication Network 333 West Wacker Drive Chicago, IL 60610	**Address**
Dear Mr. Allison:	**Salutation**

The introduction *connects* you to your reader and *connects* your reader to the purpose of your letter. With a *direct message*, state your main point in the first paragraph.

The body *tells* the reader basic information that supports your purpose. In the body of a letter, include details, descriptions, examples, and rationale. The body could be one paragraph for a short letter or any number of paragraphs for longer letters. The body should be as long as necessary to make your point, but no longer. With an *indirect message*, your main point would come toward the end of the body or beginning of the conclusion.

The last paragraph. or conclusion, defines *action* or next steps. Inform the reader of any action that you will take or that you request the reader to take. Invite the reader to contact you for additional information; if you choose, include your phone number and Web address.

Sincerely,	**Closing**
Reginald D. Piper Instructional Designer	**Writer's name** **Title**
cc: Michael Jones Enclosure Attachment	**cc stands for "courtesy copy"** **A document enclosed with the letter** **A document paper-clipped to the letter**
PS	**Postscript**

2. Leave an additional line or two between the date and the address.

3. Space down 5 to 7 lines between the closing and the writer's signature. (For an average or long letter, you would space down 4 lines.)

Your letter should have a "picture frame" of white space around it. Before printing, always use the print preview on the file menu; if it looks unbalanced, adjust the spacing until you get it in balance.

PRACTICE

Instructions: Take one of the letters you drafted for the Practice exercises on page 128 or 130 and type it in block style. (If you do not have an inside address, you may use your own or your college's address.)

Mailing Options

At times, you will fax a business letter or send it as an attachment to an e-mail. However, when putting a hard copy in the mail, you have several options. The main factors to consider when making your decision are time and money. The farther the distance and the faster the package must arrive, the more expensive the cost. In most locations, you will have several carriers from which to choose. However, automatically choosing the fastest, most expensive carrier and service can be wasteful. Consider your needs, and choose a service that meets your objective economically.

Medium-size to large corporations have mailrooms that handle all outgoing mail, so if you work for such a company, you may have less control over your mailing options. However, if you work at a small company, you will make mailing decisions and may even post your own mail at the local post office. If you need a return receipt, make sure you request it at the time you send your package; also, if your package is valuable, make sure you buy adequate insurance to cover the replacement cost.

During heavy mailing times, such as the holiday season, you may want to upgrade the service you select. Although the details are subject to change, the information below gives you a general idea of the many options you have when mailing letters and packages.

- *The United States Postal Service (USPS):* The USPS delivers most of the mail sent within the United States and to foreign countries. For an additional fee, you can insure your packages or track them by computer (the USPS Web site address is <http://www.usps.gov>. If you need documentation, purchase a delivery confirmation. The USPS offers several mailing options: first class, third class, priority, express mail, global express, and international.

- *Federal Express (FedEx):* Although the name implies that FedEx is part of the USPS, it is actually a private company. Mailing options with FedEx include FedEx Express and FedEx Ground.

- *United Parcel Service (UPS).* UPS is often identified as the "brown truck"; UPS provides various types of service, ranging from next day delivery to ground delivery.

Other major delivery companies include DHL and Emery (which is mostly freight). Depending on your location, other delivery services may be available. Check your local phone directory under "delivery services" or "packaging."

With private services, you can often designate the time of day (morning or afternoon) that your package should arrive. Although private services are generally more expensive than the USPS, the price usually includes tracking and limited insurance. Some local messenger services pick up packages at your office and deliver them directly on the same day. In large cities, bicycle messengers weave through traffic hurriedly delivering urgent packages, regardless of the weather—rain, snow, or shine!

EXPLORE

1. With a partner, discuss how you usually send your mail; also discuss the various types of services you have used to send or receive mail.

2. Check your local listings and identify a messenger or delivery service not listed in this chapter. Get a listing of its fee structure.

✓ SECTION B: CONCEPT CHECK

1. If you have bad news to share, would you write a letter or an e-mail? How would you structure the information?

2. The first part of any written document should achieve what purpose?

3. For business letters, what are the two basic types of messages?

4. The words *connect, tell,* and *act* relate to which parts of a business letter?

5. Is the most expensive mailing option always the best? How do you choose which mailing option to use?

■ SECTION C: MEMOS, FAXES, VOICE MAIL, AND CELL PHONES

Besides e-mail, other office communications that you will send on a frequent basis are memos (and "e-memos") and faxes. Each has a unique purpose and format that structure communication in a helpful way. The same is true of voice mail. Though you have used the phone casually all your life, in the business world it becomes a professional tool. Even on the phone, you are more effective with a little planning. Thus, you will apply planning techniques to phone work so that your voice mail messages contain organized information and clear requests. In addition, you will learn guidelines for using cell phones in public.

Memos and E-Memos

A **memorandum** or *memo* is a structured internal communication tool most often used to convey information, announcements, and reminders. (See the example in Figure 4.9.) Hard copies of memos are sent via interoffice mail or posted on boards.

Today most memos are sent electronically, and software packages provide templates for creating messages. These **e-memos** are sent in-house through a company's intranet system (although most corporations give employees access to the Internet, memos are not sent to outside clients). As with e-mail, you can create special mailing lists for e-memos or reports that you send to specific groups.

Though hard-copy memos are still a valuable tool, fewer hard copies are being sent through interoffice mail. Why take a day to send information when you can send it immediately via electronic mail? Electronic mail cuts down on paper and clutter. You can file e-memos and retrieve them when you need to print copies for use in meetings or for other purposes.

In examining memos, we will consider the following:

- *Purpose:* Compared with letters, e-mail, and voice mail, when is a memo your best option? What is the difference between an e-memo and an e-mail?

- *Format:* What are the basic parts of a memo? What is the best format to use?

- *Structure:* How should you structure the message?

Memos Versus E-Mail   There is a great deal of overlap in the way hard-copy memos, e-memos, and e-mail are used. All three inform, but e-mail more closely resembles a written conversation, with the participants sharing information and asking questions. E-mail encourages interaction, whereas a memo or an e-memo does not. To recap:

- *E-mail* is the least formal mode of written communication. Once again, use e-mail for both internal and external clients.

- *Memos* provide a more structured format than e-mail (they do not create an ongoing dialogue). Use memos only for coworkers.

- *E-memos* are equivalent to standard, hard-copy memos. Send e-memos only to coworkers.

FIGURE 4.9 | Office Memorandum

Memos are effective for communicating within an organization. Copies of memos can be delivered to coworkers and/or posted on bulletin boards. What are the differences between a memo and an e-memo?

M E M O

To: Chloe Harris, Alexandra King, Bill Theirs, Helna Sceine
From: Carson
Date: August 25, 2003
Subject: Reforming Credit/Exchange Policy

It's time to put on our thinking caps. I've just spent an hour in my office having my ear chewed off by a very irate customer in Idaho. It seems we've let things slip a little too far in certain areas of customer service.

Let's plan a meeting to talk about how we can do things better. Can everybody get back to me with a time and a day next week when you have an open slot for a grueling afternoon gathering. If you don't have an afternoon free, please clear one. This needs to be done.

I'll let you know a time and place as soon as all your responses are in.

Carson

Memo Format and Structure   Memos have a standard format from which there is little deviation. The memo format organizes information for readers and addresses large groups efficiently. When a writer sends a memo, the writer does not expect a reply. Thus, writers do not exchange memos back and forth the way they exchange e-mail.

- Type the heading in bold, either all-caps or caps and lowercase. Here are the two most common headings:

  To:

  From:

  Date:

  Subject:

  TO: **FROM:**

  SUBJECT: **DATE:**

- When sending memos electronically, replace *Date* with the word *Sent* in the heading. (Figure 4.10 shows an example of an e-memo.)
- Leave 2 blank lines (triple-space) below the subject line before starting the body.
- Single-space the body; leave a double space between paragraphs.
- Do not indent paragraphs.

FIGURE 4.10 | E-Memo

E-memos are the electronic equivalent of hard-copy memos.

To: Rich Spencer

From: Darlene Applegate

Sent: August 15, 2003

Subject: Updated Roster

As you requested, I am passing on the updated roster for the AMS system training. If you see discrepancies with the roster, please let me know before next Friday.

Here are the current changes:

1. Change Bill Albert's fax number to 555-4554.

2. Mary Gilbert has a new title: executive vice president.

3. Doug Sandifer is now located in our New Jersey branch.

4. Add Mathew Dwight; his e-mail address is mdwight@ourcompany.com.

5. Remove Tyler Smith from the list; he completed the training last week.

I'm sorry that the previous roster had not been updated before you needed it for distribution.

Hope your day goes well.

With a memo, do not use a salutation. Also, do not use a typed or written signature because the heading includes that information. However, with a hard-copy memo, you may place your initials at the top of the memo next to your name or at the bottom of the memo. If someone types the message for you, the typist would place his or her reference initials at the bottom.

With memos, present your message so that the reader has easy access to your information. (Readers are more likely to print out e-memos than they are to print out e-mail messages.) As with all business documents, keep your words to a minimum. Break down the information for your reader. *What are your main points?* Use bulleted or numbered items to make your main points stand out so that the reader can learn at a glance what your memo is about.

PRACTICE

Instructions: Edit and revise the following memo:

To: Project Managers
From: Josef Weintraub
Date: November 12, 2006
Subject: INSURANCE POLICY UPDATE

It appears that our current insurance carrier is working with us to reduce costs for our company and employees. In order to enable us to give accurate information to our insurance company and at the same time to make sure employees are being fairly represented in their views, I am going to ask each of you to survey your staff to understand their preferences based on costs and services.

This information should be given to me by yourself within the next week, at which time we will plan a department meeting to decide upon changes to our standard policy. Among the things you need to ask your staff is whether they are willing to pay more out-of-pocket expenses for doctor's visits to reduce the cost of the policy. We also need to know if they would accept a higher deductible for lower overall premium costs. The emergency room benefit they now receive also increases the premium greatly; would they be willing to have that dropped for lower costs?

Thank you in advance for taking the time to discuss these issues with your staff. I know insurance is an important employee benefit. Our goal is to provide the best benefits to our employees and keep expenses down. I am very much looking forward to hearing their responses and finding ways to reduce our insurance costs. As always, I am available for any questions that you might have.

JW

Faxes

In general, a **fax** is not an originally created document. Documents that have been created for various purposes are sent as "faxes." Thus, the word *fax* relates more to *the way a document is sent* than to the kind of document that is sent. A fax can be a letter, a memo, a proposal, a price list, or any other type of business document.

The word *fax* is derived from the word *facsimile* (which means "a copy"). At one time, if someone said, "We are sending you a facsimile of the correspondence," he or she would have been referring to a carbon copy. The word *facsimile* has a long history, dating back to the early part of the last century. With the advent of copiers during the 1970s, the word *facsimile* almost became extinct until fax machines became common in the 1980s.

For many types of business correspondence, the fax is still a preferred means of communication. You can fax documents with original signatures along with a time and date stamp, showing proof of the transaction. The sender does not need to scan material into a computer.

Since electronic communication has become so popular, the fax machine is being used less and less. Documents can be scanned into computers and sent as attachments to e-mail. In addition, many people now send and receive their faxes online by subscribing to a professional fax service and downloading special software.

In the discussion below, we will consider the following:

- *Purpose:* When would you use a fax?
- *Format:* What are the basic parts of a fax?

Formatting a Fax Cover Sheet   Usually, the only part of the fax that you would specifically create for the fax transmission is the cover sheet, which you should include with all transmittals.

1. Prepare a *cover sheet* for the correspondence you are faxing. (See Figure 4.11.) Include the following:

   To: Fax No.:

   From: Phone No.:

   Date:

   [Total number of pages faxed.]

2. You can include a brief message on the cover sheet explaining the material you are faxing and what you expect from the recipient.
3. Number each page you send.

FIGURE 4.11 | Fax Cover Sheet

Cover Sheet: A fax is a convenient and efficient way to send a copy of an original document, especially one that contains an original signature. An alternative to faxing would be scanning a document and then sending it via e-mail as an attachment.

TO: Juan Lewis   FAX: 800-555-9215

FROM: Jennifer Robbins   PHONE: 888-555-9242

                                         FAX: 888-555-9243

* 3 Pages Follow*

Attached is the real estate contract for the property in Long Grove. The closing is next Friday at 10 a.m. Please call me if you have questions.

Jenny

INTERNET EXERCISE 4.2

New Technologies Visit the *Foundations of Business Communication* Web site at <http://www.mhhe.com/djyoung> to find links to information about the latest in office technology.

At the home page, select "Student Activities"; then click on the Chapter 4 link to begin.

Transmitting Faxes Often a fax is sent as a result of a phone conference, so the client is expecting it. If your client is not expecting a fax, you may wish to call to let the client know that you are faxing information.

Fax transmittals are less reliable than electronic mail, although most fax machines indicate whether the message was transmitted or there was an error. Sometimes, after a fax reaches its designated location, the person to whom it was addressed never picks it up and the fax gets lost or inadvertently thrown away. In any case, if the information is important, follow the fax with a phone call to ensure that your document was received intact.

EXPLORE

Which communication tool(s) would you use to send each of the items listed below? Your options are e-mail, e-mail and attachment, standard mail, and/or fax.

1. A signed contract.
2. A short message indicating the times you will be available for board meetings.
3. An application for membership to an organization.
4. A train schedule.
5. A copy of a memo that gives details of an upcoming meeting.
6. Information welcoming a new client to your organization.

PRACTICE

1. **Instructions:** Prepare a cover sheet to send 14 pages of a contract to Jackson H. Piper. His fax number is 312.555.1212. Include a short note letting Jackson know what you are sending; also let him know that he should return a signed copy to you within one week.

2. **Instructions:** A prospective employer has asked you to fax your résumé to Alicia Whitehouse, the HR director for the company's New York office. Prepare a cover sheet with a short note informing Alicia that William Bledsoe asked you to send her your résumé. Alicia's fax number is 212-555-1213.

Voice Mail

By far, the phone is the most widely used communication tool. Business professionals spend hours on the phone every day. Many companies provide cell phones for positions that require travel or off-site work.

Voice mail has enhanced the effectiveness and efficiency of the phone as a communication tool. Some company executives use voice mail to send out announcements to large groups. Voice mail sends the same message quickly to large mailing groups of employees. Voice mail is a casual way to make company announcements; for example, a company president or chief executive officer (CEO) can use voice mail to reach every employee in a personal way.

For workers at all levels, voice mail eliminates the frustration of unanswered and missed phone calls and the wasted time of repeatedly rephoning. You will want to plan your voice mail greeting as well as voice mail messages that you leave for others.

Voice Mail Greetings

Most business professionals record their own voice mail greetings. In addition, some change their greetings on a daily or weekly basis, depending on how their schedule changes. Here are some guidelines for creating your voice mail greeting:

1. State your name at the beginning of the message and then the type of information you wish the caller to leave (such as name and phone number). Conclude by stating that you will return the call and give some indication of when you will do so.

Example: Hi, this is Jorene Richardson. Please leave your name and number and then a brief message. I will return your call as soon as I can.

2. If you will be out of the office for a day or more, you may wish to update your voice mail greeting to let callers know you will be out of the office.

Example: Hello, this is Jorene Richardson. I will be out of the office from Friday, June 18, until Wednesday, June 23. Please leave a detailed message, and I will call you when I return to the office.

3. If your schedule varies, you may change your voice mail greeting on a daily basis.

Example: Good morning, this is Jorene Richardson and today is Friday, June 18. I will be in a workshop until noon today. Leave me a brief message, including your phone number and a convenient time for me to return your call this afternoon.

If you leave a specific voice mail greeting, remember to change it as needed. In the above example, Jorene would need to change her message when she returned to her office at noon that day.

Voice Mail Messages

Too often very little thought is put into planning phone calls or leaving well-constructed voice mail messages. If you reach a person when you call, you want to be prepared to express your message confidently and clearly. However, if you reach voice mail, preparation is even more important. The last thing you want to do is leave a long, rambling message before you get to your point.

Disorganized messages are very frustrating to receive. The caller may or may not include the return phone number; many times the number is included at the end of the message and is barely audible. When that happens, sometimes the entire message must be listened to again (and again) to retrieve the number.

Sending Out an SOS: What factors should you consider when choosing the means—phone, fax, e-mail, or hand delivery—by which to transmit your message? Can the means you choose for communicating affect the way the receiver perceives the message?

When you leave a message, do not assume the recipient has your number. Many people access their phone messages without phone numbers at hand. By leaving a message that includes your number, you are making it more convenient for the recipient to contact you. Here are some guidelines for leaving voice mail messages:

1. Mind map the message before you call.
2. Start your message by stating your name, company, and phone number (slowly).
3. Prioritize the information, and give the most important details first.
4. Include a time frame. (When do you need the information you are requesting?)
5. Make sure you include the best times you can be reached.
6. Repeat your phone number *slowly* at the end of the message.

By preparing to leave a voice mail before you make a call, you are also preparing for the call itself. If a real person answers, you can confidently handle the call.

Cell Phones

Many abuses are occurring daily due to cell phone use that infringes on the public at large. At an Association for Business Communications conference, Ewuuk Lomo-David presented a list of guidelines for cell phone use.[2] Here they are:

1. Adjust ringer to vibrate when in public places.
2. Avoid loud, sensational ring tones that call attention to yourself.
3. Lower your voice when speaking.
4. Wait until you are in a comfortable place to speak.
5. Do not frown when speaking; it indicates a troubled state of mind.
6. Do not answer and speak on the phone while in a line for services.
7. Step about 20 feet away from the public when you must answer your phone.
8. Keep confidential information private (it may be overheard by someone who is familiar with the person or situation you are talking about).
9. Avoid multitasking when you are talking on a cell phone; it could be dangerous.
10. Don't make and receive cell phone calls while in meetings, the classroom, or driving.

By following these guidelines, you will remain professional in every situation.

EXPLORE

1. Have you ever left a message in which you rambled on? Have you ever received such a message? What are some differences between personal and professional telephone etiquette?
2. Identify a company at which you may someday apply for a position. Use a search engine to find its Web site. At the Web site, find the company's phone number and review basic information about the company. After you have done your research, call the company and ask if you could speak with someone in Human Resources about employment opportunities. Make sure you do a mind map of questions you will ask before you make your call.
3. You are probably used to spending time chatting with your friends on the phone. How does the informal chatting culture differ from professional phone etiquette?

PRACTICE

Situation: You have just found out that there is an opening for a part-time position, and you have all the qualifications. Mr. Alex Johnson is screening applicants for the position, and you are calling to set up an appointment. When you call, you receive his voice mail.

Instructions: Leave a message indicating your interest and briefly state your qualifications, availability, and a number where you can be reached. (Role-play this activity with a partner.)

✓ SECTION C: CONCEPT CHECK

1. Is there an advantage to sending an e-memo rather than a paper copy?
2. In writing to an external client, would you send an e-mail or a memo? Why?
3. When you send a fax, do you need a cover sheet? Why or why not? If one is needed, what information would you put on the cover sheet?
4. Imagine you are recording your own voice mail greeting at work. How would you word it?

SUMMARY

In this chapter, you have studied the basics of written business communication. All business communication is about building and maintaining relationships. Base your communication decisions not only on efficiency but also on effectiveness. Don't hide behind technology when you need personal contact to solve a problem.

A shortcoming of technology is that it allows you to react to a situation without analyzing it thoroughly. By analyzing situations, you are more likely to use your decision-making skills to solve problems objectively. In time, with experience, you will reach a flow with communication, and the most effective method will be obvious without thinking about it.

In the next chapter, you will gain experience in producing a variety of other types of writing such as persuasive letters and marketing letters. In addition, you will learn how to write manuals and instructions as well as reports, proposals, minutes, and other documents.

Following this chapter is Handbook at a Glance, Part 3, on formatting. That at-a-glance section contains specific information on how to format information professionally so that the reader has access to it at a glance. Now you want to prepare yourself for the advanced work in coming chapters by completing the checklist and activities below.

CHAPTER 4 CHECKLIST

___ For your business letter, have you followed the "connect, tell, act" format?
___ For your longer e-mail message, have you followed the "connect, act, tell" format?
___ With your direct message, have you stated your purpose clearly at the beginning?
___ With your indirect message, have you stated the rationale before presenting your main point?
___ Have you given thought to whether a hard-copy memo or an e-memo would be best?
___ In responding to controversial e-mail messages, have you taken the time to become objective?
___ For your voice mail greeting, have you updated your greeting as needed?
___ Have you taken the time to plan your voice mail message before making a call?

END-OF-CHAPTER ACTIVITIES

ACTIVITY 1: PROCESS MEMO

Instructions: In a memo or an e-memo to your instructor, discuss three points about written communication or voice mail that you learned in this chapter. Why are these points important? Did they change your mind about what to expect on the job? (Use the reflect/respond/revise process strategy to write your message.)

ACTIVITY 2: TEAM ACTIVITY

Situation: When the Recording Industry Association of America (RIAA) sent this e-mail to users of illegal Internet file-sharing services, copies appeared in several electronic mailboxes in your workplace. Your employer has put together a team with the long-term goal of establishing a company policy in regard to conduct on the Internet and with the short-term goal of dealing with online activities considered illegal and/or inappropriate for the workplace.

> COPYRIGHT INFRINGEMENT WARNING: It appears that you are offering copyrighted music to others from your computer. Distributing or downloading copyrighted music on the Internet without permission from the copyright owner is *illegal.* It hurts songwriters who create and musicians who perform the music you love, and all the other people who bring you music.
>
> When you break the law, you risk legal penalties. There is a simple way to avoid that risk: *don't steal music,* either by offering it to others to copy or downloading it on a "file-sharing" system like this.
>
> When you offer music on these systems, you are not anonymous and you can easily be identified. You also may have unlocked and exposed your computer and your private files to anyone on the Internet. Don't take these chances. Disable the share feature or uninstall your "file-sharing" software.
>
> This warning comes from artists, songwriters, musicians, music publishers, record labels and hundreds of thousands of people who work at creating and distributing the music you enjoy. We are unable to receive direct replies to this message.[1]

Instructions: Work with a partner or partners on each of the following activities:

1. Develop a message for companywide distribution that outlines a policy on acceptable Internet use in the workplace and includes the consequences for failure to follow the policy guidelines.

2. Discuss the most effective method for distributing the message to your coworkers.

3. Once you have decided on a format, create a rough draft of the letter to give to your employer for review.

ACTIVITY 3: ALL PRO TEMPS

Situation: This week you are working as a receptionist at a doctor's office. You have just learned that Dr. Ferretti was called out on an emergency and will need to cancel all his morning appointments. Patients have two options: they can either reschedule with Dr. Ferretti for the afternoon or see his partner, Dr. Duffy, this morning. Of course, Dr. Duffy's schedule will be overbooked, and there will be long waits.

Instructions: Mind map a phone message to prepare yourself to speak with patients or leave a voice mail. Since it is an important message, take the time to organize and prioritize the information for your phone call. Thus, you will end up with a numbered list of points to cover with patients.

ACTIVITY 4: CONNECTING WITH YOUR READER

Instructions: Revise each of the following sentences so that it is more effective as part of a business letter opening.

1. I received your letter last week asking for information about our services and products.

2. Enclosed please find the brochure you requested about the 401(k) plans offered by our company.

   _____

3. I am pleased that you are interested in our new line of jeans, and I am also pleased that you are interested in becoming a distributor for them at your store.

   _____

4. I am following up on our telephone conversation from last week concerning our company's interest and ability in handling all of your insurance needs.

   _____

5. I am writing you to let you know that we are still working on solving the discrepancies in your account and to give you an update on the progress we are making with solving the problems in your account.

   _____

ACTIVITY 5: USING BUSINESS COMMUNICATIONS EFFECTIVELY

Instructions: Your manager, Marcus, has left you an urgent message that Miguel Alvarez, from your Mexico City office, needs a copy of an employment contract within two days. You have the contract in hand as well as the Mexico City phone number and address. What steps do you take to ensure the contract gets there in time? What procedures do you use? Do you need to contact Marty or Miguel for more information?

ACTIVITY 6: REFLECT/RESPOND/REVISE

Instructions: Select one of the questions below to answer, and then follow these steps:

1. Take 3 minutes to think about the question and map your response (use a brainstorming tool).
2. Take 6 minutes to write a brief response.
3. Spend 3 minutes editing and revising your response.

- Listening is an important communication skill. What are the qualities of a good listener?
- Attitude often determines the difference between success and failure. What attitudes help a person become successful on the job?
- What are your career objectives? (For example, what do you want to be doing five years from now?)

ACTIVITY 7: DIRECT AND INDIRECT MESSAGES

1. Instructions: To prepare for a company meeting on customer service guidelines, Carson D'Anca, president of Here Today Gone Tomorrow Clothing, has asked you to rewrite two messages from Chloe Harris, customer service representative, to use as handouts. Carson says to you, "Although Chloe understands company policy, which is to attempt to avoid refunds and returns if at all possible, she has not yet mastered the art of delivering that news to the customer." Rewrite the messages in Figure 4.2 and Figure 4.7 (pages 121 and 131) so that they respond more effectively to the client's needs.

2. **Instructions:** Following repeated complaints from clients, Carson D'Anca, president of Here Today Gone Tomorrow Clothing, has changed company policy in regard to refunds and returns. Carson has asked you to rewrite the letter in Figure 4.7 (on page 131) to let Elaine Gonzales at Adulation Clothing know that her return authorization has been approved. She can mail the pieces to the company address for a full refund. Carson has also authorized you to offer Ms. Gonzalez up to 20 percent in discounts on her next HTGT order to smooth things over.

3. **Instructions:** A crowd of late season shoppers has cleared the summer racks at Adulation Clothing, including all of the disputed pieces from Here Today Gone Tomorrow Clothing. Elaine Gonzalez has just received the return authorization from HTGT for those pieces and the discount offer. She has asked you to compose a letter to Chloe Harris at HTGT thanking her for the return authorization and the discount offer and letting her know that Adulation is very interested in ordering the HTGT line again in the future. (Use the reflect/respond/revise process strategy to write your message.)

ACTIVITY 8: CONNECT/TELL/ACT

Instructions: Edit and revise the following letter. When you revise, pay special attention to the way you structure information—use the CTA (connect, tell, act) format.

Dear Mr. Westin:

I am following up on our conversation from last week concerning services offered by our financial services group.

In that conversation you requested information about our 401(k) plans. I am happy to say that you can find that information in the enclosed brochure. Several options are available to you and your employees. After you review the brochure contact me at 555-4297 so that we can begin to identify specific ways to implement a plan at your company.

Sincerely,

Geraldine Adams

ACTIVITY 9: PLANNING VOICE-MAIL MESSAGES

Instructions: Hampshire Telecommunications has an opening for a part-time position as a communications assistant, a support position for three of its sales representatives. The position entails making phone calls and writing messages in response to customer inquiries about Hampshire's services. Plan a message for Ronda Madera, Hampshire's director of human resources, in which you cover the following:

• Why would you like the position?

• What are your unique qualifications?

• How can Ronda get in touch with you?

Mind map your message; then with a partner role play and critique your message. If either you or your partner has voice mail, leave an actual message so that you can listen to it before you critique it. What would you do differently the next time you call?

REFERENCES

1. Recording Industry Association of America, April 20, 2003.

2. Ewuuk Lomo-David, "Cellular Phone Use and Erosion of Decorum on Campus: A Need for Etiquette and Civility," Association for Business Communication, Greensboro, North Carolina, April 22, 2005.

KEY FOR LEARNING INVENTORY

1.	F	**6.**	T
2.	T	**7.**	a
3.	F	**8.**	F
4.	c	**9.**	T
5.	a, b, e	**10.**	c

Handbook at a Glance, Part 3:

Formatting Standard Business Documents

Formatting gives your document credibility, speaking to your reader before your message does. When documents are framed beautifully with balanced margins, the difference formatting makes is obvious with just a glance. Formatting also provides visual cues to the reader by prioritizing key ideas and making them stand out from the rest of the text.

Some elements of formatting are headings and subheadings, bullets and numbers, font, color, bold, underscore, and italics. However, at times the most important element may be the unused portions of the page, often referred to as *white space*. For an effective finished product, all elements must work together harmoniously to present a balanced picture.

The Plan

1. Answer the questions in the Learning Inventory.
2. Review the at-a-glance material, and do the exercises.
3. If you need a more thorough review of key ideas, turn to the Writer's Handbook, Part 3.

Learning Inventory

1. Readers appreciate visual cues that allow them to understand key points at a glance.   T/F
2. White space assists the reader in understanding the meaning of a document.   T/F
3. For vertical spacing, 6 lines equal 1 inch.   T/F
4. With block-style letters, indent paragraphs five spaces.   T/F
5. Bulleted lists must be displayed with parallel structure.   T/F
6. An enclosure notation and an attachment are the same.   T/F
7. For prioritizing ideas, bulleted lists work better than numbered lists.   T/F
8. In e-mail messages, use all-caps to make an idea stand out.   T/F
9. In any type of message, use quotation marks to make an idea stand out.   T/F
10. Side headings should be displayed in parallel structure.   T/F

Formatting Basics: Special Features and White Space

To effect an instantaneous rapport between your reader and your document, break your message into manageable chunks and then display your key ideas prominently. Visual cues allow your reader to scan the document for key points.

Here are some elements that provide visual cues for readers:

- Bullet points or numbered lists.
- Centered, side, and run-in headings.
- Special features (bold, underscore, and italics).
- Fonts.
- White space.

Even short documents can be improved by making key ideas stand out.

Bulleted and Numbered Lists

Bullets and numbers organize and prioritize key points. For items of equal importance, bullets create strong visual cues. For items with different degrees of value, use numbers; list the most important items first.

Items in lists must be displayed in parallel structure. Here are some grammatical structures for list items:

- Active verbs
- Nouns
- Complete sentences
- Phrases (gerund or infinitive)

For example, if the above list were *not* presented in parallel structure, the items might have been written as follows:

- Verbs should be in the active voice.
- Using nouns consistently.
- Use complete sentences.
- Gerund and infinitive phrases are acceptable.

This nonparallel list is understandable, but the words do not flow. The reader must stop to read each bulleted item to digest its meaning. In contrast, parallel structure supports the meaning and does not draw energy away from it.

PRACTICE

Instructions: Apply parallel structure to the two lists below. Rewrite each list three times changing the list items into (1) active verbs, (2) nouns, and (3) gerund or infinitive phrases. For example:

Here are items to add to the agenda for our upcoming team meeting:

Incorrect:
- The proposal for environmental upgrades.
- Selecting a location for managerial retreat.
- Topics for retreat agenda.

Corrected:

Active voice:
- Discuss proposal for environmental upgrades.
- Select a location for managerial retreat.
- Identify topics for retreat agenda.

Nouns:
- Proposal for environmental upgrade.
- Location for retreat.
- Topics for retreat agenda.

Gerund phrases:
- Discussing proposal for environmental upgrades.
- Selecting a location for retreat.
- Identifying topics for the retreat agenda.

Infinitive phrases:
- To discuss proposal for environmental upgrades.
- To select a location for our retreat.
- To identify topics for the retreat agenda.

List A

The topics we need to discuss at our next team meeting are as follows:
- The employee vacation schedule must be developed.
- Smoking policy.
- Changing monthly report format.

Active voice:

- _____

- _____

- _____

Nouns:

- _____
- _____
- _____

Gerund or infinitive phrases:

- _____
- _____
- _____

List B

Our department requests the following from Human Resources:

1. What are the current health insurance benefits?

2. A list of vacation days for each employee.

3. Giving each employee a current policy manual.

Active voice:

1. _____
2. _____
3. _____

Nouns:

1. _____
2. _____
3. _____

Gerund or infinitive phrases:

1. _____
2. _____
3. _____

Centered, Side, and Run-In Headings

Break up memos, papers, and long letters with headings. Cohesive chunks of information make your text more manageable. Create centered and side headings during the composing phase, and use them as a page map.

There are various patterns to follow for headings; once you choose a pattern for your document, remain consistent with spacing, font, and display. Here is one pattern to follow:

- *Document title:* Type the title of your report in all-capital letters and boldface 2 inches from the top of the page (space down 6 lines from the default top margin in your computer template).

- *Centered headings (for sections and parts): A section or part represents a major break in content.* Display a centered (section) heading title in 12-point all-capital letters. Center section headings between the left and right margins, and follow them with a double space (1 blank line). Triple-space before your next section head (or start it 2 inches from the top of a new page).

- *Side headings:* A side heading, or *subheading,* starts at the left margin. Type the heading in bold, all-caps, or caps and lowercase. (For caps and lowercase, capitalize the first letter of every main word but not of a preposition or article with fewer than four letters unless it is the first or last word.) Start the content a double space below it.

- *Run-in headings:* Indent *run-in (paragraphs) headings* 1/2 inch from the left margin. Put the run-in heading in bold cap and lowercase letters followed by a period. (At times, you may use a colon instead of a period.) Space twice and begin your text.

- *Second pages:* Use a correct and consistent pattern to identify second, or additional pages. The preferred method is placing the page number in the upper right-hand corner. Unless you start a new paragraph, make sure you carry over at least 2 lines of the last paragraph to the next page.

When you do a final screening of your document, make sure that the document is consistent and balanced. Present each level of headings in parallel structure.

Special Features and Marks

Special features include **bold,** <u>underscore,</u> and *italics;* special marks include parentheses and quotation marks. For these elements, follow specific guidelines, and use the elements consistently within your document. The bold and underscore features serve a similar purpose; in the body of a document, use one or the other, not both at once. Here is a brief explanation of each:

- *Bold:* Make words or key ideas stand out by putting them in boldface type.
- *Italics:* Stress words; display book titles or foreign terms in italics.
- *Quotation marks:* Enclose direct quotes and jargon presented for the first time.
- *Parentheses:* Put parentheses around information that gives a brief explanation.
- *Caps:* Follow traditional capitalization guidelines; all-capital letters (all-caps) should *not* be used to make words stand out.

PRACTICE

Instructions: Edit the following sentences, incorporating special marks.

1. The word attention can be used in business letters addressed to a company.

   _____

2. He said in his message NOT TO SEND the information by regular mail.

   _____

3. For business writing, use the Latin abbreviation etc. sparingly, if at all.

   _____

4. I avoid using terms such as et al. and e.g. in my writing.

   _____

5. Chart A see page 22 demonstrates the difference between the two approaches.

   _____

Font Size and Color

For most business documents, select conservative fonts, such as Times New Roman, Arial, and Helvetica, and keep them to traditional sizes. Almost all business documents are written in a 12-point font. For e-mail, the default font size is usually 10 points, which is smaller. If you are writing to someone who has difficulty reading small print, increase the size and use the bold feature to enhance the print. The recipient will appreciate the extra care you take.

The traditional color for print and e-mail messages is black. However, for e-mail, a conservative color such as blue also looks professional.

White Space

The term *white space* refers to the unused areas of a document, such as top and side margins and spacing between lines. Standard guidelines dictate the minimum to maximum number of line spaces to leave between the parts of a document. After you learn the guidelines for spacing, you will develop a trained eye for heading and text placement within documents.

White space controls the way your document looks at a glance. Before you finalize your document, ask yourself the following questions:

- Does this document look balanced, appealing, and professional?
- Does it look as if too much information is crowded into too little space?
- Does the document look lopsided, or does it look as if it has a picture frame of white space?

For vertical spacing, 6 lines equal 1 inch. Keeping that measurement in mind, consider these basic guidelines for controlling white space in letters and reports:

Letters:
- Start most letters 2 inches from the top margin of the paper (after the 6 blank lines that your computer automatically leaves, space down 6 lines from the top of your computer page template).
- Use the default margins for most letters.
- For short letters, add more space before the dateline, between the date and the address, before the signature line, and before the reference initials.
- For long letters, leave less space between letter parts and at the top and bottom.
- Do not justify right margins (readers find justified lines more difficult to follow).

Reports:
- Start your first page 2 inches from the top margin (down 6 lines from the default top margin).
- Type the title in 14-point all-caps or bold caps and lowercase; type the body in a 12-point font.
- Use 1-inch margins or the default margins.
- Type the second-page continuation heading 1 inch from the top of the page; after the heading, space down 3 lines before continuing the body of your paper.

Memos:
- Most companies (and personal software packages) provide a memo template.
- To start the body of the memo, space down 3 times (leaving 2 blank lines) after the heading.

Follow established guidelines for research and academic papers. These rules vary slightly from source to source, so consult the reference source your instructor recommends for specifics.

Basic Parts of Letters

Letters are used for formal communications when the topic demands more attention than is possible with a phone call or an e-mail message. Two basic letter styles are the *blocked style* (also referred to as the *full-block style*) and the *simplified style*. The block and simplified are efficient and together provide writers with enough versatility for most purposes.

Block Style

Every letter, regardless of the style, contains basic elements or parts. With the block style, each part starts at the left margin (see Figure HG3.1). Thus, writers have no decisions to make about indenting lines or paragraphs.

1. *Letterhead:* Corporate letterhead contains the company's name, address, phone number, and fax number. Many letterheads also include a logo, an e-mail address, and a Web address, and some show an executive's name and title.

2. *Dateline:* The date appears 3 lines below the letterhead or no more than 2½ inches from the top of the page. (Most software programs give a 1-inch top margin; space down 6 to 9 lines to type the date; check placement with the print preview before printing a copy.)

FIGURE HG3.1 | Block-Style Business Letter

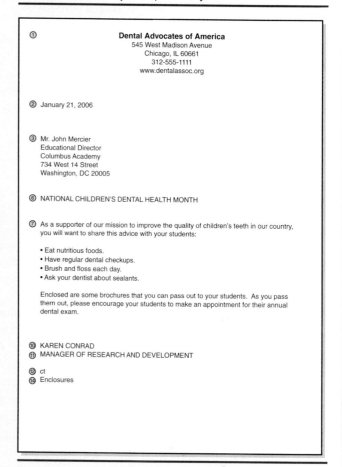

① **Valence Records**
1057 Discovery Court
North Hollywood, CA 90045
877-555-9025 phone
877-555-9021 fax
www.valencepictures.net

② March 18, 2005

③ Ms. Suzanne Colissee
Account Executive
The Pressing House
56 Cavalier Lane
Mosswood, TN 67104

⑤ Dear Suzanne

⑥ CHALICE MUSIC CD PRESS DATE

⑦ Thank you for your close attention to our files. Of course, we are glad to have had the opportunity to make the adjustments you suggested.

However, we are now at what we call the "drop deadline," after which we cannot hope to have the music CD available in conjunction with the video release. Very simply, Suzanne, we need to have the CD master disc within two weeks.

Please contact me immediately. I am keeping my fingers crossed and waiting by the phone to hear from you.

⑧ Sincerely

⑨ VALENCE RECORDS

⑩ Mahmet Singh
⑪ Production Coordinator

⑫ blk
⑬ colissees.10
⑭ Enclosures: Disc with files
⑮ Attachment Notation: New Label Copy
⑯ cc: Kevin Alder, Chalice Productions

⑰ PS: You can reach me at the home number indicated on the new label copy.

FIGURE HG3.2 | Simplified-Style Business Letter

① **Dental Advocates of America**
545 West Madison Avenue
Chicago, IL 60661
312-555-1111
www.dentalassoc.org

② January 21, 2006

③ Mr. John Mercier
Educational Director
Columbus Academy
734 West 14 Street
Washington, DC 20005

⑥ NATIONAL CHILDREN'S DENTAL HEALTH MONTH

⑦ As a supporter of our mission to improve the quality of children's teeth in our country, you will want to share this advice with your students:

• Eat nutritious foods.
• Have regular dental checkups.
• Brush and floss each day.
• Ask your dentist about sealants.

Enclosed are some brochures that you can pass out to your students. As you pass them out, please encourage your students to make an appointment for their annual dental exam.

⑩ KAREN CONRAD
⑪ MANAGER OF RESEARCH AND DEVELOPMENT

⑫ ct
⑭ Enclosures

3. *Inside address:* The inside address contains the name of the recipient, his or her title, and the company name and address.

   • Space down about 4 lines from the dateline before typing the address. (For short letters, space down 6 or 7 lines; for long letters, space down 3 lines.)

   • Type the recipient's name and title (if available).

   • Avoid abbreviating in addresses unless you are following a specific abbreviation system (when in doubt, spell it out).

   • Use two-letter state abbreviations along with the appropriate zip code.

     Type the abbreviation in capital letters, and do not follow it with a period.

     Space one time between the two-letter state abbreviation and the zip code (for example: Chicago, IL 60611).

   • Double-space after the inside address.

   Use the inside-address format on the envelope exactly as it appears in the letter.

4. *Attention line (optional):* If a letter is addressed to a company rather than an individual, direct your letter by using an attention line. The attention line appears a double space below the inside address or as the first line of the inside address (preferred): Attention Credit Department. (If you are writing to an individual, do *not* use an attention line; address the letter directly to that person.)

5. *Salutation or greeting:* The traditional greeting for letters starts with *Dear.* Thus, start your letter with "Dear Ms. Jones" or "Dear Client Representative" (if you do not know the addressee's name). If you are using an attention line, the salutation must refer to the company, not the individual (for example, "Ladies and Gentlemen").

For business correspondence, salutations are followed either by a colon (or a comma if it is a social business letter) or by no punctuation at all. After some contact, you can generally use the person's first name ("Dear Albert") rather than title and last name ("Dear Mr. Clark:"). Double-space after the salutation.

6. *Subject (optional):* The subject usually appears a double space below the salutation. If preferred, the subject can appear above the salutation. You can precede the subject with the word *Subject, In re,* or *Re.* You can also type the subject without labeling it. (The colon after the word *Subject* is optional; use a colon after *In re* or *Re.*) Double space after the subject line.

7. *Body:* The body of your letter can be as short or long as needed to convey your message. The *introductory* paragraph connects your reader with your purpose. The *middle* paragraphs contain the information, explanation, and evidence. That is, the body contains the details and provides examples, if needed. The *closing* paragraph states any needed action.

8. *Complimentary closing:* Business letters are formal and use complimentary closings (e-mail messages are informal and do not need formal complimentary closings). The complimentary closing is typed a double space below the last line of the body. For business letters, use *Sincerely* or *Sincerely yours.* Follow the complimentary closing with a comma if you followed the greeting with a colon (standard punctuation). Space down 4 times from the closing to the writer's name to leave the writer space to sign the letter.

9. *Company signature (optional):* A company signature emphasizes that the letter represents the views of the company as a whole, not just the individual who wrote it. Type the company name in all-capital letters a double space below the complimentary closing.

10. *Writer's name (required):* Type the writer's name 4 lines below the closing (or the company signature, if used), leaving enough space for a handwritten signature.

11. *Writer's title (optional):* For formal correspondence, it is recommended to use a title. Type the title on the line below the name. Double-space before a notation or postscript.

12. *Reference initials (optional):* Reference initials are needed only if the typist is *not* the writer. Since most people now type their own messages, reference initials are not as frequently used as they were in the past. If you type a letter for someone else, put your reference initials in lowercase or caps a double space below the writer's signature.

13. *File name notation (optional):* Documents created with word processing software sometimes need a file name so that they can be retrieved from storage. Follow your company's guidelines for creating file names; file names usually have three components: a name, a separator dot, and an extension consisting of 1 to 3 characters. Place the file name notation below the reference initials.

14. *Enclosure notation (optional):* If you are enclosing something with the letter, make reference to the enclosure in the body of the letter and include an enclosure notation. If you are enclosing several items, list the items.

15. *Attachment notation (optional):* If you paper-clip an item to your letter, use the attachment notation instead of the enclosure notation. In the body of your letter, refer to the document you are attaching.

16. *Copy notation (optional):* A *cc* (courtesy copy) notation appears on all copies and indicates to whom copies are being sent. Some people prefer to use *c* rather than *cc*. A *bcc* (blind-courtesy-copy) appears only on its recipient's copy and not on the original copy or courtesy copies; the addressee is unaware the blind copy was sent. (Obviously, a *bcc* notation on the addressee's copy could cause serious problems.) Single-space between copy notations.

17. *Postscript (optional):* Use a postscript (PS) for an afterthought. Position your postscript a double space below the last notation. You can begin the postscript with *PS* followed by either a period or a colon, or you can omit the *PS*. Here are some examples:

PS. It was great to see you at the meeting!

PS: Thank you for inviting Jorge to the meeting.

The agenda will arrive next week.

Simplified Style

The simplified style streamlines correspondence by replacing the salutation with a subject line. (See Figure HG3.2.) Thus, it is the style of choice when you are not writing to a specific person. The simplified differs from the block style in only a few ways. To type a letter in a simplified style, apply the block-style format with these exceptions:

- Do not use a salutation.
- Place the subject line in *all caps* 3 lines (2 blank lines) below the address; triple-space again before starting the body.
- Do not use a complimentary closing.
- Type the writer's name in *all caps* 5 lines after the body.

Basic Parts of Memos and E-Mail

1. *Heading:* The necessary elements for a memo heading are the following: *To, From, Date,* and *Subject (Re),* as well as *cc* notation if appropriate. The order in which these elements are placed can vary. (If you are not sending copies, do not type in the *cc* notation.)

2. *Salutation:* Memos do not require a salutation; however, many writers prefer to add one. Adding a salutation, such as "Dear Marge:" or "Marge," makes a memo seem more personal.

3. *Body:* Start the body of the memo 2 or 3 lines below the end of the heading. Single-space within paragraphs, but put a double space between them. Block paragraphs at the left. For long memos, use a heading for additional pages, which your software will provide.

4. *Closing:* Memos do not require a signature; however, adding a writer's handwritten initials next to the name at the top (or at the bottom) also personalizes a memo. If you are distributing hard copies of a memo, put a check mark next to each recipient's name as you put the memos into interoffice envelopes or place them in distribution bins.

FIGURE HG3.3 | Memo/E-Memo Template

E-MEMO

① **To:**   [Click here and type name]
   Cc: [Click here and type name]
   From: [Click here and type name]
   Date: [Current date will be inserted automatically]
   Re: [Click here and type subject]

A memo is often used as the cover page to a report that will be distributed internally (a letter would be used as a cover page to a report distributed to external clients).

② More and more frequently, memos are sent as e-memos with different templates used for different purposes. For example, for an e-memo announcing a phone conference, the template would show "Phone Conference" instead of "Memo" for the heading. A specific heading like this alerts the reader immediately to the nature of the message.

FIGURE HG3.4 | E-Mail

To: Receiver@email.com
Cc:
From: Sender@isp.net
Subject: E-Mail Tips

When you write an e-mail, do not take unorthodox shortcuts: follow standard
rules for grammar, punctuation, and capitalization. Also, resist the urge to add
"personality" to your business communications by using *emoticons* such as
smileys or sad faces [:) or :( ], for the same reason you should not use slang
or abbreviate unnecessarily. Since your message can be forwarded up the
chain of command without your knowing it, always keep your messages
professional in tone and appearance.

E-Mail Format

E-mail format is very similar to that of memos or e-memos. With e-mail, software templates
provide the heading; writers need only fill in the necessary information. However, there is still
room for error; the most commonly misused parts are the *cc* and subject lines. Here are a few
guidelines:

- When you expect several recipients to take action on your message, list their names after
  the guide word *To,* not *cc.*
- Use an accurate *subject line,* and update it as your correspondence evolves.
- Use a *greeting,* even if it is only the person's name.
- Keep the *body* (or message) short.
- Use a simple *closing.*
- Include a *sign-off* that lists your company name, address, and phone number. (This infor-
  mation would typically be displayed in a letterhead.)

Envelopes and Labels

There are two basic styles for envelope addresses:

- Capital and lowercase letters with punctuation (referred to as the *inside-address style*).
- All-capital letters without punctuation. (This style is used primarily for labels prepared
  for mass mailings.)

The following guidelines can be used for typing addresses directly on an envelope or on a label:

1. Block each line at the left and single-space.
2. The information in an address starts with the most specific and leads to the most general:

   Addressee's Name

   Title

   Company

   Street Address

   City, State, and Zip

Thus, the last line of the address contains the most general information, which would usually be the city, state, and zip. For international addresses, replace the zip code with the postal code and type the country of destination in all-caps on the next line.

3. For state names, spell out the name of the state or use the two-letter abbreviation of the state name, the preferred method.

4. Leave one space between the two-letter state abbreviation and the zip code.

Envelope Sizes

Envelopes come in various sizes: small, large, and letter size.

1. *Small envelopes:* The official name for small envelopes is *No. 6 ³/₄*. Small envelopes are most frequently used for personal business. Position the mailing label or typed address $2\frac{1}{2}$ inches from the left edge and 2 inches down from the top edge.

2. *Large envelopes:* The traditional business envelope is known as *No. 10*. This larger size accommodates letters nicely when they are folded in three. Position the address on a No. 10 envelope 4 inches from the left edge and 2 inches down from the top edge. Thus, the mailing address will look slightly off center (to the right) when it is positioned correctly.

3. *Letter-size envelopes:* When you do not want to send folded correspondence, use a 12-inch envelope. The 9×12 letter-size envelope is used frequently, along with even larger envelopes provided by professional couriers. Position the mailing label or typed address about 6 inches from the left edge and 5 inches down from the top edge.

To place a letter in a No. 10 envelope, follow these folding instructions:

1. Fold the bottom third of the letter upward.

2. Fold the top third downward.

3. Place the creased edge from step 2 into the envelope first, with the open side toward you.

Key to Learning Inventory

1. T	6. F
2. T	7. F
3. T	8. F
4. F	9. F
5. T	10. T

Persuasive Communication

You never know till you try to reach them how accessible (people) are; but you must approach each (person) by the right door.—Henry Ward Beecher, preacher and writer (1813–1887) ■

When you write persuasively, you are writing to prompt understanding and action. **Persuasion** affects the way people think, act, and feel. You may think that most of your persuasive writing will relate to getting a stranger to adopt an idea, product, or service, but that kind of persuasion in business is rare. More common is the persuasion you will use daily to influence your coworkers. Thus, this chapter distinguishes informal persuasion from formal persuasion:

- **Informal persuasion** is an everyday activity that relates to the way you interact with coworkers and customers. You will use informal persuasion at team meetings as well as in memos and e-mail.

- **Formal persuasion** is less common and is used in customer letters and proposals as well as formal presentations to your customers and coworkers.

Persuasion is not a one-way street marked with road signs leading only to your ideas: effective persuasive writing demands that you understand the concerns, positions, and needs of your audience. Without this understanding, you cannot successfully persuade anyone to take the action you have in mind, whether that action is buying your products and services or accepting your ideas and solutions.

In other words, when you write persuasively, your audience and their expectations, needs, and objectives must shape your communication. When you communicate to persuade, keep these tips in mind:

- *Persuading a customer to buy a particular product or service:* You will be persuasive if you clarify the benefits of your products and services for the particular client. Usually, the benefits a customer finds most persuasive involve products and services that help the customer achieve goals, whether increasing profits, efficiency, and productivity or reducing costs. Focus on specific ways your product, idea, or service will be useful to the client. Be sure to avoid the common mistake of assuming that clients are interested in you, your years of experience, or the size of your company. Clients are instead interested in *how* you can help them overcome obstacles to achieve *their* goals.

- *Persuading a coworker to take a particular action or agree with you on some point:* As with persuading a customer, you must consider your coworker's position relative to your message. Whether you think your coworker will be negatively or positively inclined to your message, always do your best to identify some benefit for her or him. For example, if you are suggesting that certain procedures be changed, highlight the improvements that will be created for those involved.

Many suggest that if you think your audience has a negative bias, you must craft your message using an indirect approach. Perhaps there are highly political circumstances in which this approach may be the best. However, most businesspeople are so busy and so stressed that they will be more receptive if you don't beat around the bush: they want the facts straight and the explanation without frills.

Being straightforward, however, doesn't mean forgetting good manners. Sometimes you will need to persuade in subtle ways, such as offering an apology or making a complaint. With apologies and complaints, you are persuading the recipient to take action because you have taken ownership for your own actions: you persuade by acknowledging and correcting your mistakes.

Persuasion isn't the act of coaxing or encouraging to try to get individuals to do something they don't want to do. Persuasion is the process of finding meaningful benefits and developing creative solutions. Then you encourage your clients—in subtle or obvious, formal or informal, direct or indirect ways—to accept your position.

OBJECTIVES

When you have completed Chapter 5, you will be able to:

- Structure subtle persuasive messages such as apologies, requests, and favors.
- Understand how to shape persuasive messages.
- Describe the difference between formal persuasion and informal persuasion.
- Identify and use the elements of persuasive writing.
- Tailor a persuasive letter to address the needs of the audience.
- Compose sales and marketing letters.

Learning Inventory

1. In business, the most common way to persuade is through formal proposals.   T/F
2. Persuasion should be indirect when your client is negatively biased.   T/F
3. Formal persuasion is more common than informal persuasion.   T/F
4. At team meetings when discussing new ideas with peers, use formal persuasion.   T/F
5. In a persuasive discussion, evidence relates to facts and benefits relate to value.   T/F
6. The first part of a sales or marketing letter usually:
   a.   presents the purpose.
   b.   grabs the reader's attention.
   c.   develops the reader's interest.

7. Before stating the main point of a direct persuasive message, provide evidence. T/F

8. Persuasion relates more to customers than it does to coworkers. T/F

9. Persuasion relates as much to client relationships as to written communication. T/F

10. Which of the following communication options is ineffective if you are persuading coworkers?

    a. memo   c. phone call

    b. meeting   d. business letter

■ SECTION A: THE PROCESS OF PERSUASION

Persuasion is all around you in small and large ways. You persuade others, and they persuade you even when you are not aware of it. Think about your family and friends. When have you tried to affect someone's decision—going out to eat, deciding on a movie, making plans for a trip, buying a new car or clothes?

Here are some on-the-job situations in which you will use persuasion and examples of why you will use it:

Interviews: to prove you are the best candidate based on motivation, skills, and expertise.

Team meetings: to share insights and ideas that will improve projects and systems.

Memos: to explain to coworkers how an idea or policy will improve operations.

Phone calls and e-mails: to show interest in clients and support them in their goals; to answer questions.

Letters: to demonstrate how your services solve clients' problems; to write apologies or respond to complaints.

Clients: to assist clients in achieving their goals; to improve the way the job gets done.

In large part, persuasion relates to what you can do for others by means of your skills and experience, knowledge, leadership qualities, and team abilities. Persuasion involves demonstrating that you will use everything within your power and expertise to get the job done, that is, to serve others in reaching their goals. In getting the job done, you must always remember that persuasion is an *interactive process:* what you offer must intertwine with what others need and want. In each situation, your skills are important only to the degree to which they support your clients, solve their problems, or help them reach their goals.

Because persuasion affects how someone thinks, acts, or feels, persuasion involves change. Any change—good or bad—can create resistance. Identifying resistance and working with it in a positive way is an important aspect of persuasion. Thus, persuasion can be complicated, and the approach you use must remain interactive.

The Role of Trust in Informal Persuasion

Informal persuasion takes many forms, both written and social. Critical to persuasion is establishing good rapport that leads to relationships based on trust. Develop a mind-set that focuses on assisting your clients to reach *their* goals; attending to your clients' needs is the best way to build relationships that lead to trust.

What are some specific strategies for building relationships? Politically and culturally accepted methods change as the corporate culture changes. About 15 or 20 years ago, the best way to build business relationships was to invite clients out to lunch; people commonly joked about the "two-martini business luncheon." Today, busy executives don't often have time for leisurely lunches, and, in most circles, having a martini on company time is *not* acceptable.

The business world is now more competitive than ever, with most jobs requiring more and more effort. One way to establish deeper trust with clients is to have *briefer, more frequent contact.* Thus, set up periodic phone conferences to share valuable information. Compared to on-site meetings or luncheons, short phone meetings require a minimal time commitment. One busy trade executive, when contacting clients to set up a phone conference, says that he has information on the changing market. Rarely does a client turn him down because he proves in each conference that his information is in fact valuable.

VOCABULARY BUILDERS

Convince/Persuade These two words have a slight distinction in meaning but are often used interchangeably. When you *convince* someone, you try to get the person to think the way you do. When you *persuade* someone, you try to get the person to take action.

Thus, you are not trying to convince someone to use your product; you are trying to *convince* the person that your product is the best. In the process, you may *persuade* the person to actually use your product.

COACHING TIP

Who Are Your Clients?
Your clients are those you serve in the process of getting your job done.
An Outdated Way of Thinking:
• Clients are customers who purchase goods or services.
A Current Way of Thinking:
• Clients are customers.
• Clients are coworkers: peers, subordinates, superiors.
Since ultimately you serve the mission of your company, you also serve everyone involved in achieving the mission. Thus, don't limit your view of who your clients are: your coworkers are internal customers.

Relationships are built on mutual exchange. Though people are paid to do a job, they do it with more enthusiasm and expertise when they are treated well. All of us are more likely to treat others well when we realize their connection to us in getting the job done effectively.

Another way to establish good rapport is to show that you appreciate what others do for you. Clients feel your sincerity when you do something as simple as send out a thank-you note. One successful consulting partnership makes it a point to send out two handwritten thank-you notes a week. By acknowledging those who support and assist them, they show that they genuinely appreciate efforts on their behalf.

With customers, you are using persuasion informally when you call or send an e-mail requesting updates on progress and satisfaction. With coworkers (your internal clients), you are using persuasion informally when you present ideas at a team meeting and link them to team and corporate objectives. These informal persuasive touches help strengthen your relationships with your clients, and this leads to deeper *trust,* the central quality of a successful business relationship.

Guidelines for Informal Persuasion

To be persuasive, you must establish good rapport and make your commitment to your clients clear through your attention to their needs. A friendly, reliable business relationship with a predictable track record does more to persuade than a well-written letter or e-mail. Let's start by examining a few basic guidelines for the persuasive process:

1. *Know as much about your client as you do about the idea, product, or service that you are "selling."* To begin learning about your client, consider the following:

   • What is your client's mission?

   • What are your client's immediate needs as well as short-term and long-term objectives?

   • What is your client's budget?

   • How are you and your client associated? Do you have common interests or friends?

   • Does your client have a bias (negative or positive) toward you or your "product"?

   • What level of trust have you and your client established?

   If you are presenting your idea to coworkers, you will be familiar with their needs; however, you will still want to show how your proposal benefits your coworkers and your organization. You can put your understanding of your clients and their mission to good use by clarifying how your products, services, or solutions will help achieve individual and corporate objectives. To meet this challenge, help the clients understand how your proposal will:

   • Increase productivity, efficiency, or effectiveness.

   • Create something new that enhances the way the job gets done.

   • Motivate employees to do their best or train them in a new skill.

   • Solve or alleviate a current problem.

   • Encourage team members to work together cooperatively.

2. *Understand all aspects and implications of your proposed idea, product, or service.* Before you bring your proposal to a decision maker (even your own manager), familiarize yourself with all aspects of it. Discuss your idea with a peer, and transfer your creative insights to paper. Collaborating with a peer helps you anticipate and respond to difficult questions; developing your thoughts on paper helps you organize your proposal logically and effectively so that you are prepared when you share your ideas verbally. Address these questions:

   • What is your product, system, or service? How does it work?

   • How much will it cost? How much time will it save?

   • What problem will it solve or alleviate?

   • How will it affect those who use it? What kind of change does it involve?

   • How long will it take to learn?

   • Why is it better than or different from what was tried before?

- What are the short- and long-term effects of adopting your proposal? What are the consequences of *not* adopting your proposal?

3. *Develop trust.* Your clients are more likely to be receptive to your message if you've established trusting relationships with them: *trust doesn't mean others will listen, but a lack of trust ensures they won't.*

   Whether you are working with coworkers or customers, realize that your daily actions contribute more to your credibility than your formal education, your work experience, and your training. Despite its higher fees, a small writing firm in Chicago won business from a nationally recognized, published writing consultant. The Fortune 500 corporation was tired of working with the more widely known consultant, who was "too difficult and demanding to work with." Another small firm, in business for more than 20 years, has established an extensive client list through only word-of-mouth advertising because its principals have adopted this philosophy: "We promise our clients everything, and then we deliver more than we promise."

   What is your track record? What successes have you created?

   - Do you respect others and listen to their ideas?

   - Are you objective, fair, and consistent in the way you manage yourself and your relationships?

   - Who supports your efforts and trusts your recommendations?

   - Are you accountable for your words and actions?

   You build trust daily through your words and actions. Look beyond your own needs and focus on the needs of others: show respect for subordinates as well as superiors, be consistent and fair in your decisions, and listen patiently even when you are not interested. You cannot force trust; trust takes time to build.

4. *Recognize that resistance tugs at decision makers from many directions, including emotion, logic, trust, attitude, beliefs, priorities, time, costs, and politics.* What keeps decision makers from moving forward? Often, there are complex obstacles that impede action, but sometimes decision makers can't act because proposals don't reflect the most fundamental courtesies, such as *brevity.* For instance, a national commercial real estate corporation sent out a request for proposal (RFP) for a large project and received five proposals: four were an inch and a half thick. The winning proposal was three pages long. The firm's senior vice president remarked, "I didn't even read the long ones: I just didn't have time."

   Some of the more complex obstacles that make it hard for decision makers require that you consider:

   - Do the decision makers have a belief or an assumption that holds them back?

   - Is there a lack of trust in you, your product, or your proposal?

   - Are other priorities creating conflicts?

   - Is the cost or time involved prohibitive?

   - Are the decision makers attached to a less effective product due to habit?

   Some of the less complex issues of getting your proposal adopted relate to presenting your ideas clearly. *Is your proposal simple, clear, and concise?* That is, have you gotten rid of background thinking and unnecessary details? Unless decision makers ask for minute details, prioritize and simplify your proposal.

   If a client is resisting your message, the only way to move forward is to discover the cause of the indecisiveness or lack of enthusiasm. Use communication to uncover resistance, and then stay positive and objective as you offer solutions. Probe deeply to find out the root causes of resistance, or else resistance is likely to resurface at an unexpected and inconvenient time. Remain flexible and open-minded, with the attitude that *every problem has a solution.*

You can counter resistance and dispel confusion by producing evidence that your product or service has benefits that exceed the client's reservations. For example, if the client objects to the cost, show how much money your product or service will save in the long run. If the concern is that the product is good but not needed, show how much more effective operations will be if it is adopted. If decision makers are attached to another product out of habit, demonstrate how easy it is to adjust to yours.

Sometimes these kinds of antidotes help dissolve resistance and move the process forward. However, real reasons for resistance are not easily uncovered, and you won't always have a solution to counteract it. By seeing the situation clearly and then developing an honest response, you know you have done your best regardless of whether you get the business or your ideas adopted.

EXPLORE

1. Identify some situations in which you have used informal persuasion. For example, consider your family and friends. Has a friend or family member asked you to do something you didn't want to do? Have you tried to persuade someone to do something for you? What methods generally work for you?

2. In one of the situations identified in question 1, discuss the dynamics of the persuasive strategy that was used. What resistance was involved? After the discussion, write a few paragraphs explaining the resistance you encountered and how you dealt with it. What were the results?

3. What are some of the ethical issues involved in persuasion? Is it always necessary to provide all relevant information to the decision maker, or is it better to supply only information that will convince him or her? What would be the characteristics of an unethical business communication? Discuss and/or write about your conclusions.

Client Relationships

As discussed, the most critical aspect in persuasion is the relationship you develop with your clients. To some extent, you redefine your relationships each day. Your behavior and the way you think contribute to the way others perceive you; you also influence perceptions by the degree to which you are accountable for your words and actions.

Establishing good working relationships with subordinates, supervisors, and customers contributes to your success in persuading. When you take the time to smile and acknowledge others, they notice. When you treat colleagues with respect and kindness, they treat you well in return. When you go out of your way for team members, they remember your consideration.

Listening to the needs of others and responding to their needs gives you a certain kind of respect that translates to power. Unfortunately, some business professionals leave communication mishaps unresolved. In a shortsighted way, they think that they can ignore people who have no influence or control over them; they walk away without taking responsibility for their role in a communication breakdown. Then they find out (sometimes years later) that the colleague with whom they have an unresolved conflict has been promoted; their "nemesis" is now a decision maker having great influence on whether their proposals are accepted or rejected or even considered. To prevent such situations, use persuasive skills in an informal way on an ongoing basis:

- Establish good rapport and trust with *everyone* with whom you work.
- Understand your clients' needs and interests, and respond to them.
- Determine how your proposal meets your clients' needs *before* you present it.
- Be aware of resistance and embrace it by showing how your product or service benefits your clients and produces value.
- Be accountable for your words, actions, and commitments.

PRACTICE

1. **Background:** In updating your company's computer system, the network coordinator devised a complicated coding system for naming company files and folders. Files that were once listed alphabetically by vendor and customer are now color-coded and numbered according to a system only the network coordinator thoroughly understands. Although it is six months since the changeover, it still takes employees twice as long to access information as it did before the changes were made.

   Instructions: Write a memo to the network coordinator attempting to persuade him to rethink either the coding system or the manner in which it was implemented.

2. **Background:** The last construction job you did for Cadence Developers didn't turn out as expected. For reasons beyond your control—bad weather, a flu bug that infected most of the work crew, and land and title issues that were Cadence's responsibility to resolve—the job was completed late and with cost overruns. But Cadence appreciates the quality of your work; in fact, your perseverance through the initial effort has convinced the company to consider you for another job.

   Instructions: You've prepared your proposal. Now write a letter persuading Cadence to hire you for another job.

3. **Background:** A misplaced decimal in an office memo has led one sales representative in your company to expect a 25 percent bonus commission on high-volume orders, to be paid on top of the standard 10 percent commission, rather than the 2.5 percent correctly identified in several other office documents related to this particular sales incentive program. The company cannot afford to pay more than the 2.5 percent. This situation has come to your attention just days before the commission checks are to be issued.

   Instructions: Compose a message explaining the situation to the sales representative. Would you put the message in an e-mail or a memo? Would you talk to the person on the phone before or after sending the message?

SECTION A: CONCEPT CHECK

1. What are some elements in the persuasive process?
2. What is informal persuasion?
3. Who are your clients?

■ SECTION B: FORMAL PERSUASION

You set the foundation for formal persuasion through informal persuasion, collaborating with your team about ideas and how to implement them. With formal persuasion, you need to go through various stages to adapt your product or service to your client's needs. Identifying your product's value to your client will help you identify the client's motivations, but you must also identify your client's resistance. The credibility and trust that you establish will open a dialogue so that you can deal with resistance head-on. As you examine these issues, rough out your plan in writing.

Regardless of your proposal, when it is finally adopted, it is likely to be different from when you initially present it. Remember that persuasion is a process, and change is an integral part of the process. As you learn more about your client's needs, adapt your proposal specifically to meet those needs.

Dismiss an "all or nothing" mind-set. Understand the boundaries of your proposal before you even speak with your client. What are the limits for each aspect of your proposal? Most resources are negotiable; create a compromise and embrace change to make the transaction flow smoothly. By adapting your proposal, you can sometimes turn an initial

FIGURE 5.1 | The Process of Formal Persuasion

Fact Sheet or White Paper? When you are formally marketing a product or service, develop a fact sheet or white paper to use during meetings or to send to interested customers. A **fact sheet** gives all the pertinent details in anticipation of questions customers may ask. A **white paper** gives more than facts; it contains a discussion of relevant issues, often including marketing strategy and research information to support that strategy. Whereas a fact sheet is more likely to be laid out with bulleted lists, a white paper contains a narrative.

Fact sheets and white papers are useful tools to support marketing and can also provide the foundation for formal proposals.

Fact Sheets Contain:

- *Purpose:* What is your product or service?
- *Evidence:* How have you demonstrated its effectiveness?
- *Benefits:* What value have others experienced from it?
- *Testimonials:* What comments have your clients made to support your mission?

White Papers Contain:

- A *narrative* that discusses relevant issues.
- The *benefits* of a course of action.

After you develop these promotional materials, you will be prepared to discuss your product or service even in spontaneous, informal encounters with potential customers.

---

rejection into a win-win situation. See Figure 5.1 for an overview of what to consider for formal persuasion.

Next we'll examine how you can more clearly define the "object" of your persuasion: your product, service, or idea.

Product, Service, System, or Idea

What are you trying to persuade others to adopt or buy? When the product or idea is developed well enough and meets an identified need, it may sell itself. As you outline and give details about the "what," consider whether your client has tried something similar. Did it succeed or fail, and why? How is your product, service, or idea different? Anticipate questions your client will ask, and then answer them.

Purpose

One way to increase the likelihood that your client will respond to your proposal as you hope is to explore your purpose and relate it to your client's perspective. How does your proposal fit into your broader mission?

Curry-Young Associates, a Chicago-based firm that assists major corporations with improving their employees' writing skills, focuses its purpose on client satisfaction. By equating success with client satisfaction, Jane Curry and Diana Young tell their clients up front, "Our success depends on your satisfaction." As a result, they have a solid foundation of major corporations that use their services, based primarily on word-of-mouth advertising. To focus on client satisfaction, here are some questions that you can ask:

- What are the client's needs? What does your client want to achieve?
- What problem does your product, system, or service solve?
- What are the benefits of the proposed product, system, or service?

Your purpose can be defined by keeping service to others at the center of your operations.

Once you think you understand purpose, probe to identify deeper issues. Explain how your product or idea fits into the larger picture. For example, by offering employees on-the-job training, a company helps its people become more productive. In the process, employees may

COMMUNICATION CHALLENGES

Hierarchy of Needs Psychologist Abraham Maslow developed a **hierarchy of needs** that humans seek to fulfill. The hierarchy prioritizes needs from those at the most basic level—the survival needs—to those at the highest level—the needs for emotional, intellectual, and spiritual fulfillment. In general, humans do not seek to fulfill higher needs while lower needs are threatened. Maslow's hierarchy, with lower-level needs at the bottom of the list, is as follows:

> *Self-actualization:* emotional and spiritual growth.
> *Esteem:* self-respect and respect for others.
> *Social ties:* love, affection, belongingness.
> *Safety:* security.
> *Physiological:* physical survival.

When you are identifying the benefits your proposal offers your client, these five broad categories can give you insight into the kinds of needs that corporations and business-people address. *Where do your ideas fit into the broader scheme of goals and objectives?*

also become more loyal and be less likely to seek jobs elsewhere. Thus, training improves not only skills and morale but also retention. In the long run, the company saves money and has more control over quality; these are some of the deeper purposes served by training.

Audience

Persuading—or selling—can create anxiety. One of your primary responsibilities is to ensure that your client, that is, your audience, feels at ease and confident that you have his or her best interests in mind. In other words, you can have the best product in the world, but *if you don't know your clients, you can't link your proposal to their needs* or identify the most persuasive benefits of the product. Analyze your client's needs and interests, and adapt your proposal to ensure you've put your client's needs first. Once you put your client's needs first, you will alleviate your anxiety as well. Here are some questions you can ask to understand your audience:

- Who is the decision maker? You will save yourself time and energy by identifying the key decision maker early in the process.
- What are your client's needs, objectives, and interests?
- What is your client's corporate mission?
- How does your client's profile mesh with your proposal?

You'll respond better to your clients if you remember that they are human beings. Clients will respond better to you if you remember that *you* are a human being too—and not an aspiring corporate robot. In other words, be friendly, be courteous, be thoughtful, and be responsive. Develop a flexible, welcoming, and problem-solving attitude.

Most important, whether you are communicating with the CEO of a large corporation or a division secretary, the language you use should always clarify that you value and respect your audience. If you adopt this perspective, you will soon find yourself surrounded by people who want to do business with you or want to help you.

Sometimes before you've even won any business, but always after you've established working relationships with clients, you can strengthen those relationships socially. *If schedules permit,* consider social events, such as luncheons. You can get to know your clients informally and thank them for their business. Exploring their needs over pasta and cheesecake expands your comfort zone, as it gives you valuable insights about how you can improve your services for your client.

If you have an interest in learning how to be more social and friendly, read Dale Carnegie's book *How to Win Friends and Influence People.*[1] It is a classic for anyone preparing to make a career in sales.

Motivation

You cannot motivate clients simply by impressing them with your educational degrees, your years of experience, or the company you keep. Get beyond yourself and focus on what your product or service means to your clients.

Your approach should always be grounded in how your offering can benefit your clients, but consider whether logic alone or logic mixed with an emotional pitch will work best. What will it mean if your proposal works or doesn't work? Ask the question "What's in it for me?" from your *client's perspective.* Your proposal's value relates to how it benefits your client: if your client is satisfied, your ideas are a success.

Consider the company's needs or objectives, and ask how your proposal supports them:

- What value and specific benefits does your proposal offer your client?
- What needs does your proposal satisfy? (Consider safety and security, social ties, self-esteem, and career or personal development.)

INTERNET EXERCISE 5.2

More on Maslow To learn more about Abraham Maslow and other thinkers whose work influenced this text, visit the *Foundations of Business Communication* Web site at <http://www.mhhe.com/djyoung>. Once you have accessed the Web site, select "Student Activities" and then click on the Chapter 5 link.

Resistance

Have you ever tried to make a decision listing all the pros and cons associated with it?
The cons side of the list is where you will find **resistance.**

Resistance is a factor in all persuasion. Some resistance is tangible and apparent,
such as having an inadequate budget or needing to address other priorities. Other types
of resistance are intangible, such as your client lacking trust or seeing little merit in the
proposal. Attitudes and emotions are often involved. For example, management may
fear employee reaction, or perhaps decision makers don't want to bother with the kind
of effort the changes will entail. To understand resistance, consider these questions:

- What attitudes or beliefs are involved? What myths do you need to dispel?

- What behavior do you expect to change, and why will the change be difficult?

- What are the costs? Consider costs other than money, such as time and resources.

- Do you need to adjust your way of thinking: are you too eager about your
  proposal?

- Are you too easily discouraged? Do you have the energy to move things forward?

To find out what is blocking commitment to your proposal, ask questions and then
listen. Identify feelings, beliefs, and attitudes—yours and your client's. What are the
reasons your client is reluctant to move forward? Does your client have preconceived
ideas or biases? If you are very excited about your own ideas, is your excitement pushing others away? Are you listening with an objective ear?

Even when you have a good proposal and do everything correctly, resistance is
somewhat unpredictable. You will encounter people who are sold on your ideas before
you even present them as well as those who resist anything new or different without
valid reason. If your client is resisting for *valid* reasons, do *not* try to talk the client out
of his or her position. Forging forward in the presence of valid concerns can create serious, complicated problems. Beyond that, doing so is unethical and will not lead to long-
term, mutually beneficial business relationships.

When a decision maker believes wholeheartedly in a product or idea, nothing can
stand in the way of making it happen. In Rome, there is the saying, *Tutto é possible:*
"All things are possible." That's also true in places other than Rome when everyone is
committed and passionate.

If your client favors your proposal, you can be direct and start talking about how
to implement it. If your client is unfavorable, try to identify the roadblocks and address

*Control Issues: Persuasion isn't
about control; similarly,
overcoming resistance isn't about
forcing people to do something
against their will. The first step in
the persuasive process,
developing your clients' trust,
begins with showing respect for
their needs. Do you remember
the last time someone persuaded
you to do something that wasn't
in your best interests? How did
that incident affect your
relationship with the person?*

concerns directly; to achieve that, you need evidence of success and how that success translates to your client. Thus, the antidote to resistance is the *benefit* your proposal will create.

PRACTICE

Background: Most decisions have pros and cons associated with them. One way to address resistance is to identify a pro to offset every con.

Use structure to help get your ideas across. Put the resistance in the first part of the sentence as a subordinate clause, and then place the idea that offsets the resistance in the main clause. In the following sentence, the resistance is *cost* and the antidote is *time:*

> **Example:**
>
> **Poorly Worded:** I know that you are concerned that the initial costs will be high. I'd like for you to consider that you will save money in the long run because of the reduced time the procedure will take.
>
> **Revised:** Although you are concerned that initial costs will be high, you will save money in the long run because the procedure will save you time.

Instructions: Revise the following sentences to downplay the resistance and highlight the benefit. Use subordinating conjunctions (such as although, since, even though) and adverbial conjunctions (such as however or fortunately) to show contrast.

1. Employees are used to the current procedure and do not want to change. They will praise the new method once they try it because it will save them two hours a day.

    _____

    _____

    _____

2. You mentioned that the cost for the materials is prohibitive. I would like to tell you that the quality of the product will improve customer satisfaction and sales will increase.

    _____

    _____

3. You are concerned about the time and effort it will take for managers to learn a new appraisal system. You may want to consider that employee morale and retention will improve with the new system.

    _____

    _____

COMMUNICATION CHALLENGES

The Specialists
Consultants consider themselves problem solvers. Before they try to solve a problem, they analyze it thoroughly. Part of their research includes interviewing the people involved, designing surveys, and observing behavior over time. A good consultant seeks to develop an honest understanding of company dynamics before proposing changes; in fact, consultants do their research before they even define the real problem.

Ask yourself: *As an employee, are there ways I can incorporate research and an open mind into the manner in which I serve my clients? What are the benefits of remaining objective when confronting problems on the job?*

Evidence

For **evidence,** use data, facts, and figures. Do informal and formal research to test your premises so that your claims are accurate. Evidence is objective and cuts through bias effectively. For example, "When employees take our training course, their average skill improvement is 55 percent." Identify tangible evidence to support your proposal:

- Have others used your product, system, or service? What were their results?
- Do you have any formal or informal research?
- Are other clients willing to give testimonials to support your claims? Often, comments from other clients are your most convincing and motivating evidence.

Benefits

Evidence relates to facts; **benefits** relate to the *value* your proposal will produce for your client. A benefit is derived from evidence. Break down your idea, product, or service into its individual components. What value will each component produce? Identify tangible, objective value as well as intangible, subjective value:

- How does your evidence translate to benefits?
- What value (measurable and intangible) will your proposal produce for your client? In short, what benefits can your client expect?

To identify benefits, ask how results will change for your client if your advice is followed. Translate evidence into benefits; for example, "When employees improve their skills by 55 percent, they will save approximately 2 hours a day because of improved efficiency. They will also reduce errors by about 20 percent, resulting in improved customer satisfaction."

Use your words to paint a picture for your client of how things will look after your proposal is adopted. Visualizing effectiveness can be more persuasive than using words to *convince* someone about a product's effectiveness. With the above example, you might say, "Imagine how relieved you will feel when customer complaints are cut by 20 percent because of your employees' improved efficiency. Picture your employees feeling less stress and more satisfaction with their jobs."[2]

Credibility

Credibility relates to believability, which develops through your accountability. Credibility equates to trust, and trust is a critical element in all relationships. Trust does not mean that your client will accept your ideas, but lack of trust ensures that your idea or product will not be adopted.

- Have you built credibility?
- What evidence can you use to show that clients can trust you to carry out the mission?

Credibility and trust develop over time; you build both by being accountable through your words and actions. By providing evidence, follow-through, examples from similar situations, and referrals from respected colleagues, you can expedite the process. Also provide examples of previous achievements, and explain how your background supports the success of your mission.

Everything you say and do contributes to your credibility. You must establish your credibility *before* you even present your proposal. If your client does not find you credible, your product or idea is inconsequential.

Action Plan

Action comes in stages, and an **action plan** consists of tasks along with specific due dates. Before you actually send a persuasive document, you are likely to have a phone conversation, followed by an e-mail or meeting. Define a plan so that you stay in contact with your client:

- Who or what will be involved?
- What is the time frame?
- What costs are involved?
- What steps can I take to network with my client?

By interacting with your client, you will identify the steps to include in your action plan. Use every contact to research your client's needs and identify resistance; use this information to tailor your proposal to your clients and their current circumstances.

Beyond Customer Service: Building Customer Loyalty

Persuasion relates to serving customers through your ideas, services, and products. Thus, persuasion plays a role in developing a client base that keeps a company fiscally strong. However, persuasion is *not* an event: persuasion is a process. When companies regard persuasion as an event, they spend extraordinary amounts of money and energy on recruiting new clients while systematically losing others.

Many companies lose a high percentage of customers because they are dissatisfied with some aspect of a business transaction.

Think about your own experience. When was the last time you were "rubbed the wrong way" by a business establishment? Was it a restaurant that gave you bad service or food? Was it a corporation whose phone number linked only to recorded messages with no "real" person to answer your question? Was it an understaffed store with no one available to assist you with a purchase? Now think about how that experience changed your views and possibly your behavior: Are you likely to deal with the company in the future? How many people have you told about your bad experience?

According to Paul Timm, author of *Building Customer and Employee Allegiance,* businesses would fare much better if they focused on developing loyalty or allegiance among their customers and employees: A 5 percent increase in customer retention can yield 25 to 100 percent increases in profit. Instead, many companies rely on marketing or advertising to bring in new business while overlooking ways to keep old business from walking out the door.[3]

Now let's go back to your experience as a consumer being treated badly. Did the particular business establishment spend massive amounts of money and effort to recruit your business? Probably so. But it's the little things that have a big impact on customers. And it's the little things that make or break a business relationship.

APPLY

Instructions: Imagine that you are a distributor of a vitamin or sports product. Draft a one-page letter to a friend recommending the product. (Decide whether you will use the direct or indirect method to structure your message.) Make sure that you end the letter with some sort of action—should you give the friend a number to call to order the product, or do you think it would be more effective to set up a meeting to discuss the product?

Customer Feedback   One way to develop customer loyalty is through feedback. By giving customers an opportunity to say what is on their minds, you have an opportunity to change lemons into "lemon-aide." In other words, rather than avoid the negative, embrace it. Let your customers lead you to effective solutions and better customer relations.

By enabling customers to give feedback, you may diffuse their negative feelings. By responding effectively to their feedback, you may not only keep them as customers but also turn their complaints into a source of growth and change for your organization.

Customer feedback will open your eyes to what is turning business away; it will help you retain more of your hard-earned customer base. According to Paul Timm, asking customers three simple questions can give you the insight you need:[4]

1. How satisfied are you?
2. Do you intend to keep doing business with us?
3. Would you recommend us to a friend?

Soliciting feedback in this way creates a dialogue between you and your customers and establishes an active-listening process. Learn what turns customers off, and then reduce the things that cause them to feel discounted, mistreated, frustrated, or angry.

Disenfranchised Customers   Customer dissatisfaction often occurs when customers' expectations are not met. Once you know that a customer is disappointed, what can you do? The important thing is to act quickly to solve the problem. Here is a three-step process Paul Timm suggests:[5]

1. *Feel empathy for the customer.* Realize the customer is in "pain" over the situation, and say something such as, "I understand how you could feel that way."
2. *Resolve the problem.* Ask the person what he or she thinks you could do to solve the problem (which might be something quite different than you would initially consider). Then take the necessary steps to solve the problem.
3. *Offer something that exceeds the customer's expectations.* If you can compensate the customer in some way for time and money lost (such as paying for his or her parking or throwing in a little extra compensation), you are more likely to regain the person's business.

Initially, this approach might sound expensive, but consider the long-term effects of losing one customer. If that customer spends $1000 in one year on your products or services, that's more than $10,000 in ten years. Also, consider the damage that one dissatisfied customer can do when he or she tells several friends about poor service or bad products.

Spending funds to build customer loyalty is at least as effective as (if not more effective than) spending funds on advertising or marketing. Once again, it's the little things businesses do to keep their customers feeling important that make the difference. The human touch restores balance to even the most difficult situations.

EXPLORE

Identify a company that you once dealt with but will no longer patronize or recommend, and then respond to the questions below:

1. What caused your dissatisfaction? What could the company have done to keep your business?
2. What feedback would you have given the company if someone had asked?
3. Could the company have retained you as a customer if it had compensated you fairly?
4. Now when you see that company's advertisements, what thoughts or feelings come to mind?

SECTION B: CONCEPT CHECK

1. Describe some of the differences between formal persuasion and informal persuasion.
2. Name at least three things you should know about your client before you present the idea, product, or service that you are "selling."
3. When speaking of client relationships, whom do you consider to be clients?

■ SECTION C: PERSUASIVE WRITING

Persuasive writing presents your reader with the value and benefits of what you have to offer. Whether you are sending a request to a coworker or a marketing letter to a customer, manage your information flow to get the best results. Make your meaning accessible and your priorities stand out.

For persuasive writing, you have exceptional tools to convey your message, which you may not have considered. By using *formatting tools* such as headings and boldface, you enable your readers to see your key points at a glance. These tools and others are the basis of *visual persuasion.*

Even when you are dealing with negative bias (resistance), you want your document to reflect your position clearly. Your client will either agree with you or disagree, but by putting forth your best effort, you have done your job. Using persuasion, you will not "win" 100 percent of the time. You don't need to *win,* but you do need to move forward with grace and integrity.

Here are some types of persuasive messages you will work on in this section:

- Routine requests
- Requests for favors
- Feasibility reports or memos
- Complaints or claims
- Apologies
- Sales and marketing letters

Common Sense: *While selling your "product" may not change lives or the course of history, displaying integrity and clarity in your dealings speaks volumes about your character and trustworthiness. Is it ever more important to win the argument or make the sale than to honor your sense of integrity?*

Visual Persuasion

Persuasion involves understanding. You can help your client understand your message by using **visual persuasion** to package your ideas. Visual persuasion is the application of formatting tools and techniques to shape your message for your reader in an economic and appealing way. As you produce documents in this section, experiment with visual persuasion so that your client can see your key points instantly.

Tools for visual persuasion include white space, bullets and numbers, and boldface and italics. Some techniques for visual persuasion are the use of headings and the use of subject lines. (See the Writer's Handbook, Part 3, on formatting, for detailed information on using special features.)

Visual persuasion takes your writing beyond the standard of "simple, clear, and concise." When you apply visual persuasion to your well-crafted message, your reader can look at the page and quickly know your main points. Visual persuasion is one more way to serve your client; it saves time for a busy professional who is barraged with reading and decision making.

White Space, Bullets, and Numbers

Create *white space* for your reader by breaking information into readable chunks. One way to ensure adequate white space is to limit the number of lines in each paragraph. Just as a sentence is more readable when it has fewer than 22 words, so is a paragraph easier to read when it takes up fewer lines. In general, for papers, consider 8 lines the maximum length for a paragraph; for letters, consider limiting paragraph length to 6 lines; for e-mail, keep your paragraphs to 4 lines or less.

To further enhance your message, display your key points as lists:

- Use *bullets* to set off important points of equal significance.
- Use *numbers* to prioritize ideas or present a sequence of steps.

As you compose a document, it is unlikely you will see what needs to stand out. Thus, as you edit and revise, select information to display.

Headings

In shorter pieces of writing, such as letters and memos, writers are hesitant to use headings. However, *headings* highlight key points so that the reader begins to understand the message at first glance. The worst kind of writing causes readers to struggle just to understand the message!

When writers state their purpose clearly and up front, the reader digests information more easily. When the main point is clear, necessary details add effective support. In contrast, details can be tedious when they build to a main point.

To develop a heading, pull out the main point from the topic sentence of a paragraph. If you turned it into a heading, would it add value for your reader? Does it enable you to cut out other detail in your paragraph, making your message more concise?

Subject Lines

Whether you are writing an e-mail, a memo, or a letter, use a *subject line* to enhance reader understanding. A subject line also enables your reader to file your message for future reference.

Every e-mail message should have a subject line. Don't get stuck trying to think of a subject line before you write your message. Pull out the main point after you have written the message. Short, descriptive subject lines are the best.

You must use a subject line in memos, but also consider using a subject line in letters, especially letters that you send to clients you don't know well. A subject line enhances understanding for your reader, and readers are more likely to agree with you when they understand what you are saying.

Let's see how to apply visual persuasion and editing to the following short letter to make it more effective.

Dear Chuck:

Bob and I enjoyed meeting with you and Marcie and appreciate the time you spent with us so that we could learn about your company. You and your staff have done a great job expanding your business.

I'm sure your background and experience led you to know how important a good banking relationship is for any company. We would be glad to help you explore banking and financing opportunities that could benefit your company. Please feel free to call me at any time. The resources of the First Bank network are here for you to use.

We wish you continued success in your company ventures.

Sincerely,

Grace

Here is the revision:

Dear Chuck:

We enjoyed meeting you and Marcie today and learning about your company. You have all done a superb job expanding your business.

I know you understand the value of a good banking relationship, and we'd like to help you look at banking and financing options to benefit your company. We specialize in serving the commercial banking needs of companies like yours, and I'm confident our products and services can help you:

- **Reduce** your costs.
- **Increase** your liquidity.
- **Provide** the capital you need to meet your growth objectives.

I will call you in the next few days to discuss the possibility of our working together. In the meantime, please call me at 630.555.6630 if you have questions.

We wish you continued success; thank you again for your time.

Sincerely,

Grace

PRACTICE

Instructions: Take some time to compare and analyze the two letters above. What differences stand out? What forms of visual persuasion were used?

Routine Requests

By far, the most common kind of persuasive document you will write is an e-mail that makes a routine request of a team member. Routine requests are part of taking care of business; when you are not expecting anything out of the ordinary, you don't need to apologize for asking for a colleague's help.

When making routine requests via e-mail, get right to the point and keep your message short (see Figure 5.2):

1. Present requested action and due dates close to the beginning of the message. If a due date is critical, mention this in the subject line.

2. Supply only necessary supporting information. Include a comment explaining why the request is important or what the request will help you accomplish.

3. Express appreciation at the end of your message. Also include next steps, if relevant.

In addition to writing routine requests to coworkers, you will often write routine requests to customers. For example, you may have to ask a client to fill out papers so that a signature is on file. Another type of request to clients might ask them to consider additional services your company provides.

When writing letters for routine requests, begin by stating your purpose for writing and then specify the requested action near the end (see Figure 5.3). Follow this pattern:

1. Connect to the reader and state the purpose of your letter.

2. Explain the reason for the request.

3. Tell the reader what to do, and supply a due date.

4. Show appreciation for action taken, and let the reader know that you are available to answer questions.

If a customer prefers, you can send correspondence as an attachment to an e-mail. Thus, your e-mail would function as a cover letter for the correspondence you are attaching. See Figure 5.4.

When you are writing to someone within your corporation who is not a team member, take extra care with routine requests. Though you both support a common mission, someone who is not on your team may not immediately understand the relevance of your request. You may want to treat your request more like a "favor."

FIGURE 5.2 | Routine Request via E-mail

Does this e-mail use a thinker or a feeler approach? Is the tone appropriate?

To: George
CC: John Silvers
Subject: February 11 Presentation

George,

John Silvers has asked that you and I make a presentation at the February 11 client conference.

The presentation should cover all changes that we expect to include in the next policy revision. If we identify how the new procedures will benefit clients, our sales staff will be more motivated to make the changes.

Let me know if you can work this into your schedule and when we can meet to plan the presentation.

Alessandro

FIGURE 5.3 | Routine Request via Letter

What kinds of visual persuasion does this letter apply? Did "breaking the rules" get your attention? What response would this letter evoke from you? Are there any changes you would make?

Banking Solutions, Ltd.
1444 West Orchard Avenue
Manchester, RI 02835

October 2, 2006

Mrs. Georgia Roberts
1456 West Maple Avenue
Manchester, RI 02835

Dear Mrs. Roberts:

I am pleased to inform you that we have honored your request to add your daughter Alicia Roberts Grey to your checking and savings accounts. She now has full privileges as a joint owner with full rights of survivorship.

To validate this request, we ask that you and your daughter please:

1. **Sign your names below** where indicated.

_____   _____
Georgia Roberts   Date

_____   _____
Alicia Roberts Grey   Date

2. **Return the signed letter** to us in the enclosed, self-addressed envelope or drop it off at the bank. As soon as we receive your signed form, we will finalize the changes to your accounts.

If you have questions, please call us at 800-555-5555 or stop by the bank. We value our relationship with you, and thank you for this chance to be of service.

Sincerely,

Tammy Higham
Account Specialist

Requests for Favors

A favor goes beyond what would be considered a routine request because you are expecting the reader to do something out of the ordinary. Your favor may take little or great effort, but it is effort that may not benefit the reader directly.

For example, if you ask a coworker to attend a meeting, that is a *request*. If you ask the same colleague to make a presentation in your place, that is a *favor*. For routine requests, you may include why the request is helpful, but for favors you should also include how the favor will benefit the person doing it for you.

Thus, when you write an e-mail requesting a favor, explain its importance as well as the benefit to the reader for granting the favor. (See Figure 5.5.) When writing to someone external to your company, you would be more likely to draft a formal letter. In a letter, also indicate to your reader the significance of the favor. (See Figure 5.6.)

FIGURE 5.4 | Routine Request via E-mail With Attachment

Is there anything in this e-mail message that you would highlight or change?

To: Georgia Roberts
CC:
Subject: Account holder update

Mrs. Roberts:

I enjoyed speaking with you this afternoon.

We were pleased to make all the changes you requested to your accounts. To complete the transaction, however, we need your signature on the updated files. Please take a moment to read the attached letter and return it to us with your signature.

Thank you for attending to this request. If you have questions, please call me at 800-555-5555. I will always be glad to hear from you and to help you in any way I can.

Tammy Higham
Account Specialist
Banking Solutions, Ltd.
1444 West Orchard Avenue
Manchester, Rhode Island
800-555-5555

FIGURE 5.5 | E-Mail Requesting a Favor

Is this an effective persuasive message? What changes would you make?

To: Julianna Janulewicz
Cc:
Subject: November 3 HR Presentation

Julianna,

You know more about human resource trends than anyone I know. On November 3, I am scheduled to present HR trends at our department's annual retreat in Kohler, Wisconsin. Although I was looking forward to the presentation and retreat, I suddenly found myself unavailable due to a family emergency.

Would you consider making the presentation in my place? I would supply you with all the data along with PowerPoint slides. Also, if you are able to present at the retreat, I will add your name as a major contributor when the report is published in *HR Journal Today*.

Please let me know as soon as possible (Friday at the latest) if you can grant me this significant favor.

Matthew Young

PS: Our new CFO will be at the meeting, and I'm sure he'll be impressed by your presentation!

Feasibility Reports

Sharing important, complex ideas in writing rather than verbally improves their prospect of being adopted. At times, you may even turn your idea into a project by presenting it as a **feasibility report** or **feasibility memo.**

Because you build friendly relationships with coworkers, you may not consider turning your ideas into informal proposals. However, your team and superiors will give your ideas more credence when you put them in writing. A feasibility memo can suggest ways to solve a problem as well as suggest ideas for change: developing a new process or procedure, buying a new product, or revising plans already in progress.

A feasibility report is an abbreviated form of proposal, containing two basic parts: The first part presents the project and gives details about how it would work. The second part urges the project's adoption by outlining its benefits. See the example in Figure 5.7.

As you write, you understand your proposal more clearly and present it more concisely. More important, your memo (or report) addresses some of your readers' questions before they even ask them; hence this approach removes some of the "devil's advocate" type of challenges. If you give

FIGURE 5.6 | Letter Requesting a Favor

This letter makes a personal appeal based on a business relationship. Is this appropriate?

September 7, 2006

Mr. Nikolai Kalamatros
Prudential Security Incorporated
One Prudential Plaza
Chicago, IL 60606

Dear Nick:

For several years, our business association has provided me with everything I have needed in terms of quality securities and advice. Now I am going to ask you for a favor.

I know that you share my passion for environmental causes. However, you may not be aware than I am on the board of the Hoosier Environmental Group. This wonderful not-for-profit association has helped save forests and streams in our region for the past two decades.

Needless to say, they run their operation on a shoestring. That's why they are having a fund-raiser this fall. They need funds to support their efforts in reducing toxins in Lake Michigan. Would you consider buying a ticket or two to their gala event, which will be held on October 22? Not only will you enjoy a gourmet meal, but you will also have the opportunity to socialize with the top environmental scientists in our region. Of course, your contribution is tax-deductible.

Your association with this group will go a long way to promote environmental progress, which also helps leave a valuable legacy to your children. I'll call you in a week or two to find out if you will be able to attend the event or make a contribution.

Sincerely,

Denise Baker

team members a copy of your memo before a meeting, you can incorporate subtle changes and eliminate some concerns *before* your team discusses the merits of your proposed project.

So remember, if you want others to apply your ideas, consider putting them in writing. No one may officially recognize your memo as a feasibility report, but your memo nonetheless serves a purpose similar to that of a proposal. Most important, it improves the likelihood that the group will adopt your ideas or turn them into projects.

Complaints or Claims

Making a complaint can be an emotional experience. Agreements or expectations have been violated, and you may have experienced some harm, financial or otherwise. When you have a legitimate complaint, you can handle it in various ways. Depending on the situation and the action you expect, you can make a phone call or write an e-mail or letter.

Realize that when you take the time to complain, you are actually doing a favor for the ones to whom you are complaining: you are giving them an opportunity to right a "wrong." You are also giving insight into a problem that can then be corrected before others experience your "pain."

A letter is the most formal means of making a complaint and will receive the most attention. Letters command action; recipients take formal, written communication seriously. In fact, a letter can be used as legal documentation for evidence, as it contains the details and demonstrates that all parties have been informed. In addition, writing will put the issue into perspective and clarify how to resolve it. (Once you have written about your experience, you may find that you no longer have strong feelings about the issue; you may even feel that you are partly responsible.)

Letters of complaint have traditionally followed an indirect pattern. However, the business world has changed dramatically in recent years: professionals are deluged with correspondence and heavy workloads. Companies are also more service-oriented. In most situations, you can effectively use the direct approach with complaints. (See Figure 5.8.) However, *direct* does not equate to *unprofessional* or *rude;* being direct means stating the

FIGURE 5.7 | Feasibility Memo

> **To:**   Jacob Morgenstern
> **From:**   Roberta Edwards
> **Subject:** Expanding Our Coffee Market
>
> ───────────────────────────────
>
> Though our sales for all coffee products are high, we're always looking for ways to improve our bottom line. Here's an idea we might want to discuss at our next marketing meeting.
>
> We established our niche in the market by restricting sales only to corporate clients. This policy has worked very well for us because it is a strong selling tool; corporations like buying a product that can't be purchased by private consumers.
>
> However, I am getting more and more inquiries from customers who want to put a brewer in their homes. They are disappointed to hear that they cannot buy our brewers because they don't own a corporation. In the past, our policies worked very well because they have firmly established us in the corporate market. However, we no longer need that restriction now that we have enough loyal customers who won't care if we expand.
>
> By developing a home market, we can be ahead of the game in case other "Starbuck quality" brewers come on the home market. We can afford to enter this market by changing some of our "sampling" policies.
>
> Let me know what you think and whether we can address this idea at our next marketing meeting. I will be happy to work out a more detailed proposal or head a team to do market research.

FIGURE 5.8 | Letter of Complaint

Internet Provider, Inc., like other ISPs, has worked diligently to prevent spam from reaching the electronic mailboxes of its clients by employing the latest in antispam technology. But the senders of junk e-mail have worked just as diligently to overcome such antispam efforts. The company's optimistic goal is to reduce spamming by 85 percent before year's end, but, like any other ISP, it cannot promise spam-free service. What are the company's choices in responding to this letter from J. B. Rittier?

February 28, 2006

Internet Provider, Inc.
2003 Bell Drive
Twin Oaks, MI 44508

ATTENTION CUSTOMER SERVICE

For the past several months, I have been receiving tons of unwelcome spam in my e-mail account.

Your customer service department recommended that I open a special spam account, which would intervene so that I do not receive these bothersome messages. Unfortunately, their remedy has not helped the problem but instead made it worse. I still get as much spam as ever; the only messages the spam account intervenes are from friends and associates.

For the past five years, I have been a loyal customer of your corporation, paying my bills regularly and recommending my friends to your service. Please let me know as soon as possible the changes you can make to my account.

Sincerely,

J. B. Rittier

---

purpose clearly and up front instead of in a roundabout way. Here is how you sequence information for each approach:

Indirect Method	**Direct Method**
Identify your expectations and the agreements.	State the problem.
Give examples of how expectations and agreements were violated.	Summarize violated expectations and agreements.
Summarize key points.	State the actions you expect.
State the actions you expect.	

Assume that the party to whom you are complaining will respond, so you want to remain objective. Objectivity will help ensure that the problem is resolved to your satisfaction.

INTERNET EXERCISE 5.3

Collection Chain When dealing with customers who have overdue accounts, what is the best approach for collecting on the bill? Some clients simply need a reminder, while others may require more effort. To find examples of the chain of collection letters you can send before hiring a professional collection agency, visit the *Foundations of Business Communication* Web site at <http://www.mhhe.com/djyoung>.

Once you have accessed the Web site, select "Student Activities" and then click on the Chapter 5 link to get started.

Remember, you are dealing with human beings who have feelings; most people do not make mistakes intentionally. Your objective is getting the problem solved, not making those involved feel bad. Thus, do not use language that you will feel embarrassed by later. Revise your initial emotional response to an objective one:

| **Emotional:** | I am angry and upset about the way your bank is handling my account. |
| **Objective:** | An inaccurate transaction was posted to my account on June 30, 2005. |

Consider using the passive voice for "pointed" sentences:

| **Emotional:** | You made a serious mistake in my account. |
| **Objective:** | A serious mistake has been made in my account. |

Be honest and do not exaggerate. After you have drafted your letter, wait a day or two before sending it. The old saying "You will get more bees with honey than vinegar" applies to complaints. Also, let the reader know you are an asset and a valuable ally when business flows smoothly. You will create less resistance to your cause and be more likely to encourage corrective action. *Even when you are correct and another is wrong, you are not justified to act without dignity.*

Apologies: Responding to a Complaint

As Duke Ellington once said, "A problem is a chance for you to do your best."

Whether you receive a complaint by letter, phone, or e-mail, your response will determine the future of your business relationship with the customer making the complaint. It is normal to feel defensive when someone is telling you that you did something wrong. The truth is, mistakes happen. Someone is responsible, and at times that may be you. An *honest mistake* is one in which you inadvertently break an agreement or misread the situation.

When someone complains directly to you about a broken agreement or unfulfilled expectation, freewrite your response to reach clarity. Then determine whether you need to make a phone call or draft a letter. Depending on the situation, a formal apology may be in order. (See Figure 5.9.) To make a formal apology to a customer, either call, write a letter, or do both. If the situation warrants doing both, you may call first or call as a follow-up to the letter—whichever best suits the circumstances. To make a formal apology to a coworker, either call, write an e-mail, or do both.

Making an apology implies only that you are a human being. Being able to apologize for your mistake without being defensive is a mature character trait. Here are some guidelines to follow:

- Take all complaints seriously; take extra care if the person drafted a letter.

- Read and then *reread* the complaint so that you are sure of what is being said.

- Respond only when you have regained your balance—and you need to regain it quickly.

- Understand the other person's perspective *before* you make contact.

- Assure the person that you understand what has happened and why it is important.

- Do not go into great detail about *why* you made the mistake; doing so could sound defensive.

- Properly acknowledge the person for letting you know about the problem:

| **Poorly worded:** | I received your letter about the problem in your account. |
| **Revised:** | Thank you for taking the time to inform me about the problem in your account. |

FIGURE 5.9 | Letter of Apology

Suppose you wrote the letter in Figure 5.8 to Internet Provider, Inc. Would you be satisfied with the reply shown here? Why or why not?

Internet Provider, Inc.
2003 Bell Drive
Twin Oaks, MI 44508
616-555-1234

March 5, 2006

Mr. J. B. Rittier
5101 Roosevelt Road
Dearborn, MI 44802

Dear Mr. Rittier:

Thank you for taking the time to let us know about the problems you are having with your Internet account.

Our customer service department has received similar complaints recently, and we have taken immediate action. Our software was not picking up new types of spam that were developed only recently to go "under our radar." When spammers do find new ways to break through, information we receive from valuable customers like you helps us to gain control of the situation quickly.

Management also approved more stringent procedures to combat the unwelcome bombardment of such ads. Thus, we are proud to inform you that we can now offer the best protection available, including firewalls, subject line detectors, and methods to ban specific addresses and domains.

Because you are a valued customer, we are crediting two months of service to your account. If you need assistance in adding these features to your computer setup, call me or my associate Mabel Johnston at 800-555-1234, extension 43.

Sincerely,

C. S. Cooper
Customer Service Manager

- Avoid using adjectives and adverbs, such as *truly* and *really,* or you may sound insincere:

Poorly worded:	I am truly sorry that your account was overdrawn and really appreciate your patience.
Revised:	I am sorry that your account was overdrawn and appreciate your understanding and patience.

- Keep a positive tone, and don't make excuses:

Poorly worded:	The mistake should not have happened.
Poorly worded:	I was very busy and not able to meet the deadline.
Revised:	I apologize for the mistake and any inconvenience it has caused you.

- Remain humble, and try to reestablish the relationship and regain trust and respect:

Poorly worded:	I will not let this happen again if you give me another chance.
Revised:	I hope that you will give me a chance to regain your confidence.

When you are dealing with someone who is reasonable, most apologies will dissolve bitter feelings. When you are dealing with someone who is not reasonable, any apology—whether written or spoken—will not suffice. In such situations, you have to acknowledge that you did your best and then dust yourself off and move on.

Use the direct approach for letters of apology:

1. Start by stating your apology.
2. Let the reader know that you value the relationship.
3. Solve the problem and compensate the reader, if appropriate and possible.
4. Invite the reader to call you to discuss the issue further.
5. Encourage the reader to let you know if the problem resurfaces.
6. Follow up with a phone call to make sure that the problem is solved.

Sales and Marketing Letters

By learning how to construct a sales letter, you may become not only a better writer but also a more enlightened consumer.

You have learned that persuasive writing taps into the logic of ideas and may touch on the emotions. With most persuasive writing, you are familiar with your readers, understand their needs, and tailor your proposal to each situation. With sales and marketing letters, you communicate with an abstract, unfamiliar audience. Unlike other types of persuasive writing, sales and marketing letters go beyond logic and primarily tap into the emotions of the reader. Marketing letters focus on a discordance or imbalance between the way things are for the reader and the way the reader would prefer them to be. (See Figure 5.10.)

In order to reach emotions, you must present a topic so that it "hooks" your reader. That assumes some sort of "preexisting condition," such as fear, discomfort, or dissatisfaction. The reader may not be aware of the preexisting condition before you present it, but if you tap into something real with the reader, you may provoke the reader to respond.

Think about advertising. Some advertising presents information in such a way that the reader sees a problem—which may or may not have been realized before—and then an instant solution: quenching thirst, eliminating odors or bacteria, cleaning stains, saving time, improving productivity, losing weight, gaining stamina, providing security, saving money—and the list goes on.

In general, advertising offers products and services that make people feel better about themselves or their lives. Advertising targets specific issues and translates them into problems that people need solved to be happy. Thus, marketing and sales letters solve problems; they focus on the reader's dissatisfaction and then offer an immediate solution. As they present the solution, they must also build the reader's trust. The reader must be led to believe that the solution is the best available at the most reasonable cost. Finally, they tell the reader what action to take.

COACHING TIP

AIDA Model The **AIDA model** provides a traditional approach to developing sales letters:

- *Attention:* Grab the reader's attention with a catchy, flashy claim, question, or statement.
- *Interest:* Develop the reader's interest by making the claim relevant.
- *Desire:* Explain how the change will benefit your reader.
- *Action:* Make it easy for your reader to contact you; keep actions simple and convenient.

FIGURE 5.10 | The AIDA Model

Analyze this letter according to the AIDA model by identifying the following parts: attention, interest, desire, and action. How would you edit or revise the letter? How could you use visual persuasion to improve the letter? What key points would you highlight?

Enterprising Cat Enterprises
44 Paw Paw Lane
Catopolis, MI 77903
1-800-555-CATS

June 7, 2006

Ms. Kallie Branzdat
1437 Calabash Drive
Livonia, MI 77902

Dear Ms. Branzdat:

Do you spend your days worried that your feline family members at home aren't getting the stimulation and attention they need and deserve? Does it distract from the quality of your time away from the house? Imagine the peace of mind that comes with knowing that in your absence, you've provided entertainment and stimulation for their ever-curious minds.

New from Enterprising Cat, the Entertain Kitty DVD Series offers lush landscapes with lots of movement to capture the imagination of your feline companions. Your cats will be mesmerized by the aquatic action in our best-selling See Undersea environment, which takes them to the depths of the Great Barrier Reef. Our newest title, Rainforest Canopy, will provide hours of fascinating entertainment focused on hundreds of species of birds in their natural habitat. You can even run different discs simultaneously on different TVs throughout the home while you are away!

You can select any video from the Entertain Kitty DVD Series, or join the Enterprising Cat DVD Club and receive a lush, new title from the Entertain Kitty DVD Series every month for a year. Simply fill out the attached postage-paid response card, indicate the form of payment, and mail the form to complete your order.

Act now and you and your cat friends will have a little more peace of mind every time you step out the door.

Sincerely,

Tom "Cat" Carruthers
President

rs

When you see how your cats react to the Entertain Kitty DVD Series, you'll never feel guilty for leaving them home alone again.

Here is breakdown of what you are trying to achieve with your marketing letter:

1. Draw attention to how your product relates to your reader's "dilemma."
2. Offer a solution; show how your proposal offers unique benefits to the reader.
3. Build trust and credibility for your product and company.
4. Make it easy for your reader to take action to contact you.

This process goes on all around you, but you may not have noticed it. Have you ever seen a TV infomercial that uses this format? Most infomercials are patterned the same way: they make listeners aware of a problem and then talk about how much more wonderful life would be with their product. In fact, an effective infomercial gets the listener to think that life just wouldn't be worth living without the product or service being advertised.

Attention-Getters

For persuasive writing (and speaking), a common approach is to develop an opening that will get your audience's immediate attention. Some common types of attention-getters are questions, quotes, and testimonials.

When you pose a question, you speak directly to each reader. Questions form connections and activate readers' minds. Once you pose the question, your audience cannot help becoming engaged. For example, "When is the last time you left a store angry?" turns a complaint letter from your point of view to your reader's, thus invoking your reader's experiences, emotions, and interest.

Though attention-getters can assist you in getting your message across, do not feel compelled to use one: *it is your message that counts*. First spend your energy developing your message effectively, and then work on finding the best type of opening.

APPLY

Instructions: Watch an infomercial on TV or think of one you have recently seen. Analyze the contents of the infomercial according to the AIDA model. Define the audience and their needs, and then write a letter promoting the product from the infomercial.

 SECTION C: CONCEPT CHECK

1. What is visual persuasion?
2. What is a feasibility memo or report? Why might it be more effective than a phone call for presenting ideas?
3. What are some attention-getters that you have used? Give an example.

SUMMARY

Proposals, presentations, and sales letters are types of formal persuasion. Though these play a major role in persuasive writing in some positions, they play a minor role in most careers. Regardless of your position, you will use informal persuasive skills every day with your manager, employees you supervise, your customers, and your coworkers.

You have examined how to develop messages that convey a complaint or an apology as well as messages that make a request or ask for a favor. Writing these subtle, persuasive communications may never become easy, but you will feel more confident knowing you are structuring them well.

When you persuade someone to buy your product or service, be sure that it serves your client well. You can win by getting a client to adopt your proposal but then lose the relationship because the objective did not meet your client's need. There is a difference between selling your product to a client once and selling your product to a client over and over again. You achieve repeat business by understanding your clients' needs and assisting them in solving problems, enhancing efficiency, or improving productivity.

In contrast to general persuasive writing, advertisements tap into customers' needs more through their emotions than through logic. Most sales and marketing materials are developed by specialists. However, knowing the "template" for the advertising process helps you become a more educated consumer.

In the remaining chapters in this unit, you will apply your persuasive skills to oral presentations and speeches. You will also learn how persuasive techniques differ in other cultures, some of which have a tendency to be more formal than the U.S. culture. As you grow in your career, you will also grow in your understanding of the role persuasion plays in getting your ideas accepted.

CHAPTER 5 CHECKLIST

Persuasive Elements:
___ How have you connected your proposal to your client's needs?
___ How does your proposal benefit and add value to your client?
___ Have you established trust with your client?
___ What evidence have you accumulated to demonstrate that you are trustworthy?
___ Are you treating coworkers and customers with respect?
___ What are the pros and cons of your proposal from your client's point of view?
___ Have you considered how your proposal fits with Maslow's hierarchy of needs?
___ Have you examined ways to build customer loyalty?
___ Have you used visual persuasion effectively?

END-OF-CHAPTER ACTIVITIES

ACTIVITY 1: PROCESS MEMO

Instructions: Write your instructor a process memo or e-memo describing your understanding of the informal persuasive process. Give an example of how you have negotiated a win-win outcome through persuasion. Your example can come from an experience with a friend, family member, or business establishment. Keep your memo to three paragraphs or less. (Use the reflect/respond/revise process strategy.)

ACTIVITY 2: TEAM ACTIVITIES

Instructions: With a partner, analyze informal and formal persuasion. What are the elements of each as well as their similarities and differences? What is the difference between *convince* and *persuade?* How do ethics relate to persuasion? Also discuss the kinds of things that motivate you and the people you have worked for. (As you discuss these concepts, do a mind map of your ideas or take detailed notes; use this information for Activity 8, on page 188.)

ACTIVITY 3: ALL PRO TEMPS

Background: At times corporations create form letters for specific purposes, thinking their employees will spend too much time composing letters and make too many errors. If you have ever received one of these prefabricated letters, you know they can be rigid and often fail to serve the purpose for which they were designed.

However, if you were sending out a similar message to a large number of clients, you might find a form letter to be necessary. The best solution in most other situations is to draft a letter to suit the specific need as it occurs. If you come across letters that are well written, keep a file of them handy so that you can refer to them as models.

Situation: Bottoms' Boots, maker of the "four-wheelers of outdoor footwear," has announced a recall of two styles of steel-tipped leather boots that appeared on last year's product list. The steel tips have been setting off metal detectors in airports, libraries, and courthouses in several northeastern states where the boots are popular gear. All Pro Temps has been hired to assist the main office with the recall-related issues.

In response to the recall, several thousand customers have already sent items to the warehouse. The items fall into three categories: packages containing the Bottoms' Boots models described in the recall notice, packages containing boots not included in the recall notice (including pairs that aren't even made by Bottoms), and a great number of letters of support from Bottoms' Boots' loyal customers.

Instructions: In order to respond to these packages and letters, your team needs to draft several form letters that will be mailed to each customer who returned an item because of the recall. Bottoms' management wants to emphasize that the recall has been instituted voluntarily to better serve its customers. The form letters should also push the new product line: each letter will be delivered along with a copy of the Bottoms' Boots new fall catalog. Prepare the following messages:

1. Form letter acknowledging receipt of the recalled boots, apologizing for any inconveniences caused by the error, and promising to have the repaired boots redelivered within 10 days.

2. Form letter explaining to clients who have sent boots not covered by the recall that their boots are being returned. This letter should invite recipients to review the catalog and visit the company's Web site to learn more about Bottoms' newest product line.

3. Form letter thanking supportive clients for their kind messages in regard to Bottoms' Boots and inviting them to review the company's newest product line.

4. Form letter asking vendors to hold on to warehouse deliveries for two weeks while the bulk of the recall returns are being processed.

ACTIVITY 4: STRUCTURING SUBTLE PERSUASIVE MESSAGES

Instructions: You have used the same credit card company for over 20 years and have had an unblemished payment history until recently. Although you mailed the last three payments to your credit card company 7 to 10 days before the due date (the last day of the month), each of these payments was recorded as arriving late, and each time you have been charged both a finance charge and a $50 late fee. A phone call was all it took to get the late fees removed the first two times; however, this month the credit card company is refusing to waive the late fee, telling you that you have abused the privilege and should be responsible for the late fee. Write a letter to Platinum Services asking that the late fee be removed from your account.

ACTIVITY 5: USING DIRECT AND INDIRECT APPROACHES

Situation: You have been offered a part-time position working for the dean of your college, Ms. Evans. Though you would like to accept the position, you have other obligations that prevent you from accepting.

Instructions: Craft two different replies to this offer, one using the direct approach and the other using the indirect approach.

ACTIVITY 6: THE ELEMENTS OF PERSUASION

Part A

Instructions: Turn the facts below into benefits. For example:

Fact: The art of persuasion relates to understanding the needs of an audience.
Benefit: By understanding the needs of an audience, a person becomes more effective at finding solutions and negotiating successful outcomes.

1. **Fact:** A college education develops critical thinking skills.
   Benefit: By developing critical thinking skills,

2. **Fact:** Some companies work on building customer loyalty.
   Benefit: By building customer loyalty,

3. **Fact:** The 540 XKE can reach 60 miles per hour within 5 seconds.
   Benefit: By reaching 60 miles per hour within 5 seconds,

4. **Fact:** Our makeup will cover your most unsightly blemishes.
   Benefit: With even your most unsightly blemishes covered,

5. **Fact:** Our company offers employees full health coverage.
   Benefit:

Part B

Instructions: Think of five facts about yourself that relate to your skills—things that would be good to bring up on a job interview. Express each fact in a sentence, such as the following:

Fact: My keyboarding skills are 50 wpm with fewer than 2 errors.

1. *Fact:* _____
2. *Fact:* _____
3. *Fact:* _____
4. *Fact:* _____
5. *Fact:* _____

Now turn your five facts into five benefits. For example:

Benefit: By typing 50 wpm accurately, I am productive and efficient.

6. *Benefit:* _____

7. *Benefit:* _____

8. *Benefit:* _____

9. *Benefit:* _____

10. *Benefit:* _____

ACTIVITY 7: ACCENTUATING THE POSITIVE

Instructions: Use subordinate conjunctions to revise the sentences below so that they are more concise and the positive feature stands out. In other words, subordinate the resistance and put the positive in an independent clause. For example:

Weak:
I know the price is higher than you expected. Our research indicates that customers are able to recapture 100 percent of their initial cost within the first year.

Revised:
Even though the price seems high now, within the first year you will recapture 100 percent of your initial cost.

1. You have indicated that your employees are resisting the software training. Their skills will improve, and they should save an hour a day by being more efficient on routine tasks.

   _____

   _____

2. You are concerned that the new X-copier produces fewer copies per minute than your previous copier. You will find over time that it has a higher-quality image and costs much less than the copier you have replaced.

   _____

   _____

3. Your major hesitation in buying this car is that it costs more than the other models. One thing you should consider is that the luxury features do more than make riders comfortable; they make them safer.

   _____

   _____

ACTIVITY 8: FORMAL AND INFORMAL PERSUASION

Instructions: Complete *one* of the following:

- Write a one-page report summarizing the elements of informal *or* formal persuasion.
- Write a one- to three-page paper that compares and contrasts formal and informal persuasion.

ACTIVITY 9: IDENTIFYING AUDIENCE NEEDS

Instructions: Interview a peer or family member.

1. What are the interests, goals, or dreams of the person you are interviewing?
2. Identify your interviewee's short- and long-term goals or a problem on which he or she would like to work.
3. How do your interviewee's objectives relate to Maslow's hierarchy of needs?
4. What are the challenges associated with making progress toward the objectives?
5. What does your subject need from friends or family to achieve his or her goals?
6. What can you do as a peer or family member to support your subject's mission?

ACTIVITY 10: INVENTING A SOLUTION

Instructions: With a partner, identify a need that either or both of you would like to address. Losing weight? Finding a mate? Becoming instantly wealthy? Getting rid of the clutter in your life? Now assume there is a product that would solve your problem. What would the product be? How would you market it?

Now that you've defined the problem and solution, write a marketing letter using the AIDA model. Be outrageous and funny as long as you also remain focused and ethical.

ACTIVITY 11: SHAPE PROPOSALS

Instructions: Edit the following persuasive letter. Add elements of visual persuasion, and revise the structure so that it follows the direct approach.

Dear Joe:

We are a leader in providing retirement and 401(k) plans to individuals who waited until they were in their 40s before thinking about the costs of retirement. Though you may have put off thinking about retirement, it is not too late to plan for your future.

Our firm is considered a conservative money manager. We have provided excellent returns to our clients while taking less risk than most money managers. We plan and design services based on your needs at no extra cost. We offer you an option of having a report sent to you monthly, and you can also check your investments online through a secure server.

Enclosed please find our latest brochure. In the brochure you can see more details on how we assist our clients plan for secure retirements.

Please call me at 555-5292 if you would like additional information. Once again, thank you for taking the time to consider the options we provide.

Sincerely,

Manny O'Brien
Investment Consultant

REFERENCES

1. Dale Carnegie, *How to Win Friends and Influence People,* Simon & Schuster, New York, 1964.

2. Dale Carnegie sales courses, given throughout many areas of the country, help participants develop expertise in clarifying benefits, evidence, and painting a visual picture.

3. Paul Timm, *Building Customer and Employee Allegiance,* Communication Solutions, Orem, Utah, 2004.

4. Ibid., p. 15.

5. Ibid., pp. 35–55.

KEY FOR LEARNING INVENTORY

1.	F	**6.**	b
2.	T	**7.**	F
3.	F	**8.**	F
4.	F	**9.**	T
5.	T	**10.**	d

Verbal Communication Skills

A word in earnest is as good as a speech. —Charles Dickens, novelist (1812–1870) ■

In a world focused on relationships, how you manage interpersonal communication in the workplace can determine your success or failure. This chapter explores various aspects of speaking skills—from casual conversations to formal presentations. Other communication skills that help shape your career are your ability to give and receive feedback and your ability to conduct meetings.

    You may dread speaking in front of an audience. However, you do not need to enjoy an activity to do it well. Even professionals who speak publicly for a living started their careers dreading presentations. The one quality that made them successful was their *persistence*. Your persistence will allow you to push through your resistance to become successful in all aspects of speaking in public.

Formal presentations may provoke the most anxiety, but they are not necessarily your most important speaking engagements. Every time you answer a phone or make comments at a team meeting, you are speaking in public. The way you speak in these casual settings is just as important as, if not more important than, your ability to give a formal presentation. The language of communication is more than words: it includes the nonverbal side of communicating, such as gestures, eye contact, and other types of body language. Thus, the first part of this chapter discusses aspects of informal public speaking. The second part discusses researching and planning a formal presentation and finally preparing a PowerPoint presentation.

OBJECTIVES

When you have completed Chapter 6, you will be able to:

- Understand the difference between Edited American English and community dialect.
- Practice refining the *lagniappe* of communications.
- Examine the qualities of informal communication, such as tone and body language.
- Understand that subtle, unspoken meanings can be conveyed through micromessages.
- Learn how to give and receive feedback for personal and career growth.
- Demonstrate the difference between evaluation and feedback.
- Learn how to give constructive feedback.
- Develop and organize informational presentations.
- Plan a meeting by creating an agenda.
- Lead and/or participate in a roundtable discussion.
- Adapt a presentation to PowerPoint.

Learning Inventory

1. In business, your informal speech patterns are just as important as a formally prepared presentation.   T/F

2. The *lagniappe* of communications is which of the following?
   a. community dialect
   b. slang and fillers
   c. the little something extra thrown in

3. Direct eye contact is always preferred regardless of whom you are speaking to.   T/F

4. Fillers such as *like, just,* and *uh* are acceptable for informal speech in an office.   T/F

5. To improve your enunciation immediately, speak more slowly.   T/F

6. Which *two* of the following language patterns are spoken by the majority of people in the United States?
   a. Edited American English (also known as *Standard English*)
   b. a community dialect
   c. Creole

7. The language of corporate America is Edited American English.   T/F

8. Most people speak a community dialect with friends and family.   T/F

9. A meeting occurs anytime two or more people come together to discuss an issue.   T/F

10. Which of the following is the *least* relevant to achieving a successful presentation?
    a. an interesting topic
    b. making the topic relevant
    c. using appropriate vocabulary
    d. an attention-getting opening

■ SECTION A: INFORMAL SPEECH

Knowing your audience is important, but first you must know yourself. This section covers several concepts of language use: dialect, vocal elements, and body language. Some qualities related to your speech are under your control and easy to change; other qualities are more difficult to change. Just as no one writes perfectly, no one speaks perfectly either: try not to judge yourself and others, and you will make much more progress.

Language Patterns

Linguists have revealed that most people speak more than one dialect and adapt their language depending on the situation.[1] The **language pattern** you use depends partly on the person with whom you are speaking and the social setting. Two common language patterns are Edited American English and community dialect.

Edited American English

Edited American English (EAE) is the most formal language pattern and is commonly referred to as *Standard English*.[2] EAE can be described as the language spoken by newscasters and journalists. Rules of grammar are followed; for example, spoken subject-verb agreement adheres to the rules for the written language (for instance, *he doesn't,* not *he don't*). Word pronunciation reflects phonetic guidelines that appear in dictionaries. This text and others apply Edited American English. In contrast, novels and short stories often incorporate dialects or slang into dialogue and, at times, even the narrative.

Community Dialect

Community dialect (CD) is a term used in reference to any variety of language pattern that differs from Edited American English.[3] Informally known as "home talk" or "talkin' country," community dialect is the language pattern spoken with family and friends. To a greater or lesser degree, a community dialect differs from Edited American English in the following three ways: grammar, word usage, and pronunciation. Community dialects vary dramatically across the nation, with "valley girl talk" and "ebonics" being examples.

EXPLORE

1. How does your language change in different social situations? Do you speak differently in class than you do with friends? When you are at a family reunion, do you speak differently than you do when you are on a job interview?

2. A universal language pattern is "baby talk." People naturally use a special dialect when speaking to babies or their pets. Think about it. Are you even capable of speaking to a baby the way you speak to an adult?

COACHING TIP

Focused Speaking Everyone has anxiety about speaking in public. When you answer a question in class—whether you get the answer right or wrong—let go of the emotional residue quickly. Only a moment after you answer, no one else is thinking about *your* response. Rather than replaying your response in your head, stay focused on the present moment. You learn more by keeping your attention on the group and not on yourself.

A guiding principle: Think *before* you speak. Many of the techniques used to get words on paper can also be used to organize what you plan to say. By writing your ideas on paper, you will have more clarity and control over your words.

Ask yourself: *What qualities make a speaker more effective? Does the success of a presentation have more to do with the content or with the presenter?*

Edited American English and Community Dialect

Most Americans speak a slightly different variety of language with family or friends than they speak at work or school; they speak yet another variety when they communicate with infants. When people are relaxed, they use **informal speech:** they do not pay attention to using proper subject-verb agreement or correct pronouns. They do not pronounce words clearly and distinctly, and they may use slang. Also, with informal speech, people tend to say what is on their minds rather than thinking things through. In reality, most people speak both language systems: Edited American English and a community dialect (or two).

Though community dialects are more accepted today than they were even ten years ago, Edited American English (EAE) is still the language of corporate America. EAE gives speakers a common ground so that meaning is clearer and speakers can identify with each other. EAE also makes understanding easier for English-as-a-second-language speakers and speakers from diverse community backgrounds. Without doubt, job applicants find more success when they speak EAE comfortably in stressful situations (such as job interviews). As a result, many people must adjust their speech patterns when they enter professional environments.

If you speak community dialect more often or more fluently than Edited American English, expand your comfort zone with EAE. Force yourself to speak deliberately until you feel comfortable and fluent in all situations. Find a partner to work with on practicing difficult words or phrases. Do not wait until you are ready to go on interviews; finding a job will be hard enough. Take small steps now to refine your Edited American English, and your job search will be less overwhelming.

However, just as being bilingual has benefits, so does being **bidialectual** (speaking EAE and a community dialect). Before being critical of community dialects, examine some of the benefits. People express certain feelings and emotions far better in a dialect than in EAE; for example, extreme sadness, joy, or anger. Family and friends identify with one another through language patterns. You can find affinity even among strangers who speak the same variety of language you do. And remember, to a greater or lesser degree, *everyone* speaks a dialect. No one speaks Standard English perfectly—it isn't even possible to do so.

EXPLORE

1. Language patterns vary throughout the country. Think about your background: Did you grow up in an urban or a rural community? A city, suburb, or small town? In the North, South, East, or West (or variation thereof)? How does your speech vary from that of friends who grew up in other parts of the country?

2. What are some qualities of your community dialect? Look for differences in verb conjugation (for example, *I seen, she done, the manager had went*) and word usage (for example, using slang such as "fittin'," "yous guys," "all y'all", or "you'ins").

3. With a partner, list at least five words and phrases you now commonly use but would not say at a job interview. Also, discuss a strategy for making changes in your speech pattern.

Vocal Elements

Beyond dialect, vocal elements such as fluency, tone of voice, rate of speech, and enunciation also play a role in speech patterns. To improve your vocal presentation, practice the various elements until you have control over them when you speak. If you feel you need more assistance, find out if your college offers speech coaching through a special services department or some other student auxiliary department.

Fluency   **Fluency** occurs in the absence of distracting vocal habits. Listen to the speech patterns of those in your immediate circle of friends. In a communication exchange, how many times do **filler words** such as *um, uh, you know, er, like,* and *just* pop up in the conversation? What are some other fillers that you sometimes hear?

Tone of Voice   Your **tone** should reinforce the verbal message you are relaying. Whether you are speaking casually or doing a formal presentation, your inflection should be appropriate. With informal speech, be conscious of the emotion in your voice. With a formal presentation, vary the tone subtly so that you are not putting your audience to sleep with a controlled monotone.

Enunciation   Proper **enunciation** ensures that you are saying words clearly and distinctly. *By speaking slowly,* you can enunciate words more clearly.

When people are nervous, they naturally speak faster and their pronunciation sounds slurred. As a result, listeners have difficulty understanding what they are saying. In addition, *speaking quickly actually makes the speaker feel more anxious.* The first thing many speech pathologists teach their clients to do is *slow down.* For pronunciation, speaking slowly solves many speech problems:

1. The speaker pronounces words clearly and distinctly.

2. The listener becomes more engaged because the message becomes easier to understand.

3. Both the speaker and the listener relax when the rhythm is slower.

When you are feeling nervous about speaking in public, concentrate on your breathing. Turn shallow, fast breathing into slow, rhythmic breathing. For each inhale and exhale, breathe slowly to a count of eight through your diaphragm (your "belly," not your chest). By breathing deeply and concentrating on your breath, you are taking your focus off what makes you nervous. In summary, to control vocal elements of your speech:

- Speak slowly to enunciate clearly.
- Cut out fillers to achieve fluency.
- Control your tone, *especially loudness,* to suit the circumstances; use tone and inflection to reinforce your verbal message.
- Practice diaphragmatic breathing.

EXPLORE

Discuss the following statement, attributed to an unknown source: "Am I running because I am scared or am I scared because I am running?"

1. How does this apply to speaking in public?
2. What can you do to speak more effectively in a group setting?

PRACTICE

1. **Instructions:** In class, select a partner. Decide who will be the first speaker and who the first listener. As the speaker, spend 2 minutes describing something funny that happened to you within the last year. As the listener, identify filler words and make a check mark each time your partner uses one. Now switch roles and repeat the exercise. Do you use any filler words that your partner didn't use?

   What did you discover about yourself in this exercise? How many times did the words *like* or *just* creep into the conversation? Don't be surprised if you log in a filler word as many as 30 times in 2 or 3 minutes.

2. **Instructions:** Identify aspects of your enunciation that you can improve, such as pronouncing word endings like *ing* or *ed.* Make a list of words that end in *ing* and practice saying them out loud until you feel comfortable saying *dancing* instead of *dancin'* or *talking* instead of *talkin'.*

COACHING TIP

Signal Anxiety Not all anxiety is bad. Some forms of anxiety assist in getting a job done effectively. For example, **signal anxiety** not only alerts a person to a task that needs attention but also provides the energy to achieve it. Signal anxiety is the little tug you feel—that sense of urgency—about an assignment that is due. Instead of "cleaning your closets" or having lunch with a friend, respond to the anxiety by taking care of business. (*After* working on your assignment, you may still have enough energy left to get to your closets!)

Many actors have said that the worst performances of their lives came at times when they felt *no anxiety* about their performance. The best occurred when their signal anxiety provided just enough adrenaline to put an edge on their performance.

Ask Yourself: *Think back to the last time you felt signal anxiety regarding an oral or written communication. How did you respond to the signal? Did your reaction reduce or increase your anxiety?*

Body Language

Communication is more than words. Your **body language** speaks to listeners through visual elements, such as eye contact, physical distance between the speaker and the listener, gestures, posture, and body orientation. Body language is as much a part of casual communication as it is of formal presentations. (However, people do not usually consider the message their body language sends unless they are giving a formal presentation.)

Some aspects of body language, such as eye contact, have a cultural dimension. For example, in the United States, many assume that lack of direct eye contact connotes distrust or dishonesty and that the speaker is hiding information. In many Asian cultures, eye contact is a sign of disrespect. Looking someone in the eyes who is superior in status is an affront and is considered rude; in contrast, looking away when communicating with someone who has status over you is considered a sign of respect.

Physical distance is another dimension that differs among cultures. In the United States, a comfortable distance while communicating is an arm's length. Standing closer is likely to create discomfort for one or both parties. In some Middle Eastern cultures, the appropriate distance is less than 10 inches—more face-to-face, nose-to-nose. With rapidly increasing diversity, encounters among people from different cultures can result in cultural collisions because of a lack of understanding about basic communication differences. (You will find more about intercultural and global communication in Chapter 7.)

Other nonverbal elements such as facial expressions and posture add extra meaning to a message, as does the tone of voice; these less tangible aspects of communication are known as the ***lagniappe*** of communications. *Lagniappe* (pronounced lan-yap) is a New Orleans Creole custom of throwing in a little something extra. In informal interactions, the *lagniappe* of communications contributes significantly to

COMMUNICATION CHALLENGES

Speaking in Gestures Do you use your hands when you communicate? Human resource managers have their own codes for interpreting behavior such as tapping your fingers or fiddling with a piece of string during an interview.

Likewise, people from other cultures may have different interpretations of your gestures than what you intend. In England, for example, flashing the V-for-victory symbol with the palm facing inward is considered an insult; in Japan, giving someone the "thumbs up" might bring you an order of five of something; in Brazil, the "OK" sign is considered obscene.

Ask yourself: *Am I conscious of how I use my hands in face-to-face conversation? Do I use my hands differently when I am speaking to a group? What do I think I am communicating with these gestures?*

the message. Think of a recent conversation and how the *lagniappe* contributed to the message; consider sighs and facial expressions (a smirk, a smile, or perhaps an expression of defeat).

For both casual speech and formal presentations, pay attention to the following:

- Appropriate eye contact.
- Physical distance suited to the occasion and the cultural differences.
- Facial expressions that match the words you are speaking.
- Suitable gestures (no fidgeting or other distracting mannerisms).
- Posture that shows you are alert yet relaxed.
- Body orientation that is relaxed and nonconfrontational.

You will violate these guidelines most often when you are nervous or under stress. At those times, take a deep breath and relax into the situation. *If you can look calm, you will begin to feel calm.* Remember this advice when you get in front of an audience to present.

Micromessages

At a recent Association for Business Communications conference, Barbara Davis and Bobbie Krapels presented information about micromessages in the workplace. Micromessages are the silent "subtle, semiconscious, universally understood behaviors that communicate to everyone what the speaker really thinks."[4]

Micromessages can either lead to microadvantages (positive results) or microinequities (negative results). For example, imagine a team of three people working on a project. Two members of the team meet for lunch and then develop a plan for the project, assigning duties and due dates. At the next team meeting they share the plan with the third member, who hears the information for the first time. What was the micromessage to the person who was left out? Was it a microadvantage or a microinequity? How would you feel if you were that third person?

The target of a microinequity feels the repercussions strongly, but others do not necessarily feel the slight or even understand it. That's because the microinequity is difficult to verbalize and deal with professionally. Here's another example. Let's say your boss asks for your input on an important decision, uses your advice, and then credits you in public; the result is that you feel as if your expertise is appreciated (a microadvantage). In turn, let's say your boss uses your input but then overlooks you and instead credits someone else for the advice; you are likely to feel slighted (a microinequity). Clearly, micromessages can be very powerful and lead to serious communication issues.

Microinequities often relate to discrimination in the workplace because they often occur when people are perceived as being different on the basis or race, gender, or culture. Diversity consultant Stephen Young suggests the following four-step approach to dealing with microinequities using the acronym TALK:[5]

1. Talk to yourself and decide if the problem is really a misunderstanding.
2. Approach the person about the perceived inequality.
3. Listen to the person and let him or her explain the perceived problem.
4. Keep communication open.

Keep in mind that the person sending the micromessage is not necessarily aware of it. Regardless, being treated unfairly is a personal as well as professional issue. Most companies take diversity issues seriously because they have a negative impact on employee morale, the corporate culture, and the company's bottom line.

Anxiety

Most people are afraid to speak in public. If you feel fear and anxiety, you are not alone. One successful consultant and author confided that when she was in college, her face broke out in hives and her hands trembled at the thought of speaking in class. As she worked to overcome

Communicating Without Words: *Although nonverbal communication is usually easy to recognize, understanding the exact message is difficult because the meaning depends on interpretation.* List five examples of ways that you communicate nonverbally (for example, "I touch my brakes lightly when a car is driving too close behind me in morning traffic," or "When I put on my red walking shoes, my dog Reggie runs to get his leash"). In these instances, how clearly do you think you communicated your message?

INTERNET EXERCISE 6.1

Oral Authorities For more information on speaking in public, there are books and Web sites that offer additional resources, strategies, and support tools to help with both your presentation and your presentation style. Visit the *Foundations of Business Communication* Web site at <http://www.mhhe.com/djyoung>.

At the home page, select "Student Activities"; then click on the Chapter 6 link to find instructions for getting started.

her fears, this weakness led to strengths and created the foundation for her career in public speaking.

She noticed early on that if she used her anxiety to propel her into action, the anxiety quickly dissipated. To this day, she admits that anxiety is a part of every speaking engagement: "When I don't feel anxiety, I become concerned that I'm not realizing the importance of the event." Her solution is using the extra energy anxiety provides to prepare meticulously: "When all of my materials are ready, so am I." This type of anxiety is known as signal anxiety—use it to your advantage.

Rest assured, no matter how afraid you are, you can overcome your fear. One essential ingredient is being prepared; another is realizing that you are not perfect and that mistakes are part of the growing process. You may never like to speak in public, but you can get the job done anyway. As with every other skill, the more you practice, the better your skills will become and the more confident you will feel. The key to success in public speaking is *persistence.*

Aim for *quality,* not perfection. When you set unreasonable standards (such as being perfect or the best), you become more afraid than you need to be; that's when you are more likely to make mistakes. When you prepare a speech, your speech may inform your audience or maybe even persuade or entertain them. However, your speech will not change people's lives. In other words, the fate of the world does *not* hinge on what you say to your audience. Take your speech for what it is realistically, and then do your best.

No one (including you) is perfect at anything. When you realize that quality is what matters, *not* perfection, you will have learned an important lesson in speaking and in life. (And that's when you are likely to do your best.)

EXPLORE

1. With a partner, discuss a disappointing experience. What are some of the *lagniappe* of communications that your partner expresses? Now discuss something very exciting. What are the "little extras" that you and your partner express?

2. In class, turn to a partner and stand an arm's length apart. Take turns telling each other one thing you learned in class today. Next, move to within six inches of each other and repeat the exercise. Discuss your reaction to this change in proximity.

3. Are you afraid to speak in front of a group? Take a few minutes to write about your feelings and experiences, and then discuss them with a partner.

4. What habits do you have when you speak in front of a group? Think about the last time you were in front of an audience. What did you do? What changes (in body language or something else) would you like to make the next time?

SECTION A: CONCEPT CHECK

1. What are the two language patterns that most people in America speak?

2. List several ways people communicate information nonverbally.

3. List three of the vocal elements that influence a person's oral presentation.

4. What is a micromessage? Identify a micromessage that you have received recently. Now identify one that you have given. What were their effects?

■ SECTION B: FEEDBACK

So far, we've discussed language patterns and body language, important aspects of communication. Now we turn to the content of office communications. Almost every day someone asks you for **feedback,** how you think or feel about a specific topic. On the job, you will need to give *formal feedback,* the kind of feedback that will help others shape their skills and performance. When someone asks for your feedback on a task, do your words reflect *effective* feedback? Only one of the following can be defined as effective feedback. Which one is it?

- State that the job was well done and the person should feel great.

- Give accurate details about how a task was carried out and its results.

- Tell the person how you would do the task differently so that better results could be achieved next time.

This section will help you understand the difference between feedback and evaluation as well as distinguish effective feedback from other types of comments or directives. Just as giving effective feedback is important, so is receiving constructive feedback effectively. Let's start by exploring the difference between feedback and evaluation.

Feedback Versus Evaluation

Often, people think they are giving feedback when instead they are evaluating a person, product, or event. Feedback and evaluation have different purposes:

- Feedback *describes.*

- Evaluation *rates* or *ranks.*

Feedback describes through observation, giving facts and details; however, feedback stops short of using labels and vague terms to "sum up" the person, event, behavior, or product. In contrast, **evaluation** does not indicate the details of something; evaluation rates it. Here are some evaluative terms:

- Good, great, wonderful, well done, excellent

- Bad, poor, ineffective, lazy, unmotivated

Evaluative terms can engage a person's feelings without indicating the *specifics* of what occurred. For example, if someone tells you that you did a *great* job, you immediately feel

COMMUNICATION CHALLENGES

Anger Management It's a fact that people don't always follow through on what they say they're going to do. The world is a bustling, busy place where many factors are often at play that affect a person's ability to follow through. For example, a contractor may quote you a price and a deadline and then run over on the costs and fall behind on the schedule.

Wrestling with mixed emotions is challenging enough, but deciding how to communicate them is even more complex. If you fire the contractor, the work isn't likely to be finished any sooner and the job is probably going to cost you even more. If you simply vent your frustration, you might not see the work crew again for three weeks. Consider: *Do you have an effective process for resolving emotional issues? What does it involve?*

Situation: A business friend calls and invites you to lunch. Though your schedule is busy, you agree to meet your friend at a popular restaurant at noon the following Friday. You show up at the restaurant on time, and you wait but your friend never arrives. You call from the restaurant but get voice mail. Later in the day when you call, you still get your friend's voice mail.

Ask yourself: *What are my feelings? Do I leave a message on voice mail? What do I say? What will I say when I actually speak to my friend? When we do communicate, will I have a purpose in mind? What will my purpose be?*

wonderful (that is, if you did your best and deserved the comment). However, evaluation does not tell you *what* about your effort worked especially well. Evaluation does not indicate the gaps or analyze the aspects that could become stronger; feedback performs these tasks. Feedback mirrors reality without labeling it. For example:

Evaluation: Your letter is good.
Feedback: Your letter states its purpose clearly and directly, but you include too much background information in the body.

Feedback and evaluation are two different tools, and each has a vital role in communication. At the end of a task, sometimes feedback *and* evaluation are necessary; at other times, one *or* the other will meet the needs. In general, evaluating often seems easier than giving detailed, accurate feedback. To give feedback, most people have to force themselves to analyze the situation, whereas evaluating seems to come as a reaction or an immediate response. Analyzing is more difficult than reacting, but analyzing gives the details that lead to effective change. For example:

Evaluation: Our team is doing a poor job.
Feedback: Our team does not have an accurate understanding of the problem because team members do not listen to one another.

Feedback, not evaluation, provides the directive for change. Though evaluation (positive or negative) can be accurate and motivating, evaluation does not indicate details. Feedback provides the road map for change that leads to growth: *What about the method worked well? What didn't work? What do we need to do differently next time?*

Objective Feedback Versus Subjective Evaluation

As discussed, feedback involves giving details rather than rating behavior through evaluative comments. Another aspect to consider is whether comments are objective or subjective:

- When you describe behavior in terms of *facts and observations,* you are giving **objective feedback.**

- When you state your *personal interpretations* of behavior and personality traits and use labels, you are giving a **subjective evaluation.**

Subjective comments are often taken personally; in fact, when comments are negative, the recipient may feel criticized or even attacked. However, objective feedback includes examples of observable behavior and doesn't address personal traits. Objective feedback focuses on tangible evidence that anyone involved could describe in a similar way. For example:

Subjective: George, you did a poor job on your report.
Objective: George, your report was late and had several errors.

In the above example, George may disagree that he did "a poor job" on his report. In fact, he may feel as if the comment *you did a poor job* is a personal attack. However, he could not disagree about the errors the report included. Hearing the objective comments, George is more likely to understand that the *report* is being discussed, not George as an individual.

Here's another example of a subjective comment:

Subjective: I don't think that you're motivated.

This comment interprets the person being addressed more than the behavior, and the person could respond in a defensive or argumentative way. In addition, the subjective comment may not be true; it is an *interpretation* of how the observer perceives behavior. A more objective approach would describe details of the behavior first and then offer an evaluative comment, if appropriate. Any evaluative comment should be phrased so that it is clear that the interpretation is coming from the speaker's point of view. For example:

Objective: You have arrived at work every day this week after 8:15, but your starting time is 8 o'clock sharp. That makes me question your motivation. Is there something you need to discuss with me?

In the above scenario, the person addressed may have had a valid reason for being late; perhaps there was a transportation problem or a sick child who needed tending. An important purpose of feedback is not only improving work performance but also improving the relationship among coworkers. *Objective feedback opens up a dialogue to gain an accurate understanding.*

In general, and especially with negative feedback, the best time to evaluate is *after* you provide accurate, thorough feedback. Then the listener is more apt to understand how you reached the evaluative comment. If you say something is "great," *why* is it great? If you start out by telling someone that a job was done poorly, the person may not hear much of what you say afterward. In addition, once you give accurate details about a poorly done task, an astute listener can figure out that it was a "bad job" and shouldn't be surprised when you say so. In fact, you may not need to add an evaluative comment; the point can be made through an accurate description.

You may want to refer to this section when you examine how to do job appraisals. Good job appraisals include detailed feedback that then leads to evaluative comments.

EXPLORE

Think of an experience in which you were given feedback, subjective or objective.

1. What about the experience was effective, and what was not effective?
2. Did you grow from the experience? How?

PRACTICE

Instructions: Select a document (letter, memo, e-mail message) that you completed for this class or another. Make sure it is an original with no comments or corrective marks. With a partner, exchange papers.

1. Give feedback on why the document was effective or ineffective.
2. Give an evaluative term to sum up the feedback.

Specific Feedback Versus General Comments

In addition to being objective, effective feedback gives specific details and examples rather than general comments. A general comment does not provide the listener with concrete information, so the main point often remains misunderstood. For example, if you were giving feedback to an employee about team relationships, the person might not understand what you meant if you said the following:

General: You don't treat people with respect.

Challenging Communication With communication, "recipes" usually don't work well. That's because communication must remain interactive; at its best, communication is an honest exchange between human beings. However, since giving constructive feedback can be difficult, here's a "formula" to keep the discussion focused when you are addressing something that affects you personally:

- First, state the problem and how it affects you; for example:
  > When you give me reports late, I cannot complete my work on time; and as a result, I feel as if you are not respecting my time.
- Next, state what the person can do to solve the problem; for example:
  > My request is that in the future you meet the deadlines or let me know in advance if you cannot meet them.
- Finally, open a dialogue by asking whether the person could change the behavior; for example:
  > Would you do that for me?

Here's another example:
> When you make sarcastic remarks about me, I feel hurt. Regardless of whether we are in a meeting or alone, I would appreciate it if you would stop making such comments about me. Would you be willing to stop making those sarcastic remarks?

Now think of a current situation and fill in the blanks below:
> When you _____, it makes me feel _____.
> Therefore, I would appreciate it if you would _____.
> Would you be willing to _____?

It takes courage to give (and receive) constructive feedback, but doing so can change ineffective behavior and put relationships back on the right track.

The person receiving this comment may have started the discussion feeling good about personal and professional relationships and be confused by such a vague statement. When people don't know how to respond, they are more likely to become defensive and defiant: "That's not true! I respect everyone and get along very well with others!" However, if you describe specific incidents that illustrate the behavior in question, the person will know what you are talking about. For example:

Specific: You seemed to interrupt Janet unnecessarily several times during our last team meeting. I felt as if you weren't really listening to her points.

This type of specific example might allow the listener to gain insight into how others perceive him or her. It might lead to an apology and a change in behavior, which is the ultimate goal. Here's another example:

General: You never turn in your reports on time.
Specific: You turned in your last report two days late; the one before that was a day late.

Allow the details to speak by focusing on observable behavior; the discussion will remain more objective. Next, we'll identify the difference between negative and constructive feedback.

Negative Feedback Versus Constructive Feedback

So far, we have stressed the importance of giving feedback that is objective and specific rather than subjective and general, focusing feedback on the behavior, not the person. Another distinction is that between negative feedback and constructive feedback:

- **Negative feedback** identifies the problem but not the solution.
- **Constructive feedback** identifies the problem, offers a possible solution, and opens a dialogue.

Constructive feedback doesn't point an accusing finger at an offender; it gets the involved persons talking. *The goal of feedback is to change behavior, not to hurt the person receiving it.* However, if feedback is not conveyed effectively, the person receiving it can feel attacked. To help ensure that your motives are in the right place, before you give any kind of negative feedback, ask yourself the following: *What is my purpose in giving this feedback? What do I want or intend to achieve?*

The way feedback is given (and received) can enhance or destroy a relationship between colleagues as well as an individual's career at a specific place of employment. Be cautious about giving negative feedback or avoid it altogether by turning your comments into constructive feedback. If you have any doubts about how to convey constructive feedback, role-play the situation with a peer or your manager.

The best time to address inappropriate behavior is soon after the behavior occurred. However, constructive feedback must also be given at a time when neither the speaker nor the listener feels emotional about it. For example, if either party is upset, that is not the time to address the behavior or incident: the speaker will not be objective and constructive, the listener will not hear the important points, and the response may be defensive rather than responsible. When emotions are high, call a "time out" until things settle down and an objective discussion can occur.

An Example of Constructive Feedback

When inappropriate behavior occurs, constructive feedback is in order; even so, constructive feedback can be difficult to give. That may be one reason why feedback sometimes turns personal by the time it is expressed. A person holds in the feedback until it explodes. Giving small bits of constructive feedback as incidents occur can sometimes correct performance concerns *before* they turn into problems.

Even though it may be objective, constructive feedback can still be difficult for the recipient to accept. One way to give constructive feedback is to start out with a truthful, positive comment. The reason for starting with something positive is to focus on changing the behavior, not hurting the person. For example:

> Gerry, I notice that your reports are thorough and accurate. However, the last two reports have been late. Will you be able to meet next month's deadline? What kind of support do you need from me so that your reports get done on time?

Notice that Gerry's supervisor gives directives through questions. As Gerry and the supervisor discuss this problem in more detail, the supervisor might find out that Gerry has been waiting for information from another department and that's why the reports have been late. Then again, maybe Gerry has no valid reason for being late. If that is the case, the two could develop a system of accountability to ensure the reports get in on schedule.

When you give constructive feedback, be especially conscious of what you are doing:

- Discuss challenging issues in private so that the recipient need not feel concerned that the conversation is being overheard.
- Do not put your concerns in writing until *after* you meet with the recipient to discuss them—you may clarify misunderstandings while discussing the issues together.

If you put the information in writing after your discussion, you have documentation; but more important, your summary helps ensure that you and the recipient both have the same understanding. Gerry's supervisor might write a constructive message to document their meeting; for example:

> Gerry:
>
> This note is a follow-up to our meeting on Wednesday, April 12, regarding your monthly reports. You have agreed to the following:
>
> 1. For data that you have not received three days prior to your report due date, send a message to department managers letting them know the urgency of getting their numbers to you.
>
> 2. If your report still cannot be completed on time, let me know in advance and give me the details as to why.
>
> Should you need additional support from me, please let me know.

As a result, Gerry will know the urgency of getting the report done on time and may also feel motivated and supported in meeting that goal.

By remaining objective and descriptive in difficult situations, you will build respect and trust among your coworkers, even those who seem to challenge your authority.

PRACTICE

1. **Instructions:** Select two or three projects you completed recently. For each, attach an evaluative comment to it. Then turn those comments into specific, detailed feedback.

2. **Instructions:** Think of a time when you gave someone subjective comments that the person did not understand or agree with. Revisit that experience by developing detailed feedback that you could have given instead. Do you think the situation might have been different?

3. **Instructions:** Identify a behavior that you would like to change in yourself and do the following:

   a. Imagine a discussion about that behavior between you and someone you respect.

   b. Write yourself a memo summarizing the changes you plan to make.

Positive Feedback

Have you ever felt that you deserved credit but your efforts were not recognized? **Positive feedback** is one of the most overlooked, underused types of feedback. Possibly competition, or even fear, inhibits people from recognizing others for their achievements. However, positive feedback plays a critical role in relationships and encourages cooperation. At times, positive feedback is even more valuable than constructive feedback. The words you use on a daily basis help form your culture, the environment around you.

Every human being has some needs and desires similar to yours. Everyone needs to feel appreciated and recognized for her or his strengths. As you communicate honestly with your colleagues about their strengths and achievements, you will build mutual respect and relationships based on trust.

Most people need their paychecks in order to survive, but they also need a nurturing environment in which to thrive. Achievement-oriented people are special because they get their satisfaction from doing a job well. Their biggest rewards relate to recognition, and their biggest hurts result from not meeting the grade or not being acknowledged for their successes. Thus, do not withhold positive feedback. Use it to affirm, validate, motivate, and inspire your team and others around you. However, make sure the positive feedback is authentic, or it may not mean much. If you are achievement-oriented, give yourself a pat on the back. Caring about getting the job done well ensures your success at whatever you pursue.

APPLY

Instructions: Think of someone whom you appreciate, and then do the following:

1. Make a list of a few things that person does to affect your life in a positive way.

2. Draft a memo stating your appreciation and why.

3. Deliver your message verbally or in writing.

4. What were the results? Discuss them with a partner who has also done the exercise.

Guidelines for Receiving Feedback

What happens when someone gives you feedback, especially the negative or even the constructive kind when it is unwelcome? How do you react? Whether you receive feedback from a peer, subordinate, or supervisor, the message is important and can lead to significant growth. That's because at times we humans see limiting behavior more objectively in others than we see it in ourselves.

Even though you know intellectually that feedback leads to growth, it doesn't always feel that way *emotionally.* Therefore, how can you receive feedback and respond in a professional way? Here are some guidelines:

- First, *thank the person* for taking the time to point out the behavior. You may or may not agree with the feedback, but that is not the immediate issue.

- *Refrain from arguing* with the person conveying the information, and do not immediately discount the feedback (even if you do not agree with it at that moment).

- *Clarify the information* by restating what you heard. At times, the message that a person receives is not the same as the message the sender intended.

- *Ask questions* so that you get as many details as possible, especially if the feedback seems vague or general.

- *Take a moment to reflect* on the comments, and open your mind to understanding *how* your actions could have led to the other person's perceptions.

Once you've had enough time to think about the feedback, consider the following:

- *If the feedback is accurate,* accept responsibility for your actions and avoid placing blame on others. If appropriate, say that you are sorry. (However, do *not* express self-pity or self-deprecation, such as "I'm always making mistakes and can't seem to get anything right.")

- *If you can refrain from being defensive,* offer valid information to explain why the behavior happened. Do not try to *convince* the other person you were justified in your actions; simply offer your explanation and leave it up to the listener to come to his or her own conclusions.

- *If you feel the feedback is not accurate,* you may want to wait longer or seek input before you respond. In the meantime, you can say something such as the following: "Thank you for your feedback. Before I respond, I need to think about it. If you don't mind, I'll follow up with you later today or tomorrow."

When you receive constructive feedback from someone, the best outcome is to define what you alone or both you and the other person can do to solve the problem. Receiving honest, constructive feedback doesn't mean that you are a failure; however, it might mean that you need to make some changes in the way you do your work. (You may need to improve your skills or change the way you think about certain things.) When you receive constructive feedback, don't act on it immediately:

- Reflect on the experience, and put it in perspective.

- Write about it; analyze your behavior and what you could do differently.

- Get a good night's rest before you make any important decisions.

However, *when a situation is emotionally charged, avoid responding in writing.* Whatever you put in writing can follow you throughout your career at a corporation. (And you will feel differently once you've had a chance to process the information and get some rest.) When you feel calm and objective, meet with the person face-to-face, if possible.

No one is immune from receiving feedback on how to get a job done. Throughout recent years, we have seen wealthy, powerful people publicly owning up to their mistakes. The key to turning the situation around is responding appropriately.

Unfortunately, many people make a situation or relationship even worse by the way they respond to unwelcome constructive feeback or negative feedback. However, all feedback when dealt with constructively can be the turning point for positive results. Worse than receiving negative feedback is not receiving accurate feedback that could lead to your growth. It's like the story about the emperor's new clothes. Do you remember the story? The emperor walked around without clothes because no one was brave enough to tell him the truth.

When people withhold constructive feedback, this does not mean that a situation is all right; the situation will continue to worsen as long as the problem persists. The great thing about constructive feedback is that it can open the door to dealing with a problem honestly. When you deal with negative results constructively, you are more likely to succeed in your relationships and on the job.

Perfection

Most human beings find it difficult to accept their own mistakes. It seems easier to give the other guy a break than to be kind and gentle with oneself. Why is that? Part of the reason may be overly high expectations. Are you a perfectionist?

- Do you expect yourself to be perfect and become frustrated when you are not?

- Do you expect yourself to know all the answers?

- When you make a mistake, do you replay it over and over again in your head, "beating yourself up" over it?

VOCABULARY BUILDERS

Contrition/Remorse When you hear the word *contrite,* what images come to mind? Being contrite means being humble in the midst of being wrong, graciously accepting responsibility.

However, some people do not act contrite when faced with their mistakes. Have you ever seen someone act very upset about having committed a crime, but those around the perpetrator say that he or she expresses "no remorse"? That's because there's a difference between being upset with oneself for doing something wrong and then being caught compared to feeling bad for the people who might have been affected. *Remorse* does not happen until a person is truly sorry that his or her behavior caused harm to another person.

If he truly felt *remorse,* he would act *contrite.* If she would act *contrite,* everyone would forgive her for the mistake.

Feedback becomes easier to digest when the recipient accepts that *mistakes are a vital part of learning.* In fact, accepting responsibility for a mistake can be the first step in making positive changes. When you make a mistake, remember that you are a human being and mistakes are a normal part of living. As you receive feedback, you will learn to make continual adjustments and will grow into doing your job effectively. If you accept mistakes graciously and learn from them, you will set yourself apart from others who have difficulty accepting that they are not perfect.

When people continually develop and improve, their lives become more satisfying (as do the lives of those they affect). Part of maturity (a fancy word for *growth*) relates to accepting more of reality by letting go of the "could've, should've, and would've" excuses. When you no longer see perfection as a possibility, you can drop impossible expectations. Constructive feedback then becomes palatable.

Now use the information you've learned about feedback to support your peers in conducting meetings and doing presentations, which you will review next in this chapter.

EXPLORE

1. Identify a question about yourself that you wish to explore, such as:
   - What kinds of things do I exhibit that are negative?
   - What patterns of thinking bring me unproductive results?
2. Spend 10 to 20 minutes writing about your question.
3. Spend another 10 to 20 minutes focusing on the positive and constructive side:
   - What changes would I benefit from making?
   - What are my strengths? What do I express that is positive and that I should continue?

SECTION B: CONCEPT CHECK

1. State the difference between feedback and evaluation.
2. What are some of the qualities of effective feedback?
3. How does constructive feedback differ from negative feedback?
4. Is positive feedback as valuable as constructive feedback?

■ SECTION C: MEETINGS, AGENDAS, AND ROUNDTABLE DISCUSSIONS

Meetings

A **meeting** occurs anytime two or more people get together (face-to-face or through telecommunications) to give and receive or gather information. In the professional arena, meetings are common: informal gatherings, phone conferences, scheduled brainstorming sessions, and formal presentations, to name a few.

Some meetings are well planned; others, impromptu. You may attend weekly, biweekly, or monthly meetings as a routine part of your job. Different meetings have different purposes; knowing the purpose up front enhances the group's ability to make progress. Here are some purposes for having a meeting: to inform, to plan, to brainstorm, to solve problems, and to evaluate performance.

In addition, meetings enhance the social aspects of working in a group by giving participants an opportunity to exchange small talk and share personal stories. In fact, some meetings focus specifically on the social aspects of working together and celebrating accomplishments. Working teams become stronger as members meet to solve problems and learn together.

COMMUNICATION CHALLENGES

Corporate Culture/Office Politics Each company has its own formal and informal processes for conducting meetings. When you start working at a new company, rather than learning a lesson the hard way, ask trusted peers about the basics of how your company conducts meetings. Also inquire about management styles and preferences. Every company has its own political process: good or bad, there is a political way that things happen. The more you learn informally, the more prepared you will be to handle new situations; the cliché "Don't buck the system" may take on new meaning for you.

Ask yourself: *Have I ever joined a group late and overstepped my bounds? Have I ever worked in a company and found myself doing or saying the wrong thing? What are the benefits of asking a peer for inside information on how a company conducts business before I "stick my neck out"?*

Planning a Meeting   Unfortunately, people are not always clear about why they are at a meeting. To keep expectations in line with reality, Wilson Learning, an executive training corporation, uses an established approach called "Purpose, Process, Outcomes" to plan meetings:

- *Purpose:* Inform participants ahead of time about the meeting's purpose. (Is the meeting informative? Are participants making decisions? Is it a brainstorming session? Is it a planning meeting?)

- *Process:* Give an overview of the plan and expectations of what will be accomplished. (How will the meeting be conducted? For decisions, do participants need to reach consensus, does the majority rule, or does the leader determine the outcome based on the group's input?)

- *Outcomes:* Identify the meeting's intended outcomes. (What's in it for the participants? What will participants walk away with? What results do we expect?)

To avoid frustration and confusion, inform participants about the purpose and process before the meeting begins. For example, a busy executive shared that she was looking forward to a meeting at which she expected to give input on an important company issue. She spent time preparing for the discussion; but when the meeting began, the leader told the group of a prearrived-at decision and explained how each person should implement it—no discussion, no input. She left disappointed and a bit angry. However, had she known in advance that the purpose of the meeting was to announce the decision (not discuss it), her expectations would have been different, and so would her response.

The purpose and process can be conveyed in the memo that is sent out to announce the meeting. (See Figure 6.1.) If people know the purpose of a meeting is to inform, they are not going to expect to give input on decisions that are already made. People feel embarrassed when they go outside their boundaries; by knowing their roles ahead of time, participants arrive more prepared and focused and less likely to give unsolicited input.

FIGURE 6.1 | Meeting Announcement

Does persuasion play a role in the development of a meeting announcement? Why make the effort, if you can simply give an order?

To: Manoli Quieros; Martin Lucas; Thyla Walters; Corinne Elbs
From: Jim O'Neill
Subject: Strategy Review

Could we get together for a quick review before we meet with the Brody board members at 11 a.m.? I'm not sure everyone is clear on the sort of support we're going to be looking for during the discussion after the presentation.

We can walk through each of the four sections we intend to present and try to identify the unanswered questions that will come our way. It will also give each of you a bit of a dress rehearsal. *I want to see each of you with your best foot forward!*

We need to project confidence, and we need to let the board know we have strong fallback positions in each division should things not work out as planned; this will also be a good opportunity for all of us to iron out any kinks in our arguments.

Let's make it at 8 a.m., Thursday, July 25, in the Presidio Conference Room.

VOCABULARY BUILDERS

Regardless/Irregardless
Only one of these words is correct, and many people mistakenly believe it is *irregardless*. However, *irregardless* has an obvious flaw. The word *regard* becomes negated by adding the suffix *less*. By then adding the prefix *ir*, which means "not," the speaker is creating a double negative all built into one word.

So the next time you find yourself saying *irregardless*, drop the prefix and simply say *regardless*.

Regardless of the difficulties, our plan will succeed.

Regardless of the problems we will face, the project is worth doing.

Conserving Time   Long, drawn-out meetings frustrate busy professionals; they sit in a conference room feeling tugged by priorities back at their desks. You can respect people's time in different ways:

- Invite only those individuals who really need to be there.
- Be flexible by allowing people to leave after they fulfill their role or to arrive late if they do not need to be there at the beginning.

Managers who consistently conduct ineffective meetings lose credibility with their staff. However, when meetings address topics effectively, they propel individuals into action and organizations into growth.

Before you schedule a meeting, ask yourself: *Does a meeting need to be scheduled at all? Can business be transacted in a more efficient way?* One busy manager said that when a subordinate requests a meeting, he first discusses the purpose and asks for details, sometimes even an agenda. When the subordinate returns to his office with the information, the manager sometimes asks, "How about talking about it right now?" If a decision can be made sooner rather than being delayed days or weeks until a scheduled meeting, those affected can move forward without remaining in a holding pattern.

Many professionals automatically schedule hour-long meetings, which can waste time. However, with a shorter time frame, participants are more likely to arrive on time and stay focused.

Establishing Ground Rules   When a team is formed, that's a good time to develop procedures and systems so that communication stays balanced and controlled. In their book *Working in Groups,* Isa Engleberg and Dianna Wynn discuss how certain behaviors can inhibit group process and progress.[6] They identify the following behavioral types:

- *Nonparticipant:* A person who always participates minimally, arriving unprepared and acting uninterested.
- *Loudmouth:* A member who talks so much that others do not get a chance to speak.
- *Interrupter:* A person who continually interrupts others while they are speaking.
- *Whisperer:* A person who carries on a private conversation with another member while the meeting convenes.
- *Latecomer and early leaver:* A member who walks in late unexpectedly or one who leaves early because of outside obligations.

These types of behaviors become problems when individuals repeat them often enough to establish them as patterns. When repeated behavior has a negative effect on meetings, team leaders will make more progress by addressing the problem rather than letting their meetings suffer. Thus, a team leader might want to "interrupt" the interrupter or loudmouth so that other speakers have adequate, uninterrupted time to speak. At times, just a lingering glance and cough can curtail whispering.

More difficult to address are the nonparticipants and those who consistently arrive late or leave early for personal reasons. When a member works on a different project during the meeting, this distracts and even annoys other team members. When members arrive late, they interrupt the flow of the meeting; when members consistently leave early, they indicate to the group that other obligations are more important than the group's task. For these kinds of issues, individual discussions might be in order; supportively question why the individual isn't participating fully. By encouraging and reminding that person that he or she is a valuable team member, you might see a change. (If you act angry or negative, do not expect a good response.)

Teams can discuss these unwanted behaviors openly before they occur, and this can help keep group dynamics in check. One approach is to establish ground rules so that all members understand group expectations and responsibilities. Here are examples of some ground rules to support effective communication:

Meeting Ground Rules

1. What we discuss in the meeting, we keep in the room so that people are free to talk.
2. We agree to manage our time effectively, appointing a timekeeper if necessary.
3. We will stay on track by bringing in only issues that are relevant.

Each group is unique. You will find that ground rules are most effective when team members develop their own and tailor them to the needs of the individual group. The next time you are in a group or team meeting, do you think it would be worthwhile to suggest your group take a few minutes to establish communication boundaries through ground rules? (Chapter 8 discusses team building strategies in more depth.)

EXPLORE

1. For the third time this month, the team member assigned to prepare and distribute the minutes of the team's meetings has not completed the work before the next meeting. The result is wasted time and some resentment among the other team members. Explore ideas for resolving the problem without alienating any of your team members.

2. Ask a manager to refer you to someone who has a reputation for doing a great job leading meetings. Ask that person if you can observe a meeting over which he or she presides. Ask your "meeting mentor" for tips on how to conduct successful meetings.

Agendas as Planning Tools

The purpose of a meeting drives the **agenda;** and the agenda, in turn, drives the discussion during the meeting. By getting people involved in developing the agenda together, asking for their opinions and input, you increase the likelihood that they will be positive contributors. By taking a participative approach to developing the agenda, you also deal with resistance indirectly.

The agenda is a planning tool. In fact, until you fill in the details of your agenda, you may not have a clear idea of what you expect your meeting to achieve. In addition, use the agenda to estimate the amount of time it will take to introduce and discuss each topic. Also use the agenda to identify roles. If each member understands his or her role, the meeting will run more smoothly and the objectives are more likely to be accomplished. (See Figure 6.2.)

FIGURE 6.2 | Agenda for a Meeting

CORE TEAM MEETING

Date: February 5, 2006

Place: Executive Conference Room

Time: 2 to 3 p.m.

Subject: CORE Clarifications

Attendees: Jumilla Yu, Process Engineer
                Calen Falak, Project Manager
                Sarah York, Enterprise Technical Architect
                Sanjay Alonanki, Business Analyst
                Rose Alonso, Financial Analyst/Strategy SME
                Oliver Walker, Business Lead

AGENDA

1. Document review and sign-off process	Calen, 10 minutes
2. Feedback on All CIO meeting	Calen, 5 minutes
3. Schedule business architecture workshops	Sanjay, 10 minutes
4. NBAC drafts update	Rose, 10 minutes
5. Relationship of architecture components	Sarah, 15 minutes
6. Status by Workstream Station	Oliver, 5 minutes
7. New business	Team, 5 minutes

Once you have identified the specific points, prioritize the items by listing the most important items first. If other items are brought up during the meeting, discuss them as "new business" at the end of the meeting or put them on the agenda for the next meeting.

An effective agenda keeps meetings moving forward and also helps participants feel closure when the meeting ends. If people are still brainstorming for solutions at the end of a meeting, they will not feel closure (that is, unless it was a brainstorming meeting). Thus, if you do not expect people to reach a conclusion, tell them that you are brainstorming possibilities, not resolving issues.

Assign a Timekeeper   When meetings are not productive, they are a waste of time. To keep meetings focused and productive, use the agenda to keep track of time; set a time limit on how long to discuss each item. If necessary, assign a timekeeper (other than the group leader) so that participants know when time boundaries are not being respected. In fact, just assigning the role of timekeeper makes participants more focused and less likely to bring in irrelevant issues or dwell on one topic too long.

One last point about time: you have much more credibility with your coworkers if you start and end meetings on time.

Roundtable Discussions

A **roundtable discussion** is more formal than an informative meeting and less formal than a presentation. At a roundtable, a group leader presents a topic and leads the discussion, keeping participants focused and engaged. For the event to be successful, participants must come prepared so that they are able to partake in a substantial discussion. A roundtable discussion can be an exciting learning event.

Here are the roles and responsibilities involved in roundtable discussions:

Leader:	Determines the discussion topics
	Assigns readings (if appropriate)
	Creates the agenda
	Leads the discussion
Participant(s):	Arrive(s) to meeting prepared
	Participate(s) in the discussion
	Evaluate(s) the leader's presentation
Evaluator:	Observes the discussion
	Keeps track of time
	Writes an assessment memo

Each member in the group actively participates to make the discussion a success. Participants play a vital role in preparing for the discussion and commenting when appropriate. However, not all groups appoint an evaluator to observe group dynamics and take notes.

Group Debriefing

At the end of any meeting, take about 5 minutes to evaluate how the meeting went. Did the group follow its agenda? Did the group achieve what it expected to achieve? What could the group do differently next time to be more effective? A group would conduct a debriefing by starting with the evaluator's comments and then allowing all participants to say a few words, keeping the discussion to a minimum. This type of discussion brings closure for participants, making them more ready to participate fully in their next task.

COACHING TIPS

Process Facilitator   A process facilitator leads a group but is not the same as a group leader. When confronted with difficult decisions or conflict, the leader of a working group sometimes brings in a process facilitator to ensure the group members express themselves freely in an unbiased environment.

Process facilitators do not have a preference or stake in decisions or outcomes, whereas a group leader may. Process facilitators are able to ask questions of group members and remain objective regardless of their answers.

Ask yourself: *How do you identify when a decision or conflict is beyond your ability to manage effectively? Have you ever been involved in a group situation in which a process facilitator would have been helpful? What were the group dynamics?*

COMMUNICATION CHALLENGES

Team Building   Everyone likes to be part of a winning team. But what is the formula for building successful group dynamics? When forming a team, often the impulse is to find people of a like mind, that is, people who are likely to work together agreeably and without conflict. While this method for team building might make the team experience more enjoyable, it is not a guarantee of success.

Some would argue that teams should represent a variety of perspectives and skill sets. Additional perspectives, even those diametrically opposed to your own, can help clarify your understanding of the team's challenges. Conflict can raise tempers and try patience, but conflict can also lead a team to solutions the members might never have otherwise considered.

Ask yourself: *If I were to select a team from my class for a group presentation, how would I go about choosing my teammates? If my goal is to get the highest possible grade, what would be my criteria? For example, would I choose my friends or the students with the best overall grades in the class?*

EXPLORE

Every Sunday morning, you will find several political roundtable discussions on various television network and cable stations (for example, NBC, ABC, CNN). Select a weekly roundtable discussion, and analyze the discussion to assess its strengths and weaknesses. Did the group stay on task or bring in irrelevant topics? Did the meeting flow from one topic to another? What were other observations? How would you have conducted the meeting differently?

 SECTION C: CONCEPT CHECK

1. Describe the "Purpose, Process, Outcomes" approach to meetings.
2. Why are ground rules and agendas helpful for presentations and meetings?
3. Describe the roles played by participants in a roundtable discussion.

SECTION D: PRESENTATIONS

Why is speaking to an audience so difficult? Do you feel as if the audience judges every word and movement you make? No one in the audience realizes how you feel; they cannot feel your palms sweating, your knees shaking, and your heart palpitating (to say nothing of your dry throat). Rest assured that any feelings you have are private.

However, the more prepared you are, the more relaxed you are likely to be. Just as writing is a process, so is developing a presentation. In fact, writing is the foundation for preparing a presentation. Until you can write about a topic, you probably don't know it well enough to talk about it. Whether you use a formal outline, a concept web, or a mind map, your first task is choosing a topic that you have a burning desire to learn about in depth.

Choosing a Topic

Interest determines motivation. If you choose a topic that you have a passion to learn about, you will have the energy to prepare sufficiently. If you choose a topic that you don't care much about, you will not have a good enough reason to push through your resistance.

For an informative speech, if it is an option, choose a topic that relates to a change you want to make in your life or career. For example, if you want to become more organized, choose a topic that gives insight into time management or getting rid of clutter. If you want to develop stronger relationships, perhaps examine gender differences. What about building a stronger financial base? Explore budgeting or investment strategies or perhaps learn more about emotional spending.

EXPLORE

Assume you've been asked to give a 10-minute presentation tomorrow on any topic with which you are familiar—a hobby, a job you perform in the workplace, the steps in a favorite recipe.

1. What topic would you choose? Take 5 minutes to brainstorm a list of discussion points on the topic. Is your list long enough to fill the allotted time?
2. Do an online search for your topic, and review at least three links related to the topic.
3. Review your list of discussion points. Have you discovered anything in your research that you might also include in your presentation?

Organizing Your Message

Organize your presentation much as you would organize a written document. (See Figure 6.3.) Here is a traditional saying to help you remember the format: "Say what you are going to say, say it, and then tell them what you said."

With writing or speaking, the first and most significant piece of information relates to purpose. You can be creative in the way you present the purpose, but you must make it relevant to your audience if you want to keep their interest. You can use the PEER model for organizing an informative presentation:

Purpose: Present the purpose, making it relevant to the audience.

Evidence: Provide examples and details.

Explanation: Explain what your supporting details mean.

Recap: Summarize your main findings, relating them back to your introduction and your audience.

FIGURE 6.3 | Organizing Your Presentation

PREPARING FOR YOUR PRESENTATION: WRITING IT OUT

1. *Introduction:* Present your purpose and explain its relevance.
2. *Body:* Give evidence and examples.
3. *Conclusion:* Summarize how your purpose has been proved; identify next steps (if relevant).

Start with questions:

What am I writing about?

Why? What is my *general purpose?*

What is my *specific purpose?*

What are my main points?

Who is my audience?

INTRODUCTION

State your purpose, making it relevant and important to your audience.
- Give an overview of the topic.
- Connect your topic to your audience.
- Pose questions for your audience.

BODY

Focus on concepts, and avoid giving intricate details that will be difficult for your audience to remember and use.
- Break your topic into component parts.
- Provide evidence/examples/explanation.
- Answer questions posed in your introduction.
- Cover all main points thoroughly.

CONCLUSION

Relate final comments to the introduction, drawing conclusions for your audience.
- Summarize.
- Clarify.
- Finalize.
- If relevant, identify next steps.

To get the audience's attention, use a creative opening:

- A question or list of questions.
- A quotation or "short story."
- An attention-getting statement.

However, do not feel pressured about using a unique opening. The substance of your presentation is far more important than the opening; many speakers waste time and energy fearing their opening will not be "catchy" enough. Focus on developing a presentation that offers good, solid, relevant information, and then reorganize the opening sentences after you write your conclusion. If you try to get a good opening before you have written your speech, you may give yourself writer's block!

Knowing Your Topic

For the most part, giving an excellent presentation relates to knowing your topic. That means doing research, reading, taking notes, identifying key points, organizing, reorganizing, and finally practicing until you know your material without hesitation. After doing the necessary groundwork, you will gain confidence: your level of confidence equates to your level of practice.

You are the best judge of how to practice. What works for your best friend may not work for you at all. Here are a few techniques:

- *Audio or video recording:* Tape your presentation, and then listen to it. Hearing your own voice will help you memorize the content as well as refine your tone and articulation. (This method is superb for most; try it.)
- *Mental recitation:* Silent recitation builds skill in a dramatic way. This method might even be superior to actually practicing out loud.
- *Mirrors:* If audio- or videotaping is not an option, rehearse your presentation in front of a mirror. You can get an idea of your facial expressions and other body language (if looking at yourself does not distract you).
- *A mock audience of peers or family:* Some people find practicing in front of a mock audience helpful; others find it distracting. If your listeners stop you to ask questions every few sentences, you may lose more confidence than you gain. Also, helpful remarks sometimes sound like criticism, so you may want to avoid practicing in public until after you make your presentation "debut."

Presenting

Many presenters get extremely nervous because they think their presentation must be perfect. Perfection is an unrealistic expectation; perfection isn't even an option. When you get nervous, focus on the details of preparing yourself: plan your appearance, think about your facial expressions, and practice making eye contact as well as projecting your voice.

Your posture and dress are important. You want to stand tall and dress comfortably and appropriately. Consider also your facial expressions; you want to look pleased to be presenting, so smile as you greet your audience. Your body language should convey both enthusiasm and confidence: many a presentation has been saved by an enthusiastic and confident presenter.

Next consider eye contact. With a group of 20 to 25 people, you should be able to look at everyone and make eye contact at least once throughout the presentation. With a larger audience, individual contact is more difficult. Regardless of the size of the audience, look around as you speak and try to make contact with as many people as possible.

In preparing for your presentation, consider your voice projection, pronunciation, and speed. You want to project your voice so that the people in the back of the room can hear it. You also want to practice pronouncing any words that you anticipate having difficulty saying. Also, plan to modulate your speed—speaking slowly at times, pausing, and also speaking somewhat quickly.

Confidence will develop naturally when you have practiced sufficiently. Allow enough time to prepare; work on your topic a little chunk at a time so that it doesn't seem overwhelming. If you present information or ideas that help your listeners become more efficient, productive, or self-confident, they will like your speech.

Challenging Your Fears: *Facing up to a communication challenge, whether it's giving a presentation or placing an important phone call, is usually easier than avoiding it; procrastinating doesn't make it go away, but it can increase the pressure you feel.* List three concerns you have about speaking in front of an audience (for example, "I'm afraid I'll start talking too fast and lose my train of thought"); then come up with a strategy for addressing those concerns (for example, "bring a glass of water, and pause every once in awhile to sip at it to pace myself").

When you present to an audience, use an outline, notes on cards, or topic sentences. The worst presentations are those that the presenter reads verbatim. In addition:

- Speak to your audience at *their* level: adapt your language and make your topic relevant.
- Speak clearly and slowly. What seems slow to you may sound just right to your audience. The information is new to them, and they need time to digest your message.
- Do *not* read your speech, or you will bore your audience.
- Present concepts supported by examples and explanation.
- Be aware of your body language; maintain good eye contact and a relaxed posture.
- Keep your voice clear; vary your tone appropriately.
- Be prepared for questions, if time allows.

One final point: Use self-talk to keep yourself calm. When you feel especially nervous, go over the content in your mind. You will do an excellent job if you are prepared—do not even consider anything less.

Establishing Ground Rules for Feedback

One of the biggest fears we all have is making a mistake and then being criticized for the mistake. When you give others feedback, stress the positive and discuss only a point or two. If you tell colleagues everything they did wrong, they might become overwhelmed and not know where to start to improve.

1. Give constructive feedback before you make evaluative comments, especially about behavior you are encouraging the speaker to improve.
2. Do not make personal comments: remain professional even if you have an outside conflict with the presenter.
3. Follow the Golden Rule: "Do unto others as you would have them do unto you."
4. Be objective and specific with your comments, and give examples.

Example: You had good, consistent eye contact; try to work on keeping your arms relaxed. The topic you chose was intriguing; I would have liked to hear a few more examples.

A positive comment should also include details describing why you commented favorably. For example, "The introduction captured my attention because of the detailed questions." A more general comment is less helpful: "The introduction was great." (Review Section B, "Feedback.")

EXPLORE

What's so difficult about presenting? Mind map and do a 10-minute focused writing on this question. Then discuss the question in small groups.

Using Technology for Visual Support

Presentations are learning experiences for presenters and audiences alike. The best presentations provide information, concepts, and tools that the audience can use in making better decisions or being more effective. Since presenting involves learning, and some people learn best through the visual mode, consider using visual support.

PowerPoint is the most popular audiovisual aid used today, replacing the overhead projector and slides. However, many presenters still use the overhead, and it is an excellent backup in case PowerPoint equipment fails. In addition, do not overlook using a flip chart or whiteboard to capture audience comments in an interactive presentation.

Whether 5 people or 100 people will be in your audience, do a dry run of your presentation using the available equipment. Ensure that good visibility exists in all places in the room. If people cannot read your presentation visuals, you will lose their attention; they will leave disappointed, even if you talk them through the materials.

Whether you use PowerPoint or an overhead, consider providing your audience with copies of your presentation before you begin. Your audience can then use your handouts as an aid in taking notes while you speak from the podium. Having handouts also serves as a backup in case the equipment malfunctions. Now let's examine how to prepare the actual slides for your presentation.

Preparing a PowerPoint Presentation

With its enormous popularity, why do concerns about PowerPoint abound? The answer is that people often do not prepare PowerPoint presentations the way they prepare other forms of communication. According to Dolores Lehr, a communications professor, you will produce superior, lively presentations if you take time to follow these seven steps:[7]

1. Determine your purpose.
2. Identify your audience.
3. Plan the overall structure and content of each slide.
4. Compose with text and graphics.
5. Format each slide.
6. Edit text and graphics.
7. Deliver the presentation.

Determine the Purpose   As with other forms of communication, you first need to determine your *general purpose* and then your *specific purpose*. While your general purpose might be to explain, instruct, persuade, or entertain, your specific purpose will emanate from it. Examples of specific purposes might be to explain the history of a project and what you deduced, instruct your colleagues on a new procedure, or persuade your audience to adopt your recommendations. You may find it useful to write a purpose statement before constructing your slides.

Identify the Audience   Your purpose, of course, will be linked closely to your understanding of your audience:

Who is this audience?

How many people will be part of it?

What is their background? What do they know about the topic?

How receptive are they to the topic?

What kind of typeface and graphics will they be comfortable with?

In order for your listeners to enjoy your presentation, the topic and content need to relate to their interests. Also, the vocabulary should be at a level that facilitates their understanding of the material. Follow these language guidelines:

- Define words that are out of the ordinary.

- Avoid acronyms and initialisms; jargon can cause confusion even when an audience is familar with the terms.

- Respect cultural differences by using common words, not slang.

Ask a few peers what they think of your topic, and try to focus it toward a general group. If you choose a topic that interests only a few people in your audience, those are the only ones whose interest you will keep.

Plan the Overall Structure and Content of Each Slide

After you have determined your purpose and analyzed your audience, you are ready to plan the organization and content of your slides. When you prepare a written document, you often plan by brainstorming or mind mapping (jotting down ideas in a free-form manner). For your presentation, you can do something similar, or you can start to outline your topic. Here are a few steps to follow:

1. Decide on your *major headers,* which will each become the title of an individual slide.

2. Divide each header into *subtopics* or *second-level headers.* Remember, you need at least two subtopics under each header. If you have only one subtopic under a header, change the wording of that header so that it includes the subtopic.

3. Divide each of your subtopics further, if necessary.

Generally, you will create one slide for each major header. You can also create additional slides for subtopics (second-level headers and even third-level ones).

Since your presentation is a visual one, consider planning your slides by **storyboarding,** or sketching them out on paper. To storyboard, turn your paper horizontally so that its layout is "landscape." Then draw a line down the middle, and put your text on one side of the sheet and a sketch of a graphic on the other. In planning your graphics, consider browsing for clip art.

Also consider the *tone* you wish to convey in your graphics. For a more professional tone, you might use only photos; for a lighter tone, you might use cartoons. In any case, jot down the image or the file name in your storyboard across from your text.

Compose with Text and Graphics

After you have outlined or created storyboards, you can begin generating text and graphics for your slides. Limit the amount of your text to *no more than eight words per line* and *no more than eight lines per slide;* some guidelines recommend even fewer. Be sure to create an introduction and a conclusion, and supply *transitional slides* that introduce new sections or summarize what preceded them.

For large groups, be more succinct and use large print. If you choose to add animation for entertainment value, keep your presentation balanced; too much animation can be worse than none at all.

Format Each Slide

As you compose each slide, consider formatting your text and graphics. Decide which type *font* you will use. Many presenters just convert the text from their printed documents to their slides. On the printed page, a font such as Times Roman (or another serif font) is quite readable; however, on a screen it is more difficult to read than a *sans-serif* font such as Ariel or **Impact**.

The size of the font should be set so that the slides can be read by those in the back of the room. If enough words are added to a slide, the font will automatically become smaller; if it appears too small, consider editing your text down or moving some of it to the next slide.

Since you want a sufficient amount of *white space* around your text for readability, limit the number of words and even the size of your graphics. If you want to change the color of your type, keep in mind that light colors may look fine on your computer screen but can seem washed out and be difficult to read when projected on a large screen.

Decide what *effects* you want to use for your slides and text. Most software programs have numerous effects to choose from, but be wary of choosing too many and changing them too often. Having your words fly in from the left or having slides change like vertical blinds can work well, but if you mix too many effects, they will distract your audience. For example, if you have the words fly up from the bottom and then down from the top with the slides changing like blinds and then dissolving and fading, your audience may not be able to focus on what you are saying.

Edit Text and Graphics   As with other assignments, you should edit ruthlessly. Begin by checking the overall organization of your slides. (*Note:* Go to "Slide Sorter" on the View drop-down menu. If any slide seems out of place, just left-click on it, right-click for "cut," point the cursor where you want to place the slide, left-click, and right-click for "paste.")

In editing the organization, you want your slides arranged logically. Also make sure that you place transitional slides appropriately and that your transitional effects are working properly. (*Note:* You can check the transitions between slides and effects by going to "Slide Sorter" and left-clicking on the star icon in the lower left corner of each slide. If any slides are not functioning, then go to "Slide Show→Slide Transition" and make the necessary changes.)

Next, edit the text and graphics of each slide for accuracy, clarity, consistency, and conciseness:

- Are your facts all correct?
- Is your text free of grammatical and mechanical errors?
- Have you selected the best graphic to illustrate your concepts?

After checking for accuracy, make sure that you have written what you intend to say in the clearest, most concise way. *Are your text and graphics clear enough so that your entire audience can see your key points instantly?*

Along with checking for clarity, look for consistency in your use of punctuation, capitalization, color, type font, and effects. Ensure that lists on each slide have the same grammatical structure; if not, change them so that they are parallel. Finally, eliminate any unnecessary words, and condense your phrasing so that you have more white space. Also ask yourself if you can eliminate any excess graphics. Once again, your goal in this step is to be concise, clear, consistent, and accurate. See Figure 6.4 for examples of slides that meet these criteria.

Deliver the Presentation   Allow time to prepare for delivering your presentation. As with all presentations, consider your appearance, eye contact, and voice as well as your interaction with both your slides and audience.

Since the audience will read your slides from left to right, you will create a better flow by standing on the right side of the screen (from your audience's perspective). When you deliver your presentation, do not "hide behind" your slides but interact with your slides and audience. Since effective PowerPoint presentations are those which involve the audience, *use the slides as part of your conversation with the audience:* do not read word for word but rather refer to your slides and elaborate on parts of each. Remember, *reading PowerPoint slides is no more effective than reading a typed speech.* Keep the audience aware that both the visual and verbal aspects are one.

You can interact effectively with your slides by pointing to them and commenting on individual terms. You can interact with the audience by asking questions, whether or not you expect an answer. To get the audience more involved, you can present your listeners with a question or controversial comment and then give them 2 to 3 minutes to discuss it with a partner or small group.

Only do this kind of activity if you feel confident about your audience and the topic. If you are not confident or well prepared, the effect can be disastrous: you may have difficulty regaining

---

COACHING TIP

Graphic Designs   You can add spice to your PowerPoint presentation with pie charts, bar graphs, illustrations, or photographs that emphasize, highlight, or reinforce important points. Cartoons can also be used to inject some lightness or humor into the proceedings, though this is most effective when it is not overdone.

Some artwork that you find on the Internet, such as **clip art,** is easy to use—a simple cut-and-paste operation—and in the **public domain,** meaning you can use the graphics without paying a fee or crediting the illustrator. Many software programs come with a cache of clip-art icons for you to use.

Other artwork on the Internet, including some illustrations and photographs, is copyrighted, meaning you must get the copyright holder's permission to use the art and you may have to pay a fee or credit the artist. Similarly, pictures scanned from books or other sources may or may not require permission, a credit, or a fee.

It is your responsibility to research the source of any material you use in your presentations. Whether or not there is a copyright notice, you should get permission from the Web site owner before downloading any graphics (unless the site invites people to download).

FIGURE 6.4 | PowerPoint Slides

These slides are part of a PowerPoint presentation entitled "Closing the Gender Gap" by Trisha Svehla, a diversity consultant. Trisha presented it at a luncheon for college faculty. As she prepared the presentation, she wrote main points on Post-it notes. This enabled her to organize her ideas as she did her research. Trisha created her PowerPoint slides first and then developed her narrative around the slides.

Closing the Gender Gap	Group Discussion Questions	One Change	Empathy Vs. Solutions
❖Acknowledge differences between men's and women's communication styles. ❖Understand gender-specific motivations. ❖Adapt your communication style to create successful relationships. ❖Reduce gender-related conflicts. ❖Improve working relationships.	❖ What one change could men make to improve communication with women? ❖ What one change could women make to improve communication with men?	❖Women: – Get to the point !! ❖Men: – Listen !!	❖ Women tend to seek an empathetic response. ❖ Men tend to offer solutions. 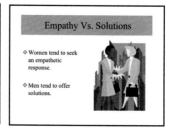

Details vs. Big Picture	Cooperation vs. Competition	Asking for Help vs. Not Asking for Help	Rapport vs. Invasion
❖Women want complete details. ❖ Men want only the big picture and find details irritating.	❖Women focus on areas of agreement. ❖Men tend to express disagreements openly.	• Women generally ask for help if they need it. • Men consider asking for help or information as a sign of weakness.	❖ Women tend to be participative and indirect ❖ Men tend to be authoritative and direct 

INTERNET EXERCISE 6.2

From Draft to PowerPoint For links to more information about developing slides for a PowerPoint presentation, visit the *Foundations of Business Communication* Web site at <http://www.mhhe.com/djyoung>. You will find the full PowerPoint presentation of "Closing the Gender Gap," by Trisha Svehla, including her complete presentation notes, and activities to help you hone your slide-writing skills.

At the home page, select "Student Activities" and then click on the Chapter 6 link to begin.

control and the presentation will seem chaotic. However, if you can orchestrate it well, getting your listeners involved will make your presentation an enjoyable experience that they will appreciate and remember.

By following these guidelines, you can produce and deliver a very lively PowerPoint presentation and thus avoid the pitfalls that so often characterize this popular means of communication.

APPLY

Research a topic of interest to you, and prepare the text for a PowerPoint presentation on that topic.

 SECTION D: CONCEPT CHECK

1. List the parts of the PEER model used in developing a presentation.

2. What are some qualities of a good PowerPoint presentation?

3. How do editing and revising skills apply to developing presentations?

4. How can you overcome your anxieties about giving a presentation?

S U M M A R Y

In this chapter, you have examined personal aspects of your communication style as well as how to conduct a meeting and give a formal presentation. You may now be more aware of language patterns and community-dialect qualities in your speech, which you will reserve for social situations. By examining the *lagniappe* of communications and the meaning of micromessages, you have become more aware of the impact of nonverbal communication.

Meetings play a central role in the lives of all business professionals. Meetings can propel people and organizations into action, but they can also waste time. Even worse, meetings can violate participants' expectations, creating frustration and confusion. Having the confidence to be an active participant is just as important as being a dynamic group leader.

Being able to prepare a formal PowerPoint presentation is an important skill. To develop a successful presentation, you not only need to understand your topic but also must transform key points into slides that you can talk your audience through. Stay confident by preparing meticulously!

CHAPTER 6 CHECKLIST

Presentation Evaluation:

Content

Opening:

___ Gains attention, creates interest.
___ Identifies *what* (clearly states purpose of speech).
___ Reveals *why* (proves relevance to audience).
___ Covers *how* of speech (gives agenda or overview of speech).

Body:

___ Has an appropriate topic.
___ Shows thorough understanding of topic.
___ Proves credibility of subject through research.

Closing:

___ Summarizes main points.
___ Brings closure to topic.

Delivery

Voice:

___ Has good volume.
___ Stays well paced.
___ Pauses effectively.
___ Varies tone; remains upbeat and animated.
___ Articulates clearly.
___ Limits use of distracters and fillers.
___ Remains professional and conversational.
___ Talks *to* rather than *at* the audience.
___ Interacts with audience as appropriate.

Body language:

___ Makes good eye contact with entire group.
___ Uses natural and appropriate gestures.
___ Limits random movement, swaying, extraneous steps.
___ Moves deliberately and effectively.
___ Appears poised and confident.
___ Uses appropriate facial expressions.

END-OF-CHAPTER ACTIVITIES

ACTIVITY 1: PROCESS MEMO

Instructions: Write a memo or an electronic memo to your instructor giving details on what you have learned about giving presentations. What steps did you go through to prepare? What would you have done differently as you presented? How could you have improved your overall presentation? Overall, what would you do differently the next time you present? (Use the reflect/respond/revise process strategy to prepare your message.)

ACTIVITY 2: TEAM ACTIVITY

Situation: Every year, Masthead Corporation turns to its staff of employees to generate ideas for new magazine titles. Teams are formed by combining members from every department (editorial, art, photography, production, marketing, sales, administrative, and general staff). Each team is asked to develop titles for two new magazines. You and your partner(s) have been chosen as organizers for Team Gemini.

The organizers' duties center on getting the team together for the first meeting, at which a team leader will be elected, a team plan will be generated, and various other responsibilities will be divided up. The meeting will also be a great opportunity to lay down ground rules for getting individuals from different divisions to work together successfully.

Instructions: Working with your partner(s), generate the following communications to get Team Gemini off to a strong start:

1. Write an e-mail to the team members regarding the first team meeting. You'll need everyone to agree on a time and place.

2. Write a meeting announcement.

3. Write an agenda for the meeting.

4. Write a short introduction to open the meeting, at the end of which the team members will elect their leader. At this point, your duties as organizer(s) end.

ACTIVITY 3: ALL PRO TEMPS

Situation: It's time to consider the identity of All Pro Temps. The company has grown quickly into a competitive business. It is your impression that the informality that worked so well for a small company isn't working as well for a large company. Though you have yet to hear any complaints about the quality of any completed job, you have heard some comments from clients about lapses in customer service at the home office, employees' inappropriate attire at job sites, and use of inappropriate language on the job. You've decided it is time to create a company handbook.

You've also decided to have a company meeting to discuss what sort of company the employees want All Pro Temps to be and what guidelines they all feel will benefit the company. At the same time, you want to make it clear to all the employees that regardless of the atmosphere they're hoping for, there are going to be basic guidelines for office conduct that cover ethics, dress, work hours, customer service procedures, and other issues.

Instructions: Do the following:

1. Prepare a letter to All Pro clients promising improved service.

2. Prepare a memo to employees announcing the meeting time and location.

3. Create an agenda that describes the topics to be focused on during the 2-hour-long session.

4. In preparation for leading the discussion at the meeting, outline ten basic rules of conduct that you expect every employee to follow (for example, no sexually explicit language or no taking of other people's lunches from the refrigerator).

ACTIVITY 4: EDITED AMERICAN ENGLISH AND COMMUNITY DIALECT

Instructions: In a small group, identify at least ten community-dialect words or phrases that members of your group commonly use. What are the equivalent expressions in Edited American English (Standard English)? For example, *I'm fittin' a* means "I'm getting ready to"*; I'm all over it* means "I've got the situation under control." Compare your group's list with other groups' lists.

ACTIVITY 5: THE *LAGNIAPPE* OF COMMUNICATIONS

Background: The *lagniappe* of communications relates to the "little something extra" thrown in, such as facial expressions, sighs, and tone of voice. As you become more aware of your own communication style, you may identify unique ways you communicate nonverbally.

Instructions: With a partner, spend 3 minutes communicating without speaking. Try to convey information to each other with your eyes and gestures. When the 3 minutes have passed, discuss your experience. On a daily basis, how do you use the *lagniappe* of communications effectively to improve communication? How do you use it ineffectively?

ACTIVITY 6: MICROMESSAGES AND MICROINEQUITIES

Background: Micromessages are the hidden, unspoken messages conveyed by "reading between the lines." When micromessages are negative, they result in microinequities, which are demoralizing slights to the individual at whom they are directed. (For example, you and a coworker completed a project together, but your boss gives all the credit to your partner and ignores your efforts.)

Instructions: With a partner, develop three different scenarios that demonstrate microinequities. Select the best one and then role-play the situation. After the role-play, discuss how each of you felt on the giving side of the communication as well as the receiving side.

ACTIVITY 7: BUSINESS CARDS AND INFORMAL MEETINGS

Instructions: Design a business card that you can use when you go on job interviews. Make sure it contains your name, phone number, and address as well as e-mail address. You may even have a caption that describes your objective. Print out a few "mock" copies, and cut them down to size. (Use a higher-quality paper if you want your cards to have a better effect.)

Now, with a peer, role-play exchanging business cards and information. Imagine that you are at a networking meeting. Talk about the kind of position you will be looking for when you graduate.

ACTIVITY 8: PLANNING AND LEADING A ROUNDTABLE DISCUSSION

Instructions: This roundtable discussion activity is designed for groups of four or five participants. If time permits, each member will have an opportunity to be the group leader. All group participants are expected to arrive prepared to discuss the article that the group leader selects. The instructions below relate to leading the group. (This activity corresponds with Section C in this chapter.)[8]

1. Select an article from a reputable periodical that deals with a business-related topic; specifically, choose an article about a business experiencing a conflict.

2. Give a copy of your article to everyone in your group a few days (or class periods) before the group will meet for the roundtable discussion.

3. Do additional research to inform yourself more fully on the topic.

4. Prepare an agenda that includes the main topics discussed in your article; distribute your agenda to the group and your instructor on the day that you lead the discussion.

5. Prepare key questions to trigger a good discussion and to focus on coming up with persuasive solutions and recommendations for the company in your article.

6. Lead a 20-minute discussion based on your article.

7. Once the discussion is finished, prepare a 5-minute presentation that summarizes the key issues and explains your group's recommendations for the business.

8. Present your findings to the entire class.

ACTIVITY 9: IMPROMPTU SPEECHES

Instruction: Impromptu speeches are an effective whole-group activity. Each member of the class should identify a topic, write it on a piece of paper, and put the paper in a hat. (Your instructor will select the order in which students will present their speeches, and write the names on the board.) As you get up to give your impromptu speech, select a topic from the hat. Spend a minute (no more than 2 minutes) giving your impromptu speech.

Your instructor may repeat this activity a few times so that everyone feels comfortable getting up and speaking to an audience about a topic that is unfamiliar. (As a variation, the class can select one topic that is of interest to everyone in the class, and everyone can speak on the same topic.)

ACTIVITY 10: CREATING A POWERPOINT PRESENTATION

Instructions: Choose a topic from the list below, and create the text for a PowerPoint presentation. (Your instructor may give you the option of selecting a topic not on this list.)If you have access to PowerPoint software, input your text and develop a finished product. You will need to go online or to a library to conduct research on your topic. Your presentation should be as long as necessary to get the point across; however, it should not include more than 15 slides.

Applying for a U.S. product patent.

Shipping oversized packages overseas.

Using prewriting techniques.

Buying and selling at an online auction.

Creating a job portfolio.

Catching plagiarists: online advances.

Responding to a computer worm attack.

REFERENCES

1. Robbins Burling, *English in Black and White,* Holt, Rinehart and Winston, Inc., New York, 1973.

2. Lynn Troyka, *Simon and Schuster Handbook for Writers,* 6th ed., Pearson Education, Upper Saddle River, NJ, 2002.

3. Constance Gefvert, Richard Raspa, and Amy Richards, *Keys to American English,* Harcourt Brace Jovanovich, New York, 1975.

4. Barbara Davis and Bobbie Krapels, "Micromessages in the Workplace," Association for Business Communication, 2005 Spring Conference, Greensboro, NC.

5. Management News, www.swlearning.com/management/management_news/com_0904_001.html, South-Western, 2004. (Accessed April 26, 2005.)

6. Isa Engleberg and Dianna Wynn, *Working in Groups: Communication Principles and Strategies,* Houghton Mifflin, Boston, 2003.

7. D.B. Du Frene and C. M. Lehman, "Concept, Content, Construction, and Contingencies: Getting the Horse Before the PowerPoint Cart," *BCQ,* Vol. 67, No. 1, 2004, pp. 84–88.

8. Holly Littlefield and JoAnn Syverson, "Running Meetings, Presenting Results—Developing Real World Communication Skills," Association for Business Communication, 68th Annual Conference, October 24, 2003.

KEY FOR LEARNING INVENTORY

1. T	**6.** a and b
2. c	**7.** T
3. F	**8.** T
4. F	**9.** T
5. T	**10.** d

Global Communication and Technology

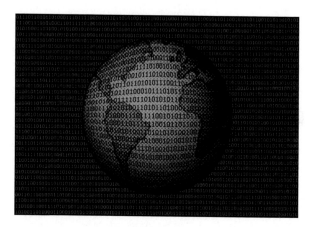

We don't see things as they are . . . We see them as we are. —Anais Nin ■

On any given business day, marketing teams in Japan discuss how best to package products for sale in North America and Europe; team members in Argentina have a Web conference with their manager in London; and inventory managers in Côte d'Ivoire use e-mails to inquire about an overdue shipment from Singapore.

As companies expand their presence abroad, markets once limited by geography, language, and culture are opening to firms ready and willing to compete. What will your role be in the global economy of the twenty-first century? Have you considered the opportunities available to you?

Whatever your career path, to be effective you will need special skills for communicating in the ever-changing world economy. This chapter provides the foundation for effectively navigating business communication challenges in the age of globalization. You will learn to distinguish the context in which business communications take place and will explore the importance of cultural contexts.

You will first become familiar with your own communication style and examine the hidden, unintentional messages your style may send to other language and national groups. You will review best practices in global settings and apply proven techniques for greetings, business cards, e-mails, phone conferences, presentations, and relationship building. By exploring international business and cross-cultural communications, you will also glean details about enhancing your skills and marketability in this sector.

OBJECTIVES

When you have completed Chapter 7, you will be able to:

• Recognize and critique global communication styles.

• Practice exploring nonverbal cues for unspoken cultural meanings or micromessages.

• Connect outward business behaviors with culturally held values, assumptions, life experiences, and concepts of self-awareness.

• Rewrite low-context communications for high-context communicators.

• Apply the major concepts of authenticity, the Platinum Rule, and cultural informants.

• Choose between indirect and direct communication styles when communicating globally.

• Plan a global conference call.

• Send a global e-mail.

Learning Inventory

1. The terms *global* and *international* are interchangeable.   T/F
2. Differences in culture relate only to differences in national background.   T/F
3. Attitudes and values make up about 10 percent of cultural differences.   T/F
4. In global communications, being aware of your own culture is more important than listening
   to and observing other cultures.   T/F
5. How you feel about others is based *less* on their behavior and *more* on your own perceptions
   and norms.   T/F
6. An indirect style is one in which context (or situation) is not important.   T/F
7. When compared with other nationalities, Americans are generally considered indirect
   communicators.   T/F
8. The Platinum Rule states, "Treat others as *they* want to be treated."   T/F
9. In some cultures, writing on the back of a colleague's business card is considered offensive.   T/F
10. As a group, Americans tend to be more individualistic and informal than other national groups. T/F

■ SECTION A: GLOBAL COMMUNICATION AND CAREER OPPORTUNITIES

Many opportunities are available for you to participate in the daily rhythms of global business, both in international and in domestic markets. More and more U.S.-based businesspeople are working with virtual teams to serve colleagues, customers, and markets outside the United States. Though they never set foot outside their home office, employees at nonprofit organizations, government agencies, and multinational corporations require global skills to accommodate multicultural communication styles.

For example, consider for a moment the case study in Figure 7.1. Here, a not-for-profit center outlines its thoughts regarding the best way to work across language barriers with patients and their families in U.S. medical centers. Being effective in such situations requires a special and critical cross-cultural skill set.

Besides having domestic opportunities that involve global business, you can pursue a career in **global communications** by working for one of the world's more than 60,000 transnational corporations. Examples include the Ford, Coca-Cola, and IBM corporations. Many such companies offer internships and special entry-level programs that are worth pursuing.

FIGURE 7.1 | Communication in Multilingual Settings: U.S. Hospitals

The challenge of working with multicultural, multilingual groups is not restricted to international settings. These guidelines were developed by a national coalition to help medical staff and social workers overcome language barriers in U.S. hospital settings. Ask yourself: Do I think I have the skill sets necessary for a career in a multilingual environment? What can I do to improve my qualifications?

GUIDELINES FOR OVERCOMING LANGUAGE BARRIERS

1. Bilingual/Bicultural Professional Staff
- Recruit and retain **bilingual/bicultural** staff at all levels of the organization.
- Provide significant additional compensation for bilingual ability.

2. Interpreters
- Establish minimum standards for interpreter training and competency.
- Make a concerted effort to increase and foster medical interpreter training.
- Provide courses designed to train providers to work with interpreters.
- Reimburse for interpreter services.
- Allow providers more time with patient when using interpreters.

3. Language Skills Training for Existing Staff
- Support the development of bilingual skills for all staff members.
- Establish clear goals and realistic expectations for Spanish language courses.
- Offer classes in conversational and medical Spanish to all staff.
- Utilize training programs that have a demonstrated track record.

4. Internal Language Banks (only as a back-up measure)
- Hire supervisors to oversee and assess the language and interpretation capabilities of language bank members.
- List interpretation as a secondary responsibility of language bank members.
- Compensate members who do a significant amount of interpretation.

5. Phone-Based Interpreter Services (emergency back-up measure for brief follow-up questions only)
- Use simple or common terms when using phone interpreters.
- Inform health care providers that phone-based interpreters may not be proficient in medical terminology.

6. Written Translations (emergency stop-gap measure and in simple conversational use only, never as the sole means of communication)
- Develop mechanisms to promote the sharing of bilingual written materials, such as consent forms and patient education pamphlets.

Source: "Navigating Language Differences," *Proyecto Informar Trainers Manual,* National Coalition of Hispanic Health and Human Services Organizations (COSSMHO), 1998, pp. 107–123.

A point of entry into these corporate giants for a graduate from a U.S. college or university is one of their U.S. offices. International assignments are well paid, very demanding, and highly competitive. If you prove yourself to be a valuable resource at home, in due time you might be a strong candidate for an overseas position.

International nongovernment organizations (NGOs) and government sectors offer another range of possibilities for students interested in global communications. Organizations such as the International Red Cross, Habitat for Humanity, and Doctors Without Borders do important work. They have both volunteer and professional positions available to the right

VOCABULARY BUILDERS

Global Terms When you are dealing with global issues, your vocabulary needs to include some common terms that are used with meanings specific to the global context:

International: selling goods or services in, or having suppliers from, more than one country.

Multinational: having business functions established in more than one country.

Global: combining local know-how with a multinational presence, leveraging the opportunities presented by different world regions and their markets in a systematic way.

Culture: the norms, beliefs, behavior, and ways of thinking that form a similar background, holding groups of people together.

Ethnocentric: seeing the world primarily from the eyes of one's own culture, not incorporating other cultures and their ways of doing things.

candidates. You might also consider government agencies such as the U.S. State Department, the Foreign Service, a branch of the military, or even the Peace Corps. The Foreign Service and military can be career paths unto themselves. Joining the Peace Corps is an excellent way to gain some international experience that you might later leverage when pursuing jobs in the global arena.

While you are still in school and exploring your career interests, opportunities exist in the form of exchange programs. Both the American Field Service and Youth for Understanding have been supporting international exchanges and trips abroad for dozens of years. Both organizations have a broad mission and strong base of support in the United States and many other countries throughout the world.

Your own university may offer semesters abroad that allow you to receive college credit toward your degree. If you are interested in international exchanges of any type, a good source of information is your school's study abroad or international programs office.

EXPLORE

1. Do you communicate globally now, either at work or school, or in your personal life? Do you write letters, send e-mails, or place phone calls to people outside the United States? What barriers have you encountered in global communications?

2. As you consider your future career, what possibilities do you foresee to apply global communication skills?

3. Why must business professionals who "never set foot outside their home office" understand global communications?

Culture and Communication

Nearly all business interactions involve diverse communication, yet many people worldwide have yet to learn how to approach the differences effectively. For people born in the United States, this communication gap often appears when they communicate with people who have not been raised in U.S. culture.

In the global setting, communication can get very complicated. The major reason for this complication is that to a large degree *culture determines communication.* In addition, *culture takes many forms.* Examples of different cultures include nations, ethnic groups, regions, industries, companies, families, religions, and even small groups. A majority of the world's population associates culture with the way people behave, speak, or dress. However, these factors are only the tip of the iceberg among the qualities that actually determine culture.

The iceberg provides a useful framework for studying communication styles and cultural patterns. (See Figure 7.2.) When you communicate globally, your attention is initially drawn to the iceberg tip: in your first experience with a culture, you usually notice how people act, talk, dress, dance, and greet one another. These are the outward manifestations, the **observable behaviors.** However, 80 percent of the iceberg remains below the waterline. This bulk consists of the **attitudes** and **values** that serve as the foundation for communication; these intangibles provide the unobservable *context* in which the communication is held. To become competent in managing intercultural situations, pay more attention to the cultural foundations beneath the waterline. Thus, the iceberg base is a tool; it allows you to explore the role that values and attitudes play in shaping the way you and everyone else behaves.

You will find that culture affects how you address business letters and the way you exchange business cards. Culture also helps determine your body language (such as facial expressions), the distance you stand from the person you are communicating with, and the kind of topics that are acceptable conversation. Your expectations and the expectations that others

COMMUNICATION CHALLENGES

Clichés and Idioms A *cliché* is an overused, worn-out phrase that has lost its capacity to communicate effectively. An *idiom* is a word or phrase that has a different meaning from its literal meaning. Clichés and idioms are used as fillers in day-to-day communications, and here are some examples:

Clichés	Idioms
run of the mill	pass the buck
general rule of thumb	shotgun approach
better late than never	down the tubes
it could be worse	shoot from the hip
time will tell	needle in a haystack
no news is good news	the last straw

Think about the difficulty of trying to explain the meaning of each of these to individuals whose first language is not English. How do you explain *pass the buck* when you are not literally referring to passing around a dollar bill or a deer! If you think that one is hard to explain, try *shoot from the hip* or *shotgun approach* when you aren't discussing weapons.

Make a list of clichés and idioms that you use regularly in your speech. How might these expressions be misinterpreted?

FIGURE 7.2 | The Cultural Iceberg

The tip of the iceberg represents a culture's observable behaviors—what we notice first about other cultures. The part of the iceberg beneath the waterline represents the foundations of those behaviors.

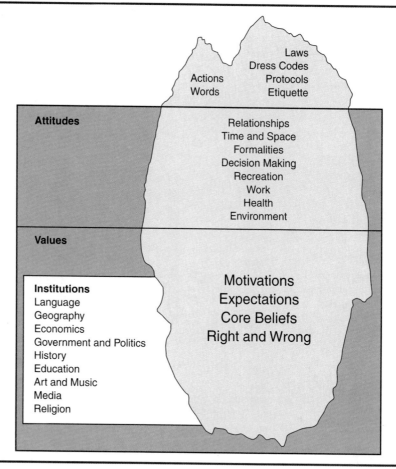

Source: Used with permission from Language and Culture Worldwide, LLC.

have of you are primarily based on culture. *Have you ever thought about communication in this way?*

Here is a main principle of global communications: To be effective globally, you need to look "below the waterline" to understand how others interpret your verbal messages. Use the insights gained from this understanding to adjust your communication style. Put another way, adapt your communication style to the context in which you find yourself.

Success Across Cultures

A panel of 50 global communication specialists was shown the list below and asked which item was most important for succeeding across cultures:[1]

- Listen and observe.

- Learn from interacting.

- Be aware of one's own culture.

- Respect the other culture.

- Be able to communicate.

Now stop for a moment to consider each item, and then select the one you think would be most important.

Which did you choose? The specialists chose "Be aware of one's own culture." Although you can learn a great deal with reflection and listening and observing, the challenge lies in

Cultural Guide: Developing an understanding of your own culture and style can provide you with both a compass and an anchor in the process of communicating globally. Why is self-awareness important when communicating across cultures?

INTERNET EXERCISE 7.1

Cultural Resources Where can you turn when you need more information about a particular culture? Visit the *Foundations of Business Communication* Web site at <http://www.mhhe.com/djyoung> for a list of cultural references, including books, newspapers, and online resources.

Once you have accessed the Web site, select "Student Activities"; then click on the Chapter 7 link.

COMMUNICATION CHALLENGES

Eyes Have It? How do you feel when someone does not meet your steady gaze with a similar level of eye contact? You might feel or interpret that behavior to be a sign of disrespect. You might even feel offended.

Now consider that *you* have been *conditioned* to interpret eye contact in this way and that, conversely, some *others* have been *conditioned* to believe that matching the gaze of a superior or someone they hold in esteem is a sign of disrespect. With this feedback about the other culture, you have a new insight and new advantage.

Ask yourself: *Do I maintain eye contact when I am in a conversation with someone? Why or why not? Does my answer vary, depending on the person with whom I am speaking or the context of the conversation? Why?*

knowing how to *interpret* what you are seeing. For example, is the shift manager wearing the same outfit to work every day because he is sloppy or because it is the nicest thing he owns and he is trying to make a good impression?

Learning to "respect the other culture" and "be able to communicate" are also valuable. However, first you must know what respect *means* to people in the other culture as well as the language and styles of communication they *prefer and use* locally. Language is a powerful tool for communicating globally, and speaking a foreign language is a definite advantage. However, the power of language is diluted when you do not understand the micromessages (nonverbal messages and hidden meanings) and broader contexts involved in any given interaction. *Are there different connotations associated with specific actions and words?*

The key factor in developing global communication skills is understanding your own culture and style. Though you are not born with culture, once cultural norms are taught to you, you see the world through your selective perception. The more you learn about your own culture and communication style, the more you will understand how other styles compare and combine with your own. To reinforce this idea, let's take a look at the following fable developed by Michael C. Mercil, a global consultant:

Sunglasses Analogy

Imagine that in your country . . . everyone . . . was born with two legs, two arms, two eyes, a nose, a mouth, and a pair of sunglasses. The lenses in the sunglasses are yellow. No one has ever thought it strange that the sunglasses are there, because they have always been there, and they are a part of the human body. Everyone has them. What makes them yellow are the values, attitudes, ideas, beliefs, and assumptions that all people in your country have in common.

. . . Thousands of miles away in another country . . . everyone . . . was born with two legs, two arms, two eyes, a nose, a mouth, and a pair of sunglasses. The lenses in the sunglasses are blue . . . everything that people see, learn, or experience is filtered through the blue lenses.

A traveler from the yellow sunglasses country . . . realize[d] that, to learn about the blue sunglass country and the people more thoroughly, he would have to acquire some blue sunglasses so that he could "see." When the traveler arrived, he wore the blue glasses, stayed for two years, and felt that he really was learning about the attitudes, beliefs, and values of the people he actually "saw" wearing the sunglasses. He came home to his own country and declared that he was now an expert on that country . . . and that their culture was green![2]

In global communications, your *selective perception* or *filter* will cause you to see things one way, whereas your overseas colleagues will see them another way. The number of filters will increase with the number of countries and cultures involved. When communicating globally, recognize that *you* perceive and project behaviors according to your filters. Also recognize that others possess filters different from your own.

These filters are rooted in long-standing experiences that began in childhood. How you feel about others——their qualities and faults, as well as the respect you assign them—is based on *your own perceptions and norms.* If you are fortunate enough to encounter behavior similar to your own when in another culture, this allows you to relax. No change is necessary (a rare experience in global communication encounters). However, if on a gut level you do not like the behavior you encounter in another culture, you obviously face a challenging situation.

Global Diversity

When faced with the many language and cultural patterns in the world—**global diversity**—you would not be alone in hoping for tips to make communicating in this environment easier. If you could magically have a "universal translator," language barriers would be manageable. Even better would be a single set of "right" techniques to apply wherever and with whomever you do business.

However, with 6,800 languages spoken in the world's nearly 200 countries, global communications truly defy any quick fixes. International markets require dynamic, complex approaches where the *context* of the communication is everything.

Thus, any simple list of do's and don'ts for all unknown territories is unreliable. That's because what is a "do" in one set of circumstances is a "don't" (not only inappropriate but possibly insulting) in another. Just ask the student who thought Spanish skills honed in Mexico would universally carry her through in Chile. As many who have traveled in Spanish-speaking countries can attest, the same word can mean one thing in Mexico and entirely different things in other parts of Latin America, depending on the local dialect and context. Of course, Spanish will get you only so far in Latin America regardless: many indigenous peoples have their own native languages, and Brazilians speak Portuguese.

EXPLORE

Interview someone from a culture different from your own. Compare and contrast attitudes, beliefs, and core values. What did you learn about yourself from this experience?

PRACTICE

Instructions: Rewrite the following e-mail message sent to Tseng Nguyen, inventory disbursement manager at the Pol Ten clothing manufacturing plant in Thailand, from his counterpart Dale Patterson, inventory controller at Casualty Riding Gear, Ltd., in Colorado, Utah.

Tseng:

Hey, homeboy! What's shakin'? Listen, I just wanted to give you a heads up on some issues with the last shipment you sent us. I'm trying to nip this in the bud before my manager catches wind of the situation and pops his lid. The problem is still the same: colors. Even after five years of working together, you and me still have communication mishaps in the trenches and it almost always goes to color. Sometimes it's like you guys are working in a different color spectrum on your side of the planet!

We agreed on the phone that the helmets and the riding jerseys were supposed to be Ocean Blue and Gray; the ones we got were Navy Blue and Sea Foam. I asked you to increase the red on the pants by 10 percent, and instead of deepening the color you expanded the colored area. And the Elgian thermals are nowhere in the vicinity of the flesh color we discussed.

COACHING TIP

Word Variations You can rewrite nearly any sentence a different way—sometimes better, sometimes not.

When you edit and revise in your own language, you have an advantage. Can you be that effective in other languages?

Remember this when you receive documents that originated in another language: style and personal preferences can vary. Try not to criticize or judge the writer by his or her language style, especially if the writer was not born in your country.

I'm thinking we don't have this kind of hassle when everything is down on paper and you have color samples instead of color printouts . . . computers never print in true colors. Maybe we should just stick to doing this on paper from now on instead of over the phone?

Anyway, we bounced the delivery back to you, and we still need to line our shelves with new goodies. I'll round up swatches to overnight to you right after I give you the forms to get the gears turning on the re-do: if you can turn this around on a dime no one will skip a beat and this will just be water under the bridge.

I know you can make this right! Thanks, Tseng.

Don

SECTION A: CONCEPT CHECK

1. What is a starting point of successfully communicating across cultures?
2. Explain what is meant by the statement "culture determines communication."
3. Explain the concept of the cultural iceberg and what it represents.

■ SECTION B: DIRECT AND INDIRECT COMMUNICATION STYLES

You worked with *direct* and *indirect* letter styles in Chapter 4. With a direct letter style, you get right to the point; with an indirect letter style, you first give background information or a rationale that leads to your main point. Now you will extend your understanding of these terms by working with them in conjunction with communication styles. With communication, direct styles find meaning primarily through words; whereas with indirect styles, the context sometimes speaks louder than the words themselves.

Some of the greatest miscommunications occur by not understanding the "why" or *context* surrounding a behavior. **Context** refers to the amount of innate and largely unconscious understanding a person brings to a particular communication setting. Here's how context relates to direct and indirect styles of communication:

- A **direct style** is low-context: the *words* are more important than the situation.
- An **indirect style** is high-context: the *situation* is highly important and can even define the encounter; thus, the words alone may not convey the meaning of the communication.

The proverb "A picture is worth a thousand words" points to indirect, high-context communication styles. The words hold little meaning, and one must search for seemingly hidden meanings that exist in facial expressions or other nonverbal behavior.

Conversely, the adage "Mean what you say and say what you mean" points to direct, low-context communication. The words themselves contain the full meaning of what is being conveyed; no importance should be placed on unspoken circumstances surrounding the communication. Generally speaking, Americans are considered direct (low-context) communicators when compared to other cultures and styles.

A high percentage of human communication is affected by **nonverbal cues.** This means that in all cultures—high and low context—people communicate to some extent through unstated means. However, in high-context (indirect) cultures people transmit more information nonverbally than through conversation. A smile in high-context Japan, for example, could mean happiness, amusement, confusion, anger, embarrassment, sadness, or *nothing.*

Thus, words can sometimes play less of a role in communication than do nonverbal cues. Even in the relatively low-context United States, consider the role that gestures, eye contact, facial expressions, personal space, touching, and dress can play. Silence, too, is a natural and expected form of expression. Distances are maintained between people, and what people consider an appropriate amount of touching can vary even in business contexts.

Specialists say a comfortable distance is measurable; for example, some people feel at ease 12 inches apart, whereas others need 18 inches of distance. In the United States, respecting one's personal space is important; an appropriate distance between two people is considered "an arm's length." Standing too closely or speaking a few inches from someone's face is not considered appropriate.

Indirect communicators, such as the people in high-context Thailand, generally carry highly developed and refined notions of how most interactions will unfold. With their indirect style of communication, they have less need to be explicit and they do not always rely on the literal meaning of the spoken word. As an example, the word *yes* does not always mean "yes" in the traditional "I agree" sense; it can also mean "I hear and acknowledge you." The difference lies in understanding the context and implied meaning. If circumstances dictate that a subordinate not openly contradict his or her boss in front of others, a "yes" might signify "Yes, I hear you" rather than "Yes, I agree."

Thus, in indirect, high-context settings, people often express messages without words; nonverbal communication may be enough. People tend to infer, suggest, and imply rather than say things out loud. At least that is how it seems to people from more direct cultures (though not, of course, to one another). People in indirect cultures tend to work closely together and know what everyone else knows. The overriding goals of the communication exchange are maintaining harmony, strengthening relationships, and saving face; therefore, the people have a natural tendency to avoid confrontation.

The Role of Context

In the United States and Canada, direct, low-context communication is dominant. Direct communicators tend to be more individualistic. Accordingly, with a direct style, the situation and context do not play as major a role. Less can be assumed about a person in a heterogeneous society of individuals, a society where difference is the norm. In a culture where people prefer independence:

- Less is known about others.

- More value is placed on self-reliance.

- A greater emotional distance is maintained from others.

People need to spell things out and be explicit, to say exactly what they mean rather than suggest or imply. The spoken word carries most of the meaning, and you should read little into what is *not* said or done. Getting or giving information is the goal of most communication exchanges.

Applying frameworks developed by Farid Elashmawi and George Simons, we can explore the role of context in four common types of business communications:[3, 4]

Business Introductions:

- *Indirect communicators* will generally start by giving their company names and their titles, followed by their own personal names. Identifying seniority and role in the organization is a priority.

COMMUNICATION CHALLENGES

Understanding the Concept of "Face" Generally **face** is defined as "the measure of one's internal quality, status, good name, and good character." Face is much more than personal pride. Face is a concept that:

- Involves the entire group: family, school, neighborhood, workplace, city, and country.
- Keeps relationships intact.
- Preserves group harmony and promotes group solidarity.
- Measures the social standing of the person within the group and the social standing of the group.

Key attributes associated with face include being:

- Honest but tactful.
- Kind without being weak.
- Honorable and integral.

Behaviors that can be associated with promoting a "lack of face" include:

- Asking questions in a large group meeting.
- Speaking up in class.
- Challenging teachers.
- Saying no frankly to friends.
- Criticizing parents.

Face cannot be underestimated: if one loses face, the whole group loses face; the effect is much deeper and stronger than that of a simple personal embarrassment. Face plays a prominent role in Hispanic, Asian, and Middle Eastern cultures, among others.

- *Direct communicators* will generally begin by providing their full names, after which they get to the purpose relatively quickly. Stating their own seniority or role does not seem important, nor does focusing on their associate's seniority or role.

Business Disagreements:

- *Indirect communicators* are highly sensitive to conflict but do not outwardly express their feelings; however, conflict must be resolved before work can progress (unless it is avoided because it is so personal). They express disapproval through **implicit** rather than explicit means.

- *Direct communicators* are often **explicit** about what they find bothersome in their colleagues' behavior; they tend to depersonalize disagreements and get on with the task.

Business Information Processing:

- *Indirect, high-context groups* look for knowledge embedded in a situation, approaching information as interconnections. They prefer processing information and solving problems in groups, using multiple sources of information, and thinking deductively (from general to specific). Learning occurs by modeling, practicing, and demonstrating.

- *Direct, low-context groups* tend to view information as fragmented and compartmentalized, often with single sources. Thinking is inductive, moving from small pieces of information to the general, and the focus is on detail. Things are specifically spelled out and contain explicit explanations.

Business Letters:

- *Indirect, high-context groups* expect formal written correspondence to convey information somewhat indirectly regardless of whether the communication conveys good news or bad news. Thus, the writer would not immediately state the purpose or main point. The first paragraph of a letter might state appreciation for the reader's time and give background information on the purpose of the letter.

- *Direct, low-context groups* expect even formal written correspondence to get to the point quickly and efficiently unless the information is bad news. Although the first part of a business letter can connect with the reader on a personal level, the writer would get directly to the point with a minimum of formality. Background information is screened for relevance and cut when possible.

Best Practices for Communicating Globally

At this point, you may be asking yourself a few questions about global communications: *Can I remember all this? If I make mistakes, will colleagues understand? What about authenticity—can I still be "me" and be effective?*

Generally, the only way to develop competence in global communications is to practice your knowledge and skill in real-world environments. As your awareness and respect grow for your international colleagues' perspectives, your sensitivity will generate more understanding from them; as a result, you will overlook unintended insults. Beyond that, effective global communications depend on tools that can be applied almost universally in all contexts. Primary among them are authenticity and the Platinum Rule.

The Platinum Rule   *Treat others as they want to be treated.* You may be familiar with the Golden Rule, which states, roughly, "Treat others as you want to be treated." This idea works in contexts of homogeneity, where others define respect and values in the same way that you do. In global contexts, however, this principle has limits. The **Platinum Rule** helps us take another step toward accommodating the needs of others. This suggests identifying and working toward appreciating your colleagues' preferences, cultural patterns, and communication styles. The challenge, of course, lies in knowing *their* styles and preferences.

Authenticity   Sincerity, humility, and a considerate attitude can take you a long way in global communications. Ask yourself: *How would I react if an international exchange student somehow insulted me?* What if, right after the insult, the exchange student was obviously

COMMUNICATION CHALLENGES

Enter the Cultural Informant A **cultural informant (CI)** is a credible, qualified resource person who can filter information about a given group or culture and provide you with insight as to what is considered appropriate.

The informant is usually someone who was born in the culture and has recent, relevant experience in it. To use the sunglasses analogy, your cultural informant can offer a perspective with a native lens. The informant can help you to understand appropriate behavior in a given culture. The caveat or warning is to remember that an informant is only one resource. Your CI may not necessarily represent everyone or even the majority within the culture.

Ask yourself: *Why is it important to get information from multiple sources? Why should I not interpret one individual's perspective as indicative of a whole group?*

uncomfortable about what happened and was eager to discover the nature of the offense. You would probably place less importance on the insult itself and more importance on the student's considerate attitude and interest in accommodating you in the future. Your colleagues, especially those who are high-context communicators, can likewise sense the difference between sincerity and insincerity. Your effectiveness depends on your **authenticity,** in other words, on being yourself.

EXPLORE

Imagine you are going to study in France for two years. Think about differences between the cultural patterns where you study now and those you are likely to encounter in France. Specifically, consider factors such as education systems, national economics, social welfare structures, and the roles of business, government, and religion.

1. What differences are you likely to encounter?
2. What could you do to prepare yourself before you go?
3. How might your experience there influence you upon your return?

PRACTICE

Instructions: In the space before each of the statements below, write *I* if the statement applies to a culture where communication is indirect, high context or *D* if it applies to one where communication is direct, low context.[5]

___ People are reluctant to say no.

___ You have to read between the lines.

___ Use of understatement is frequent.

___ It's best to tell it like it is.

___ It's okay to disagree with your boss at a meeting.

___ *Yes* means "yes."

___ *Yes* may not mean "yes."

___ People tell you what they think you want to hear.

___ Business first, then small talk.

___ Small talk first, then business.

___ The rank/status of the messenger is as important as the message.

___ Letters state the objective in the first paragraph and get to the point.

Differences in Business Values

Remembering that culture influences and shapes communication, let us now take a deeper look at some of the dimensions of differences encountered in global business settings.

First, return again to the iceberg framework in Figure 7.2 on page 229. The bottom third of the diagram identifies some of the institutional forces that help define or influence a person's core values. Put another way, these institutions are doing the "cultural programming," creating the "lens in the sunglasses," so to speak. Among others, cultural forces also include the following:

- The native tongue or home language.
- Geography and history.
- Government and politics.
- Education, arts, and music.
- Media (radio and television).
- Religion.

Their influence can be on a personal, national, regional, or even corporate culture level. The extent of their influence on value systems will vary, sometimes even among people in the same family. Still, some general trends appear across cultures that are useful in helping us navigate global business communications.

With regard to business values and behaviors, consider the impact that coming to the United States has on the mind-set, value system, and workplace behavior of immigrants. How might the behavior they exhibit in the workplace (which is shaped by their deeper base of attitudes and values) be different from that of coworkers born in the United States? Furthermore, how might the persons working with these immigrants be affected by such differences? On occasions when the immigrants' value system is compatible with the value system of their adopted workplace, few or no adjustments are required. In contrast, if major differences exist, everyone may need to make behavioral and style adjustments to ensure that communications and business interactions are effective.

EXPLORE

1. Think of someone whom you respect professionally and complete the following:

   a. What is one specific thing you have seen this person do in a business setting (an observable behavior) that you respect?

      Behavior: _____

   b. What values do you think might underlie this person's professional behavior? What is important to this person that motivates her or him to behave in this way?

      Value(s): _____

      Motivator: _____

   c. Speculate about this person's value system. Where and how was she or he raised? What life or environmental experiences have had the most influence? Check off each of the following that you think may have influenced or helped to shape the value(s) you listed above for this person:

      _____ Language or mother-tongue

      _____ Geography

      _____ Government and politics

      _____ History

      _____ Education

      _____ Arts and music

      _____ Media

      _____ Religion

2. If you choose, think of someone whom you do *not* respect professionally and repeat the exercise above (but be discreet and keep the name anonymous).

Individualist Versus Collectivist Thinking

Interestingly, although people *learn* most of their behavior, they come to regard that behavior as natural and normal for everyone. Social scientists and communication specialists have done studies to quantify the degree and nature of cultural differences. To understand the major ways that values can affect business relationships, take a look at the cultural value continuum in Figure 7.3 on the next page. Read the descriptions of the two value pairs in the figure. Where do you think businesspeople from the United States tend to be on the continuum?

As a group, Americans tend to be more **individualistic** and informal than other national groups. Of course, many people in the United States do not fit that description. Perhaps you had a boss who was more relationship-focused than task-focused, for example. In addition, certain traditions in the United States foster hierarchy in families, organizations, and companies. For each of the value pairs, you are likely to know some people who are at each extreme and some who are in the middle. However, viewed as an entire cultural group, people from

Culture Club: *Cultural awareness can have an impact on your mind-set, value system, and workplace behavior.* Beyond improving business communication, what benefits are there in developing a better understanding of other people's cultures and values?

FIGURE 7.3 | Cultural-Value Pairs

On both continuums, the United States tends to exemplify a culture on the left and Japan tends to exemplify a culture on the right.

INDIVIDUALIST	COLLECTIVIST
Identifies primarily with self; individual needs satisfied before those of the group; taking care of oneself and being self-sufficient guarantee well-being of the group; self-reliance is stressed; one may choose to join groups, but membership is not essential to success.	Identity is in large part a function of one's membership and role in a group; survival and success of group ensure well-being of the individual; considering needs and feelings of others protects oneself; harmony and interdependence are stressed; distance psychologically and emotionally from nongroup members.
INFORMALITY	FORMALITY
Body language, attention to ritual, and dress are less important; using first names with people you've just met is fine, suggesting openness; people may slouch down in chairs or lean on walls or furniture when they talk, rather than observing strict postures; the atmosphere is often informal, with joking, teasing, and wandering around offices; greetings are extended casually to passersby and strangers and to groups as a whole; titles such as "Dr." for someone with a PhD are sometimes seen as pretentious and too formal.	Etiquettes and protocols are used to ensure a sense of order and to demonstrate respect; protocol of rank is observed and defines situational behaviors and appropriate responses; preservation and use of titles is important for showing respect; naming conventions are observed; posture, dress, gestures, and body language are used to evaluate one's credibility and to demonstrate respect for others; a high value placed on personal space; handshakes, bows, kisses, and so on are used to open and close encounters.

Source: Portions of this continuum have been drawn from *Culture Matters: The Peace Corps Cross-Cultural Workbook.* Peace Corps, 1997.

the United States tend to fall on the left-hand side of the continuum in business settings. (In contrast, Canadians are more **collectivistic** in their thinking, and cooperation among them is more of a tradition.)

Let's consider the fact that Americans tend to value individualism. Where does this trait come from? Why are independence and self-initiative, even at work, so important? In part, the answer lies in the following influences on workplace value systems in the United States:

- A democratic form of *government* that promotes the importance of the individual.

- A pioneer *history* in which survival depended on providing for oneself.

- A tradition of *religion,* beginning among the early settlers, that has promoted individual hard work (for example, the "Protestant work ethic").

- A capitalistic *economy* that rewards individual achievement financially.

Looking at these influences on our cultural programming in the United States, you can see how the role of the individual has been reinforced and rewarded. At work, self-initiative is considered a good thing.

Cultures that emphasize individualism contrast sharply with cultures where group harmony is most important. In cultures that value group harmony, self-initiative is interpreted as an overstepping of boundaries and can be considered insubordinate behavior. These cultures value hierarchy and order. Thus, taking the initiative is deemed less important than doing one's prescribed duty and honoring one's role in the larger scheme of things. Individualism can even be viewed as a threat to group harmony; initiative is something to be avoided and minimized in the workplace. Anyone who places a high value on self-initiative is likely to experience substantial miscommunication in cultures where values and priorities focus on group harmony. When an individual acts contrary to an established norm, it sends micromessages that can result in miscommunication and microinequities.

The concepts of **formality** and **informality** relate to the value placed on tradition. As a group, Americans tend to be more informal than other cultures in business interactions. In contrast, much of the world is formal in business dealings. Formality dictates that there is a respectful way to behave in every setting and situation. Formality takes the form of **protocols** (or rules of order and etiquette) regarding how the following are handled: greetings, introductions, names and titles, business cards, business gifts, business letters, e-mails, and dining. Once again, the "right" thing to do will vary by country, region, company, individual, and situation.

EXPLORE

Review the cultural-value continuum in Figure 7.3, and think about each one. Where do your own tendencies lie regarding each value pair? Consider the following questions:

1. What accommodations could you make to your personal style when communicating with people whose value-pair orientation is substantially different from your own?

2. What resources might be helpful for finding more information about the differences regarding informality and formality?

3. How do differences in communication relate to micromessages (see Chapter 6 to review information on micromessages)?

VOCABULARY BUILDERS

Explicit/Implicit These two words relate directly to communication style; one approach is used with direct communication styles, and the other is predominant with indirect styles.

Explicit relates to stating a point distinctly and clearly in language that can be easily understood. The meaning of the communication does not depend on the context.

Implicit relates to implying or inferring a point that is not expressed entirely in words; the context of the communication is important in deciphering the message. An implicit communication could take the form of a nod of agreement or a shrug of the shoulders. The communicators would interpret the meaning on the basis of their relationship and the context of the behavior.

John gave *explicit* directions to the meeting site.

Jasmine stated *explicitly* that we were not to jeopardize the contract.

The committee member showed his disagreement *implicitly* by the look on his face.

Though Melvin did not state that he approved of the project, his smile was an *implicit* indication that we would go forward.

As you explore direct and indirect communication styles, use these terms to gain deeper understanding of the cultures you are studying.

  SECTION B: CONCEPT CHECK

1. Explain the role of context in direct and indirect communication styles.

2. In what ways do people in the United States demonstrate their individualism? Describe some of the influences that have led to the individualistic perspective that is prevalent in the United States. Do you see yourself as an individualistic or collectivistic thinker?

3. What is the Platinum Rule? Do you think this rule can be (or should be) applied to your personal as well as your business communications?

■ SECTION C: MEETINGS AND PRESENTATIONS

Communication expresses culture. And nowhere does the range of expectations and style differences present itself more than at international meetings, training programs, and presentations. These events are full of cross-cultural communicators reflecting vast differences in background and culture. Understanding and adapting to cultural differences will help you build stronger business relationships across cultural lines.

As a direct communicator, you can adapt your style by learning to be more comfortable with silences and placing a greater priority on listening and observing than on talking. Direct communicators can also accommodate other styles by recognizing that their own preference for informal, casual settings may make others uncomfortable. When norms have programmed indirect communicators to expect formal protocols, anything different may defy their comfort zone. Consider two miscommunications that often arise:

- *To indirect communicators,* direct communicators may seem to be ruled by agendas, as if they forget that people are meant to rule over timelines, and not the other way around.

- *To direct communicators,* indirect communicators may appear to either talk around the point or embellish it, as if they are more interested in communication as an art than as a business tool.

Of course, these perceptions depend on the filter of expectations one brings to the encounter. Indirect communicators do care about time, and direct communicators can appreciate stories or allegory; the difference lies in the priorities and emphasis involved for each.

Culture dictates other issues that can be a source of miscommunication in meetings and presentations. Some of these issues are the seating arrangements for senior managers and elders, the order and level of formality of introductions, the means for achieving harmony, and the honor given to hierarchies in the group. Thus, it is difficult to generalize a universal strategy that will serve you well across the wide range of cultures and contexts that you will encounter. To illustrate the role of culture in international meetings, imagine the following scenario:

You are an American preparing to deliver a presentation in a high-context setting. Your audience members speak English very well, but they are largely unfamiliar with Americans and work in a hierarchical organizational pattern. Wanting to show respect and build relationships with the group, what are some things you could do to adjust your own style to accommodate theirs?

Now that you've given it some thought, here are some proven strategies to improve rapport in high-context settings:

- Gain respect from participants by seeking a high-level management endorsement for your objectives before the meeting. This collaboration would help improve the chances that your ideas will be well-received by the group.

- If possible, participate in a social activity with the group before the meeting. This would enable you to forge relationships, and it would allow others to assess your credibility and style in an additional context.

- Share your handouts or PowerPoint slides ahead of time, preferably translated. Participants would have a chance to read them and formulate questions in their native language.

- Arrange to have yourself formally introduced to the group by a high-level manager, again implying senior endorsement.

- Start your presentation in a formal way. Work on projecting a calm confidence regarding your subject-matter expertise, and speak with a sense of authority.

- Offer ways for indirect communicators to get their questions answered outside the presentation, such as at follow-up meetings. (You will thereby protect participants from situations that may cause them to look ill-informed or foolish in front of their colleagues.)

- Pay attention to the tone of discussion during breaks, and incorporate any necessary changes.

- Make yourself available and approachable outside the presentation.

- Tap into informal feedback that indirect communicators may provide over time through indirect channels.

In general, an unfortunate but likely assumption is that many of your international colleagues may expect your approach to be ill-informed, ethnocentric, and possibly "too American." There are some things you can do to counter such impressions, however, and also increase your effectiveness globally:

- Read about the country's or organization's culture, economics, and politics *before* the encounter.

- Integrate any relevant points from your cultural readings into your dialogue.

- Incorporate or make reference to materials from local, in-country authors, universities, and thinkers.

- Read orientation materials that your hosts have read about *you;* this information will expand your understanding of how Americans are perceived.

- Learn and practice a few basic phrases in the local language, and review greeting and naming protocols.

- Consider the accommodations your hosts make for you, including their attempts to accommodate you with English.

- Be open, and do not act as though the "best ideas are from America."

PRACTICE

Situation: You are a sales representative for an American company that produces database and storage systems. Your good friend Peter works for an Israeli company that is planning to upgrade its equipment and has invited you to his country and company to make a sales presentation. Peter believes your product is exactly what is needed; though he doesn't want to put pressure on his supervisors for fear it might jeopardize the sale, he's offered to do what he can to help.

Instructions: Write an e-mail to Peter explaining what kind of help you will need from him to prepare your presentation and trip to Israel.

Interpreters

If you prepare for an international meeting, you may find it necessary to use an interpreter, either in person or via video- or teleconferencing. In such settings, note that there is a difference between translating and interpreting:

- A **translator** transfers written texts into another language.

- An **interpreter** transfers the spoken word into another language.

Two types of interpreting are simultaneous interpretation and consecutive interpretation. In **simultaneous interpretation,** the interpreter interprets the target language at the same time that the speaker delivers the speech; the interpreter usually sits in an interpreting booth and uses a microphone and headset. During **consecutive interpretation,** the interpreter interprets chunks of no more than 1 to 3 minutes of speech each time the speaker finishes a sentence or a paragraph. Knowing these few simple facts will help you in many situations.[6]

Unless the meeting or presentation is short, quality interpreters usually work in pairs. To ensure effective interpretation, consider the following points:

1. Select interpreters/translators who are accredited or certified by a professional association. Such associations include the American Translators' Association (ATA) or the Bund Deutscher Übersetzer/innen (BdÜ).

2. Prepare the interpreters carefully. Give your interpreters a thorough briefing on your goals, objectives, and desired outcomes. Also give them instructions on all technical details, such as terminology, word lists, and presentation materials.

3. Allow time for the interpreters to rest and catch their breath between meeting segments. Also, speak slowly and pause often. Give them a chance to clarify highly technical or complicated subject matter before, during, or after the meeting.

4. Since the grammar and syntax of languages vary, your interpreters may need additional time to relay what was said. English sentences tend to be considerably shorter than, for example, their equivalents in most European languages.

5. Avoid looking directly at the interpreters during the meeting or presentation; the interpreters professionally facilitate but are not part of the audience and do not participate. Thus, look directly at the speaker or audience and speak to them, *not* the interpreters.

6. Seat the interpreters in a visible and central position, not in a corner of the meeting room.

7. Best practice dictates that you give the interpreters a chance to debrief after the meeting. Thank your interpreters publicly for their efforts.

If you and the interpreters are a good match, consistently use the same interpreters. Over time you and your interpreters will develop a rhythm. The better your interpreters know you and your communication style, the better they are able to represent your message accurately to others.

Business Cards, Greetings, and Naming Patterns

In many parts of the world, presenting business cards is a first step during introductions. In these regions, the card exchange—particularly with businesspeople from high-context cultures—is more formal than in the United States. Proper business cards furnish critical and practical information such as the spelling of your name, your company, and your position (or place) in the company. If you think of a business card as *an extension of the person* presenting it, the logic behind other cultures' business-card protocols becomes clear. Here are some guidelines for exchanging business cards with international colleagues:

- Exchange cards with consideration. Take time to study the card and acknowledge the person presenting it.

- Treat cards with care. Keep your own cards in a well-conditioned card case. Do not bend cards or put them inside front pockets or loosely into bags.

- Use professionally translated bilingual cards where appropriate.

- Do not use the back of business cards to make notes about the person you are meeting. High-context communicators may interpret this as disrespectful.

During introductions, notice the roles that respect for gender and respect for seniority play in communications. These can vary substantially from one setting to the next. For example, in China greet the oldest, most senior person before any others. Groups should line up according to seniority, with the senior people at the head of the line. Among Indian cultures, some traditional men do

Not *Lost in Translation:* *A growing number of technological solutions are available for those in need of translation services, including voice recognition software that translates the spoken word into computer text and language translation software that translates electronic documents.* If you were in a situation where interpretation or translation was necessary, would you prefer to work with a person or a computer program? Why?

COACHING TIP

Accents and Colloquialisms Within the United States, there are many differing accents and **colloquialisms.** In a multicultural world, these language variables become a barrier to the communication process. Consider this scenario:

Pretik, originally from India, is in a business meeting in one of the southern states. He is making a presentation to Sam, vice president of sales. He thinks things are going smoothly; then Sam stops his presentation, leans over, and says "That dog won't hunt." Unless Pretik is familiar with the meaning of *that dog won't hunt,* he may not know how to respond.

By the way, if someone tells you "that dog won't hunt," the person may be saying either of the following in a polite way: he or she doesn't buy what you are selling; or he or she already tried what you are recommending, and it doesn't work.

Accents may also be a barrier in the communication process. When English is spoken as a second language, biases may prevent a listener from really hearing what the speaker is saying. As you likely know from your own experience, people may nod or smile as if they understand when an accent creates a barrier to understanding.

not touch women when meeting or greeting. However, Western women may offer their hand to a westernized Indian man, but not normally to others. Educated and more modern women in India may also offer their hand to a man and shake hands with women when appropriate.

When trying to establish a relationship with a new international colleague, do some research regarding the most basic greeting in that person's native language. Practice the proper pronunciations of the greetings in advance. Also consider how greetings may vary, even within the same country. An Indian Hindu would be greeted with *namaste* (na-mass-TAY), while Indian Muslims are generally greeted with the phrase *salam alaikum* (sah-LAAM a-LEH-come). Sikhs in India are greeted differently again, with the phrase *sat sri akal* (sut shree ah-kaal). Likewise, there are different language patterns by gender in some countries.

Business communications may also vary in respect to naming patterns. In some cultures, women continue to use their maiden names (also called *surnames* or *family names*) after marriage. In these cases, women may indicate marital status by using their local language equivalent of *Mrs.* In China, for example, Mrs. Wang may be married to Mr. Li; and in Mexico, the American Dr. Anne Coleman may be married to Mr. Juan Rodriguez. Mexicans who know that Dr. Coleman is married would generally refer to her as *Señora* ("Mrs."), indicating her marital status, instead of *Señorita* ("Miss"): "Señora Coleman's husband's name is Rodriguez."

Other challenges evolve around naming, particularly regarding the placement of given names (or first names) with respect to surnames (last names). Again, let us examine norms in Mexico. Extended names are common. For both men and women, the two names following a first name represent parents' surnames: father first and then mother. A married Delphina Buendia Arrieta de Rodriguez is generally referred to as "Mrs. Buendia" or "Señora Buendia"; *Buendia* is from her father's family, and *Arrieta* is from her mother's family. Her son, Juan Rodriguez Buendia, would generally be referred to as "Juan Rodriguez," "Mr. Rodriguez," or "Señor Rodriguez." (Señora Buendia's husband's name is Rodriguez.)

As many variations for these conventions exist as there are cultures in the global market. Such diversity makes it difficult to know the best practice for each situation. When possible, research naming practices for expected encounters. In general, here are a few tips that will get you through most situations:

- Observe and follow the lead of your international colleague regarding how introductions are done.

- Do not use your colleague's first name until invited to do so. Using a first name can be interpreted as a sign of disrespect or an inappropriate breach of formality.

- Be prepared with a large number of business cards, professionally translated on the second side.

- If your colleague is introduced with a title such as "Doctor" or "Director," use the title until you are invited to drop it.

- Show respect by being mindful and conservative in your dress, body language, tone of voice, and attitude.

COACHING TIP

Card Tips To ease introductions and language barriers, prepare business cards for international occasions. Bilingual cards with one side printed in the language of the country in which you are doing business and the other in English are very helpful. A title printed on the cards makes each person's rank clear, thereby clarifying respective roles and status within a company.

In some Asian cultures, the exchange of business cards is a formal process. Two colleagues give and receive cards with both hands, give a slight bow, and show the utmost respect. Each most likely practices pronouncing the other person's name while reading the card and then checks to make sure the pronunciation is correct. When the two are seated, each may place the other's card squarely in front of him or her during the meeting for easy reference (especially when there are multiple people and multiple card exchanges in a given meeting).

Ask yourself: *How do I manage my business introductions? Do the issues of formality and respect play a role in my behavior?*

Résumés and Curricula Vitae

In the United States, graduating students use **résumés** to present themselves in what can be a very competitive job market. Students are taught how best to use the résumé to impress and persuade potential employers by highlighting their

**INTERNET
EXERCISE 7.2**

Curriculum Vitae You've
seen a résumé, but what does
a curriculum vitae look like?
Visit the *Foundations of
Business Communication*
Web site at <http://www.
mhhe.com/djyoung> to view
samples and find out more
about formatting CVs.

skills. Common advice for preparing résumés includes keeping the document to one page and using strong action words. Often résumés are tailored for a specific position, and only the most relevant background information is included. Though résumé styles vary, most people in the United States would agree that the résumé is a tool used to "sell yourself" to your potential employer. (Chapter 9 provides guidelines for résumés.)

In the global market, a contrasting style is the use of a **curriculum vitae,** or **CV.** The CV is a history of one's professional and academic credentials. A CV is less a marketing tool than it is a chronological record of where you have worked. The CV starts with your most recent position, and it includes what you have studied, publications you have authored, awards you have earned, and so on. In cultures valuing context, a midcareer professional's CV might run on for many pages. In some parts of the world, CVs include photographs, marital status, age, and number of children; these attributes are considered important qualifying and "contextual" information.

On the other hand, American managers can be disappointed and confused when they review the CVs of highly recommended international candidates. Conditioned to expect high-impact, concise bullet-pointed résumés, American managers can misconstrue CVs as being long-winded, bland accounts of seemingly mediocre careers. Some international professionals respectfully understate credentials so that (high-context) readers can infer a candidate's desirability based on prestigious schools and industry stature; this approach is ineffective with low-context Americans.

In your own career, best practice in using a résumé or CV dictates that you get to know your audience and then rely on the Platinum Rule (treat others as *they* want to be treated). When applying for a position at an international company, gain insight into your audience by asking cultural informants about its norms and protocols for hiring and documenting performance. Review documents from candidates who have been successful in the organization that you are approaching. Use insights gleaned from your understanding of cultures to anticipate where miscommunications might occur, and then accommodate different expectations accordingly.

EXPLORE

Situation: A young professional applies for a job with an established, conservative European firm that is the clear leader in its industry. Excited about the opportunity, the candidate prepares what she considers to be a hard-hitting, concise résumé. In addition to part-time work while she was in school, she highlights her work experience over the last four years at a large industry giant, including as many positives as she can.

Consider: What type of reception do you think her résumé will receive from a midcareer, traditional European human resource manager with little exposure to the United States? Would you be surprised if the manager thought the candidate was demonstrating an inappropriate arrogance, even an inflated sense of her value, particularly for one so early in her career?

 SECTION C: CONCEPT CHECK

1. Why is understanding another culture's traditions for introductions and naming important?

2. Why should you adjust your style to accommodate the style of your audience? What are some things you can do to accomplish this?

3. What is the main difference between a résumé and a curriculum vitae?

■ SECTION D: TRENDS IN TECHNOLOGY

The process of making a product culturally appropriate to the country in which it will be marketed and sold is known as **localization.** When it comes to the Internet, *localization* is a hot word.

According to Bill Dunlap, managing director of Euro-Marketing Associates and an expert in Web site localization, two major reasons for localizing Web messages are (1) to get Web surfers' attention in the first place and (2) to convince them to spend time looking into a given product/service.[7] Dunlap continues:

> Do not assume "they speak English in other countries, so there is no reason to translate our marketing materials or Web site." Even if some Europeans can read English, they have a tendency to ignore advertising in English. . . . Willy Brandt, the former German chancellor, put it this way: "If I'm selling to you, I speak your language. If I'm buying, dann müssen Sie Deutsch sprechen ['then you must speak German']."[8]

Online Translation Services

On the Internet, you will find free, online translations available. However, these services may not be very helpful in routine global communications. Generally, online translations are most helpful when you translate another language into your native language or translate a few key words for personal use. With more expansive applications, you may find that literal meanings and differences in grammar pose major obstacles in generating understandable translations.

In October 2000, *The Wall Street Journal* tested two free, online automatic translation services and concluded: "These services are passable for travelers or for those wanting to translate a letter from a distant cousin. I definitely wouldn't use them for business or anything that remotely requires accuracy."[9]

International Conference Calls

Global businesspeople regularly arrange international conference calls across borders and time zones. There are several techniques for ensuring such calls go as smoothly as possible for all those involved.

Obviously important is coordinating the time of the call at your location and all the international locations. U.S. daylight saving time and the International Date Line can cause confusion, and adjacent international time zones can differ by 15, 30, and 45 minutes, as well as by an hour. Be sure you determine the correct time for each international location by using scheduling and time-check tools, which are available free online.

Here are a few more effective practices:[10]

- *Share the responsibility.* When multiple calls are involved, share the burden and inconvenience of having to be available for late nights or early mornings among participants. Also, the "chairing" of the call should be rotated among different participants and different cultures. Everyone involved will appreciate these courtesies.

- *Check for complete phone numbers.* International telephone numbers have a country code and a city code before the local number. These codes vary in length, so accuracy is difficult to determine at first glance. Confirm all international numbers directly with the participants before the call.

- *E-mail the agenda and translations.* Before the call, e-mail an agenda and a copy of any presentations or notes. Also include translations of key terms and concepts; technical "business speak" and jargon can pose major challenges; translations will minimize miscommunications. Participants with language barriers can then prepare ahead for the call; preparation will give them more confidence to ask questions.

- *Be on time.* If you are late, apologize and explain your tardiness. However, the best rule of thumb is to be on the phone ahead of your guests.

- *Make introductions.* When participants do not know one another, spend the first minutes going around to all participants in turn (alphabetically). Have them introduce themselves and say where they are calling from. Also, do not assume that you should use first names; do research ahead of time to determine whether the formal approach of using last names is appropriate.

COACHING TIP

Time Zones Dates and times are written differently in different countries and can be a source of confusion. In some countries (and even in the U.S. military), 6/9/06 would be September 6, not June 9. And remember, 7 a.m. occurs at a different time in Chicago than it does in Paris.

The military uses a 24-hour clock. When you get to 1 o'clock in the afternoon, military time is 13:00 hours; at 6 p.m., it's 18:00 hours.

If you want to be clear about a meeting time, be specific about times *and* locations.

- *Outline protocols.* Even with an agenda, an international conference call can be confusing. Use the first few minutes to have the chairperson outline the protocols. To discourage people from talking at the same time, have participants identify themselves before asking questions; for example, "This is Monica Marcel, and I have a question for Rita about the deadlines she mentioned. Is now a good time?"

- *Slow down and articulate.* Nonnative speakers consistently rate telephone conversations among the most difficult challenges faced in international business communications. Furthermore, Americans typically speak faster than others. Be aware of how fast you speak, especially if a language barrier is present. Make a conscious effort to speak very clearly and at a reasonable pace. Stop periodically to check for understanding, and politely ask your colleagues if they are following along.

- *Introduce changes in topic.* As you move through your agenda, formally introduce each new topic so that participants do not lose their place in the conversation.

- *Be conscious of humor and slang.* Humor and colloquialisms do not translate well. In addition, avoid terms such as "domestic," which can have different meanings for different callers.

- *Provide alternate access.* At times a convenient calling time cannot be arranged for all international parties. If this is the case, arrange for international participants to have access to a recording of the conference in a format that allows them to leave messages for response at a later time.

As a matter of best practice, you can do a few more things a day or two after the call. First, send an e-mail to participants thanking them and encouraging them to follow up with you if they have questions. Second, send out minutes to confirm action items, negotiated points, and decisions made during the call. If language barriers are an issue, pay special attention to this postcall follow-up; translated versions of the minutes can ensure consistent understanding and avoid costly and embarrassing miscommunication.

Global E-Mail

Jeremy Solomons, an intercultural coach and trainer, has explored the use of e-mail as a global communication tool. He points out that even though English is widely spoken in global business circles, it may not be your counterpart's first language. Among his pieces of advice for global e-mail, or "g-mail," are the following:[11]

- Use short, simple phrases and uncomplicated sentence structure. Explain acronyms, initialisms, and technical terms. Avoid clichés, idioms, and slang, as well as humor.

- Realize that some people still do not know how to use some e-mail features or do not check their e-mail frequently. Always check that your message arrived and got to the right person. Follow up regularly and check often for understanding.

- Keep it simple and boring. Different countries use different systems and many people have trouble reading rich-text, colored-screen formats. Even quotation marks and apostrophes can come out looking different. Block capitals are difficult to read and denote SHOUTING in other cultures, too!

- Many people have difficulty downloading attachments. At times, you may find it advisable to separate long documents into "bite-size chunks." You can also cut and paste information into the body of clearly labeled e-mails and send them out separately.

- Be aware of the fact that antivirus protection might be much less widespread in some countries.

- Err on the formal side, especially with someone you do not know well. Use titles such as "Dr." or "Professor," and do not rush to first names or abbreviate them without permission.

- Use salutations (such as "Dear Mr. Rossi") and a friendly opening paragraph ("I hope things are going well in . . .") before launching into business. Make sure to end on a friendly, proper note ("I look forward to hearing from you again soon. Best regards").

- Confidentiality means different things in different cultures. Thus, a "blind copy" may be forwarded to others. Compose e-mails on the assumption that anything you write may be seen by the person you least want to see it.

- When receiving correspondence from a nonnative English speaker, read closely between the lines of what is being said or not said. Avoid correcting spelling or usage. By using the correct term in your next communication, you are using an *indirect* approach to assist your colleague.

As you can see, global e-mail has a few additional guidelines to add to those you already follow for sending e-mail within the United States.

SECTION D: CONCEPT CHECK

1. List steps you can take to manage a global conference call effectively.

2. Why is follow-up on conference calls and e-mails important?

3. How are the "rules" of communicating globally by e-mail similar to those for communicating locally by e-mail? How are they different?

SUMMARY

Over time, global communicators tend to adopt a mind-set reminiscent of a Taoist philosophy: the more you know, the more you realize there is to learn. Your greatest chance for successful and meaningful interactions among people of different backgrounds, cultures, and languages lies in your ability to be self-aware.

Given the role that context plays in global communications, you cannot avoid all mishaps. Thus, the challenge is managing your communications and even anticipating where miscommunications might occur so that you can prepare. Instead of spending your time looking for universals and shortcuts in global communications, learn to communicate on terms your colleagues can understand.

Above all, remember that true leverage comes from accommodating different communication styles. That, combined with authenticity, the Platinum Rule, and the use of cultural informants, will take you as far as you need to go.

CHAPTER 7 CHECKLIST

___ Have you considered how attitudes and values influence communication?
___ Are you aware of how using slang or colloquialisms can confuse meaning?
___ Have you considered that your filters may distort communication across cultures?
___ Are you a direct or indirect communicator?
___ How will you adapt when communicating with someone who has a diverse style?
___ Are you ready to exchange business cards with international associates?
___ Have you prepared your curriculum vitae?
___ Have you clarified the time differences for your international conference call?
___ Have you used the appropriate salutation in an e-mail that is going overseas?
___ Have you considered the micromessages you may be sending to indirect communicators?

END-OF-CHAPTER ACTIVITIES

ACTIVITY 1: PROCESS MEMO

Instructions: Write a memo or an e-memo to your instructor explaining at least three insights you had about global communications while reading this chapter. How will your behavior or attitudes change as a result of what you have learned? (Use the reflect/respond/revise strategy to develop your message.)

ACTIVITY 2: TEAM ACTIVITY—MEETING STYLES[12]

Background: A meeting was scheduled at the U.S. headquarters of a multinational company in Ohio. Executives from Belgium were asked to brief the U.S. management team regarding new customs and export regulations affecting a major product line. Wanting to convey the importance of the research he had just completed, Stijn Streuvels, the VP of sales, took extra care preparing his 25-page report for the management team.

On the day of the meeting, things started 20 minutes late, and several agenda items took longer than their allotted time. Finally, it was Streuvels' time to present. After ensuring that each person sitting at the table had received a copy of the report, he began walking his colleagues through the analysis and calculations.

During the presentation, the chairperson noted that the calculations and analysis were included in the report documentation. The chair politely interrupted Streuvels to suggest that perhaps the findings could be summarized with a few key points for the group.

Taken aback, the Belgian said that it would be quite impossible to summarize his work of the past month in a mere few words. At this point, the chair of the meeting smilingly replied, "Mr. Streuvels, if it cannot be summarized in a few words, it is possibly not worth considering. Let us move on to the next item on the agenda."

Instructions:

1. Discuss the following among your teammates:

   a. How would you describe Streuvels' understanding of his role during the meeting?

   b. What were the chairperson's expectations?

   c. What is a basic principle that would explain the difference in approach between Streuvels and the chair of the meeting and participants?

2. Assume you and your partners are members of the Belgian delegation represented by Streuvels. As a team, compose a message to the chairperson that acknowledges the misunderstanding and requests a second opportunity to present Streuvels' findings.

ACTIVITY 3: ALL PRO TEMPS

Instructions: All Pro Temps is going global with the opening of its first overseas office in Seoul, South Korea, which will serve branch offices of American companies in several Asian countries. There are just a few last things to settle:

1. You've had many discussions with a knowledgeable colleague, Hang Lee, whom you would like to have working as the manager of the new office. While Hang has seemingly been very supportive of the idea, saying such things as "It's a wonderful idea" and "A man would be crazy not to hope that such a position might come along in his lifetime," he's never actually accepted your offer or asked any of the questions you would expect if he were seriously considering it. You have another potential candidate lined up for the

job, but you feel the offer to Hang hasn't been resolved. Compose a letter that asks for Hang's response so that you can move on one way or the other. Consider: *Do you need to know more about South Korean business traditions before you send the letter? Where can you turn to find the necessary information?*

2. Compose an e-memo to the employees in the Seoul office, most of whom are recently transplanted Americans, titled "The Five Most Important Things to Remember When Communicating Globally."

ACTIVITY 4: LOOKING FOR COMMUNICATION CLUES[13]

Instructions: For this exercise, find a workplace where people of different cultures or countries congregate. Your task is simply to watch and listen to what is going on around you and record what you see. Below is a list of questions to prompt or guide your observations. Take note of the sometimes subtle differences between behaviors you see, and consider how the behaviors compare with your own norms of behavior. *Alternate instructions:* Interview someone you know who comes from a different culture. Record her or his responses, and compare them with your norms of behavior.

Nonverbal Communication:

What do people do with their arms, hands, and fingers and with their head, eyes, mouth, and eyebrows?

How does eye contact vary among people of different ages, genders, or professional levels?

How do people dress?

How do they greet one another in the morning?

What is the protocol for going into and out of someone's office?

Do people maintain eye contact when they talk?

How far apart do people stand?

Time Behaviors:

Do people come to work on time? Who does and who doesn't?

What happens when someone gets a phone call while talking to someone else?

What does a third person do when approaching two others who are already in conversation?

Do meetings start on time?

How long do people with appointments have to wait?

Feedback Styles:

How is conflict handled?

How is disagreement expressed?

How long does one person speak before allowing the other to speak?

How is bad news or a negative concern communicated?

How important does saving face seem to be?

Are people generally direct or indirect in their conversation?

Other Norms:

When people interact, do they get to the point right away or begin by talking more generally?

Do people work closely together or more independently?

Are women treated differently from men? If so, in what way?

What kind of behaviors in workers seem to be rewarded? What are people praised for?

What does the prevailing attitude seem to be about rules and procedures and the need to follow them?

The two exercises below give you a chance to practice the direct and indirect communication styles. The direct communicator's way of saying certain things may strike indirect communicators as too harsh, while the actual meaning of an indirect communicator's words may be a poor guide to what he or she is saying. If possible, do the exercises below with a partner.

Part A

Instructions: Listed below is a series of *direct* statements. While these statements could be appropriate in some situations, the setting here is a meeting at which allowing people to save face is important. Try to rephrase the statements to make them more indirect, writing one or two suggestions in the blank spaces below each one. Suggested rephrasing of the first statement is offered as an example:

Direct statement: I don't think that's such a good idea.
Indirect suggestions: Do you think that's a good idea?
                            Are there any other ideas?
                            I like most parts of that idea.

1. *Direct statement:*   That's not the point.

   Indirect suggestions: _____
                                _____
                                _____

2. *Direct statement:*   As the assistant, what do you think, Ms. Wong?

   Indirect suggestions: _____
                                _____
                                _____

3. *Direct statement:*   Those figures are not accurate.

   Indirect suggestions: _____
                                _____
                                _____

4. *Direct statement:*   You're doing that wrong.

   Indirect suggestions: _____
                                _____
                                _____

5. *Direct statement:*   I don't agree.

   Indirect suggestions: _____
                                _____
                                _____

Part B

Instructions: In communicating across cultures, you need to explore the possibility that the speaker may mean something other than what he or she has said. Thus, this exercise is the opposite of the one you just completed. Listed below is a series of *indirect* statements. Try to "decode" them by explaining in direct language what the speaker probably means. Looking at the example, remember that the person may mean exactly what the statement says but sometimes may use the statement as an indirect way of saying "I disagree with you."

Indirect statement: That is a very interesting viewpoint.
Decoded meanings: I don't agree.
We need to talk more about this.
You're wrong.

1. *Indirect statement:*   This proposal deserves further consideration.

     Decoded meanings: _____

_____

_____

2. *Indirect statement:*   I know very little about this situation, but . . .

     Decoded meanings: _____

_____

_____

3. *Indirect statement:*   We understand your proposal very well.

     Decoded meanings: _____

_____

_____

4. *Indirect statement:*   We will try our best.

     Decoded meanings: _____

_____

_____

5. *Indirect statement:*   I heard another story about that product.

     Decoded meanings: _____

_____

_____

6. *Indirect statement:*   Can we move on to the next topic?

     Decoded meanings: _____

_____

_____

ACTIVITY 6: INFORMALITY AND FORMALITY

Situation: The poster in Figure 7.4 was originally designed for distribution in Europe. It was part of a series done for each of the company's world regions, encouraging employees to

FIGURE 7.4

explore the deeper meaning behind corporate values and the company's code of ethics. After an initial pilot review done by the human resource manager in Europe, the company canceled plans to distribute the poster in Europe. Why? It was decided that the informal, "fun" tone—intended to encourage creative, outside-of-the-box thinking—would be misinterpreted and counterproductive in Europe. Europeans interpret comics differently than Americans do.

Instructions: You are the human resource manager in Europe and have just received the notes from the pilot reviews of the poster, which were quite negative. Among the objections voiced most often in focus groups were the childlike and patronizing tone and the idea of forcing family members to participate in work-related activities. Compose a memo to your counterpart, the human resource manager in the United States, explaining that you don't think the poster will be effective in Europe. He will be disappointed to hear the news because he helped develop the campaign, and it has been used quite effectively in the United States.

ACTIVITY 7: LOW-CONTEXT AND HIGH-CONTEXT MESSAGES

Situation: Manatee Aquatics has survived a challenging business year. Managers have met their goals by laying off 50 percent of the company's employees, closing sales offices throughout the United States, freezing employee salaries, and canceling employee charge accounts. At the company's plant in Canada, employees have been hard hit by the layoffs. They have responded to the hardship by working longer hours and by developing innovative methods to increase their productivity and to improve the quality of their products. As a result of these combined efforts, the company has returned from the brink of bankruptcy and has a positive outlook on the future: jobs are more secure.

Instructions: Compose two messages of appreciation to the groups of employees who brought Manatee out of its slump. One memo will be sent to the company managers in the United States; the other, to factory workers in Canada. The memos will thank each group for their contributions to the company's success. Consider: *Would it be more effective to distribute one memo to all employees? What are the benefits of tailoring each message for its specific audience? Is this ethical? Why or why not?*

ACTIVITY 8: GLOBAL CONFERENCE CALL

Situation: Your task is to organize and schedule the first conference call to plan a session for an upcoming European conference in The Hague. Though you have never met the participants before, you have been collaborating with them individually by telephone and e-mail for a few months now. Your virtual team members include:

> Bob and Emily (Atlanta Headquarters)
>
> Anne (Hamburg, Germany)
>
> Sirawan (Bangkok, Thailand)
>
> Doug (London, England)
>
> Semra (Ankara, Turkey)
>
> Antonio (Milan, Italy)
>
> Kone (Abidjan, Africa)

Instructions: Prepare your background notes before you start making contacts to set up the meeting. Answer the following questions:

- What are the issues and who are the people involved?
- What resources might you need?
- What will your steps be?
- What else will you keep in mind?
- What other information do you need?

ACTIVITY 9: GLOBAL E-MAILS[15]

1. **Situation:** Jerry is an American manager working for a U.S.-based company. He sends the following e-mail to a colleague in the company's European headquarters in Madrid:

   Hi, Esme. What's up out there?

   Listen, I am following up on my e-mail I sent you the other day. I really needed a response ASAP and am wondering what in the h . . . happened to it! I'll bet you've been busy in the sunshine again!!

   Unfortunately, my guys are getting on my case and I have to have something pronto.

   So can you get the info together, run it by your team and let me have it by the end of the day today? About 4:00 would be great.

   Hasta la vista!

   Jerry

Instructions: Rewrite Jerry's message, considering the following:

- What message(s) is Jerry trying to convey to Esme?
- How effective is he? Why?
- How could he be more effective?

2. **Situation:** In the following e-mail exchange, Monica, who is from the United States, is requesting information from Sonia, a colleague in South America.

Instructions: Edit only Monica's messages. What should be added, deleted, or corrected so that Monica's e-mails are more effective global messages? Also, analyze Sonia's messages. Identify points in her e-mail messages that might indicate Sonia is from another country.

From: Monica F. Marcel

Sent: segunda-feira, 3 de dezembro de 2005 16:13

To: Sonia Verita

Subject: RE: additional help

Sonia:

As you know, we are asking the senior managers at each of the locations to complete an evaluation form. We only have a contact person's name—and I doubt that the contact is in fact the senior manager.

Please provide me with the e-mail address and name for the senior location manager at each of the locations in the attachment. I have already sent the form to other locations (in Spanish for Spanish-speaking sites, and Portuguese for Brazil.)

Thank you,

Monica Marcel

------Original Message------

From: Sonia Verita

Sent: Friday, November 30, 2005 3:52 PM

To: Monica Marcel

Subject: RE: additional help

Hi! How are you feeling? I have some doubts about who need answer this form. We have in each plant a General Manager and Manager for each area (ex: Human Resources, Fertilizer, Finance, etc). These people are "senior managers"? Would you like send this form to him or can I send? Anyway you can find the principals managers.

I'm going on vacations after dec 15th maybe I'll go to Bahia (I'ts a nice place!) You need visit us. I would like you know our country. If you like sun and friendly people, come on!

Have a nice weekend!

Sonia

------Original Message------

From: Monica F. Marcel

Sent: segunda-feira, 3 de dezembro de 2005 16:13

To: Sonia Verita

Subject: RE: additional help

Sonia:

I received the contact managers' information you sent. I will send the evaluation form to each of the managers you provided, since there are several "senior" managers at each location.

I understand you and my colleague Randy will be meeting when he is in South America.

Regards,
Monica Marcel

------Original Message------

From: Sonia Verita
Sent: Monday, December 03, 2005 4:10 PM
To: Monica Marcel
Subject: RE: additional help

I am glad that my information was good for you.

I understand it snow where you live. I've never seen snow in my life. I think it's nice!

Me, Ana and Randal will have a nice time!

Warmest regards
Sonia

3. **Instructions:** First, edit and revise the following e-mail message, which is from a German plant manager. Second, draft a thank-you response. Consider the following:

   a. How would you match the style and tone?

   b. Is the writer a man or a woman? Does it matter or affect the greeting?

   c. What other considerations do you have for your response?

-------Original Message------
Sent: Tuesday, November 06, 2005 11:03 AM
To: communication and training coordinator
Subject: training

GOOD MORNING;
TODAY WE HAVE HAD THE COMPLIANCE TRAINING IN HAMBURG / GERMANY.

THE TRAINING WAS GOOD AND EVERYBODY WAS FOLLOWING THE WHOLE TIME.

SPECIALY THE DIALOG WITH THE AUDIENCS HELPED TO KEEP THE MOOD UP.

THE DISCUSSION AT THE END SHOWS THAT WE HAVE TO IMPROVE ON SOME DETAILS.

EMPLOYEE NEEDS MORE INFORMATION ABOUT THE TELPHON NUMMBERS.

WE HAVE ALSO CONTACT PEOPLE FOR ENVIRONMENT / SAFETY / FOOD SAFETY IN EUROPE TO BE CONTACTED IF THERE IS ANY CONCERN.

EMPLOYEE NEEDS MORE INFORMATIONS ABOUT THE ACTIONS AFTER CALLING COPLIANCE #.

IT IS GOOD TO SEE THAT ADM IS CONSDERING MORE AND MORE THE CULTURAL ASPECTS OF EACH NATION.

WE ARE VERY PLEASED TO HAVE FIRST TIME GERMAN TRAINING ABOUT COMPLIANCE.

KIND REGARDS

L. von Schreiber
Plant Manager
Hamburg, Germany

REFERENCES

1. Monica Francois, Language & Culture Worldwide, LLC, taken from U.S. Peace Corps Office of Staging, 2001.

2. Adapted with permission from "How to Learn about a Culture" by Michael C. Mercil.

3. Farid Elashmawi and Philip R. Harris, *Multicultural Management 2000: Essential Cultural Insights for Global Business Success,* Butterworth-Heinemann, 1998.

4. *Global Competence: 50 Training Activities for Succeeding in International Business,* Jonamay Lambert, Selma Myers, and George Simons, eds., HRD Press, Amherst, Mass., 2000.

5. Portions of this exercise have been adapted from *Culture Matters: The Peace Corps Cross-Cultural Workbook* by Craig Storti and Laurette Bennhold-Samaan, Peace Corps, 1997.

6. Monica Francois and Rita Wuebbeler, *Building Bridges: Working and Communicating Effectively with Europeans* (Manual), Language & Culture Worldwide, 2003.

7. "Why Your Company Should Go Global Now More Than Ever," unpublished article by Bill Dunlap, <http://glreach.com/eng/ed/art/rep-eur23.php3>, accessed on October 5, 2003.

8. Ibid.

9. *The Wall Street Journal.* "A Closer Look," October 2000, as quoted by A4 Translations online at <http://www.a4translations.com/english/services.htm>, accessed on June 25, 2005.

10. Francois and Wuebbeler, *Building Bridges.*

11. Jeremy Solomons, adapted with permission from an article for Jeremy Solomons & Associates, 2003.

12. Francois and Wuebbeler, Training Materials.

13. Ibid.

14. Ibid.

15. Adapted with permission from an exercise developed by Jeremy Solomons of Jeremy Solomons & Associates.

KEY FOR LEARNING INVENTORY

1.	F	6.	F
2.	F	7.	F
3.	F	8.	T
4.	T	9.	T
5.	T	10.	T

Applications And Careers

BusinessWeek

For UPS Managers, a School of Hard Knocks
Execs share the gritty life experiences of some workers.

At United Parcel Service, Inc., rules are religion. Without them, UPS could never move 13.5 million packages to their destinations on time each day. But two years ago, Mark J. Colvard, a UPS manager in San Ramon, California, had to decide whether to buck the system. A driver needed time off to help an ailing family member, but under company rules he wasn't eligible. If Colvard went by the book, the driver would probably take the days anyway and be fired. If Colvard gave him the time off, he would catch flak from his other drivers. Colvard wound up giving the driver two weeks, took some heat—and kept a valuable employee.

Six months earlier, Colvard admits, he would have gone the other way. What changed his approach? A month he spent living among migrant farmers in McAllen, Texas, as part of an unusual UPS management training experience called the Community Internship Program (CIP). After building housing for the poor, collecting clothing for the Salvation Army and working in a drug rehab center, Colvard said he was able to empathize with employees facing crises back home. And that, he says, has made him a better manager. "My goal was to make the numbers, and in some cases that meant not looking at the individual but looking at the bottom line," says Colvard. "After that one-month stay, I immediately started reaching out to people in a different way."

CIP began in 1968 as the brainchild of UPS founder James Casey, who wanted to open up the eyes of UPS's managers to the poverty and inequality exploding into violence in many cities. By now, nearly 1,200 current and former middle managers have moved through the program. It has evolved into an integral part of the UPS culture, teaching managers the crucial skill of flexibility at a company that is trying to fit a diverse base of employees into its rigid rules-based culture.

Therefore, each summer UPS plucks 50 of its most promising executives from the company's 2,400 managers and brings them to cities across the country, where UPS partners arrange for daily community service projects aiding local populations. The problems encountered there—from transportation to housing, education, and health care—are the kinds of issues many UPS employees confront every day.

In New York this summer, eight managers visited the emergency room at Bellevue Hospital, tutored inmates at Sing Sing in interviewing skills, and provided meals to the homeless.

Patti Hobbs, a division manager in Louisville who spent a month on New York's Lower East Side in 1998, remembers being impressed by the creative ideas of uneducated addicts for steering teens away from drugs. Realizing that the best solutions sometimes come from those closest to the problem, she immediately started brainstorming with the entire staff instead of just senior managers. Says Hobbs: "You start to think there's no one person, regardless of position, who has all the answers. The answers come from us all."

Source: July 22, 2002, Management column by Louis Lavelle in New York. For a full transcript of the article and additional questions, see the *Foundations of Business Communication* Web site at <http://www.mhhe.com/djyoung>.

EXPLORE

1. Do you think leadership is a skill that can be learned or a natural-born talent? What characteristics do you think define an effective leader, and how do you attain them?

2. Why is it important to incorporate a "you" attitude when communicating with your coworkers as well as your customers and vendors?

3. Many companies have rules covering everything from proper business dress and preferred spelling to proper interpersonal communication. From a business standpoint, what are the pros and cons of flexibility in enforcing such rules? What are the pros and cons of strictly enforcing the rules?

Team Communications

Team work is neither "good" nor "desirable"—it is a fact. Wherever people work together or play together they do so as a team. Which team to use for what purpose is a crucial, difficult, and risky decision that is even harder to unmake. Managements have yet to learn how to make it (work). —Peter Drucker ■

Most of the time, in the educational arena, you solve problems alone. You don't have to negotiate duties because you're managing projects in your own way and on your own time. Thus, you need argue only with yourself over priorities and deadlines, and you accept total responsibility for the outcome (even though you may not always like the result).

    In business, however, *working alone* takes on new meaning: individual projects are only a part of the whole. Even a project depending entirely on one person's expertise connects to others within the organization, directly and profoundly or indirectly and subtly. In addition, projects often cross departmental lines, with diverse talents joining forces to solve problems from various perspectives. Teamwork is integral to business, and team communication is a dimension of many performance appraisals.

-     A *team* consists of a group of people who work together *to achieve a mutual objective.* People communicate differently on teams than they do in other environments; the team process brings out the best and, at times, the worst in communication behavior. For example, team members may not value diverse styles or be aware of how their personalities mix with others'. Hence, at times differences disrupt a group's flow and efficiency, having less than optimal outcomes.

- With *effective teamwork,* everyone supports the objectives of the team, *not* the individual. Rather than be distracted by differences, successful teams treat diversity as an asset that can strengthen their outcomes. Just as some teams lose focus, others thrive on differing viewpoints and approaches to create richer, more innovative solutions to the problems they are solving.

To learn about teams, you will first examine qualities of successful teams and what you already know about team communication. Then you will explore a process for group planning. Finally, you will bring your diverse talents together in a team by writing a proposal. Let's start by examining the characteristics of successful teams and build from there. By the end of this chapter, you may even be equipped to be a "team consultant."

OBJECTIVES

When you have completed Chapter 8, you will be able to:

- Understand how to communicate in a team and function as a team.
- Identify the characteristics and mechanics of successful teams.
- Develop a purpose, plan, and results for team projects.
- Establish team ground rules and roles to produce a team project.
- Analyze team dynamics and make recommendations for effectiveness.
- Work in a team to produce a successful proposal.

Learning Inventory

1. With effective teams, members think alike and seldom disagree.	T/F
2. With a collaborative leadership style, the team leader makes the decisions.	T/F
3. When time for a project is short, planning is the first area to cut.	T/F
4. Identifying tasks and deadlines creates positive stress.	T/F
5. The American culture encourages cooperation more than competition.	T/F
6. Regardless of the task, a collaborative approach is better than an autocratic one.	T/F
7. When giving feedback, use the active voice and get right to the point.	T/F
8. Building trust among team members is an important part of working together.	T/F
9. A team facilitator would take minutes to meetings and distribute them to the group.	T/F
10. A record keeper develops the meeting agenda to keep the team on track.	T/F

■ SECTION A: WORKING IN TEAMS

What is a team? You have probably worked on more teams than you realize. A **team** can be loosely defined as *people who come together to work on a common goal.* Whenever you work with even one other person on a project, you may consider yourselves a team. Likewise, a team does not necessarily have a limit on its number of members—the number depends on how people define their goals and work to achieve them.

A team can be a *committee,* a *task force,* or a *work group.* Teams can consist of members who work closely together at the same location or members who never meet one another in person. For example, *virtual* teams function through online meetings or phone conferences; their team members can be throughout the world, in different countries and time zones, or they may simply be in different branch offices at opposite ends of the same town. (See the Communication Challenges sidebar on virtual teams, page 265.)

FIGURE 8.1 | Making Teams Work

Outlining desired outcomes is a strategy that can improve a team's performance.

To:	Staid, Marta; Fallon, Cyrus; Elbe, Kyle; Fareed, Elka; Flanjak, Alice
From:	Colin
Subject:	Company newsletter

Hi, folks.

It's our division's turn to produce the company newsletter. I've just received word that final copy has to be turned in to the printer by May 15. This might be a good time to get the team together for a first meeting to figure out who is going to be responsible for each section and how we're going to meet that deadline.

I can reserve the conference room at 10 a.m. on either Thursday or Friday. Please e-mail me back ASAP to let me know what day works best for your schedule.

Colin

COMMUNICATION CHALLENGES

Service Learning In service learning, individuals and/or businesses undertake community projects. These unique alliances effect positive changes in individuals, organizations, neighborhoods, and even larger systems in a community. Schools incorporate service learning into their curricula as a method of combining real-world experience with academic learning, while businesses may use service learning as a method of strengthening ties to local communities.

Although some service-learning projects consist of work that an individual can perform, an element of teamwork is inevitably involved. For example, a typical service-learning assignment might entail interviewing residents at a local retirement hotel, keyboarding their stories into your computer, and creating a book of their experiences to share with coworkers or classmates. You can do all the work yourself, but without the participation of the residents of the hotel and the support of the hotel's management—your "team" on this assignment—your project will never get off the ground.

Visit the *Foundations of Business Communication* Web site at <http://www.mhhe.com/djyoung> for a list of suggestions for service-learning projects. As you review the list, consider whose support and assistance you would need to accomplish each project.

Some teams are a permanent part of a company, such as management teams, quality assurance teams, and boards of directors. Other teams come together only for as long as it takes to solve a specific problem, such as develop a proposal or update policies. These types of teams dissolve naturally when their project is completed. With teams, the central focus is on their common *purpose.*

Team composition may change based on needs; however, that does not necessarily mean that members can leave if they don't like team dynamics or other members. In **captive teams,** members have an ethical obligation to fulfill their roles, like it or not. Examples of such teams are a group of attorneys representing a client or a team of doctors pooling their expertise for the benefit of a particular patient. What about sports teams? Team members sign contracts and must stay through the season even under the most excruciating circumstances.

Characteristics of Effective Teams

At first glance, a successful team might seem to be one in which everyone thinks alike, agrees easily, and makes decisions without effort. However, what happens when team members do not agree with one another? How teams function when members *disagree* gives more insight into successful teams than how they function when members *seem to agree*. In fact, the freedom to disagree openly is an important quality of successful teams. Successful teams also share the following:

- *Purpose:* The team members have a *clear and unified sense* of what they are trying to achieve; everyone shares ownership of goals and objectives and their importance.

- *Process:* The team establishes leadership and decision-making strategies as well as ground rules; team members discuss team dynamics openly, periodically doing self-checks. Diverse views are explored rather than thwarted.

- *Participation:* Members are active and engaged; they have a clear understanding of their tasks and take responsibility for their share of the work; members participate equally in discussions and receive feedback if they are slacking (also known as *freeloading* or *social loafing*).

- *Feedback:* Members give feedback about ideas and processes without criticizing one another personally. They avoid backbiting and hurtful comments and take responsibility for their shortcomings rather than look for a scapegoat to blame.

Team Machine: *Effective teamwork requires balancing respect for the diverse experiences of individuals on the team with an understanding of the need for the parts of the team to function as a cohesive unit to achieve its purpose.* As you have worked your way through this text, you have been asked to work in teams on many occasions. List three things you have learned from your team experiences that you can apply to future team experiences.

- *Diversity:* Members respect and even embrace differences in thinking and style; members also accept that at times disagreement is integral to the process and a possible catapult to deeper understanding and higher quality.
- *Decision making:* Members know how decisions are made and accept the leadership structure. For participatory groups, members make decisions at a point of consensus, with participants feeling as if their views were heard, respected, and incorporated when feasible.

Teams conduct their business primarily through meetings, scheduling them to keep a steady momentum in progressing toward achieving their goals. In effective teams, members discuss controversial issues, stay focused, and remain productive. When teams establish ground rules, members understand their boundaries and are more likely to stay on task. When teams keep minutes of their meetings, they can establish major decisions as benchmarks. Minutes help ensure that teams move forward consistently toward their goals rather than backtrack to rehash controversial issues.

An informal indication that a team is effective occurs when team members have the same conversation in the meeting as they do in the hallway after they leave. In other words, are individual team members open and honest during the meeting? If they are, the way they think and feel about team issues will be the same when they informally discuss outside the meeting what happened inside the meeting.

Leadership and Management Style

Teams are structured in various ways, and their structure is often determined by their function, which relates to the types of problems they address. Some teams have a designated leader, others share leadership, and some even rotate leadership. Depending on what they need to get the job done, teams may shift their structure from time to time.

Leadership style combines with individual personalities to determine team dynamics. Each leader manages in a unique way; however, most leaders have a management style that can be categorized in the most basic way as being either **participatory** (also known as *participative* or *collaborative*) or **autocratic** (also known as *authoritative* or *heroic*). The various management styles or models (of which there are many) can generally fit within one of these categories or represent a blend of them.

With a **participative** or **collaborative** leadership style, team members share in the decision-making process. In other words, rather than carrying out top-down mandates and delegated tasks, individuals take control of managing their areas of responsibility; as a result, problem solving occurs at the grass roots. Collaborative management styles have been acclaimed as liberating creativity and motivation and are more common today than they were in the past. When upper managers trust individuals to participate in making decisions, their employees are more likely to take ownership of a project and invest themselves deeply in the outcomes. Thus, collaborative leadership can elicit team members' strengths and motivation.

With an **authoritative** or **heroic** leadership style, team members carry out assigned tasks in prescribed ways. Though this top-down leadership may not sound as appealing, at times a heroic style is undeniably the most effective. When a critical job needs to be accomplished, a leader can make difficult decisions quickly and without debate, taking full responsibility for the outcome. For example, in the military a heroic style works well when time does not allow discussion. Everyone knows everyone else's role; the team members can work together as precisely as clockwork to maintain order and efficiency. Another example is a surgical team: the lead surgeon directs the process with team members meticulously following the directives.

Most leadership styles are a blend of the participative and authoritative styles. An effective leader applies a *situational* leadership style by adapting to what the team members need according to their culture and the type of problem they are solving. Thus, even a lead surgeon or military commander becomes collaborative depending on the events at hand.

EXPLORE

1. What kind of leaders have you worked for? Think of current and past managers and supervisors; describe their leadership styles.

2. What kind of leader are you? Give examples of your leadership experiences and how you got a group working effectively toward a goal.

3. With what kind of leadership style do you do your best work? Can you explain why that style motivates you or brings out your best?

Decision Making

The leader of a group may or may *not* make final decisions; however, the team leader will determine *how* the group makes decisions. Typically, group decisions are made either by the leader, by majority rule, or by group consensus. Whatever the process, participants should know at the start of a discussion how the decision will be made. Here are the choices for making decisions:

- *Decision by leader:* Even when a leader makes the decision, input from the group is often sought. However, leaders may lose credibility by giving the impression that input counts when it does not affect the outcome. When a group knows ahead of time that their input will not influence the outcome, they have less to react to if the decision does not go their way.

- *Majority rule:* Some groups follow formal parliamentary order: motions are made and seconded, the group votes, and the majority decides. Few groups are this formal; an example of a formal group following parliamentary order would be the board of directors of a public corporation or not-for-profit organization. However, even informal groups make decisions on a majority basis by taking a tally of opinions. For controversial decisions, a group can tally votes anonymously.

- *Consensus:* To reach **consensus,** everyone in the group must agree with a decision, at least to some degree. Reaching consensus has drawbacks; getting everyone to agree may sometimes result in a watered-down outcome. Then again, when team synergy is strong, divergent ideas often crystallize into clear and innovative choices; heated discussions break through walls of misperceptions and open the way to fresh approaches.

Active and Engaged Team Members

Teams need more than members who show up and follow directions well. Teams need engaged members who care about the issues and their outcomes. When members actively engage, diverse talents and viewpoints contribute to the group's energy, developing a *synergy* that at times can feel intense and at other times, serendipitous.

When team members do not carry their own weight, this brings down the entire group; group dynamics can even become unmanageable. For example, team members may show up for a meeting, but their minds may be somewhere else; they may be more concerned about personal problems than they are with the group's objectives. At other times, members may not consider the team's purpose important enough to remain focused or may not complete tasks on time. Hence, a team can fail in an endless number of ways.

An effective team goes through various stages to reach the point of becoming a well-functioning unit, but ineffective teams seem to get stuck along the way. In 1965, Bruce W. Tuckman created a model of team development, and his model has become a classic in the field.[2] Let's examine Tuckman's model to see how a team develops from being a group of strangers to being a synergistic body of problem solvers.

VOCABULARY BUILDERS

Synergy *Synergy* is the energy team dynamics create. You have often heard the saying "The whole is more than the sum of its parts." In other words, when individual ingredients combine, they can produce a profound outcome. As an example, consider the different elements that Thomas Edison brought together to produce a lightbulb. Edison experienced a great deal of failure but passionately experimented until he discovered the right combination of elements used in the right way. Once he brought the elements together correctly, the result was *light.*

Diverse individuals working together in a group combine their talents, insights, experiences, and vision to solve a problem. When the process works well, the result is creative energy, inspiration, flow, and innovation: all of these reflect the group's synergy.

COACHING TIP

Formal and Informal Groups Whether a group is formal or informal is not an absolute, but a matter of degree:

- In the most *informal* settings, meetings occur without planning or even an agenda. (These types of meetings can be successful, especially if the objective is brainstorming.)
- In the most *formal* meetings, group members not only have an agenda but follow parliamentary order.

Parliamentary procedure is outlined in *Robert's Rules of Order.*[1] This book contains hundreds of rules for conducting business. Organizations select specific rules to use in conducting their meetings and then write them into their bylaws. By selecting specific rules, each group makes progress and maintains order in its own way.

Team Process

In his article "Developmental Sequence in Small Groups," Tuckman outlined four stages of team development:[3]

- *Forming:* getting to know one another, valuing acceptance, gathering perceptions, but avoiding confrontation and not getting much work done.

- *Storming:* starting to address important issues, with conflict rising to the surface; addressing conflict and differences over the work of the group or roles and responsibilities; trying to suppress conflict and keep issues below the surface.

- *Norming:* listening, understanding, appreciating, and supporting one another's skills and differing views; being willing to change preconceived views; developing into a cohesive, effective group.

- *Performing:* reaching a state of interdependence and flexibility; accepting roles and trusting one another in completing independent activities; feeling good about one another and the task; directing energy toward getting the task done.

About ten years after his original work, Tuckman added a fifth stage:[4]

- *Adjourning:* completing the task and disengaging from group members; acknowledging achievements and feeling a sense of pride; also feeling a sense of loss and mourning.

These stages do not necessarily occur in a linear way: groups can go back and forth between forming and storming or storming and norming. Even after a team reaches the stage of performing, members can regress to earlier stages when they confront change, such as getting new members. Unfortunately, some groups never make it to performing. An experienced leader or facilitator can keep a group progressing toward performing by addressing conflict and diversity effectively.

Teams have a difficult time reaching the performing stage because they must deal effectively with conflict to get there. Even the best communicators find it challenging to handle irresponsible behavior in a professional, growth-oriented way. When people find it difficult to confront conflict or differences in thinking, they may react by being subjective and emotional, remaining superficial, or even disengaging from the group.

When team dynamics get out of control, group members can lose trust and credibility. Once these qualities are lost, they may *never* be regained. To keep your team focused, remain engaged and embrace differences. Meet your commitments, and also have the courage to be honest and objective with teammates who act irresponsibly. Here are some tangible ways to ensure active participation:

- Develop ground rules to which all team members can commit.

- Identify tasks and assign deadlines.

- Publicize deadlines not only among team members but also among decision makers outside the group.

Ground rules provide appropriate boundaries and expectations. Clearly defined tasks and deadlines create pressure or *positive stress* to get the job done, which is more effective than criticism from team members. This approach will reduce conflict and help teams get to the stage of performing.

However, if things do not go as planned, which can happen, take responsibility for your actions *and* accept the apologies of others. An honest, contrite approach generally evokes understanding and keeps the team members focused on their goals. According to Voltaire, an eighteenth-century philosopher and writer, *love truth, but pardon error.*

EXPLORE

Log onto the Internet to find out more about Bruce W. Tuckman's model on group development. Also explore other models that can give you insight into working in groups. *Can you relate these models to your own experience?*

Gender Differences in Team Communications

Another consideration in team communications is gender differences. According to Trisha Svehla, a specialist in diversity, men and women react differently in groups.[5] These differences

COMMUNICATION CHALLENGES

Conferring in Virtual Teams Corporations carry out their mission worldwide through *virtual teams*. Through Webcasting, videoconferencing, and text messaging, team members hold virtual meetings at which they follow some of the same guidelines they would use if they were meeting in person.

For example, in a **videoconference,** all participants would receive a copy of the agenda before the meeting. They would be able to see one another through monitors as they speak on the phone.

A **Webcast** is the most inclusive type of virtual meeting. A Webcast consists of a phone conference, online dialogue, and online presentation—*all at the same time.* Participants can view a PowerPoint presentation as the group facilitator talks them through the presentation. Participant names are listed on one side of the screen; team members can communicate with one another privately through instant **text messaging** by clicking on another participant's name. Webcasting offers many dimensions of communicating, which can even include body language if videoconferencing is also a component.

Webcasts and videoconferences save companies millions of dollars a year by enhancing operations significantly.

CHALLENGE:

Situation: Your supervisor, Alex Morton, is responsible for organizing bimonthly reports from 11 satellite offices in the Midwest. Alex, who is not very technologically savvy, heard a news item on the radio about Webcasting and videoconferencing, and she wants to know more.

Instructions: Working with a partner, write the body of a memo that describes the basics involved in Webcasting and videoconferencing. Specifically address the following:
- What equipment would be required?
- What would be required of participants?
- What might be the benefits and drawbacks of using these techniques as opposed to making a simple conference call?

Remember, *keep it simple.*

relate partly to brain chemistry and partly to experience and socialization. The following points indicate some differences in how women and men approach various issues; however, these points are only tendencies, *not* absolutes.

- *Cooperative versus competitive styles:* Women tend to be more cooperative, and men tend to be more competitive. In fact, women can be too accommodating by worrying too much about others' feelings. On the other hand, men see situations as "win or lose," and feelings may not be a consideration.

- *Collaborative versus heroic management styles:* Women tend to have collaborative styles, and men tend to have heroic (or authoritative) styles. Thus, men are more comfortable delegating and giving directions, whereas women are more comfortable in situations in which everyone is treated equally, without a hierarchy of power.

- *Indirect versus direct communication:* Women communicate in an indirect way; men get right to the point. Men feel more comfortable with confrontation than do women, who prefer that things run smoothly. Men can have difficulty understanding women who give signals about how they feel and think rather than coming right out and stating their point. Women tend to be good listeners; men have difficulty tuning in to the fine points, which may seem irrelevant to them.

- *Detailed versus global picture:* Women want the details, but men prefer the big picture. Men can become impatient when women give many details without stating the big picture; men prefer that speakers get right to the point.

- *Questions and answers:* Women use questions and questioning very differently than do men. Women ask questions to build rapport, whereas men take the questions literally and can be offended by the "small talk" women use to build relationships. In addition, women find it easier to ask questions when they need help or directions; men prefer finding their own way and solving their own problems. In fact, when women ask questions to be social, men often respond with answers that attempt to "solve" the women's problems.

Most people use a blend of both masculine *and* feminine communication styles—and use a different blend under different circumstances. One successful executive shared that he had a female boss who communicated in a way that was probably an 80-20 blend of masculine and feminine when she spoke with the division as a whole. However, she used the opposite communication style in one-on-one and small-group conversations. The executive commented, "Before I understood the whole picture, communications with my boss seemed unpredictable and confusing."

Certainly gender differences have been the topics of many comedians and popular books, such as *Men Are From Mars, Women Are From Venus* by John Gray. By understanding differences, you can create bridges when communication gaps first surface. *How does your communication style blend? Does it change according to circumstances?*

Cooperation Versus Competition

Though this topic has gender implications, it is broader than a gender issue. In Chapter 7 you learned that the U.S. culture promotes individuality more than a collective identity. Americans naturally have strong work ethics related to working alone rather than in groups. Individual tasks may seem more motivating than group tasks because assigning credit and recognition to individuals is easier. When working in groups, people may not get recognition even for their most creative ideas.

Individuality even appears in *team* sports. Consider basketball. Every player has an assigned role, and all roles function best in synchronicity. Even Michael Jordan, one of the most acclaimed players of all time, had to make changes to become a strong team player. Team spirit reflects team dynamics, and Jordan received criticism about his dominant role even when games were won. It didn't take long before Michael shared the ball more, and the result is history.

In such situations, the way team members communicate with one another on and off the "court" makes a difference in how they work together to achieve common goals. At times, professional ethics must rise above communication differences in the quest to achieve the team goal. There is a time and a place to be competitive, but neither is with your own team.

To be a successful team player, let go of the need for individual recognition. Share your ideas and talents freely to accomplish the group's mission (and if you must change your thinking to achieve this quality, realize that you are not alone).

Resistance and Team Thinking

Discussing ideas in team meetings can be challenging for many reasons. At times, creative ideas can be shut down with only a comment or an intimidating glance. A team may even fall into *groupthink*, which happens if a need for approval (or a fear of disapproval) exists

FIGURE 8.2 | Team Politics
Are there circumstances in which it would or would not be appropriate to send the following e-mail message? Assuming you are the team leader, compose an e-mail in response to Julie's request.

To: marcusw@twotreescabinetry.org
From: juliek@twotreescabinetry.org
CC:
Subject: Team dynamics

Marcus,

Can we arrange a meeting tomorrow or Friday to go over some of this stuff that was left unresolved at the last team meeting after Jeanie decided to turn the event into her vacation travelogue?

The situation seems desperate to me. Ron is being obstructionist because he doesn't want to add to his workload; Collette is enthusiastic and full of great ideas, but won't be back for ten days; and Gil is on his own planet, as usual. I know you're worried about our progress, as well.

The way things are going, we'll have a hard time hitting the deadline unless *someone* decides to take heroic measures. It'll be a feather in our caps and everyone (except Ron) will be pleased with the results. Why can't we just step up to the plate and knock it out of the park?

Let me know what you think.

Julie

COMMUNICATION CHALLENGES

Groupthink Groupthink is a phenomenon that occurs when everyone "goes along" just to "get along." The quality of decisions deteriorates because no one in the group challenges decisions that could be controversial.

Members feel pressured for one reason or another. For example, groupthink might develop in a group that has an outspoken member or powerful, autocratic leader who views opposing opinions as disloyal.

It might also develop in a group in which personal interests take priority over the integrity of the group's mission. Once group members act without integrity in one situation, they are likely to act without integrity in other situations—members develop an "I'll scratch your back if you'll scratch mine" mentality.

A symptom of groupthink is any situation in which people are criticized or harassed for coming forward to tell the truth. This symptom characterized the Enron debacle.

Ask yourself: *Can I think of other examples of groupthink? What does it feel like to be in a group that falls into groupthink?*

---

among members. When team members do not remain independent and assertive, groups can accept convenient, but mediocre or even harmful, solutions. Here are three of the many ways in which teams express resistance:

- Good ideas are dismissed without exploring or understanding them; individuals feel shut down by the process.

- Superficial ideas are adopted without seriously considering alternatives, possibly to avoid debate and discord.

- Self-promoting decisions profit a select few, compromising the integrity of the group's aims.

When these actions occur, they may relate more to attitudes and the relationships among team members than to the ideas themselves. To transcend these pitfalls, team members must focus on the *quality of ideas* rather than on their relationships with other team members, and they must give up unproductive patterns of thinking.

Another important element of group problem solving is brainstorming, or "thinking out loud." This type of group reflection must be *embraced* rather than dismissed. John Dewey, a twentieth-century educator, said:

> Thinking is a process of inquiry . . . it is seeking, a quest, for something that is not at hand. We sometimes talk as if "original research" were a peculiar prerogative of scientists or at least of advanced students. But all thinking is research, and . . . all thinking involves a risk.[6]

Even when you cannot see the merit of your teammates' ideas, the creative group process thrives when you support teammates in expressing their views freely. Each of us has a unique style as well as personal limits. Thus, we all need to be tolerant at times; it's the professional approach.

An Open Mind

Whether working alone or in teams, you will achieve more success by remaining open to innovative ideas. Your mind is open when you consider possibilities, adapt to change, and give people a chance to prove themselves before drawing a conclusion. Focus on suspending your judgment until you hear the facts so that you can explore the possibilities.

It is easy to become overly attached to what "you assume" that "you know." Here are some examples:

- At one time, it was believed that the world was flat. Galileo was condemned for heresy and publicly humiliated because he challenged that belief.

- In 1982, two Australian physicians, Dr. Robin Warren and Dr. Barry Marshall, identified a link between *H. pylori* bacteria and peptic ulcers. Few listened to Drs. Warren and Marshall, and in 1995, the majority of physicians in the United States still treated ulcers as if they were caused only by stress. Only 5 percent of ulcer patients were being treated with antibiotics. It wasn't until one of the physicians induced ulcers in his own stomach by swallowing *H. pylori* that the theory was taken seriously. In 1997, the Centers for Disease Control launched a campaign to educate physicians and change their attitudes about ulcers.

Can you think of other examples? Are there times when you have an insight but no one can see what you see? Are there times when you don't listen because the message does not fit into the way you view the world?

How many squares can you find in Figure 8.3? Are there only 16? How about 20? Can you find 22? 25?

FIGURE 8.3 | Testing Perceptions

Think outside of the box to find the number of squares.

When you listen with an open mind, you may experience a *paradigm shift*. The word *paradigm* can be illusive to comprehend: a paradigm is the *context* in which a person holds information. Here's a more developed definition:

> A paradigm is a set of rules and regulations (written or unwritten) that does two things: (1) it establishes or defines boundaries; and (2) it tells you how to behave inside the boundaries in order to be successful."[7]

Paradigms, or models, help shape the way we view the world; as such, they determine how we analyze and interpret relationships. Most of us are not even aware of our own paradigms. A paradigm shift changes the context of how we perceive reality. The examples presented above led to paradigm shifts:

- With the discovery that the world is round and not flat, many aspects of reality simultaneously changed. Voyagers were no longer afraid that they would fall off the earth into an abyss.

- With the discovery that bacteria causes ulcers, patients no longer felt that their uncontrolled stress was the sole cause of their disease and doctors began prescribing antibiotics, a treatment that usually cures the illness.

As you solve problems, you go well beyond your immediate objective if you also shift the way you perceive the world around you. Think of problem solving as occurring in different layers: the deeper you go, the more profound your understanding. At times, contradictory ideas become harmonious when perceived from a broader, more inclusive view. Such insights generally occur through intense discussion and reflection and only by chance occur through pleasant conversations.

EXPLORE

Have you had an effective or an ineffective team experience? For example, have you participated in team sports, the Boy Scouts or Girl Scouts, a 4-H club, informal play activities, church functions, or volunteer organizations? What have you learned about teams from your experience?

 SECTION A: CONCEPT CHECK

1. What are some qualities of effective teams?

2. When team members disagree, is this a sign that team dynamics are not good? Which stage of Tuckman's model does open conflict reflect?

3. What is a paradigm shift?

■ SECTION B: DEVELOPING A TEAM STRATEGY

An effective team can develop through any number of approaches. The guidelines presented in this section are only suggestions of how a team *might* operate. Each team must develop its own strategy, deciding what works and what doesn't work at each step. Team members should pick and choose from this framework to define their team's *purpose, plan,* and *results,* creating their own team style as they work together.

If you have an assigned project for this chapter, become familiar with this section *before* your first team meeting. Let's get started by examining how to develop a common understanding among team members and establish some trust in the process.

Developing a Common Understanding

Many teams make the mistake of being too task-oriented too soon, letting the anxiety of an impending deadline overwhelm them. Some individuals do not like to plan, preferring to operate intuitively and spontaneously, which is fine when working alone. However, team projects rarely consist of completing a simple series of linear tasks; so without developing a plan, team members may not be working on the *right* tasks.

Effective teams start the planning process by establishing a common understanding about what they are doing—*getting everyone on the same page,* so to speak. This approach gives a team focus and direction, avoiding unnecessary work and frustration that leads to a waste of time (a prescription for failure). Thus, by establishing its purpose and plan up front, a team will have sufficient time to achieve its goals.

Before discussing the project together, every team member may interpret the project differently. By developing a *common and cohesive understanding,* team members eliminate misperceptions before they pull the group in diverse directions. As President Lincoln once said, "A house divided cannot stand."

To develop cohesion, first define *what* your team will do and then *how* the team will do it. Use questions to reach that common understanding: reframe the six basic questions—*who, what, when, where, why,* and *how*—to establish goals that lead to objectives and an action plan:

- Develop **goals,** which are broad, general intentions of what your group plans to achieve.
- Develop **objectives,** which are narrow, precise statements of what your group will do.
- Develop an **action plan,** which states specific action steps or tasks along with due dates.

As your team answers the six questions, create a **concept map** (see Figure 8.4) that shows the major parts of the project. A concept map is similar to a mind map; however, the concept map accommodates major parts of a project that group members will work on simultaneously. The concept map provides flexibility as it captures ideas the group generates; a facilitator can fill in details for each leg of the map as the group discusses the project.

Instead of a concept map, you could use columns with headings for each part or a separate page for each part. Regardless of how the group records the details, putting them on paper is important. Recording preliminary discussions as a map or chart establishes progress and aids those whose dominant learning style is visual.

Establishing Purpose, Plan, and Results

Defining your *purpose, plan,* and *results* develops a framework for any type of team project. Included in this section are a number of questions that will help you define these basic elements. You may decide not to use any of these questions or to use some but not others. That's your choice: groups remain interactive and vibrant by making their own choices, *not* by following a recipe in a linear way. Therefore, though these questions will provoke your thinking, tailor them to your team in a unique way. Then spring into your own creative process.

Defining Purpose *Purpose* relates directly to a problem that you are solving; the purpose embodies the "what and why" of the problem. A **purpose statement** defines your project. From a purpose statement, team members can develop goals and objectives, clarify the methods they will use to solve the problem, and even identify the results they will achieve. Start the process with questions:

FIGURE 8.4 | Team Planning
The concept web works for teams as well as individuals when it comes to planning a project. Is it a good idea to involve team members in the planning phase of a project? Why or why not?

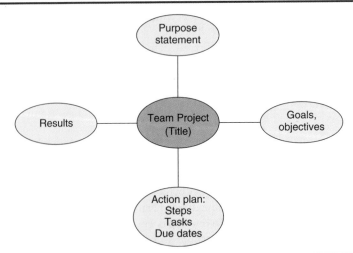

1. *What is the critical problem that your team is solving?* State the problem *and* how your team intends to solve it in one sentence, which will be your purpose statement. For example, if All Pro Temps has high absentee rates for its employees and your job is to help them solve the problem, your purpose statement might read:

   > Develop a plan for All Pro Temps to improve employee attendance.

   Develop two or three statements before selecting the best one as your working purpose statement.

2. *What is the topic that you are researching?* Don't assume you know what your topic is upon hearing it for the first time. Identify your topic or subject in *broad* terms first; then when you need to narrow it, your knowledge base will not be superficial. For example, will the team need to do research in different *content areas* or *disciplines?* By crossing content lines (such as psychology and sociology) to answer your questions, you develop a deeper, more comprehensive response.

   In the All Pro example above, finding a solution partly depends on understanding *why* employee attendance is poor; hence, your team's research might entail theories that relate to sociology, social psychology, or management theory. The team may also want to collect data and conduct on-site interviews. (*Note:* See the Writer's Handbook, Part 4: "Research—Collecting, Conducting, Displaying, and Citing," for research techniques and tools.)

3. *What are your project goals?* The project goals relate to accomplishing the purpose statement. *What are three to five goals that support your purpose statement?* Drawing from the example about employee attendance, here are some goals:

   1. Identify root causes of employee absentee behavior.
   2. Develop recommendations to management for policy change.
   3. Implement a system to improve employee attendance.

Whereas goals are broad and somewhat abstract, objectives are specific and tangible. From your goals, you will develop *specific objectives* that will serve as the road map for achieving your purpose.

Planning Logistics or Group Operations   Your plan identifies **methods** for achieving team objectives: it connects the questions *how, when, what, where,* and *who* to group operations (logistics), the tasks, and the time frame.

Your group should answer these questions after you have discussed the project enough to understand what it entails but still early in the process:

1. *What are our team's objectives?*

   What are our requirements and expectations?

   What is our deadline?

2. *How will we conduct meetings?*

   How will we establish decisions: consensus or majority rule?

   What are our ground rules?

   What roles (leader, evaluator) will members play, and will the roles change periodically?

COACHING TIP

The Fishbone   Also known as the "root-cause diagram" or "Ishikawa diagram," the fishbone is a brainstorming tool companies use to discover root causes. In using the fishbone, start by identifying your problem, and then identify major components of it. For each component, ask "why" five different times.[8]

The Fishbone

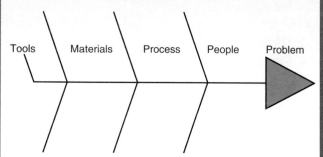

Here's an example of asking *why* in a series:
   Problem statement: I was late to class today.
   Why? I stopped to buy a sandwich.
   Why? I had run out of sandwich fixings.
   Why? I didn't remember to go to the store.
   Why? I went out with friends after class.
   Why? I feel as if I'm under stress and need a break.
Now go to an Internet search engine and type in "fishbone brainstorming technique." *What kinds of variations have you found? How will you adapt this tool for your own use?*

Fixing the Weak Link: *Being flexible allows a team to adjust its process when the job becomes more complicated than anticipated. This can happen when a teammate contributes less than expected or when the workload is not distributed equally within the group.* When you are part of a team, do you find it easy or difficult to voice honest opinions about the group and the way it functions? Why or why not?

Will we use an agenda or keep minutes for each meeting?

How will we keep one another informed (especially if a team member misses a meeting)?

3. *What is the time line?*

What is the deadline?

What are some milestones or intermediary deadlines?

How often will the team meet and where (including phone and online conferences)?

4. *What tools or resources do we need to accomplish our tasks?*

Do we need a laptop, whiteboard, or flip chart for brainstorming sessions?

Does our research demand that we develop surveys?

Do we need to conduct interviews?

5. *How will we know if we are accomplishing our objectives?*

How will we give one another feedback?

What happens if someone doesn't fulfill his or her role?

What degree of flexibility will be allowed or tolerated when someone is late or absent from a meeting or when deadlines are not met?

Obviously, your team will come up with its own questions, and you will answer many of them informally as you develop rapport and build trust.

Forming an Action Plan: Steps, Tasks, and Time Frame   An action plan will anchor your team's activities and give you tangible touchstones by which you can measure your progress. Here are some questions to get you started:

1. *What are the team's objectives?* After defining goals, your team is ready to identify individual objectives and tasks or action steps to achieve its objectives. Continuing with the All Pro example about employee attendance, here are some objectives relating to the first goal:

   1. To identify root causes of employee absence, we need to conduct focus groups, surveys, or individual interviews with the employees.
   2. To conduct focus groups or survey employees, we need to develop a list of relevant questions.

   From these objectives, tasks will unfold naturally as the team develops *flow* with the project. However, some tasks won't become apparent until the team does deeper work on the project. Thus, rather than try to identify all the tasks at once, keep an ongoing *task log.* Some teams use charts on which they put Post-it notes—devise your own creative way to keep track of your ideas.

2. *What are the specific tasks or action steps?* Once you identify tasks, turn them into **action steps** by determining who will complete each task and by what date. Continuing with the example on employee attendance, here are some action steps:

   1. Develop employee survey. (Joe and Alice; due date: October 15)
   2. Distribute survey by November 1 and collect by November 15. (Marcie)
   3. Tabulate results. (Joe, Alice, and Marcie; due date: November 18)

   Your task log will change as your project develops: you will drop some items, add others, and possibly change some due dates. Be flexible in the way you accomplish your goals.

Accept your team members' unique styles and ways of thinking: use diversity to enrich your project, not destroy it.

Determining Results **Results** are your **outcomes:** *What will you accomplish?* The types of outcomes depend on the type of project you are working on. What products will fulfill the project requirements? What kinds of things will change as a result of the project? Consider all types of outcomes, including policies, behavior, and attitudes:

How will those affected by the project change or grow?

Will people develop new skills through training?

What new policies will be implemented?

Will new products be developed?

How will the new products help people, improve systems, or change operations?

You could, as an extra step, relate your results to a broader vision or mission. By doing this, you are placing your project into a context, thereby highlighting its importance in a broader scheme. Also, if your research uncovers next steps or leads to new topics for examination, include these in your results.

There is one final, important question: *What do team members expect to gain personally as a result of participating?*

The more invested team members are in achieving outcomes, the more driven they will be to achieve group objectives. Teams can nurture individual investment by discussing how members can benefit personally by achieving group goals.

Before jumping into a project by working on questions from this framework, learn more about team roles and building trust, which are addressed next.

Assigning Team Roles

A team may choose not to assign roles, preferring not to add structure to the team's dynamics. If a team chooses to assign roles, the most basic roles are facilitator, record keeper, and evaluator (also discussed in Chapter 6).

- A **facilitator** leads the group discussion, creating an agenda if feasible. The facilitator can take an active role with the group by capturing their ideas on a flip chart or whiteboard. In a less active role, the facilitator directs the discussion by giving one speaker the floor at a time rather than having everyone speak at once. The facilitator also determines when the group is ready to make a decision or move on to a new topic. Effective facilitators remain objective and use open questions to solicit responses.

- A **record keeper** takes notes during the meeting, recording the group's decisions and other important details. If the facilitator writes ideas on a flip chart or whiteboard, the record keeper makes a permanent record of the information. If the group members decide they want copies of the minutes of their meetings, the record keeper compiles the minutes and presents copies before or at the beginning of the next meeting.

- An **evaluator** assists in assessing the group's progress and proposes changes the group could make so that future meetings are more effective. The evaluator leads a feedback discussion at the end of the meeting for a specific time, perhaps 5 minutes. The group can do a *plus-delta feedback* assessment in which the evaluator records the group's feedback in two columns: on the plus side, things about the meeting that worked; on the delta side, things that should be changed (see the Coaching Tip on page 274).

   The goal of this exercise is to bring the group members closer to their ideal even though they may not be able to achieve it. Since the team and its leader may not be able to make all the changes suggested for future meetings, members should be realistic about their requests.

If the team members want to delineate roles further, they can appoint a *timekeeper* who would subtly inform the facilitator when the time allotted to a topic has expired and the group needs to move on. Another role that could be filled is that of *devil's advocate,* a person who would provide reasons why some of the group's choices might not work as planned.

COACHING TIP

Plus-Delta Feedback To organize feedback and keep it balanced, the evaluator could facilitate a *plus-delta activity*. The *plus* stands for "what worked" and *delta* stands for "what should be changed." On a flip chart or whiteboard, put a plus sign (+) at the top of one column and a delta sign (Δ) at the top of a second column. The group first fills in the *plus* column and then seeks to keep balance by putting items in the *delta* column. For example:

Plus-Delta Feedback Figure	
+	Δ
The agenda was clear and kept us on track.	We went on and on about the topic, and the facilitator should have moved us on sooner.

COMMUNICATION CHALLENGES

Text Conferencing Teams can use text conferencing alone or as part of a Webcast. In a **text-based conference,** members first check in online. They then write in an informal and immediate style (without taking time to correct grammar, punctuation, and spelling).

One of the biggest drawbacks of this type of communication is the lack of nonverbal cues. Since text conferencing relies on writing to communicate meaning *and* feeling, members sometimes use "emoticons." Thus, symbols such as (:-) could be used sparingly to keep the conversation light and upbeat.

Important words are sometimes put between asterisks (*) rather than italicized:

We sent the shipment to *Tokyo* not Singapore.

As with other types of electronic messaging, using all-caps is considered rude and the group might assume the writer is angry.

Although the most challenging barriers relate to language ability and time differences, members must be careful not to misinterpret a message or read more into it than was intended. *When in doubt, check it out:* before assuming a confusing or uncomfortable communication is valid, clarify the meaning through an objective, professional question. For example, "John, could you please clarify your last point; I'm feeling a bit confused about your reaction."

Here is one last point about roles, but this time *personal roles:* If you develop special relationships with group members, do *not* bring those relationships into the group. Close alliances can cause friction and develop a **split** in the group (that is, team members take sides and even small issues can become controversial). Hence, in team activities treat friends impartially; this boundary relates to keeping the trust with other members.

Building Trust

According to Patrick Lencioni, author of *The Five Dysfunctions of a Team,* the following qualities lead to dysfunctional teams:[9]

1. Lack of trust.
2. Fear of conflict.
3. Lack of commitment.
4. Avoidance of accountability.
5. Inattention to results.

Notice that *lack of trust* is first on the list. In fact, trust relates to the other issues on the list as well. When team members trust one another, they handle conflict appropriately; members feel free to disagree without turning differences into conflict. Team members who have good relationships with one another commit to a project's success because they don't want to let one another down; thus, a level of self-accountability exists.

Trust develops over time as team members get to know one another as human beings—one person to another. As members demonstrate that they keep their word and are committed to the project, respect for one another develops into trust.

When getting started (in the *forming* stage), teams can plan activities that reveal the human qualities of their members (see Internet Exercise 8.1 on page 270). The members may then have more patience with one another and more tolerance for differences in ideas and styles. Unfortunately, once trust is violated, it may take professional intervention to get members back on track (for example, bringing in a facilitator to conduct conflict management training).

Should conflict occur in your team, refocus on team goals and find mutual objectives. Each member who takes responsibility for his or her actions will contribute to reining in the discord and reestablishing constructive team dynamics.

Giving and Receiving Feedback

In teamwork, communication problems and frustrations can mysteriously appear at odd times, with no one understanding the hidden dynamics behind them. Team members will not always agree with one another, and at times some members will not be able to meet obligations. Addressing challenges effectively helps the group avoid conflict. To be fair and keep communication flowing, team members must periodically give one another **feedback.** Since this topic was discussed in Chapter 6, some of the information below may be familiar:

1. *Describe behavior rather than evaluate it.* When you describe behavior rather than evaluate it, team members may listen more receptively. *Describing* relates to giving specific details as to what happened; *evaluating* relates to judging (or criticizing) the behavior. To avoid evaluating, focus on what happened without interpreting the behavior or implying how it affected team dynamics. For example:

Evaluating: George disrupted the meeting and created problems when he was late.
Describing: George was 10 minutes late for the meeting.

2. *Use "I" statements.* You have learned that effective writing focuses on the reader by using the "you" point of view. However, when giving verbal feedback or responding to it on challenging issues, it is important not to sound accusatory. You can achieve this by focusing on how the behavior affected you. For example:

"You" statement: You blamed me for the entire problem.
"I" statement: When that comment was made, I felt as if you were blaming me for the entire problem.

3. *Use the passive voice.* In regard to style, the active voice makes writing clear and direct. However, the passive voice is preferred when you are pointing out a mistake or problem. This is true whether you are writing or speaking. Thus, if you are communicating about a sensitive issue, consider using the passive voice.

With the passive voice, you can leave the "actor" out of the statement and keep the focus on the issue. This approach allows those involved to take responsibility or make amends without feeling unduly targeted. For example:

Active voice: You were wrong not to bring the information to the group.
Passive voice: The information should have been brought to the group.

You can even add an "I" statement, which will further cushion the information:

I feel that the information should have been brought to the entire group.

4. *Beware of the micromessages your nonverbal behavior conveys.* Team members are sensitive to **nonverbal behavior.** When a member rolls his or her eyes, shrugs shoulders, or nods in disapproval, a dynamic may be set in motion that creates hidden conflict. Even a member's tightly folded arms during a heated discussion give the impression that the person is closed or angry. Keep your body relaxed, and refrain from gestures that might display a negative attitude. (Even if your gestures mean no harm, you have no way of knowing how others will interpret the communication.)

When a team member personally attacks those who do not agree, this affects everyone on the team. When team members do not feel free to voice their opinions, the communication flow can stop, stifling the creative process. More important, by ignoring or condoning disruptive behavior, the entire group can lose credibility and trust.

PRACTICE

Part A

Instructions: Turn the following evaluative statements into appropriate feedback:

1. Sue went on and on about the topic and used up all our time.

_____

2. You should have come to the meeting prepared to discuss the topic.

_____

3. Stop interrupting me when I'm trying to make a point.

_____

4. You shouldn't be telling me which tasks to do on the project.

_____

Part B

Situation: Your company has outgrown its office space, and management has formed a committee to pursue the details of moving operations to a new location. Duties range from identifying a proper location to finding a moving company that can handle the job at a reasonable price. One member of the committee, Pat, has been late to every committee meeting and has failed to apologize for the tardiness, much to the consternation of some team members. During meetings, Pat interrupts others when disagreeing with their opinions; Pat also treats you as if you were not the team leader of the committee.

Instructions:

1. Write a message to Pat about the disruptive behavior in meetings, and suggest changes.
2. Next, meet with a partner to role-play this situation.
   a. One partner should read the message to the other partner, who assumes the role of "Pat."
   b. You and your partner should now describe how it felt to play your respective roles: How did it feel to receive the message? How did it feel to give someone that kind of feedback?
3. Now switch roles and repeat the exercise.

Team Writing

From rough draft to final copy, you can do team writing projects in various ways. Here are a few suggestions for getting the task accomplished:

1. _Map out the various parts or sections._ Start with a concept map for the entire project, and then work together to do mind maps and page maps for individual parts. (With certain types of documents, such as proposals, standard parts can be identified immediately.)
2. _Research and become familiar with the content and topics._ Fill in details as you go along, using Post-it notes or any other creative tool you can devise.
3. _Brainstorm ideas together._ Assign a team facilitator to lead brainstorming sessions at any phase of the writing venture. (If feasible, use a laptop, flip chart, or whiteboard to capture ideas.)
4. _Coordinate writing assignments with task assignments._ In this way, team members and partners write about tasks they complete and about topics they are familiar with.
5. _Map pages and compose together or alone._ Then compare notes.
6. _Respect differences in working and learning styles._ Some team members work better alone than they do in a group; a team can respect that style through individual tasks rather than forced partnerships.
7. _Establish reasonable due dates_ so that team members have clear expectations. Allow room for error in case unforeseen circumstances arise—that means setting **internal due dates** in ample time to meet **external due dates.**
8. _Evaluate and revise your draft together:_
   • Agree ahead of time that every draft will need at least one revision.
   • Allow a few minutes for silent reading _before_ you discuss a section.
   • Give suggestions for improving the document rather than criticizing its current state. (In other words, every time you find something wrong, point out how to make an improvement or correction. Avoid criticism that points blame without adding anything constructive.)

9. *Bring the parts together for a final editing.* An important outcome is that your team write the project in a consistent voice even if several members contribute portions of it. Early on, your team may want to identify the member who is the most competent editor and reserve that individual's time for the final edit.

10. *Recognize one another for effort that results in work well done!*

COMMUNICATION CHALLENGES

Romance, Precision, and Generalization
Around 1900, a British mathematician and philosopher named Alfred North Whitehead believed that there was a *rhythm* to learning and that it was *cyclical*. Whitehead identified three distinct parts to the cycle of learning.[10] Here's how he described them:

- **Romance:** Exploring without being graded or evaluated; engaging the subject in a playful manner: *having fun.*
- **Precision:** Repeating something until you have mastered it: *practice, practice, practice.*
- **Generalization:** Applying the learning in a new and different way: *expressing creativity.*

Whitehead believed the critical part of the cycle was *romance*. Without romance, a learner would never reach generalization, which is the phase in which significant outcomes occur. By engaging with a subject in a playful manner, the learner may become passionate about it. This passion will carry the learner through the difficult stage of precision and lead to generalization.

Ask yourself: *Is this cycle of learning true in my own life? Do I have a hobby or sport that I feel passionate about, or did I have one in the past?*

INTERNET EXERCISE 8.2

Alfred North Whitehead To find out more about Alfred Whitehead and other thinkers whose work has influenced the development of this text, visit the *Foundations of Business Communication* Web site at <http://www.mhhe.com/djyoung>.

At the home page, select "Student Activities"; then click on the Chapter 8 link to begin.

Of course, every team is unique, developing its own team dynamics. Work on understanding one another's strengths and weaknesses, and then interact in constructive ways to get the job done. Use your communication skills to divide the project into manageable tasks and then pull all the parts together; every team will do this in its own unique way.

A Problem-Solving Strategy: Explore, Practice, Apply

This textbook breaks most activities into one of the following three categories: *explore, practice,* or *apply.* These concepts are an extension of the learning theory developed by Alfred North Whitehead, a British mathematician and philosopher (see the Communication Challenges sidebar). Here is how to apply these concepts to a problem-solving strategy:

- *Explore* involves considering ideas without evaluating them. Drop expectations and notions about what you should achieve. Let innovative, creative ideas enter the mix of topics that pertain to solving the problem.

   Exploration involves becoming familiar with a problem *before* you consider how to solve it. Exploration bypasses the serious aspect of problem solving and allows a bit of fun to enter the process. When group members explore a topic, they should not feel pressured to produce an answer—they are acquainting themselves with one another and their topic; they are developing interest and motivation, connecting to the project's mission in a personal way. Exploration leads to *thinking outside the box.*

- *Practice* involves precision: getting the precise details down correctly—the cold, hard facts, so to speak. Practice takes focus and determination. Practice also relates to developing specific skills by repeating a concept until you thoroughly learn it and can use it confidently in new situations.

   Practice also pertains to research: developing details about the difficult concepts you discovered through exploration and building the body of knowledge you need to solve the problem. Practice is the tedious, mechanical part of any project; but once a team explores a topic and connects with its mission, the practice phase becomes palatable. In addition, the practice phase provides the *foundation* for developing a solution.

- *Apply* involves creating an innovative, unique solution drawn from the knowledge and skill you acquire in the practice phase. To reach the best answers, you (and your team) should not consider responses final until you have explored and practiced sufficiently.

Are all three of these phases necessary in solving a problem? Alfred North Whitehead thought so. In fact, Whitehead believed the most critical phase was *exploring.* Unless team members buy into the mission or importance of a project (which usually occurs during *explore*), they may not commit to the intense work that leads to creating an innovative, quality outcome. *Explore* opens the door to creativity (and possibly passion); *practice* provides the details; and *apply* assembles the pieces in a novel way to generate a truly effective result.[11]

These phases are cyclical and not meant to be experienced in a linear way. As you work through your project, take note of which phase describes where you are at various points. For example, you may find yourself exploring ideas in the application phase of the cycle. By using these concepts in a creative way rather than a linear 1-2-3 approach, you will achieve good results. (At the end of the chapter, you will find activities relating to each of these concepts.)

SECTION B: CONCEPT CHECK

1. What steps can a team take to clarify its mission? When should this occur?

2. What questions does a team need to resolve to determine its methodology?

3. List ways that you can buffer negative feedback or criticism.

■ SECTION C: WRITING A PROPOSAL

COACHING TIP

Company Mission Statements Most companies develop a statement that expresses their mission and sometimes their vision. The company **mission statement** is published in brochures and on Web sites as well as posted on walls in places where employees meet, such as cafeterias or conference rooms.

The following example could be a mission statement:

Our business is customer service leading to customer satisfaction.

Employees remain in sync with their company's philosophy by referring to it as they work with clients or write their performance objectives. Some employees use the mission statement as their motto; by focusing on the company mission, employees ensure that they carry out the directives of their company's leadership.

As you write proposals, do your research by identifying the client's company mission statement and link your proposal to it.

As a blend of informative and persuasive writing, **proposals** are important business tools. However, the word *proposal* can intimidate writers. This might be because formal proposals require adherence to rules and protocols or because the word *proposal* implies acceptance as well as *nonacceptance*. Beyond that, some proposals involve inordinate planning and research, which can be the most difficult aspects of writing. However, the most important aspects of proposal writing are the following:

- Establishing that a problem exists and that you are the best one to solve it.
- Knowing who the key stakeholders are and what they are seeking.
- Incorporating into your plan solutions tailored to your key stakeholders.

A team may find itself writing a proposal for various reasons: for example, to persuade members of its own organization to make changes or to persuade external organizations to adopt a product. One common type of proposal is written to request funds from a not-for-profit foundation or government agency to implement a project.

Define the scope of your proposal:

- Is the team developing a proposal for a current customer or prospective one?
- Does the proposal need to include every aspect of a formal proposal?
- Can the proposal be a short letter or memo that addresses a few pertinent questions?

Different types of proposals have different types of requirements, some more rigid than others.

Client Relationships

Writing proposals is a form of listening to a client's needs and then customizing a solution. Thus, proposals emanate from your client's needs (not from what *you think* the client needs). In addition, they are often part of a larger organizational process that helps the client fulfill its mission. Hence, a writer or team is foolish to submit a proposal without tailoring *every detail* to the targeted audience. Take the following steps in developing a base for your proposals:

1. Research the philosophy, culture, and mission of your target audience.
2. Establish an honest dialogue with the decision makers and key stakeholders.

Obviously some situations will not allow direct contact with a prospective client; but when you can meet with the client, doing so is your most important work. After the client clarifies the problem, that information becomes the foundation for defining purpose, methods, and outcomes. In turn, these pieces will develop into your proposal; they answer most of the questions for the major parts of your proposal.

Cover Letter

Formal proposals include a **cover letter** that summarizes main points of the grant (often taken from the executive summary and statement of need). The cover letter is secondary to the proposal itself. Though the cover letter should be accurate and well written, it does not need to contain *new* information; you can use direct statements from the proposal or executive summary in the letter. By summarizing highlights from the proposal, the letter prepares the reader for the language and ideas that the proposal contains. (See Figure 8.5.)

Formal Proposals

Formal proposals involve considerable research and development. To be successful, the writer (or writers) must have command of the problem and its solution as well as of the formal structure for writing a proposal.

In a proposal, you are detailing a problem and showing how you would solve it. However, often you must first ignite the reader's motivation by showing that the problem

FIGURE 8.5 | Proposal Cover Letter

Can you identify the different parts of the following letter?

The Hoosier Environmental Council
1915 West 18th Street, Suite A
Indianapolis, IN 46202
317-685-8800
hec@hecweb.org

June 10, 2004

Nina Mason Pulliam Charitable Trust
222 Monument Circle
Indianapolis, IN 46207

Ladies and Gentlemen:

Thank you for reviewing our proposal for the Fall Creek Stewardship Project.

As Indiana's largest environmental organization, our mission is to use *education, advocacy, and citizen empowerment to restore and protect the natural systems upon which life depends*. The Fall Creek Project will achieve that mission by enabling middle school students to become Stream Doctors as they assess Fall Creek's physical, biological, and chemical health. As they prescribe remedies for this vital water system, they will also learn important lessons in effecting social and environmental change.

Our staff has worked diligently to develop this project and create a fit with your organization's vision and mission. Please let me know if there is any other information with which I may provide you. In the meantime, I look forward to hearing your response so that we may implement the Fall Creek Stewardship Project.

Sincerely,

Tim Maloney
Executive Director

db
Enclosure: Fall Creek Stewardship Grant Proposal

needs to be addressed. Then you must demonstrate that the manner you suggest—your plan—is the best way to proceed. Thus, your proposal must convince the reader of the following:

- That a problem exists and needs to be solved.
- That you are the best choice to solve the problem.
- That your approach is the most effective.
- That your costs are competitive and justified.

If an organization has a particular need, it may publicly announce that need in a *request for proposal (RFP)*. The RFP establishes the scope of the intended project and alerts interested parties that the company is soliciting competitive bids and formal proposals. Companies use RFPs so that responding vendors provide information that is uniform and complete. Before submitting—*or even starting*—a formal proposal, learn the organization's requirements for written proposals. State and federal governments, along with not-for-profit foundations, have the most complicated guidelines for grants and proposals.

An individual or committee may evaluate your proposal along with many other proposals; consistency in format makes it easier to determine whether the proposal is complete and to compare it with others. In fact, if a proposal does not follow the prescribed format exactly, it may be returned without being read. (Remember, proposal format varies somewhat from organization to organization.)

In Section B of this chapter, you learned how to develop a team strategy to solve a problem; you start by identifying the *purpose, plan,* and intended *results* of your project. The information you develop from considering those basic elements becomes the foundation for a proposal. (However, since each company or organization has its own preferred format and individual requirements, you will need to adapt your information to the client's structure and style.) Here's one way to shape that information into the basic parts of a proposal (also see Table 8.1):

Statement of Need:

Purpose: Start with a short statement connecting your services to your client's needs. Briefly state information about the need to solve the problem; relate confidence in developing a comprehensive or innovative solution.

Background: Give a brief history of the problem; include details that relate to individual objectives the proposal will address. Include enough information so that the reader becomes motivated to have you solve the problem. In short, *why should the client hire you?*

Project Description:

Objectives: State what you will accomplish; write individual objectives for major parts of the project.

Plan, methods, and schedule: Discuss the details of how you will achieve your purpose and objectives; identify the methods you will use and the order in which you will use them. State how long the activities will take, and give dates, if applicable (for example, "Phase 1," "Phase 2").

TABLE 8.1 | The Foundation Center Format for Formal Proposal[12]

Part	Description	Length
Executive summary	A summary of the entire proposal.	1 page
Statement of need	A description of why the proposal is necessary.	2 pages
Project description	How the program will be implemented and evaluated.	3 pages
Budget	Financial description of the project and explanation of costs.	1 page
Organization information	History and governing structure of the nonprofit; its primary activities, audiences, and services.	1 page
Conclusion	Summary of the proposal's main points.	2 paragraphs

Results: Summarize the expected outcomes your client will achieve from implementing your proposal.

Remember, *the devil is in the details* (but only include details when your client wants them).

Organization Information:

Your company: Include relevant information about your company's history, management structure, clients, and services.

Staffing and credentials: Provide the names and credentials of those who will be implementing the proposal. (For letter proposals, which are shorter, present this information in a less formal way.)

Budget:

Include a detailed breakdown of the costs. Justify any costs that may seem extraordinary.

Evaluation:

Explain how you will measure results. Indicate how you (and your client) will know if you achieve the objectives.

Authorization:

Formal proposals include an authorization statement for your client along with a signature line. (In shorter, less formal proposals, the authorization statement is often omitted.)

A formal proposal is a contract, so expect to be held responsible for performing any service you indicate that you can provide and for doing so at the cost that you list. To protect yourself, you may want to specify the time frame during which the proposal is effective. For example,

The prices quoted in this proposal are valid until the end of this year.

Proposals represent partnerships. You are using your skills to solve a problem that may affect people you have never met. Hence, early in the process, get to know your client.

FIGURE 8.6 | Formal Proposal

Nina Mason Pulliam Charitable Trust
PROPOSAL SUMMARY

Organization: Hoosier Environmental Council

Name of project/campaign: Fall Creek Stewardship Project

Amount requested: $23,644

Area served: Marion County, Indiana

Organization description and history: HEC was established as a 501(c)(3) organization in 1983. We have since become Indiana's largest environmental organization, with more than 20,000 individual and 60 organization members.

Mission statement: *Through education, advocacy, and citizen empowerment, we restore and protect the natural systems upon which life depends.*

Proposed grant activities: Middle-school students will become *Stream Doctors* and assess Fall Creek's physical, biological, and chemical health. Students will write and fulfill their prescriptions for restoring Fall Creek.

Dates of proposed grant activities: September 1, 2001 to August 31, 2002

Proposed grant outcomes: Students will demonstrate increased knowledge and appreciation of Fall Creek's wildlife and habitat. Their activities will protect animals and nature in our community. Adopted sections of Fall Creek will display improved appearance and wildlife habitat.

Grant partners/collaborators: Rosseau McClellan Montessori School 91, the Center for Inquiry, and Merle Sidener Middle School.

FIGURE 8.6 | Formal Proposal *(Cont.)*

APPLICATION FOR FUNDING

PROGRAM INFORMATION

Need
The Fall Creek Stewardship Project stems from a need to restore Fall Creek. According to the Indiana Department of Environmental Management's Office of Water Quality, Fall Creek is one of 208 impaired waterways in Indiana. Furthermore, 26 combined sewers drain into Fall Creek, according to the City of Indianapolis.

Despite these threats, Fall Creek provides important urban wildlife habitat. As a tributary of White River, it composes part of a major flyway for many waterfowl and songbirds. This creek is a treasure for the city of Indianapolis, improving the quality of life for urban dwellers.

Primary Audience
The Fall Creek Stewardship Project will focus on middle-school students within Indianapolis public schools and will serve approximately 240 students. The *Community Assessment* states, "Communities need to develop a philosophy and theoretical framework which involves a vision of youth development and its relationship to school/home/community linkages."

The Fall Creek Stewardship Project embraces such a vision, and even extends that vision into practical application. The project will open students' eyes to bountiful nature in their own community. The hands-on experience will also foster a sense of connection, ownership, and pride. Such action encourages the human psyche to transform from despair to caring citizenship.

Time Frame
The project will span from September 1, 2004 to August 31, 2005. After launching the project this first year, we hope to make the project ongoing.

Goals, Strategies, Outcomes, Indicators
The project's goals are to protect animals and nature by improving the physical quality of Fall Creek within the given time frame. It also seeks to educate middle-school students about protecting this life-sustaining natural system.

Strategies involve taking middle-school students on monthly field trips to their adopted section of Fall Creek. Students will become *Stream Doctors* and diagnose Fall Creek's physical, biological, and chemical health. (The Izaak Walton League designed *Stream Doctors* as a watershed restoration program in 1994.) Students will report their findings to local officials, the Indiana Department of Environmental Management, and the Indiana Department of Natural Resources' Riverwatch program. During every field trip, students will also clean up litter.

Students will then write a prescription for restoring Fall Creek. Fulfilling their prescriptions may include planting trees and shrubs. These activities will improve wildlife habitat and food, reduce stream bank erosion, filter runoff pollutants, and enhance aesthetic quality. Students may also work with local officials to design a city plan to improve water quality.

By June 15, 2005, at least 70 percent of students involved will be able to name at least three species depending on Fall Creek habitat. Also, at least 60 percent of students will report feeling closer to nature as a result of engaging in the project. These statistics will be reflected in year-end student evaluations. Adopted sections of Fall Creek will have 50 percent less trash. Each adopted section of Fall Creek will possess at least one new element that improves wildlife habitat, such as a native fruit-bearing bush.

Staff
Tricia O'Neil, HEC's education coordinator, will lead the project. From time to time, curriculum input may be given by Denise Baker, former education director. Of course, teacher and student involvement will also shape the evolution of each class's prescription.

FIGURE 8.6 | Formal Proposal *(Cont.)*

FINANCES

Future Funding
HEC's Environmental Education Explorations has been successful in attracting corporate community support. Besides receiving direct financial support from the Indiana Pacers, it has received in-kind support from Marsh, Emmis Broadcasting, Bank One, Galyan's, and the U.S. Postal Service. In the long term, we believe the Fall Creek Stewardship Project will also have strong appeal to corporate donors. However, the project may require another year or two of support from the foundation community before it becomes fully funded through corporate contributions.

Revenues and Fiscal Agents
No revenues will be generated as a result of Fall Creek Stewardship Project activities. However, if student prescriptions for Fall Creek involve planting numerous trees or bushes, they may have to undertake small fund-raising initiatives to purchase such items through bake sales or car washes. If student prescriptions call for extensive tree planting, they would submit a grant to the Indiana Department of Natural Resources.

Operating Results and Budgets
Attached is HEC's year 2002 income and expense statement, with our actual income and operating expenses. Also attached is our 2003 and 2004 budget.

BUDGET

FALL CREEK STEWARDSHIP PROJECT

Hoosier Environmental Council
Proposed budget for September 1, 2001, to August 31, 2002
Year 1 of one-year project

	Amount Requested from NMPCT	Amount Supported by Add'l Sources	Amount Supported by Earned Grants	Amount Supported by HEC	Total Proposed Budget Income
Direct Costs:					
A. Salaries and benefits	$17,347				$17,347
B. Consultants	240				240
C. Supplies				$1,509	1,509
D. Transportation	993				993
E. Equipment purchase/rental	674	$500			1,174
F. Printing and publication costs	483				483
G. Miscellaneous	300	2,000			2,300
Subtotal—Direct Costs	$20,037				$24,046
Indirect Costs:					3,607
(e.g., administrative overhead charged to this project)	$3,607				$3,607
Subtotal—Indirect Costs	$3,607				$3,607
Total Project Costs	$23,644				$27,653

PROJECT LEADER BIO
Tricia O'Neil is HEC's education coordinator, who has been heading HEC's Environmental Education Explorations project since April 2001. Ms. O'Neil is also a peace education facilitator at the Peace Learning Center. She teaches conflict resolution and environmental education to fourth- and fifth-graders in Indianapolis public schools.

Letter Proposals

Many corporations do not require formal proposals. When this is the case, a two- or three-page letter proposal will generally suffice. The letter proposal contains most of the same information that a longer, formal proposal contains. However, the client is likely to be familiar with the problem and convinced it needs to be addressed. The client may also be familiar with the services and solutions you offer.

FIGURE 8.7 | Letter Proposal

This proposal follows a slightly different format from that of a formal proposal. What about this approach? How does Comerford Consulting adapt this proposal to All Pro Temps' needs?

Comerford Consulting
555 Onyx Circle
Indianapolis, IN 46237

E-mail: comerford@tcon.com
Website: comerfordconsulting

February 21, 2006

Mr. James Riley, CEO
All Pro Temps, Inc.
600 North McClurg, Suite 304
Chicago, IL 60611

Dear James:

Congratulations on your desire to improve the writing and speaking skills of those in your organization. As we discussed, your goal to help All Pro employees write more effectively, efficiently, and correctly are commendable.

Comerford Consulting looks forward to helping you meet those needs. Since you want to achieve the highest-quality training for a price that meets your budget, I am including various training and coaching options. The two workshops I recommend you consider for your 100 employees are the following:

• "Professional Writing Skills at a Glance"
• "Taking the 'Grr' Out of Grammar"

TRAINING

Professional Writing Skills at a Glance

Class Size: Although we discussed a class size of 16 to 17 participants per session, you could save an additional day of training by breaking the participants into groups of 20 instead of 16.

Option 1: 16 to 17
participants in 6 sessions

Option 2: 20
participants in 5 sessions

Taking the "Grr" Out of Grammar

Class Size: You proposed one day of grammar and punctuation training to help all 100 employees learn to write and edit more correctly. The larger the class, the more challenges involved to meet everyone's needs concerning both course content and participant scheduling. An alternative for you to consider is offering two sessions of 50 each.

Option 3: 100 participants
in 1 session

Option 4: 50 participants
in 2 sessions

FIGURE 8.7 | Letter Proposal *(Cont.)*

James Riley   2   February 21, 2006

PRICING OPTIONS

Training Fee: $1800 per session (this represents a 10 percent discount for a 100-person volume).

Training Manuals: The price per participant is $20 for *Professional Writing Skills at a Glance* and $20 for *Taking the "Grr" Out of Grammar;* participants can receive both for $30 (a $10 discount). Should you wish to save even further, you may duplicate those manuals from a .pdf file for which you would pay a royalty fee of $15 per participant.

Price per participant
for both manuals: $30

Price per participant
for .pdf files: $15

Training Fee Totals for Both Workshops

Option 1	o r	Option 2	+	Option 3	o r	Option 4
Professional Writing Skills at a Glance		*Professional Writing Skills at a Glance*		*Taking the "Grr" Out of Grammar*		*Taking the "Grr" Out of Grammar*
16 Participants 6 Sessions		20 Participants 5 Sessions		100 Participants 1 Session		50 Participants 2 Sessions
$10,800		$9000		$1800		$3600

Mr. James Riley   3   February 21, 2006

Training Manual Totals for Both Workshops

	Option 5	o r	Option 6
Training Materials for 100 Participants	**Comerford Consulting Provides Manuals**		**All Pro Temps, Inc. Copies Manuals**
Royalty	$15 each		$15 each
Reproduction Fees	$15 each		$0.00
Total for Materials	$3000		$1500

Train the Trainer: For future employees, a "train-the-trainer" option could work; however, an easier alternative would be for you to purchase the video versions (tape or CD) of both workshops. Once you determine which options would work best, we can tabulate a price-per-person cost for your on-site workshops that meets the distance learning equivalent.

Your employees can receive additional assistance through coaching sessions. We can discuss this option as a follow-up to one or both of the trainings proposed. Please note that the pricing options in this proposal are designed with flexibility in mind to fit your budget requirements; these prices are valid for the remainder of this year.

Comerford Consulting prides itself on having the expertise and experience to meet the writing needs you described. We look forward to working with you toward a win-win situation by improving your employees' skills and, thus, the credibility of your corporation.

Sincerely,

Linda Comerford
President

Comerford Consulting: from the workshop to the workplace and beyond

Though all proposals need to be tailored to the specific audience, here are general guidelines for a two-page or three-page letter proposal:

Statement of Need:

Start with a short statement connecting your client's needs with your expertise. Once again, *why should the client hire you?*

With letter proposals, the statement of need may be very short or omitted because the proposal is often written at the client's request. The client may be asking that details be put in writing to grant approval or finalize authorization.

Description of Project:

Objectives: State what you will accomplish; write objectives for major parts of the project.

Plan and schedule: Discuss only important details of your plan. Identify each phase of the proposal, and give prepared dates, if applicable. If feasible, give your client options.

Results and evaluation: State the results your proposal will accomplish and how you will measure them.

Budget:

Include a detailed breakdown of the costs. If you have given the client options, make sure the costs for each option are clear.

The information on proposal writing in this chapter is meant to complement the information on persuasive writing that you learned in Chapter 5. All persuasive writing, including proposals, is challenging and exciting at the same time. You are forming a partnership with your client to solve problems and effect important change.

PRACTICE

Instructions: Analyze the Comerford letter proposal according to the AIDA model, a traditional approach to developing sales letters that you learned in Chapter 5. Here's the *AIDA model:*

Attention	Grab the reader's attention.
Interest	Develop the reader's interest by making the claim relevant.
Desire	Explain how the product will benefit the client.
Action	Make actions convenient and simple for your reader to take.

Identify three or four ways this proposal adapts to All Pro Temps' needs. Can you give suggestions to make this proposal even more effective?

 SECTION C: CONCEPT CHECK

1. What are some differences between a formal proposal and a two-page letter proposal?

2. How does the process of defining purpose, methods, and outcomes relate to writing a proposal?

S U M M A R Y

Working on teams challenges even the most talented professionals. Everyone communicates in an individual style and solves problems in an individual way. Developing synchronicity starts by developing a common understanding of a problem and agreeing on a creative approach to solving it. The melding of differences among team members generally occurs through planning followed by action (rather than completing tasks without a plan).

You have had the opportunity to write a proposal through a team project; the more proposals you write, the more success you will have. Persistence is the key to winning in the proposal marketplace, and, to some extent, winning is a matter of statistics: if you don't try, you have no chance to win a bid. If you learn something each time you fail, your likelihood for success increases.

Every team has its own set of challenges and rewards. Change is inevitable; keep the team process vibrant by giving honest and professional feedback along with the best of your talents. Now you are ready to move on to Chapter 9, "Getting a Job"; use your new teamwork skills to enhance your résumé and job qualifications.

CHAPTER 8 CHECKLIST

Team Communication
___ Has your team developed a common understanding of its project?
___ Has your team written a purpose statement?
___ What are your team's objectives?
___ What are your team's project goals and objectives?
___ What action steps has your team planned?
___ Has your team assigned a due date for each action step?
___ Has your team developed ground rules?
___ Has your team developed methods and broken them down into tasks?
___ Has your team established clear internal and external deadlines?
___ What results will your team's project accomplish?
___ Has your team established trust?
___ Have team members given one another honest, objective feedback as needed?
___ Has your team developed a strategy for team writing?
___ Has your team incorporated "explore, practice, and apply" into team activities?

END-OF-CHAPTER ACTIVITIES

ACTIVITY 1: PROCESS MEMO—ARE YOU A TEAM PLAYER?

Instructions: Write a process memo or e-memo to your instructor. Start by defining teamwork, and then give some insight into your own qualities in regard to working in teams. Do you work well with others? What about decision making: are you comfortable with others making decisions, or are you more comfortable in a leadership role? Do you prefer to participate in a discussion or prefer to facilitate it? Do you find yourself sitting back and listening to a discussion or find yourself driving the discussion?

In light of the information presented in this chapter, what characteristics do you bring to a team project? Examine your own behavior in team situations, and describe it honestly. (Use the Reflect/Respond/Revise process strategy.)

ACTIVITY 2: ALL PRO TEMPS

Instructions: Mr. James Riley, the CEO of All Pro, has asked you to develop a proposal check sheet. It seems he will be soliciting proposals from consultants to do some team building for the entire company. To compare the different proposals, he would like a tally sheet that indicates the various parts of a proposal. As he reads the different proposals or watches the consultants' PowerPoint presentations, he can tally their scores on the sheet you prepare.

You need to decide how he will tally results. Will he use a scale? What will each number on the scale represent?

ACTIVITY 3: TEAM MEETING

Instructions: If you have been assigned a team project, this activity gives you an overview of steps to follow. Since teams accomplish projects through a series of meetings, the first goal for you and your teammates is to get to know one another and get focused on the project. Attend your first team meeting, and as a group see which of the following you can accomplish:

1. Do a warm-up activity or check-in. (See Activity 4.)
2. Develop ground rules. (See Activity 5.)
3. Identify how your group will facilitate meetings and make decisions. Will the team appoint a facilitator, recorder, and evaluator? (See Activity 8.)
4. Select a group project and analyze it. (See Activity 9.) Identify the topic, and determine content areas for researching the project.
5. Compose a rough purpose statement (which can be revised at the next meeting).
6. Develop a timeline and a meeting schedule.
7. Assign tasks. What preparation should each member make for the next meeting?
8. What products will the team generate to meet the project's requirement?

By the end of the first meeting, a team has accomplished a great deal if the members leave feeling as if they are "all on the same page." Has your team developed a common understanding of the project? Which of the listed items do you need to carry over into your next meeting? Will someone prepare an agenda for the next meeting?

ACTIVITY 4: WARM-UP ACTIVITIES OR CHECK-IN

Background: Beyond doing simple introductions, you may want to use a warm-up activity (or *check-in*) so that you and your teammates can learn more about one another's background and interests. A warm-up activity gets team members focused on the meeting and builds respect and trust, qualities that contribute to a team's success. Here are samples of questions that you can use:

- What three words describe your mood or how you are feeling about the project?
- What's up with you right now?
- What is something people would not know about you just by looking at you?

Instructions: Develop a question or two of your own:

1. _____
2. _____

Specify a maximum amount of time your team will spend on each step or question; for example, tell members they each have about 1 minute to speak. You may be surprised to learn that some team members will speak for only a few seconds and others, well . . . *Staying within boundaries helps everyone!*

ACTIVITY 5: UNDERSTANDING HOW TEAMS FUNCTION

Background: Just as successful meetings depend on shared expectations, so do team activities. In fact, most team activities take place in meetings, with team projects being accomplished through a series of meetings. Thus, successful teams often set ground rules so that members share expectations through established boundaries. Here are samples of ground rules:

1. People are free to express feelings as well as ideas.
2. Members agree to give objective feedback relating to ideas rather than give personal criticism.
3. Members agree to follow through on their responsibilities or inform the group when they are not able to meet their obligations.
4. Members agree to keep controversial issues in the open.
5. Members agree to keep what's spoken in the room among the members.
6. Members give the facilitator permission to manage the meeting process.

Instructions: Your group should meet to adopt its own ground rules. The team can refer to this list, but by creating its own list (even if the ideas are similar), your group will take ownership of the rules.

What are your team's ground rules? Before the team adopts them, your team facilitator should ask if anyone has anything to change or add. When the team is finalizing the ground rules, silence does not mean agreement; each member should either give a nod or raise a hand to show agreement.

ACTIVITY 6: UNDERSTANDING THE CHARACTERISTICS OF SUCCESSFUL TEAMS

Background: What are the characteristics of a successful team? How is a team's success measured? It isn't always the winning team that garners admiration and respect; sometimes an underdog team that performs beyond expectations is seen as the greater success. A team might be involved in a project whose wisdom and success might not be judged for years to come, such as a NASA mission to Saturn or a Supreme Court majority ruling on a controversial topic. From the Founding Fathers to the Olympic dream team, each team offers its own dynamics, mission, and measure of success.

Instructions:

1. Identify a successful team that interests you. If possible, obtain information about the team's dynamics. In an e-mail to your instructor, describe what you believe are the team's "secrets of success," and explain whether its secrets can be applied to your team's communication dynamics.
2. Attend a team meeting (the team doesn't have to be one you identified in Item 1, above), and analyze it. Identify three characteristics of a successful team, and assess the team you selected on those characteristics. Describe the behavior the team displays that reflects each characteristic (or lack of it). Put the information in a memo to your instructor.

ACTIVITY 7: PERSONALITY STYLE AND TEAM DYNAMICS

Instructions: Go to the *Foundations of Business Communication* Web site at <http://www.mhhe.com/djyoung> to learn about different personality types and the Myers-Briggs Personality

Type Indicator (MBTI). As you read through the information, identify what you think are your dominant traits.

1. Discuss your profile with a partner and compare notes.

2. How does understanding your profile expand your understanding of working with others?

3. How will this understanding assist you in becoming more patient and cooperative with team members whose styles differ from your own?

ACTIVITY 8: ANALYZING TEAM DYNAMICS

Instructions: At a team meeting, play the role of evaluator. At the end of the meeting, facilitate a plus-delta activity. After the meeting, compare your perceptions with your teammates' perceptions. Who was the natural leader? Who was a note taker? Who sat back and said or did nothing? Do you agree or disagree with the group's assessment? Do you have other points to add? Type a memo to your instructor in which you summarize the group's feedback and then present your insights.

ACTIVITY 9: TEAM PROPOSAL

Situation: You are part of a consulting firm that offers training on human resource and organizational development topics. All Pro Temps has called your firm saying it needs help with team building. All Pro has a total of 50 full-time employees working at five different branch offices (all located within your state).

Lately, there has been unprofessional behavior at some of the branch offices, and some branch managers are not being effective team leaders. Employees are showing up late and not following up on client requests. Clients have even called the home office to complain, saying that some of the temps All Pro is sending over do not meet the specifications they requested.

Instructions: All Pro's managers have decided to implement a new evaluation system. Before they do, they would like to do some team-building activities. They have asked your firm for a proposal that outlines the type of team-building plan it could provide for them. Your proposal should be between 5 and 10 pages long and include the following parts:

- Purpose statement, goals, and objectives.
- Instruments your team would use (such as the Myers-Briggs or other assessment methods).
- Expected outcomes or results.
- Strategy and timeline for implementing your plan.
- Features that distinguish your firm and proposal from others.
- Your firm's credentials as a consulting agency.

For part of your proposal, research team dynamics: what works and what doesn't work. Once the proposal is written, you and your team will have an opportunity to give it in person. All Pro will make its vendor-selection decision after you and representatives from several other consulting firms have presented proposals. Your instructor will define the requirements and logistics; for example, PowerPoint, roundtable discussion, role play, or group presentation, and so on.

You and your teammates may want to spend the first project meeting developing your own team-building approach by establishing how the team will make decisions, discussing team roles, scheduling team meetings, and establishing a timeline. By the way, don't forget to spend part of the time in your first meeting getting to know one another! (See Activities 3, 4, and 5.)

Alternative-Project Instructions

1. A Denver-based business that sells copiers has expanded its operations overseas and is having difficulty in its relations with the local community. Its managers need some training in global communication skills. In six months, they are having a three-day meeting in Japan. The business has asked your firm to present a proposal outlining the training program it could offer the management team before they go to Japan.

2. Return to the list of service-learning activities presented on the *Foundations of Business Communication* Web site at <http://www.mhhe.com/djyoung> (see Communication Challenges on page 261). Choose an activity on the list, or create one of your own. With your partner or partners, develop a proposal describing the service-learning activity, its benefits, and the duties members of the class, working in teams, will be expected to perform to participate.

ACTIVITY 10: DEVELOPING NEWSLETTERS

Instructions: This activity is an extension of Activity 9. Go to the *Foundations of Business Communication* Web site at <http://www.mhhe.com/djyoung>, and read about constructing newsletters. Using your team project as the basis for this assignment, write a newsletter about team building. Specifically, mold some of your research into a 2-page print newsletter. How would you present the same information in an electronic newsletter? Would you organize it differently?

REFERENCES

1. General Henry M. Robert, *Robert's Rules of Order,* Scott Foresman, 1978.

2. Bruce W. Tuckman, "Developmental Sequence in Small Groups," *Psychological Bulletin,* No. 63, 1965, pp. 384–399.

3. Ibid.

4. Bruce W. Tuckman, and Mary Ann Jensen, "Stages of Small Group Development Revisited," *Group and Organizational Studies,* No. 2, 1977, pp. 419–427.

5. Trisha Svehla, (secondary source), diversity consultant, Managing the Mosaic, Spring, 2003. Primary sources: Diana Booher, *Communicate with Confidence,* McGraw-Hill, NY, pp. 331–356. *Hardball for Women,* Lowell House, Los Angeles, 1992, pp. 331–356; (or RGA Publishing Group, Inc.)

6. John Dewey, *Democracy and Education,* The Free Press, A Division of Macmillan Publishing Co., Inc., New York, 1966, p. 148.

7. Joel Arthur Barker, Whole Systems Glossary, <http://www.worldtrans.org/whole/wholedefs.html>, accessed July 22, 2004.

8. Jodie Solow, A specialist in organizational development, Solow recommends the fishbone as a problem-solving tool. Until problems are solved at their root level, they are likely to persist.

9. Patrick Lencioni, *The Five Dysfunctions of a Team,* Jossey Bass, San Francisco, 2002, pp. 180–220.

10. Alfred North Whitehead, *The Aims of Education,* The Free Press, New York, 1968, pp. 15–29.

11. Ibid.

12. The Foundation Center, <http://fdncenter.org/learn/shortcourse/prop/.html>, accessed February 11, 2004.

KEY FOR LEARNING INVENTORY

1.	F	6.	F
2.	F	7.	F
3.	F	8.	T
4.	T	9.	F
5.	F	10.	F

Handbook at a Glance, Part 4:

Research—Collecting, Conducting, Displaying, and Citing

Research is an organized attempt to answer a specific question: *the goal of scientific research is to explain, predict, and/or control phenomena.* Valid research commands respect because the results take away misleading assumptions and point humanity onto a more genuine path.

This Handbook at a Glance covers four different aspects of research:

- *Collecting research* through a review of the literature.
- *Conducting research* through quantitative and qualitative methods.
- *Displaying research* in graphs and charts.
- *Citing research* in a standard format.

When you use research to shape the way you think, your decisions become clearer and more objective and your outcomes become more predictable. The key is letting the research lead to your conclusions rather than having your predispositions determine the conclusions of your research. As Fred Menger, a chemistry professor, once said, "If you torture data sufficiently, it will confess to almost anything."[1] Nowhere is integrity more critical than in dealing with research.

As you work through this chapter, you may find yourself *applying* more research as you make decisions, and that's the key to making any kind of research worth the effort.

The Plan

1. Answer the questions in the Learning Inventory.
2. Review the at-a-glance material, and do the exercises.
3. If you need a more thorough review of key ideas, turn to the Writer's Handbook, Part 4, "Research—Collecting, Conducting, Displaying, and Citing."

Learning Inventory

1. The first part of any formal research is "a review of the literature."   T/F
2. Qualitative research deals with probability.   T/F
3. The most credible research comes from online sources.   T/F
4. When you ask people how they think or feel about a topic, you are doing informal qualitative research.   T/F
5. Action research can combine qualitative and quantitative methods.   T/F
6. You can count on all proven research to be true.   T/F
7. Focus groups provide valuable information in qualitative research.   T/F
8. You can use the APA style to cite research regardless of the field of study.   T/F
9. Qualitative research cannot involve quantitative methods.   T/F
10. A works-cited list is the same as a bibliography.   T/F

Collecting and Conducting Research

There are two broad categories of research: *quantitative* and *qualitative*. Below are brief explanations so that you can understand the basics of each:

- *Quantitative research* collects numerical data to explain, predict, and/or control phenomena of interest. Quantitative research employs the scientific method to test research designed to predict whether an event happened by chance or whether there is a *cause-effect relationship*. It starts with a *hypothesis*, or "an explanation that can be tested." Quantitative research is rigorously applied in the medical field, but it is also used in education and the social and physical sciences, as well as business and economics.

- *Qualitative research* collects narrative data to gain insight into phenomena of interest. Qualitative research entails gathering information through *surveys, questionnaires, focus groups*, and *interviews*. It identifies beliefs and opinions that businesses can use to identify the needs of clientele, make marketing decisions, and develop new products. Qualitative research does *not* seek a cause-effect relationship; it simply seeks to identify the current state of a specific topic.

The primary goal of all research, quantitative or qualitative, is to obtain *unbiased, objective* results. Credible research does *not* take a position and then seek proof to confirm it. Rather, credible research asks a question and then objectively evaluates evidence, with the data determining the conclusions.

EXPLORE

Think of the last time you used a piece of quantitative or qualitative research. Did you agree with the findings or find flaws in the way the research was conducted or the conclusions it made? Did the research help shape your thinking?

A Review of the Literature

The first step in any type of formal research is reviewing information that others have already discovered; the work of specialists provides a springboard for your thesis or hypothesis. To be credible, your research must include information from reputable, *established* publishing houses, periodicals, associations, and organizations.

A thorough review of the literature includes all types of sources. Use print and electronic sources as well as microfilm or microfiche. If your library does not have what you need, you may request material through an interlibrary loan—a reason to start your research early.

In addition to books and periodicals, many Web sites contain important information. However, *some* online sources are not credible because no authority screens information posted on the Web. To ensure the credibility of online sources, follow these tips:

- Look for impartial sites sponsored by large, credible organizations, such as the American Medical Association and the U.S. Bureau of Labor Statistics. (In other words, individuals or small private organizations that have been around for only a short or indiscernible amount of time may *not* be credible.)

- Identify how long the site has been in operation; the longer, the better.

- Identify how often the site is updated. Some sites are posted and left unchanged for years.

- Check to see whether the site is linked to other sites you consider reputable.

- Evaluate whether the site provides information that answers your questions accurately and objectively.

Also consider doing the following:

- Use sources your library has already screened *before* you put your topic into an outside search engine. (Your library has screened many sources through online subscriptions, databases, and CD-ROMs.)

COACHING TIP

Brainstorming Revisited
When you brainstorm with a team, do the following to ensure that you are productive:

1. Inform everyone of the topic before the meeting: minds start working as soon as a problem is defined.
2. Divide into small groups if your group has more than ten members.
3. Add ground rules: do not judge or evaluate ideas; remain open to all ideas, even odd and "crazy" ones.
4. Build on other people's ideas: extend a line of thought.
5. Use whiteboards, flip charts, and Post-it notes to capture ideas.
6. Appoint a note taker, if necessary.
7. Encourage your team members to have fun while they are brainstorming.

As you and your teammates meet to define and research problems, do you find yourselves going in and out of brainstorming sessions? Next time, be aware and let the creative energy flow— it's part of the process.

- Compare how information on a Web site meshes with the print materials in your research. (Since print materials are scrutinized heavily during the publishing process, online sources that agree with print sources can be considered more seriously.)
- Discuss your source with your local librarian if you have a question.

Action Research

The types of qualitative research that you are likely to use are *surveys, focus groups,* and *interviews.* These tools are part of a qualitative approach to research known as *action research.* Action research is a method that assists the researcher in collecting information to use in an immediate application. Thus, the researcher "takes action" *as* the improved understanding (or research) occurs.

According to L. R. Gay and Peter Airasian, action research is carried out in a *cyclical* manner; here are the four basic steps of action research:[2]

1. *Identifying a problem* or question.
2. *Conducting a meeting* or brainstorming session to gain information.
3. *Analyzing research data* or information.
4. *Taking action* to rectify the problem or illuminate the question.

Action research provides feedback that assists in making decisions that lead to effective change. In addition, action research can involve both quantitative (numbers, statistics) and qualitative (feelings, beliefs, opinions) data.

Consider ways you can include action research in your personal and professional life to get better results. For example, if you wish to improve team communication, ask for feedback about what works well in getting a job done and what creates barriers to making progress. This informal "testing of the water" can make a difference.

EXPLORE

How does conducting action research differ from problem solving in general? How can you incorporate action research into the way you conduct your business?

Surveys, Focus Groups, and Interviews

The most popular type of qualitative research involves asking people their opinions about an issue or product. Surveys, focus groups, and interviews are important *listening tools.*

Depending on the purpose and the types of questions, information can be collected from individuals or from small groups. Let's examine each approach.

Surveys   You can develop simple surveys without advanced science. People generally like to share their opinions because they feel more important when they think their views matter.

Determine what you would like to ask, and then construct your survey. Keep your survey brief and focused; be honest about why you are asking for the information and how it will be used. To design a survey, first figure out what's important to know versus what isn't important. Setting priorities is a recurring issue; much time is wasted by addressing unimportant issues that camouflage the real ones. Here are some things to consider:

1. Meet with colleagues to discuss the issues and brainstorm a list of questions.
2. Wait a day or two before you edit your list, but then edit it ruthlessly.
3. Keep your survey as simple as possible.
4. Depending on the topic, your survey may be more effective if respondents remain anonymous; choose the approach that will produce the most accurate results.
5. If time permits, do a pilot test of your survey with a small sample to ensure the design meets your needs.
6. Set a time frame, and then distribute the surveys.

7. Do not expect all surveys to be returned, and expect some to be late.

8. Tally results.

9. Report the results in an unbiased, honest way (whether you like the results or not).

Focus Groups Companies often hire outside consultants to facilitate focus groups because of intricate interpersonal dynamics. If you are not using a trained facilitator, here are some tips for running a focus group:

1. Develop a clear purpose and objectives.

2. Identify issues and brainstorm questions to ask.

3. Edit your list of questions so that you do not collect too much detail.

4. Select a group large enough to provide diversity of thought but small enough to let everyone feel free to participate in the discussion. (The average number is often between 8 and 15 participants. Also, the only accurate way to recruit a focus group is through random sampling of a defined population.)

5. Solicit input through open-ended questions and statements.

6. Keep the tone of questions neutral:

Incorrect: What do you think is wrong with the climate in the company?

Corrected: Describe the climate within the company.

7. Collect data.

8. Identify common themes.

When you report the information, do so without interpretation or bias. Consolidate *common themes* and reactions while respecting the importance of anonymity. If you betray a group's trust, you may lose your credibility; also, your indiscretion may cause someone to experience serious repercussions.

Interviews Individual interviews consume more time than other types of qualitative research and provide less generalized feedback; that's because the information relates to one individual and not a group. Interviews are a good method to use when you are working with a population of 20 or fewer people.

Interviews are used for many types of informal research, such as making hiring or promotional decisions and doing job performance appraisals. Another way to collect important information is to interview an expert in the field.

In the next section, you will be asked to display your information in a simple chart, graph, or table.

PRACTICE

Instructions: In this exercise, you will practice your interviewing and listening skills. An interview is not a two-way conversation: as an interviewer, do *not* present your own thinking; instead, solicit opinions, beliefs, experiences, and information from your interviewee. (Thus, you shouldn't find yourself "disagreeing" with anything the interviewee says.)

Keep your interview brief and focused, or else it will be difficult to consolidate your information and find common themes. Choose a topic that you want to learn more about, such as losing weight, buying a new or used car, or finding a job. In other words, select a topic in which you have a genuine, immediate interest.

Here's a process to follow:

1. What is your topic?

2. Develop a list of questions to solicit information, experience, and recommendations from your interviewees.

3. Interview four or five people.

4. Tabulate your results:

    a. What common themes can you identify?

    b. What did you learn from those you interviewed?

5. What results or questions are conducive to being displayed in a chart, graph, or table?

6. What did you learn about yourself as a result of conducting your research?

Displaying Research

Displaying research spans different levels of complexity: you are displaying research when you put someone else's words in quotation marks or when you turn complicated data into charts, graphs, or tables. Before discussing charts, graphs, and tables, we'll examine how to display quotations.

Quotations

To display quotations, you often must use other sorts of punctuation besides double quotation marks, such as ellipsis marks, brackets, and single quotation marks. Below are some guidelines for displaying quotations.

Short Quotations   Incorporate direct quotes that are *less than four lines long* into your narrative and set them off by using quotation marks. When placing punctuation, here are a few rules to remember:

*   *Commas* and *periods* (including ellipsis marks) always go inside quotation marks.

    Examples: According to Robert Browning, "Less is more."

    Robert said "Less is more," but I don't know whether he was referring to the pasta or the sauce.

*   *Semicolons* and *colons* always go outside quotation marks.

    Examples: When it comes to writing, Browning believes "less is more"; however, according to Mies van der Rohe, the statement also applies to design.

    Robert explained the statement "Less is more": simplicity trumps complexity.

*   References to *footnotes* are placed directly after the closing quotation mark (no space added).

    Example: According to the Infectious Disease Clinics of America, the virus can spread quickly: "Insects, birds and some species of animal are carriers . . . across the Australian continent."[10]

*   The placement of *question marks* (and *exclamation points*) depends on the meaning. That is, does the quotation itself pose the question, or is the quotation within a sentence that poses the question?

    Examples: Did Browning really say "Less is more"?

    It was Elizabeth who said "What are our options?"

Long Quotations   For a quotation of *four or more lines,* display the quotation as an extract, set off from the text, by doing the following:

- Indent ½ inch from both left and right side margins. (Do not use quotation marks; the indentation signals the reader that you are displaying a quote.)

- Single-space the quotation.

- Leave one blank line before and after the displayed quotation.

Quotations Within Quotations   How to display a quotation within a quotation depends on whether you are starting with a long quote or a short quote:

- *Short quotes* (two or three lines of quoted material within text): Display the main quote between double quotation marks, and display the internal quote between single quotation marks.

  Example: According to Kegan, "Carl Rogers's 'client-centered' or 'nondirective' therapy has had an enormous influence on the training and practice of three generations of counselors and therapists."[15]

- *Long quotes* (four or more lines displayed as an extract):

  Example: *Feeling* is the function by which one comes to decisions by weighing relative values and merits of the issues. Feeling relies on an understanding of personal values and group values; thus it is more subjective than thinking. Nevertheless, "Feeling, like thinking, is a *rational* function, since values in general are assigned according to the laws of reason." (Jung, 1921/1971, 9.435)

Indirect Quotes or Paraphrases   Do not use quotation marks for indirect quotes, such as paraphrases of someone's words. Credit the source by using the person's name in the text and/or providing a footnote or endnote.

Omissions in Quotations   Use ellipsis marks to show omission of a word or words. Ellipsis marks consist of three spaced periods.

If one or more sentences are omitted between other sentences, use three spaced periods after the terminal punctuation of the preceding sentence.

  Example: We have recommended a course of action that will bring good results. . . . The choice is theirs.

As an example, consider again the fable developed by Michael C. Mercil (which appears in Chapter 7 of this text). The first quote below is Mercil's original text; the second quote is an abridged version in which ellipsis marks were added where information was taken out:

  Original: Imagine that in your country, from the time of the first people, today, and far into the future, everyone that was ever born or will be born, was born with two legs, two arms, two eyes, a nose, a mouth, and a pair of sunglasses. The lenses in the sunglasses are yellow.[4]

  Abridged: Imagine that in your country . . . everyone . . . was born with two legs, two arms, two eyes, a nose, a mouth, and a pair of sunglasses. The lenses in the sunglasses are yellow.

If the omission comes at the end of a sentence of quoted material, add one more period to indicate the end of the sentence.

Additions in Quotations   At times, it is necessary to add a word or two to quoted material so that the reader can make sense of it, especially when words have been taken out. When you add a word or two of your own, put them between brackets: [ ].

PRACTICE

Instructions: Insert punctuation into the sentences below. For example:

Incorrect: It was Ruth Gordon, an actress, who said, courage is like a muscle. We strengthen it with use.

Corrected: It was Ruth Gordon, an actress, who said, "Courage is like a muscle. We strengthen it with use."

1. According to Hippocrates to do nothing is sometimes a good remedy.

     _____

     _____

2. To quote Nhat Hahn at any moment, you have a choice, that either leads you closer to your spirit or further away from it.

     _____

     _____

3. Think not those faithful who praise all thy words and actions but those who kindly reprove thy faults was the sage advice given by Socrates.

     _____

     _____

4. In The Little Prince by Antoine de Saint-Exupéry, you will find the quote it is only with the heart that one can see rightly; what is essential is invisible to the eye.

     _____

     _____

     _____

5. Another quote by Antoine de Saint-Exupéry is What saves a man is to take a step. Then another step. It is always the same step, but you have to take it.

     _____

     _____

     _____

6. To quote Helen Keller Security is mostly a superstition. It does not exist in nature, nor do the children of men as a whole experience it. Avoiding danger is no safer in the long run than outright exposure. Life is either a daring adventure, or nothing.

     _____

     _____

     _____

Graphics: Charts, Graphs, and Tables

At times, visual displays speak more loudly than words. Displaying numbers and other concepts in charts and graphs clarifies meaning at a glance. Words can include excuses or explanations mixed in with the numbers, thus making it difficult to illuminate real trends.

   As you display your research, keep in mind that the information is the important issue, not a fancy display. Don't try to impress your audience with "smoke and mirrors." Let your concepts and ideas lead the way, with the displays remaining secondary to the information they support.

Bar Charts   Use a bar chart to compare and contrast up to six different items. You can show relationships over a period of time by clustering several different groups in the chart.

FIGURE HG4.1 | Bar Charts

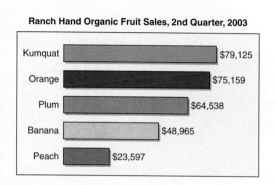

Ranch Hand Organic Fruit Sales, 2nd Quarter, 2003

(a) Horizontal

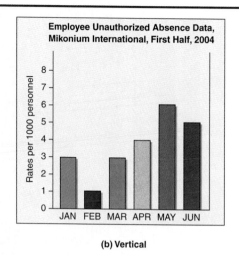

Employee Unauthorized Absence Data, Mikonium International, First Half, 2004

(b) Vertical

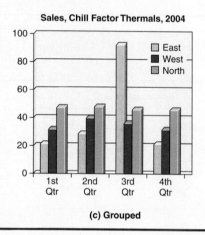

Sales, Chill Factor Thermals, 2004

(c) Grouped

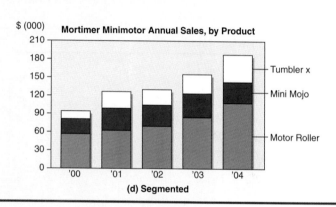

Mortimer Minimotor Annual Sales, by Product

(d) Segmented

Examples of bar charts are shown in Figure HG4.1. The following guidelines apply to any type of bar chart:

- Display relationships horizontally or vertically.
- Limit the number of bars to six.
- Make sure bar widths and the space between bars are equal.
- Arrange bars in a logical order (by length, by age, by date) to make comparisons easier.

Pie Charts   Use pie charts when the various components add up to 100 percent. (See Figure HG4.2.) Follow these guidelines:

- Limit the number of categories to six; if you have more than six, try to combine them.
- Label categories directly and add percentages. (Avoid using a key, if possible.)
- Place the most important section at the 12 o'clock position to emphasize a point.

Line Graphs   Use line graphs to show trends. (See Figure HG4.3.) Follow these guidelines:

- Use left-justified, 10- or 12-point bold for line graph titles.
- State what data the graph illustrates.
- Label each axis clearly.
- Start the vertical axis with zero (unless there is a good reason not to).
- In a time graph, indicate time on the horizontal axis, and display units of measurement on the vertical axis.

FIGURE HG4.2 | Pie Chart

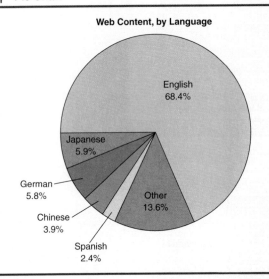

Web Content, by Language

Source: Vilaweb.com, 2001, as quoted by emarketer.

FIGURE HG4.3 | Line Charts

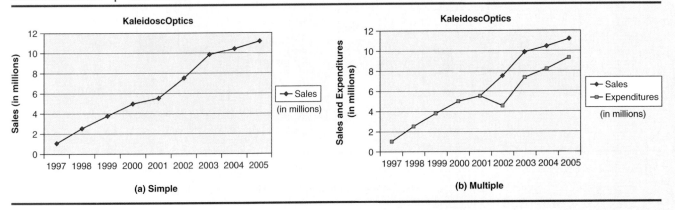

PRACTICE

Instructions: For this exercise, use the data you gleaned from the interviews you conducted in the Practice exercise on page 295. Choose two or more variables from the interviews, and construct charts that summarize the response data from those you interviewed.

For example, if your interview topic was "buying a used car," you could compare how many interviewees bought used cars in the past with how many would buy a used car in the future.

Citing Research

There are four common systems for citation in business, social sciences, and humanities. Usually, the person or organization commissioning your work will specify the documentation system you are to use. You are likely to follow the system outlined in one of the following:

- *The Gregg Reference Manual* (GRM)
- *The Chicago Manual of Style* (CMS)
- The *Publication Manual of the American Psychological Association* (APA)
- The *MLA Handbook for Writers of Research Papers* (Modern Language Association—MLA)

COACHING TIP

Plagiarism When you use someone else's words and present them as your own, that's *plagiarism*. Plagiarism is a unique form of stealing. At best, it can result in loss of credibility; at worst, it can result in academic punitive action or a lawsuit.

Using even part of someone else's sentence without crediting that person is plagiarizing. *Paraphrasing,* or putting someone else's words into your own words, can be a form of plagiarism if you do not give proper credit for the idea the words express. The same holds true for summarizing someone else's idea. However, you do not have to document general knowledge.

Proper citation adds credibility as it improves your confidence. For more specific details about referencing, consult *The Gregg Reference Manual* or another authoritative source for guidance.

But that's not the complete story. While *The Gregg Reference Manual* presents guidelines for business writing applications, *The Chicago Manual of Style* offers two sets of guidelines: one for fine arts and humanities (academic) applications, the other for social and physical science applications. If you go on to study in medicine or the physical sciences, you are likely to cite references in the Council of Biology Editors (CBE) style. Before you turn in any work, check to make sure you are using the correct referencing style.

Plagiarism

With the use of computers and the Web, taking the words of others and patching them in as your own has become easy but remains unethical. The only way you will learn the important concepts and principles that research reveals is by *developing your own ideas.*

The same advances in technology that make plagiarism easier to accomplish also make it easier to detect. Many instructors screen for plagiarism *before* they even read a paper. With only a partial sentence, your professor can immediately identify the real source. If you have any doubts about whether you should cite a source, go ahead and cite it.

Unfortunately, every year many students find out the hard way that plagiarism costs too much in terms of personal shame and lost credits. By making the effort to do your own work, you will not only improve your knowledge and skills but also get the appropriate credit for your work.

What to Credit

Not all information needs to be documented. For example, information that is considered common knowledge (something generally known to everyone) or facts available from a wide variety of sources need not be credited. According to *The New St. Martin's Handbook,*[3] the following information needs to be documented:

- Direct quotations and paraphrases.
- Facts that are not widely known or assertions that are arguable.
- Judgments, opinions, and claims of others.
- Statistics, charts, tables, and graphs from any source.
- Help provided by friends, instructors, or others.

Let's first take a look at the two most common uses of formal credits, for *direct quotations* and *paraphrases,* and the use of informal credits. Then we will examine how to assign legal claim to information in business.

Words and Ideas

Formal Credit:

- *Direct quotation:* Using someone else's exact words requires that the words be set off; for short quotes, use quotation marks; for quotes of four or more lines, set off the quotation by indenting the margins at least $1/2$ inch on either side. You can use an in-text reference along with a footnote or endnote.

- *Paraphrase:* Paraphrasing is putting someone else's idea into your own words. When you paraphrase and cite your source, you add credibility to your work. *Note:* Making a few changes in word order, leaving out a word or two, or substituting similar words is not paraphrasing—doing so amounts to plagiarism.

Novice writers have the most difficulty with paraphrasing. "Incorrectly paraphrased" information usually ends up with a similar sentence structure. With a bit of deconstructing, the original source can be identified. True paraphrasing occurs when you read material, digest it, and then write about the concepts in your own words. However, the idea still belongs to the original author and needs to be credited. Paraphrasing incorrectly can be considered a form of "cut and paste" plagiarism.

Informal Credit:

• When sharing someone else's original idea, mention the person's name in connection with the idea. In the business world, information isn't tracked as it is in the academic world. Most of your writing will involve solving current problems, conveying immediate information, and developing informal proposals for action. Thus, most business writing involves no citation (though at times, citation can be a powerful way to persuade your reader or audience).

Trademarks, Patents, Copyrights, and Incorporation   In business, instead of citation, ideas that merit ownership go through any one of a number of formal, legal processes. To protect themselves, individuals and businesses can register names, ideas, designs, logos, slogans, and complete works with the federal government to obtain trademarks, patents, or copyrights; they can register with state governments for incorporation.

Working Bibliography

As you collect and use information that others have discovered or developed, compile a *working bibliography*. Though each system of documentation has slight variations from the others, the references in each all contain similar information. Record references on note cards, in a small notebook, or in a special file on your computer as you collect your research. Here is the kind of information you will need regardless of the style you use:

Books:

• Author
• Title
• Page number
• Publisher and location
• Year of publication

Periodicals:

• Author
• Title of article
• Title of periodical
• Volume and issue number and page number
• Date of publication

Web sites:

• Author (if known).
• Title of document.
• The uniform resource locator (URL) network address (including any path and file names), enclosed in angle brackets.
• Date the information was posted on the Web site (if available, this is often at the bottom of the home page).
• Date on which you accessed the information.
• If the source was previously published in print, also include the publication date.

Because electronic sources are relatively new in the world of communication, the standards for documenting them are not yet fixed and are sometimes confusing. To save yourself time and energy, print out a hard copy or download the accessed information.

Some Common Elements

All citation systems require that sources be cited in the text where the material appears and be fully referenced elsewhere as footnotes, endnotes, or a bibliographic list. This cross-referencing provides the reader with complete information. Each referencing system uses its own set of terms, as shown below:

GRM	Footnotes, endnotes, textnotes, bibliography
CMS	Footnotes, endnotes, bibliography
MLA	In-text citation, works-cited list, works-consulted list
APA	In-text citation, references list

Footnote information is placed at the bottom of the page; endnotes are displayed on a separate page at the end of each chapter or the end of the work. For footnotes and endnotes, a raised number (superscript) is placed at the end of the sentence in which the reference occurs.

For all citation methods, you may cite one source several times in your manuscript (showing that you are paraphrasing, quoting, or drawing ideas from its content in several places). However, you need to include a full reference note for the source (author, title, publisher, and so on) only one time in your bibliography, works-cited list, or references list.

In a bibliography or references list, you can include sources that you consult but do not actually cite in your work. Note that if you are using the MLA system, you list noncited sources in a separate works-consulted list. Only include significant noncited sources on this list.

If you can, find a passion for research and incorporate it into your daily life. You will find yourself making more educated decisions that lead to better results.

References

1. Fred Menger, quoted from "Aphorisms about Models," <http://www.chebucto.ns.ca/science/AIMET/models>, accessed December 7, 2004.

2. L. R. Gay and P. Airasian, *Educational Research, Competencies for Analysis and Applications,* 7th edition, Merrill Prentice Hall, 2003, pp. 263–273.

3. Andrea Lunsford and Robert Connors, *The New St. Martin's Handbook,* Bedford/St. Martin's, Boston, 2001, pp. 495–497.

Key for Learning Inventory

1.	T	6.	F
2.	F	7.	T
3.	F	8.	F
4.	T	9.	F
5.	T	10.	T

Getting a Job

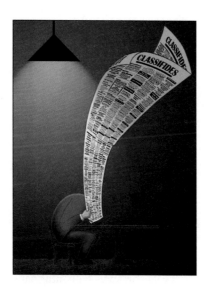

It is not the strongest of the species that survive, nor the most intelligent, but the one most responsive to change. —Charles Darwin ■

No matter how smart, talented, and skilled you are, looking for a job can make you question everything you have ever achieved. That's because the job search process is different from other activities and projects. It's not just that you are using your talents to solve a problem: it's that your skills, talents, achievements, and attitude become the *central theme* of the project. Like it or not, you are at the center of your job search project; the job itself is secondary.

If you are like most people, you take your skills and personal qualities for granted. However, now you need to create your unique *job search profile* so that you can showcase it in your quest to start your career.

Let's explore how you can get in the driver's seat to *manage your career* (not just find a job). The first step to success is identifying your *transferable skills;* you will then be prepared to develop a résumé and prepare for interviews. Though these activities might be some of the most challenging you will confront, they will also be the most satisfying. Think about it: everything you have achieved until this moment can contribute to your career.

OBJECTIVES

When you have completed Chapter 9, you will be able to:

1. Identify your transferable skills.
2. Develop your job search profile.
3. Use networking as a job search strategy.
4. Design your résumé and cover letter.
5. Incorporate electronic communication in your job search.
6. Prepare for a job interview.
7. Use follow-up tools to reinforce a job application.

Learning Inventory

1. Job survival skills encompass your skills and experience, but not your attitude.	T/F
2. Networking is not an important activity when you are not looking for a job.	T/F
3. Send a thank-you letter within two days after an interview.	T/F
4. The first part of looking for a job is developing your job search profile.	T/F
5. Always be prepared with a question or two of your own when on a job interview.	T/F
6. A contact letter is used as a letter of application.	T/F
7. Even if you do not have formal work experience, you have a solid background on which to build.	T/F
8. Transferable skills are job survival skills.	T/F
9. Volunteering in a professional organization is an unpaid career opportunity.	T/F
10. Before speaking to a hiring manager, prepare a 10-second script describing your qualifications.	T/F

■ SECTION A: JOB SURVIVAL SKILLS

Verbalizing your job survival skills amounts to marketing yourself; to do that, you first need to identify your unique qualities so that you establish your **job search profile.** Your job search profile provides base information for your résumé and prepares you for interviewing.

Confidently verbalizing your skills and abilities is different from applying them. In fact, you probably feel more comfortable using your skills than you do talking about them. Well, that will change: It's time to *sing your own praises*—but before you do, you have to *compose the lyrics and the melody.*

Skills, Not Titles or Degrees

Have you ever been asked this question: *What do you want to be when you . . . ?* Most of us fumble with this question until we can answer it with a job title: teacher, accountant, mechanic, doctor, nurse, lawyer, engineer, and so on. In fact, life can feel a bit uncomfortable until settling on a college major and ultimately a job title. But titles and majors are *labels,* and they do not accurately capture who you are or what you are capable of doing.

Because shifts in the job market are now common, labels (job titles and college majors) limit a job seeker's opportunities. New job titles are created every day as traditional titles are eliminated or reduced. People who have had a certain title all their lives may now find that specific job title no longer exists in their locale. As a result, talented and skilled people are discovering that they must relocate, retrain, or repackage themselves to earn a living.

COACHING TIP

Lateral Transfers Promotions are not the only route to success in the business world. **Some Career Myths:**

- Career changes must be upward.
- Promotions come within two years.
- Success means job security until retirement.

Lateral transfers are job changes that do not include a promotion, and they are *good* for your career. By broadening your skill base, you prepare yourself for a wider range of job functions. If your company reorganizes or goes through downsizing, you will have more flexibility for being placed in a new position.

Thus, be a *jack of all trades:* the more you know, the more valuable you are. This flexibility opens doors to numerous organizational opportunities.

Though a title will not follow a person throughout a career, a person's skills, talents, attitudes, and achievements will. Versatility has never been more important in achieving career success and then maintaining it. Thus, though you may have started this chapter thinking you would learn about job search techniques, you were only partly correct. You will actually begin your job search by identifying your skills and seeing how they transfer to *any* business environment. Then you will apply your skills to finding a specific job.

Transferable Skills

Until this point, you have worked toward your degree; now you are working toward your career. Though your degree is essential, you must now "reframe" your academic achievements to focus on your skills. Here's why: Your degree will get you in the door, but your **transferable skills** will get you the job and lead to career growth.

You may be thinking to yourself that you don't have experience or transferable skills, but that simply is *not* true. Even without work experience, you have developed valuable abilities through your studies; you have also demonstrated a winning attitude by completing difficult projects under stressful conditions. Now, by dissecting your experiences, you will identify the skills, attitudes, and knowledge that have led to your current success; those same skills will go with you on your journey to attaining success in the business world.

Defining marketable skills is a challenge (especially when you think that you don't have any), so approach this task with an open mind. Some of your skills have come from interests or hobbies, and you may not even be aware of what you learned. As you compile your list of skills, ask your friends, family, and colleagues to assist you in developing your job search profile. After you demonstrate your skills, you will set goals, write your résumé, and pursue your dream job. Part of the reason for developing a job search profile is to open your mind to possibilities from which you might otherwise walk away. Once you join the business world, one thing will lead to another. By being flexible, you will have access to more opportunities.

Let's start to develop your job search profile by exploring four basic skill areas: people, knowledge, tasks, and personal qualities.

EXPLORE

1. Before you get started defining your skills and doing your résumé, take a moment to write about how you feel about searching for a job.
2. What aspects of searching for a job or starting your career will present challenges?
3. Write a few objectives that relate to your job search—what are some things you need to accomplish to secure your "dream job"?

Working With People *How do you work with people?* Consider formal and informal experiences at your school and place of worship, in part- and full-time jobs, in group sports, and in associations and volunteer groups. Below are some terms to provoke your thinking; go through the list slowly, and notice your impressions as well as the specific experiences that some of the terms bring to mind.

> Communicating / Working on teams / Working independently / Leading / Managing / Evaluating / Giving feedback / Supervising / Receiving feedback / Teaching / Training / Facilitating / Selling / Soliciting / Phoning / Marketing / Motivating / Organizing events / Delegating / Counseling / Advising / Negotiating / Caretaking / Serving / Mediating / Entertaining / Expressing humor / Being compassionate / Listening

Now take a few moments to start your job search profile. First, identify three terms listed above that describe you and seem to stand out from the others. For each of these terms, recall

COMMUNICATION CHALLENGES

Changing Lanes Even after you secure your first "permanent" job, you may find yourself reapplying for jobs throughout your career. According to the U.S. Department of Labor, Americans change jobs on average about every 4.5 years. Statistics predict that people in their twenties just starting out in the job market will have had three jobs by the time they turn 30.

Some professionals suggest that changing jobs and companies is a necessary part of the process of advancing a career. However, companies still value longevity, so try to stay on your first full-time job a minimum of one year.

Consider your own work history. How many jobs have you had? Have you stayed on a job long enough to develop a track record even though there may not have been room for advancement? Have you tried to learn aspects of the business other than your own job? Every good decision you make contributes to a successful career.

CHALLENGE:
Assume you've been working as an assistant to Elliott Campbell, the president of a company that manages and operates snack bars in gyms and health clubs. You're interested in many aspects of the business and see more interesting work, more opportunity, better pay, and a chance to get away from a desk in the company's sales and marketing division. Elliott values and depends on the work you do for him and has openly discouraged your aspirations to move into another position.

Strategize an approach, and then compose a message to Elliott explaining your position. Ask yourself: *Are there any decisions I need to make before I write my letter?*

an experience in which you used your people skills successfully. For example:

> *Giving feedback:* When I worked on a team project, I gave objective feedback even though it was difficult. Some team members did not agree with me, and I needed to defend my position until they understood my point. As a result, we ended up with a stronger team and a better project.

> *Serving:* I work part-time at the local diner and take pride in assisting customers in whatever way I can. Sometimes they can't make up their minds, and I'm honest about the best things to order.

For each of the three terms you chose, give a specific example of how you used your people skills successfully.

1. _____

   _____

2. _____

   _____

3. _____

   _____

Identifying Knowledge You Can Apply   In which subjects or areas have you developed knowledge? In addition to formal learning, consider hobbies and interests. Circle three or more of the terms below that reflect your abilities:

> English / Literature / Writing (composing, editing, revising) / Communication skills / Languages (speaking, writing, translating, interpreting) / Global communication / Business / Organization and management / Financial accounting / Math / Statistics / Accounting / Budgeting / Calculus / Science / Physics / Biology / Medicine / Pharmaceuticals / Music / Instruments / Voice / Theater / Filmmaking / Art / Archeology / Artifacts / Anthropology / Law / Criminal / Civil / Police science / Political science / History / Social sciences / Psychology / Sociology / Social work / Counseling / Physical sciences / Sports / Nutrition / Cosmetology / Physical therapy / Organizational development / Human resource development / Fund-raising / Child care / Early child development / Elementary or secondary education

What other subjects or major areas can you identify? Look through your college catalog, and list specific classes and assignments that were particularly meaningful. Can you come up with three or more subjects in which you feel competent? For example:

> I feel confident with my *writing* skills. I can compose, edit, and revise e-mail messages, letters, and reports.

> I like working with *numbers.* I make a budget, follow it, and balance my checking account online; I also have good *computer skills.*

> *Nutrition* and *sports* have always been major interests. I *coach* my friends when we're at the gym, and they've seen good results.

In the spaces below, identify three subjects, and write a sentence describing your experience or competence with each one.

1. _____

   _____

2. _____

   _____

3. _____

   _____

Working on Tasks   *What kinds of tasks can you perform?* Consider all the classes you have taken as well as your job experience (paid or volunteer). Also consider your *hobbies* and *interests:* these activities are important to employers. *Which tasks can you perform well? Which tasks do you enjoy?* As you go through the list below, circle the ones that you do well or enjoy. (This part of your job search profile relates to *tasks;* later in this section, you'll list part- and full-time jobs.) Use the mix of nouns and verbs below to generate a list of tasks you do well:

> Computers / CAD / Keyboarding / Drafting / PowerPoint / Web design /
> Automotives / Machinery / Repair / Design / Paint / Draw / Sketch / Sculpt /
> Construct / Build / Maintain / Restore / Analyze / Solve problems / Troubleshoot /
> Survey / Landscape / Gather information / Organize and file / Spreadsheets / Tables /
> Graphs / Letters / E-mail / Memos / Agendas / Minutes / Reports / Proposals /
> Set goals / Canvass / Meet quotas / Read / Write / Edit / Work with children /
> Counsel / Wait tables / Caddy / Greet and receive / Clean houses, cars, or offices /
> Play music / Compose / Cashier / Style hair / Drive / Walk dogs / Care for children /
> Coach / Groom horses / Manage / Supervise

(You'll put your final list in parallel form before the final draft of your résumé.)

What other tasks (not listed here) relate to your experience? _____

Even though some tasks may not seem directly related to your future employment, every task you do well contributes to your unique profile. Employers like to hire people who have broad interests. Thus, while you may not put some of this information on your résumé, it might come up during an interview.

In the spaces below, give five examples of successful experiences you've had in connection with your hobbies or interests. (An experience may include more than one task, as in the second example below, which involves taking minutes, organizing and filing papers, and making phone calls.) For example:

During my free time, I enjoy walking dogs. I posted an announcement in my neighborhood about my dog-walking service and get several jobs a month. The dogs are fun to work with, and their owners are grateful that I can help them out in a bind.

My mother is a member of an organization that helps raise funds for the disease lupus. I helped the director by taking minutes at one of their meetings and then organizing and filing papers in their office. I even made some calls to solicit money for fund-raising. Every part of it was fun because I was helping people.

My phone work is good. I enjoy making follow-up calls to tell someone about a meeting or let a member know what we did at a meeting that she or he missed.

Examples of successful experiences:

1. _____
   _____

2. _____
   _____

3. _____
   _____

4. _____
   _____

5. _____
   _____

In addition to itemizing the specific tasks you performed, you should also describe what you learned about yourself and others from performing these tasks. This is difficult to do because most people are used to "doing a task" rather than analyzing what they learned from it. Select three of your tasks or "work experiences," and in the spaces below record what you learned about your skills and attitudes. For example:

When I volunteered at the lupus organization, I acted friendly and confident, even though I didn't feel secure at first. I was also patient with clients on the phone. When I made mistakes, I took responsibility for them and corrected them quickly.

When I posted the sign for my dog-walking business, this showed initiative and courage. I didn't know if I'd get any business and was very excited when people started to call.

Tasks and learning experiences:

1. _____
   _____

2. _____
   _____

3. _____
   _____

The unfamiliar is challenging for everyone—until it becomes *familiar.* Reviewing tasks you do well will build your confidence, remind you of your competence, and put your job search into perspective. Thus, you are spending your time well by identifying specific tasks that you are good at *and* that you enjoy.

Identifying Personal Qualities   You are unique whether or not you realize it. *What are the personal qualities that shape you into who you are? Which of the following qualities describe you?*

Reliable / Dependable / Motivated / Persistent / Optimistic / Self-reliant / Strong / Independent / Capable / Supportive / Eager / Focused / Purposeful / Task oriented / Disciplined / Friendly / Persuasive / Artistic / Committed / Easygoing / Encouraging / Flexible / Well balanced / Open-minded / Accepting / Prompt / Courteous / Patient /

Dedicated / Supportive / Loyal / Adaptable / Credible / Ethical / Competent / Kind / Helpful / Determined / Confident / Decisive / Creative / Enthusiastic / Honest / Responsible

You may have outstanding qualities not listed here. Close your eyes and reflect for a moment. *What adjectives come to mind when you think of yourself?* _____

Write three of your positive qualities below, and give examples of situations in which you displayed them to get a job done or help someone.

1. _____

_____

2. _____

_____

3. _____

_____

Now that you've established several good qualities, you will need to think of one or two weaknesses that you want to improve; call them your **growing edges** if you wish. When prospective employers ask about your weaknesses, you need to answer honestly. Human resource (HR) professionals interview hundreds of applicants and can see through insincere answers. If you are honest yet focused and optimistic about your weaknesses, you will actually score points. (You see, we all have weaknesses, whether we like to admit it or not.)

State your weakness in a positive way. For example:

Incorrect: I'm always late getting my work done, and I need to get control of my schedule.
Corrected: Sometimes I get so involved in solving a problem that I lose track of time. I'm working on structuring my time so that my schedule is more balanced. Overall, it feels as if I have more time and more control over my time.

Incorrect: When I work on a project, I'm a perfectionist. Because I want everything perfect, I worry about it and then put things off till the last minute; sometimes I miss deadlines.
Corrected: I'm a bit of a perfectionist. Rather than working on a project to get it perfect, my goal now is to achieve "good quality," which is a more realistic aim. As a result, I am getting better at producing good work and then moving on to other projects. My schedule is getting more balanced, and I'm getting better results.

What are some changes you are making or growing through? State one weakness below; be honest, but don't dwell on the negative. Focus instead on the results you are achieving.

_____

_____

_____

Now that you've thought about your unique skills and qualities, it is time to seek objective input. When you are on a job interview, one of the questions that you may be asked is, "How do others perceive you?" The following exercise prepares you for that question.

Ask three friends or associates who know you well to describe your skills and attitudes. Choose people who are positive and supportive. Let them know that you are doing research for your job search profile. If feasible, ask them to give you something in writing via a short note or e-mail. By getting some feedback in writing, you can build a discussion around it and refer to it later.

What's Your Track Record? This question isn't about your ability in track and field events—it is about your patterns of success and achievements.

When you go on an interview, be prepared with an example that shows your success over time and two or three achievements. You can even relate their significance; for example, perhaps you are the first person in your family to graduate from college or maybe you recently won an award. These types of notable experiences give prospective employers insight into your personality and interests as well as into the way you apply your skills.

Though it may seem irrelevant to you, the prize you won in a 4-H club, the scouts, or a competition for building classic car models might be the hook that connects you to an employer. The interviewer might see your patience, attention to detail, or commitment; or maybe it will be your pride in workmanship or teamwork that shows through—desirable traits in a new hire.

Of course, use some discretion in citing your achievements. A prospective employer doesn't want to hear about personal milestones such as engagements or weddings; and no matter how cute your children are, save those stories for your friends and relatives.

Here are some questions you can ask:

- What are three adjectives that you would use to describe me?
- What are some tasks that you have seen me do well?
- In your eyes, what achievements have I made?
- Do you consider me a team player? A leader? A self-starter?
- What do you think are my growing edges or areas in which I can improve?

What are two or three additional questions that you can use when asking someone for feedback?

_____

_____

_____

You may be surprised at how positively others perceive you. If you have difficulty hearing good things about yourself, do not get into a debate over your skills or negate what is said; simply thank the person for the input. The same advice is true if you hear negative things—try to keep an open mind, and use the feedback to develop objectives for self-growth.

Take a few moments to reflect on the input and your accomplishments. In the spaces below, record the feedback you receive, especially if it is all verbal (rather than a written note or e-mail); otherwise, you are likely to lose the essence of your respondents' valuable information.

_____

_____

_____

PRACTICE

Instructions: After you have developed your feedback questions (above), identify three people from whom you can request feedback.

1. Send each of them a short e-mail explaining that you want his or her input. Include a few questions so that the person knows what you are asking.

2. In your message, ask when it would be a good time to have a short phone conference or meeting so that you can discuss the feedback.

3. After you meet, send each a short note thanking the person for his or her time and feedback.

Work Experience

Make a list of all paid or volunteer jobs you have had. For each, specify when you had the job. Instead of giving exact start and end dates, you can list just the months and years. You also want to have an idea of the amount of time you spent on each job, so *quantify* your experiences in terms of years, months, or even weeks. The quantity of time should accurately reflect the time you worked, so if you started toward the end of January and left at the beginning of March, you would put "7 weeks" rather than "3 months." For example:

Part-time Cashier, Market Store	January to March 1999	7 weeks
	July to August 1999	6 weeks
	December 1999	3 weeks
		(about 4 months)

Quantifying your experience in this way will give you an accurate estimate of your experience, especially with jobs that you start and stop at intervals, such as summer or holiday jobs. After you tally the specifics (as in the part-time cashier position listed above), your experience can be listed as follows:

Part-time Cashier, Market Store   January to December 1999   4 months

Now take a moment to record the jobs you have held and tally your job experience in months and years:

Job 1: Title/Company   **Dates**   **Time**

_____   _____   _____

                                              _____   _____

                                              _____   _____

                                      Total time: _____

Job 2: Title/Company   **Dates**   **Time**

_____   _____   _____

                                              _____   _____

                                              _____   _____

                                      Total time: _____

Next, for each position write three to five sentences that explain how you applied skills. Write _active sentences with strong verbs_ (see Table 10.1 on page 360 for a list of active words), and avoid filler verbs and phrases such as "I learned how to" or "I gained experience doing." For example:

Incorrect: While working as a cashier at the Market Store, _I learned how to communicate_ with all types of clients.

Revised: While working as a cashier, _I communicated_ effectively with all our clients.

Incorrect: While volunteering at the hospital, _I gained experience from helping_ nurses distribute medication.

Revised: While volunteering on the children's ward, _I helped_ nurses distribute medicine to children.

Incorrect: As an apprentice at the Car Exchange, _I was able to learn how_ to make minor repairs.

Revised: As an apprentice at the Car Exchange, _I assisted_ in minor repairs as well as changed oil, brake, and transmission fluids.

JOB EXPERIENCE SUMMARY

Example:

Cashier, Market Store   While at the Market Store, I communicated effectively with

From   1/99   to   12/99   customers and corrected my mistakes with confidence.

Total time: about 5 months   _____

1._____   _____

From_____to _____   _____

Total time: _____   _____

2._____   _____

From_____to _____   _____

Total time: _____   _____

3._____   _____

From_____to _____   _____

Total time: _____   _____

In this section, you have prepared extensive information about yourself. You will use this information on your résumé and for job interviews, topics that will be covered later in this chapter. In Section B, we'll explore networking, the informal aspect of a job search that contributes to your career in major ways and helps you manage your career at all levels.

EXPLORE

1. As you highlighted your work experience, what did you learn about yourself?
2. What did you learn about yourself from the feedback you received from friends and family?

 SECTION A: CONCEPT CHECK

1. What are job survival skills?
2. Why are transferable skills important in today's job market?
3. Why is it important to identify your weaknesses, or growing edges?

■ **SECTION B: NETWORKING**

In any labor market, a good job can be hard to find. However, people who are motivated, talented, and flexible will always find a place. Only a small part of job seeking entails responding to an ad; some of the extra activities relate to networking. Through networking, you can take initiative and get your job search moving in many directions.

Building a Network

Finding a job is partly a numbers game: the more exposure you have, the more contacts you have and the more career opportunities you encounter. **Networking** may be the *best* way to make new contacts, and many new jobs are attained every day through networking. Let's look at how to build an effective network.

• Connect with people who have interests similar to yours or who can support you in your objectives. Your network can include everyone you know through peers, organizations (such

COMMUNICATION CHALLENGES

The Business Profile Card A new approach in conducting a job search is to print business cards to include with your letters and résumés. These business cards list a few simple bulleted points about your accomplishments. For example:

James Reeder	312.555.1212

BS, Marketing, Best College
- Three years of part-time marketing experience
- Creative, dedicated, and motivated
- Excellent GPA and references

References are available upon request.

A **profile card** is a useful tool for networking; it provides your contact information and reminds associates of your skills. This card is just one more way to make it convenient for contacts to assist you in your search.

CHALLENGE:

Use your computer skills to create a business card that highlights your job search profile. Either have your card printed by a local printer, or buy a few pieces of high-quality, hard-stock paper and print your own cards; use a good-quality paper cutter (the type sold in art supply stores) so that the cards look professional.

Global Networking: *Before the Internet, the price of long-distance phone calls and the time constraints on postal service usually meant that the most cost-effective and efficient networking happened locally and by word of mouth. In the digital age, communication happens at the touch of a button, and networking has taken on a global dimension.* What efforts do you make to maintain contact with the people you consider part of your network? Do you speak with them regularly or usually only when you need something?

as your place of worship), past or current jobs, friends of your family, club memberships, associations, volunteer groups, and so on.

If you are currently not involved in any organizations, find some with which to become involved. By going to meetings and introducing yourself, you have a safe place to practice your interviewing skills. As people find out more about you, they may even give you leads for jobs, along with a recommendation to the person making the decision.

Though your current purpose in networking is finding a job, you may continue networking after you find a job. Networking will keep you current on issues in your field and will build your reputation and credibility within that field. It will also keep you visible within your community. Networking is about staying active and involved.

- *Build your network before you need it.* Many people make the mistake of looking for ways to build a network *after* they already need it. It generally takes a period of weeks or months to find a job; and after you have sought employment for a period of time, your optimism and motivation may decline. Since some network associates will have similar goals, your network will partly function as your support group. Thus, start your networking now, and do it on an ongoing basis so that you make contacts, remain visible, and get the support you need.

- *View networking as a communication exchange, not a one-sided dialogue.* Before you meet with someone to network, articulate why the meeting will be *mutually* beneficial. Look for common interests, experiences, or shared acquaintances. A word of caution: When you call someone, don't say that you want "to network" (or you could sound needy). Instead, focus on mutual interests; your associate will get the point.

Example: I noticed that you are looking for a job now too. Would you like to get together to brainstorm options or join a professional organization together?

- *Reciprocate favors: when you ask people in your network for help, also ask what you can do for them in return.* As well as finding mutual interests, ask those with whom you come into contact how you can help them. You may find that an opportunity that did not work out for you is perfect for someone else.

- *Use professional organizations as career opportunities.* Professional organizations within your field provide a steady stream of new people with whom to network and can also enhance your managerial and leadership skills. In addition to providing career opportunities, professional meetings help you keep pace with changing technology and see how others solve complex problems. Professional organizations rely on volunteers for tasks ranging from setting up tables at meetings to serving as officers. Look at volunteering as an unpaid window of opportunity. You will not only expand your networking base but also demonstrate your leadership ability.

- *Don't stop looking until you find your niche: one organization leads to another.* Go to meetings; use your connections at those meetings to find out about other organizations. You may arrive at an organization that sounded perfect for helping you achieve your goals; once you get there, however, it may not offer you what you thought. As you mingle, tell other professionals

INTERNET EXERCISE 9.1

Group Challenge To find tips for identifying groups, organizations, or meeting places of people who share your career goals or interests, visit the *Foundations of Business Communication* Web site at <http://www.mhhe.com/djyoung>.

Once you have accessed the home page, select "Student Activities" and then click the Chapter 9 link to get started.

about your goals; ask them about other organizations to which they belong. One thing leads to another; remain patient until you find *your* organization. You will know it by the camaraderie among employees, the way it meshes with your goals, and the way it motivates and inspires you.

- *Continue to network within your organization.* Networking is typically associated with contacts outside the company for which you work. However, once you secure your first position, consider networking *within* your organization to promote your visibility. Volunteer to serve on task forces, participate in focus groups, and attend company activities. Find new friends in the company cafeteria. Treat everyone at your organization with respect, including the support staff (such as mailroom and cleaning personnel).

    When you participate in company events, remain professional—when in doubt, leave it out. Many young people have overindulged at office parties and picnics only to find themselves regretting their return to work. Another caution: Networking does not necessarily include getting personally involved. Maintain a professional distance with coworkers; if you choose to participate in an office romance, find out your company's policy first. Private information has a way of becoming public, so don't get involved unless you can afford to lose your job as a result of breaking company policy. (At times, there is a fine line between dating activities and sexual harassment.)

- *Become visible and establish a track record.* Don't assume your terrific track record will speak for itself. To climb the corporate ladder, you must at times be assertive about your achievements. Look for formal and informal ways to get yourself known by top executives. Stay abreast of new business developments, and use your creativity and innovation to analyze how to enhance the success of your team and employer.

    Put your ideas in writing for your manager; when you achieve success with a project, be specific about outcomes. **Quantify** your achievements where you can. Instead of saying your idea brought in more customers, keep track of *how many* new customers came in.

Example: The new process brought in 20 new customers; it increased our client base by 5 percent.

Your idea then becomes an achievement that you can list on your résumé or use in a job interview. Getting to the top of any organization requires bottom-line accountability. If you do not show how your ideas contribute to the bottom line, it is unlikely that anyone else will. Keep a file of memos or e-mails that state your accomplishments in terms of results that can be measured in dollars and cents. This file will come in handy when you prepare for an evaluation or apply for a promotion.

COACHING TIP

Networking Basics If you are introverted or a bit shy, a networking event is a great time for you to practice introducing yourself to new people. Don't focus on trying to impress people by letting them know who you are. Instead, focus on what you can learn about the other person. Other people feel just as intimidated as you do. If you take the lead and show genuine interest, you will arrive at a mutual exchange of information.

Smile warmly and offer your hand as you introduce yourself; you will break the ice and get a smile back. Make sure your name tag is clearly visible to help those who are bad with names. If an easy topic for conversation doesn't come to mind, talk about the event itself. Don't feel offended if you speak to someone only a few minutes before each of you move on. Feel free to excuse yourself politely to get an hors d'oeuvre or speak to someone else.

Find a mentor and ask if you can attend a networking event together. Shadow your mentor at the event to observe how to "schmooze" at such events.

EXPLORE

Select a group on campus or a professional organization in your field, and do the following:

1. Attend a meeting and do some informal networking.
2. Write about your experience; was there anything about the situation that created anxiety? What will you do differently next time?
3. Within five days, follow up with anyone you said you would contact.

PRACTICE

Instructions:

1. Select an achievement at school and quantify your results.

    Example: I completed my résumé 2 days before the due date. I identified 9 months of part-time job experience.

COMMUNICATION CHALLENGES

Office Politics and Backstabbing   A well-known business author, Andrew J. DuBrin, defines **office politics** as "informal ways of gaining professional advantage other than through hard work, talent, and luck."[1] Manage office politics to your advantage; companies promote people who can anticipate the needs of the boss as well as show creativity, innovation, and self-promotion.

However, being politically savvy also relates to the "dark side" of business relationships. When advancement opportunities are limited, internal competition can spawn a behavior known as **backstabbing**: making negative, exaggerated comments about a coworker. Don't confuse office politics with backstabbing; backstabbing is *never* part of a success strategy. Prepare yourself to identify this tactic when it is applied against you, or you may unexpectedly find yourself unemployed. Here are the best ways to defend yourself against unscrupulous backstabbers:

1. Maintain a positive work record.
2. Manage your work relationships effectively through good ethics and professional conduct.
3. Confront known backstabbers when you encounter their aggression toward you.
4. Avoid getting involved in the office gossip mill.

Ask yourself: *How effectively do I manage my work relationships? Do I involve myself in office politics? How would I describe my conduct in terms of office politics?*

2. Now think of an achievement from some sort of work experience. Can you quantify it?

   Example: When I volunteered at the local food pantry, I put together 30 bags of groceries each hour.

3. Now repeat steps 1 and 2 above five more times or until you have a solid list of achievements that you can quantify.

Nurturing Network Relationships

Use social opportunities to get to know your peers, colleagues, and management. Like friendships, networks have to be nurtured. Though networking is a powerful tool, it competes with other obligations. Let go of your apprehensions about taking the time to build a strong network. If you currently don't have a network, resolve now to build one. If you have an existing network, make at least one call today. Here are a few more networking ideas:

- Call someone to share ideas with over coffee or solicit advice from about your job search.
- Find out about the next meeting of a professional organization in your field, and plan to attend.
- Meet five new people, and use their business cards to begin your networking data bank.
- Reciprocate favors: when asking someone in your network for help, also ask if you can help that person in any way.

EXPLORE

1. Throughout this section, you have been given several suggestions for networking. Consider:
   - Have you made a networking call today?
   - Have you identified or attended a meeting at a new organization in your field?
2. Is anything holding you back from pursuing your job search more aggressively? Write about your anxieties related to finding a job. What can you do to take charge of your job search?

 SECTION B: CONCEPT CHECK

1. When is the best time to begin establishing a network?
2. What are three things you can do to develop a network?
3. What is meant by "*quantify* achievements"?

SECTION C: JOB SEARCH LETTERS AND RÉSUMÉS

Letters are important tools for initiating, developing, and following up on contacts and job prospects. Whether you are writing a letter to send with a résumé or to use as a marketing tool for a specific position, your prospective employer's first impression may come from your letter. Here are three types of letters related to the job search process:

1. Cover letter
2. Contact letter
3. Follow-up or thank-you letter

Every letter you write must be specifically tailored to the company that will receive it. In addition, some companies prefer that *all application letters and résumés be submitted online;* other companies prefer to receive hard copies. Make sure you know each company's preference as you engage in your job search. Let's review how to get the information you need to customize your letter.

Researching Companies

Tailor everything in your job search process to the specific job for which you are applying. Therefore, write an original letter every time you inquire about opportunities or send your résumé. Though each letter may contain basic facts and key accomplishments, parts of each letter must be new and specific to the occasion. Finding the information you need may take some research.

Researching companies is now easier than it has ever been. In the past, an applicant relied on information given over the phone or in company brochures that arrived through the mail. Now you can find detailed information about major firms online. In fact, even if you intend to call, often the easiest way to get a company's phone number is through its Web site.

Though the human resource department does most of the screening, it is usually an advantage to speak directly to the hiring manager, who can work in any department in the company. However, don't ask to speak to the hiring manager until you are prepared to state why that person should be interested in you. Of course, *you don't want to sound scripted,* but you need to have your facts at hand and to state them without hesitation. For example:

> Hi. My name is Kerry Young. I'm a recent graduate of Best College, with a degree in computer science. I not only specialize in computer software design but am a good team player with strong leadership qualities. Would you be interested in receiving my résumé, or do you have any jobs that I might apply for?

Your "script" should take no more than 10 *seconds.* Give the listener enough honest information to highlight key reasons why you could contribute to their company. (By the way, sound natural; if you sound as if you are reading a script, the person is unlikely to want to meet you.)

Before you end your call, you need to get the name (including the exact spelling) and address of the person to whom you should address your cover letter. If the company prefers that you send your information via e-mail, make sure you also get that address. Follow the preferred company process, and you will get the best results.

PRACTICE

Instructions: Write a short script highlighting your achievements. With a partner, practice it a few times. If you want your experience to reflect reality, you and your partner should go to separate rooms and use cell phones, if available, to call each other.

Basic Guidelines for Job Search Letters

Your letter may not get you the job, but a poorly written letter will keep you from getting in the door to apply. Let's start with some guidelines that relate to all types of job search letters, including cover letters and contact letters:

- *Know the name and title of the person to whom you are writing; do not address a letter to "Dear Sir" or "Dear Madam."* Go to the company Web site or make a phone call to find out the addressee's name and its correct spelling; clarify the spelling with the person who tells you the name (even if it is a common name such as "Smithe"). Do not feel intimidated as you get the information that you need to make a good impression on your intended party.

- *Respect the company culture.* Find out the company preference for receiving résumés: online or through regular mail. If you are submitting an application letter and résumé online, e-mail them to yourself first and print them to make sure they look as professional on paper as they do on the screen.

INTERNET EXERCISE 9.2

Online Career Resources
To find a list of links to online resources that may prove integral to your job hunt—online career Web sites, placement services, and temporary agencies—visit the *Foundations of Business Communication* Web site at <http://www.mhhe.com/djyoung>.

Once you have accessed the home page, select "Student Activities" and then click the Chapter 9 link to get started.

- *Stress what you can offer the organization.* Rather than writing a letter that focuses on you and what you are looking for in a position, stress how your skills can benefit the organization. Once again, that means doing a bit of research to tailor your skills to the industry or company mission.

- *Take responsibility for follow-up and develop a plan.* When you search for a job, you need to take charge of the process. Therefore, do not expect others to contact you after they receive your information. If you say you will follow up to inquire about setting a time for an interview, do so. Otherwise, you are wasting your time and creating unnecessary frustration for yourself.

- *Aim for perfection with all job search letters: they create first impressions.* Though all written correspondence should be accurate and well written, a cover letter may be one of the most important letters you will write. Errors will reflect on your ability and potential, and a prospective employer will assume that you either do not have the necessary skills or do not pay attention to detail. Employers expect that you are on your best behavior when seeking a position, so they take mistakes seriously.

- *Write in a simple, clear, and concise way.* In this textbook, Chapter 2 presents thorough guidelines for achieving simple, clear, and concise writing. You have been applying those guidelines for some time now. At this time, your challenge is to apply what you have learned about using the active voice, using the "you" viewpoint, and being concise. Work with a colleague to proofread and edit your letters so that you have extra assurance that they are perfect.

Cover Letter

Whether you send your résumé through regular mail or e-mail, include a **cover letter** stating why you would be right for the job and highlighting your accomplishments. A strong cover letter has an opening that captures the reader's attention but also identifies the job for which you are applying.

Examples: The opportunity listed in Sunday's *Chicago Tribune* for a marketing associate is a great fit with my background and qualifications.

Our mutual colleague Jennifer Lopez suggested that I have the talent and qualifications that you are looking for in a marketing associate.

In the next paragraph of your letter, explain your special skills by listing three to six major accomplishments or qualifications that are relevant to the position you are seeking.

Example: As a recent graduate of Best University, I have knowledge of computer systems and accounting software. My grade point average of 3.8 demonstrates only part of my achievements. My degree in marketing includes a three-month internship. As an intern, I supported three vice presidents who trusted me with assisting clients and managing their portfolios.

In the last part of your cover letter, request an interview. State that you will call within a specific time frame to establish a mutually agreeable time.

Example: My enclosed résumé summarizes the skills and abilities you are looking for in a marketing associate. I'd appreciate the opportunity to meet with you to discuss how my background can benefit your corporation. I will contact you during the week of October 12 to arrange a time that we can meet.

FIGURE 9.1 | Cover Letters

The public relations firm Toye and Bhee is accepting résumés for an opening in its publications department. Which letter do you think will evoke a better response from the HR manager? Have you already started forming an opinion about the senders? What would you do to improve either or both of the letters?

3048 Stang St.
Tampa, FL 45623
813-555-2304

January 5, 2006

To Whom It May Concern:

Please consider my application for the position of Publications Traffic Coordinator, this sounds like a fun and exciting project be involved with. My Bachelor of Arts Degree from MSU is in Communications and my minor was Economics. I have worked for two local schools as a librarian, as a Substitute Teacher, and interned for two years with the local newspaper. My passion and many of my past positions have always been with using computers programs. I am a whiz at Microsoft Word, have an eye for detail and love reading books, newspapers and articles.

I am a quick learner and work well independently and with others. I would be a great asset for your position!

Sincerely,

Kenny Laine

Melanie Wayko
1212 Cache
Tallahassee, FL 35319

January 5, 2006

Eileen Karuso, HR Manager
Toye and Bhee
8100 Avenue Constellation
Tallahassee, FL 35316

Dear Ms. Karuso,

I enjoyed talking to by phone yesterday. Here, as promised, is my résumé and a business card. As you can see, I've worn a number of hats in the publishing field—writing, editing and managing—almost all in the areas of marketing and advertising.

I hope to hear from you in the next few weeks. In the meantime, best wishes for the New Year!

Sincerely,

Melanie Waykow

On a cover letter, the first paragraph identifies the job, the second paragraph explains your special skills, and the third paragraph is the call to action. Be sure to follow up on your commitment to follow up with a phone call. If the party is not available, ask if there is another time that would be convenient for you to call. Leave your name and number, but don't feel slighted if you don't get a callback. That's part of the reason why finding a job is difficult: *the major responsibility for communication is on your shoulders.*

PRACTICE

1. **Instructions:** Make a list of five types of jobs for which you are qualified.
2. **Instructions:** Draft a cover letter that highlights three to five of your key achievements.

Employment Ads

For entry-level jobs, responding to newspaper, journal, or online ads is a feasible way to search for a job. For higher-level positions, a job search focused on ads is not as productive. In fact, many higher-level jobs never get posted; if they are posted, often they are filled through networking (which is another term for "word of mouth"). If you have a connection or contact within a company, you have an advantage over those who do not. Many companies post jobs on their Web sites as well as in local and national publications.

The purpose of writing a letter in response to an ad is to get an interview. When responding, include the ad's language in your response letter. Coordinate your key accomplishments with those outlined in the ad. Focus on how your qualifications match the organization's needs. For example:

Dear HR Manager:

Your advertisement in the *Chicago Sun-Times* for a manager trainee in banking is a great match with my background. My bachelor of science degree in business management along with quality experience in the banking industry provide a solid foundation for a trainee at your bank.

Here are my key accomplishments:

*   Part-time teller during summers and while attending college.
*   3.5 grade point average.
*   A team player with strong leadership qualities.
*   "Teller of the Month" on four separate occasions.

I am confident that my knowledge, skills, and professional approach will meet both the technical and the people challenges in your intense banking environment.

I welcome a meeting to explore this opportunity further. Please call me at 555-1212 so that we can set a convenient time for an interview.

Sincerely,

John A. Bryant

Notice that John did not say that he would contact the interviewer. That's because in responding to ads, applicants often reply to an e-mail box (such as Careers@Allprotemps.com); the name of the company or person screening applicants is not listed. If that is the case, use a generic salutation or simplified letter style; avoid using a "Dear Sir or Madam" salutation. However, if the company name is listed, John should call to find out more details before putting a letter and résumé into the mail or sending them electronically. It is possible that a phone call could at least get him the name of the person screening applicants. A phone call might even get him an interview.

PRACTICE

1. **Instructions:** Look through at least two newspapers or magazines (one local and one national, such as *The New York Times*), and pull out two ads from each one. Draft a cover letter that tailors your experience to one of the ads.

2. **Instructions:** Do an online search for a position you could fill. Check out some of the Web sites that list openings. You will find a list of job search links at the *Foundations of Business Communication* Web site (see Internet Exercise 9.2 on page 318).

3. **Instructions:** Make a list of at least ten companies for which you would like to work (list small and medium-size companies as well as large Fortune 500 companies). Go to the Web sites of three of your choices. Find out if the companies have career or employment information on their sites.

Contact Letter

A contact is not necessarily a person who has a job opening for which you can apply. A *contact* is someone referred to you by someone in your network. The contact may become part of your network or know other people who can help you in your job search.

Writing letters or e-mail messages to contacts (also known as *referrals*) is critical in building your job-search network. Even though your contact may not know you personally, feel confident in asking for assistance with your job search. As discussed in the section on networking, your letter should have a mutual objective for you and the recipient. Personalize your message to show that you know something about this individual or his or her company.

Here is an example of a **contact letter:**

Dear Mr. Randolph:

Ruble Newcomb has suggested that I send you a message because I am in the midst of a challenging job search.

Our mutual friend Ruble also tells me that you are an avid golfer. I would welcome the opportunity to meet you for a quick cup of coffee to discuss golf as well as to get your valuable advice on my job search.

Would there be a convenient time at which I could call you? (By the way, I've taken the liberty of attaching my résumé so that you can take a quick glance at it.)

I look forward to hearing from you.

Trisha Sveitla

A contact letter or e-mail may or may not result in a meeting. When Trisha calls Mr. Randolph, they might accomplish what they need during the phone call. Alternatively, Mr. Randolph might be unable to provide tangible help in the job search. If that is the case, Trisha has nothing to lose by asking Mr. Randolph if he knows of anyone else who can help.

Part of your goal in speaking with any contact or referral is to inquire whether that individual can provide you with other networking contacts. Having one contact lead you to more contacts builds a great networking database. As the conversation proceeds, if you learn that your contact does not know of any specific jobs available, your next question should be, "Do you know someone who might know of something available or someone who would be willing to talk with me?"

> **COACHING TIP**
>
> **Small-World Phenomenon:** The **small-world phenomenon,** a Columbia University sociology experiment, is based on the hypothesis that everyone in the world can be reached through a short chain of acquaintances. The idea for this ongoing experiment resulted from the work of Stanley Milgram, a Harvard social psychologist. Milgram's research led Duncan Watts and Steven Strogatz to the famous phrase "six degrees of separation."[2]
>
> The idea is that everyone you know has many friends, and those friends in turn have many other friends. At one degree of separation is the person you know directly. At two degrees of separation is someone known by the person you know. Each "someone" represents a degree. By the time you get to the sixth layer—or sixth degree—you theoretically have the potential of contacting everyone in the world, including presidents, royalty, and celebrities. This phenomenon helps explain why networking can be so effective in finding the right job.
>
> Be creative in managing your network contacts. Someone, somewhere in your network, might have a connection—if only a phone number—to your next job.

In general, people like to be helpful. They actually appreciate being a bridge between you and people who can use your talents. Think of it this way: looking for the right person to fill a position is challenging for the person doing the hiring. When that person finds someone good, this solves a problem for him or her too. Thus, *don't be shy about asking for help* (and do include your résumé with any written or electronic communication).

Follow-Up and Thank-You Notes

Two of the most powerful tools in your job search toolkit are a follow-up e-mail and a hand-written thank-you note. Human resource professionals appreciate a thank-you note, and the best way to provide any requested follow-up information is through an e-mail message. Your contacts also appreciate a thank-you note when they provide networking assistance, as well as a follow-up e-mail message letting them know how things turned out for you.

A thank-you note that is handwritten may have the most impact. (You can buy a stack of thank-you cards at any stationery store.) Your note will make your new networking associate feel good about having to rearrange a schedule to meet with you or having placed a call or two on your behalf. The next time your name comes up, that person is likely to react positively.

If you choose to write a formal thank-you letter, you have another opportunity to sell yourself. It allows you to restate your skills or accomplishments. Make the letter simple, friendly, and genuine. For example:

Dear Ruble:

Looking for a job in today's job market is extremely stressful, but meeting such helpful individuals like you makes the journey easier.

I have contacted Randy, as you suggested, and will keep you informed on my progress. If I can assist you in any way, do not hesitate to contact me. I would be pleased to put my strong computer skills to use on your behalf!

Again, thank you for your valuable time and advice.

Sincerely,

Trisha

Don't use a boilerplate, *one-size-fits-all* message. Customize each letter, e-mail message, or handwritten note by specifically referring to something you and the recipient discussed. (Some people use software to generate letters and résumés; this approach is not recommended. However, if you use software, it is very important that you customize your final product—remember, you're not the only person who bought the software!)

Make sure you get a business card from each person who gives you time and attention so that sending a note or e-mail takes less effort. Surprisingly, no matter how often the advice is given or how good the results are when followed, few letters or notes expressing "thank you" are actually written. Make a decision right now to upgrade that statistic.

PRACTICE

1. **Instructions:** Identify two or three people who have assisted you in your job search.
2. **Instructions:** Write a thank-you letter to each of them, letting the person know how her or his assistance helped you in your job search.

The Résumé

Human resource executives and hiring managers typically receive hundreds of **résumés** for dozens of different job openings. What will make your résumé stand out among others?

To start, being brief is critical: your résumé should not exceed two pages. If you can highlight your experience effectively in one page, that's even better. (As noted in Chapter 7, an

American résumé is quite different from a **curriculum vitae,** which lists everything a person has accomplished in life.)

Human resource professionals start the process of job selection by sorting résumés. Consider that your résumé may be put into one of three piles:

- Category A: The résumé shows a clear fit with the job requirements.
- Category B: The résumé may fit some requirements, but not as clearly.
- Category C: The résumé does not fit requirements for the job opening.

In all likelihood, the applicants with résumés in category C will get a letter stating, "We have received your résumé and do not have any openings at this time for a person with your qualifications." How do you make sure your résumé ends up in the A pile?

Whatever you do, don't use flamboyant fonts or fancy paper; use conservative fonts (such as Times New Roman or Arial) and crisp, white, heavyweight bond paper. Concentrate on substance, style, and consistency: your résumé should reflect your values and achievements. Thus, even though you may start the process by using a résumé *template* from your computer software, make sure you *individualize* your résumé before you send it out. As one employer said, "Many times, when we have job openings, all the résumés look alike because all of the applicants use the same template." In the past, résumés were more difficult and expensive to produce. Today, applicants can easily tailor a résumé for each job interview.

Let's consider how to organize your information. The two basic formats for résumés are the chronological format and the functional format.

Chronological Format   The **chronological format** lists your education, positions, and accomplishments in order of occurrence, starting with the most recent and working backward. (See Figure 9.2.) With chronological formatting, the first job listed would be your most recent; the last job listed would possibly be your first job. This format has the advantage of being the more traditional; it is easy for the reader to evaluate your background quickly and see a history of steady promotions or increased responsibility. The disadvantages of this format are that it may appear routine and may raise questions about numerous career changes or gaps. This type of order also emphasizes age.

Basic Parts of a Chronological Résumé

1. *Heading/contact information:* Create a letterhead with your name, address, phone number, cell phone number, e-mail address, and a number where you can be reached during normal work hours (if that doesn't infringe on other commitments). Use a larger font size, such as 14 points, and use bold type for your name or the entire heading. (For the phone numbers you list on your résumé, make sure you have a voice-mail message that sounds professional.)

2. *Objective/summary:* Whether to use a summary or an objective is a personal choice. Consider the following:

   - A **summary** lists your experience and achievements and tells a company at a glance your skills and attributes. It enables an interviewer to see instantly the strongest skills you bring to the job and your greatest strengths and abilities. An interviewer knows immediately whether you should be called for an interview for a current job opening or whether your résumé should be filed for future consideration. Some interviewers use the summary to glean more information about specific skills, so make sure your summary is accurate and you have examples to back up your statements.
   - An **objective** helps an interviewer sort your résumé. If you are applying for a specific type of job, it identifies whether your objective matches a current job opening. A general objective says less than a specific objective but will keep more doors open.

   An objective can be meaningless to an interviewer; even worse it can eliminate you from being considered for a good job opening. Most interviewers do not need to see your objective: they assume that the job they have open meets your objective or you would not be applying for it. Rather than list an objective on your résumé, discuss your objective in

FIGURE 9.2 | Chronological Résumé

For more examples of chronological résumés, visit the Foundations of Business Communication *Web site at <http://www.mhhe.com/djyoung>. Once you have accessed the home page, select "Student Activities" and then click the Chapter 9 link.*

---

① **DAISY BRITO**
1728 Celes Street
Pittsburgh, PA 42108
926-555-5655 (H) • 926-555-9328 (cell/voice mail)
daisybrito@mymail.com

② **SUMMARY**

Dedicated administrative professional offers versatile skills and experience supporting key executives. Extensive experience in office and facilities management, meeting planning, and computer applications. Good organizer who can lead, train, and motivate others. Energetic team player with strong interpersonal and communication skills. Excellent analytical ability in dealing with complex problems and issues. Self-starter and quick learner with a willingness to take on extra responsibilities and new challenges.

③ **EXPERIENCE**

TEMPORARY ASSIGNMENTS, Pittsburgh, PA   *3/02 to Present*
Various temporary assignments through employment agencies in Pittsburgh. Experience with financialinstitutions, consulting firms, a publishing house, and a large hotel corporation (Marriott Corporation).(I have also helped a friend close his business.) Most positions held were as an administrative assistant.

PULLMAN EAR AND NOSE, Pittsburgh, PA   *4/99 to 2/02*
Executive Assistant to Dr. Graydon Pullman
• Functioned as liaison between Pullman and Orlando Hospital.
• Scheduled and maintained calendar, appointments, files, and travel.
• Coordinated luncheon meetings.
• Contacted attorneys, doctors, and patients.
• Renewed state and federal licenses.
• Coordinated building issues, such as furniture, office machines, moves.
• Ordered office supplies.
• Composed correspondence and completed monthly reports.

COMPUTER CONSULTANTS, LTD., Pittsburgh, PA   *8/97 to 3/99*
Office Manager
• Assisted accountant and various levels of support staff.
• Served as liaison between corporate and branch offices.
• Supervised clerical staff.
• Typed contracts, agreements, and proposals
• Maintained files for legal counsel.
• Dealt with vendors.
• Evaluated monthly performance reviews.
• Coordinated and updated companywide telephone book every two weeks.
• Ordered and proofread business cards for over 400 employees.

④ **EDUCATION AND TRAINING**

Office Management and Organizational Courses, Louden University
Training Seminars: Time Management, Communication Skills, Motivating Employees
Accounts Receivable and Reconciliation, Pittsburgh Technical Institute

Computer skills include Windows, Word, Excel, PowerPoint, WordPerfect, Lotus Notes and 1-2-3,
Harvard Graphics, AIM, Calendar Creator Plus, Pegasus and Outlook E-mail,
Internet (Orbitz & Expedia)

⑤ **ACHIEVEMENTS**

Employee of the Month at Pullman Ear and Nose, March 2002
Team Captain, National Volleyball Champions, 2001

⑥ References available upon request.

your cover letter. A summary can be far more beneficial than an objective. (If you write an objective, use the heading "Objective" in the place where you would put "Summary.")

3. *Work experience:* The easiest way to list your work experience is in chronological order, starting with your most recent job and working backward. For each job, list either exact dates of employment or month and year (which is common and looks less cluttered). (If you don't have a lot of job experience, you may instead do a functional résumé, which stresses specific job categories; you would then give detailed information on your qualifications in each area.)

4. *Education and training:* If you have sufficient job experience, list your education information after your work experience. However, if you have very little job experience, you can highlight your education by listing your education experience directly after your objective or summary (then follow it with work experience). Give the names of colleges you have attended and major areas of study. List your GPA if it is 3.0 or higher; otherwise, list only the GPAs in your major and minor areas.

5. *Achievements, awards, and affiliations:* Do you have special achievements from your educational experience, volunteer work, sports, or part-time jobs? Your special achievements exemplify your character. One of the reasons organizations give awards is so that winners can use the achievement to set themselves apart in competitive situations. Thus (especially if your résumé lacks sufficient job experience), find a place to include clubs, sports, other associations, and achievements that demonstrate your leadership quality.

6. *References:* It is preferable not to list references on your résumé. (It is not even necessary to state that references are available upon request.) However, be prepared with a list of three or more references, with their titles, phone numbers, and even e-mail addresses. Always check with your references *before* you put them on your list and discuss the kind of job you are seeking; review your major strengths and accomplishments with your references. Also, alert them each time a reference call is certain to come their way. Briefly tell them about the position for which you are applying and how your strengths can contribute to the position. Employers usually contact references only as a final stage in their hiring process to confirm details you've already given.

Functional Format   The **functional format** highlights your experience and accomplishments in each technical area of expertise. (See Figure 9.3.) The advantage of the functional format is that it is brief and quickly identifies strengths and accomplishments. In addition, this format can hide lapses in work history or demotions. The disadvantages are that it is not the traditional style and biased readers may dismiss accomplishments that are not directly related to their interests. Thus, the biased reader may skip entire technical areas in which you make important achievements.

Basic Parts of a Functional Résumé

1. *Heading/contact information:* Create a letterhead with your name, address, phone number, cell phone number, e-mail address, and a number where you can be reached during normal work hours (if that doesn't infringe on other commitments). Use a larger font size, such as 14 points, and use bold type for your name or the entire heading.

2. *Objective/summary:* Since a functional résumé highlights your skills in particular areas rather than your work history, write a summary based on your experience and abilities. If you use an objective, your objective should be specifically tailored to the job for which you are applying (but not be a verbatim description taken from the job posting).

   A brief summary of your experience and qualifications keeps your options open. You can be more specific in your cover letter, which you also need to tailor to each job and company to which you apply. Thus, summarize your educational and work experience by giving a brief overview. (If you have an extremely short résumé, you can include an objective *and* a summary.)

3. *Skills:* If you have very little or no job experience, identify the skills you can perform. You can use bulleted lists of words so that employers can easily recognize any skills they need.

FIGURE 9.3 | Functional Résumé

For more examples of functional résumés, visit the Foundations of Business Communication *Web site at* <http://www.mhhe.com/djyoung>. *Once you have accessed the home page, select "Student Activities" and then click the Chapter 9 link.*

---

① **NOAH TRENTON**
1010 South Island Court, Apt. 8
Galveston, TX 64102
426-555-7555 (H) • 426-555-9328 (voice mail)

② **Objective**

A highly motivated college graduate with a passion for art and history seeks an administration position in which I can complement the existing environment while developing new avenues for growth.

③ **Skills**

- Fluent in English, Spanish, and French (trilingual).
- Strong organizing skills: oversaw monthly campus lecture series on Renaissance artists.
- Good planning skills: coordinated two 3-week workshops on diversity issues in the arts.
- Excellent lecturing and interviewing skills for media environment: lecturer for semester-long workshop on communication.

④ **Education**

Master of Arts, Communication Consultancy with Cultural Diversity Emphasis
Degree Conferred: May 2004
Oklahoma State University
Stillwater, Oklahoma

Bachelor of Arts, Communication Consultancy
Degree Conferred: May 2002
Oklahoma State University
Stillwater, Oklahoma

⑤ **Work Experience**

August 2002–August 2004
Supporters of Art
Program Assistant (Internship)

- Prepared press and action alert releases.
- Reviewed position papers published by private collectors.
- Created art information packets for grade-school students.

September 2000–October 2001
Institute for Art Conservation
Assistant to Collections Manager (Internship)

- Collected research of historical collections in conjunction with the National Art Institute Conservation Branch.
- Maintained database on endangered artworks.
- Copyedited press releases, in-house documents, and reports.

June 1998–Present

Artwalk Docent

Conducted bimonthly artwalk for traveling exhibits.

---

4. *Education:* If you have very little job experience, list your education experience next. Give the names of colleges you have attended and major areas of study. Include clubs, sports, and other associations that demonstrate your leadership ability. List your GPA if it is 3.0 or higher; otherwise, list only the GPAs in your major and minor areas.

5. *Work experience:* Even with a functional résumé, list your work experience in chronological order for each skill area. Once again, you can list either exact dates of employment or only month and year (which looks less cluttered). If you don't have a lot of job experience, do some volunteer work. Learn to use as many different types of office machines as you can, including fax machines and copiers.

Résumés That Work   To make their résumés eye-catching, some applicants resort to using colored paper; use this approach only if you are applying for a creative type of position in a field other than business. However, for most professional business positions, remain conservative. Bright white is appropriate, as is an off-white or buff color.

To produce a clean, crisp résumé, do the following:

- Be concise; prioritize information and include only the most important.
- Be specific about your accomplishments; quantify them when possible.
- Apply parallel structure (represent words in a consistent form).
- Edit ruthlessly; then proofread to perfection.
- Honestly state your educational and professional background.
- Keep your résumé to one page if you can, two pages if you can't.

Write your résumé so that it answers questions before they arise. Use your cover letter to fill in gaps of unemployment that might appear on your résumé. Realize that employers assume you are telling the truth until they find out otherwise. Employers do check specific details, but usually only after they have already decided to hire you.

COMMUNICATION CHALLENGES

Scannable Résumés and E-Résumés A job search trend is the use of "cyberspace résumés." According to Diane Wilson, president of Grimard Wilson Consulting, Inc., a good e-résumé is a good traditional résumé. Thus, your e-résumé should include an inventory of your skills and accomplishments. Here are a few specific tips:

- The e-résumé should have no more than 65 characters per line.
- Omit italics and underlines.
- Include a *keyword summary* at the top of the page that highlights your experience or duties you have performed.
- Adhere to parallel structure; if you choose verbs, end verbs in their "ing" form.
  Example: Answering phone and e-mail messages.
  Interviewing prospective clients.

The keyword summary allows organizations to pair résumés with available positions on the basis of word matches.

A scannable résumé is a hard-copy document that is designed to be scanned by an optical character reader (OCR). Scannable résumés are fed into a database for screening based on keywords.

A word of caution about e-résumés: Because applying for a job online involves little more than the click of a mouse or the push of a button, many employers have reported receiving thousands of résumés for jobs listed online. Experts agree that unless the job advertisement states "Apply by e-mail only," it is best to respond with a traditional résumé and cover letter.[3] And, if you are producing a scannable résumé, include as many keywords as you can to maximize your chances for a match.

Electronic Résumés   What are electronic résumés, or **e-résumés**? They are résumés that are sent through e-mail, attached as part of online applications, or posted on the Internet within personal Web pages. The most common type is the résumé sent in an e-mail (not as an attachment), with more and more employers requesting that applicants send their résumés this way.

How do e-résumés differ from traditional ones? Though similar in many ways, traditional résumés and e-résumés differ in two important ways: First, an e-résumé includes an additional section called a "Keyword Summary." Second, the e-résumé should *not* include many of the special features typically included on a traditional résumé. (See Figure 9.4.)

Creating Keyword Summaries   The keyword summary should appear at the top of the page after your name and contact information. The summary should consist of 20 to 30 words and phrases that relate to your education and experience.

Use this summary as an opportunity to emphasize any knowledge, experience, and skills you have that are likely to attract prospective employers. On a traditional résumé, you would describe your work experience in verb phrases that begin with strong action verbs (such as *managed, supervised, processed*). However, on an e-résumé, such summaries usually consist of noun and adjective phrases. Some examples might be "fluent in Spanish" or "team-oriented" or "strong communication skills."

Companies increasingly use software programs (such as Resumix and BrassRing) that allow them to scan résumés for words that match those that the employer wants to see. These programs give an applicant a numerical score based on the number of matches or "hits."

FIGURE 9.4 | Electronic Résumé

VANESSA A. GODOY

School: 211 Butler Hall, Philadelphia, PA 19141, 215-555-8221
Home: 377 Tree Lane, Ambler, PA 19083, 215-555-2308
E-mail: Godoy@larson.edu

KEYWORDS

digital arts, marketing, knowledge of Spanish, Web design, leadership ability, willing to travel, customer-oriented, Office 2003, Illustrator, PhotoShop, XHTML, Flash MX, Dreamweaver MX, JavaScript, Sound Forge, FTP, PDF, written and oral communication skills, MIS, database maintenance, resolving problems, analytic, researcher, instructor, community service

OBJECTIVE

A position that will allow me to use and develop my digital arts, business, and communication skills.

EDUCATION

Larson College, Philadelphia, PA
BA—May 2005
Major: Digital Arts and Multimedia Design
Minor: Business
Related Courses: marketing, computer science, digital arts, economics, business law, management information systems, developmental psychology

Assumption Academy, Jenkintown, PA
Diploma—June 2001

WORK EXPERIENCE

Box Office and Reservation Assistant, weekends, 2004
National Constitution Center, Philadelphia, PA
Process ticket orders and assist customers.

Lab Assistant, 2001–Present
Larson College, Philadelphia, PA
Assist students with logging on to computers, using programs, and finding missing files; fix printer problems in the computer lab.

Cashier, Floral Consultant, and Team Leader, 2000–2004
Genuardi's Family Markets, Roslyn, PA
Processed food orders for customers, prepared flower arrangements, supervised cashiers to ensure sufficient sales support.

Asst. Tennis Instructor, summer 2000
Abington Township, Abington, PA
Assisted in teaching three classes of tennis lessons for children 10–16.

ACTIVITIES

Larson Singer 2001–Present (Secretary)
Appalachian Service Project, spring 2002 and 2003
Organization of Latin-American Students, 2002–Present (Representative)
New Media Club, 2001–Present
Larson Gospel Choir, 2001

Formatting   Whereas traditional résumés contain tabbed indents and bold or italic type (as in headings, such as "Education" and "Work Experience"), e-résumés lack these features. Because e-mail programs usually have difficulty reproducing such features, do not use them or else your résumé may appear differently to your recipient than you intend it to appear. To change your traditional résumé into an electronic one, follow these steps:

1. Remove all boldface, italics, and underlining.
2. Eliminate bullets, and replace them with dashes, small o's, or asterisks.
3. Move all your text to the left.
4. Remove returns except for those separating major sections.
5. Use all-caps for headings.
6. Provide an additional line or two of space between sections.
7. Save the file in ASCII or rich-text format.

Sending Your E-Résumé and Cover Letter   To send your electronic résumé, start with a subject line that states the title of the job for which you are applying, such as "Trading Assistant Applicant." Then copy and paste your cover letter followed by your résumé into the e-mail. In your cover letter, refer to the résumé that follows.

Do not send your traditionally formatted résumé as an attachment. With the proliferation of viruses and the fear of infecting computer systems, employers are more and more reluctant to open attachments from applicants they do not know.

Career Portfolios

Everything you've done so far in this chapter has prepared you for your job search. To attain a higher level of preparation, organize and expand your job search toolbox by putting together a career **portfolio.**

Your portfolio can be as simple or thorough as you choose. Most professionals recommend using a three-ring binder; if you choose one with a zipper or some other closure, you can secure loose items. (Try to find one that has a secure pocket for business cards.) Use tabs to organize the various parts. Here are some suggestions:

- *Purpose statement:* Give serious consideration to writing a purpose statement and objectives to use as part of your portfolio. A purpose statement can enhance your job search as it gives you clarity in making career decisions; a purpose statement also assists you in intertwining your professional career goals with your personal objectives. (Chapter 10 gives specific guidelines for developing a purpose statement and objectives.)

- *Résumé:* You may want to prepare different types of résumés (a chronological and a functional résumé) that are tailored to the specific jobs for which you apply. You may even want to prepare a curriculum vitae just in case you apply to an international corporation.

- *Work samples:* Select two or three exhibits of your best work from classes or previous jobs: a letter you drafted, a report you wrote and formatted, a paper that highlights your part of a team project. A sample of your work demonstrates your skill and commitment to quality.

- *Reference letters:* Working on a portfolio gives you a specific reason to ask for letters of reference *before* you need them. Thus, your references will have more time to draft a letter and give it to you, and having reference letters as part of your portfolio will give you more confidence in your job search. Ask your references to use the salutation "To whom it may concern."

- *Networking contacts:* Keep your business cards in a secure pocket; this will keep you organized so that you can follow up with contacts.

- *Business profile card:* Design your own job search card with your name, address, phone number, and a few vital points about your skills. (See sidebar, page 315.)

Bring your portfolio with you on job interviews. Your portfolio will speak for you by demonstrating your motivation and organizational skills. Though you will probably compete with other applicants who also bring a portfolio, your portfolio will definitely set you apart from those who arrive without one.

Now that you've done all the work to create your traditional portfolio, consider reformatting select pieces to create an *e-portfolio*. You will then have the information ready to paste into an e-mail. Another option is to create your own Web site. (You will find information about developing a Web site in Chapter 10.)

Interviewers are impressed to see a candidate who takes searching for a job seriously. Your career portfolio demonstrates your enthusiasm, strong organizational skills, and commitment to being prepared.

EXPLORE

1. **Instructions:** Go to a career Web site. Check out employment possibilities.

2. **Instructions:** Contact a temporary employment agency in your area. What kinds of testing do they do? What kinds of positions are they currently filling?

3. **Instructions:** Take an employment test from one of the organizations you researched, and find out how they rank you.

PRACTICE

Background: In previous chapters, you reviewed the concept of parallel structure, which relates to putting terms in the same grammatical form. Parallel structure is especially important for listing duties on résumés.

- The most common grammatical form to use in listing duties is the gerund (formed by adding *ing* to the base form of the verb); for example: *arranging, putting, coordinating.*

- Another common form is the base form of the verb; for example: *arrange, put, coordinate.* You can also use the past-tense form of the verb; for example, *arranged, put, coordinated.*

- The key is to remain *consistent* throughout your résumé regardless of the form you choose. For example:

Inconsistent	**Gerund Form**	**Base Form**
Arrangement of travel	Arranging travel	Arrange travel
Put in expense accounts	Putting in expense accounts	Put in expense accounts
Coordination of vacation schedule	Coordinating and keeping track of vacation schedule	Coordinate and keep track of vacation schedule

Instructions: Put the following terms and phrases in parallel structure:

Sort and disperse payroll checks _____

Assisted staff _____

Backup to the president's assistant _____

Copied, faxed, filed office correspondence _____

Profit and loss reconciliation _____

Renewal of licenses _____

Heavy phone contact with clients and attorneys _____

Maintenance of library _____

Ordered office supplies _____

Sort and distribute mail _____

Spreadsheet creation _____

Online order shipment _____

Calendar, appointment scheduling _____

Travel arrangements and coordination of luncheon meetings _____

✓ SECTION C: CONCEPT CHECK

1. What is the difference between a chronological and a functional résumé?

2. Which is more effective, applying online with an e-résumé or sending a hard copy through the mail?

3. What is a contact letter, and when would you use one?

■ SECTION D: THE INTERVIEW

Everything you've done until now—your résumé, cover letter, networking—is for the sole purpose of getting to meet a hiring manager. Now you must be ready for the most important step in finding a job: *the interview.*

Preliminary Considerations

Dress for Career Success   The first thing anyone notices about you is your appearance. According to William Thourlby, contributing author of *You Are What You Wear,* people decide the following ten things about you within the first 10 seconds of meeting you:[4]

1. Economic level
2. Educational level
3. Trustworthiness
4. Social position
5. Level of sophistication

6. Social heritage
7. Educational heritage
8. Economic heritage
9. Successfulness
10. Moral character

One way to rank high on your image is to dress appropriately (and conservatively) for the position for which you are applying. Interviewers complain that job applicants show up in t-shirts, tattered jeans, and wrinkled clothing; in addition, the interview is not the time to flaunt a tattoo or body piercing. Know the proper etiquette; prospective employers interpret anything less as disrespectful of the organization and the position. After you have been hired, you can dress according to the company dress code. However, for the interview, wear conservative clothing and jewelry; in other words, wear nothing that would call attention away from you or your interview.

Both men and women succeed in conservative business suits. Avoid extreme colors and styles. There is a saying in business, "The more skin a person shows, the less power the person has." Though you want to express your personality, you want your prospective employer to remember you for your smile, not your skirt length, baggy pants, or loud tie.

Be Prompt   Being prompt means arriving about 10 to 15 minutes before your scheduled appointment. *Never show up late for an interview.* The interviewer will interpret late behavior as an indication of your potential work habits.

COMMUNICATION CHALLENGES

Growing Edges   Earlier in the chapter, you identified a weakness or two, which we labeled your "growing edges."

Keep in mind that identifying your *strengths* and confidently verbalizing them will get you the job. However, to keep the job and be consistently promoted, you may need to pay more attention to your growing edges than to your strengths. That's because *people are usually fired for their weaknesses,* not their strengths. Thus, by honestly working on your growing edges, you will be taking control of your career success.

In addition, most people find a direct connection between their biggest weakness and their biggest strength. Even a good quality expressed in its extreme has both a positive and a negative side. Thus, if you are always on time, you may display a lack of patience or become annoyed with others who are occasionally late. Another example is developing creative or innovative solutions to problems: though some of your ideas may dramatically improve the bottom line, others may be a waste of time and money.

Identify your growing edges, and develop an action plan to minimize your weaknesses and express them in a balanced way.

Ask yourself: *What are my greatest strengths, and how do they sometimes express themselves as weaknesses?*

Though being late is out of the question, being too early can also affect a prospective employer's impression. Thus, do not arrive an hour (or even a half hour) before your scheduled appointment. To get there *on time,* you might need to drive or walk around the block once or twice. As you do, reflect on the points you will make in the interview.

EXPLORE

1. What does being on time tell you about a person?
2. What micromessages are you giving when you are late?
3. Do most excuses for lateness actually excuse the behavior?

Be Prepared   An important part of your interview is the interpersonal communication you establish with the interviewer. One way to achieve a good rapport is by going to the interview prepared. Know about the company, the position, and the industry; have two or three key questions that you can ask the interviewer. The interviewer will know that you have done your research on the organization by the questions you ask. Greet the interviewer with a warm smile and a firm, but not bone-crushing, handshake. Exhibit a positive and enthusiastic demeanor.

Be aware of your body language, as your nonverbal messages can shout volumes about you. Nervous habits (such as nail biting, hair twirling, extreme hand movements, or rocking in your chair) are distractions and signal insecurity. Make good eye contact; looking away during key questions could signal to an interviewer that your answer is not honest.

When you become skillful at being interviewed, you will work the discussion toward the organization's needs (the driving force for the interview) rather than focus on your own needs. Apply your listening skills so that you read the interviewer's nonverbal messages. If the interviewer stares at the clock or glances at it too often, this could indicate that you are talking too much and not staying on track with the interview. Active listening will help you develop flow with the interview.

Demonstrate how your skills and experience counteract any issues or concerns the interviewer may express. For example:

Build a Garden: *Just as you need to put thought and planning into the process of selling a product, an idea, or yourself, so should you also develop a process for dealing with the challenges that often go hand in hand with career building. What strategies can you use in your job search to maintain your focus and relieve pressure when you encounter obstacles, setbacks, or rejection?*

Interviewer's statement: I'm concerned that you don't have enough experience for this position.

Your response: Though I may be short on formal experience, I am a very quick learner and enjoy all the tasks this job entails.

Be prepared with at least two or three questions that you can ask during or after the interview. For example:

Whom do I report to?

How will my performance be monitored?

What is the busy time of year?

What immediate projects are pending?

At the end of the interview, you can get an idea of how you did by asking the following question before you leave:

WORKING AND LEARNING IN TEAMS

Selection Process Interviews occur under a variety of circumstances, but here is a general process: Most employers begin with a **screening interview,** which allows them to sort through the applicant pool to find the candidates who are best qualified for the job.

The screening interview may occur over the telephone, online, or in person. The screening interview usually involves answering a few simple questions or taking an exam that covers skills basic to the job.

The best candidates culled from the applicant pool face one of three interview scenarios:

- *One-on-one interviews:* These are the most common types of interviews, usually focused on specific and job-related questions.
- *Group interviews:* These can involve a meeting with either a small hiring committee or members of the team with whom the job candidate will be working. On occasion, the candidate might meet with each member of the team in a succession of short, one-on-one sessions, also known as *consecutive interviews.*
- *Stress interviews:* Characterized by intense questioning and quick subject changes intended to throw a person off balance, a **stress interview** tests the candidate's response to pressure. Slowing things down is the best response to pressure techniques such as rapid-fire questioning and confusing questions: repeat the question in your head slowly, and carefully consider your answers before you speak.

TEAM EFFORT:
With a partner, discuss the challenges you would anticipate during the three interview scenarios described above. Discuss ways that an interviewee can make the best impression in each interview scenario.

How do my skills and qualifications match what you are looking for?

This question will give you one last chance to overcome concerns and sell your skills before the interview ends as well as give you a more realistic impression of how you did.

The Traditional Interview

At the beginning of this chapter, you developed your job search profile. Use what you learned in answering the traditional interview questions below. Work alone or with a partner. As you answer these questions, give examples that demonstrate your abilities. Your examples do not need to be job-related. If a question doesn't apply, you may skip it; however, keep in mind that you may be asked any or all of these questions on a job interview.

Interview Questions:

Tell me about yourself.

Describe your ability to solve problems.

Are you a team player? Give me some examples of how you work on a team.

How have you demonstrated leadership?

Are you an independent self-starter?

What special talents or gifts do you have? (Consider sports, music, and hobbies.)

Tell me about your communication skills.

Are you a good listener? Tell me about your listening skills.

How are your writing skills? What kinds of documents do you feel confident writing?

Describe your presentation skills: Do you feel comfortable presenting to a group or facilitating a meeting? (Give examples.)

Which is stronger, your people skills or your technical skills? Why?

How are your computer skills? What software programs do you know well?

Are you capable in global communications or foreign languages? (Give examples that demonstrate your ability.)

Can you negotiate?

Describe your management skills and philosophy—have you ever supervised or directed others in completing tasks?

What are your people skills like? Do you enjoy working with people? Are you easy to get along with?

Do you take responsibility for your actions?

How about mistakes? Do you take responsibility for your decisions when things don't turn out as planned?

If I were to ask your best friend to describe you, what would he or she say?

What are your weaknesses or growing edges?

Often, a person's attitude helps secure a position and contributes to promotions throughout a career. Thus, you may feel uncomfortable answering some questions, especially about mistakes or growing edges (weaknesses). However, your honest and positive approach will demonstrate that you are not defensive but instead have a good, realistic way of thinking.

Even when a question sounds as if it needs only a yes or no answer, embellish your response with examples that demonstrate your answer. Interviewers feel most comfortable in a communication exchange; they find it difficult to be in a situation in which the applicant speaks either too little or too much. Balance is the key.

The Behavioral Interview

Though preparing for the traditional interview is essential in a job search, it isn't the final step. Many companies are now applying more sophisticated approaches to finding out about candidates. The behavioral interview provides the depth and sophistication companies need to predict behavior more successfully.

Behavioral-interview questions probe into a person's self-perceptions and ability to think critically and work well in teams, among other qualities. The answers are found by placing an applicant in a context and then asking for specific information about experiences. The various scenarios necessitate that the applicant place the experience in a broader context and give more intricate detail about the experience. One piece of the puzzle connects to another, and the interviewer has better insight into an applicant's likely behavior on the job. Here are a few behavioral-interview questions:

> *Tell me about a specific situation in which you had to work with someone you didn't like or who didn't like you.*
>
> *Tell me about a time when you were rushed to meet a deadline and had other priorities to manage at the same time.*
>
> *Give me an example of a situation in which you used your problem-solving skills to make a difficult decision.*
>
> *Describe a situation in which you were called on to use your leadership skills.*
>
> *Tell me about an experience dealing with an upset customer or colleague.*
>
> *Tell me how you deal with conflict, and give a specific example.*
>
> *Give me an example of a situation in which you used your persuasive communication skills to convince someone to do something your way.*

Katharine Hansen, of Quintessential Careers, recommends that one way to handle a behavioral interview question is to use the *STAR technique,* breaking the answer into the following:[5]

1. Situation or task
2. Action
3. Result

Since it is difficult to predict the questions an interviewer will ask in a behavioral interview, preparing is a challenge. However, Hansen recommends that you equip yourself with a few specific examples that you can apply to a number of different questions. Think of yourself as telling a concise, highly focused story about the event.

Obviously an interviewer is more interested in negative events than positive ones. Search your background for difficult situations you were able to turn around or handle so that you achieved positive outcomes. These examples show strong character traits, even though you might prefer forgetting the experiences!

The traditional interview and the behavioral interview are not mutually exclusive: as you prepare for one type of interview, you also make progress with the other. The more you prepare, the better you will do (as long as you do not have rehearsed answers). You can find more information online about behavioral interviews, or pick up a book specifically about interviewing, such as *Landing the Job You Want: How to Have the Best Job Interview of Your Life* by Byham and Pickett.[6]

PRACTICE

Instructions: You will need to do this mock interview with a partner. Start by making two lists of questions. Have fun with this exercise as you get valuable practice preparing for a job interview.

1. Compile a list of five questions that you might be asked on an interview.

2. Compile a list of three questions that you could ask the interviewer.

3. Now role-play an interview with a partner; as your partner asks each question, give interview-quality answers.

4. After you have answered your five interview questions, ask your partner the questions you developed for the interviewer. Your partner can "improvise" answers.

5. Switch roles and repeat the interview.

Salary Requirements

Most prospective employers prefer that they initiate the issue of salary. Even if you are impatient, realize that the topic will come up eventually—they know that you do not expect to work for free. Also realize that how you handle this subject gives a strong impression about your goals and character. Are you solely interested in working for the highest salary you can get, or are other issues (such as potential to learn and develop versatile skills) just as important as salary?

In addition to not asking about salary too soon, also do *not* ask about any of the following too soon:

• How long will it take to get promoted?

• What benefits do you offer?

• How much vacation time will I get?

These types of questions can lead employers to think that you really aren't interested in the job for which you are applying. They may think that you overestimate your value and will become bored easily. If you do ask about salary directly, ask about the "salary range" rather than the exact salary.

At some point, a company will either request your salary history or ask your salary requirement. Supply this information when it is requested. If you are in doubt about what salary to specify, state that your salary requirement is flexible. However, if salary data is required when you submit your résumé, list your last salary along with the statement that "salary is negotiable based upon the right opportunity."

Follow-Up

After an interview, focus on two types of follow-up:

1. Thank the interviewer for meeting with you.

2. Reflect on your interviewing skills to make them stronger for your next opportunity.

For every interview, send a thank-you letter within the first day or two following your meeting. A thank-you letter provides you with an opportunity to restate your skills and put your name once more in front of a decision maker.

After the interview, develop a follow-up strategy that relates to reflection and self-growth. Evaluate how you think you did in the interview process, and consider how you can do even better next time. What questions do you wish you had asked? What pertinent information did you leave out? What was the most positive or negative thing that occurred in the interview?

The bottom line: The more you interview, the better you are able to hone your interview skills. As the adage goes, *practice makes perfect.* After an interview, do *not* beat yourself up over what you *should* have done; this is the time to look optimistically to the future.

Job Offers

Accepting a Job Offer   Getting a job offer is always exciting, even if you do not accept the position. Usually, employers make job offers through a telephone call. That phone call is the perfect time to ask about salary, if it has not already been discussed. If the salary sounds low, ask whether it is negotiable.

You do not need to accept on the spot, but you should give a definite time frame in which you will convey your answer. Sound positive, even enthusiastic. You don't want your prospective employer to have doubts about you at this stage of the process. If you need it, take a day or two to think about the offer and give a response. (However, before you give the employer a time frame, ask how much time you can have to consider the offer.

If you are positive that you want the position, it is perfectly all right to accept during the same phone call in which the position is offered. Be excited about the offer. Also realize that the company is excited about you or the employer wouldn't have offered you the position. Savor the moment. It won't be long before your first day on the job, when you will have a new set of challenges (exciting ones, though).

Resigning from the Old Job   When you resign from your current company, do your best to give two or more weeks' notice. Your company may ask you to put your resignation in writing. In your resignation letter, get right to the point and don't include any reasons or excuses. Simply state that you are resigning, and give the effective date. However, you should be prepared to leave sooner than your resignation date, as many companies let people go as soon as they receive their resignation. On the other hand, many companies count on your giving them enough time to fill the position. By acting as a true professional regardless of the situation, you will have fewer regrets and will retain a better reputation.

Rejecting a Job Offer   If you are offered a position that you choose not to accept, start by thanking the representative for making the offer. Then be honest, yet tactful and professional, as you decline the offer. You do not need to say whether you accepted another position (or where or why), but you may offer that information if you choose.

PRACTICE

Background: You've just had a great interview for an assistant buyer position with Troy Orato at Media Consultants, a public relations firm. It turned out that you and Troy have the same breed of dog, so there was a comfortable topic to talk about during the conversation. You want to follow up with a thank-you note.

1. Would a faxed message be appropriate? An e-mail or an e-memo? A phone call?
2. Compose a brief message to Troy thanking him for his time.

SECTION D: CONCEPT CHECK

1. Why is it a good idea to dress conservatively for a job interview?
2. Describe the difference between a traditional interview and a behavioral interview.
3. What questions should you avoid asking during a first interview?

SUMMARY

You have made a commitment to developing a successful career; securing a good job is only your first step, not your final one. Especially in the beginning, don't be overly concerned about salaries or titles: focus on what you can learn to become even more valuable as your career progresses.

You may think that the most difficult parts of any job search are putting your résumé together and going on interviews. Those aspects are difficult, but the most difficult part of any job search is rejection. When you do not get an offer, especially if you really wanted that particular job, disappointment is a natural reaction. Everyone gets rejected: it's not a matter of *if* as much as *when* and *how often*. Every time you go on an interview, prepare yourself for that possibility and realize that finding the right job is partly a matter of statistics. The more interviews you go on, the better your job-seeking skills will become.

In the process, try not to compare yourself with your classmates or other job seekers; however, do use them for support. No one has a better idea of what you are going through than other job seekers. Focus on developing your strengths and improving your growing edges. The outcome of your job search depends as much on the way you think as it does on your skills—keep your attitude positive and realistic, and *you will succeed.*

CHAPTER 9 CHECKLIST

___ Have you identified your transferable skills?
___ Have you developed your job search profile?
___ Have you made a list of networking opportunities?
___ Is your résumé complete and professional?
___ Have you created a business profile card?
___ Have you made a list of interview questions and practiced them?
___ What is your greatest weakness?
___ Have you researched your company?
___ What questions will you ask on your interview?
___ Have you written a thank-you note to someone recently?
___ Have you spoken with each person whom you plan to use as a reference?
___ Have you examined specific situations that you could use for examples in behavioral interviews?
___ Have you assembled your career portfolio?

END-OF-CHAPTER ACTIVITIES

ACTIVITY 1: PROCESS MEMO

Instructions: Write a message to your instructor explaining your ideal job—one for which you believe you are qualified (not necessarily your dream job). Identify a salary range for your starting salary; in other words, what is the least amount that you would accept, and what is the upper limit that you think you could be offered? What kinds of duties will you be performing? Have fun on this assignment but be realistic. (Use the Reflect/Respond/Revise process strategy.)

ACTIVITY 2: TEAM ACTIVITY—MOCK INTERVIEWS

Instructions: Refer to the Working and Learning in Teams sidebar on page 334 to select an interview scenario: screening, one-on-one, group, group-sequential, or stress interview. With a partner (or partners), develop a list of 15 interview questions. Put each other through a mock interview, with the interviewer(s) taking notes on the interviewee's performance. When the interviews are completed, it's time to share your feedback. What suggestions do you have for your partner to improve his or her performance?

ACTIVITY 3: ALL PRO TEMPS

Situation: You are currently working the front desk at All Pro, and your manager wants you to do the first screening of applicants. In other words, if you don't think someone has the potential to be an All Pro temporary, the applicant will not go further in the application process. Though you can informally ask questions, your manager doesn't want prospective applicants to know that you are doing any kind of screening—he is using you as an undercover agent, so to speak.

Instructions: Decide what criteria you will use to determine whether an applicant will have a personal interview with your manager. What makes a person an All Pro temp? Appearance? Attitude? Work experience? You've been given a lot of power. Develop notes and a one-page script you can use with the applicants.

ACTIVITY 4: PERSONAL AND CAREER OBJECTIVES

Instructions: What do you want to achieve 6 months from now? 1 year? 5 years? Objectives are always challenging to write, but people who write them tend to be more focused on achieving meaningful goals. Either before or after you have written your personal and career objectives, imagine that you are going to your retirement dinner. What do you want the speaker who introduces you to say about you?

1. *Personal objectives:* Take some time to identify your dreams, goals, and aspirations. When you define your personal and financial goals, you can identify how your career goals can help you achieve them. Do you want to own your own car, house or condo, or business? How about vacations—are there places in the world that you want to see? Do you want to get married? Have children? How many and when? Do you need more education and training? Will you start your master's degree or doctorate?

2. *Career objectives:* Now that you have a clearer idea about your personal objectives, compose a statement that reflects your career objective (or several different statements if you have more than one career goal).

ACTIVITY 5: DEVELOPING YOUR RÉSUMÉ AND CV

Instructions: Prepare the following items:

1. *Résumé:* Determine whether a chronological or functional résumé would present your skills in the best light. Use the information you prepared in the pages of Section A of this chapter; make sure that you apply parallel structure to terms you list on your résumé.

2. *Curriculum vitae:* In Chapter 7, "Global Communications and Technology," you learned that a curriculum vitae (CV) is often used in an international job search. Summarize all your job experience, education, awards and honors, clubs, and references that you chronicled earlier in this chapter. Collect all relevant details, and develop them into a CV. The more details, the more depth and thus the more effective your CV will be. To see an example, visit the *Foundations of Business Communication* Web site at <http://www.mhhe.com/djyoung>. Once you have accessed the home page, select "Student Activities" and then click on the Chapter 7 link.

ACTIVITY 6: PREPARING FOR AN INTERVIEW

Instructions: Use your research skills in each of the following:

1. Develop a list of at least five different companies for which you would like to work. Go to each one's Web site to find out more about the company, such as its mission statement,

size, and location. Also print a copy of the company's job application form, if available. Put the information into a short report to share with your peers and instructor.

2. What are some of the most common mistakes that occur on job interviews? Go online to research this topic. You can also call human resource executives at local companies and ask them about the kinds of behavior and attitudes that immediately eliminate applicants from the pool of prospects. Once again, put the information into a short report to share with your peers and instructor.

3. Research behavioral interviewing techniques. Develop a list of at least 20 possible behavioral-interview questions, and develop 5 to 10 tips for succeeding on a behavioral interview.

ACTIVITY 7: INTERVIEW FOLLOW-UP LETTERS

Instructions: Write the following letters:

1. *A letter rejecting a job offer:* Although you will experience rejection as part of your job search, you will also be on the other side: you will not accept every offer you receive. Draft a letter gracefully explaining that you are not accepting a company's offer at this time. Remember, it is never good to burn bridges. (Also keep this in mind when you resign from a job.) Focus on the positive, and show your appreciation for the offer.

2. *A thank-you letter to an interviewer:* Have you gone on an interview recently? If so, draft a letter highlighting a few positive points about the company or the interview. If you have not gone on an interview recently, write a mock letter, one that models statements you could use in a real letter.

3. *A letter of resignation:* Congratulations! You've gotten the new job! You start in three weeks. The only loose end to tie up is letting your current employer know that you'll be moving on. Once again, don't "burn any bridges"—you may need this employer as a reference or contact in the future.

4. *A letter responding to a job denial:* Imagine that a company has denied you a position but you would still like to work for that company someday. Write a letter thanking the interviewer for his or her time. Let the interviewer know you still have a keen interest in the company and would be interested in upcoming opportunities. This type of letter ranks among the rarest responses to rejection, so you will definitely make a strong, positive impression.

ACTIVITY 8: UNDERSTANDING HUMAN RESOURCES

Instructions: One step to include in preparing for your job search is to interview an HR professional. When you are the one asking the questions, you will feel more in control and thus less intimidated. Follow the directions below:

1. Develop a list of questions that you would find interesting; for example:
   - What kinds of qualities do you look for in prospective employees?
   - What kinds of positions are available?
   - What are some things that real candidates have done that immediately take them out of your pool of prospects?

2. Call the human resource department of a company in your area. Let the HR professional know that you are doing research on finding a job, and ask if you could briefly discuss a few of your questions.

ACTIVITY 9: CREATE A PORTFOLIO

Instructions: It's time to assemble a portfolio. You can prepare either a class portfolio, which will include documents you have created during your work with this textbook, or a career portfolio for use in your job search.

Throughout this chapter, you have gathered and prepared much of the information necessary to complete this task. You will find step-by-step information about assembling career portfolios at the *Foundations of Business Communication* Web site at <http://www.mhhe.com/djyoung>. Once you have accessed the home page, select "Student Activities" and then click on the Chapter 9 link.

REFERENCES

1. Andrew J. DuBrin, *Human Relations: Interpersonal, Job-Oriented Skills,* 8th ed., Prentice Hall, 2003.

2. "Six Degrees of Separation," <http://whatis.techart.com/definition/0,,sid9_gci932596,00.html>, accessed November 10, 2004.

3. Diane Wilson, *Back in Control: How to Stay Sane, Productive, and Inspired In Your Career Transition,* Sentient Publications, Boulder, 2004.

4. William Thourlby, *You Are What You Wear,* Forbes/Wittenburg and Brown, New York, 2001.

5. Katherine Hansen, *Behavioral Intervewing Strategies,* <www.quintcareers.com/behavioral_interviewing.html.>, accessed November 30, 2004.

6. William C. Byham, Ph. D., with Debra Pickett, *Landing the Job You Want: How to Have the Best Job Interview of Your Life,* Three Rivers Press, 1999.

KEY FOR LEARNING INVENTORY

1.	F	6.	F
2.	F	7.	T
3.	T	8.	T
4.	T	9.	T
5.	T	10.	T

Communicating on the Job

We become what we learn. —John Dewey, twentieth-century educator ■

You've been learning all your life and have developed good skills and a strong knowledge base; now you are ready to join the workforce. You may have thought that after graduating you could take a break from learning. To the contrary, when you start your career, you will learn new things every day. Sometimes it will be about a task; other times it will be about people; and *on important days, you will learn something about yourself.*

In this last chapter, you will learn tools to shape your skills as well as your career. First, you will examine leadership and your role as a leader. Then you will develop an understanding of job performance appraisals. Used effectively, feedback from appraisals can propel people into action and growth. As a result, a job performance appraisal is a powerful communication tool for achieving positive change in an individual and a corporation.

You will also have an opportunity to develop a written *purpose statement*. Your purpose statement will enhance, and possibly complete, your career portfolio, as it intertwines your personal and professional goals. Your purpose statement will also focus your energies and gauge your career decisions. A purpose statement draws on all your communication skills to produce a directive that reflects your goals and aspirations.

Finally, you will work on a team project that taps into all your communication skills: the *entrepreneur project*. Let your dreams pave the way as you create a vision of possibilities.

Thus, the book ends by helping you open the door to a future that fulfills you both personally and professionally. Let's get started by exploring leadership.

OBJECTIVES

When you have completed Chapter 10, you will be able to:

• Understand the difference between leading and managing.

• Identify your leadership experiences, qualities, and values.

• Examine two major performance feedback systems.

• Compose a purpose statement to complement your career portfolio.

• Analyze life experiences through reflective writing exercises.

• Write a job description.

Learning Inventory

1. When a person becomes a manager, that person becomes a leader.	T/F
2. If you do not manage others, you cannot be considered a leader.	T/F
3. Leadership qualities are determined solely by a person's experience.	T/F
4. The heroic leadership style is more effective than the collaborative style.	T/F
5. The main purpose of job appraisals is to determine salary increases.	T/F
6. Leading and managing are similar activities requiring similar qualities.	T/F
7. Once a leader makes a decision, he or she must "stay the course."	T/F
8. MBO performance appraisal systems include 360-degree multirater feedback.	T/F
9. Most people expect to be evaluated as above average or exceptional.	T/F
10. Performance feedback is an event, not a process.	T/F

■ SECTION A: LEADERSHIP

Right now, you may not consider yourself a leader, but it is your leadership qualities that will set you apart from others and determine the quality of your future—and that's true whether your goal in life is to become a "stay-at-home" parent or the CEO of a major corporation. What is a leader anyway?

- The word *leader* does not just refer to someone who holds a high-level corporate or government position.

- A **leader** is someone who *influences the way people think and act.*

This text takes the approach that leadership is developed from within, from a person's own set of qualities, values, and character. Though you will learn important lessons from profiles of

The "Truth" About Leadership *Have you already formulated ideas about leadership?* As you read the items below, consider what each myth means before you read the dialogue that follows.

Myth 1: *The leader is always right.* Many people do not question their leader's judgment, assuming their leader is always right. But leaders are human, and human beings make mistakes. When you idealize your leaders, at some point you are destined to be let down. *Identify strength as well as weakness in those you admire.*

Myth 2: *Leaders have all the answers.* A person becomes a leader partly because of highly developed decision-making skills. However, even the best leaders run into situations that have no clear answers, and, once again, sometimes leaders choose the wrong answer. You can avoid some fallout from a leader's mistakes by staying in tune with your own values: whenever you follow a leader's directive, make sure it is consistent with your values. *When in doubt, do a values check.*

Myth 3: *My ability to lead is determined by what I know about leadership.* Right now you might feel insecure about your leadership skills because you are somewhat unclear about what leadership entails. However, most of the best leaders throughout history had no formal training about leadership. *Your ability to lead is determined by your leadership actions, not your leadership knowledge.* To become a more effective leader, first learn about yourself: know the qualities that make up *your* character, and get in touch with your values.

Myth 4: *If I am a manager, I am automatically a leader.* To *lead* means to influence others in the way they think and act. Sadly, some people believe that getting a title automatically makes them a leader. Just because people follow someone's directives does not mean they consider that person a leader. A title gives you a certain kind of authority, but it does not give you power to influence people. People follow those whom they trust and respect, qualities that are *earned,* not assumed.

Myth 5: *I am not a leader because I don't manage people.* Leadership is a broad concept. Everyone needs to lead within his or her own life. *To what degree do you influence those around you on a daily basis?* That's what a leader does: influence people. Organizations are loaded with *informal leaders.* Look behind yourself and see if anyone is following: *do friends or family ask your opinion and then follow your direction?*

Myth 6: *All leaders have the same leadership abilities.* It's easy to go into the corporate world and assume that everyone who has an impressive title has effective leadership skills. However, every leader has a different profile with different strengths *and* limitations, and not all people in leadership positions display effective leadership qualities.

Myth 7: *Once leaders make a decision, they need to stay the course.* Too often people and organizations stay the course of action when it is going in the wrong direction. A sign of strong leadership is doing the right thing at the right time, even if that means making a change (or admitting a mistake). Limiting severe consequences by taking responsibility reaps superior results in the long run.

CHALLENGE:
As you read the chapter, record insights that change what you think about leadership. At the end of the chapter, you will have an opportunity to record some of your own myths along with your new ways of thinking.

leaders and the principles they live by, it's how *you* apply principles in your life that will make a difference in your life: even the best knowledge achieves little when it is not applied effectively. Consider the following questions:

- How do you know a good leader when you encounter one?
- Do you define leadership through a person's professional position or personal qualities?
- Are some people natural-born leaders, or do people develop into being good leaders?
- Do you have leadership qualities?

Theories about leadership abound, but exactly what good leadership is, how leadership skills are developed, or how you can identify a good leader when you see one—all of these are open for debate. The goal here is to open your thinking about leadership and then assist you in uncovering your own leadership qualities: ways of thinking and acting (that reflect both strengths *and* weaknesses) that you can use to shape your profile as a successful leader.

Aspects of Leadership

Is Leading Different From Managing?   Before considering qualities of leadership, let's examine the difference between leadership and management. According to Bostrom Solutions, the difference between "doing the right thing" and "doing things right" gives insight into how the two roles differ: [1]

- **Leadership** is about *doing the right thing* by providing vision and direction.
- **Management** is about *doing things right* by coordinating and balancing resources.

Whether you are a better manager or a better leader probably depends on the task and the circumstances. Both roles involve making effective decisions, but this chapter delves more into leadership qualities than management qualities. For now, just realize that on a broad, general level the two can be considered different types of roles.

Every person is a leader in his or her own life, whether or not that person feels like a leader in a group or work situation. In addition, roles change during a lifetime. Who you are today is different in many ways from who you will be tomorrow.

Who Is an Effective Leader?   At times, people confuse their feelings about a person with that person's leadership qualities. In other words, you can hold a person in high esteem as a leader, but that doesn't mean the person achieves effective, or even honest, results. Consider the high-profile leaders who through the years have fallen from their positions in shame. Most of them rose to their positions through what appeared to be good leadership qualities, at least on the surface. Afterward, people who trusted them felt violated by their influence.

When a leader "misleads," it is difficult for those outside the situation to know the truth. Part of being a good, effective leader is *demonstrating behavior to the outside world that is consistent with the leader's internal values.* In other words, an effective leader has solid values and consistently portrays those values:

1. *An effective leader is someone who is the same on the outside as on the inside; the person's actions directly reflect his or her values.* **Integrity** exists when there is no difference between a person's internal set of beliefs and his or her actions. Therefore, from the outside, it is not always possible to determine whether a person has integrity—that judgment is valid only to the degree to which a person's values align with his or her actions, which is not always readily apparent.

   People admire leaders who seem to hold the same values as their own, and people judge their leaders based on trust. Thus, *trust* is a critical element of leadership. So how does a leader develop trust?

2. *When leaders are consistent and predictable, they develop trust.* In contrast, inconsistent and unpredictable behavior causes people not to trust; when leaders contradict themselves, they appear untrustworthy. Inconsistent decisions do not seem to be drawn from a solid rationale that drives the decisions, and the integrity of the leader can come into question. Think about a time when a colleague said one thing one day and then the opposite the next day (with no valid rationale to explain the change)—how did that make you feel about the person?

3. *Effective leaders are clear about purpose, and they focus on it.* Effective leaders have defined the vision and mission of their domain. They have also communicated that purpose to those carrying it out. Thus, a good leader is more loyal to the cause than to personal interests or friendships. Leaders get the right job done in the right way, making difficult decisions even if some people will not be pleased.

4. *Effective leaders value strengths and understand their own limitations.* As discussed, no one is exceptional at everything. Effective leaders understand their own strengths and honestly accept their own limitations. By realistically defining their own qualities, leaders maintain more control. By honestly accepting their own shortcomings, they build teams that have the diversity to counteract the leader's own weaknesses through the strengths of the team members.

   For example, if a CEO knows that his or her weakness is finance, that CEO will take extra care in hiring an expert in that area who can be trusted. Effective leaders maximize their ability to use their strengths and manage limitations by bringing others on their teams who complement their abilities.

How Do Leaders Influence?

Whether a group is aware of it or not, their leader influences in *spoken* and *unspoken* ways. By *words* and *example,* the leader lets the group know how seriously he or she takes certain kinds of behavior or ways of thinking. When group members go outside those parameters, they violate group norms and usually know it.

Leaders set the tone of how a company operates. Hence, if everyone in a company sees the boss spending company money frivolously, others in the company feel justified in taking extra liberty with their spending also. If the company president orders a tuna fish sandwich at a company luncheon, everyone at the table will be influenced by the lunch order—it's unlikely that anyone will order filet mignon.

Leaders influence the moral tone of an organization. Leaders unconsciously give others permission to do or not to do specific behaviors through the actions they take. Therefore, when we discuss leadership, ultimately we must also discuss integrity and ethics.

COMMUNICATION CHALLENGES

Misleading Conduct Some of the most challenging communication moments in the workplace happen when leaders falter. Whether it is over a leader's lack of integrity, failure to assume responsibility, or inability to change course, communicating your discomfort can be precarious. When you know you are communicating with someone who lacks ethics or integrity, do not assume your complaints will be welcomed or dealt with fairly.

Many companies have policies that allow employees to request, through the human resources department, that a third party mediate a discussion between those involved; through HR, complaints about misconduct can be filed, though there is no guarantee they will be acted on. When you are faced with challenging behaviors, keep a daily log of your workplace activities and what objections you had. You cannot change the way others behave, but you can protect yourself for the day their behavior comes to light.

CHALLENGE:

Although it is well known within your company that it is the supervisor's job to negotiate contracts with new vendors, your supervisor has asked you to take on that responsibility. You are assigned a new vendor who has developed an exciting product that would mesh perfectly with the company product line.

The problem is that you are new to the company, unfamiliar with the contract process and without a lot of experience in negotiating. You're worried not only about scaring the vendor away but also about what that loss might mean to your career at the company.

After listening to your concerns, your supervisor responds, "I want every one of my people to be capable of doing the work I'm expected to do in this chair because someday you might be sitting in it. Now go to it." *You don't think you can. How do you proceed?*

To some degree, people prefer approval; they prefer to do things right and be acknowledged for it. That's one way leaders inspire and motivate. However, all people have a range of undesirable behavior that they may express under the "right" circumstances. That's why leaders tend to bring out *the best* and *the worst* in their followers.

In addition, just because a leader asks or implies that you do something doesn't mean that your actions are automatically right. When a leader expects you to do something that's clearly wrong, following that leader is a poor choice. When people fall into the trap of doing something wrong because of a leader's instructions, the defense of "I couldn't help it; it was what I was told to do" doesn't usually hold up in court.

How Do Leaders Move an Organization Forward?

For an organization or team to be effective, all the various parts and people need to align. When everyone is focused on achieving the same outcomes, success is much more likely. One way leaders achieve focused alignment is through developing a mission and vision:

- A **mission statement** expresses a company's reason for being, its purpose.

- A **vision statement** is broader and establishes the context in which the business exists.

For example, here are the mission and vision statements for Wilson Learning Worldwide, a company that provides various types of corporate training:

Mission statement:	Helping people and organizations achieve performance with fulfillment.
Vision statement:	Recognized as a premium provider of human performance improvement solutions that work.

Once a company has developed its mission and vision statements, the next step entails putting the mission and vision into action. How does an organization lead the group toward fulfilling the company mission and vision?

Communicating a Strategy

To accomplish the vision, a leader can create a strategy through planning that identifies specific actions.

A **strategy** consists of *goals, objectives,* and *action plans* that align with the company mission and vision statements:

- **Goals** are broad statements of what you'd like to achieve.
- **Objectives** are specific and measurable actions.
- An **action plan** consists of specific tasks along with due dates.

For example, a manager may decide that one way to increase effectiveness is to upgrade the financial software system (the goal). This strategy could then be turned into an action plan by identifying objectives, the various tasks involved, and assigning due dates.

Any group can look at an organization's vision and use it to create a strategy consisting of goals and action plans. If they guide their decisions by the vision and mission, they know they are doing work to advance the company.

Vision and mission statements are tools that leaders can use to focus energies, build momentum toward achieving goals, and shape their corporate culture. However, not all companies have written vision and mission statements. When they do, they develop them in their own ways. For example, some companies hire consultants to help their managers develop statements; others develop the statements behind the scenes and then communicate the statements to their employees.

When you start a new job, read your company's vision and mission statements and then consider how your job is an extension of them. These statements can play a vital role in driving a company forward, as they give employees a cohesive understanding of purpose.

Peering Into the Future: *Although it is impossible to know what the future will bring to a business, vision and mission statements offer an opportunity to present an idealized goal to guide employees to that future.* Is it important for a company to update vision and mission statements over time?

VOCABULARY BUILDERS

Micro and *Macro* Have you ever heard the term *micromanaging? Micromanagers* are meticulous, getting down to minute details of how to do a job. In contrast, *macromanagers* deal only with the big picture. "Minor" details frustrate them; macromanagers feel that if the people they supervise need microscopic details, they are in the wrong job.

Whether you are a micro- or macromanager may already be evident, even if you don't manage anyone right now. When you give someone instructions, do you provide every tiny detail for fear the listener won't get the job done correctly? Or do you prefer to give only the basics, believing the listener will ask a question if more details are needed?

Ask yourself: *What's my style? Will I be a micro- or macromanager? Do I know someone who has an opposite style? Am I able to adapt, giving details when asked and providing a global picture when someone feels frustrated with all the details?*

INTERNET EXERCISE 10.2

Testing Yourself The Myers-Briggs Personality Type Inventory is only one tool for gauging leadership and personality styles; there are many different measurement tools available. For more information about social styles or personality assessments, visit the *Foundations of Business Communication* Web site at <http://www.mhhe.com/djyoung>.

Once you have accessed the home page, select "Student Activities" and then click the Chapter 10 link for instructions on getting started.

However, when leaders view vision and mission statements simply as tasks to accomplish so that they are available upon request, employees generally view them as interesting wall hangings to be read in passing. As a leader, you will decide the role vision and mission statements will play in your operations.

Collaborative Versus Heroic Leadership

Two basic questions all leaders must answer are:

- What are our goals and objectives?
- How are we going to achieve them?

Some leaders take a **collaborative** approach (also referred to as *participative* or *democratic* approach) to answering these questions; they involve their teams in defining goals and objectives and allow the teams freedom in deciding how to accomplish them. Others take a **heroic** approach (also referred to as *authoritative* or *autocratic* approach) by defining objectives and directing how employees should carry out their jobs. With a collaborative approach, managers and employees work together to identify their department's objectives; individuals write their own objectives and quotas and use them as a standard for evaluation. With a heroic approach, top management makes the decisions; directives are then passed down to lower levels.

Under most circumstances, collaborative leadership is considered more effective. That's because all leaders have certain strengths and limitations; one person cannot possibly do everything. A collaborative leader is more prone to recognizing limitations and building a team that has strengths to shore up limitations. In general, collaborative leaders build much stronger teams.

However, there are times when a leader needs to be collaborative and other times when the situation demands that the leader decide important issues without collaboration: leaders cannot bring everything to the team.

Nature or Nurture?

Is leadership determined by nature or nurture? If you did research, you could find evidence to back up either position. However, whenever there is an either/or choice relating to issues of nature versus nurture, the answer does not lie in one *or* the other. The answer inevitably relates to the percentage of influence: to what degree does nature (genetics, biology) influence versus to what degree does nurture (education, experience) influence?

Everyone has a unique biological inheritance, just as everyone has a unique set of experiences. Think of nature as *predetermined social or personality tendencies.* To become a good leader, you will want to know your personality tendencies or social style so that you can reach for balance, nurturing some tendencies and subduing others. The key is using experience to bring out the best in your or someone else's nature.

One popular way to learn about personality and social style is through the Myers-Briggs Personality Type Inventory (MBTI). The MBTI divides variables into four major categories; two of those categories are introverts/extroverts and thinkers/feelers. (See Activity 7 in Chapter 8's end-of-chapter activities for more on Myers-Briggs.)

Knowing that everyone has a unique style allows you to work more effectively with differences without being defensive about your own style or trying to change or control others. For example, imagine you are an extrovert who is working with an introvert. If your introverted colleague is always quiet, it helps to understand that being quiet doesn't mean something is wrong. By being sensitive to other people's styles, you will be more accepting and able to work with their strengths.

So remember, there are aspects of your personality or social style that are determined by your nature, your genetic composition. By understanding your nature, you can nurture your strengths as you work on balancing your weaknesses or compensating for them.

The Leader in You

So far we've discussed broad aspects of leadership. As you make decisions daily, you shape the environment around you, but you also shape yourself. You have your own unique leadership qualities and experiences.

To develop your own leadership qualities more fully, you must first understand who you are and then take actions based on what you know about yourself as a leader:

- Understand your purpose.
- Identify your values, strengths, and limitations.
- Take actions that are consistent with your values.

Becoming an effective leader is a lifelong process; you build your leadership ability by the way you think and the actions you take. The remainder of this section assists you in identifying some of your current leadership qualities.

Your Leadership Qualities   A person doesn't wake up one day and find that he or she is a strong leader. Leadership skills develop over a lifetime. In many situations every day, you have opportunities to exercise your leadership skills.

What leadership qualities do you express? Consider formal and informal experiences at school, at your place of worship, in part- and full-time jobs, in group sports, and in associations and volunteer groups. Below are some words and phrases that describe qualities of strong leaders; go through the list slowly and notice your impressions as well as the specific experiences that come to mind.

Risk taker / Ambitious / Good listener / Excellent communicator / Problem solver / Confident / Pushes through fear / Brings out the best in others / Focused / Energized / Motivator / Passionate / Clearheaded / Sees the big picture / Thinks outside the box / Tries new ideas / Gives credit where credit is due / Gives honest feedback / Collaborative / Shares responsibility / Takes responsibility / Admits mistakes / Committed / Dedicated / Open-minded / Visionary / Communicates the mission / Deals with root causes not just symptoms / Optimistic / Energizes / Mobilizes team toward achieving goals / Understands consequences (immediate and long-term) / Expresses initiative / Self-starter / Embraces diversity / Team player / Cooperative / Decisive / Entrepreneurial / Strong / Courageous / Brave / Calm under pressure

First, identify three qualities listed above that describe you. For each quality, recall an experience in which you used your leadership skills successfully. Summarize each in the spaces below. For example:

Mobilizes team toward achieving goals: My high school basketball team was at the end of the season with no chance of winning the conference. It would have been easy to give up, but I played as strong and tough at the end of the season as I did at the beginning. As a result, my teammates played harder too, and surprisingly we won a game against the state champions.

Entrepreneurial: I work as a hairstylist part-time, and I have developed a clientele. Even though I am away at school, I maintain contact with several clients and do work for them when I am home during school breaks. Some clients like my work so well that they say they would travel 50 miles just to have me cut their hair.

Leadership Qualities:

1. _____

_____

2. _____

_____

3. _____

_____

Your Peak Leadership Experiences   Think about your peak leadership experiences—situations in which you acted with integrity to influence another person or group. Include anything from grade school to the present. Describe one of these experiences below, and explain what it was about the experience that drew on your leadership abilities. What did you learn about yourself as a leader?

_____

_____

_____

_____

_____

_____

Here are other questions to provoke your thinking:

- Describe a time when a group depended on you to get a specific job done.
- Describe a time when you were in a group and a wrong decision was being made: how did you handle it?

Your Values   Frederick M. Hudson and Pamela D. McLean discovered, after studying hundreds of biographies of successful adults, that people evaluated their lives based on some combination of six core values:[2]

- *Personal mastery: to know yourself* (self-esteem, confidence, identity, inner motivation, a positive sense of self, courage, sense of being a distinct person)
- *Achievement: to reach your goals* (working, winning, playing in organized sports, getting results and recognition, being purposeful, focusing on "doing")
- *Intimacy: to love and be loved* (bonding, caring, making relationships work, feeling close, being a friend, being connected)
- *Play and creativity: to follow your intuition* (being imaginative, spontaneous, original, expressive, artistic, funny, curious, or childlike; not being purposeful)
- *Search for meaning: to find wholeness* (spiritual integrity, unity, integrity, peace, an inner connection to all things, spirituality, trust in the flow of life, inner wisdom, connecting with nature, connecting with a higher power, focus on being)
- *Compassion and contribution: to leave a legacy* (improving, helping, feeding, reforming, leaving the world a better place, serving, social and environmental caring, institution building, volunteering, engaging in activism)

Hudson and McLean also found that as people grow and change, the order of priority of these core values tends to change as well. Thus, what was a priority at age 20 may not be as important at 40 or 70.

Which core value is most important to you? That's your key source of energy and passion. By focusing your energy on activities that are congruent with your most important values, you find more energy and satisfaction. In turn, when you focus on activities that are incongruent with your values, your energy and passion are sapped.

In the following exercise, you have to make difficult choices; but in the process, you will prioritize your core values. Rank-order the core values listed above to identify which are most important to you at this point in your life (1 = most important, 6 = least important). Also, write a few comments to describe how you express each value. For example:

Personal mastery: Right now my most important goal is doing things to build my confidence so that I get a good job that leads to a great career. Every day, I try to learn more about who I really am compared to what people expect from me.

Core Values:

1. _____

_____

2. _____

_____

3. _____

_____

4. _____

_____

5. _____

_____

6. _____

_____

Feedback on Your Leadership   How others perceive you as a leader is different from how you perceive yourself. The only way to find out how others perceive your leadership qualities is to ask them.

Select three people from different areas of your life (family members; long-time, personal friends; peers or associates at school; coworkers). Ask each of them how he or she would describe your leadership abilities: *What do you see are my strengths as a leader? What growing edges should I work on to become a stronger leader? What other suggestions about leadership can you give me?* Record the feedback you receive, and identify common threads (similar comments that surface among all of those you interview) and list them below. For example:

> I interviewed my older brother, my best friend, and a member of my communications team. They all had different things to say, but agreed that my strengths were that I was highly motivated and committed to achieving my goals. They also seemed to agree that I sometimes got too excited about reaching a goal and stopped listening to what others had to say.

Whom did you interview? _____

Leadership strengths: _____

_____

_____

_____

Growing edges: _____

_____

_____

Your Heroes You may not be totally aware of your beliefs about what effective leadership is, but your beliefs can be revealed by examining the individuals you respect and admire (as well as those you don't).

1. Select a famous person whom you consider to be a *great leader.* Consider presidents, business leaders, spiritual leaders, and athletes. Now ask, *what are his or her characteristics?* Consider accomplishments, leadership styles, communication abilities, and other attributes.

_____

_____

_____

2. Select a famous person whom you consider to be an *ineffective leader: what are his or her characteristics?*

_____

_____

_____

3. Now write about someone who is a personal role model or mentor. *Why do you consider your role model or mentor a strong leader? What have you learned from that person?*

_____

_____

_____

Your Ability to Motivate One quality of good leadership is inspiring others to carry out their tasks with dedication and passion. It's one thing to be able to do that yourself; it's quite another thing to find a way to inspire others. How do you motivate others?

1. Describe a situation or problem you were working on in which someone inspired you. What words or actions did that person use to motivate you?

_____

_____

_____

2. Describe a situation in which you needed to get others involved to get a job done. What words and actions did you use to motivate your team?

_____

_____

_____

EXPLORE

1. What is integrity? Spend 10 minutes developing your ideas about what you think integrity is: Where does integrity come from—within or without? What factors encourage integrity and what factors stifle it? Use the reflect/respond/revise process strategy.

2. What are some major theories of motivation that you have studied? Some names associated with motivation theory are Douglas McGregor (theory y), Frederick Herzberg (two-factor motivation hygiene theory), Abraham Maslow (hierarchy of needs), and David McClelland (achievement motivation). Select one and log onto the Internet to do some research. Write a paragraph summarizing the theory, and then state what aspects of the theory you agree and/or disagree with.

COACHING TIP

Time Management Do you find yourself running as fast as you can but still not getting everything done? It may be that you need to use your time more wisely.

Planning is a process. Your priorities change on a daily basis, so you need to do some sort of planning every day:

1. Start your day by *doing a mind map* to identify what you need to work on that day.
2. *Prioritize your list.* What is essential versus nonessential? What is urgent versus less urgent or even trivial? Work first on the items that are essential and urgent.
3. Finally, *learn to say no.* How much of your time is taken up with things you do simply because you don't want to hurt someone's feelings? Though being kind and being compassionate are important qualities, saying yes for fear of disapproval is neither kind nor compassionate: it's needy behavior, and people will take advantage of your fears.

Structure might also help you with your time. Get in the habit of doing certain things at the same time every day, and set a time limit. You will then do those things automatically, and they won't drain you of precious mental or emotional energy. As established advice goes, repeat the desired behavior 21 days in a row and it will become a habit.

Focus on developing useful habits to support your routine, and you will have more time to do your essential, urgent work.

Ask yourself: *What new, productive habit do I want to incorporate into my daily routine? To what kinds of activities or requests do I need to start saying no?*

Results: Your Major Achievements People often use words to paint a picture of their achievements; whether their words paint a truthful picture is another story. However, outcomes cannot be denied—they are tangible results of honest effort.

Describe two situations in which you achieved excellent outcomes. At least one of your examples should have occurred within a team or leadership setting. What qualities, values, or characteristics does each achievement reveal?

Achievement 1: _____

_____

_____

_____

_____

Achievement 2: _____

_____

_____

_____

_____

EXPLORE

1. Identify a question about yourself that you wish to explore, such as "What qualities do I exhibit that do not demonstrate good leadership?" First do a mind map and then spend 10 to 20 minutes writing about your question.

2. Now spend another 10 to 20 minutes focusing on the positive and constructive side; for example:

   • What changes would I benefit from making?

   • What are my strong leadership qualities?

   • What do I express that is positive and that I should continue?

SECTION A: CONCEPT CHECK

1. How is managing different from leading? How are they similar?
2. What are some commonly held misconceptions about leadership?
3. Describe the difference between a collaborative approach and a heroic approach to leadership.

■ SECTION B: PERFORMANCE FEEDBACK, JOB DESCRIPTIONS, AND ACTION PLANS

Performance Feedback

Since you may not have your first job yet, you may be asking yourself: *why do I need to learn about writing performance feedback or appraisals?* Here are some reasons:

- Even in an entry-level position, you may write part of your own evaluation as well as your job description and objectives.

- In any position, you may provide performance feedback for others.

- By understanding basic concepts about performance feedback, you acquire an advantage in achieving career success.

Being evaluated in business differs dramatically from being evaluated in education. For the most part, you are accustomed to completing individual projects that lead to a grade in a course. However, in the business world, you will be evaluated on a number of different things simultaneously and possibly from all directions—from your supervisor as well as your peers and clients. Your "grade" will not generally hinge on one particular project or paper; part of your evaluation may relate to teamwork, another part to leadership.

Since performance feedback systems vary somewhat from company to company, this chapter provides only basic points so that you have a foundation on which to build. Nevertheless, this section provides enough information to prepare you for your first encounter with performance feedback on the job.

A Process, Not an Event   Many people consider performance feedback to be an annual event (see Figures 10.1 and 10.2). That may be because many corporations require an annual review (at minimum). However, perceiving performance feedback as an event—rather than understanding it as a process—overlooks the most important aspect of performance feedback: the purpose of performance feedback is to improve on-the-job performance.

Effective performance feedback enhances relationships as it brings perceptions more in line with reality. However, many people, as well as businesses, identify performance feedback primarily with an annual raise. It is important to point out that even when money is linked to performance, *the greater significance of feedback relates to professional growth.*

When you view performance feedback as an avenue toward growth, you have the advantage of feeling less fearful about it. You also have the advantage of taking more control of it.

Self-Directed Feedback and Growth   You do not need to wait until you have an annual review to ask your manager how you are doing. Often young professionals are hesitant to ask for feedback because they fear hearing the worst. According to M. Scott Peck, a psychiatrist and author, the feedback we don't want to hear can be a powerful impetus for growth:

The truth is that our finest moments are most likely to occur when we are feeling deeply uncomfortable, unhappy, or unfulfilled. For it is only in such moments, propelled by our discomfort, that we are likely to step out of our ruts and start searching for different ways or truer answers.[3]

Thus, even *if* the feedback is not initially good, honest feedback expands the opportunity for significant change and growth. Seeking an honest perception early on gives the opportunity for turning things around before a formal, written appraisal occurs. In all likelihood, the feedback you receive will not be as bad as you fear, but you may not have a clear understanding until you ask.

Another point to remember is that even the best managers find giving constructive feedback challenging. By being receptive to

---

COACHING TIP

Start/Stop/Continue One effective way to receive balanced feedback is to apply an exercise called *start/stop/continue*. When asking your manager for feedback, the following questions will point you in the right direction:

Start:	What am I currently not doing that you would like for me to start doing?
Stop:	What am I currently doing that I should stop doing?
Continue:	What am I doing that I should continue to do?

By asking for one to three examples for each question, you will get a balanced view. By answering the questions about yourself before you meet to discuss the answers, you will enhance the process.

When all parties to a discussion explore these questions about how they get the job done, feedback sessions stay focused and productive. If you are leading the discussion, provide the questions ahead of time.

The benefit of following this pattern is that everyone involved knows what to expect and understands that the approach is based on a system.

FIGURE 10.1 | Traditional Performance Appraisal Form

Job Feedback: A traditional performance appraisal covers a specific time period—the last year, the last quarter—and is usually tied to an employee's salary review. A developmental performance appraisal includes an additional section in which the employee describes job-growth goals, ambitions, or expectations for the future. If your employer or instructor were to use the following form to rate your performance on the job or in class, what responses would you anticipate in Sections A and B?

Performance Appraisal

Employee's Name   Division:
Soc Sec No.   Work Location:
Job Title

Supervisor's Name   Supervisor's Title
Review Period

A. Responsibilities for Review Period
1.
2.
3.

B. Description of Overall Performance
❏ *Performance Substantially and Consistently Exceeded Expectations:*
    Results substantially and consistently surpass all defined expectations. Employee
    regularly contributes beyond current job responsibilities.
❏ *Performance Exceeded Expectations:*
    Results frequently surpass all defined expectations. Employee consistently demonstrates
    an ability to excel in the widest variety of assignments within the scope of the job.
    Learning progress exceeds expectations.
❏ *Performance Achieved Expectations:*
    Results consistently achieve the defined expectations. In some areas, results may
    exceed the expectations whereas in others, they may occasionally fall short; however,
    the overall composite is solid performance. The rating means meeting the high standards
    of our company, and most employees will typically achieve this rating. Learning
    progress meets expectations.
❏ *Performance Needs Improvement to Meet Expectations:*
    Results indicate that the employee met some but not all of the performance standards for
    the position. Occasionally, the employee may not have completed assignments on time
    or comprehensively. Performance was generally sound, but usually in the highly routine
    or structured areas of the job. Learning progress minimally meets expectations.
❏ *Performance Substantially Below Expectations:*
    Results missed achieving the defined expectations to a degree that cannot be allowed
    to continue. Learning progress did not meet expectations.

C. Approvals

_____
Supervisor's Signature   Date

_____
Human Resource Representative's Signature   Date

FIGURE 10.2 | Self-Appraisal Form

Look at Yourself: A **self-appraisal** *form can be a useful communication tool for both the employer and the employee. Effective performance review that leads to job growth depends on both the employer's ability to deliver a constructive and objective assessment and the employee's willingness to honestly assess his or her own work.* Why might an employee be unwilling to provide a completely honest yearly self-appraisal of his or her own work to a supervisor?

YEARLY SELF-APPRAISAL

Employee's Name
Title:

Directions: Please complete the Self-Appraisal on your key responsibilities for the year in review. You should respond in bulleted summaries and indicate your projects.

Self-Appraisal

1. Job skills:
_____
_____
_____
_____

2. Completion of assignments as given:
_____
_____
_____
_____

3. Communication-organization skills:
_____
_____
_____
_____

4. Professional development goals:
_____
_____
_____
_____

5. Include your specific strengths:
_____
_____
_____
_____

6. Include your specific areas for improvement:
_____
_____
_____
_____

---

all types of feedback, you lighten a serious task your manager may dread performing. Your open attitude shows leadership as well as commitment to your own success.

Input For Your Performance Feedback Most entrants into the business world believe that their immediate supervisor is responsible for their performance feedback. Though this belief is true, it is also misleading: believing their managers' perceptions are the most important, professionals may focus their energies on trying *to please* or *impress* their bosses.

Sometimes this is done at the expense of other people and things that are just as important, sometimes more important.

In observing how an employee gets the job done, an astute supervisor takes into account more than her or his own relationship with the employee. The supervisor cares how the employee treats peers and clients, even when no one else is there to observe. To make a company work, everyone needs to report to somebody; however, it is a fallacy to believe the immediate supervisor is the only one who counts when it comes to measuring performance.

It is doubtful that you will report to the same supervisor or manager for your entire career. In the business world, change occurs rapidly, and you are more likely to have several supervisors during your career. Instead of trying to impress your immediate supervisor, focus on developing your growing edges and learning important lessons at each stage of your career. Each manager can teach you something valuable and unique, but only if you pay attention and learn from his or her actions as well as words.

By going beyond your own perceptions and learning from others, you are letting go of self-limiting, egocentric behavior. Try to see your performance from all perspectives by asking: *Who are my key stakeholders? Who are the people most affected by my work?* Know who they are, and consider each of them important. Align your performance with expectations, and you will succeed. First, however, you must understand what others expect from you; asking for their feedback periodically helps ensure that your expectations are aligned.

EXPLORE

Who is affected by how you do your work? In other words, if you were to seek input from those you affect, whom would you approach for feedback?

Performance Feedback and Expectations   Ideally, performance feedback leads to improved relationships as well as improved skills and ways of getting a job done. However, when performance feedback is linked to salary increases, the stakes seem higher and the focus can become displaced.

Though unrealistic, most people expect to be rated *above average* or *exceptional* for job performance.[4] The problem is that everyone cannot be rated above the standard. Looking at a bell curve, only 50 percent are average and above. Though a bell curve is not exact, it demonstrates that a high proportion of people are likely to feel disappointed because their expectations did not match their reviews.

Going into a performance feedback session, don't try to convince yourself that you are doing your job perfectly. Align your expectations with feedback that you have received throughout the year. Even if salary is tied to your performance rating—or *especially* if salary is tied to it—keep your focus on *development,* not money. If you can tie performance feedback to development rather than money, you will be ahead in the long run.

EXPLORE

Think of an instance when you received feedback that was very different from what you expected. How did you feel? How did you work through your feelings? What is the "bigger lesson" you learned from the experience?

PRACTICE

Instructions: In a team of two or three, observe one another in class for a week (or another specific amount of time) and take turns playing the roles of the manager and the employee.

1. Before the observation, develop performance feedback criteria (for example, class participation, completion of assignments on time, focus, motivation, attendance), along with a scale to measure or rate the behavior.

2. At the end of the week, write feedback for each member of your group, giving specific examples for three or four behaviors; balance positive feedback with constructive feedback.

3. Deliver your feedback to one another. (See the Coaching Tip on page 354; if feasible, use the start/stop/continue approach when giving feedback.)

4. After everyone has received feedback, discuss what you learned from the exercise.

Feedback Systems

So far we have discussed job performance feedback as a process; now we will discuss job performance feedback as a *system.* Two common systems are managing-by-objectives (MBO) and 360-degree multirater performance feedback. Though the framework for each of these systems is discussed below, how they are implemented will vary from company to company and even from manager to manager.

Because each corporation has its own system, as a new hire you will want to learn about the system your company employs so that you can apply it effectively. Many young employees are apprehensive about being appraised on the job, even though a job appraisal can be a most powerful guide for growth.

Managing by Objectives

Companies started using managing-by-objectives (MBO) systems in the 1960s, and these systems have been used to some extent ever since; MBO represents a classic approach to job performance appraisal. When using an MBO system, the *outcome* becomes the focus, not *how* the objective will be achieved. There are a multitude of variations of MBO systems; here we will cover the basic model.

To start, a direct report (employee) and supervisor negotiate the direct report's objectives. The direct report has a degree of freedom in determining how to achieve the objectives. Of course, all objectives are written as an extension of the company mission.

One way to implement an MBO system is to start with a written job description. The job description identifies key elements of the job and basic job duties. From that job description, key result areas (or major areas of responsibility) can be identified. For each key result area, one or more measurable objectives are written. At the end of the year, performance feedback focuses on the extent to which the objectives were achieved.

An advantage of MBO is that the system primarily focuses on tangible outcomes that everyone understands. Rewards may be given according to how closely objectives are achieved; thus, MBO systems generally tie money to performance.

Here are the major components of an MBO system:

- Company mission statement.
- Job description: key result areas and job duties.
- Measurable objectives.
- Performance feedback to assess objectives.

Keep in mind that these are the basic elements of an MBO system; however, there are as many different ways of implementing an MBO system as there are companies that use them. Also, within each company, managers add their own individual approaches. Performance feedback and appraisal systems are complicated because they deal with sensitive issues that are extremely important to most people.

360-Degree Multirater Feedback

As early as the mid-1990s, companies started using a feedback system called *360-degree feedback.* This system appraises or evaluates competencies that are important to the job. Competencies are measured from all directions; hence, the term *360 degrees* indicates the scope of the feedback.

A person's manager as well as peers, clients, and customers (raters) all give input through forms that are tailored to the competencies needed for the person's job. Each rater compares the person's current performance on a specific competency to what the rater thinks it should be. A critical piece is the person's self-assessment, to which rater perceptions are compared.

- When raters' scores are *consistent* with the self-score, this shows that perceptions are aligned and indicates that individuals are working together to solve mutual issues.
- When perceptions *differ,* it is important to discuss the *why* and *how* so that needed changes can be identified.

Here's how it works: Let's imagine Bill is conducting a 360-degree feedback on himself. Together, Bill and his manager identify who will give Bill feedback. They select the following:

Bill's manager (Sue)

Sue's manager (Terry)

Bill's peers and team members (Al, Marge, Jose, Ahmed)

Bill's direct reports (George, Marjorie, Katlyn, Sandro)

Bill's customers (5 clients chosen randomly from among 20 possibilities)

When more than one person is in a grouping (such as Bill's peers, direct reports, and customers), the feedback is given anonymously. It can take about two weeks from the time the forms are distributed to the time they are tallied. The feedback form includes questions grouped in various behavioral competencies, such as teamwork, leadership, decision making, planning, and follow-through, among other categories.

Here are Bill's overall results on a scale of 1 to 5 (with 1 being the lowest score and 5 being the highest):

Bill's self-assessment	4
Sue (Bill's manager)	2
Terry (Sue's manager)	3
Peers and teammates	4
Direct reports	2
Bill's clients	4

This sort of feedback takes individual perceptions and assigns numbers to them; however, the numbers still need to be interpreted. Where Bill's perceptions are aligned with those giving him feedback, little discussion is needed. However, where there is a discrepancy, Bill may want to schedule a meeting to understand and learn from the feedback.

Some companies bring in professional coaches from outside the company to help interpret results and develop a plan. Feedback at its best has positive outcomes, not destructive and hurtful ones. However, sometimes a person must hear honest feedback before developing the significant motivation that it sometimes takes to change the way work is performed.

To benefit from the feedback, Bill would probably want more information from his direct reports and his immediate supervisor. He might begin the meeting by saying something like the following:

I am a bit confused by the results and am really interested in learning from this. I would appreciate if you would tell me more about why you rated this competency the way you did and how I can improve.

The 360-degree feedback approach is comprehensive and can give honest, credible results when implemented in a professional manner. In this case, if Bill can open himself to listen and understand the various perspectives, he can then set goals for himself that lead to dramatic change in his relationships and the results he achieves.

Many software programs for 360-degree multirater feedback are now available, and many companies conduct the feedback online. As you learn more about this type of feedback, you will realize that it takes courage to hear what others actually think about how you perform your job. One point to remember is that although this system can be implemented professionally and successfully, many things can go wrong if it is done without adequate planning and controls.

Job Descriptions

Regardless of the type of performance feedback system your company uses, you are likely to have to write a job description. Though you may inherit a job description from a predecessor, you will have to review the description and adapt it to current circumstances.

Even if you think you understand what your job will be like when you accept a job offer, the reality can be quite different. Your employer's description of the challenges you will face is one thing; coming face-to-face with the "real deal" is quite another.

INTERNET EXERCISE 10.3

Group Analysis Are you interested in seeking input from your peers, instructors, or family about how you complete tasks? You can examine a 360-degree feedback form at the *Foundations of Business Communication* Web site at <http://www.mhhe.com/djyoung>.

Once you have accessed the home page, select "Student Activities" and then click the Chapter 10 link for instructions on getting started.

TABLE 10.1 | Action Words for Active Job Descriptions

Analyze	Edit	Interpret	Produce
Apply	Enhance	Invent	Promote
Appraise	Establish	Inventory	Propose
Arrange	Estimate	Launch	Provide
Assemble	Evaluate	Lead	Rate
Assist	Examine	Learn	Rearrange
Break down	Explain	Listen	Recognize
Build	Focus	Monitor	Reconcile
Compile	Formulate	Motivate	Reinforce
Complete	Fortify	Negotiate	Reorganize
Compose	Generate	Observe	Report
Compute	Guide	Operate	Review
Construct	Help	Organize	Revise
Consult	Illustrate	Orient	Rewrite
Coordinate	Implement	Outline	Score
Create	Incorporate	Participate	Simplify
Demonstrate	Increase	Perform	Solve
Describe	Influence	Persuade	Summarize
Design	Initiate	Plan	Support
Develop	Inspect	Predict	Teach
Devise	Inspire	Prepare	Train
Devote	Install	Present	Write
Direct	Instruct	Process	

Your objective in writing a job description is to identify your major areas of responsibility and give some details on your daily, monthly, and yearly responsibilities. Table 10.1 lists examples of active words you can use in developing your job description. By writing out what is expected of you, you may come to a deeper understanding of your position in the company. Here are two sample job descriptions:

Market Research Analyst

- Focus on a product's or service's potential sales. Study statistics to predict market share, conduct research on competitors, and provide strategies for producing, marketing, distributing, and pricing products or services.

- Develop processes and procedures, including telephone, personal and mail surveys, and focus groups and public opinion polls, to assess market preferences.

Management Accountant

- Record and analyze information about budgets, costs, and assets.
- Participate in strategic planning and/or product development.
- Prepare financial reports for stockholders, creditors, and government agencies.

PRACTICE

Instructions: Identify a paid or unpaid job that you have held. Write a few objectives that relate to the job. (Use action verbs and write in the active voice.) For example, if you ever held a job as a baby-sitter, your objectives might be:

1. Keep children involved in a safe play activity for 1 hour.
2. Prepare and serve a nutritious meal.
3. Get everyone ready for bed, and make sure they are tucked in by 9 p.m.

When you begin writing job descriptions and objectives, you will find that they are difficult to write but enhance your understanding of what you are attempting to achieve.

Action Plans

When you set a specific goal, an **action plan** can help you achieve it. Your action plan lists everything you need to do to achieve your goal, as well as the things that will get in your way. An action plan consists of the following:

- A specific, measurable goal.
- A deadline with periodic checkpoints.
- Individual tasks to complete that lead to the goal.
- Obstacles that need to be overcome or addressed.
- Outside support in the form of reminders or encouragement.

Let's say you want to complete your **career portfolio** for your job search. Here is a rough example of how your action plan might look:

> **Objective:** Compile a complete career portfolio within 6 weeks.
> 1. Individual tasks include:
>
>   Get a binder (zipper or snap) with tabs.
>
>   Identify the parts that I will include:
>
>   Purpose statement
>
>   Résumé
>
>   Writing samples
>
>   References
> 2. Complete résumé:
>
>   Determine style (chronological or functional).
>
>   Make a list of part- and full-time jobs.
>
>   Check dates.
>
>   Make a list of possible references; check with references.
> 3. Select sample work from group projects; update for binder.
> 4. Write my purpose statement.
> 5. Ask Marcus and Pat to check with me every two weeks on progress.
> 6. Obstacles: what will get in my way?
>   For starters, I don't like details and need to set time aside to complete the portfolio. Maybe we can all work together and compare results. Other obstacles? I better write about what's holding me back every time I get stuck so that I can get this finished before my first interview in June.

Keep your action plan alive by updating it with details as you go along. When you get stuck, break a larger task into smaller ones. If you can work together with others who have similar goals, you will have more incentive to achieve your goal within your deadline.

What goals would you like to achieve? Do they relate to budgeting and handling finances, losing weight, improving nutrition, getting organized, completing course requirements?

PRACTICE

Instructions: Identify a goal and write an action plan. Build in a method for holding yourself accountable, such as getting a friend involved with keeping track of your progress.

✓ **SECTION B: CONCEPT CHECK**

1. How does on-the-job feedback encourage growth?
2. Are feedback systems the same from company to company?
3. What can you do to make progress on an important task? What is the process called?

■ **SECTION C: PURPOSE STATEMENTS**

Today most corporations have a mission statement that guides their decisions. A mission statement brings focus and cohesion to a company; a **purpose statement** can do the same thing for an individual. This section explores the subject of *purpose* and how to use it for guidance when making personal and professional choices.

Since this section comes at the end of the book, you may or may not complete it as part of class requirements; but it is here for you when you are ready to use it. Though defining purpose may not help you acquire a job, it will assist you in developing a touchstone to use in making career decisions.

Many successful business professionals in their forties and fifties wake up one day to discover that they feel unfulfilled in a career to which they have dedicated their lives. By getting in touch with purpose early on, you help ensure that your career objectives will intertwine with your life objectives and that each will enhance the other. As you deepen your understanding of purpose, you will apply it more fully to your career and life.

The end-of-chapter activities include a number of reflective writing exercises to help you develop your written purpose statement. (Your purpose statement can then become a valuable part of your career portfolio.)

What Is Purpose?

Purpose answers the deep questions of life, such as:

- Who am I?
- Why am I here?
- What am I meant to do?
- How do I lead a meaningful life?

While these questions are not easy, you may find that they tug at you until you answer them; that's because humans are purpose-seeking beings. While some of us might imagine that these questions were developed in recent times, ancient tribal rituals of indigenous peoples tell us that the search for purpose has been with us for centuries. Understanding purpose has been on the hearts of humans throughout recorded history.

Twentieth-century mythologist Joseph Campbell discovered an uncanny similarity among unrelated native tribes from different parts of the world.[5] These unrelated tribes told similar stories about sending young adults on a quest for meaning to find their own purpose. It was considered a right of passage to adulthood for a child to leave the tribe on a journey in quest of uncovering his or her purpose. The newly christened adult would return to the tribe, ready to live purposefully within the local community.

Today people who do not live in tribes and do not participate in these ancient rituals are often at a loss about how to uncover their own life purpose. After you explore the subject of purpose as presented in this section, complete the reflection activities at the end of this chapter so that your purpose statement can guide your work choices.

COMMUNICATION CHALLENGES

Prioritizing What is important to you? What is the most valuable thing in your life right now?

Take a moment to rank the items below. Assign a numerical value to each one, and then organize them according to their priority.

Career goals
High grades
Family relationships
Friendships
Status in social groups
Dating relationships
Sports activities
Spiritual growth
Personal possessions (such as car, clothes, jewelry)
Personal growth

Ask yourself: *Which ranks the highest for me? How do I think my values and goals will change throughout my life?*

Purpose Is Unique

You may believe that there isn't anything unique about you or your life. At one point or another, most people doubt the unique qualities of their lives. A starting point with purpose is for you to realize that no one can offer to the world exactly what you can, done in the way that you can do it. No one else has the same set of gifts, values, life experiences, and passionate concerns that you possess. As a result, your purpose is uniquely yours and different from everyone else's.

After reflecting on your gifts, values, life experiences, and passionate concerns, you will come to realize that it is not even possible for another human to be the same as you are. In a world filled with billions of people, you and your purpose are unique (whether you realize it yet or not).

Purpose Is Uncovered, Not Discovered

Your attempt at writing a purpose statement could be a disaster if you are more concerned about constructing something that sounds good to others rather than writing a statement that really describes you. Thus, don't look for something outside yourself that sounds impressive but has little to do with the real you.

Purpose is uncovered by looking inward, engaging in a process of self-reflection. You are not finding something new; it's a matter of uncovering what is already within you. Raising your own awareness of what feels fulfilling and gives your life meaning isn't easy. Self-reflection is challenging because it requires quiet—real silence. Most of us find it difficult to focus on *feeling* and *being* instead of the *thinking* and *doing* that typically dominate our lives.

Real quiet can be a particular challenge if you have integrated technology into your way of living. Most of us crave constant stimulation, and technology-driven interruptions are part of life. When everything is turned off, the real quiet that results can feel overwhelming.

Technology has become so ingrained in our way of living that we have a hard time separating from it when we finally take the time to reflect. People work on laptops while "reflecting" in nature preserves, and they even answer pagers while attending religious services. Experiencing real quiet involves making your life a high priority: you must be willing to shut everything off in order to open the space needed to explore your purpose.

Purpose Evolves Over Time

Regardless of your current age, your purpose will continue to evolve over time. It is not too early for a 10-year-old to consider purpose, nor is it too late for a person approaching 90. Some people have a clear sense of direction right away; others are in a fog for many years before clarity comes.

Start from where you are regardless of your age and continue to reflect on the question of purpose, raising your consciousness of it in all aspects of your life. Your sense of purpose will evolve and deepen if you are willing to commit to working on it over the long term. Purpose is a series of continual adjustments over the journey of a lifetime.

Purpose Guides Work Choices

The word *purpose* comes from the Latin word *proponere,* which means "to put forward." When you are clear about your purpose, you are putting forward your intention to live your life in a particular way.

Being intentional means making choices. Consciously consider all possibilities, and make deliberate choices instead of letting possibilities choose your direction. Making a choice is powerful because choosing one direction means excluding another.

Sometimes people don't want to make a choice because they want to keep their freedom and their options open. However, the opposite is true: trying to live with all possible options can be a heavy load to bear. *Full commitment to a conscious decision can feel liberating.* A great deal of attention is required to keep two different expressions of purpose going at the same time. Narrowing possibilities is a source of freedom, so commit to your purpose and lighten your load.

Digging for Purpose: *Uncovering purpose is a process of sifting through your writing, finding what is valuable, and clearing away what is not. Through this process, purpose becomes better defined.* How does the writer's cliché, "The magic is in the rewrite," relate to this concept of uncovering purpose?

VOCABULARY BUILDERS

Inspire The root of the word *inspire* comes from the Latin word *inspiro;* which literally mean "to breathe." For example:

When you *inspire* others, you literally breathe new life into the situation.

While you can express purpose through work, *purpose isn't job-specific.* Thus, you can express your unique purpose through many different kinds of work. For example, if one of your purposes is to add humor to people's lives, you could express that purpose through nearly any kind of work or experience imaginable. However, if you seek to express humor through a role, such as being a comedian, you have put a limit on the kinds of work available to express that purpose. What is important is ensuring that your chosen work gives you the opportunity to express your purpose, even if that is done in a less direct or nontraditional way.

After you settle on the type of work that represents the best expression of your purpose, your next choice is whether you will join an organization or work independently through forming your own company. If you form your own company, you will have an easier time ensuring that your purpose remains aligned with your work. If you choose employment, assess whether your purpose will fit under the umbrella of the organization's purpose, or mission. If your purpose and your company's purpose are aligned, this increases the possibility that you will be able to express your purpose at work.

Most companies commit their organizational purpose to writing and include it with promotional materials about the company, such as marketing brochures, press releases, and Web sites. The mission statement for the Wondra Group is:

To help business leaders radically expand their ability to take action and achieve future visions that are compelling for themselves and their organizations.

The way that the company helps people expand their ability to take action and acheive their visions is through coaching and learning. Those of its employees who have "learning" at the heart of their own purpose will feel aligned with the company's mission. Alignment with purpose and a company mission leads to more work fulfillment and satisfaction.

Once you determine that there is some level of alignment between your purpose and the stated mission of a company you're interested in, verify whether or not the company lives its mission statement. Not all companies "walk their talk," so you want to find out if the corporate culture exudes the mission before accepting a position. Here's a comment from someone who learned this lesson the hard way:

> Early in my career I wanted to switch employers; I read about a company's mission statement and felt that it was a perfect match for me. After I joined, I learned that in reality the company had drifted away from its stated mission years ago, and it turned into a place that was nearly opposite its stated mission. If I had known about this, I never would have taken the job.

To find out whether a company carries out its mission, ask these questions during the interview process:

- Describe the company mission statement. What are some examples of how it is put into action on a daily basis?

- Describe the company culture. How does it support the company mission? Is there anything about the company culture that needs to change?

- What would most employees want to change about the company mission statement?

- Who talks about the company mission statement, when do they talk about it, and how often?

- On a scale of 1 to 10, rate the extent to which the company mission statement matches the current beliefs of people within the company.

Answers to these questions will give you insight into whether or not the company mission statement is authentically "lived" within the organization.

On your first job, you may or may not work for a company that lives its mission statement, but finding one that does is a goal for which you can strive. In addition, you may someday want to form your own company. Keep these points in mind as you develop your business. By the way, most successful businesses start with an idea and a passion to bring the idea to life. The first thing many young entrepreneurs do is write their company mission statement.

Purpose Drives Companies

To start your own business, you need a winning idea and the willingness to take a risk on something you believe in. Business ownership no longer needs massive overhead to thrive—it is now a common practice to run a business from one's home (not so long ago, this was a stigma).

You can develop your own product and ship it from home and still have worldwide recognition through your Web site. Thus, you don't need a building or massive overhead to be important in today's market, but you do need a novel product or service that meets people's needs. As far as creativity is concerned, often *the obvious is overlooked.*

Kathy Ireland, a former *Sports Illustrated* swimsuit model, started her business in the mid-1990s by making a better pair of socks. Today her company generates a billion dollars of revenue annually. What's her company mission? ". . . finding solutions for families, especially busy moms." Her company's motto is "Life is messy." That motto may give you some insight into how she jumps into the creative process.

A lesser-known entrepreneur is Dorothy, who lives in northwest Indiana. Dorothy's passion was making apple strudel, and everyone loved her strudel. Suddenly in the 1960s, her husband died and she was the sole support of her family. To earn a living, she started making large batches of strudel in her own kitchen and then going door-to-door to sell it. In time, the local stores were commissioning her on a regular basis. As her daughter grew older, Dorothy taught her how to make strudel, and now Dorothy's granddaughter helps with the family business as well. They still make their strudel in Dorothy's kitchen.

The best activity you can do if you are thinking about starting your own business is writing its vision and mission statements, as well as its motto. Below is a brief description of each, along with an example.

Writing a Vision Statement

What broad statement captures the nature of the work and the values of your company? The vision statement focuses on the ends, not the means to those ends; some authorities suggest including a pictorial description of what things will look like when the vision is accomplished, along with a time frame for accomplishing it. Here is the Hoosier Environmental Council's vision statement:

> By 2025, Hoosiers will embrace a conservation ethic that values long-term sustainable use and preservation of our natural heritage.

Writing a Mission Statement

What kind of business are you in, and what kind of end results do you seek to achieve? Unlike a vision statement, a mission statement does not have a time frame attached to it. Instead, it is a short, active declaration of *continuing business focus.* An organization communicates its mission statement internally, and employees use it daily as a benchmark for their decision-making process. Here is the mission statement of the Hoosier Environmental Council:

> Through education, advocacy, and citizen empowerment in Indiana, the Hoosier Environmental Council works to protect and restore the natural systems upon which life depends.

A shorter version might read,

> To protect and restore the natural systems upon which life depends.

Developing a Working Motto

What catchphrase captures your culture? A motto does not describe something you'd like to achieve; it describes how you achieve it. For example, "The customer is always right," or "We do our best to achieve our best."

In the end-of-chapter activities, you have an opportunity to work on an entrepreneurial project in which you develop a product or service and then create a company to produce it. If you do the exercise as part of this class, your instructor will have additional guidelines for you to follow. Maybe one day your dream will become your reality. As the artist Marc Chagall is credited with saying, "If I create from the heart, nearly everything works; if from the head, almost nothing." But maybe the key is connecting the two, which is what defining purpose will help you do.

EXPLORE

The activities at the end of this chapter contain reflective writing exercises to help you begin to uncover your own purpose. When working through the reflection activities, minimize anything that will distract you. Consider taking a walk or sitting quietly before writing to help quiet and focus your mind. Find a peaceful writing location conducive to concentration, such as a library, empty classroom, coffee shop, place of worship, or city park. Turn off communication devices such as your phone and start writing.

Take a moment now to follow these instructions and write about the ideas that came to you as you read this section of this chapter. (You may want to review these instructions as you complete Activities 4 to 8 at the end of the chapter.)

 SECTION C: CONCEPT CHECK

1. How can a person become conscious of meaningful choices?

2. Is it important for a person's purpose statement to be congruent with a prospective employer's mission statement? Why?

3. Why is purpose important in the business world? Is your purpose always the same?

◼ SECTION D: WEB WRITING AND DESIGN

Regardless of the position you seek, it is to your advantage to know more about Web writing and design. You may end up having your own Web site one day (or maybe you already do). Even if Web writing is not part of your job duties, you will be able to save your company time and money by knowing the basics of Web design.

Writing for the Web

When you are writing for the Web, some of the rules of effective writing change. Many of these changes are also true for other forms of online writing, such as online help files or intranets. Here is how Web writing differs from print writing:

1. *Web writing contains hyperlinks.* Hyperlinks are places (often words) that can be selected on a Web page that take you elsewhere on the page, site, or Internet.

2. *Web writing is easier to change.* Web sites can be constantly revised and updated. In contrast, once something is printed and distributed, such as a book, a magazine, or a catalog, it does not change. It can be revised and a new edition distributed, but doing so takes major effort and does nothing to change the existing versions. With a Web site, the second a change is made, the site is different.

3. *Web sites are interactive.* Web sites can keep track of information about a user and develop suggestions for that client. For example, Amazon.com suggests action DVD titles to customers who have previously bought other action DVDs.

4. *Web sites offer more options.* Print text can include only graphics, such as pictures or tables, and using color in print documents greatly increases their printing costs. However, with Web sites, you can integrate various media relatively easily—they can include color, graphics, animations, video, and sound. To achieve these special features, creators of Web sites may have to develop new skills or hire someone to create needed multimedia effects.

5. *Web sites are not as portable.* To use print materials, people need few resources. To read Web sites, people need appropriate electronics (such as a computer), a connection, and electricity.

6. *Web sites aren't carefully read.* Studies show that people do not read Web sites carefully—they generally skim them. Thus, you have to write differently for the Web.

7. *Web design is harder to control.* Once it is produced, a print document looks the same to most readers, barring such things as vision or lighting problems or physical damage. Web sites are different. Variations in screen sizes, operating systems, browsers, installed fonts, and video card settings can cause Web sites to display very differently.

Web writing has much in common with print writing. When creating Web sites, don't forget everything you have learned about print writing. You'll still compose, edit, and revise. You will still need to *establish your purpose* and *connect with your readers.* And everything you have learned about tone—such as the "you" point of view, positive attitude, and gender-neutral language—still applies, but sometimes in different ways. Lastly, Web sites can and will be read by global audiences, thus making cultural concerns crucial.

Creating Web Sites

Web sites are created using hypertext markup language, or HTML, a coding system that tells computers how to display Web pages. To view the HTML code using your Web browser, go to a Web site and select "Source" within the View menu. If you are going to be creating a lot of Web pages, you will need to learn some HTML. There are many Web sites with tutorials for learning HTML; they can easily be found by using Internet search engines. For example, using Google, conduct a search for "learning HTML." Various print sources are also available.

Luckily, while it is useful to understand HTML, you don't have to know HTML to create Web pages. Most people use HTML editors, which automatically insert the HTML code as pages are created. Many editors exist, with varying costs and levels of quality. One common editor, Microsoft FrontPage, is often included as part of Microsoft Office and is available in many college computer labs.

While they do not offer as many features, other programs can be used to create Web pages. For example, Microsoft Word and PowerPoint can save files in HTML. The procedure for doing this depends on the version but generally is as follows: Select "Save As" on the File menu. Then in the save-as-type option select "Web Page." When using a program such as Word to create Web pages, the process is pretty much the same as that for creating anything else with the program. One difference is that you will want to create hyperlinks. To do so, highlight the text that you want to be a link, and then select "Hyperlink" on the Insert menu.

One important difference between regular Word files and HTML files (such as Web pages) is how items such as graphics are handled. Word files typically save a copy of the picture itself within the file—that is why a Word file with pictures in it becomes so large. HTML files save the picture separately and merely include a pointer telling the browser where to find the picture. When moving Web files (such as from a hard drive to a disk), be sure that any picture files are moved with them. Otherwise, the pictures may not display. It is a good idea to locate pictures in the same folder as the HTML file for a Web page, or in a nearby folder, before inserting them into your Web pages. This keeps the links intact and makes them easier to move.

Designing Web Sites

Web sites should be easy to use and thus follow basic design concepts and established conventions.

Make Web Sites Usable   One central concept in writing for the Web is usability: Web sites should be easy to navigate and use. Steve Krug, in *Don't Make Me Think,* suggests that the key to a good Web site is that users should spend as little time as possible thinking about how to use the site.[6] Usability is important, because usable Web sites:

- Save users time.
- Create a good impression of the owner or creator of the site.
- Are more likely to be used again.
- Make users feel better about themselves.

Follow Basic Design Concepts   Robin Williams and John Tollett, in *The Non-Designer's Web Book,* list four basic principles of design:[7]

- *Proximity:* Related items should be closer to one another than unrelated items. For example, there should be more space above a heading than below it so that the heading ends up closer to the text for which it is a heading.
- *Alignment:* Items should be aligned on the page. Nothing should be placed thoughtlessly on a page—everything should align with something. You can use alignments such as indentations to organize items on a page. And be consistent with alignment—for example, you can't align some things on the left and center other things. In general, avoid centering.
- *Repetition:* Repeat design choices from page to page on a site. In general, pages on a site should all look like they are part of the same site, and repeating design choices allows you to achieve this. Repeat fonts, colors, logos, and even layouts.
- *Contrast:* Elements on your page should be either the same or clearly different. Nothing should be similar. This goes for colors, fonts, and other elements. Headings, for example, should look clearly different from body text.

Every page should have a clear focal point—the point that first draws a reader's eye. There are many other basic issues for Web writing and design, and numerous books have been written on this topic. Here are several important ones:

- *Choose common fonts.* When you choose fonts for a Web page, they may not display the same way on someone else's computer. One reason for this is that if the person does not have the font installed on his or her computer, a different font will be substituted. So try to stay with the most common fonts, such as those that come with Windows (Arial, Times New Roman, Verdana, and so on).
- *Use tables to control layout.* By default, text in HTML will rearrange itself to fit into the available space. This can make it very difficult to design a page properly, as the layout will change according to the size of the window the Web browser is in. To get around this, most Web designers use tables. Create tables of absolute widths (measured in pixels or inches). No matter how the screen is resized, the table will not change in size. Professional designers precisely control Web page layouts by using several tables, often placing tables within tables, and then placing text and graphics within the table cells.
- *Give every Web page a descriptive title.* The title displays at the very top of the browser window, above the icons. This text is used by the browser to record the name of a bookmark or favorite and is used as a title by search engines when they display results. It is important that this text be descriptive, like "ABC Corporation—Employment Opportunities." In many HTML editors and in programs such as Microsoft Word, this text can be set by selecting "Properties" on the File menu.
- *Know the difference between paragraph breaks and line breaks.* When you are using an HTML editor (such as Microsoft FrontPage or Macromedia Dreamweaver), the enter key skips a line and then starts a new paragraph. To simply start on a new line without skipping a line first, hold the shift key down while pressing the enter key.

Follow Web Conventions   Conventions are generally accepted ways of doing things and exist for many forms of writing, including that for Web sites. For example, most Web sites have an identifying logo on the upper left-hand corner of each page. Clicking on it will take you to the site's home page. Sites that follow Web conventions often have increased usability because users know what to expect. To learn Web conventions, look at successful sites, such as Amazon.com, and see what they do right. Here is a list of some of the most common Web site conventions:

- *Don't make users scroll to find something important.* People rarely scroll down on Web pages, so the most important things should display without scrolling.

- *Use running navigation.* Most Web sites have the same major links on the top of every page. This repetition establishes site identity and also makes it easier for users to get around the site. Directly below the major links are, usually, navigation links for that section of the site; if even more navigation is needed, links are placed along the left margin.

- *Make links clear.* Anything that is a link should be clearly indicated as a link, and what it links to should be clearly evident.

- *Chunk text.* Since people usually skim Web writing, it is important to keep text in short chunks of related information. These chunks will usually not be more than a few sentences long.

- *Use headings and subheadings.* Chunks of text should be labeled with clear headings or subheadings, allowing users to skim easily.

- *Be concise.* Since people do not want to read a lot of text on a screen, be as concise as possible. Cut half of your words, if possible.

For links to more resources concerning Web writing, check the Web site for this text.

EXPLORE

Though you may have looked at hundreds or even thousands of Web sites throughout your career, have you ever taken the time to analyze consistent components among them—in other words, the navigation links that appear. Go to five different professional Web sites, and list the three most common navigation links.

 SECTION D: CONCEPT CHECK

1. Do you need to know HTML to create a Web site?
2. What are the four most important concepts to follow in Web page design?
3. Why should you choose common fonts when designing your Web site?

SUMMARY

Everyone is a leader in his or her own way: your leadership skills started to develop when you were too young to remember and will continue developing for the rest of your life. By learning more about who you are and who you want to be, you have more control over exercising your leadership qualities.

Job performance appraisals present challenges for everyone. However, the feedback they provide fuels and directs growth. If you learn to communicate feedback effectively both verbally and in writing, you have a tool that will serve you well every day of your career.

Everyone receives constructive feedback at some time in a career. Be careful about taking feedback too personally; being too hard on yourself over a mistake does not necessarily help you overcome the behavior or the faulty thinking that caused it. Once you learn to use job performance feedback as an avenue to growth, you have a significant career advantage.

Define your purpose statement early in your career. By merging your personal and career goals, you are likely to feel more satisfied with your work; to go one step further, use your individual purpose statement to connect with a company (or develop your own company) that has a congruent mission statement. Once you achieve that goal, you are even more likely to find your career, and life, fulfilling.

Take control of your own growth and success. Sometimes, what you need to learn will be obvious; it will come from within through insight and be carried out through motivation. At other times, it will come through feedback that others provide. According to Ralph W. Tyler, a twentieth-century educator:

> Sometimes it isn't what you are currently doing that you need to do better; sometimes it is what you are not doing at all that you need to begin to do.[8]

Good luck in achieving your career goals—and enjoy a fruitful journey on the path on which your life leads you.

CHAPTER 10 CHECKLIST

___ Have you noted the qualities of effective leaders?
___ Have you identified new myths about leadership?
___ Have you identified your leadership qualities?
___ What are your peak leadership experiences?
___ Who are your heroes?
___ What gets you motivated?
___ How do you inspire others?
___ Have you ranked your six core values?
___ Have you identified your goals and objectives?
___ Have you developed an action plan with specific action steps and due dates?
___ Have you written your purpose statement?

END-OF-CHAPTER ACTIVITIES

ACTIVITY 1: PROCESS MEMO

Instructions: Write your instructor a memo or an e-memo giving feedback on the course you've just completed. Focus on your goals, and explain how the course has or has not helped you get closer to achieving them. After you give detailed feedback, you can add an evaluative comment or two. (Use the reflect/respond/revise process strategy.)

ACTIVITY 2: TEAM ACTIVITIES

Background: At the end of Section B, you were instructed to identify a goal and write an action plan; in Section C, you were instructed to write your purpose statement. To review, an action plan consists of the following:

- A specific, measurable goal.
- A deadline with periodic checkpoints.
- Individual tasks to complete leading to the goal.

Instructions: For steps 2 and 3 below, you will meet with three to five class members to discuss your action plan.

1. Complete an action plan for a goal that is important to you.

2. After completing your plan, meet with your team members to discuss one another's action plans. First, give feedback about each plan: identify what about the plan works and what doesn't work. Is it detailed enough? After you have given detailed feedback, including changes that might improve the plan, go ahead and attach an evaluative comment.

3. Now discuss what *purpose* means to you at this point in your life. Will your action plan relate to your purpose statement (which is discussed in Activity 8)?

ACTIVITY 3: ALL PRO TEMPS

Instructions: The CEO of All Pro, James Riley, stopped by your desk to let you know that many new job opportunities will be opening up soon. He would like you to describe your "dream job." Write him a short memo or letter giving a few details.

Activities 4 to 8 relate to building your purpose statement.

ACTIVITY 4: STEP 1—WRITING YOUR STORY

Instructions: To begin, write a six- to ten-page paper on the story of your life. In particular, explore the following areas:

- Recall the earliest instance when you declared what you wanted to do when you grew up. Write about how your vocational declarations deepened or changed over time.

- Describe the influential people in your life and the impact they had on your life.

- Explain the major events that had a life-changing effect on you.

- Describe the natural talents that other people notice in you (go as far back as you can remember). We all have gifts, or natural talents. Since they are natural, they are often overlooked because they come easily to us.

ACTIVITY 5: STEP 2—LEAVING A LEGACY

Instructions: Write your responses to the following questions:

1. How old do you believe you will live to be?

2. Imagine that you have reached that age and are looking back on your life. What do you want to be able to say about the legacy of your life?

3. What might you do with your remaining time between now and then so that when you look back on your life, you have no regrets about how you lived it?

ACTIVITY 6: STEP 3—PEAK EXPERIENCES

Instructions: Write about one or two work experiences (paid or unpaid) that had a deep impact on you. Describe the situation, your contribution, and the end result, as well as how the experience made you feel. What parts of that experience were energizing for you? Why?

ACTIVITY 7: STEP 4—ABOUT WORK

Instructions: Write your response to the following questions:

1. Why do you want to work (other than to earn money)?

2. What are your expectations of work? Is work something to be suffered through and endured, or should it be more than that? Why?

3. Describe your dream job. If you had no constraints (money, family, or geography requirements), what work would you love to do?

ACTIVITY 8: STEP 5—WRITING A PURPOSE STATEMENT

Instructions: The first step in writing your purpose statement is to read through everything you wrote in the previous exercises, looking for *themes from your passionate concerns, deep interests, and natural talents.* Make notes about what you notice, and follow these steps:

1. Based on your notes, write several different drafts of a purpose statement. Begin each sentence with "My purpose is to . . ." (an action verb will follow, such as "My purpose is to design . . ."). Simply let the words flow, and do not be concerned about writing coherent sentences. You will have an opportunity to edit later.

2. Over the period of a few days, reread your purpose statement drafts, noticing how they feel to you. Notice any words or phrases or clauses that are emotionally appealing. Read the drafts out loud. Take note of any words or phrases that quicken your heartbeat when you hear them.

3. Write a new draft of your purpose statement, incorporating the words that you emotionally connected with in step 2.

4. Read your revised draft to a partner and get feedback (or read it to the entire class with no feedback; see Activity 2 on page 370).

ACTIVITY 9: THE ENTREPRENEUR, AN INDIVIDUAL OR TEAM PROJECT

Background: When you think of employment, you inevitably think of large Fortune 500 companies, but less than 25 percent of workers are employed in these large companies. The rest find jobs at small companies. Thus, more people are self-employed or work for small businesses and "mom and pop" operations than they do for the large firms.

You may not have the desire or ambition to start your own business, but take a moment to dream: *If you could create any kind of business you wanted, what would it be?* Do you spend your free time on one special activity because you have a passion for it? What about social or environmental problems—do you have a vision for a different kind of world? What about producing renewable or solar energy? Do you play sports and have insight into a better kind of running shoe or jersey? How about a sports center? Do you love young children and know how to develop a day-care center with a cutting-edge approach to child care? What about animals—is there a pet care service or product the market is just waiting for? Do you love organizing and getting rid of clutter? Maybe you want to develop a consulting firm or temporary employment agency. If you got into retail, would you be interested in selling clothes, electronics, or automotive products?

From the practical to the innovative, the world has room for more products and services to serve a growing marketplace. What business venture would you be willing to take risks to develop? Although the vast majority of small businesses fail in their first year, those built on passion and authentic need are more likely to succeed: creativity is listening to the obvious and then responding with a good plan. **Here is your final project:**

Instructions:

1. Define the problem: what genuine need, interest, or service needs attention?

2. Develop a product or service to address the need.

3. Gather and analyze data about your problem and product or service: do research online or do some original qualitative research (surveys or interviews) to find out if your idea has merit.

4. Identify and analyze your target audience: is one generation or age group more likely to be interested than another? Why?

5. Develop a "company": what is your company name?

6. Define a vision statement, a mission statement, and a working motto.

7. If time permits, develop a storyboard of the home page for a Web site. Include all of the vital information for your project. (The home page will describe your company and your product or service. It may also contain tabs for other information, but you need not post information on those pages.)

8. Pull everything together in a 10 to 15-minute PowerPoint presentation. Your presentation can be an advertisement for your product or a presentation to potential investors in your company. Provide your audience with at least one piece of marketing material: a fact sheet, white paper, brochure, or copy of the home page from your Web site.

Identifying Your Target Audience

Who are the major stakeholders?

What age group or generation are you speaking to?

What are their needs, interests, likes, and dislikes? Their defining qualities or attitudes?

Why serve this group?

Developing a Product or Service

What is your product or service? Describe it in as much detail as possible.

Who are your competitors? What are their strengths and weaknesses?

How will you differentiate yourself from your competitors? How will your product or service differ?

Building a Brand

In what ways can you *brand* your identity?

From your company name to its mission, vision, motto, and logo, how are you unique?

How can you set yourself apart from others and make the public remember you?

Where are you located and why? Do you even need a physical locale or can you operate from the Internet?

Here is your final commission: *have fun doing this project*. Yes, work can be fun. If it is not, then you might be in the wrong place. As Richard J. Leider says, "Each life has a natural built-in reason for being . . . the integration of who we are with what we do is one of the true joys of life."[9] Now go for it!

REFERENCES

1. Randy Lindner, *Role Definitions: Leading Versus Managing*, Bostrom Solutions, <http://www.bostrom.com.Solutions/Solutions1-1.htm>, accessed March 2004.

2. Frederick M. Hudson and Pamela D. McLean, *Life Launch: A Passionate Guide to the Rest of Your Life*, The Hudson Institute Press, Santa Barbara, CA 1995.

3. M. Scott Peck, *A Bounty of Happiness: A Treasury of Wisdom,* Andres McMeel Publishing, Kansas City, 2003.

4. David Wondra, The Wondra Group, October, Chicago, 2004.

5. Joseph Campbell, *Joseph Campbell and the Power of Myth*, Mystic Fire Video, Prince Station, NY, 1988.

6. Steve Krug, *Don't Make Me Think: A Common Sense Approach to Web Usability*, New Riders Press, 2000, pp. 10–29.

7. Robin Williams and John Tollett. *The Non-Designer's Web Book*, 2nd Edition, Peachpit Press, 2000, pp. 105–122.

8. Ralph W. Tyler, *Basic Principles of Curriculum and Instruction*, The University of Chicago Press, Chicago, 1949. Quote shared by Dr. John Ginther, The University of Chicago, Principles of Curriculum, July 1984.

9. Richard J. Leider, *The Power of Purpose*, Berrett-Kowhler Publishers, Inc., San Francisco, 1997, pages 25, 55.

KEY FOR LEARNING INVENTORY

1.	F	**6.**	F
2.	F	**7.**	F
3.	F	**8.**	F
4.	F	**9.**	T
5.	F	**10.**	F

The Writer's Handbook: Part 1

The Writer's Handbook

The Mechanics of Writing

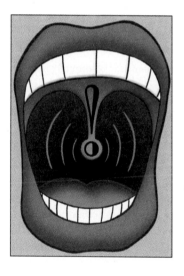

The writer who neglects punctuation, or mispunctuates, is liable to be misunderstood.
—*Edgar Allan Poe* ■

Punctuation is the glue that holds language together. Without punctuation, language lacks meaning because it lacks order. Punctuation provides clarity, but it does more than that. Punctuation communicates with the reader, adding energy and excitement as it packages words into logical bundles that make sense to the reader.

Commas are only tiny little scratches on the page, yet they wield great power when you don't know the correct way to use them. With a little practice, commas will make sense and so will the semicolon, another powerful punctuation tool.

Electronic communication has increased the use of less traditional punctuation, such as the dash, ellipsis marks, and the colon. Since many writers are unaware of how to use these marks correctly, this Handbook part also includes information on using these marks to add variety and flair to your writing.

Learning the mechanics of punctuation means you can stop guessing and instead move forward with confidence. You will no longer be confused about fragments or run-on sentences: punctuation is the key to solving these problems.

OBJECTIVES

When you have completed the Writer's Handbook, Part 1, you will be able to:

- Describe basic sentence structure.

- Identify the core elements of sentences.

- Understand the roles of coordinating, subordinating, and adverbial conjunctions.

- Demonstrate the correct use of the comma and semicolon.

- Apply basic comma and semicolon rules in composition.

- Demonstrate the correct use of colons, dashes, and ellipsis marks.

- Revise fragments and run-ons into complete sentences.

Learning Inventory

1. Commas are placed in sentences based on pauses.	T/F
2. Placing a period after a subordinate clause creates a fragment.	T/F
3. A semicolon creates a "full stop" and can often be used where a period would be used.	T/F
4. Placing a comma where a period or semicolon is needed creates a run-on.	T/F
5. Conjunctions build bridges between thoughts and clauses.	T/F
6. The word *but* is a coordinating conjunction, and a semicolon is rarely placed before it.	T/F
7. Conjunctions signal how to punctuate a sentence.	T/F
8. One comma can be correctly placed between the subject and the verb of a sentence.	T/F
9. The subject and verb are the core of a sentence.	T/F
10. Commas are not placed based on pauses.	T/F

■ SECTION A: THE COMMA

What is your main reason for placing a comma in a sentence? Think for a moment. What popped into your mind? If you suddenly thought of "to pause," you are not alone. That's what most people say. Another common response is "to take a breath." You may be surprised to learn that neither of these responses is a valid reason for using a comma.

Based on this misconception, have you ever reread the same sentence several times, each time pausing at different places while searching for the perfect place to put a comma? The pause approach turns punctuating into a guessing game. Actually, there should be no guessing about punctuation—sometimes educated choices, but no guessing.

Punctuation is based on sentence structure. **Syntax**—a word for *grammar* that refers to "the orderly arrangement of words"—creates natural breaks at the end of clauses. Comma rules provide guidance on where to look for the separations or natural breaks in structure.

The bottom line: readers do pause at a comma, but that is not why the comma was placed there. Comma placement is based on rules (or theory). The rule came first, the comma came second, and the pause came third. That brings us to our starting point.

COACHING TIP

No Pause, Please Punctuation is based on rules, not on pauses. Placing a comma where a reader might pause is based on myth, but it is close enough to the truth to cause problems for writers. Placing commas according to pauses is so alluring that it is a difficult habit to break.

Once you know the rules, you will place commas consistently and correctly on the basis of structure. You won't be rereading the same sentence trying to guess the perfect pause! Remember: The structure determines the comma, and the comma creates the pause.

Basic Comma Rules (Rules 1 and 2)

This section presents 12 basic comma rules. The first two rules stress when *not* to use a comma; the remaining 10 stress when to use a comma. Be aware that there are more comma rules than those listed in this part, and some rules have exceptions. The goal of Part 1 is to develop a foundation in punctuation; this simplified approach will help you become conscious of the structure and rhythm of the language.

Once you learn the basic rules, your foundation will be solid; you will be ready to learn exceptions to the rules as well as some advanced rules. For additional work with commas, refer to *The Gregg Reference Manual*.

Comma Rule 1: The Golden Rule

When in doubt, leave it out.

Comma Rule 1 tells you to stop putting in commas unless you have a valid reason. *Remember, pausing is not a valid reason for using a comma.* If you don't know a reason for using a comma that is based on a rule, you have three choices:

- Don't use the comma.

- Do additional research. (Refer to *The Gregg Reference Manual.*)

- Rewrite the sentence in a way that you know is correct. (This works when you are doing your own writing but not when you are proofreading someone else's work.)

This first rule tells you when *not* to use a comma, as does Comma Rule 2. By using commas only when you are sure, you will avoid making many serious grammatical errors.

Comma Rule 2: The Cardinal Rule

Do not separate a subject and its verb with one comma.

When a subject and verb come together, they form an important grammatical unit: the **clause.** Two basic types of clauses are **independent clauses** and **dependent clauses.** Their names describe their functions: independent clauses can stand alone; dependent clauses cannot stand alone (they need support from an independent clause).

- An independent clause has a subject and verb and expresses a complete thought; an independent clause is a **sentence.** (*Note:* In the examples in this section, simple subjects are underlined once, simple verbs are underlined twice, and conjunctions are italicized.)

Incorrect:	The <u>trees</u>, <u><u>were blowing</u></u> in the wind.
Corrected:	The <u>trees</u> <u><u>were blowing</u></u> in the wind.

- A dependent clause has a subject and verb but does not express a complete thought; it cannot stand alone. A dependent clause is a *fragment* of a sentence and needs to connect with an independent clause to be complete. (Dependent clauses often begin with subordinating conjunctions, such as *when, if, although,* and *because.*)

An independent clause becomes a dependent clause if a subordinating conjunction is added to it:

although the <u>trees</u> <u><u>were blowing</u></u> in the wind   *because* the <u>trees</u> <u><u>were blowing</u></u> in the wind
even though the <u>trees</u> <u><u>were blowing</u></u> in the wind   *while* the <u>trees</u> <u><u>were blowing</u></u> in the wind

A major grammatical mistake is ending a dependent clause (which is a fragment) with a period, question mark, or exclamation point. These marks are known as "terminal marks" of punctuation and indicate the end of a sentence. (For more information on terminal marks of punctuation, see *The Gregg Reference Manual,* Section 1.) Thus, do not place a period at the end of a dependent clause:

COACHING TIP

Identifying Subjects and Verbs In statements, the subject almost always precedes the verb. However, the verb is usually easier to identify. If you identify the verb first and then the subject, you are more likely to be correct. Here is the most efficient way to identify subjects and verbs:

1. *Identify the verb first.* Verbs express action (*identify, analyze, gain, precede*) or state of being (*is, are, was, were, seem, feel*). Underline the verb twice so that it stands out.
2. After you identify the verb, *work backward to identify the subject.* Underline the subject once. If you read the subject and verb out loud, they should make sense together (*you identify, you read, they should make*).
3. If you have difficulty finding the subject, consider whether it is an "understood" subject. In English, the pronouns *you* and *I* can sometimes be omitted; this happens with commands or requests. For example:
   (You) Please assist me with the project.
   (You) Start with the first list.
   (I) Thank you for your assistance.
4. In English, a question is formed by inverting the subject and verb of a statement. To identify the subject and verb in a question, invert the order to statement form so that the subject comes before the verb:
   Will you go to the meeting with me?
   You will go to the meeting with me.

Incorrect: *Although* the <u>trees</u> <u><u>were blowing</u></u> in the wind.

To recap Comma Rule 2: This rule tells us that one comma should *not* be placed between the subject and the verb in any clause, independent or dependent. When commas are used between a subject and its verb, they are most likely a **set of commas,** which we'll get to with Comma Rule 5, which relates to nonessential elements.

PRACTICE

Instructions: In the following sentences, identify the simple subject and verb of each independent clause. First identify the verb and underline it twice; then work backward in the sentence to identify the subject and underline it once. If you have difficulty finding the subject, ask yourself if it is "you understood" (you) or "I understood" (I). For example:

> **Sentence:** Each sentence needs a subject and verb to be complete.
> **Answer:** Each <u>sentence</u> <u><u>needs</u></u> a subject and verb to be complete.

1. The proposal will require a detailed analysis.

   _____

2. My newspaper arrived after I had left for work.

   _____

3. When my manager researched and analyzed the data, he was pleased with the results.

   _____

4. In the summer, some companies implement a shortened schedule on Fridays.

   _____

5. Can you report to Human Resources before going to your desk?

   _____

6. Our director and placement counselors met for two hours discussing the strategy.

   _____

7. Thank you for the report.

   _____

8. Did your elevator stop on the fourth floor?

   _____

9. Please give me your budget for the next quarter.

   _____

10. Will you have time to listen to his employee's request?

    _____

More Comma Rules (Rules 3 to 12)

The remaining comma rules (Rules 3 to 12) are more specific than the first two rules. Each comma rule names the reason for the comma's use and has an abbreviation. For example, the next rule is *comma conjunction,* with the abbreviation *CONJ.* Applying a name to each comma rule will help you analyze the reason for using the comma. If you don't know the reason for using a comma, you may *not* need a comma. If that is the case, either do more research or leave out the comma.

As you work through the comma rules, you will also identify the core elements of independent clauses. The core elements are the subjects and verbs. You will be asked to identify conjunctions because they play a major role in punctuation as well as style. Don't take time to identify elements of minor clauses, such as *who, which,* or *that* clauses or subordinating clauses that come at the end of a sentence.

Identifying core elements is different from diagramming sentences. The core elements directly influence structure and style. Once you can easily identify core elements, you are one

COACHING TIP

Finding Verbs In many of the exercises in this text, you are asked to identify the verbs in sentences. You may be feeling rusty about which words are verbs, so here are some guidelines:

1. The following are common verbs that are used alone or as helping verbs:
    is are was were
    has have had
    do did done

2. The word *will* is usually a verb (unless you are referring to someone named "Will" or using it as a noun, as in "Last Will and Testament"). When used as a verb, *will* is almost always followed by another verb:
    I _will_ go to the store.
    Mary _will_ do that tomorrow.

3. The word *not* is an adverb (not a verb); you will find a verb on one *side* or both sides of *not*. (Unless the verb is *cannot*, in which case *not* is then part of the verb because it is part of the word.)
    George _does_ *not* _have_ the answer.
    The _dog_ _did_ *not* _bark_ at the mail carrier.
    The _manager_ _is_ *not* available.

step closer to gaining control over your writing style. The following points cannot be stressed too much:

- Each time you correctly place a comma and identify the reason, you are applying theory to practice. The **theory/practice method** not only ensures that you are correct but also develops your analytical, critical thinking skills.
- You will be tempted to place the comma and not bother to put the reason. Forcing yourself to analyze the sentence and identify the reason for the comma ensures that you are practicing the theory correctly. This alone will make the difference between whether you learn to use commas correctly or whether you continue putting them in haphazardly.
- Once you understand punctuation, you will also understand structure. You will then be able to manipulate sentence elements and have greater control over your writing style.

Comma Rule 3: Comma Conjunction (CONJ)

Use a comma to separate independent clauses when they are joined by a coordinating conjunction.

By placing a comma before the conjunction, you are showing the *separation* between the independent clauses. There are only seven **coordinating conjunctions:** *and, but, or, for, nor, so, yet.* You may use the abbreviation *CC* to refer to coordinating conjunctions.

In the example in this section, the subjects are underlined once, the verbs are underlined twice, and the coordinating conjunctions (CCs) are italicized. The name of the comma rule, or reason, is shown in parentheses after the sentence.

Bob _went_ to the meeting, *but* he _arrived_ late. (CONJ)
Mary _summarized_ the report, *and* she _did_ a good job. (CONJ)

PRACTICE

Instructions: Correct the sentences below by applying the comma conjunction (CONJ) rule. (*Note:* Watch out for compound verbs.) For each sentence, do the following: (1) Insert any missing commas. (2) In each main clause, underline the verb twice and the subject once. (3) Circle each coordinating conjunction (CC) that joins two independent clauses. (4) Even though it may seem redundant, write the reason *(CONJ)* after the sentence. For example:

Incorrect: My manager asked for input so I told him what I thought.
Corrected: My _manager_ _asked_ for input, (so) I _told_ him what I thought. (CONJ)

1. The meeting lasted for six hours and we were all very tired.

_____

2. My manager and I agreed to cut the budget but we could not agree about which items to cut.

_____

3. Joseph arrived late but was still able to participate in the decision.

_____

4. The announcement was made early so our department left at noon.

_____

5. Mary gave me the report but not the supporting documents.

   _____

   _____

6. The convention was held in Dallas last year and will be held in Boston this year.

   _____

   _____

7. The stockbroker gave accurate information and he should be commended.

   _____

   _____

8. The annual report was published recently so you should receive yours soon.

   _____

   _____

9. Ms. Barton returned the signed copies and she requested to be notified when you received them.

   _____

   _____

10. The mail carrier did not leave the package yesterday so it may arrive today.

   _____

   _____

Comma Rule 4: Comma Introductory (INTRO)

Place a comma after a word, phrase, or dependent clause that introduces a main clause.

To learn the comma introductory (INTRO) rule, you must first be familiar with subordinating conjunctions (SCs) and adverbial conjunctions (ACs).

Subordinating conjunctions are words or phrases that introduce dependent clauses; for example, *if, when, as, although, because, as soon as, before, while, after, since, even though, unless,* and *whereas.* There are too many subordinating conjunctions to memorize. However, you can tell whether a word is a subordinating conjunction by placing it at the beginning of an independent clause. If the independent clause becomes dependent, then the word is a subordinating conjunction. (See pages 379 and 380.)

Adverbial conjunctions are words or phrases that introduce or interrupt independent clauses. Adverbial conjunctions build bridges between ideas and help the reader understand the writer's intention; they provide **transitions.** Here is a list of some common adverbial conjunctions:

therefore	hence	in summary	that is	furthermore
however	as a result	moreover	in contrast	on the contrary
for example	in addition	of course	as usual	in general
fortunately	in conclusion	otherwise	unfortunately	consequently

If you place an adverbial conjunction at the beginning of an independent clause, the clause will still be complete.

George <u>was offered</u> the job of his choice.
Fortunately, George <u>was offered</u> the job of his choice.

In each of the following, an adverbial conjunction (AC) introduces a main clause:

> *However,* <u>Bob</u> <u><u>went</u></u> to the meeting alone. (INTRO)
> *Therefore,* the <u>change</u> in the agenda <u><u>created</u></u> controversy. (INTRO)
> *As usual,* <u>we</u> <u><u>followed</u></u> the new schedule exactly. (INTRO)

In each of the following sentences, a dependent clause that begins with a subordinating conjunction (SC) introduces a main clause:

> *Although* <u>we</u> <u><u>went</u></u> to the store, <u>we</u> <u><u>did</u></u> not <u><u>remember</u></u> to buy notebooks. (INTRO)
> *Because* <u>Juan</u> <u><u>is</u></u> the chairperson, <u>he</u> <u><u>will determine</u></u> the agenda. (INTRO)
> *Even though* the <u>report</u> <u><u>was</u></u> late, my <u>manager</u> <u><u>was</u></u> happy to receive it. (INTRO)

COACHING TIP

Parts of Speech as Functions There are different approaches to learning parts of speech. In the past, students were taught to memorize lists of words for the various parts of speech. In schools today, students learn that a word can change its part of speech based on its function in a sentence.

However is an adverb, but it can also function as a conjunction; as a conjunction, *however* can be either a subordinating conjunction (SC) or an adverbial conjunction (AC). In the following examples, note the different functions of *however:*

> *However* <u>you</u> <u><u>respond</u></u> to the question, your <u>answer</u> <u><u>will be</u></u> acceptable. (SC)
> <u>Margaret</u> <u><u>should respond</u></u> to the message *however* she chooses. (SC)
> *However,* the <u>committee</u> <u><u>met</u></u> yesterday and <u><u>did</u></u> not <u><u>discuss</u></u> the issue. (AC)

When placed at the beginning of a sentence, both adverbial conjunctions and subordinating conjunctions signal that a comma is needed. As the first word of a sentence, an adverbial conjunction (AC) is usually followed by a comma.

Example: *Therefore,* <u>we</u> <u><u>were</u></u> late.

When a subordinating conjunction (SC) is the first word of a sentence, a comma is placed at the end of the subordinating clause. (Do *not* place a comma immediately after the subordinating conjunction.) For example:

Incorrect: *Although,* <u>we</u> <u><u>were</u></u> late, <u>we</u> <u><u>did</u></u> not <u><u>miss</u></u> anything.
Corrected: *Although* <u>we</u> <u><u>were</u></u> late, <u>we</u> <u><u>did</u></u> not <u><u>miss</u></u> anything.

PRACTICE

Instructions: Correct the sentences below by applying the comma introductory (INTRO) and comma conjunction (CONJ) rules. For each sentence, do the following: (1) Insert any missing commas. (2) In each main clause, underline the verb twice and the subject once. (3) Circle each adverbial conjunction (AC) and subordinating conjunction (SC). (4) Even though it may seem redundant, write the reason (*INTRO* or *CONJ*) after the sentence. For example:

Incorrect: If you are able to assist John you should.
Corrected: If <u>you</u> <u><u>are able</u></u> to assist John, <u>you</u> <u><u>should</u></u>. (INTRO)

Incorrect: However do not compromise your position.
Corrected: However, (<u>you</u>) <u><u>do</u></u> not <u><u>compromise</u></u> your position. (INTRO)

1. Furthermore the cost of the computer included all software.

_____

2. Although we purchased the computer we did not need it.

   _____

3. In addition the new software was not compatible with our computers.

   _____

4. Even though we are pleased with the results we do not recommend this approach.

   _____

5. The idea of a merger is refreshing but it soon loses its appeal.

   _____

6. So that you may make a wiser decision please read our report thoroughly.

   _____

7. James is not responsible for the decision yet he is willing to accept the consequences.

   _____

8. However he did not indicate when his manager would return.

   _____

9. The phone rang several times and the intern walked away without answering it.

   _____

10. If you arrive early will someone be there to greet you?

    _____

11. Because they were dissatisfied with our product their answer did not surprise us.

    _____

12. As soon as George hears from his attorney he will call us.

    _____

Comma Rule 5: Comma Nonessential Element (NE)

Use commas to set off a nonessential (nonrestrictive) element.

Though nonessential elements add value, a sentence does not need them to be clear and complete. Thus, when nonessential elements are taken out of a sentence, the sentence will still make sense.

   A word of caution: Focus on identifying *who* and *which* clauses that are not essential for clarity; do not set off phrases in a sentence just because the sentence makes sense without them (for example, do *not* set off prepositional phrases). In the example below, the sentence will still be *clear and complete* if the *who* clause is removed:

   My uncle John, who currently lives in Dallas, has been a police officer his entire career. (NE)

Without the *who* clause, the sentence still makes sense:

   My uncle John has been a police officer his entire career.

   If the *who* clause is essential to the meaning, do not set it off with commas. (With grammar, the word *essential* basically means the same as *restrictive*.) **Essential elements** are not set off with commas. Here's a sentence with an essential *who* clause:

The <u>person</u> who gave you that information <u>should have known</u> it was not correct.

Taking out the *who* clause leaves the sentence unclear:

The <u>person</u> <u>should have known</u> it was not correct. (*Which person?* The meaning is not clear without the *who* clause.)

The comma nonessential element (NE) is one of the few comma rules that calls for a decision based on meaning rather than structure. That makes this rule trickier than some of the other rules.

PRACTICE

Instructions: Correct the sentences below by applying the comma nonessential element (NE) rule. Also look for comma introductory (INTRO) and comma conjunction (CONJ). For each sentence, do the following: (1) Insert any missing commas. (2) In each main clause, underline the verb twice and the subject once. (3) Circle each adverbial conjunction (AC) and subordinating conjunction (SC). (4) Even though it may seem redundant, write the reason (*NE, INTRO,* or *CONJ*) after the sentence. For example:

Incorrect: Did you advise the woman who chairs the meeting that you would be late?
Corrected: <u>Did</u> <u>you</u> <u>advise</u> the woman who chairs the meeting that you would be late?

Incorrect: Did you advise Marla Jones who chairs the meeting that you would be late?
Corrected: <u>Did</u> <u>you</u> <u>advise</u> Marla Jones, who chairs the meeting, that you would be late? (NE)

1. The sales representative who sold you the product should answer your questions.

   _____

2. Mr. Jacobs who is our team leader will plan the upcoming retreat.

   _____

3. My employee who manages the service department is now visiting our European facility.

   _____

4. Bill Riley who manages the service department is now visiting our European facility.

   _____

5. The quarterly report which is always completed on time will be sent to you on June 15.

   _____

6. Furthermore the new account will need to be paid in full each month.

   _____

7. Of course we have a complete listing of services on our Web site.

   _____

8. Ms. Applegate is a good friend of mine and she will attend the workshop.

   _____

9. While the supervisor reviewed the evaluation his employee seemed optimistic.

   _____

10. Did they say that it was Martin Bradley who gave you the package?

    _____

11. The general manager who usually has weekends off is here today.

    _____

12. Global Express which is known worldwide accepted my résumé.

    _____

Comma Rule 6: Comma Independent Comment (IC)

Use commas to set off a nonessential word or phrase that interrupts an independent clause.

This rule primarily relates to *adverbial conjunctions* that are interjected into an independent clause, expressing the writer's attitude and slightly interrupting the flow of the sentence. These independent comments can often be removed without affecting the sentence.

I will, *however,* call you when I receive the new report. (IC)
Margaret, *therefore,* will be the next committee chairperson. (IC)
We will, *of course,* look forward to your reply. (IC)

There are times when you must determine whether the adverbial conjunction plays a *vital role* in the sentence or is a *nonessential independent comment.* For example, in the following, the word *however* would not be set off with commas:

My supervisor said that the project would be acceptable *however* it was completed.

In this example, *however* functions as an adverb and is restrictive (essential): the sentence would not make sense if *however* were removed: *My supervisor said that the project would be acceptable it was completed.*

A few decades ago, adverbial conjunctions were commonly used in the middle of sentences. However, now they sometimes sound out of place there. When you edit, try moving the adverbial conjunction to the beginning of the sentence. Your sentence may sound better, and your reader will have an easier time understanding your message. For example:

George, *however,* gave the report to Sam.   *However,* George gave the report to Sam.
Their efforts, *thus,* eventually showed results.   *Thus,* their efforts eventually showed results.

According to *The Gregg Reference Manual,* there are times when you must say a sentence out loud to know whether an adverbial conjunction is essential or nonessential. If your voice rises as you say the sentence, leave it in; if your voice drops, leave it out.

PRACTICE

Instructions: Correct the sentences below by applying the comma independent comment (IC) rule. Also look for comma nonessential element (NE), comma introductory (INTRO), and comma conjunction (CONJ). For each sentence, do the following: (1) Insert any missing commas. (2) In each main clause, underline the verb twice and the subject once. (3) Circle each adverbial conjunction (AC) and subordinating conjunction (SC). (4) Even though it may seem redundant, write the reason (*IC, NE, INTRO,* or *CONJ*) after the sentence. For example:

Incorrect: Our policy however prohibits us from joining the organization.
Corrected: Our policy, however, prohibits us from joining the organization. (IC)

Incorrect: If your policy changes please call us.
Corrected: If your policy changes, (you) please call us. (INTRO)

1. Jim however will not attend the team meeting.

   _____

2. Their efforts fortunately showed results by the end of the quarter.

   _____

3. They too wanted to implement the program in their department.

_____

4. My manager asked me to complete the report however I saw fit.

_____

5. We will therefore make another offer for the contract.

_____

6. Even though the meeting went well we did not receive the proposal.

_____

7. The attorney encouraged us however to drop the case.

_____

8. In addition Jimmie Adamczek received an exciting call from our major competitor.

_____

9. Our team will of course conduct informal research before committing to a plan.

_____

10. Maricel said that she was going to the meeting and I will attend it with her.

_____

11. George Kramer who shares my office received my mail in error.

_____

12. My entire team received an invitation but my manager said that I could not attend.

_____

Comma Rule 7: Comma Direct Address (DA)

Use commas to set off the name or title of a person addressed directly.

This rule needs little explanation. When you see a person's name or formal title, this is a signal that you may need a comma. The context of the communication will help you distinguish whether the person is being _spoken to_ or _spoken about:_

> George, <u>will</u> you <u>assist</u> me with the project? (DA)
> (I) <u>Thank</u> you, sir, for allowing me to use the parking spot. (DA)
> <u>Everyone</u> <u>expected</u> that you would do the follow-up report, Marcus. (DA)
> Doctor, (<u>you</u>) please <u>call</u> the pharmacy with my prescription. (DA)
> <u>Would</u> <u>you</u>, professor, <u>allow</u> me to turn in my report late? (DA)

In the above examples, notice the following:

- The **direct address** can occur anywhere in the sentence: beginning, middle, or end.

- The direct address is not the subject of the sentence. In fact, it cannot be the subject because it is set off with commas. (Remember Comma Rule 2?)

- If you have difficulty finding the subject in a direct-address sentence, consider whether the subject is "I understood" (I) or "you understood" (you).

Commas are *not* used to set off the name of a person being spoken about or referred to indirectly:

George <u>assisted</u> me with the project.
The <u>professor</u> <u>allowed</u> me to turn in the report late.
Marcus <u>completed</u> the follow-up report.

PRACTICE

Instructions: Correct the sentences below by applying the comma direct-address (DA) rule. Also look for comma independent comment (IC), comma introductory (INTRO), and comma conjunction (CONJ). For each sentence, do the following: (1) Insert any missing commas. (2) In each main clause, underline the verb twice and the subject once. (3) Even though it may seem redundant, write the reason (*DA, IC, INTRO,* or *CONJ*) after the sentence. *Note:* With direct-address commas, often the subject is implied ("you understood" or "I understood"). For example:

Incorrect: Doctor thank you for giving me the results quickly.
Corrected: Doctor, (<u>I</u>) <u>thank</u> you for giving me the results quickly. (DA)

1. Margo would you assist me with the minutes of the board meeting?

   _____

   _____

2. Niki ask Miguel for his report.

   _____

   _____

3. Niki asked Miguel for his report two weeks early.

   _____

   _____

4. Thank you Mr. Levin for taking the time to speak with me.

   _____

   _____

5. Bill therefore informed the clients that the issue was open for discussion.

   _____

   _____

6. Your nurse gave me the report doctor.

   _____

   _____

7. The secretary of the board arrived late for the meeting and he had forgotten the agenda.

   _____

   _____

8. Would you Jorge go to the meeting in my place?

   _____

   _____

9. If Martino cannot accept the position should he inform Human Resources immediately?

   _____

   _____

10. The account executive did not give the report to me Marge.

_____

_____

11. Milton you can find your account information online at our Web site.

_____

_____

12. They gave you the wrong information Sue.

_____

_____

Comma Rule 8: Comma Appositive (AP)

Use commas to set off a word or phrase that describes or identifies a preceding noun or pronoun.

An **appositive** is a "restatement." When a brief explanation follows a noun or pronoun, it is considered a restatement; this restatement is usually a nonessential appositive. Here are some examples:

John, my brother, will plan the family reunion this year. (AP)
Mr. Jackson, the bank's president, is responsible for the policy change. (AP)
(You) Please speak to Janet, my assistant, if I am not available. (AP)

Some appositives are essential (restrictive), which means that they should *not* be set off with commas. An **essential appositive** occurs when more than one person fits the category and the meaning would not be clear if the appositive were removed:

Debbie's brother Charles plays golf well. (Debbie has more than one brother.)

This is an essential appositive because Debbie has more than one brother. If Charles were Debbie's only brother, his name would be set off with commas because the meaning would be clear *with* or *without* her brother's name:

Debbie's brother, Charles, plays golf well. (Debbie has only one brother.)

PRACTICE

Instructions: Identify each appositive, and then determine whether the appositive is essential or nonessential. When the appositive is nonessential, put in a set of appositive (AP) commas. Also look for other types of commas, and identify each with the appropriate abbreviation. For each sentence, do the following: (1) Insert any missing commas. (2) In each main clause, underline the verb twice and the subject once. (3) Even though it may seem redundant, write the reason (*AP, DA, IC, INTRO,* or *CONJ*) after the sentence. For example:

Incorrect: Reggie my personal assistant will join us at 10 a.m.
Corrected: Reggie, my personal assistant, will join us at 10 a.m. (AP)

1. My instructor Mr. Jones prefers to test on Fridays.

_____

_____

2. Mrs. Ramirez my English teacher never tests on Fridays.

_____

_____

3. Alicia the president will give us a bonus based on performance.

_____

_____

4. We should consult with Allison Roth our financial adviser before removing the account.

_____

_____

5. I have full confidence in Jorge my assistant.

_____

_____

6. Mrs. Francois our director of accounting will be available until noon.

_____

_____

7. The building manager Frank Sanders will complete the report.

_____

_____

8. You can ask Elaine my cousin about the job opening because she works at that company.

_____

_____

9. My colleague Susan preferred that we meet on Friday.

_____

_____

10. Ms. Alvarez the bank's president is on vacation in London.

_____

_____

11. John my friend will play in the basketball game this week.

_____

_____

12. My friend John will play in the basketball game this week.

_____

_____

Comma Rule 9: Comma Address/Date (AD)

Use commas to set off an address or a date.

Many writers make mistakes with this rule because addresses and dates usually occur in places other than within a sentence (for example, in the dateline or inside address of a letter). When a complete date occurs within a sentence, use commas to set off the day, month, and year:

Lexi agreed that Friday, May 29, 2007, would be a good date for the opening.

Never put a comma between the month and the day. For example, the following is incorrect: *August, 15, 2006.* It stands corrected as follows: *August 15, 2006.* When a date includes only a month and year, do not separate the month and year with a comma:

The target date for the merger is April 2009.

When an address occurs in a sentence, use commas to set off the city and state (and country, if applicable):

Jonathon will relocate to Boise, Idaho, as a result of his new position.

Here are a few more examples:

My first <u>day</u> on the job <u><u>was</u></u> Friday, October 12, 2002. (AD)
<u>Monday</u>, November 3, 2007, <u><u>is</u></u> the day that the project will officially begin. (AD)
My favorite <u>cities</u> <u><u>are</u></u> San Diego, California, and San Antonio, Texas. (AD)
The <u>meeting</u> <u><u>was scheduled</u></u> in Springfield, Massachusetts, not Springfield, Illinois. (AD)
<u>Rome</u>, Italy, <u><u>is known</u></u> as the eternal city. (AD)

PRACTICE

Instructions: Correct the sentences below by applying the comma address/date (AD) rule. For each sentence, do the following: (1) Insert any missing commas. (2) In each main clause, underline the verb twice and the subject once. (3) Even though it may seem redundant, write the reason *(AD)* after the sentence. For example:

Incorrect: Boston Massachusetts is the perfect city for our satellite office.
Corrected: <u>Boston</u>, Massachusetts, <u><u>is</u></u> the perfect city for our satellite office. (AD)

1. My manager has lived in Salt Lake City Utah for two years now.

   _____

2. Did he say the date for the meeting was Tuesday December 5 or Wednesday January 6?

   _____

3. Was it Friday December 24 2004 that the package arrived?

   _____

4. Arlene has lived in Dallas Texas during the entire investigation.

   _____

5. Norbert believes that New Orleans Louisiana is the best city for the convention.

   _____

6. The International Trade Show will be held in Chicago Illinois in 2008.

   _____

7. Did Michael say that Omaha Nebraska was his favorite city?

   _____

8. Please complete the form and send it to us before Friday April 10 2006.

   _____

9. Is Sally's birth date August 15 1978 or September 7 1979?

   _____

10. The December 2007 meeting in Tucson Arizona has been canceled.

    _____

Comma Rule 10: Series (SER)

When three or more items occur in a series, separate each item with a comma.

This comma rule offers an option: the comma before the *and* is optional. In some cases, the meaning of a series can be misinterpreted without the comma. Since one purpose of punctuation is to achieve clarity, this text recommends that you place the comma before *and*.

(You) Please <u>complete</u> Parts 1, 2, and 3 before you leave. (SER)
The <u>menu</u> <u>listed</u> potatoes, peas, and carrots, for the daily special. (SER)
<u>Mr. Jordan</u> <u>has divided</u> his estate among Bob, Rose, Chuck, and Lisa. (SER)

Here are some questions to ponder:

- In the second example above, how will the peas and carrots be prepared? If the menu had instead listed the items as "potatoes, peas and carrots" how do you think they would have been prepared?

- In the third example, what if Mr. Jordan's will had omitted a comma, and it read "Divide the estate among Bob, Rose, Chuck and Lisa"? Should each get an equal share, or should Chuck and Lisa split one share? (With the comma before *and,* there is no question.)

PRACTICE

Instructions: Correct the sentences below by applying the comma series (SER) rule. Also look for comma introductory (INTRO) and comma address/date (AD). For each sentence, do the following: (1) Insert any missing commas. (2) In each main clause, underline the verb twice and the subject once. (3) Even though it may seem redundant, write the reason (*SER, INTRO,* or *AD*) after the sentence. For example:

Incorrect: Would you be able to provide lodging meals and transportation?
Corrected: <u>Would</u> <u>you</u> <u>be able</u> to provide lodging, meals, and transportation? (SER)

1. They need to change the margins font and color.

   _____

   _____

2. The applicant listed his goals as finding a job establishing a track record and securing financial independence.

   _____

   _____

3. Although our department usually orders supplies the accounting department ordered palm pilots cell phones and laptops for everyone.

   _____

   _____

4. The insurance company filed a complaint collected evidence and prepared for a trial.

   _____

   _____

5. Bob's interests include golfing bowling fishing and hiking.

   _____

   _____

6. Defining your goals practicing daily and remaining positive will ensure success.

   _____

   _____

7. You may need to buy salad beverages and desserts for the Tucson Arizona retreat.

_____

_____

8. Did Brenda Marco and Sylvia attend the annual conference?

_____

_____

9. The applicant said that her strengths were honesty enthusiasm and dependability.

_____

_____

10. The best players and highest scorers were Larry Miranda and Miko.

_____

_____

11. Before agreeing to the merger they need records that are accurate complete and unchallenged.

_____

_____

12. Marvin said that on Friday June 13 2003 he made a cold call about a job opening went downtown for an interview and accepted his first job.

_____

_____

Comma Rule 11: Comma Words Omitted (WO)

Use a comma for the omission of a word or words that play a structural role in sentences.

At times, words that play a structural role in sentences are omitted. Although omitting words is common and can be grammatically correct, omitted words can also create a _gap._ When a gap occurs, use the words-omitted comma to fill the gap. Here are some instances when the words-omitted (WO) comma is needed:

- And _omitted:_ When two adjectives modify the same noun, they should be separated by _and;_ if _and_ is omitted, separate the adjectives with a comma. For example:

  The _long and boring_ <u>speech</u> <u>seemed</u> to go on forever.
  The _long, boring_ <u>speech</u> <u>seemed</u> to go on forever. (WO)

- That _omitted:_ The word _that_ sometimes functions as a conjunction. When the omission of _that_ breaks the flow of a sentence, use a comma to fill the gap. (Most often, omitting the word _that_ does not create a break in the flow, and a comma would not be placed in its absence.) Here's an example of _that_ removed with a comma added to take its place:

  The <u>truth</u> <u>is</u>, we never received the contract. (WO)
  The <u>truth</u> <u>is</u> that we never received the contract.

- Here's an example of _that_ removed without a comma added:

  <u>Sally</u> <u>recommended</u> the meeting start on time even though all were not present.
  <u>Sally</u> <u>recommended</u> that the meeting start on time even though all were not present.

- *Repetitive words omitted:* Sometimes words are omitted when their restatement would be obvious. For example:

> The annual <u>report</u> <u>should be sent</u> to our corporate office; the proposal, to the New York branch. (WO)

> The annual <u>report</u> <u>should be sent</u> to our corporate office; the proposal should be sent to the New York branch.

Comma Rule 12: Comma Contrasting Expression or Afterthought (CEA)

Use a comma to separate a contrasting expression (often beginning with but, not, *or* rather than*) or an afterthought that is added to the end of a sentence.*

This rule is more complicated than the other basic rules because it applies in different situations. It also involves structures that are more common among experienced writers. Thus, as you write more and your skills advance, you may find yourself referring to this rule.

> My <u>friend</u> <u>asked</u> me to go to the theater, not the ballgame. (CEA)
> The board <u>meeting</u> <u>is</u> on Tuesday; (<u>you</u>) <u>bring</u> up the issue at that time, but only if you wish. (CEA)
> The <u>heckler</u> <u>interrupted</u> the speaker, creating chaos for a brief moment. (CEA)
> <u>We</u> <u>would like</u> to fill this position by the end of the week, meaning that time is of the essence. (CEA)
> The <u>leader</u> of the group <u>asked</u> that we report back at 1 p.m., not 2:30 p.m. (CEA)

 SECTION A: CONCEPT CHECK

1. State the comma rules designated by at least three of the following abbreviations: CONJ, INTRO, IC, DA, or AP.
2. What comma rules do the following abbreviations represent? AD, SER, CEA, or WO.
3. Suppose you've decided that for business communications, you are going to write only short, easy-to-understand sentences that require no punctuation other than a period. Try doing this for a while, and see how it works. Is there anything wrong with this approach?

■ SECTION B: THE SEMICOLON

Many people don't like to use semicolons and avoid using them by relying totally on commas. One of the most common errors in writing is to use a comma where a **semicolon** (or period) is

VOCABULARY BUILDERS

Principle/Principal These words are both nouns but mean dramatically different things. Unfortunately, many of us misinterpreted their meaning while in elementary school because the principal was supposedly our "pal."

- *Principle* is a noun and means "a theory or rule of conduct":
  Live by your *principles.*
  Principles of Accounting is an excellent course.
- *Principal* can be a noun or adjective. As an adjective, principal means "chief" or "leading." As a noun, principal means "capital sum of money" or "chief official of a school."
  My *principal* objective is to start a career in advertising. (used as an adjective)
  The *principal* of my school wrote a letter of recommendation for me. (used as a noun)
  The *principal* of my loan is due in two years. (used as a noun)
  I'd rather pay my *principal* (the main part of my loan) than my interest. (used as a noun)

To avoid confusion, remember that *principle* relates to your conduct, not your money. The *principal* on your loan is as much of a "pal" as the *principal* of your school. Pay off your *principal* to save on interest.

needed. When a comma is used where a semicolon belongs, the result is a *comma splice.* A comma splice creates a run-on sentence and is a serious grammatical error.

Besides avoiding mistakes, here are some other reasons to use the semicolon:

- Semicolons add variety and keep writing from getting choppy when sentences are short.
- The semicolon communicates to readers that ideas are close in meaning. Thus, the writer gives the reader a subtle cue that ideas are related.

Learn the semicolon rules; stretch your skills and experiment using a semicolon or two. If you still don't like semicolons, you never need use one. However, after you know how to use them correctly, you may actually like semicolons!

Semicolon Rule 1: Semicolon No Conjunction (NC)

Use a semicolon to separate two independent clauses that are joined without a conjunction.

This rule is sometimes referred to as *semicolon in place of a period.* In fact, you can tell that you are using a semicolon correctly if you can substitute a period for it. A semicolon is not as strong as a period, which is a terminal mark of punctuation. Usually, a semicolon is used when one or both statements are short and related in meaning; the semicolon helps the reader infer the connection between the ideas. For example:

Jodie <u>wrote</u> the marketing report; <u>Christopher</u> <u>will edit</u> it. (NC)
Jodie <u>wrote</u> the marketing report. <u>Christopher</u> <u>will edit</u> it.
The <u>chairperson</u> <u>resigned</u> yesterday; the <u>president</u> already <u>appointed</u> a replacement. (NC)
The <u>chairperson</u> <u>resigned</u> yesterday. The <u>president</u> already <u>appointed</u> a replacement.

PRACTICE

Instructions: Correct the sentences below by applying the semicolon no-conjunction (NC) rule. Some sentences may need a comma conjunction (CONJ) instead, so stay on the alert. For each sentence, do the following: (1) Insert any missing semicolons or commas. (2) In each main clause, underline the verb twice and the subject once. (3) Even though it may seem redundant, write the reason (*NC* or *CONJ*) after the sentence. For example:

Incorrect: We went to the meeting the chair did not ask for our opinion.
Corrected: <u>We</u> <u>went</u> to the meeting; the <u>chair</u> <u>did</u> not <u>ask</u> for our opinion. (NC)
Corrected: <u>We</u> <u>went</u> to the meeting, but the <u>chair</u> <u>did</u> not <u>ask</u> for our opinion. (CONJ)

1. The meeting went as planned the chairperson was relieved.

   _____

   _____

2. Alan's computer is down he has already called the technician.

   _____

   _____

3. The meeting was canceled unexpectedly and we found ourselves with nothing to do.

   _____

   _____

4. The instructions were not clear most of us did the project incorrectly.

   _____

   _____

5. A report must be filed the deadline is Friday.

   _____

   _____

6. The package arrived late I have informed the shipping company that this was a problem.

   _____

   _____

7. Michael did not report to the meeting Mr. Johnson was not pleased.

   _____

   _____

8. A typical response would have been appreciation but he acted annoyed.

   _____

   _____

9. Minutes are due within a week of the meeting a short delay is acceptable.

   _____

   _____

10. I have only 20 minutes for lunch so carryout is my choice.

    _____

    _____

11. Martha did her report on the consequences of insecticide Mary Jean chose that topic also.

    _____

    _____

12. The business office opens at noon on Friday but it is closed on Saturday.

    _____

    _____

13. All attendees should bring registration forms those without them will not be admitted.

    _____

    _____

14. Jeffrey Ballen was appointed vice president Shakira Mason was appointed sales manager.

    _____

    _____

Semicolon Rule 2: Semicolon Transition (TRANS)

Place a semicolon before and a comma after an adverbial conjunction when it acts as a transition between independent clauses.

This rule applies when adverbial conjunctions provide transitions between independent clauses. Once again, a semicolon implies that the clauses are related in meaning.

> Michael <u>went</u> to the market; *however,* <u>he</u> <u>forgot</u> several items on the list. (TRANS)
> My <u>supervisor</u> <u>asked</u> for my resignation; *fortunately,* <u>he</u> <u>was</u> only <u>joking</u>. (TRANS)
> There <u>will be</u> a meeting after work on Friday; *however,* <u>it</u> <u>will be</u> short. (TRANS)
> The <u>proposal</u> <u>arrived</u> late; *therefore,* <u>we</u> <u>should apologize</u>. (TRANS)
> Their <u>governor</u> <u>has</u> already <u>solved</u> many problems; *for example,* <u>he</u> <u>has</u> solved their energy crisis.

PRACTICE

Instructions: Correct the sentences below by applying the semicolon transition (TRANS) rule. Also look for semicolon no conjunction (NC) and comma conjunction (CONJ). For each sentence, do the following: (1) Insert any missing semicolons or commas. (2) In each main clause, underline the verb twice and the subject once. (3) Circle each adverbial conjunction (AC). (4) Even though it may seem redundant, write the reason (*TRANS, NC,* or *CONJ*) after the sentence. For example:

> **Incorrect:** The meeting started late however it ended on time.
> **Corrected:** The meeting started late; however, it ended on time. (TRANS)

1. The meeting began on time however several key people were late.

   _____

   _____

2. A new agenda has been posted on the intranet refer to it before finalizing your plans.

   _____

   _____

3. They are no longer our client thus you may wish to reconsider your options.

   _____

   _____

4. Our president changed the tuition policy fortunately most employees appreciated the change.

   _____

   _____

5. Fortune 500 companies generally offer good benefits however do not base your job-search strategy solely on that.

   _____

   _____

6. This year's annual report contained many errors therefore we needed to have it reprinted.

   _____

   _____

7. Seth attended the conference however he did not attend the closing session.

   _____

   _____

8. Ramona created the brochure consequently she is responsible for its contents.

   _____

   _____

9. You will find the information on our Web site for example we list all products and codes.

   _____

   _____

10. The package was returned unopened but we could never locate the owner.

    _____

    _____

Semicolon Rule 3: Semicolon Because of Commas (BC)

When a sentence needs major and minor separations, use semicolons for major breaks and commas for minor breaks.

Major and minor breaks don't occur very often when the writer keeps sentences simple, clear, and concise. Most often this rule applies when several cities and states or names and titles are listed:

> This year's meetings will be held in Chicago, Illinois; Boston, Massachusetts; Dallas, Texas; and Pittsburgh, Pennsylvania.

> The following employees should meet with Human Resources to complete their benefit package: Mary Hopkins, director of sales; George Martini, accounts receivable; Antonio Hernandez, vice president; and Miki Tonio, sales representative.

PRACTICE

Instructions: Correct the sentences below by applying the semicolon because of commas (BC) rule. For each sentence, do the following: (1) Insert any missing semicolons or commas. (2) In each main clause, underline the verb twice and the subject once. (3) Write the reason (BC) after the sentence. For example:

> **Incorrect:** There are extra materials in Dallas Texas Atlanta Georgia and Greensboro North Carolina.
>
> **Corrected:** <u>There</u> <u>are</u> extra materials in Dallas, Texas; Atlanta, Georgia; and Greensboro, North Carolina.

1. Next year's sales meeting may be held in Orlando Florida San Francisco California or Phoenix Arizona.

   _____

   _____

2. The plan was to meet at the Civic Center so unless I hear otherwise I will see you there later today.

   _____

   _____

3. We need to allow time on the agenda for Charles Cecil regional sales manager John August district sales manager and Robert Lindsey sales associate.

   _____

   _____

4. The manual was available while we were doing the report but since pages were missing from the manual we could not complete the report.

   _____

   _____

5. The presentation was excellent and although it started on time it ended 15 minutes late.

   _____

   _____

This rule also applies when sentences are long and complex, containing independent clauses with subordinate clauses that require a comma or commas:

> Dr. Axelrod applied for the position; but because his references have not yet replied, we have not scheduled him for an interview.

> The best time of the year for marketing campaigns is September; and since we have that time available, we should schedule a meeting to develop a plan.

INTERNET EXERCISE WH1.1

Punctuation Online There are many places you can go online to find answers to your punctuation questions, exercises to hone your skills, and more detail on punctuation usage. Visit the *Foundations of Business Communication* Web site at <http://www.mhhe.com/djyoung> for a list of online reference links.

Once you have accessed the home page, select "Student Activities" and then click the Writer's Handbook, Part 1, link for instructions on getting started.

The semicolons in the following example are needed because of the commas, which relate to Comma Rule 11 (repetitive words omitted):

> The photos will be taken in groups of ten. Employees from the fifth floor will have their photos taken at 10 a.m.; from the seventh, at 11 a.m.; and from the ninth, at 12 p.m.

This example could be simplified by removing the semicolons and using only commas:

> **Revised:** Employees from the fifth floor will have their photos taken at 10 a.m., from the seventh at 11 a.m., and from the ninth at 12 p.m.

 SECTION B: CONCEPT CHECK

1. Describe the semicolon rules referred to by the following abbreviations: NC, TRANS, BC.
2. If periods and commas serve just as well, why use semicolons at all in your writing?
3. What is the difference between commas and semicolons?

■ SECTION C: OTHER MARKS

Through the years, most business writing has been conservative. The comma and semicolon have been the traditional, basic punctuation marks of business writing. However, writing has changed dramatically during the last few years. Business now depends on more casual forms of writing, such as e-mail. With e-mail, people are more likely to incorporate less traditional marks, such as *colons, dashes,* and *ellipsis marks,* and these marks are often misused.

The colon, the dash, and ellipsis marks can add variety and flair to your writing, but only if you use them correctly. Unfortunately, many writers throw them in e-mail and other documents haphazardly. Using these marks correctly does not take much effort; and even simple, casual messages deserve accuracy. Even when you are using the colon, the dash, and ellipsis marks correctly, remember to use them sparingly.

Less common terminal marks of punctuation include the *courteous-request period,* the *exclamation point,* and the *question mark.* Terminal marks cause the reader to come to a full stop. They are generally used at the end of complete sentences but can be used after words or phrases, especially when you are transcribing dialogue.

The Colon

The **colon** is a traditional mark of punctuation, and it can add power to your writing. Colons alert the reader that information will follow to explain or illuminate the information that preceded it.

- A colon can be used to indicate a series or numbered list. Often the colon is preceded by one of the following terms: *these, the following,* or *as follows.*

  Example: These are the items to add to the agenda: annual meeting schedule and draft report changes.

- Use a colon after the words *note* and *caution.*

  Example: Note: If a complete sentence follows the introductory word *note* or *caution,* capitalize the first word of the sentence that follows it.

- Use a colon in business letters after the salutation. **Standard punctuation** style calls for the placement of a colon after the salutation and a comma after the complimentary closing. In **open punctuation** style, no punctuation appears after the salutation or the greeting.
- Use a colon at the end of one independent clause to introduce the next independent clause; the first word of the second independent clause can be capitalized if it requires special emphasis or is presented as a formal rule. In general, do not capitalize the first word of an independent clause after a colon. This punctuation practice should not be overused: use it sparingly, no more than one time for a short document.

  Example: LaSalle Bank is a great place to have an account: it ranks number one in customer service.

The colon has several other uses. See Section 1 of *The Gregg Reference Manual* for details.

PRACTICE

Instructions: Insert a colon where needed. For example:

  Incorrect: My favorite publisher is McGraw-Hill they just accepted my book proposal.
  Corrected: My favorite publisher is McGraw-Hill: they just accepted my book proposal.

1. The CEO's objectives are these decrease spending and consolidate holdings.

   _____

   _____

2. The following items should be added to the agenda revising the budget, improving communication among departments, and upgrading corporate software.

   _____

   _____

3. The job offer was better than I expected they offered me double my current salary and a company car.

   _____

   _____

4. Note items that are not shipped by Federal Express should be sent priority.

   _____

   _____

5. These are the issues that the president will address at the board meeting delays in product development and problems with new acquisitions.

_____

_____

Ellipsis Marks

Ellipsis marks (also known by its plural form *ellipses*) are used formally in business and academic documents and informally in e-mail messages. For formal use, writers should familiarize themselves with the rules and stay within those boundaries. For informal writing, writers should be selective on the latitude they give themselves in straying from the rules. (Ellipsis marks are also covered in the Writer's Handbook, Part 4.)

Let's start by explaining what ellipsis marks mean and how they are represented in printed form:

*   Ellipsis marks indicate an omission of a word or several words.

*   Ellipses are represented by three periods with a space before and after each period (. . .).

*   When ellipses occur at the end of a quoted sentence, a fourth period is added.

In formal business and academic documents, ellipses are most often used with quoted material. When only selected parts of a quotation are relevant, the material that is left out is indicated by ellipses. However, ellipsis marks may be used informally to indicate that a sentence trails off before the end, creating an effect of uncertainty or abrupt end of thought.

Ellipses can be found in the most unusual and incorrect forms: two, three, or four periods without spaces between the periods. At all times—whether a document is formal or informal—ellipsis marks should be typed correctly.

Here's an example of a long quote followed by its shortened version applying ellipsis marks.

A formal quote:
Most people live, whether physically, intellectually or morally, in a very restricted circle of their potential being. They make use of a very small portion of their possible consciousness, and of their soul's resources in general, much like a man who, out of his whole bodily organism, should get into a habit of using and moving only his little finger. Great emergencies and crises show us how much greater our vital resources are than we had supposed.[1] *William James*

Quote shortened by using ellipses:
Most people live . . . in a very restricted circle of their potential being. . . . Great emergencies and crises show us how much greater our vital resources are than we had supposed. *William James*

In informal documents, writers use ellipsis marks to indicate they are not completing their thoughts in writing. Used this way, writers assume the reader will infer what was omitted. Here's an example of using ellipses in an e-mail:

Jan,

How are you feeling about the proposed changes in our department? The impact on upper management will be dramatic . . . people will complain like crazy!

Talk to you later.

Donna

PRACTICE

1. Find three pieces of writing that use ellipsis marks—an article from a newspaper, an e-mail, a letter from a friend, an office bulletin, and the like. Identify whether or not the

ellipsis marks are used correctly. Ask yourself: *Is it always easy to figure out what has been left out and replaced with ellipses?*

2. Turn to the *BusinessWeek* article on page 1. Assume you are writing a paper on the topic "Communicating Leadership in a Crisis." Choose two paragraphs in the article to quote from, and then practice shortening the quotes by using ellipsis marks.

The Dash

The **dash** is the most versatile of all punctuation marks and can be used in both formal and informal documents. It can be a substitute for a comma, semicolon, period, or colon. A single dash places emphasis on the information following it; a pair of dashes emphasize the information between them. For example:

Trisha hosted the charity gala dinner—it raised more money than any other event in the history of our organization.

Charlie Richards—our new CEO—invited me to apply for the position of senior VP.

The dash has traditionally been represented by two hyphens without a space before, between, or after them. When you key in a dash as two hyphens without a space before, between, or after them, your computer software is likely to display an "em dash" (one solid line about the width of a capital "m").

A word of caution: Use dashes sparingly. Though the dash is a traditional mark of punctuation, it is less conventional than the other marks it replaces (the comma, semicolon, period, and colon). If you want to be a bit flamboyant, use some dashes. Just make sure you express your flamboyancy in a conservative way by restricting your dashes to no more than one or two a page.

Terminal Punctuation Marks

A terminal mark of punctuation occurs at the end of a sentence and brings the reader to a full stop. In fact, in Great Britain, the term *full stop* is used instead of the word *period*. Below are brief discussions of some of the less common terminal punctuation marks, which include the courteous-request period, the exclamation point, and the question mark.

The Courteous-Request Period A **period** indicates the end of a statement. However, a period can also be used to indicate the end of a **courteous request,** that is, a question that prompts action rather than a written response. When a writer asks such a question, the sentence ends in a period, not a question mark.

Example: Would you return the enclosed form by Friday.

The recipient would not respond, "Yes, I would." The statement is phrased as a question because a request sounds more polite than a command. Thus, if you do not expect a question to be answered, consider whether it might be a courteous request.

The Exclamation Point   The **exclamation point** indicates surprise. An exclamation point can occur after a word, phrase, or complete sentence.

Examples: Stop!
Congratulations on your promotion!

Exclamation points are highly overused, especially in e-mail. Whenever you use an exclamation point, consider whether it adds value to your writing or instead makes your writing sound too casual or too full of emotions. You will be safe using the exclamation point only if you use it sparingly.

The Question Mark   The **question mark** indicates a question the writer expects the reader to answer. As with exclamation points, under some circumstance, question marks can occur after individual words as well as complete sentences structured as statements or questions.

Examples: What next?
He said that he would do what?
What did he say?

Questions that end in prepositions are considered grammatically correct. (Note: At this writing, some statements ending in prepositions can also be considered correct. For example, "Please tell us what the meeting is about." Make your decision based on natural versus stilted-sounding language.)

Example: Whom would you like to attend the meeting with?

SECTION C: CONCEPT CHECK

1. What are the different uses of the colon?

2. Do you think it is appropriate for business writing to include punctuation that is less formal stylistically, such as the dash and ellipsis marks? Why or why not? Would your answer be different for messages written to coworkers than it would be for letters written to clients? To the president of the company?

3. Do you use punctuation to make your writing resemble your conversational style? How does using dashes and ellipses affect the tone of your writing?

■ SECTION D: COMMON PUNCTUATION ERRORS

Now that you have learned how to use basic punctuation marks, let's examine the kinds of errors that result when commas and semicolons are not used correctly. Incorrect use of punctuation results in fragments or run-on sentences.

Fragments

A **fragment** is a group of words that is punctuated as a sentence but does not meet the qualifications of a sentence. (A sentence has a subject and a verb and expresses a complete thought.) Fragments usually come in the form of dependent clauses or phrases.

Dependent Clauses as Fragments   A clause is a unit of words that has a subject and verb, and it comes in two forms:

• *Independent clause:* It can stand alone.

• *Dependent clause:* It doesn't express a complete thought, so it can't stand alone.

The example below is a simple sentence; it has a subject and verb and expresses a complete thought:

Bill advised our department the policy had changed.

Here are the fragments that result when a subordinating conjunction is added to the beginning of the independent clause:

Although Bill advised our department the policy had changed.
Even though Bill advised our department the policy had changed.
Because Bill advised our department the policy had changed . . . what happened?

When you read a fragment, the question that may pop into your mind is "What next?" That's because a fragment leaves the reader wondering where the sentence is going.
    Here are ways to correct dependent-clause fragments:

1. *Turn the dependent clause into an independent clause.* You may be able to do this simply by removing the subordinating conjunction.
2. *Attach the dependent clause to an independent clause.* Often the sentence before or after the dependent clause completes it nicely. By connecting the dependent clause with the sentence that precedes or follows it, the correction is made. For example:

INTERNET EXERCISE WH1.2

Practice Sheets Need more punctuation practice? You will find additional worksheets covering all the punctuation topics in this chapter at the *Foundations of Business Communication* Web site at <http://www.mhhe.com/djyoung>.
    At the home page, select "Student Activities" and then click on the Writer's Handbook, Part 1, link to find instructions for getting started.

Incorrect: Bob did not complete the report prior to the team meeting. *Even though* his supervisor gave him the morning to work on it. He could not interpret the data and needed to return to the project later in the day to make final decisions.

Revised: Bob did not have enough time to write the report *even though* his supervisor gave him the morning to work on it. He could not interpret the data and needed to return to the project later in the day to make final decisions.

Or: Bob did not have enough time to write the report. *Even though* his supervisor gave him the morning to work on it, he could not interpret the data. He needed to return to the project later in the day to make final decisions.

Of course, you could have removed *even though*, which would have turned the dependent clause into an independent clause. However, the sentences sound choppy without a transitional word:

Weak: Bob did not have enough time to write the report. His supervisor gave him the morning to work on it. He could not interpret the data and needed to return to the project later in the day to make final decisions.

Phrases as Fragments   Fragments can also be formed when a **phrase** is punctuated as a sentence. Unlike a clause, a phrase does not have a subject and a verb. Nevertheless, long and involved phrases can be mistaken for sentences:

To communicate effectively on the job regardless of the situation
Speaking to Giorgi about the situation before noon so that the problem can be avoided

To avoid fragments, punctuate only independent clauses as complete sentences. You can correct the above phrases by making sure each has a subject and a verb:

Managers must communicate effectively on the job regardless of the situation.
You should speak to Giorgi about the situation before noon so that the problem can be avoided.

Infinitive phrases and gerund phrases are two common types of phrases that are mistaken for sentences:

- *Infinitive phrase:* An **infinitive** is formed by adding *to* the base form of the verb. An infinitive can act as a noun, an adjective, or an adverb. The following are examples of infinitives: *to go, to see, to be, to follow, to communicate, to speak.* An **infinitive phrase** is formed when a group of words follows the infinitive. Here are some long infinitive phrases that could be mistaken for sentences:

To go to the store before going to work because it was on my way
To see you at the meeting later today with all the necessary forms
To be there all day without having breakfast or lunch
To follow the directions precisely as posted on the board in the conference room
To communicate effectively on the job every day regardless of the situation
To speak to Giorgi about the situation before noon

- *Gerund phrase:* A **gerund** is formed by adding *ing* to the base form of the verb. Gerunds function as nouns. The following are gerunds: *going, seeing, being, following, communicating, speaking,* and so on. Here are the infinitive phrases shown above represented as gerund phrases:

Going to the store before going to work because it was on my way
Seeing you at the meeting later today with all the necessary forms
Being there all day without having breakfast or lunch
Following the directions precisely as posted on the board in the conference room
Communicating effectively on the job every day regardless of the situation
Speaking to Giorgi about the situation before noon

Run-On Sentences

"Run-on" does not refer to long and rambling sentences. "Run-on" is a grammatical term that describes independent clauses that are connected without adequate punctuation. A **run-on sentence** can consist of two independent clauses that are joined with a coordinating conjunction but without a comma to separate them. Another type of run-on consists of two independent clauses that are connected without a comma or conjunctions (also called a fused sentence).

To correct these kinds of run-on sentences, do one of the following:

- Place a period after each independent clause.
- Use a comma and coordinating conjunction to separate the independent clauses.
- Use a semicolon to separate the independent clauses.

Run-on: Each session is limited to 22 participants call today to reserve your space.
Corrected: Each session is limited to 22 participants. Call today to reserve your space.

Run-on: The sales department will start their campaign in August and the marketing department will continue to support their efforts.
Corrected: The sales department will start their campaign in August; the marketing department will continue to support their efforts.

VOCABULARY BUILDERS

To/Too/Two These words are frequently used incorrectly.

- *To* is a preposition and part of an infinitive:
  Mark went *to* the store.
  To whom it may concern . . .
  Tell them *to go* to the meeting.
- *Too* is an adverb relating to quantity:
  We have *too much* work.
  This has happened *too many* times.
  They have given us the wrong order *too often.*
- *Two* is a number:
  Please provide *two* packets of materials.
  I would like *two* cheeseburgers.
  It is *too late* for the *two* of us *to* argue.

To avoid confusion:

- Follow *to* with a noun or a verb.
- Follow *too* with an adverb.
- Use *two* when you can substitute the numeral 2.

Run-on: Opponents say the president's plan would do little to solve the problem acres of forest land would still be lost to fire.

Corrected: Opponents say the president's plan would do little to solve the problem, and acres of forest land would still be lost to fire.

Run-on: In response, several states have adopted their own provisions and several more are considering similar measures.

Corrected: In response, several states have adopted their own provisions, and several more are considering similar measures.

Another type of run-on is a comma splice. A **comma splice** occurs when two independent clauses are joined with only a comma.

Incorrect: The department received explicit instructions, everyone agreed to participate. Family values are a critical issue, every candidate needs to take a position. This year's congressional campaign is important, a change in one representative could influence the entire power structure.

To correct a comma splice, do one of the following:

- Change the comma to a semicolon.
- Add a coordinating conjunction.
- Change the comma to a subordinating conjunction.

Corrected: The department received explicit instructions; everyone agreed to participate. Family values are a critical issue, and every candidate needs to take a position. This year's congressional campaign is important because a change in one representative could influence the entire power structure.

 SECTION D: CONCEPT CHECK

1. What are the differences between a dependent clause and an independent clause?
2. Describe methods for correcting run-on sentences.
3. When fragments and run-on sentences appear in business writing, what is their effect on the reader? Do you believe errors like these can affect the message in a communication?

SUMMARY

You may have discovered that the best way to improve your grammar and punctuation skills is to apply the principles you are learning in your own writing. As you write more, all your skills will become stronger. You may also have discovered that by improving your punctuation skills, you also improve your writing style.

You now have some options for how to proceed. You can either do more work on improving the accuracy of your writing *or* work on improving your writing style. Based on your instructor's guidance and how you did on your assessment, design a learning strategy for achieving your goals. Here are your options:

1. You can work on Chapter 2, "What Is Good Business Writing?" which covers style in depth. Chapter 2 explains principles for achieving simple, clear, and concise writing.

2. You can skip Chapter 2 for the moment and work on Part 2 of the Writer's Handbook (page 422), which reviews the use of verbs and pronouns. Since most grammar mistakes relate to verbs and pronouns, you will want to gain mastery of them early in your career: your speech will sound more sophisticated and your writing will be more respected.

   Your goal is to *change patterns,* not just correct isolated mistakes. You may find this very difficult in the beginning. However, you will progress very quickly.

WRITER'S HANDBOOK, PART 1 CHECKLIST

Basic Comma Rules

1. *The Golden Rule:* When in doubt, leave it out.

2. *The Cardinal Rule:* Never separate a subject and a verb with only one comma.

3. *Conjunction:* Use a comma to separate independent clauses joined by a coordinating conjunction. (CONJ)

4. *Introductory:* Place a comma after a word, phrase, or dependent clause that introduces a main clause. (INTRO)

5. *Nonessential elements:* Use commas to set off a nonessential element, such as a *who* or *which* clause. (NE)

6. *Independent comment:* Use commas to set off a word or phrase that interrupts an independent clause. (IC)

7. *Direct address:* Use commas to set off the name or title of a person addressed directly. (DA)

8. *Appositive:* Use commas to set off a word or phrase that describes or identifies a preceding noun or pronoun. (AP)

9. *Address/Date:* Use commas to set off an address or a date. (AD)

10. *Series:* When three or more items occur in a series, separate each item with a comma. (SER)

11. *Words omitted:* When a word such as *and* or *that* is omitted and the omission creates a "gap," use a comma. (WO)

12. *Contrasting expression or afterthought:* Use a comma to separate a contrasting expression (often beginning with *but, not,* or *rather than*) or an afterthought that is added to the end of a sentence. (CEA)

Basic Semicolon Rules:

1. *No conjunction:* Use a semicolon to separate two independent clauses that are joined without a conjunction. (NC)

2. *Transition:* Place a semicolon before and a comma after an adverbial conjunction when it acts as a transition between independent clauses. (TRANS)

3. *Because of commas:* When a sentence contains major and minor breaks, use semicolons for major breaks and commas for minor breaks. (BC)

ACTIVITY 1 : CORE SENTENCE ELEMENTS

Instructions: The subject and verb represent the *core* of a sentence. In the sentences below, identify these core elements in main clauses and subordinating clauses at the beginning of sentences. Underline subjects one time and underline verbs two times. (*Hint:* With statements, the best strategy is to identify the verb first and then work backward to identify the subject: *Bill wrote the report.* With questions, the best strategy is to phrase the question as a statement and then identify the verb and subject: *Did Bill write the report? Bill did write the report.*)

1. The proposal required a detailed analysis.

   _____

2. The newspaper arrived after I had left for work.

   _____

3. When my manager researched and analyzed the data, he was pleased with the results.

   _____

4. In the springtime, job openings are more prevalent.

   _____

5. The director and placement counselor met for two hours discussing the strategy.

   _____

6. The teller at the bank advised me that my account was in good standing.

   _____

7. All trucks and cars need periodic servicing so that they function well.

   _____

8. If you wish to request a statement, our customer service department will assist you.

   _____

9. Will Bob advise us about the changes in the survey?

   _____

10. The program was completed ahead of schedule, and our department was rewarded.

    _____

11. The Web site gave all pertinent information; we purchased the product online.

    _____

12. Did their answer provide the information that you needed?

    _____

13. The wind blew the papers on the floor, and everything was in disarray.

    _____

14. Are there still several issues that we need to discuss?

    _____

15. It is a perfect day to sign the contract.

    _____

Comma conjunction (CONJ):   Put a comma before a coordinating conjunction when it connects two independent clauses.

Coordinating conjunctions (CCs):   and, but, or, for, nor, yet, so

Exercise A: Practice—Comma CONJ

Instructions: In each sentence below, underline each subject once and each verb twice, put a comma where needed, and circle the coordinating conjunctions. Write the reason (CONJ) after the sentence. For example:

Incorrect: The problem was apparent to everyone yet Robert refused to acknowledge it.

Corrected: The problem was apparent to everyone, (yet) Robert refused to acknowledge it. (CONJ).

1. George wanted to join their committee but he had other commitments.

   _____

   _____

2. Her manager had told her about the meeting but she refused to go.

   _____

   _____

3. Donald explained the policy effectively but the board of directors refused to listen.

   _____

   _____

4. Alex waited in the ninth-floor conference room and Martin waited for Alex in Alex's office.

   _____

   _____

5. The matter was already resolved but we needed to advise management of the problem.

   _____

   _____

6. The seminar was rescheduled at the same time so we were not able to attend the meeting.

   _____

   _____

7. The new copier does not work as effectively as the old one yet we purchased it anyway.

   _____

   _____

8. Duffy wants to assist us with conference preparations but his suppervisor is out of town.

   _____

   _____

9. Antonia did very well on the year-end report so her supervisor commended her in the staff meeting.

   _____

   _____

10. Christopher never put in any extra time yet he received a bonus for his work on it.

_____

_____

11. The product must arrive on time or they will void the agreement.

_____

_____

12. Byron will accept the job in the marketing department or he will seek employment outside of our company.

_____

_____

Exercise B: Apply—Comma CONJ

Instructions: Write three sentences below to demonstrate comma conjunction; use three different conjunctions. (coordinating conjunctions: _and, but, or, nor, for, yet, so_)

Example: My plans include more education, and I am saving money for that purpose.

_____

_____

_____

_____

_____

ACTIVITY 3: PUNCTUATION—COMMA INTRODUCTORY

Comma introductory (INTRO):	Place a comma after an introductory expression (a word, phrase, or clause) that introduces a main clause. Introductory expressions often begin with a subordinate conjunction or adverbial conjunction.
Subordinate conjunctions (SCs):	after, as, before, so that, even though, if, until, because, although, as soon as . . .
Adverbial conjunctions (ACs):	however, therefore, fortunately, for example, consequently, in summary . . .

Exercise A: Practice—Comma INTRO

Instructions: In each sentence, underline each subject once and each verb twice, put a comma where needed, circle each subordinate conjunction (SC) and adverbial conjunction (AC). Write the reason (INTRO) after the sentence.

Incorrect: If you tell me your plans while in the city I will see if I can meet you.
Corrected: If you tell me your plans while in the city, I will see if I can meet you. (INTRO)

1. As my manager advised I sent the report to everyone on the list.

_____

_____

2. Before I accept the position I need to negotiate a better employment package.

_____

_____

3. If you would like Mr. Sims to return your call you may wish to leave your phone number.

_____

_____

4. Therefore you probably should arrive before 8:30 a.m. so that you can receive your materials.

_____

_____

5. So that you can join us at the managers' meeting my assistant will fax your reports to the home office.

_____

_____

6. After they made the announcement the participants were disappointed.

_____

_____

7. In general we do not provide direct links at our Web site to our satellite offices.

_____

_____

8. Although we accepted their proposal they still continue to negotiate trivial details.

_____

_____

Exercise B: Apply—Comma INTRO

Instructions: Write five sentences below to demonstrate comma introductory. Use both subordinate and adverbial conjunctions.

Example: If I had known about the hard work, I still would have signed up for the class.

_____

_____

_____

_____

_____

Exercise C: Practice—Comma CONJ and Comma INTRO

Instructions: In each sentence, underline each subject once and each verb twice, put a comma where needed, and circle the conjunctions: coordinating (CC), subordinating (SC), and adverbial (AC). Write the reason (CONJ) or (INTRO) after the sentence.

Incorrect: If Jake scheduled the meeting how could Jesse have canceled it?
Corrected: (If) Jake scheduled the meeting, how could Jesse have canceled it?

1. As soon as we receive the material you sent we will give you a response.

_____

_____

2. When you arrive at the airport please check your messages.

_____

_____

3. I appreciate your assistance so please continue to write your comments.

_____

_____

4. If you care to call your office feel free to use my phone.

_____

_____

5. While Lois is out of the office please supervise the staff.

_____

_____

6. Unless you hear from Charles within an hour you should send the material by Federal Express.

_____

_____

7. There was not a problem with our agreement yet he refused to take delivery.

_____

_____

8. However she called to inform us the officers would arrive late.

_____

_____

9. Martha agreed to do the minutes so Mary took control of the logistics.

_____

_____

10. Although time is important it is also important to have adequate resources.

_____

_____

11. Until the president arrives we cannot begin the meeting.

_____

_____

12. Unfortunately we did not receive your bid in time to consider you for the job.

_____

_____

13. My manager agreed to go to the conference but refused help on the proposal.

_____

_____

14. The consultant completed the analysis and asked us if we agreed with the conclusions.

_____

_____

Comma conjunction (CONJ):	Put a comma before a coordinating conjunction when it connects two independent clauses.
Semicolon no conjunction (NC):	Use a semicolon to separate two independent clauses that are joined without a coordinating conjunction. This is sometimes referred to as *semicolon in place of period.*
Coordinating conjunctions (CCs):	and, but, or, for, nor, yet, so

Exercise A: Practice—Comma CONJ and Semicolon NC

Instructions: In each sentence, underline each subject once and each verb twice, place a comma or semicolon where needed, and circle the conjunctions: coordinating (CC), subordinating (SC), and adverbial (AC). Write the reason (CONJ) or (NC) after the sentence.

Examples:

Incorrect: The president set the tone of the meeting the vice president gave the message.

Corrected: The <u>president</u> <u><u>set</u></u> the tone of the meeting; the <u>vice president</u> <u><u>gave</u></u> the message. (NC)

Corrected: The <u>president</u> <u><u>set</u></u> the tone of the meeting, (but) the <u>vice president</u> <u><u>gave</u></u> the message. (CONJ)

1. I said that I could not complete that project today but Martha felt that would cause a problem.

   _____

   _____

2. We sent the proposal by Federal Express call me when it arrives.

   _____

   _____

3. He said that there was not a problem with our agreement he was eager to begin the transaction.

   _____

   _____

4. Sandra is not the only one who needs assistance George also needs help.

   _____

   _____

5. I appreciate your assistance so please continue to attend the board meetings.

   _____

   _____

6. Mr. Michaels ordered supplies for our office but the order was not complete.

   _____

   _____

7. We look forward to hearing from you do not hesitate to call.

   _____

   _____

8. The manager spoke highly of your skills he recommended you without hesitation.

_____

_____

9. Janet's auditor balanced our account and we were very grateful.

_____

_____

10. Marie likes to attend board meetings but not to participate in controversial decisions.

_____

_____

11. Volunteering is time-consuming but it can also be rewarding.

_____

_____

12. Sam should fly to Boston but take a train to Washington.

_____

_____

13. Mr. Jackson applied for the position of vice president he is still waiting for their decision.

_____

_____

14. Our local bank will become a subsidiary of the national bank and its policies will change.

_____

_____

Exercise B: Apply—Comma CONJ and Semicolon NC

Instructions: Write 2 sentences each to show the use of comma conjunction and semicolon no conjunction. In each sentence, underline each subject once and each verb twice. Put punctuation where needed, and write the reason after the sentence. Also, circle and identify the coordinating conjunctions (CC).

Example: I left for lunch early; but, I still did not have enough time. (NC)

_____

_____

_____

_____

_____

_____

ACTIVITY 5: PUNCTUATION—COMMA INTRODUCTORY, APPOSITIVE, AND DIRECT ADDRESS

Comma introductory (INTRO):   Place a comma after an introductory expression (a word, phrase, or clause) that introduces a main clause. Introductory expressions often begin with a subordinating conjunction *(when, if, while)* or an adverbial conjunction (*however, therefore, for example, consequently*).

Comma appositive (AP): Use commas to set off a word or group of words that describes or identifies a preceding noun or pronoun.

Comma direct address (DA): Put commas before and after the name or title of a person addressed directly.

Exercise A: Practice—Comma INTRO, AP, and DA

Instructions: In each sentence, underline each subject once and each verb twice, place a comma where needed, and circle the conjunctions: coordinating (CC), subordinating (SC), and adverbial (AC). Write the reason (INTRO), (AR), or (DA) after the sentence.

Incorrect: Although I was not at the meeting they named me chair of the committee.

Corrected: Although <u>I</u> <u><u>was</u></u> not at the meeting, <u>they</u> <u><u>named</u></u> me chair of the committee. (INTRO)

1. Sylvia is that letter from a client or vendor?

   _____

   _____

2. As soon as we receive the brochure we will evaluate it.

   _____

   _____

3. When you arrive in Boston please call me George.

   _____

   _____

4. If you wish to call your office Kathleen you may use the phone in the conference room.

   _____

   _____

5. While Lenore runs the charity event send all applicants to my office.

   _____

   _____

6. Jennifer Gonzales a former employee requested the records.

   _____

   _____

7. Unless Charles calls me himself I cannot assist with the problem.

   _____

   _____

8. Thank you Mr. Williams for responding so quickly to our request.

   _____

   _____

9. Michelle ask Joe to take minutes at the next board meeting.

   _____

   _____

10. Alice the president of our firm is asking that you run this event.

_____

_____

11. Consequently he decided to cooperate with the merger.

_____

_____

12. Barbara you may indicate your preference by circling your choice of entrée.

_____

_____

Exercise B: Apply—Comma INTRO, AP, and DA

Instructions: Write a sentence to show the use of comma introductory, appositive, and direct address. In each sentence, underline each subject once and each verb twice. Put punctuation where needed, and write the reason after the sentence. Circle the conjunctions: coordinating (CC), subordinating (SC), and adverbial (AC).

Examples: (If) I finish the project early, can I be excused from the other work? (INTRO)
Jane, my friend since high school, will join us for lunch. (AP)
Mark, (I) thank you for your help. (DA)

INTRO: _____

_____

_____

AP: _____

_____

_____

DA: _____

_____

_____

_____

_____

_____

Exercise C: Practice—Comma AP and DA

Instructions: In each sentence, underline each subject once and each verb twice, put a comma where needed, and circle and identify the conjunctions: coordinating (CC), subordinating (SC), and adverbial (AC). Write the reason (AP) or (DA) after the sentence.

Incorrect: Rosalie please give Charles my regards.
Corrected: Rosalie, (you) please give Charles my regards. (DA)

1. We received the policy manual that you sent yesterday David.

_____

2. The new accounting manager Mark Swanson makes decisions about audits.

_____

3. My associate Katherine works in the office next to mine.

_____

4. Margaret Albertson our human resource manager is in our Phoenix office.

_____

5. Bill Gomez a good friend of mine will attend the workshop in San Diego.

_____

6. My assistant Colin will call you tomorrow with an update.

_____

7. Thank you Miles for filing the motion.

_____

8. The agenda was given to everyone before the meeting Ms. Allison.

_____

9. The new CEO Blake Evans will not agree to the merger.

_____

10. Barbara you may indicate your choice on the questionnaire.

_____

ACTIVITY 6: PUNCTUATION REVIEW—COMMA IC AND SEMICOLON TRANSITION

Comma independent comment (IC):	Put commas before and after a word or phrase that interrupts an independent clause.
Semicolon transition (TRANS):	Place a semicolon before and a comma after adverbial conjunctions when they act as a transition between two independent clauses.

Exercise A: Comma IC and Semicolon TRANS

Instructions: In each sentence, underline each subject once and each verb twice, put punctuation where needed, and circle the conjunctions: coordinating (CC), subordinating (SC), and adverbial (AC). Write the reason (IC) or (TRANS) after the sentence.

Examples:
UPS delivered the materials; however, the most important box was not there. (TRANS)
The most important box of materials, however, was not in the shipment. (IC)

1. I will not however be attending the dinner meeting.

_____

_____

2. We sent the package to the wrong address as a result we lost some time.

_____

_____

3. There was a problem with our contract consequently he refused the shipment.

_____

_____

4. We look forward to hearing from you therefore please contact my office upon your return to Baltimore.

_____

_____

5. We therefore look forward to hearing from you soon.

_____

_____

6. Suzanne did well on her evaluation unfortunately she resigned before finding out the results.

_____

_____

7. I appreciate your attention to this matter hence please continue the investigation.

_____

_____

8. Tim wanted to go to the meeting however he had to conduct a workshop.

_____

_____

9. Lionel however invited Kyle to chair the meeting instead of Helen.

_____

_____

10. Mr. Bradshaw spoke positively of the renewal plan consequently many investors changed their plans.

_____

_____

Exercise B: Apply—Comma IC and Semicolon TRANS

Instructions: Write two sentences to demonstrate each rule: comma independent comment and semicolon transition. Underline each subject once and each verb twice.

Examples: I delivered the materials; however, I forgot the most important box. (TRANS)
The most important box of materials, however, was the one that I forgot. (IC)

TRANS: _____

_____

_____

_____

IC: _____

_____

_____

_____

ACTIVITY 7: PUNCTUATION REVIEW—COMMA CONJUNCTION, INTRODUCTORY, APPOSITIVE, DIRECT ADDRESS; SEMICOLON NO CONJUNCTION

Instructions: To review the rules, write a sentence that exemplifies each rule below.

Comma conjunction (CONJ): Put a comma before a coordinating conjunction when it connects two independent clauses.
CC: *and, but, or, for, nor, so, yet*

_____

Comma introductory (INTRO): Place a comma after an introductory expression (a word, phrase, or clause) that introduces a main clause. Introductory expressions often begin with a subordinate conjunction or an adverbial conjunction.
SC: *although, because, since, after*
AC: *however, therefore, for example, consequently*

_____

Comma appositive (AP): Use commas to set off a word or group of words that describes or identifies a preceding noun or pronoun.

_____

Comma direct address (DA): Put commas before and after the name or title of a person addressed directly.

_____

Semicolon no conjunction (NC): Use a semicolon to separate two independent clauses that are joined without a coordinating conjunction. This is sometimes referred to as *semicolon in place of period.*

_____

ACTIVITY 8: CUMULATIVE PUNCTUATION REVIEW

Instructions: Insert punctuation where needed in the following sentences. Identify the reason for each comma; underline subjects once and verbs twice.

1. If you have another commitment find a replacement to chair the committee.

_____

_____

2. Should Bob Rose and Charley discuss these issues with you?

_____

_____

3. As soon as we receive your application we will process your account.

_____

_____

4. Your new checks were shipped last month therefore you should have received them by now.

_____

_____

5. Will you be sponsoring a seminar in Dallas Texas later this year?

_____

_____

6. Fortunately my manager values my ability to get the job done.

_____

_____

7. Mr. Peters would you have time to approve the check requests before noon today?

_____

_____

8. We received his resignation and promptly developed a new strategy.

_____

_____

9. Alison brought her numbers to the meeting however they were not complete.

_____

_____

10. Ms. Randall sent a letter of recommendation the direct supervisor never got a copy of it.

_____

_____

11. The merger however required that all parties agree to a compromise regarding staff and location.

_____

_____

12. Thank you Mr. Carter for supporting our quality assurance plan.

_____

_____

13. The costs for the renovation are outrageous but I recommend we consider this proposal.

_____

_____

14. We received the contract too late therefore we are not implementing the project.

_____

_____

15. You must apply for a license by July 15 2004 to meet all requirements.

_____

_____

REFERENCE

1. William James, *The Principles of Psychology,* 1890, quoted from Heartquotes, www.heartquotes.net /monthly-June2003.html, October 2004.

KEY FOR LEARNING INVENTORY

1.	F	**6.**	T
2.	T	**7.**	T
3.	T	**8.**	F
4.	T	**9.**	T
5.	T	**10.**	T

The Writer's Handbook: Part 2

The Writer's Handbook

Writing Essentials—Grammar *for* Writing

OUTLINE

Section A: Verb Basics

Section B: Pronoun Basics—Case and Point of View

Section C: Parallel Structure

Section D: Modifiers

Syntax—the arrangement of words in sentences—is the basis for . . . effective revision strategies affecting style. —William Strong ■

Experts argue that improving grammar skills will not necessarily improve writing skills. While improving grammar skills *may not* improve writing skills or the quality of one's ideas, grammar skills have a strong, direct effect on editing and revising skills:

- Grammar *for* writing involves conveying ideas in correct form.
- Grammar *for* writing also relates to syntax, or the way a writer structures ideas.

Structure, or syntax, brings flow to writing by presenting ideas in consistent forms. Correct and consistent structure, whether it is at the sentence level or paragraph level, aids the reader in understanding ideas more easily. The flow that consistent structure provides ensures that ideas are packaged in their most powerful form.

At any rate, professionals who perceive their grammar skills as poor do not write with confidence. And even if their critical thinking skills are excellent, they probably will not convey their ideas confidently until they build their skills. Though some feel overwhelmed by grammar, there are only a limited number of topics that need attention. The way to improve is to take control by identifying weak points and then getting appropriate practice.

What are the most common types of grammar problems in writing? The basic problems involve using parts of the language *incorrectly* (especially verbs and pronouns). The more advanced problems involve using the language *inconsistently* (such as verb tense, pronoun point of view, and parallel structure).

Everyone makes errors in grammar: no one speaks or writes English perfectly. Errors usually occur in patterns. Thus, if you make a particular kind of error, you are likely to repeat that error throughout your speech and writing. Since the error occurs in a pattern, it can give the impression that everything is wrong with a piece of writing when only one type of correction needs to be applied. Hence, as you gain insight into one pattern, you may simultaneously correct many errors—not only in your writing but also in your speaking.

While reviewing this chapter, you may become conscious of errors you have been making all your life. In fact, a mistake may sound better to you than the correct grammatical construction. That's why you can't judge grammar by how your words sound to you; you must base grammar on theory and rules.

OBJECTIVES

When you have completed the Writer's Handbook, Part 2, you will be able to:

- Apply past and past participles of regular and irregular verbs correctly.
- Use the "s" form of verbs correctly (third-person singular, present tense).
- Write sentences that demonstrate parallel structure.
- Place modifiers close to the word or words they modify.
- Distinguish between subjective case and objective case pronouns.
- Display consistent use of point of view in sentences and paragraphs.
- Understand the use of *who, whom,* and *that.*

Learning Inventory

1. The subject and verb are the core of a sentence.	T/F
2. All verbs have both a past tense form and a past participle form.	T/F
3. A helper verb (such as *is, has,* or *do*) must be used with a past participle form.	T/F
4. To select the correct pronoun case, determine the role the pronoun plays in the sentence (such as subject or object).	T/F
5. The verb in a sentence determines its grammatical subject.	T/F
6. For irregular verbs, add *ed* to form both the past tense and the past participle.	T/F
7. The base form of a verb is called an *infinitive.*	T/F
8. All third-person singular verbs in English end in *s.*	T/F
9. The main categories of pronouns are subjective, objective, possessive, and reflexive.	T/F
10. Reflexive pronouns can be used as objects or subjects.	T/F
11. The word *than* is a conjunction, and a subject and verb usually follow it.	T/F
12. In the subjunctive mood, use *were* (rather than *was*) with singular pronouns.	T/F

■ SECTION A: VERB BASICS

Verbs provoke action and develop power behind a message. They also create energy and direction. In fact, the verb determines the other core parts of the sentence: the subject and (when applicable) the object. Not only are verbs vital, but they can seem more complicated than they really are.

Rather than going into every detail about verbs, this section covers essential information about the most common mistakes that writers make with verbs. If you want a more detailed analysis of verbs, refer to *The Gregg Reference Manual*—it will tell you everything you ever wanted to know about verbs and more!

Verb Problems

In English, *verbs tell time:* verbs indicate whether an event happened in the past, is happening in the present, or will happen in the future. When people have problems with verbs, they often think their mistakes relate to using verb tense incorrectly. Verb tenses are complicated, but most problems with verbs can be corrected without examining the various tenses. Instead of concentrating on verb tense, focus on *verb parts.*

Verb parts (or verb forms) are developed from the **base form** of the verb, often referred to as the **infinitive.** Using verb parts incorrectly results in grammatical errors. Here is a foundation for understanding verbs:

1. Verbs are either **regular** or **irregular.**

2. For past time, the two principle parts are the **past** and **past participle.**

3. *Regular* verbs form their past and past participle by adding *ed* to the base (that's why they are considered "regular"). For example, *walk* is a regular verb; its past form is *walked,* and its past participle is also *walked.*

4. *Irregular* verbs vary in the way the past and past participle are formed. For example, *write* is an irregular verb; its past form is *wrote,* and its past participle is *written.*

5. Past participles need **helper** or **auxiliary verbs.** Common helping verbs are the forms of *be (is, are, was, were)* and *have (has, have, had).*

6. In present time, all verbs have an **"s" form,** which is constructed by adding *s* to the base of the verb. The "s" form is also known as *third-person singular* (in simple present tense); for example, *works, does, believes.*

In regard to the above points, writers and speakers make the following common errors with verbs:

- Using the past and past participle of verbs incorrectly (regardless of the tense).

Incorrect:	The manager *had ask* for the form the other day.
Corrected:	The manager *had asked* for the form the other day.

Incorrect:	An associate *would have went* to the meeting if asked.
Corrected:	An associate *would have gone* to the meeting if asked.

- Leaving off the *s* for "s"-form verbs.

Incorrect:	Bill Snyder *maintain* all equipment in our department.
Corrected:	Bill Snyder *maintains* all equipment in our department.

- Shifting tense inappropriately within a sentence or paragraph.

Incorrect:	The committee chair *informs* us the date has been changed.
Corrected:	The committee chair *informed* us the date has been changed.

Irregular Verbs in Past Time

Verb Principle 1: *When using irregular verbs in past time, do not use a helper verb with the past form; however, you must use a helper verb with the past participle.*

Below are a few irregular verbs that will be used in the examples that follow. (The helper verbs were randomly chosen.) For a more complete list of irregular verbs, see Table WH2.1.

VOCABULARY BUILDERS

Loan/Lend Can you figure out what is wrong with the following?

Please loan me $5 for lunch.

George loaned me his briefcase.

If you said using the word *loan* as a verb, you are correct. The word *loan* is officially a noun, and nouns cannot be used as verbs. Thus, you cannot "loan" anything to anyone. The correct word to use is *lend.* Both the past and the past participle of *lend* are *lent.*

Please lend me $5 for lunch.

George lent me his briefcase.

Base	Past	Past Participle
choose	chose	(has) chosen
do	did	(have) done
freeze	froze	(had) frozen
go	went	(is) gone
see	saw	(are) seen
speak	spoke	(was) spoken
write	wrote	(were) written

For irregular verbs, here are the two most common errors:

1. *Type 1 error:* Using an irregular past form with a helper.

Incorrect:	Mary *has wrote* the report. *(has written)*
	The budget *is froze* until next year. *(is frozen)*
	The director *has spoke* about that problem. *(has spoken)*
	Marty *has* finally *did* the paperwork for the proposal. *(has done)*

2. *Type 2 error:* Using an irregular past participle without a helper.

Incorrect:	Margaret *seen* Bob at the conference. *(saw)*
	They *done* the work last week. *(did)*
	Mr. Martin *chosen* the painting for our department. *(chose)*
	Alice *gone* to the store late last evening. (*went*)

Here is what you need to do to stop making errors with irregular verbs:

1. Know the correct past and past participle forms of each irregular verb.

2. When using the past form, do *not* use a helper or auxiliary verb.

3. When using the past participle, *use* a helper.

If you do not have a problem with the verbs presented above or in Table WH2.1, diagnose your own language pattern to know which verbs give you problems.

PRACTICE

PART A

Instructions: For the irregular verbs listed below, write the correct past and past participle of each. Use a helper verb with each past participle form. Remember, any form of *be (is, are, was, were)* or *have (has, have, had)* can function as a helper. Choose any helper you wish for Items 3 to 15.

	Base	*Past*	*Past Participle*
Example:	break	broke	have broken

Base	Past	Past Participle
1. bring		were
2. buy		was
3. do		
4. drink		
5. drive		
6. forget		
7. freeze		

Note: Continued on Page 428.

COMMUNICATION CHALLENGES

Error Patterns When a person's speech or writing includes errors, the errors probably occur in patterns. These patterns of errors help define a person's community dialect.

Since no one speaks or writes English perfectly, everyone has dialect characteristics. Dialect patterns are most evident in the use of verbs and pronouns. Dialect patterns also surface in word usage or pronunciation, such as "*Wa jeet* for lunch?" "*I'm fixin'* to go now," and "*Whoja* go to the meeting with?"

Ask yourself: *Have I noticed any community-dialect patterns in my speech or writing?*

TABLE WH2.1 | Irregular Verbs

Base Form	Past Tense	Past Participle
arise	arose	arisen
become	became	become
break	broke	broken
bring	brought	brought
buy	bought	bought
catch	caught	caught
dive	dived, dove	dived
draw	drew	drawn
drink	drank	drunk
drive	drove	driven
eat	ate	eaten
fall	fell	fallen
feel	felt	felt
find	found	found
fly	flew	flown
forget	forgot	forgotten
get	got	got, gotten
give	gave	given
grow	grew	grown
know	knew	known
lay*	laid	laid
lend	lent	lent
lie	lay	lain
lose	lost	lost
pay	paid	paid
prove	proved	proved, proven
ring	rang	rung
ride	rode	ridden
say	said	said
set*	set	set
sink	sank	sunk
sit	sat	sat
shine	shone	shone
shine*	shined	shined
show	showed	showed, shown
shrink	shrank	shrunk
stand	stood	stood
swim	swam	swum
take	took	taken
think	thought	thought
throw	threw	thrown
wear	wore	worn

*Transitive verbs that need an object to be complete.

Note: Past tense does not take a helper verb. Past participles must have a helper verb. Helper verbs consist of the various forms of *to be* and *to have* (*is, was, were, has, have, had*).

EXPLORE

1. Select five verbs that you find challenging. Compose three sentences for each verb using the past form correctly and then three sentences using the past participle form correctly.

2. Observe speech patterns in a public place (a restaurant, an elevator, a bus or train, on the street). Listen until you hear five community-dialect statements involving verbs, pronouns, or pronunciation. Make a list of the statements, and bring it to class for discussion.

8. go

9. get

10. lend

11. lose

12. speak

13. spend

14. throw

15. write

PART B

Instructions: Circle the correct verb in each of the sentences below:

Example: The plane had (flew, (flown)) to Tulsa.

1. We had finally (did, done) our part of the work.

2. He should not have (went, gone) to the conference on Friday.

3. Margaret has (choose, chose, chosen) the luncheon menu for the banquet.

4. She had (spoke, spoken) eloquently at the annual stockholders' meeting.

5. He (loaned, lent) me the material for the meeting.

6. You should have (wrote, written) to the office first.

7. The phone must have (rang, rung) 20 times before they answered.

8. I should have (brang, brung, brought) another copy.

9. Who has (drunk, drank) the last glass of milk?

10. The quarterly budget is (froze, frozen) until further notice.

VOCABULARY BUILDERS

Transitive and Intransitive Verbs Have you ever wondered about the difference between the verbs *lay* and *lie?* These verbs are confusing and rarely used correctly.

The verb *lay,* which means "to place," is transitive and needs an object. The verb *lie,* which means "to recline," is intransitive and cannot be followed by an object.
- **Transitive verbs** need a direct object.
- **Intransitive verbs** cannot have a direct object.

Most verbs can be used with or without a direct object, but verbs that are *only* transitive or *only* intransitive can create confusion. The verbs that are especially tricky are the ones that seem to come in pairs, such as *lay* and *lie* or *sit* and *set.* Here are some examples of transitive and intransitive verbs:

	Base	Past	Past Participle
Intransitive:	lie	lay	lain
	I felt ill, so I had lain *down.*		
Transitive:	lay	laid	laid
	I laid the *book* on the table.		
Intransitive:	sit	sat	sat
	Sue sat *down.*		
Transitive:	set	set	set
	Sue set the *book* on the table.		

In these examples, the adverb *(down)* modifies the intransitive verbs, but the direct object *(book)* follows the transitive verbs.

Regular Verbs in Past Time

Verb Principle 2: *When using regular verbs in past time, add* ed *to the base to form the past and past participle.*

With regular verbs, the past and past participle are the same; they both end in *ed.* Thus, you cannot make an error with regular verbs in past time based on using (or not using) a helper verb (with *irregular verbs,* this kind of error is common).

A common mistake with regular verbs in past time is leaving off *ed.* Leaving off the *ed* with regular past-time verbs pertains as much to speaking as it does to writing. If you have a habit of leaving off the *ed* when speaking, you will most definitely leave off the *ed* when writing. Here are some examples:

Incorrect: Yesterday the attendant *help* me.
Corrected: Yesterday the attendant *helped* me.

Incorrect: Mary *talk* too much at this morning's meeting.
Corrected: Mary *talked* too much at this morning's meeting.

Incorrect: The attorneys *negotiate* for hours.
Corrected: The attorneys *negotiated* for hours.

Incorrect: At the meeting, the committee *focus* on the report.
Corrected: At the meeting, the committee *focused* on the report.

PRACTICE

Instructions: Correct the sentences below by using verbs in the past time. For example:

Incorrect: My assistant *help* me with the project.
Corrected: My assistant help*ed* me with the project.

1. The financial analyst report the funds were misplaced.

2. My adviser ask me to submit my résumé.

3. The report suggest that our company had a fiscal problem.

4. Mr. Abbanati face some difficult decisions related to the merger.

5. When Barton went on the interview, he answer many questions well.

Present Tense: The "s" Form

Verb Principle 3: *In simple present tense, apply the "s" form correctly to third-person singular verbs.*

Linguists now refer to third-person singular verbs as the *"s" form* to draw attention to the fact that they *all* end in *s*. Many Americans consistently make errors with the "s" form. For example:

Incorrect: Bob *don't* give the directions as well as he should.
Corrected: Bob *does not (doesn't)* give the directions as well as he should.

Incorrect: Martha *have* the right attitude about her job search.
Corrected: Martha *has* the right attitude about her job search.

Incorrect: My partner *say* that the paper is due on Friday.
Corrected: My partner *says* that the paper is due on Friday.

PRACTICE

PART A

Instructions: Correct the simple present tense sentences below. For example:

Incorrect: Their sales representative call on our company.
Corrected: Their sales representative calls on our company.

1. The account representative have the reports done weekly.

2. When Marie ask a question, she does not wait for the answer.

3. Martin know the right people to talk to about a job.

4. The director don't always call in the numbers each month.

5. His expense account have not been turned in.

PART B

Instructions: Below are some sentences that have mistakes in regular verbs. Make appropriate corrections in present or past time where errors occur. For example:

Incorrect: When Jim had a problem, he ask his supervisor for advice.
Corrected: When Jim had a problem, he ask*ed* his supervisor for advice.

1. Every day Alex coach the team in leadership qualities.

   _____

2. At yesterday's meeting, our president ask the sales team to run totals.

   _____

3. Our department finish the project sooner than expected.

   _____

4. For every game, Micki pick Alice to be on her team.

   _____

5. At our last meeting, my manager shout loudly to get our attention.

   _____

6. At the meeting, the group listen carefully to every comment about the economy.

   _____

7. On most days, William focus on the objectives.

   _____

8. The attendant ask us if we had problems with the seating.

   _____

9. The professor pass out reports at the beginning of every class.

   _____

10. Bob fill out the report every time it is due.

   _____

COACHING TIP

Progressive Tenses Progressive tense verbs end in *ing*. You can refer to the *present perfect progressive* tense as the *recent past*. The recent past uses a present tense helper such as *has* or *have* and implies the action began in the past and is still ongoing.

Example: I have been walking to my office every day this week.

You can refer to the *past perfect progressive* as the *distant past*. The distant past uses the past participle *had* as the helper. This implies the action began in the past, continued for a time, and was completed in the past.

Example: I had been walking to my office every day last fall.

Try *not* to focus on tenses. Most of the time you use tenses correctly; when mistakes with verbs occur, they usually involve irregular verbs in past time. Focus on the following to improve your language patterns:

1. Do not use a helper with the past tense form of verbs (especially irregular verbs).
2. Use a helper with the past participle form of verbs (especially irregular verbs).
3. Make sure regular verbs in past time end in *ed*.
4. Do not shift verb tense unnecessarily within a sentence or paragraph.

Verb Tense and Consistency

Verb Principle 4: *Within the same sentence and paragraph, do not shift verb tense unnecessarily.*

Inconsistency in verb tense is a common error even among experienced writers because sometimes writers cannot see the logic behind the rule. In addition, this error is more difficult to find; verbs may be conjugated correctly, but it is their inconsistent use that creates the problem. For example:

Incorrect:	We scheduled the teleconference early on Monday because we *are going* to another meeting.
Corrected:	We scheduled the teleconference early on Monday because we *were going* to another meeting.

PRACTICE

Instructions: The sentences below contain errors in tense. Correct the errors. For example:

Incorrect: Yesterday the director said that the report was acceptable and that we are doing a good job to get it in on time.

Corrected: Yesterday the director said that the report was acceptable and that we were doing a good job to get it in on time.

1. Jones gave us the answer, and we are surprised to hear it.

    _____

    _____

2. John did the report today because his numbers are ready.

    _____

    _____

3. Five computer terminals were broken, so the manager is requesting all new ones.

    _____

    _____

4. My adviser informs me of class openings, but I signed up for the wrong ones.

    _____

    _____

5. The program analysis was difficult, and our team requires more time.

    _____

    _____

6. The inscription on the plaque was blurry and needs to be corrected.

    _____

    _____

More on Verbs: The Subjunctive Mood

Mood is a grammatical term used to describe a writer's attitude toward a subject as it is expressed by the form of the verb. Verbs have three moods: the indicative, the imperative, and the subjunctive. Most people do not have a problem with the indicative mood, which states a fact or asks a question; or the imperative mood, which expresses a command or makes a request. If an error is to be made, it is with the subjunctive mood.

The **subjunctive mood** expresses improbability. When a statement conveys a wish or possibility, it should be made in the subjunctive mood. The subjunctive mood is also used with certain requests, demands, recommendations, and set phrases.

*   For the past subjunctive, *to be* is always expressed as were.

    (As in, "If I *were* you, I would have gone to the meeting.")
*   For the present subjunctive, the verb is expressed in the infinitive form.

    (As in, "It is important that she *go* to the meeting.")

You may want to reserve your use of the subjunctive mood for business or formal occasions. When the subjunctive mood is used, the language sounds more formal. Read the examples below, and then decide how you plan to incorporate the subjunctive mood into your speech and writing.

Statements Following *Wish* or *If*   If something is a *wish*, it is not a fact; thus, statements following *wish* should be made in the subjunctive mood. The verb *to be* is always expressed as *were* in a subjunctive statement.

Incorrect:	**Corrected:**
I *wish* I *was* able to be there.	I *wish* I *were* able to be there.
She *wishes* he *was* able to attend.	She *wishes* he *were* able to attend.
They *wish* it *was* true.	They *wish* it *were* true.

Pronouncing Difficult Words Sometimes simple words can be difficult to pronounce. For example, the word *ask* is difficult because it ends in a *consonant cluster* (two or more adjacent consonants form a cluster).

Consonants (such as *d, k, r, s, t*) are as easy to pronounce as vowels *(a, e, i, o,* and *u)* until they form a cluster, such as *st, sts, sks,* or *rd.* With consonant clusters, the tongue and mouth have to work very hard to pronounce all the distinct sounds. Sometimes speakers drop the last consonant or two; this practice should be avoided in business situations.

Here are some words with consonant-cluster word endings that can be difficult to pronounce:

St/sts: test, tests, list, lists
Sk/sks: mask, masks, flask, flasks, ask, asks
Sp/sps: lisp, lisps

To improve pronunciation, don't focus on the consonants—instead extend the sound of the vowel that precedes them.

For example, when pronouncing the word *ask,* focus on the *a.* Say the *a* very slowly. Then gradually feel yourself pushing air through your front teeth as they come together to form the "ess" sound. Finally, feel the *k* being formed in the back of your throat. Practice each part until you get it right. (You might prefer to practice in a quiet spot with a mirror.)

If you don't have difficulty pronouncing *ask,* make a list of words that are difficult. What are they?

It's like correcting people's grammar. I don't do it to be popular. —"Frasier"
CHALLENGE:
One of the stores on your delivery route, a customer for ten years, has various signs posted inside that contain spelling errors ("Thank you for you're patronage," "Sweat relish available," "Minimun Charge of $10"). You are on good speaking terms with the owner and the head clerk. Should you mention the errors? Why or why not? If your answer is yes, how would you approach the owner?

When a sentence begins with the word *if,* very often the statement that follows is not a fact but a *condition.* As improbable or contrary-to-fact conditions, such statements should also be made in the subjunctive mood.

Incorrect:	If he *was* more positive, it would seem easier.
	If she *was* more mature, she would understand their decision.
	If I *was* you, I would go to the seminar.
Corrected:	If he *were* more positive, it would seem easier.
	If she *were* more mature, she would understand their decision.
	If I *were* you, I would go to the seminar.

The Present Subjunctive The present subjunctive is expressed by the infinitive form of the verb, regardless of the person or number of the subject. The present subjunctive occurs in *that* clauses after verbs expressing wishes, commands, requests, or recommendations.

> The manager said that it is imperative you be on time.
> It is essential (that) he take you to the meeting.
> He suggested (that) the committee be disbanded.
> Bob requested (that) Sarah repeat her answer.

Note: That is an essential element when the word *said* or *reported* precedes it. It shows that a direct quote does not follow. With other verbs, *that* is implied even when removed.

PRACTICE

Instructions: The sentences below are written in the subjunctive mood, present and past. Circle the correct form of the verb.

> **Example:** The instructions required that the director (take, takes) that approach.

1. The president requested that Mike (invite, invites) the new manager to the ball game.

2. John wishes he (was, were) in charge of the new department.

3. If Lester (was, were) on your team, would you support him?

4. It is imperative that she (complete, completes) the proposal.

5. If Tiffany (was, were) your manager, (would, will) you attend the conference?

Error Patterns

If you make a mistake with a verb or pronoun in one place, you are likely to repeat the mistake when using the word in other places. That's because errors are rarely isolated; they usually occur in patterns. As with all grammatical errors, work at *changing the pattern,* not the isolated mistake.

To make real improvement, you also need to change the way you think about errors. Instead of feeling bad about making mistakes, use your energy to fix the problem. Everyone makes mistakes with grammar. No one speaks or writes perfectly.

Here's some advice: The next time you make a mistake, look for the *pattern* and practice repeating the correct usage until the correct pattern becomes automatic.

SECTION A: CONCEPT CHECK

1. When using verbs in past time, which past tense form requires a helper and which does not?
2. For regular verbs, explain how to form the past and past participle forms.
3. In simple present tense, the "s" form applies to what person and number?
4. Can you shift verb tense within a sentence or paragraph unnecessarily?

■ SECTION B: PRONOUN BASICS—CASE AND POINT OF VIEW

In case you may have forgotten, a **pronoun** is a word that is used in place of a noun or another pronoun; for example, *I, you, he, she, it, we, they.* For speaking and writing, pronouns create at least as many problems as verbs do. However, most people are aware of neither their own mistakes nor the complexity of pronouns. Here are the most common pronoun mistakes:

- Using pronoun case incorrectly.

Incorrect:	The issue is between you and *I.*
Corrected:	The issue is between you and *me.*

- Using pronouns that do not agree with their antecedents.

Incorrect:	A *person* must do what *they* are asked.
Corrected:	A *person* must do what *he or she* is asked.
	Or: People must do what *they* are asked.

- Using pronouns inconsistently (or with an inconsistent point of view).

Incorrect:	*We* will show that *one* needs to focus on international trade.
Corrected:	*We* will show that *we* need to focus on international trade.

- Not being gender-neutral; in other words, writing with gender bias.

Incorrect:	A *manager* should conduct *his* meetings in a professional way.
Corrected:	A *manager* should conduct *his* or *her* meetings in a professional way.
	Or: Managers should conduct *their* meetings in a professional way.

If you aren't familiar with pronoun rules, the above examples of common errors may mean little to you right now. However, by the end of this chapter you should be able to understand which mistakes you were making and how to correct them.

Principles of Pronoun Usage

Four Basic Cases

Pronoun Principle 1: *Pronouns are categorized by case; the four basic cases are* subjective *(or* nominative*),* objective, possessive, *and* reflexive.

You are aware that verbs have tenses. Pronouns do not have tenses; instead, pronouns have **cases.** Table WH2.2 lists the subjective, objective, possessive, and reflexive pronouns.

Pronoun Case and Function

Pronoun Principle 2: *Pronoun case is determined by the pronoun's function in a sentence.*

Here are four pronoun cases:

- **Subjective case** (or nominative) pronouns function as *subjects* of verbs.
- **Objective case** pronouns function as *objects* (usually of verbs or prepositions).
- **Possessive case** pronouns *show possession* (of nouns or other pronouns).
- **Reflexive case** pronouns *reflect back* to subjective case pronouns.

Here is how each pronoun case functions in a sentence:

- *Subjective case* pronouns are subjects of verbs; thus, a "subject" pronoun must be followed by a verb (either real or implied).

Sylvia and *I* go to the store every Wednesday.
Mr. Jones and *he* prepared the report.
Bill is taller than *I* (am).
Alice dances better than *I* (do).

- *Objective case* pronouns are objects (and cannot be subjects of a verb). "Object" pronouns can be objects of verbs, prepositions, or infinitive or other types of phrases.

You can give *him* and his manager the report when you are ready.
The project manager assigned the task *to* George and *me.*
The problem should remain *between* you and *me.*
Human resources decided to hire *me* and Sarah.

- *Possessive case* pronouns show possession.

The book is *hers.*
You can't judge a book by *its* cover.
Their comments were unjustified.

COACHING TIP

I/Me Use the following guidelines to check whether your pronoun use is correct:

- When using *I* and another person's name, substitute the subject pronoun *we.*
  Example: *John and I* assisted: *we* assisted.
- When using *me* and another person's name, substitute the object pronoun *us.*
  Example: They gave the report *to Ivan and me:* they gave the report *to us.*
- When the pronoun *I* or *me* is part of a pair, remove the name so that the correct pronoun becomes clear. In the phrase *to John and I,* by removing the name *John,* the phrase becomes *to I.* This sounds awkward and shows clearly that the correct phrase should be *to me (to John and me* or *to us).*

TABLE WH2.2 | Personal-Pronoun Cases

	Case			
	Subjective	Objective	Possessive	Reflexive
Singular:				
First person	I	me	my, mine	myself
Second person	you	you	your, yours	yourself
Third person	he, she, it	him, her, it	his, hers, its	himself, herself, itself
Plural:				
First person	we	us	our, ours	ourselves
Second person	you	you	your, yours	yourselves
Third person	they	them	their, theirs	themselves

- *Reflexive case* pronouns can be used only when their corresponding noun or subjective case pronoun is already in the sentence. (Reflexive case is often called an *intensive case*; subjective case is the same as nominative case.)

I will wash the car *myself*.
Marty said that *he* would complete the project *himself*.
Paulette focused the attention on *herself* throughout the entire meeting.
Marty and *Paulette* found *themselves* giving all the right answers.

Pronouns Following the Preposition *Between*   Many case errors are made with pronouns following the preposition *between,* so here are some examples related to that type of error. Since *between* is a preposition, an object should follow it.

Incorrect:	The issue should remain *between Bob and I.*
Corrected:	The issue should remain *between Bob and me.*
	The issue should remain *between us.*

Incorrect:	Albert implied that the work should be split *between George and he.*
Corrected:	Albert implied that the work should be split *between George and him.*
	Albert implied that the work should be split *between them.*

Pronouns Following the Conjunction *Than*   When the word *than* comes at the end of a sentence, writers and speakers should be cautious. The word *than* is a conjunction and is often followed by a *subject* and *verb.* Since the verb is often implied, an objective case pronoun sounds correct even when it is incorrect.

The best way to correct this pattern is to include the implied verb in your speech and writing. For example:

Michelle has more time than I (do).
The accounting department thinks they are more competent than we (are).

PRACTICE

Instructions: Revise the sentences below by correcting for pronoun case. For example:

Incorrect:	When you call the office, ask for Alice or myself.
Corrected:	When you call the office, ask for Alice or me.

Incorrect:	Tobi went to the meeting because she has more time than me.
Corrected:	Tobi went to the meeting because she has more time than I (do).

1. If you can't reach George, feel free to call myself.

   _____

2. You can contact himself personally if you wish.

   _____

3. Between Alice and he, there should be enough expertise to complete the job.

   _____

4. The accounting department has more work to do than us.

   _____

5. Him and his manager have two more reports to complete.

   _____

6. The Ashburn proposal went directly to Jane and myself.

   _____

7. You can include Alyssa and I on your list of supporters.

   _____

8. There is a disagreement between my manager and I.

   _____

9. Alexi and her should have prepared for the meeting more effectively.

   _____

10. I hate to admit it, but the task is bigger than me.

   _____

Pronouns and Their Antecedents

Pronoun Principle 3: *Pronouns must agree in number and gender with their antecedents.*

An **antecedent** is a word or words to which a pronoun refers. In the following example, *managers* is the antecedent of *they* and *their.*

All managers said that *they* would submit *their* monthly progress reports on time.

Here are more examples showing a lack of agreement between pronouns and their antecedents:

Incorrect: When a *person* listens, *they* need to focus on the speaker.
When *one* listens, *he/she* needs to focus on the speaker.
When *we* listen, *you* need to focus on the speaker.

Corrected: When a *person* listens, *he or she* needs to focus on the speaker.
When *people* listen, *they* need to focus on the speaker.
When *one* listens, *one* needs to focus on the speaker.
When *we* listen, *we* need to focus on the speaker.

PRACTICE

Instructions: Correct the sentences below for pronoun-antecedent agreement. For example:

Incorrect: When an employee calls in sick, they should give a reason.
Corrected: When employees call in sick, they should give a reason.

1. A supervisor should give their employees adequate time to respond to messages.

   _____

   _____

2. When a teller does not relate well to their customers, they need more training.

   _____

   _____

VOCABULARY BUILDERS

There/Their/They're   These three words are all pronouns; however, they have distinctly different functions.

- *There* is an *anticipating subject,* also known as an **expletive form.**
  There <u>are</u> too many questions to answer.
  There <u>is</u> an interesting play at the Goodman.
  There <u>does</u> not <u>seem</u> to be a problem.
- *Their* is a *possessive pronoun* and is always followed by a noun.
  Their <u>dog</u> <u>ran</u> into our yard.
  Their <u>reports</u> <u>fell</u> out of the file.
  They <u>gave</u> us *their* answer too late.
- *They're* is a *contraction* of *they are.*
  They're giving free cholesterol screening at the clinic.
  <u>George</u> and <u>Sue</u> <u>said</u> that *they're* not interested in the antique clock.
  They're doing just fine without us.
     To avoid confusion:
- With *there,* make sure a verb follows it (unless it is used as an adverb).
- With *their,* make sure a noun follows it.
- With *they're,* stop using the contraction; spell out *they are.*

3. A mail carrier goes beyond her job description when they arrange for their clients' mail to be forwarded.

_____

_____

4. When a pilot says their work is challenging, believe them.

_____

_____

5. If a student turns their work in late, he or she should inquire about possible repercussions.

_____

_____

6. If a patient asks for more medicine, you must tell them to check with their doctor.

_____

_____

Pronoun Viewpoint

Pronoun Principle 4: *Pronouns must have a consistent point of view (or viewpoint).*

A viewpoint emanates from a subjective case pronoun; when a writer establishes a point of view, the **pronoun viewpoint** should remain consistent within sentences and paragraphs and at times throughout entire documents.

When writers do not use a specific point of view, they are forced to write in the passive voice (leaving out the actor); passive writing can be abstract and difficult to follow. By using a point of view to describe or narrate, a writer can be more direct and personal. Here are the various viewpoints:

	Singular	Plural
First person:	I	we
Second person:	you	you
Third person:	he, she, it	they
	a person	people
	one	one

Note: With the **one viewpoint,** the only appropriate antecedent for *one* is one; *he or she* is not an antecedent for *one.*

Consider these examples:

Incorrect: Listening is a skill that *we* should all improve. When *you* listen, *I* sometimes hear things that change *my* life. (shifting viewpoint)

Corrected: Listening is a skill that *I* would like to improve. When *I* listen, *I* sometimes hear things that change my life. (first-person singular viewpoint)

Or: Listening is a skill that *we* should all improve. When *we* listen, *we* sometimes hear things that change *our* lives. (first-person plural viewpoint)

Or: Listening is a skill that *all* can improve. When *people* listen, *they* sometimes hear things that change *their* lives. (third-person plural viewpoint)

Incorrect: In the East, a *person* must research cultural variables so that *they* gain insight into how values affect economic pricing decisions.

Corrected: In the East, *one* must research cultural variables so that *one* gains insight into how values affect economic pricing decisions.

Or: In the East, *we* must research cultural variables so that *we* gain insight into how values affect economic pricing decisions.

VOCABULARY BUILDERS

It's/Its *It's* and *its* cause serious problems for many well-educated writers.

- *It's: It* is a pronoun and *it's* is a contraction meaning *it is.*

  It's a great day.
  It's too early to be this dark.
  They said that *it's* too late to submit the proposal.

- *Its: Its* is the possessive form of the pronoun *it.* Though possessive, *its* takes no apostrophe.
  The dog chased *its* tail.
  The baby lost *its* bottle.
  You cannot judge a book by *its* cover.

  To avoid confusion:

- Stop contracting *it is.*
- Make sure *its* is followed by a noun.

Same Sentence, Various Viewpoints:

When *I* edit, *I* must pay attention to every detail.
When *you* edit, *you* must pay attention to every detail.
When a *person* edits, *he or she* must pay attention to every detail.
When *we* edit, *we* must pay attention to every detail.
When *people* edit, *they* must pay attention to every detail.
When *one* edits, *one* must pay attention to every detail.

PRACTICE

Instructions: Correct the sentences below for shifts in viewpoint. For example:

Incorrect: I started the project early because you never know when you will run into problems.

Corrected: I started the project early because I never know when I will run into problems.

1.   I like to eat lunch before the afternoon because it is better for your health.

_____

_____

2.   When one works hard at a task, he or she usually gets good results.

_____

_____

3.   I usually work late on Thursdays because you can get a lot done at the end of the week.

_____

_____

4.   The manager said that their department is exceptionally productive when you least expect it.

_____

_____

5.   If you listen carefully, we can hear inconsistencies in their responses.

_____

_____

Pronouns and Gender Bias

Pronoun Principle 5: *When speaking from a point of view, do not express gender bias; keep your writing gender-neutral.*

A few decades ago, people commonly used language that was gender-biased; so did books, magazines, and newspapers. That is, when speaking from the third-person singular viewpoint, most speakers and writers defaulted to the masculine viewpoint: *he, him,* and *his.*

Gender bias is a form of discrimination. You need only to think about speaking to your audience a moment to realize that you are excluding half of your listeners by speaking in *only* one viewpoint, masculine or feminine. To some degree, as language changes, so does thinking. Today, women enter professions that in the past they were blocked from solely because of their gender. Some people still discriminate on the basis of gender, and that's unfortunate.

Language has helped pave the path of gender equality. You can achieve gender-neutral language by adjusting the way you use pronouns, thereby respecting and reaching 100 percent of your audience. As a writer and speaker, consciously use language in an unbiased way not only to show respect but also to be more respected.

This task is more difficult to achieve in speaking than it is in writing. Here are some ways to remain gender-neutral:

1. Take out pronoun references when writing from a singular perspective:

Weak: A manager should give *his or her* employees opportunities to share responsibility.
Revised: A manager should give employees opportunities to share responsibility.

2. When possible, write from a plural perspective:

First-person plural (*we, our, us*):   *We* should give *our* employees opportunities to share responsibility.

Third-person plural (*they, their, them, people*): *Managers* should give *their* employees opportunities to share responsibility.

3. Use the "you" point of view:

Give *your* employees opportunities to share responsibility.

Viewpoint in Professional Writing

With professional writing, avoid overusing the pronoun *I*. Two alternatives are the "you" viewpoint and the "we" viewpoint.

The "You" Point of View

By using the "you" viewpoint, you connect with readers and focus on their needs. For example:

Weak:	I hope you respond to our questionnaire.
Revised:	(You) Please respond to our questionnaire by Friday, April 14.
Weak:	I appreciated your assistance with the Bakerfield project.
Revised:	Your assistance with the Bakerfield project contributed to its success.
Weak:	I think that you are a wonderful asset to our department.
Revised:	You are a wonderful asset to our department.
Weak:	I am hoping that you will join the committee to select new hires.
Revised:	(You) Please consider joining the committee to select new hires.

The "We" Point of View

The **"we" viewpoint** is another frequently used point of view in business today. When writing business communications that reflect your company's view as well as your own, use the "we" viewpoint. For example:

WORKING AND LEARNING IN TEAMS

Pronoun Mistakes or Hypercorrections Pronouns may create more problems for speakers and writers than verbs create. Most people who make mistakes with pronouns are not even aware of their mistakes.

There is a widespread confusion between the use of *I* and *me*. As children, many people were corrected when they used *me* as a subject: "*Me and John* are going to the store." A correction might have followed immediately: "No, that should be '*John and I* are going to the store.'"

As a result, many people use the "more professional-sounding" subjective case pronoun *I* even at times when *me* is the only correct choice. This kind of response is called *hypercorrecting*. To a trained ear, using *I* in place of *me* can sound like nails scratching a chalkboard. Using *myself* in place of *me* sounds even worse.

The improper use of *I* and *myself* in the object position is contagious, and this erroneous construction may have reached epidemic proportions. Develop immunity by using pronoun cases correctly.

With a partner, develop several examples using I, me, *and* myself *incorrectly, and then revise your examples so that they are correct.*

Weak: Your application will be processed within the next few weeks.
Revised: We will process your application within the next few weeks.

Weak: I will address your complaint to our customer service department.
Revised: We apologize for problems you had with your account, and our customer service department will address your complaint immediately.

PRACTICE

Instructions: Correct the paragraphs below by rewording them in a consistent point of view. Consider putting the first paragraph in the "I" point of view and the second paragraph in the "you" or "we" point of view. Just for fun, you may also want to put one of the paragraphs in the "one" point of view.

1. The purpose of writing from my perspective is to communicate ideas. It allows one to express ideas in a structured manner for others to review. To become a person that writes well, one must practice. In order to have good structure, I first identify my topic and do a mind map or brainstorm. Then you should write a draft, and leave your rough copy until the next day. Finally, review for content, clarity, and information. Writing can be rewarding if a person knows what they are doing. I plan to write more so that I can improve my skills.

_____

_____

_____

_____

_____

_____

_____

_____

2. Listening is an important skill that I would like to improve. When a person listens, they show respect for the person to whom they are listening. When you listen, you must hear with your ears as well as one's heart. I find that listening makes you a better person because you develop more empathy for the other person. One feels validated when others listen to them. Thus, if a person wants to be a better communicator, they should spend time improving his or her listening skills.

_____

_____

_____

_____

_____

_____

_____

_____

_____

_____

Difficult Pronouns

Who and *Whom*   The vast majority of Americans have difficulty with the pronoun *whom;* anyone who does not clearly understand how to use *whom* should not use it at all. Even people who use *whom* correctly may not use it in daily speech; instead, they reserve its use for formal occasions and written documents.

The correct use of *whom* is less important today than it was in the past. The correct use of other subjects and objects *(I* and *me)* and the use of a consistent viewpoint are important; rank these aspects of pronoun use higher on your priority list than the use of *who* and *whom.*

Here are the basics for using *who* and *whom* correctly:

1. *Who* is a subjective pronoun: *who* is the subject of a verb.
2. *Whom* is an objective pronoun: *whom* is the object of a preposition, a verb, or an infinitive or another type of verb phrase.
3. Use *who* as a subject complement following a state-of-being verb *(is, are, was, were).*

The following examples illustrate these guidelines:

Who *used as a subject:*

Who goes there?
Who gave the report?
Did she say *who* made the initial contact?
Jim asked *who* called him, but I did not know *who* (called him). (implied verb)

Who *used as a subject complement:*

The person responsible for the order was *who?* (*Who* is the subject complement of *was.*)
Who do you want to be when you grow up? (You want to be *who? Who* is the subject or complement of the infinitive *to be.*)

COACHING TIPS

Who* Versus *Whom   Here are tips for deciding between *who* or *whom:*
1. If you need a subject, the obvious choice is *who.*
2. If the word does not function as a subject, use *whom.*
3. When in doubt, use *who* and do not worry about it. (It sounds much worse to use *whom* incorrectly; *whom* used incorrectly sounds bad to everyone, even people who do not know the correct use of *who* and *whom.*)
4. If you can substitute *he* or *she,* use *who;* if you can substitute *him* or *her,* use *whom.* (This will work in most, but not all, situations.)

Incorrect:	Whom (him) goes there?
	Whom (him) did that?
Corrected:	Who (he) goes there?
	Who (he) did that?

Whom *used as an object of a preposition:*

To whom did you mail the reply?
Mary has not decided *with whom* she will go to the dance.
Whom were you sitting *with?* (*With whom* were you sitting?)
To whom did you show the report?

Whom *used as the object of a verb:*

Alice gave *whom* the information?
I should ask *whom* for assistance?

Whom *used as the object of an infinitive:*

Whom would you like to hire?
You are planning to include *whom?*

Who and *That*

Sometimes when people do not know how to use *whom* correctly, they incorrectly choose the word *that*. A better solution is to use *who* all the time, even when you are unsure. Referring to a person as *that* implies the person is an object or a thing.

Incorrect: Rosalie is the person *that* offered to help us.
Corrected: Rosalie is the person *who* offered to help us.

Incorrect: Charlie is the one *that* spoke up at the meeting.
Corrected: Charlie is the one *who* spoke up at the meeting.

When you are referring to a class or category of people, you may use the word *that*.

Examples: Suzie is *the kind of* employee *that* works diligently.
Bart is *the type of* football player *that* wins games.

In the above examples, *kind of* or *type of* is part of the antecedent, making the use of *that* acceptable. However, even in these cases, *who* would have also been acceptable; for example, "Suzie is the kind of employee *who* works diligently."

Your speech and writing will sound more sophisticated if you use *who* instead of *that* when referring to people. Another way to improve speech is to pronounce *who* correctly:

Incorrect: Whoja go to the ball game with?
Acceptable: Who did you go to the ball game with?
Formal: With whom did you go to the ball game?

PRACTICE

Instructions: Circle the correct pronoun (*who* or *whom*) in each of the sentences below. Also underline subjects once and verbs twice in all clauses.

Examples: (Who, Whom) presented the information to Alice's team?
Michael is the person (who, that) operates the machinery.

1. (Who, Whom) gave you the report?

    _____

2. (Who, Whom) are you going to the meeting with?

    _____

3. Nicole is the person (who, that) initiated the contact with union representatives.

    _____

4. Milt asked me (who, whom) wrote the report.

    _____

5. An employee (who, that) arrives late more than twice will be put on probation.

    _____

✓ SECTION B: CONCEPT CHECK

1. Pronouns can be categorized into what major cases?

2. Select a random sentence containing one or more pronouns from something you are reading. Determine each pronoun's case and function in the sentence.

3. Should pronouns always agree with their antecedents?

4. Why is it important *not* to express gender bias in your business writing?

■ SECTION C: PARALLEL STRUCTURE

Using *parallel structure* means putting similar sentence elements in the same form. Parallel structure not only creates flow and consistency but also makes your writing readable and your ideas stand out. Look for parallel structure in words, phrases, and clauses.

Writing that lacks parallel structure is choppy and disjointed. Worse than that, writing that lacks parallel structure can be difficult to understand. Let's start by reviewing how to put words, phrases, and clauses in the same form.

Words

Some sentences contain a list of two, three, or more items. Present these lists of items in the same grammatical form. For example:

Incorrect: Charley's favorite activities are *golfing, to fish,* and *going swimming.*
Corrected: Charley's favorite activities are *golfing, fishing,* and *swimming.*
                 Or: Charley's favorite activities are *to golf, fish,* and *swim.*

In the two corrected sentences above, the first list was made parallel by presenting the items as *gerunds*, the second as *infinitives.*

- A **gerund** functions as a noun: add *ing* to the base form of a verb; for example, *golfing, fishing,* and *swimming.*

- An **infinitive** also functions as a noun: add *to* to the base form of the verb; for example, *to golf, to fish, to swim.* (*Note:* The word *to* does not need to be repeated in a series of infinitives: *to golf, fish, and swim.*)

PRACTICE

Instructions: Edit the sentences below for parallel structure. For example:

Incorrect: The job duties include filing, to call back customers, and track deliveries.
Corrected: The job duties include filing, calling customers, and tracking deliveries.

1. Good writing results when writers focus on proofreading, to edit, and the revision of documents.

   _____

   _____

2. At the company picnic, employees will play horseshoes, volleyball, and a soccer match will be held.

   _____

   _____

3. Your assigment was to increase your number of new clients, retaining your old clients, and get referrals.

   _____

   _____

4. The job called for someone to freeze delinquent accounts, getting clients to bring their accounts up to date, and information provided about repayment options.

    _____

    _____

5. More time needs to be spent calling clients and to inform them of the changes.

    _____

    _____

Phrases

When related phrases appear in a sentence, they should be put in the same form. For example:

Incorrect: Meeting activities included *screening new applicants* and *a review of department policies.*

Corrected: Meeting activities included *screening new applicants* and *reviewing department policies.*

The corrected example above shows parallel gerund phrases. Gerunds and infinitives play a role in revising for parallel structure not only as words but also as phrases. Other types of noun phrases also play a role in parallel structure—the key is to remain consistent in the way you present ideas.

PRACTICE

Instructions: Edit the sentences below for parallel structure. For example:

    Incorrect: The instructions said *to correct the errors* and then *a copy should be made.*
    Corrected: The instructions said *to correct the errors* and then *to make a copy.*

1. The message referred to selling the property and a profit could be made on it.

    _____

    _____

2. The sign said that the entrance was closed to deliveries and the arrival of guests.

    _____

    _____

3. To remain competitive in the job market, pay attention to staying abreast of new technology and your résumé should be kept updated.

    _____

    _____

4. The new truck is used for delivering equipment and the transportation of supplies.

    _____

    _____

5. The new office provides applications to new clients and the current clients are given information.

    _____

    _____

Clauses

Sentences often consist of two or more clauses. For ease of understanding, the clauses should remain parallel. To ensure clauses remain parallel, focus on keeping the verbs in the same tense and voice.

Incorrect: *He caught* the flight to Denver, but then *his flight to Dallas was missed.*
Corrected: *He caught* the flight to Denver, but then *he missed* his flight to Dallas.

Incorrect: *Mr. Adams met* with their purchasing agent, and *several new computers were purchased* for our department.
Corrected: *Mr. Adams met* with their purchasing agent, and he *purchased* several new computers for our department.

In each of the incorrect examples above, the sentence starts in the active voice and then moves to the passive voice. Readers have an easier time with a consistent voice; the active voice is preferred when possible. Here are more examples in which clauses (and thus verbs) shift form:

Incorrect: *Robert and Milton presented* the information, and then *an offer was made* to follow up with the attendees.
Corrected: *Robert and Milton presented* the information, and then *they offered* to follow up with the attendees.

Incorrect: *We should hold* the annual conference in August, and *representatives* from all departments *should be required* to attend.
Corrected: *We should hold* the annual conference in August, and *we should require* representatives from all departments to attend.

PRACTICE

Instructions: Edit the sentences below for parallel structure. For example:

Incorrect: Jeff *informed* managers of the date and *would like us to respond by Friday.*
Corrected: Jeff *informed* managers of the date, and he *asked for responses by Friday.*

1.   Margarite prefers that meetings begin on time, the focus stays on the agenda, and they end on time as well.

     _____

     _____

2.   The report covered employee benefits, and changes in corporate policy were suggested.

     _____

     _____

3.   Expense reports must be current, and information should be complete and accurate.

     _____

     _____

4.   Company outings encourage social networks, and camaraderie is created.

     _____

     _____

5.   The new president will provide an enlightened corporate vision, fiscal responsibility will be encouraged, and promotions will be made from within.

     _____

     _____

Correlative Conjunctions

Correlative conjunctions come in pairs; and to use these conjunctions correctly, you must be careful where you place them in the sentence. Here are common correlatives:

> not . . . but
>
> not only . . . but also
>
> either . . . or
>
> neither . . . nor
>
> both . . . and

The following example lacks parallel structure:

We will **not only** *trade for your account* **but also** *are providing monthly reports.*

You can revise the above sentence in the following ways. Notice that the structure after each conjunction is the same:

We **not only** *will trade for your account* **but also** *will provide monthly reports.*
We will **not only** *trade for your account* **but also** *provide monthly reports.*

With correlatives such as *either . . . or, neither . . . nor, both . . . and,* pay attention to *where* you place the conjunction in relation to the information it is modifying. Here are some examples:

Incorrect: Bill will *either* go to graduate school *or* he will not.
Corrected: *Either* Bill will go to graduate school *or* he will not.

Incorrect: *Neither* Susan will volunteer to chair the meeting *nor* even attend it.
Corrected: Susan will *neither* volunteer to chair the meeting *nor* even attend it.

PRACTICE

Instructions: Edit the sentences below for parallel structure. For example:

Incorrect: Barbara will either go to the meeting or she will not.
Corrected: Either Barbara will go to the meeting or she will not.

1.   Our company will both save you time and money.

_____

2.   Martha applied both for the job and got it.

_____

3.   Phillip will either assist the manager or he will not.

_____

4.   The solution makes not only sense but also saves resources.

_____

5.   Neither my new car has a warranty nor does it run well.

_____

✓ SECTION C: CONCEPT CHECK

1. Describe some of the benefits of parallel structure in writing.

2. Name three correlative conjunctions, and use them in sentences.

3. What characteristics of verbs need to be consistent to ensure clauses in a sentence remain parallel?

■ SECTION D: MODIFIERS

A **modifier** is a word or group of words that describes a noun or a verb. Though a modifier is not a main element of a sentence (the main elements of a sentence are the subject and verb), it can be an important element.

Modifiers can add richness and depth to meaning if they are used correctly.

- **Adjectives** modify nouns and pronouns.
- **Adverbs** (which often end in *ly*) modify verbs, adjectives, and other adverbs.

In the following examples, *good* is an adjective modifying the noun *paper,* and *well* is an adverb modifying the verb *did.*

Everyone in economics turned in a *good* paper.
Everyone in economics did *well.*

Here are some common errors that writers make with adjectives and adverbs:

- Modifying action verbs with adjectives.

Incorrect: Bill drives *good.*
Corrected: Bill drives *well.*

- Modifying state-of-being verbs with adverbs.

Incorrect: I felt *badly* about the situation.
Corrected: I felt *bad* about the situation.

- Using a suffix (such as *er* or *est*) with an adjective or adverb and modifying it with *more, most, less,* or *least.* (This is called a double comparative or double superlative.)

Incorrect: We were *more busier* yesterday than today.
Corrected: We were *busier* yesterday than today.

- Misplacing modifiers in the sentence (placing modifiers away from the word they modify).

Incorrect: The *book* was placed on the shelf *with a bent cover.*
Corrected: The *book with a bent cover* was placed on the shelf.

- Dangling a modifier; that is, placing a modifier in a sentence without placing the noun it modifies directly after the modifier.

Incorrect: *Walking into my office,* my coffee spilled on the carpet. (*Who* was walking into the office?)
Corrected: *Walking into my office, I* spilled coffee on the carpet.

A gerund phrase or an infinitive phrase needs a subject; the first noun that follows the phrase is considered the subject of the phrase. Thus, in the above incorrect example, the sentence literally states that "my coffee is walking into the office." To correct a dangling modifier, either turn the phrase into a clause *(as I walked into my office)* or put the subject of the phrase immediately after it (as was done in the corrected example above).

Modifiers for Action and State of Being

Modifier Principle 1: *Modify nouns and pronouns with adjectives; modify verbs with adverbs.*

In order to understand this principle, it is necessary to review some qualities of verbs:

- Verbs have *action* or *state of being.*
- Action verbs are tagged "action" because they can transfer action from the subject to the object: *Bob* <u>threw</u> the ball.
- *Action verbs* are modified by adverbs:

The computer <u>runs</u> *well.*
The presenter <u>spoke</u> *loudly.*
(You) <u>Drive</u> *safely.*

State-of-being verbs do not transfer action. (That may surprise you because the word *verb* is almost synonymous with *action.* The English language has about 11 state-of-being verbs or **linking verbs.**)

- Common linking verbs are forms of *to be (is, are, was, were), appear, become, seem,* and at times *smell, taste, feel, sound, look, act,* and *grow.*
- The words following a linking verb modify the subject rather than the verb. Thus, a modifying word following a linking verb would be an adjective (subject complement) rather than an adverb:

I <u>feel</u> *bad* about the situation.
The proposal <u>sounds</u> *good.*
The situation <u>is</u> *bad.*

PRACTICE

Instructions: Correct the sentences below. For example:

Incorrect: When you speak too loud, you may get an unwelcome response.
Corrected: When you speak too loudly, you may get an unwelcome response.

1. Drive the rented vehicle slow until you know where everything is.

   _____

2. George feels badly about the situation.

   _____

3. The trainer spoke too loud, and our group was offended.

   _____

4. The car runs bad so drive careful.

   _____

5. The entire group felt badly about the change in management.

   _____

Comparative and Superlative Degrees for Comparison

Modifiers Principle 2: *When using adjectives or adverbs to compare, use either* more, most, less, *and* least *or* er *and* est *to show the degree of comparison (but do not use both).*

Follow these rules:

1. When you compare *two items,* use the **comparative form** of the modifier. The comparative is formed by adding *more* or *less* or the suffix *er.*

2. When comparing *three or more* items, use the **superlative form** of the modifier. The superlative is formed by adding *most* or *least* or the suffix *est.*

Speakers make some of the following kinds of mistakes more often than writers:

Brad is the *most tallest* player on the team.
I am *more hungrier* now than I was an hour ago.
This is the *most stupidest* report that I have ever been given.

PRACTICE

Instructions: Correct the modifiers in the sentences below. For example:

Incorrect: I felt more hungrier after I ate lunch than before I ate.
Corrected: I felt hungrier [*or* more hungry] after I ate lunch than before I ate.

1. Use your editing skills to make this letter more better than it was before.

   _____

2. Toni made the most silliest comment at the board meeting on Tuesday.

   _____

3. I was the most hungriest person in the room but the last to be served.

   _____

4. Of all the employees in our company, I live the most farthest from work.

   _____

5. Our committee is more further along on the project than I could have imagined.

   _____

Position of Modifiers in Sentences

Modifier Principle 3: *Place modifiers close to the word or words they modify to keep meaning clear.*

Placing modifiers away from the words they modify can create not only a grammatical error but also an ambiguous meaning. With modifiers placed correctly, your writing has better flow, and the meaning is clearer.

INTERNET EXERCISE WH2.2

Grammar References All writers need a good reference manual near their keyboards. In this text, we frequently refer to *The Gregg Reference Manual*. For more information on *Gregg* and other grammar references—both on the bookshelf and online—visit the *Foundations of Business Communication* Web site at <http://www.mhhe.com/djyoung>.

At the home page, select "Student Activities" and then click on the Writer's Handbook, Part 2, link to find instructions for getting started.

Here are some examples of *misplaced modifiers:*

Incorrect: The *report* was assigned to the Albuquerque office *with policy errors.*
Corrected: The *report with policy errors* was assigned to the Albuquerque office.

Incorrect: The *applicant* was the best candidate *arriving late to the interview.*
Corrected: The *applicant arriving late to the interview* was the best candidate.

Incorrect: Our *merger* created chaos *with the other company* for us.
Corrected: Our *merger with the other company* created chaos for us.

Incorrect: The *truck* pulled into the dock area *with huge dents.*
Corrected: The *truck with huge dents* pulled into the dock area.

Here are some examples of *dangling modifiers:*

Incorrect: *Arriving late, the presentation* ran over the time limit.
Corrected: *Arriving late, the presenter* ran over the time limit.

Incorrect: *Following my manager's instructions, the papers* were filed incorrectly.
Corrected: *Following my manager's instructions, I* filed the papers incorrectly.
                 Or: Although *I followed* my manager's instructions, the papers were filed incorrectly.

Incorrect: *Entering the conference room, the notebook* was dropped by Bob.
Corrected: *Entering the conference room, Bob* dropped the notebook.
                 Or: As *Bob entered* the conference room, he dropped the notebook.

PRACTICE

Instructions: In the senctences below, place modifiers close to the words they modify. For example:

Incorrect: George will give a presentation at this week's meeting on how to select the best cell phone package.
Corrected: George will give a presentation on how to select the best cell phone package at this week's meeting.

1. The report is due in September on policy change.

    _____

    _____

2. Major issues must be addressed at the fall meeting relating to dress policy.

    _____

    _____

3. Filling out the forms, a mistake was made by the applicant.

    _____

    _____

4. New hires within their first month must complete all personnel forms.

    _____

    _____

5. Traveling with her manager, Alice's PowerPoint presentation was left in Denver.

    _____

    _____

6. Mr. Alessandro gave the assignment to George reluctantly.

    _____

    _____

7. The letter was sent out yesterday giving details about the incident.

    _____

    _____

8. Answering the phone, my feet slipped right out from under me.

    _____

    _____

 SECTION D: CONCEPT CHECK

1. Describe the role modifiers play in sentences.
2. What are the three principles of modifier usage?

SUMMARY

This part of the Writer's Handbook reviewed grammar *for* writing. Though grammar is an immense topic, this chapter limited its grammar coverage to essential elements relating to the quality and flow of writing. Thus, only the most common mistakes writers make with verbs, pronouns, parallel structure, and modifiers were covered.

Writing is *thinking on paper,* and thinking presents ideas in rough form. Editing digests rough writing and shapes the syntax (the sentence structure) to make your words readable and correct. Without errors to interfere, your message becomes clear to readers.

Grammar skills continue to improve when integrated with writing or speaking. Therefore, make a concerted effort to apply the concepts you are learning. With practice, you will eliminate your major problems and your grammar decisions will become automatic.

WRITER'S HANDBOOK, PART 2 CHECKLIST

When composing business messages, consider the following:

___ Verb tense is consistent.
___ Structure is parallel.
___ Comparative/superlative degrees are correct.
___ Modifiers are close to the words they modify.
___ Subjective pronouns are functioning as subjects.
___ Objective pronouns are functioning as objects.
___ Reflexive pronouns refer to subject pronouns.
___ Third-person present tense singular verbs end in *s.*
___ Regular past tense verbs end in *ed.*
___ Irregular past participles are used with helper verbs.
___ Verb tense has not been shifted unnecessarily.

___ Verb voice is consistent (active or passive).
___ Pronoun point of view is consistent (*I, you, we, they*).
___ Pronouns agree with their antecedents.
___ Writing is gender-neutral.

END-OF-CHAPTER ACTIVITIES

ACTIVITY 1: REGULAR AND IRREGULAR VERBS

Part A

Instructions: In each sentence below, circle the correct word in parentheses.

Example: Our attorney had not (saw, (seen)) the docket yet.

1. We had finally (did, done) our part of the work.
2. He should not have (went, gone) to the appointment on Friday.
3. If I (was, were) you, I would (of, have) gone to the meeting.
4. She had (spoke, spoken) (eloquent, eloquently) at the banquet.
5. He had (loaned, lent) me the material for the meeting.
6. You should have (wrote, written, writen) to the office first.
7. The phone must have (rang, rung) 20 times before they answered.
8. I should have (brang, brung, brought) another copy.
9. Who has (drunk, drank) the last glass of milk?
10. We were (near, nearly) (froze, frozen) when they arrived.
11. She should have easily (saw, seen) the error in the report.
12. I wish she (was, were) my client.
13. They were (took, taken) by surprise.
14. She had (chose, chosen) the most beautiful painting.
15. (May, Can) I assist you with the project?

Part B

Instructions: The sentences below contain errors in verbs and adverbs. Make corrections as necessary. For example:

Incorrect: He and his office manager has felt badly about the project.
Corrected: He and his office manager have felt bad about the project.

1. My heart sunk when she gave the news.

_____

2. The budget is froze until next quarter.

_____

3. If he was your manager, will you attend the conference?

_____

4. George would have saw him the other day if he was there.

_____

5. Mr. Arnold often select the information for the agenda.

_____

6. Ever since I got a new manager, I always got too much work.

_____

7. I wish she was the new manager.

_____

8. If he was on your team, would you support him?

_____

9. If the bank was to loan you the money, what would you buy?

_____

10. We don't give that information to no one.

_____

11. We ate quick because we are going to the meeting.

_____

12. Try and drive more careful.

_____

13. That was the most silliest decision he ever made.

_____

14. She felt bad because he is not available to assist us.

_____

15. His assistant don't appreciate our suggestions.

_____

16. Bob and his entire team is going to the conference.

_____

ACTIVITY 2: PRONOUN PRACTICE

Instructions: Circle the correct pronouns to complete the sentences below.

Example: My boss and (me, Ⓘ) had lunch together today.

1. John and (I, me) completed the project yesterday.

_____

2. Barbara was more competent than (he, him). (Implied verb?)

_____

3. Why were the materials delivered to (she, her) and Bob?

_____

4. Dr. Jones said that (us, we) managers should do the work.

_____

5. Between you and (I, me), we have enough expertise.

_____

6. The supervisor required Bob and (I, me, myself) to attend the seminar.

_____

7. You can ask George or (I, myself, me) for the updated report.

_____

8. They are more competent to do the job than (we, us).

_____

9. The attorney asked that the case be divided among you, Alice, and (myself, me, I).

_____

10. She asked who would do the report, my secretary or (me, myself, I).

_____

11. Margaret is taller than (I, me). (Implied verb?)

_____

12. Bill likes Sue better than (I, me). (Implied verb?)

_____

_____

13. The professor told my associate and (I, me, myself) to complete our report.

_____

14. The information was sent to (she and I, her and me, her and I).

_____

15. George and (me, I) attended the meeting before (he, him) and (I, me) left.

_____

16. Upon recommendation, he gave the project to Jim and (I, me, myself).

_____

17. Bob has more time than (me, I). (Implied verb?)

_____

18. The project will be split between John and (I, me, myself).

_____

19. She asked Phyllis and (me, myself) to attend the board meeting.

_____

20. The problem should remain between Bob and (you, yourself).

_____

21. Did Allison and (I, me) cause you a problem?

_____

22. I am going to make (me, myself) an excellent dinner.

_____

23. When he asked, I responded: "It is (I, me)."

_____

_____

ACTIVITY 3: PRONOUN AND ANTECEDENT AGREEMENT

Instructions: Correct the pronoun errors in the sentences below. For example:

Incorrect: I always think a project is hard until you do some work on it.
Corrected: I always think a project is hard until I do some work on it.

1. One always thinks the grass is greener until you arrive at the other side.

_____

2. We generally follow the rules unless you are told otherwise.

_____

3. If a person is conscientious, they will do well in their jobs.

_____

4. One does not look at new words as changes in the language; we look upon them as fads.

_____

5. A person should strive to get the best education possible so that you can have a satisfying career.

_____

6. Trying one's hardest to get in good shape can ruin your health if your not careful.

_____

7. Everyone must make their own reservations.

_____

8. Neither of the trees lost their leaves.

_____

9. Both of the girls should have her work done on time.

_____

10. A pronoun should always agree with their antecedents.

_____

_____

ACTIVITY 4: PLACING MODIFIERS EFFECTIVELY

Instructions: Revise the following sentences so that modifiers are placed correctly. For example:

Incorrect: Taylor asked to use the conference room for the meeting next to his office.
Corrected: Taylor asked to use the conference room next to his office for the meeting.

1. All our managers attended the conference in Tulsa on international trade.

_____

2. Give the information to Doris about the revised plan.

_____

3. The account was lost to our competitor for new car loans.

_____

4. Mr. Jordan is the man talking to your manager with the briefcase in his hand.

_____

5. You will find the new forms in the supply closet for joint accounts.

_____

6. The driver left 20 minutes ago in the black sedan.

_____

7. The group would like to have lunch served at noon meeting in Room 202.

_____

8. You can pick up the proposal from the development office for new business today.

_____

9. The official title for the new position is development director in our New Jersey office.

_____

10. File the papers early in the day for incorporation to meet the deadline.

_____

ACTIVITY 5: DANGLING MODIFIERS

Instructions: Correct the sentences below by placing modifiers next to their subjects or by turning phrases into clauses. For example:

Incorrect: Getting return business on the new account, increased bonuses went to Spencer.
Corrected: Getting return business on the new account, Spencer increased his bonuses.

1. Following the account closely, a mistake was still made by the new sales representative.

_____

2. Applying a service fee, the account was overdrawn by the bank.

_____

3. To achieve the best results, a plan was developed by our team.

_____

4. Leaving in frustration, the meeting was canceled by our team leader.

_____

5. To open an account, these forms must be filled out.

_____

ACTIVITY 6: PARALLEL STRUCTURE

Instructions: Revise the sentences below to achieve parallel structure. For example:

Incorrect: William encouraged us to join the task force and that recommendations be given to the team leader.

Corrected: William encouraged us to join the task force and give recommendations to the team leader.

1. Your assignment was to make cold calls and questions were to be answered.

2. If the bank does not correct the error, our business will be taken elsewhere.

3. The insurance policy covers damage due to storms and also covered are floods.

4. Take their recommendation seriously, and a change should be made by you immediately.

5. I made a mistake, and the correction was made by Jerry.

ACTIVITY 7: CUMULATIVE REVIEW

Instructions: Correct the errors in the following sentences.

1. The decision is political, and it was not made with everyone's interests in mind.

2. Human Resources had finally wrote a policy to alleviate hiring complaints.

3. Between Vincent and I, we have enough expertise to develop a marketing plan.

4. The vice president of finance gave the proposal to Phyllis and myself to review.

5. Their recommendations were to improve employee benefits, making provision for internal advancement, and we should also change the sick-day policy.

6. Ramond says the report was late.

7. The account manager told Lydia that her and her assistant would be promoted.

_____

_____

8. The annual budget was officially froze due to the changes in the economy.

_____

_____

9. To correct the problem, they are issuing a report, speak to the press, and plan to hire a public relations firm.

_____

_____

10. Our corporate office has never went to outside sources for input on major decisions.

_____

_____

KEY FOR LEARNING INVENTORY	
1. T	**7.** T
2. T	**8.** T
3. T	**9.** T
4. T	**10.** F
5. T	**11.** T
6. F	**12.** T

The Writer's Handbook: Part 3

The Writer's Handbook

Formatting Standard Business Documents

Words differently arranged have different meanings, and meanings differently arranged have a different effect. —Blaise Pascal, philosopher and mathematician (1623–1662) ■

Though professionals spend an extraordinary amount of time crafting their messages, sometimes they ignore the obvious: the overall appearance, or **format,** of their document on the page. Consider this:

• *Formatting speaks to your reader* before your message is even read, and the finishing touches related to formatting give your document credibility. Lopsided documents can give the impression that the writer either did not know how to format or simply did not care. When documents are framed beautifully with balanced margins, the difference formatting makes is obvious in a glance. But well-formatted documents do more than present a "pretty picture."

• *Formatting gives visual cues* to aid the reader in understanding the material. Some elements of formatting are headings and subheadings, bullets and numbers, font, color, bold, and italics. However, at times the most important element may be none of these but, rather, is the unused portions of the page often referred to as *white space*. For an effective finished product, all elements must work together harmoniously to present a balanced picture.

Within limits, you can be creative with formatting. However, take a conservative approach until you are certain that you are improving the quality of your document rather than creating clutter or *noise*.

OBJECTIVES

When you have completed the Writer's Handbook, Part 3, you will be able to:

• Create visual cues for the reader with elements of formatting.

• Format business documents professionally.

• Use special features, such as font, color, bold, and italics.

• Understand how formatting affects the reader's understanding.

• Structure agendas and minutes.

Learning Inventory

1.	Italics are used in place of underscoring.	T/F
2.	One of the most important features to control in formatting is white space.	T/F
3.	Send memos to associates outside your company if they are good friends.	T/F
4.	Use Latin terms such as *etc.* because everyone knows what they mean.	T/F
5.	When you know that your reader has a visual impairment, use a larger font size.	T/F
6.	Use all-caps when you want the reader to know that your message is serious.	T/F
7.	To make words or phrases stand out, use bold *or* italics.	T/F
8.	To list items of different degrees of value, use numbers, not bullets.	T/F
9.	When you use numbering, list the most important item last.	T/F
10.	The block letter style is very popular because every part starts at the right margin.	T/F

■ SECTION A: FORMATTING BASICS—SPECIAL FEATURES AND WHITE SPACE

To effect an instantaneous rapport between your reader and your document, break your message into manageable chunks. Position your text so that it is well-balanced on the page, and display your key ideas prominently. Such visual cues allow your reader to scan the document and understand its meaning before actually reading it.

Here is an overview of the elements we will discuss in this section:

• Displaying key ideas with bullets or numbers.

• Organizing a topic by using headings and subheadings.

• Incorporating special features such as bold and italics.

• Setting off explanations or descriptive information with parentheses.

• Selecting fonts for ease of reading.

• Following official guidelines for white space.

Display Key Ideas With Bullets and Numbers

Even short documents can be improved by displaying key ideas. Bullets and numbers organize and prioritize key points; thus, your reader does not have to work as hard to pull them from your narrative. In addition, when the important points are highlighted, the reader does not need to reread an entire document to review the key ideas.

• For items of equal importance, bullets create strong visual cues.

• For items with different degrees of value, use numbers; list the most important items first.

Items in lists must be displayed in parallel structure. For example, if you start with an active verb, every item in the list should start with an active verb in the same tense. If you are listing nouns, all items in the list should be nouns. If your items are displayed in complete sentences, make sure they are grammatically correct. Below are a couple of examples of a list displayed in parallel structure. The first example presents the items as nouns:

Here are items to discuss at our team meeting:

- Employee dress policy
- Holiday schedule
- Summer hours

You can represent the same list more specifically by starting with verbs:

The topics we need to discuss at our next team meeting are as follows:

- Revise employee dress policy.
- Review holiday schedule.
- Implement summer hours.

Adding *ing* to the verbs turns them into gerunds (a noun form), as shown below:

At our next team meeting, we need to discuss the following:

- Revising employee dress policy.
- Reviewing holiday schedule.
- Implementing summer hours.

For bulleted or numbered items, you have a variety of different styles (size, shape, and indentation) from which to choose. Limit the number of styles you use within the same document, and maintain a consistent style based on purpose, or you will distract your reader. Thus, shift from one style to another only if you have a special purpose for changing styles; for example, use a larger bullet for a major point and a smaller bullet for a minor or subordinate point.

If you present your information in complete sentences or short phrases, you can end your bulleted or numbered points with a period. For answers to more technical questions, consult *The Gregg Reference Manual.*

PRACTICE

Instructions: Proofread and reformat the following memo to give it more visual appeal. Start by crossing out unnecessary information.

To: Margola Adams
From: Alex Guireria
Subject: Orrin Keyes' Transfer Application.

Hi Margola:

I heard through the office grapevine that Orrin wants to transfer into our department. I'd like to put in my five cents on his behalf because I think he'd be a great addition to our team. We worked together on the Corona project to link our restaurants, the busy stores and warehouses on a common data systems, and I have only good things to say about his contributions, which include: creating the daily PMIX data verification report for all U.S.

stores, producing a resturuant inventory report that is now being used to track inventory for all U.S. stores and restaurants, was an integral part of repopulating the date warehouse in December after the crash, and produced the file we used for the Action Dog promotion to determine supply and demand. Weve used that file for every toy promotion since!

I was so impressed with his work and his attitude, and really, well, you know how it is here. Hard workers don't always get the credit they deserveThere was no proper recognition of the work we did on Corona so you might not know what went into it or who was involved in the aspects of the project. Orrin never hesitated to perform data transformation products during the evenings nor coming in over the weekends as required to keep Corona up and running during daytime hours.

Something to consider.

A. G.

Create Centered, Side, and Run-In Headings

Headings are more relevant for writing memos, papers, and long letters than for short letters or e-mail. Break your text into manageable and cohesive chunks of information so that both you and your reader will have an easier time navigating your document. You can create centered and side headings during the composing or revising phase of writing.

- *Composing:* Create a *page map* of your major ideas. (Page mapping is presented in Chapter 1.) Use key words from your page map as centered (section) headings and side headings. A page map may be the most effective means for starting any document that is longer than one page.

- *Revising:* As you revise your work, you will further refine your thinking. Organize and prioritize your ideas as you pull out key terms for centered and side headings.

Levels of Headings   There are various patterns to follow for headings, with as many as four different levels considered acceptable, depending on the complexity of your document. *The Gregg Reference Manual* discusses three types of headings: a centered head, a side head, and a run-in head.

Once you choose a pattern for your document, remain consistent with spacing, font, and display. Also, for each level of heading, maintain parallel structure within that level. You may choose not to make your final decisions until the revising stage of writing, at which time you will clean up your document for *consistency*. Here is one pattern to follow:

- *Document titles and chapter openings:* Type the title of your report or chapter in all-capital letters and boldface type 2 inches from the top of the page (space down 6 lines from the default top margin in your computer template).

- *Centered headings (for sections and parts):* A section or part represents a major break in content. The **centered** (section) heading can be in 12-point all-capital letters. (For caps and lowercase, capitalize the first letter of every main word but not of a preposition or article with fewer than four letters, unless it is the first

---

VOCABULARY BUILDERS

Latin Abbreviations   Latin abbreviations are cumbersome, and too frequently writers use the abbreviations incorrectly. Avoid using them (except for *a.m.* and *p.m.*) unless you are writing a scientific paper or bibliography. Here are the correct meanings of a few common Latin terms, and English substitutes you can use for these terms:

- *Per* is an abbreviation meaning "through, by, or by means of." Use *per* correctly in common expressions such as *miles per hour* or *cost per day.* Also use it correctly in Latin phrases such as *per diem* ("by the day"). Avoid using *per* in general writing, such as "per our discussion," by substituting "as discussed."

- *Etc.* is the abbreviation for the Latin phrase *et cetera,* meaning "and other things of a like kind" or "and the rest." Avoid using *etc.* by substituting a phrase such as "and the like," "and so on," or by giving a more complete list of items.

Weak:	We will need to bring laptops, flip charts, etc., to the meeting.
Revised:	We will need to bring laptops, flip charts, and so on to the meeting.
Revised:	We will need to bring laptops, flip charts, and other support materials to the meeting.

- Other substitutions for *etc.* include *and so forth* or *among others.* However, if you still choose to use *etc.* within a sentence, make sure you precede it and follow it with a comma. Also, do not precede *etc.* with *and* because *and* is part of its definition.

- *Et al.* means "and others." Use it when you are writing a bibliography or citing a legal case, but avoid using it in sentences. Instead, write out "and others."

   Here are four more common Latin abbreviations:
   i.e. (id est) means "that is."
   e.g. (exempli gratia) means "for example."
   a.m. (ante meridiem) means "before noon."
   p.m. (post meridiem) means "after noon."
For ordinary use, the abbreviations "a.m." and "p.m." are not italicized.

FIGURE WH3.1 | Levels of Headings

Headings and subheadings can improve a document's readability. How would the content in this figure be affected if you were to remove the heads and subheads?

Peashaw Books Editing Guidelines　　　　　　**Page 7**

Proofreading
Not to be confused with copyediting, which comes earlier in the production cycle, proofreading involves catching and correcting small errors—incorrect spellings, sentence fragments, type style errors and the like—anything that slipped by the copyeditors. If you're rewriting major sections of the text at the proofreading stage, you're wasting everyone's time in production, and it's time for a sit-down conversation with your manager to determine why major errors are slipping by the copyeditors. Proofreading should be all about polishing the final product!

PROOFREADING STYLE SHEETS
Although most of the proofreading marks we use at Peashaw are in agreement with the industry standards, we do have a few variations that require familiarization on your part. The Peashaw Proofreader's Marks Chart can be accessed two ways:

Main server: In the folder titled Editing Tools, you will find a variety of forms and files that you'll be using in your daily work at Peashaw. These include, among other things, contracts, a writer's phone directory, and a folder titled Proofreaders' Grab Bag, wherein the chart can be found.

Viewpad: The Viewpad feature built into our word-processing software allows direct access to the files on the Main Server. Some prefer this option because the chart launches with the program; others dislike being unable to enlarge the Viewpad screen. The marks can be challenging to read at such a small size.

---

or last word.) Section headings should be centered between the left and right margins and followed by a double space. If you start a section on a new page, leave a 2-inch top margin (space down 6 lines on your computer template); if you do not start the new section on a new page, triple-space before your next section head.

- *Side headings:* A **side heading,** also referred to as a **subheading,** starts at the left margin. Type the heading in bold, either all-caps or caps and lower-case. Start the text content a double space below the side heading.

- *Run-in headings:* A **run-in heading** is also known as a **paragraph heading.** Indent the run-in heading $1/2$ inch from the left margin, and type it in bold cap and lowercase letters followed by a period. (At times, you may use a colon instead of a period.) Space twice and begin your text.

- **Second pages.** Use a correct and consistent pattern to identify second, or additional, pages. The preferred method is placing the page number in the upper right-hand corner. Unless you start a new paragraph, make sure you carry over at least 2 lines of the last paragraph.

When you do a final screening of your document, make sure that the document is consistent and balanced. Also make sure that you present headings within each level in parallel structure.

Incorporate Special Formatting Features and Marks

Special features include **bold,** *italics,* and <u>underscore</u>; special marks include parentheses and quotation marks. For these elements, follow specific guidelines, and use the elements consistently within your document. The italic and underscore features serve a similar purpose; italics is preferred unless you are writing a document by hand or using a typewriter rather than a computer. Before presenting more detail, here is a brief explanation:

- *Bold:* Make words or key ideas stand out by putting them in boldface type.
- *Italics:* Stress words; display book titles or foreign terms in italics. (If necessary, use underscoring in place of italics.)
- *Quotation marks:* Enclose direct quotes and jargon.
- *Parentheses:* Put parentheses around information that gives a brief explanation.
- *Caps:* Follow traditional capitalization guidelines; all-capital letters (all-caps) should *not* be used to make words stand out.

Sometimes, especially in e-messages, writers think they are making an idea stand out by putting it in all-caps. However, readers may infer that the writer is shouting or screaming at them. Once again, do not use all-caps in e-mail.

Many writers also think that putting a word between quotation marks makes the idea stand out (such as, *It's a really "good" idea*). In fact, placing a word between quotation marks does not stress its meaning. When writers use quotation marks for no valid reason, most readers infer that the writer is implying the *opposite* of what the word actually means. So be careful; do not throw quotation marks into a document unless you are clear about what you are doing. For more detailed explanations than provided here, refer to *The Gregg Reference Manual.*

Use Quotation Marks to:

1. Enclose a direct quote of three or fewer lines within the body of a document.
2. Identify technical terms, business jargon, or coined expressions that may be unfamiliar.
3. Use words humorously or ironically (if you think your reader will otherwise miss the humor).
4. Show a slang expression, poor grammar, or an intentionally misspelled word.

Use Italics to:

1. Refer to a word as a word; for example, the word *listen* has many shades of meaning.
2. Emphasize a word, phrase, or entire sentence.
3. Display foreign terms (such as *Merci, Grazie, Dobra, Domo Arigato*) and Latin abbreviations (such as *i.e.* and *e.g.*).
4. Display book titles. In the past, book titles were underscored. However, now that we have access to the variable spacing and special features of computers, using italics is the preferred method.

Use Parentheses to:

1. Include a brief explanation within a sentence.
2. Insert a sentence that does not directly relate to the topic of your paragraph.
3. Supply abbreviations.

Using parentheses de-emphasizes information. Parentheses also help to break up information flow in a positive way; the writer does not need to give a lengthy discussion of why information is being supplied. Parentheses tell the reader that the information is related to the broader topic without giving

---

COACHING TIP

Acronyms and Initialisms Abbreviations are shortened forms of words or phrases. Two commonly used types of abbreviations are initialisms and acronyms. **Initialisms** are pronounced letter by letter, such as *IBM* and *NYPD.* **Acronyms** are pronounced as words, such as *AIDS* and *SADD.*

When using an acronym or initialism for the first time in your writing, spell out the term and put the abbreviation in parentheses after it. For example:

Students Against Drunk Drivers (SADD) will hold its annual meeting in New York this year.

The American Association for Retired People (AARP) has lobbyists in Washington.

Both forms are represented by capital letters, and many, but not all, omit periods. If you have a doubt about how to write a specific abbreviation, check its correct form in a dictionary or reference manual. *When in doubt, check it out.*

Ask yourself: *How often do I use initialisms and acronyms in my communications? Which ten initialisms or acronyms do I use regularly?*

an explanation of how or why. Thus, you can sometimes avoid writing a lengthy explanation by enclosing a few words in parentheses.

PRACTICE

Instructions: Edit and reformat the following message, incorporating special marks and bullets or numbers.

Dear George,

Last month, Salaway Home Care sent out a notice regarding a problem we were experiencing with the Coordinator's Notes and the Participation Notes sections of the Profile Manual profile pages. In order to correct this problem we had to edit many of the profile page "note sections" The editing was done by eliminating unnecessary information in those two sections. For example: where Participation Notes state "White Harbor/Canton Medical of Vermont is the Canton of Vermont's active market HMO, please refer to Medicare Risk/Cost members to Senior DelawareCare (DE2M), we have revised to read Canon plus is the active Market HMO for Canton of America. Please refer Medicare members to DE2M-Canton 65." Information such as "coordinator use only" and "direct members access" has also been deleted. Immediate action is requested on your part. Take the next steps: Please visit our web site and print out the new profile pages that have already been edited. You can then review your HMO profile pages and make necessary edits. Also, please advise us of any additional information that can be edited down or deleted.

Choose Font Size and Color

For most business documents, select conservative **fonts** (such as Times New Roman, Arial, and Helvetica), and keep them to traditional sizes. Almost all business documents are formatted in a 12-point font, which means there are 12 characters per inch. This traditional size is a carryover from the typewriter, which had only two sizes (10 or 12 point). Now, with electronic processing, almost any font size is possible.

The traditional color for print and e-mail messages is black. However, for e-mail, some business professionals use blue for the body of their messages or their automatic sign-offs. Colors other than blue may be considered unprofessional; in fact, some business executives are annoyed when nontraditional colors or special features appear in an e-mail. These individuals may or may not be justified for feeling this way; however, entrants into the workforce should be aware of possible critics before sending out blazing red or purple messages (or animation), thinking they are being creative. To avoid criticism, use accents of color conservatively.

For documents that will be professionally printed, be aware that printing costs increase significantly when more than two colors are used. For documents that are copied, color copiers are now cost-effective and are used more frequently than they were in the past. However, continue to be conservative with color, using it sparingly to highlight a document. Otherwise, you may detract from your message. Consult a professional graphic designer if you have questions.

Here are a few more points to consider:

- Limit font types to two per document so that your work does not appear cluttered.

- Increase the font size if you know your reader has visual difficulty. Most e-mail templates are set for a size 10 font; increase the font size to 12 or 14. You may even use bold type to make the message especially clear.

- Use a larger-size font for the title of your document (size 14) and major text headings (chapter and section headings).

EXPLORE

1. Look through magazines, textbooks, and other common reading materials. Examine the appearance of a typical page, excluding any advertisements. How many different fonts are there? How many different type sizes? Does the page look clean or cluttered?

VOCABULARY BUILDERS

Serif/Sans Serif When someone refers to the **face** of a font, they are often referring to the name by which that font is commonly known, such as Times, Copperplate, or Arial. *Face* can also be used in reference to two descriptives that identify the look and composition of a font, *serif* and *sans serif*.

A **serif font,** such as the one used in this book (Times New Roman), features short lines at the ends of a letter, creating a pointed or sharp look around the edges of the letter.

A **sans-serif ("without the line")** font does not have the same pointed look; the top and bottom of the letters are uniform in thickness and look flat. Sans-serif fonts are considered easier to read when enlarged because of the smooth look of the characters and have thus become the fonts of choice for presentations.

Serif: **Times**
Sans-serif: Arial

2. Surveys have repeatedly shown that the inside column is the least-read section in a news-paper. Thus, a common design for the front page of newspapers places current and break-ing news stories in the right-hand column and human-interest stories in the left-hand column. When you read a newspaper, where do your eyes go first? Do you begin reading immediately, or do you examine the whole document?

Control White Space

The term **white space** refers to the unused areas of a document, such as top and side margins and the space between lines. Standard guidelines dictate the minimum to maximum number of lines to leave between the parts of a document. After you learn the guidelines for spacing, you will develop a trained eye for headings and text within documents.

White space gives your readers' eyes a place to rest and delineates the various parts of your document. It also gives readers a place to make notes and comments. The most impor-tant point to remember about white space is that it controls the way your document looks at a glance. Before you finalize your document, ask yourself the following questions:

- Does this document look balanced, appealing, and professional?
- Does it look as if too much information is crowded into too little space?
- Does the document look lopsided, or does it look as if it has a picture frame of white space?

Documents should look balanced, with top and bottom margins being roughly equal; side margins should be somewhat equivalent. The easiest mistake to make is to leave too little space at the top of a document, resulting in too much empty space at the bottom. A profes-sional rule of thumb is to aim for a picture-frame look. Use the page-preview feature on your computer to examine how your document will look before you print it. (Page preview can be found in the File menu on your toolbar.)

Here are some basic guidelines for letters and reports before you get to the specifics. (*Note:* For vertical spacing [up and down], 6 lines take up 1 inch of space.)

Letters:
- Start most letters 2 inches from the top margin of the paper. (After the 6 blank lines that your computer automatically leaves, space down 6 lines from the top of your computer page template.)
- Use the default margins for most letters.
- For short letters, add more space before the date line, between the date and the address, before the signature line, and before the reference initials.
- For long letters, leave less space between letter parts and at the top and bottom.
- Do not justify right margins (readers find justified lines more difficult to follow).

Reports:
- Start your first page 2 inches from the top margin (down 6 lines from the default top margin).
- Type the title in 14-point all-caps or bold caps and lowercase; type the body in a 12-point font.
- Use 1-inch margins or the default margins.
- Type the second-page continuation heading 1 inch from the top of the page; after the heading, space down 3 lines before continuing the body of your paper.

Memos:
- Use a memo template provided by your company or in a personal software package.
- To start the body of the memo, space down 3 times (leaving 2 blank lines) after the heading.

Research and academic papers must be written according to strict formatting rules; however, these rules vary slightly from source to source. For specifics, consult the reference source your instructor recommends.

Many companies post reference guides on their intranet systems. When you start working at a new company, ask whether the company has a corporate reference guide. Amazingly, many employees remain unaware that their companies provide this critical tool for written correspondence. Ask your human resources department or an informed coworker so that you can be on the cutting edge of your company's policies.

The remaining sections of this chapter review formatting for business letters and memos as well as other business documents.

SECTION A: CONCEPT CHECK

1. Why is it important to format your business communications?

2. What are of the two primary types of font styles?

3. Bullets and headings serve what overall purpose in a business document?

4. Why is white space important to the look of a document?

■ SECTION B: BUSINESS LETTERS

In today's busy corporate office, letters are the most formal and least frequently used business document. Generally, letters are used when the topic demands more attention than is possible with a phone call or an e-mail message.

This section covers two basic letter styles, the block style and the simplified style. Several additional styles exist (such as the modified-block style); examples are posted at the *Foundations of Business Communication* Web site (see Internet Exercise WH3.1 on page 473). The block and simplified styles are presented here because they are efficient and together provide writers with enough versatility for most purposes.

Block Letter Format

Every letter, regardless of the style, contains basic elements or parts. With the **block style** (also referred to as the full-block style), each part starts at the left margin. (See Figure WH3.2.) Thus, writers have no decisions to make about indenting lines or paragraphs.

The list below explains the parts of a business letter. Some of the parts (such as the subject line, reference initials, and postscript) do not appear as often in business communications as they used to. Others (such as the enclosure and attachment notations) are required only when other materials are sent with your message.

1. *Letterhead:* Corporate letterhead contains the company's name, address, phone number, and fax number. Many letterheads also include a logo, an e-mail address, and a Web address, and some show an executive's name and title. Also, some companies use different letterheads for different purposes, so it is common to select one type of stationery from several provided.

2. *Dateline:* The date usually appears 3 lines below the letterhead or no more than $2\frac{1}{2}$ inches from the top of the page. If the letterhead takes up little space at the top of the paper, spacing down only 3 lines will give an unbalanced look. For a short to medium letter, space down $2\frac{1}{2}$ inches from the top of the page. Other tips:

   • Use the current date; do not predate or postdate letters.

   • Space down 6 to 9 lines to type the date (since most software programs give a 1-inch top margin).

   • View in print preview and adjust the dateline so that the letter looks balanced on the page.

FIGURE WH3.2 | Block-Style Business Letter

Considered a more formal formatting method for business messages, the block style is popular because of its clean lines and uniform layout. Do you use any particular formatting style when composing business or personal messages? *(The numbers in the figure correspond with the list in the text.)*

① **Valence Records**
1057 Discovery Court
North Hollywood, CA 90045
877-555-9025 phone
877-555-9021 fax
www.valencepictures.net

② March 18, 2005

③ Ms. Suzanne Colissee
Account Executive
The Pressing House
56 Cavalier Lane
Mosswood, TN 67104

⑤ Dear Suzanne

⑥ CHALICE MUSIC CD PRESS DATE

⑦ Thank you for your close attention to our files. Of course, we are glad to have had the opportunity to make the adjustments you suggested.

However, we are now at what we call the "drop deadline," after which we cannot hope to have the music CD available in conjunction with the video release. Very simply, Suzanne, we need to have the CD master disc within two weeks.

Please contact me immediately. I am keeping my fingers crossed and waiting by the phone to hear from you.

⑧ Sincerely

⑨ VALENCE RECORDS

⑩ Mahmet Singh
⑪ Production Coordinator

⑫ blk
⑬ colissees.10
⑭ Enclosures: Disc with files
⑮ Attachment Notation: New Label Copy
⑯ cc: Kevin Alder, Chalice Productions

⑰ PS: You can reach me at the home number indicated on the new label copy.

3. *Inside address:* The **inside address** contains the name of the recipient, his or her title, and the company name and address.

- Space down about 4 lines from the dateline before typing the address. (For short letters, space down 6 or 7 lines; for long letters, space down 3 lines.)

- Avoid abbreviating in street addresses unless you are following a specific abbreviation system. That means you should spell out "suite" and "floor" *(when in doubt, spell it out).*

- Spell out the name of the state or use two-letter state abbreviations along with the appropriate zip code.

  Type the abbreviation in capital letters, and do not follow it with a period. Space one time between the two-letter state abbreviation and the zip code (for example: Chicago, IL 60611).

- List the most specific information of an address first (a person's name) and the most general last (state, zip, country). If you are having difficulty ordering information, think of the principle *specific to general.*

- Double-space after the inside address, leaving 1 blank line before the salutation.

- Use the inside-address format on the envelope exactly as it appears in the letter (unless you are using the all-cap style with open punctuation—see Section E on envelopes).

4. *Attention line (optional):* If a letter is addressed to a company (rather than an individual), direct your letter by using an attention line that contains the name of a person or department. Traditionally, the attention line appeared a double space below the inside address; the preferred method today is to place the attention line as the first line of the inside address.

- Use an attention line on impersonal correspondence; for important correspondence, call to get the name of the person to whom you should address the letter. For example:

Attention: Credit Department
Finest Department Store
1505 Sales Boulevard, Suite 401
Portage, IN 46368

5. *Salutation or greeting:* The traditional greeting for letters starts with *Dear.* Start your letter with "Dear Ms. Jones" or "Dear Client Representative" (if you do not know the addressee's name). For business correspondence, salutations are always followed by a colon (or a comma if it is a social-business letter) or no punctuation at all. After some contact, you can demonstrate familiarity by using the person's first name ("Dear Albert:") rather than title and last name ("Dear Mr. Clark:").

- When writing to a high-ranking government official or judge, check *The Gregg Reference Manual,* which covers many more specific salutations.

- After the salutation, double-space (leaving 1 blank line) before starting the body or typing a subject line.

6. *Subject (optional):* The subject usually appears a double space below the salutation. Simplified letter styles suggest putting the subject in all-caps and centering it 3 lines below the address (the colon after *Subject* is optional). Here are some examples of subject lines:

Subject: Invoice No. 4529
INVOICE 4529

COACHING TIP

Standard Versus Open Punctuation Two punctuation styles prevail in workplace letters: standard punctuation (also known as *mixed* punctuation) and open punctuation. **Open punctuation** style requires no punctuation after the salutation or the complimentary closing. **Standard punctuation** style calls for a colon after the salutation and a comma after the complimentary closing.

    Open: Dear Jana   **Standard:** Dear Mr. Nathan:

        Sincerely   Sincerely yours,

Other tips to remember:

- Use *In re* or *Re* in place of *Subject* if you prefer; these terms are commonly used for legal correspondence. (*In re* means "in reference.")
- Double-space after the subject line for a block letter; triple space for a simplified letter.

7. *Body:* The body of your letter can be as short or long as necessary to convey your message. The **introductory** paragraph connects your reader with your purpose. Allow yourself to sound as if you are one human being communicating with another: keep your writing friendly and avoid canned phrases. The **body** paragraphs contain the information, explanation, and evidence. That is, the body contains the details and provides examples, if needed. The **closing** paragraph states required actions. For letters longer than one page, use a second-page heading.

- Use the following format for a second-page heading:

    Mr. John Smithe   *(Name to whom the letter is addressed)*

    Page 2   *(Page number)*

    October 29, 2006   *(The date that appears on the first page)*

- Double-space between paragraphs (but single-space within the body of the paragraph).

8. *Complimentary closing:* Business letters are formal and use complimentary closings (e-mail messages are informal and thus do not use formal complimentary closings). Type the complimentary closing a double space below the last line of the body. For business letters, use *Sincerely* or *Sincerely yours.*

Follow the complimentary closing with a comma if you followed the greeting with punctuation (standard punctuation).

- Space down 4 lines from the closing to the writer's name so that the writer has space to sign the letter.

9. *Company signature (optional):* Use a company signature to emphasize that the letter represents the views of the company as a whole, not just the individual who wrote it. Type the company name in all-capital letters a double space below the complimentary closing.

10. *Writer's name (required):* Type the writer's name 4 lines below the closing (or the company signature, if used), leaving enough space for a handwritten signature.

11. *Writer's title (optional):* For formal correspondence, it is recommended to use a title. Type the title on the line below the name. Double-space before a notation or postscript.

12. *Reference initials:* Reference initials are needed only if the typist is *not* the writer. Since most people now type their own messages, reference initials are used less frequently than they were in the past. If you type a letter for someone else, put your reference initials in lowercase or caps a double space below the writer's signature.

13. *File name notation (optional):* Documents created with word processing software sometimes need a file name so that they can be retrieved from storage. Follow your company's guidelines for creating file names; file names usually have three components: a name, a dot used as a separator, and an extension consisting of 1 to 3 characters. Place the file name notation below the reference initials.

14. *Enclosure notation (optional):* If you are enclosing something with the letter, include an enclosure notation. State in the body of the letter the documents you are enclosing. The notation at the bottom of the letter is just as much for your benefit as for the recipient's. The notation reminds you to make sure the enclosure is sent along with the letter. If you are enclosing several items, list the items (or specify the number of enclosures). Here is an example:

Enclosures:

1. $545 check

2. Maintenance Contract

or:

2 Enclosures

An enclosure is different from an attachment; place the enclosure inside the envelope *without* stapling or paper clipping the item to the letter.

15. *Attachment notation (optional):* If you paper clip an item to your letter, use the attachment notation instead of the enclosure notation. State in the body of your document that you will be attaching the item to the letter.

16. *Copy notation (optional):* A *cc* (courtesy-copy) notation appears on all copies and indicates to whom copies of the letter are being sent. Some people prefer to use *c* rather than *cc*.

    A *bcc* (blind-copy) notation appears only on its recipient's copy and not on the original or on courtesy copies; the addressee is unaware the blind copy was sent. (Obviously, a *bcc* notation on the addressee's copy could cause serious problems.) Single-space between copy notations.

17. *Postscript (optional):* A postscript (PS) has been traditionally used for an afterthought. Start the PS a second line below the copy notation (or whatever notation was typed last).

    You can begin the postscript with *PS* followed by either a period or a colon, or you can omit *PS*. Here are some examples:

    PS. It was great to see you at the meeting!
    PS: Thank you for inviting Jorge to the meeting.
        The agenda will arrive next week.

Simplified Letter Format

Though the block style (also known as full-block style) is the standard for its efficiency, the **simplified style** streamlines correspondence even further. (See Figure WH3.3 on page 474.) The simplified style replaces the salutation with a subject line, and thus it is the style of choice when you are not writing to a specific person. (Omitting the salutation when you do not know the recipient allows you to avoid impersonal salutations such as *To Whom It May Concern* or *Ladies and Gentlemen.*)

To type a letter in simplified format, apply the block-style format with these exceptions:

- Place the subject line in *all-caps* a triple space (2 blank lines) below the address; triple-space again before starting the body.
- Omit the complimentary closing.
- Type the writer's name in *all-caps* 5 lines after the body.

The date line and inside address follow the same guidelines as those for other letter styles. Thus, you will leave about a 2-inch top margin before typing the date; space down about 4 lines to start the inside address.

Another popular version of the simplified letter format is the modern simplified letter, illustrated in Figure WH3.4 on page 475.

SECTION B: CONCEPT CHECK

1. Some parts of letters are required, and others are optional. Make a list of the standard parts of a block-style letter. Do you feel prepared to format a business letter?

2. When sending a bcc, is the notation made on the original and all copies?

3. What are the standard complimentary closings for business letters?

4. How does the simplified letter style differ from the block letter style?

FIGURE WH3.3 | Simplified Letter Format

The simplified letter does not *include a salutation. It emphasizes the subject line, so the subject of the letter jumps out at the reader.* What do you think about this style? Do you like starting with a subject line, or do you prefer including a salutation?

① **Dental Advocates of America**
545 West Madison Avenue
Chicago, IL 60661
312-555-1111
www.dentalassoc.org

② January 21, 2006

③ Mr. John Mercier
Educational Director
Columbus Academy
734 West 14 Street
Washington, DC 20005

⑥ NATIONAL CHILDREN'S DENTAL HEALTH MONTH

⑦ As a supporter of our mission to improve the quality of children's teeth in our country, you will want to share this advice with your students:

• Eat nutritious foods.
• Have regular dental checkups.
• Brush and floss each day.
• Ask your dentist about sealants.

Enclosed are some brochures that you can pass out to your students. As you pass them out, please encourage your students to make an appointment for their annual dental exam.

⑩ KAREN CONRAD
⑪ MANAGER OF RESEARCH AND DEVELOPMENT

⑫ ct
⑭ Enclosures

■ SECTION C: MEMOS AND E-MAIL

Memos are used within an organization to communicate information. If your information is going to an external client, send a letter or e-mail instead. A memo is also used as the cover page to a report that will be distributed internally (a letter would be used as a cover page to a report distributed to external clients).

E-mail is the most common form of office communication, and it is used both within an organization and with external clients.

Basic Parts of Memos

Most corporations now provide templates for memo headings. If you need to make your own heading, you can use a template provided by your software. Microsoft Windows includes the template shown in Figure WH3.5.

More and more frequently, memos are sent as e-memos, with different templates for different purposes. For example, for an e-memo announcing a phone conference, the template would show "Phone Conference" instead of "Memo" for the heading. The specific heading alerts the reader immediately to the message contained in the e-memo.

Here are the various parts of a memo:

FIGURE WH3.4 | The Modern Simplified Letter

Mona Casady's modern simplified letter style saves time and resources when used with window envelopes. Special features of this style are described in the body of the figure. An example of the format for the corresponding modern simplified memo can be found at the text Web site.

② 15 September 2004

③ MR P F HILL
INFORMATION SERVICES INC
1009-19 AVENUE NW
CEDAR FALLS IA 50613-3013 *(TS)*

⑥ ***The Modern Simplified Letter*** *(TS)*

⑦ Sharing information with you about the modern simplified letter format, Mr Hill, is a pleasure. Notice the use of Block Style and standard placement for dateline and margins, an effective and progressive format. Here are some other points:

   1 **Military Style Dateline**—compatible with global audiences and facilitates reading.

   2 **Letter Address Positioned for Window Envelope**—saves addressing an envelope, avoids mismatching letters and envelopes, and meets US Postal Service guidelines. Font size can be adjusted to accommodate window envelope.

   3 **Subject Line**—identifies the purpose of the letter and eases filing. Typefaces can be changed for emphasis. Use a larger font, italic, bold, or all cap.

   4 **Name of Addressee to Open and Close the Body**—adds personalization.

   5 **Omission of Periods After Abbreviations and Numbers**—offers compatibility with other office systems and technologies as well as saves keystrokes.

   6 **Name of Writer**—includes personal/professional title for correctly addressed reply.

You will have much success with this simplified style, Mr Hill. Your associates will be impressed with your friendly letters that are presented with this professional format.   *(QS)*

⑩ Dr Mona J Casady, Professor
Phone 555-555-4340
E-mail monacasady@emailaddress.com

---

1. *Heading:* The necessary elements for a memo heading are the following: *To, From, Date, and Subject (Re),* as well as a *cc* notation if appropriate. The order in which these elements are placed can vary. (If you are not sending copies, do not type in the *cc* notation.) If you are addressing two or three people, try to fit all the names on the same line. For longer lists, you can type the names one under the other. For extremely long lists, after *To* type "See Distribution List Below." Provide the list at the end of the memo under the other reference notations.

2. *Salutation:* Memos do not require a salutation, but you may use one. Adding a salutation, such as "Dear Marge:" or "Marge," makes a memo seem more personal. If you use a salutation, put it a double space below the heading and follow it with a double space.

FIGURE WH3.5 | E-Memo Template

Even though the memo is a less formal mode of communicating, maintain a professional tone. Have you ever written and then sent a document that in hindsight you wish had been more professional?

Memorandum

① To: [Click **here** and type name]

  cc: [Click **here** and type name] [Be sure to delete if not using]

  From: [Click **here** and type name]

  Date: [current date will be inserted automatically]

  Re: [Click **here** and type subject]

②
③ This template is only one among many provided by software companies.
  It contains the necessary elements for the heading: *To, From, Date,
  Subject (Re),* along with a *cc* notation.

  The order in which these elements are placed can vary. In fact, some companies
  now put *Subject* first because seeing that information is more important to the
  recipients than reading their own names. The entries following the guide words
  should be blocked at the left and clear the longest guide word by at least
  two spaces.

④

---

3. *Body:* Start the body of the memo 2 or 3 lines below the end of the heading or 2 lines below a salutation, if used. Single-space within paragraphs, but put a double space between them. Block paragraphs at the left. For long memos, use a heading for additional pages, which your software will provide.

4. *Closing:* Memos do not require a salutation or a signature; however, many writers prefer to add one. Adding a writer's handwritten initials next to the name at the top (or at the bottom) also personalizes a memo.

   If you are distributing hard copies of a memo, put a check mark next to each recipient's name as you put the memos into interoffice envelopes or place them in distribution bins.

Basic Parts of E-Mail

The format of e-mail is very similar to that of memos or e-memos. With e-mail, software templates provide the heading; writers need only fill in the necessary information. (See Figure WH3.6.) However, there is still room for error; the most commonly misused parts are the *cc* and *Subject* lines.

Here are points to consider about the basic parts of an e-mail:

- When you expect several recipients to take action on your message, list their names after *To,* not after *Cc.* Reserve the Cc line for use when you are copying a message to someone but *not* expecting that person to take action on the basis of the information in the message. The Cc function is misused when writers expect Cc recipients to read a message sent to someone else and then figure out the action they should take. Sound confusing? Well, it is confusing, but it happens all the time. To avoid confusion, forward the original message with a note at the top stating any expected action.

- Use an accurate *subject line* and update it as your correspondence evolves. Sometimes you will send an e-mail and get a response, and that's the end of the cycle. However, at times you will send an e-mail, and then you and the recipient

---

COACHING TIP

Personal Touch Although ready-made templates are handy, many writers prefer to create their messages in a more personalized format or in a format that better serves their needs. What look do you prefer for your business messages?

To explore the possibilities, open the template provided by your word processing software and practice reformatting the template to your satisfaction: change fonts, reduce the size of the type, space the type differently (for example, reduce the point size, change the heading, or shorten the word *Memorandum* to *Memo*). Once you've created a look that satisfies you, save the file for later use in an easy-to-access location on your computer. You have just created your own template.

FIGURE WH3.6 | E-Mail

How do you feel about the message contained in the second paragraph of this e-mail?

To: John R. Houston
Cc:
From: Sender@isp.net
Subject: E-Mail Tips

John,

Here are some suggestions for your electronic messages.

Use correct grammar and punctuation. Also, do not take unorthodox shortcuts: follow standard rules for capitalization, and do not abbreviate unnecessarily. Keep information short and to the point. Also, don't press the send button if you have any doubts about your message. If you feel unsure, either save your message as a draft or make a phone call.

Resist the urge to add "personality" to your business communications by using emoticons such as smiley's or sad faces [:) or :( ], and do not use slang or abbreviate unnecessarily. Since your message can be forwarded up the chain of command, always keep your messages professional in tone and appearance.

Tammy L. Higham
Developmental Editor
Business Careers
McGraw-Hill/Irwin
1234 Main Street
Chicago, IL 60610
ph: 555.555.5084
fax: 555.555.6944

---

will write back and forth several more times. For example, you may send a colleague an e-mail with the subject line "Update." Your colleague writes back giving you the update but then asks you about a meeting next week. At that point, one of you should change the subject line to "Next Week's Meeting" (or some other subject line that reflects your discussion).

- Use a *greeting,* even if it is only the person's name. When a person opens an e-mail, the communication seems incomplete if there is simply a message and no greeting. If you are writing to several people, use a greeting such as "Hello, team" or "Good day." If you are writing to one person, simply use the person's name followed by a comma. Then double-space and start your message.

- Keep the *body* (or message) short. If the body of your e-mail is much longer than one screen in length, consider using another mode of communication, such as a phone call.

- Use a simple *closing.* E-mail is not as formal as a business letter, so complimentary closings are not used. However, feel comfortable using a short phrase, such as "Enjoy your day" or "Take care."

- Include a *sign-off* that lists your company name, address, and phone number. (This information would typically be displayed in a letterhead.) There will be times when clients need to call you because they have urgent information that an e-mail message can't convey. By adding your contact information at the end of a message, you are making it easy for your clients to get in touch with you.

SECTION C: CONCEPT CHECK

1. If you are distributing a report to internal and external clients, what type of cover document will you attach to each?

2. Can you vary the format on memo headings? What information remains constant?

3. When you write a memo, do you prefer to include a salutation and reference initials? Why?

4. Is the subject line of an e-mail important? If you are writing back and forth to the same person, should you use the same subject line over and over again?

■ SECTION D: AGENDAS AND MINUTES

Agendas and minutes are used for meetings from the most informal and casual to the most formal. An **agenda** is a list of topics to discuss at a meeting (see Figure WH3.7); **minutes** are a written record of what transpired at a meeting. The two go together: the agenda presents the framework for the minutes.

FIGURE WH3.7 | Agenda

Agendas can be formally presented or simply be an informal list of topics to discuss; individual groups define their own tone and requirements. Think of a group you meet with regularly—does your group use an agenda? If not, would your group benefit from using one?

COMMUNITY SERVICE ASSIGNMENTS

Date: Jul 3, 2006
Place: Selma Charleston's office
Time: 3:30 p.m. to 4:30 p.m.

Coordinator: Selma

Group Leaders: Bill, Alexis, Devona, Walter, Caren, Rashid, and Selma

AGENDA

1. Review minutes from last meeting and make corrections.	5 minutes
2. Introduce community service concepts.	15 minutes
3. Identify resources we have to draw upon.	10 minutes
4. Establish assignment parameters.	5 minutes
5. Assign group projects.	5 minutes
6. Start developing brochure, "How Do I Choose a Charity?"	10 minutes
7. New business?	5 minutes

Depending on the group, the agenda can establish the purpose of the meeting and list measurable outcomes. For informal, casual meetings, an agenda keeps a group focused and organized. By knowing what to expect before going into a meeting, participants can bring pertinent materials and collect information ahead of time. For formal meetings, the agenda and minutes become legal documents, reflecting discussions and decisions made during the meeting.

Make sure participants have an agenda a day or two in advance of a meeting. Agendas enhance communication by developing a consensus of what will be discussed and achieved during a meeting. Participants can follow along with the agenda to ensure the meeting stays on track, checking off items as they are discussed. Thus, agendas function as much as "thinking tools" as they do as time management tools.

By distributing an agenda a day or two before a meeting, meeting coordinators not only help prepare participants but also allow them to help design the meeting by adding to the topics. An agenda can include all of the following information:

- The name of the organization (which could be a company, team, department, professional association, or branch of the government—county, state, or federal).
- The meeting purpose and date.
- The location (if it varies from meeting to meeting).
- A list of those who are expected to attend.
- Objectives of the meeting or what the group expects to accomplish.

The items to be discussed at the meeting could be numbered or listed as bulleted points. If a particular individual will present an item, that person's name could be listed next to the topic.

For formal meetings, minutes are a *legal record* of what transpired at the meeting. (See Figure WH3.8.) Most groups assign a secretary to take the minutes and to provide copies to all members no later than at the beginning of the next meeting. The first item of business is a reading of the minutes (either silently or out loud) to identify any needed corrections. Once all corrections are noted, the minutes can be officially approved; some minutes become part of the public record. For example, the minutes from a monthly meeting of the local board of health are available for residents to examine so that they can learn about decisions made at the meeting. Public organizations are required by law to provide copies of minutes upon request within specific time limits.

The most common type of meeting for business professionals is a team meeting. For these somewhat informal meetings, the team leader creates an agenda based on current issues and input from the group. During the meeting, participants can use the agenda to follow the discussion and check off their progress. After the meeting, a designated note taker (someone other than the leader) can use the original agenda to fill in important points and the names of significant contributors. (See Figure WH3.9.)

Most agendas end with *new business.* New business consists of ideas and issues that are brought up for the first time during the meeting. If time permits, the new business can be discussed, or it can be tabled and become an agenda item for the next meeting.

The importance of agendas and minutes relates to involving participants, keeping them informed, and recording progress. Without a written record, the same topic could be discussed, decided on, and then readdressed at the next meeting by those who didn't agree with the decision. Keeping a record of decisions—especially controversial ones—brings closure to issues and establishes a history. In addition, an agenda keeps the group focused!

EXPLORE

For a month, keep track of your own "minutes" in the workplace. Keep a work journal, or start a new file on your computer. Use it to keep track of significant discussions, ideas you would like to implement, or insights you have about improving operations. What uses might such a journal have in your professional life?

FIGURE WH3.8 | Formal Minutes

For the Record: *The board members of this not-for-profit organization meet quarterly, and their minutes are a legal record of their proceedings.*[1] Do you think it is more challenging to take notes at a meeting if you will need to turn them into minutes? Suggestion: The next time you are at a meeting, take notes as if you are going to prepare minutes from them.

HOOSIER ENVIRONMENTAL COUNCIL
BOARD OF DIRECTORS MEETING
November 22, 2003

The Hoosier Environmental Council Board of Directors meeting was called to order by President Jack Miller at 1 p.m. at the Hoosier Environmental Council offices located at the Old Centrum building. Present were board members President Jack Miller, Vice President Lori Olivier, Secretary Jeannette Neagu, Treasurer Bill Miller, John Maier, Tim Maloney, Denise Baker, Andy Knott, Clarke Kahoe, and Art Edelstein.

The July 18 minutes were presented. John Maier moved to adopt the minutes and Earl Becker seconded the motion. The March minutes were adopted as presented.

Treasurer's Report. Bill Miller reported that nothing was out of the ordinary. Denise passed out a summary of the grants. Direct mail exceeds budgeted amounts; we received $12,000 as a result of a promotion letter.

Canvass Report. Denise reported that the salary system was implemented at the end of March. We are now sending out 10 to 11 people; the base salary helps in hiring and retaining canvassers and improves job satisfaction. Their current focus is the ground water rule; they have generated 150 letters. PAN keeps canvassers more accountable, involving them in decision making. Lori agreed to follow up with PAN to ensure that canvassers achieve their goals.

Development Committee Report. Art and Clarke reported on the spring campaign. *The Monitor* is improving, and this helps in fund-raising. We are purchasing new fund-raising software. Tim will update the board on the software at the next meeting.

 SECTION D: CONCEPT CHECK

1. How are agendas and minutes used for formal meetings as compared to informal meetings?
2. What are some benefits of using an agenda for a meeting?
3. What are some benefits of completing and distributing minutes?
4. Besides the topics of discussion, what other information is included on formal agendas?

FIGURE WH3.9 | Informal Minutes

For the Team's Reference: Informal notes provide a quick overview of a meeting, recording the date, the names of those in attendance (and those missing), and a list of topics discussed at the meeting. In what situations do you think informal minutes might be more acceptable to use than formal minutes?

**Informal Minutes of Systems Consolidation
Working Group Meeting**

September 14, 2005

Present: Helen Whitman, Dylan Izumi,
          Michael Flenin, Mai Ghazo
Absent: Miller Grassner

Helen Whitman provided an outline of SCWG's current goals:

Personnel consolidation:
 • Freeze hiring.
 • Eliminate overlapping positions.
 • Update technology.

Technology consolidation:
 • Assess system compatibilities.
 • Upgrade security/encryption.

The discussion focused on gathering information. Issues raised included compensation, training, and computer system performance capabilities.

Some discussion was devoted to archiving. This task is difficult: much material is stored by individual employees and not available for long-term archiving.

Helen Whitman discussed the search for locations for the new main office.

The question arose whether management would be willing to pay for relocations. This will be referred to management.

SECTION E: ENVELOPES AND LABELS

The way you format your envelope is just as important as the way you format the document you will enclose in it. Professional-looking envelopes have never been easier to produce; now you can perfect a mailing label before you attach it to the envelope.

Using the label feature of your word processing program is the most efficient way to produce mailing labels. Your software program will provide a menu of label types and sizes. When you select the appropriate label, simply type the addressee's information into the address window. If your address does not fit neatly in the space provided on the label, either use a larger label or adjust the size of your font. Some people use boldface print on their labels because it is easier to read and makes the labels look attractive.

Address Styles

There are two basic styles for envelope addresses:

1. Capital and lowercase letters with punctuation (referred to as the *inside-address style*).
2. All-capital letters without punctuation. The United States Postal Service (USPS) recommends the all-cap style but acknowledges that the inside-address format can easily be read and processed.

COACHING TIP

International Post When mailing international correspondence, it's best to check the local customs for specific formatting instructions. In some countries, for example, the street name appears before the building or house number. As for dates, people in European countries write the day before the month: "The next review will occur 18 October."

When addressing mail to another country, remember to put the name of the country in all-capital letters on the last line of the address.

Ask yourself: *What sources can I look to for information on customs in other countries?*

Inside-Address Style:
Mr. Robert Lindsey
Manager, Human Resources
R&R Corporation
170 Sweet Circle
Winter Haven, FL 33884

All-Cap Style:
MR ROBERT LINDSEY
MANAGER HUMAN RESOURCES
R&R CORPORATION
170 SWEET CIRCLE
WINTER HAVEN FL 33884

Most people still prefer the inside-address style. Even though the all-cap style is more efficient, it can be more difficult to learn because of special abbreviations and line limits. If your company is large and has a preferred style for mailing labels, check with the mail department for specific guidelines.

Use the following guidelines for typing addresses directly on an envelope or on a label:

1. Block each line at the left; single-space addresses that consist of more than two lines.
2. Start the address with the most specific information and progress to the most general.

Example: Addressee's Name
Title
Company
Street Address
City, State, and Zip

Provide the most general information on the last line of the address, which would usually be the city, state, and zip. For international addresses, replace the zip code with the postal code and type the country of destination in all-caps on the next line.

3. Use two-letter abbreviations for state names or spell out the name of the state.
4. Leave one space between the two-letter state abbreviation and the zip code.

Envelopes

Envelopes come in various sizes: small, large, and letter size.

1. *Small envelopes:* The official name for small envelopes is *No. 6³/₄.* Small envelopes are most frequently used for personal business. If a small envelope is not already printed with a return address, place the return address in the upper left-hand corner. Use the default settings for margins. Position the mailing label or typed address 2¹/₂ inches from the left edge and 2 inches down from the top edge.

2. *Large envelopes:* The traditional business envelope is known as *No. 10.* This larger size accommodates letters nicely when they are folded in three. (See Figure WH3.10.) Position the address on a No. 10 envelope 4 inches from the left edge and 2 inches down from the top edge. Thus, the mailing address will look slightly off center (to the right) when it is positioned correctly.

3. *Letter-size envelopes:* When you do not want to send folded correspondence, use a 9- by 12-inch envelope. The 9 × 12 letter-size envelope is used frequently, along with even larger envelopes provided by professional couriers. Position the mailing label about 6 inches from the left edge and 5 inches down from the top edge.

Figure WH3.11 shows how to fold and insert a letter into No. 6 ³/₄ and No. 10 envelopes.

FIGURE WH3.10 | Instructions on Folding Letter for Window Envelope[2]

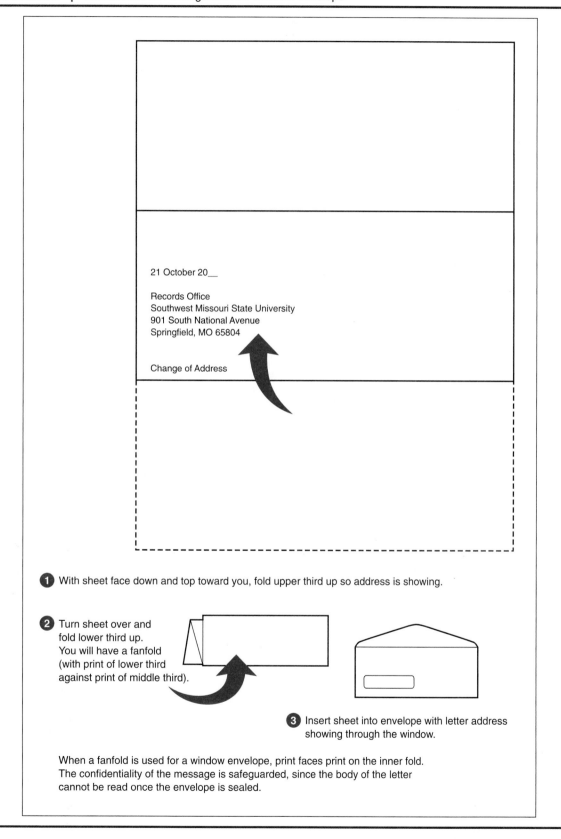

21 October 20__

Records Office
Southwest Missouri State University
901 South National Avenue
Springfield, MO 65804

Change of Address

1 With sheet face down and top toward you, fold upper third up so address is showing.

2 Turn sheet over and fold lower third up. You will have a fanfold (with print of lower third against print of middle third).

3 Insert sheet into envelope with letter address showing through the window.

When a fanfold is used for a window envelope, print faces print on the inner fold. The confidentiality of the message is safeguarded, since the body of the letter cannot be read once the envelope is sealed.

FIGURE WH3.11 | Instructions on Folding Letter for No. 6 ³/₄ and No. 10 Envelopes

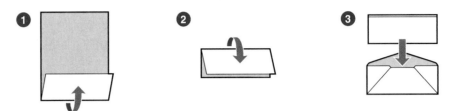

To fold a letter for a large envelope:
1. Place the letter face up and fold up the bottom third.
2. Fold the top third down to 0.5 inch from bottom edge.
3. Insert the last crease into the envelope first, with the flap facing up.

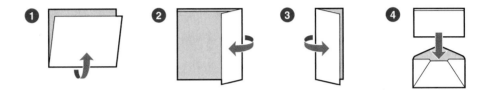

To fold a letter for a small envelope:
1. Place the letter face up and fold up the bottom half to 0.5 inch from the top.
2. Fold the right third over to the left.
3. Fold the left third over to 0.5 inch from the right edge.
4. Insert the last crease into the envelope first, with the flap facing up.

Two-Letter State Abbreviations

When addressing an envelope or typing an inside address, most businesses use two-letter state abbreviations. Do not type periods after the letters or space between them. Space only *one* time between the state abbreviation and the zip code (for example, Chicago, IL 60611).

Here is a list of two-letter state abbreviations:

Alabama	AL	Indiana	IN
Alaska	AK	Iowa	IA
Arizona	AZ	Kansas	KS
Arkansas	AR	Kentucky	KY
California	CA	Louisiana	LA
Colorado	CO	Maine	ME
Connecticut	CT	Maryland	MD
Delaware	DE	Massachusetts	MA
District of Columbia	DC	Michigan	MI
Florida	FL	Minnesota	MN
Georgia	GA	Mississippi	MS
Guam	GU	Missouri	MO
Hawaii	HI	Montana	MT
Idaho	ID	Nebraska	NE
Illinois	IL	Nevada	NV

New Hampshire	NH	South Carolina	SC
New Jersey	NJ	South Dakota	SD
New York	NY	Tennessee	TN
North Carolina	NC	Texas	TX
North Dakota	ND	Utah	UT
New Mexico	NM	Vermont	VT
Ohio	OH	Virgin Islands	VI
Oklahoma	OK	Virginia	VA
Oregon	OR	Washington	WA
Pennsylvania	PA	West Virginia	WV
Puerto Rico	PR	Wisconsin	WI
Rhode Island	RI	Wyoming	WY

✓ SECTION E: CONCEPT CHECK

1. Describe the two basic styles for addressing envelopes.
2. Where can you turn for more information on addressing and sending mail?

SUMMARY

The business world has experienced an information explosion since the 1970s, and things are not slowing down. Professionals must read a multitude of documents every day, sometimes numbering in the hundreds. Your goal as a writer is to make the paper load more manageable for your readers.

This chapter showed you how to present a message so that the content is instantly accessible. You achieve a strong format by making key ideas stand out through the use of bulleted and numbered lists. Other formatting tools to enhance meaning include centered headings, side headings, and run-in headings. Special features such as boldface and italics also make ideas stand out for the reader.

Your goal now is to experiment using these elements until you feel confident that you are using them to help the reader focus on your message. (Unfortunately, these same elements when used improperly can distract the reader rather than enhance your message.)

WRITER'S HANDBOOK, PART 3 CHECKLIST

___ Have you identified key ideas in your document?
___ Have you used bullets or numbers to make key ideas stand out?
___ Have you controlled the white space so that your document looks balanced?
___ Did you use the print preview to screen your document for a "picture-frame" look?
___ What special features have you used, such as boldface, italics, or underscoring?
___ Have you incorporated centered, side, and/or run-in headings into your longer document?
___ Is the address on your envelope the same as the inside address of your letter?

ACTIVITY 1: CREATING VISUAL CUES

Instructions: Edit and revise the memo below. Break down the information using formatting cues for the reader. (Formatting cues include side headings, bullets, numbers, bold, underscore, and italics.)

To: Weekend Employees
From: Production Supervisors
Date: March 16, 2006
Subject: Standard Procedures

Since some people are unaware of standard procedures. Therefore, take time to read the following information. It is important that you sign in as your arrive and are at your desk working at the starting time, which is 7 a.m. Do not sign in before your start time unless you have scheduled an early start with your supervisor. Next on the list is sorting mail. When fine sorting, look at every piece of mail. In the complex and high volume mail areas place mail tags to the right side of any mail in the bin. Sort mail to the right side of the mail tag. Everyone is entitled to a 15 minute break and a 45 minute lunch. You must sign out for your lunch break. At the end of the day, clean your work area. Also, empty your garbage can. Place any type of food or drink garbage in the plastic brown containers. The small black trash can by your desk should be left used only for paper. One more thing, phones are not to be used for personal calls. Calls can be made and accepted only in emergencies. Anyone found using the phone in the conference room or in someone else's office will immediately be placed on warning. Please see your production supervisor if you have questions.

_____

_____

_____

_____

_____

ACTIVITY 2: FORMATTING BUSINESS DOCUMENTS PROFESSIONALLY

Instructions: Your boss, Carolyn Lens, gave you the information below for a letter to Dave Jackson. Type the letter first in block style and then a second time in simplified style. Make sure you place any necessary notations at the end, including reference initials. Also, revise the letter for the "you" viewpoint.

I received your invitation to attend the annual session being held on May 23. I am pleased to inform you that I will be able to attend. So that I may coordinate my activities, please send me travel information and an agenda for the meeting. I have enclosed the form you requested, which finalizes the details of my attendance. I am looking forward to spending some time with you at the meeting, and I look forward to receiving your information so I can begin planning my visit to Philadelphia.

Dave's address is 2243 West Marshall, Philadelphia, Pennsylvania. His zip code is 71200. That's his company address. He works at Taylor-Heath Manufacturing Corporation, and his title is production supervisor.

ACTIVITY 3: USING SPECIAL FEATURES

Instructions: Reformat and edit the text below to make it more visually appealing. As you are working, ask yourself: In regard to special features and visual effects, how much is too much?

Eric Diaz

14 Southern Square Rd.

White Falls, ID 74512, (505) 555-5555

Objective: Seeking permanent middle-school teaching position

Employment History/Work Experience:

1995 to Present: Substitute Teacher

Working on an emergency credential for the first two years, and credentialed for the remainder of this period, my reputation for working successfully with middle-school students has had me on regular rotation at several middle schools in the area for more than 8 years: Private: White Falls Private School, contact Lynne Scrupp; Jackson Academy, contact Jed Padwa, Helen Loren; Horn Corner School, contact Bill Orman. Public: White Fall Middle School, contact Olsen Dare; Sunnybrae Middle School, contact Evelyn Hartin; Hale Junior High, contact Steve Schabow; and Timber Middle School, Arleen Fukumoto.

1990 to 1995   Playground Supervisor /Athletic Coach

Oakhurn Elementary, 6542 Elkins Ave, Boise, ID (505) 432-4534

Playground Supervisor: Initially working at Oakburn as part of a grant program to encourage development of afterschool programs in local schools, the number of students who could claim they participated in some part of the program increased to include most of the student body. Athletic Coach: A permanent staff position created as a result of the afterschool success allowed me to implement a program that fused the curriculum ongoing in the classroom with playing games, artwork, singing, learn new physical (sports) activities, and music.

ACTIVITY 4: FORMATTING AND THE READER

Instructions: Work with a partner or partners on each of the following.

1. Bring in a sample of a letter, a memo, or an e-mail that you wrote before you reviewed the information in this Handbook part. Exchange samples with your partner or partners. Discuss among yourselves the effects of the formatting on the visual presentation of the letter. Is white space used effectively? Drawing on the information in this chapter, how might you improve these samples?

2. List the elements of formatting and the various special features available to you when you are composing or editing a message. Discuss the following: Are there elements you prefer to use and others you avoid? As a reader, do you find that some elements appeal to you more than others? What do you know about white space? What are some specific guidelines you use for white space when producing letters and reports?

ACTIVITY 5: AGENDAS AND MINUTES

1. Situation: The Engagement Committee was formed to measure employees' level of "engagement" with the workplace. Alice Flanjak, the human resource director, has asked you to notify the members of the team—Rita Alsop, Richard Kilne, Amara Hodnes, Zin Tseng, Aria Stone, and Nate Hollins—of a meeting planned for the 6th of December at 9:30 a.m. in the West Conference Room. Alice wants to gather the team members, introduce them to one another, explain the thinking behind the engagement survey, and strategize an approach. She also wants to introduce the team to Martin Coleman, an independent analyst who will provide an overview of the data-gathering process and pitfalls.

   Instructions: Create an agenda for the event.

2. Instructions: Working alone or with a partner, identify some public agencies (such as the town council, the county commissioner's office, the health board, the local food pantry, the water department), from which you can request the minutes of a meeting. Collect several samples of minutes from different sources.

   Compare the various sets of minutes to identify similarities and differences. What types of topics were discussed? Did any of the decisions surprise you? Do you have a better idea of local government and the issues the agencies discuss? Which group had the most professional minutes?

3. Instructions: Attend a meeting of any organization that welcomes visitors—at your school or somewhere else in your community—and make a record of the proceedings. From this record, create minutes for the meeting.

REFERENCES

1. The Hoosier Environmental Council is a not-for-profit organization. The minutes shown were compiled from their quarterly board minutes in 2001, Indianapolis, Indiana.

2. The illustration was provided compliments of Mona J. Casady.

KEY FOR LEARNING INVENTORY

1.	T	**6.**	F
2.	T	**7.**	T
3.	F	**8.**	T
4.	F	**9.**	F
5.	T	**10.**	F

The Writer's Handbook: Part 4

The Writer's Handbook

Research—Collecting, Conducting, Displaying, and Citing

Doubting everything or believing everything are two equally convenient solutions, both of which save us from thinking. —Jules Henri Poincaré, La Science et l'hyphothèse *(1902)* ∎

Research is an organized attempt to answer a specific question. Every day you find yourself asking questions on the way to making decisions, and every decision involves at least two options (or it wouldn't be a decision). To get good results on important issues, you try not to rely on a whim or a guess. Instead, you evaluate past experiences or ask others what they have done in similar situations. These types of inquiries reveal the roots of research: *the goal of scientific research is to explain, predict, and/or control phenomena.*

The word *research* has different meanings depending on the context in which it is used. For example, when you say you are going to "do research," you generally mean you are going to *collect* what others have discovered rather than *conduct* your own research.

- In *collecting* research, you can readily find information through a variety of sources (books, periodicals, and online sources). In fact, the first phase of any type of research is a *review of the literature,* the process of collecting what others have already discovered.

- In terms of *conducting* research, you have many options for discovering new information, such as the use of surveys and questionnaires. More and more, business professionals are using action research to make effective, timely decisions that are in sync with their clientele.

Thus, you will start Part 4 of this handbook by learning how to collect and conduct research, and you will end by learning how to cite your research. By conducting your own *action research,* you gain powerful options for accessing information and adapting your decisions to what is actually needed (rather than what you *think* is needed).

Graphics convey research findings in a concise and powerful way. Used effectively, charts and graphs display some findings much more effectively than words ever could. Since most software programs allow you to create graphics somewhat painlessly, you have flexibility in using graphics. Section B demonstrates how to display your research by incorporating graphics, as well as quotations, into your work.

Regardless of what system you use to document your sources, proper citation verifies your points and gives your work credibility. Detailed citation can be challenging; it is essential to give proper credit, the lack of which can result in plagiarism. Plagiarism is unacceptable, and today it is easier to detect than at any other time in the history of writing. The last section of this part gives details on citation, including examples from the major systems.

Research can shape your decisions and the way you think. As you work through Part 4 of this handbook, you may find yourself *applying* more research as you make decisions, and that's the key to making any kind of research worth the effort.

OBJECTIVES

When you have completed the Writer's Handbook, Part 4, you will be able to:

- Understand the difference between quantitative and qualitative research.
- Develop a survey to use in conducting qualitative research.
- Apply quotations, ellipsis marks, parentheses, and brackets to reference material.
- Display research through the use of charts, graphs, and tables.
- Collect research through online and printed sources.
- Distinguish how the GRM, CMS, APA, and MLA systems differ.
- Compile critical information to use with any of the four systems.
- Apply action research tools to everyday problems.

Learning Inventory

1. The word *research* has different meanings depending on the context in which it is used.   T/F

2. Quantitative research deals with probability.   T/F

3. Research that is more than ten years old is not likely to be found online.   T/F

4. You do qualitative research every day as you make decisions.   T/F

5. Action research applies research results as they are obtained.   T/F

6. Once something is proved through research, it can be relied on as true.   T/F

7. For a focus group, an outside facilitator is more likely to get accurate results than someone the group knows.   T/F

8. Research is cited in the same way regardless of the field of study.   T/F

9. Action research involves presenting surveys and running focus groups.   T/F

10. Quantitative research involves interviewing to collect opinions.   T/F

■ SECTION A: COLLECTING AND CONDUCTING RESEARCH

There are basically two types of research: *quantitative* and *qualitative*. Below are brief explanations so that you can understand the basics of each.

Quantitative research collects numerical data to explain, predict, and/or control phenomena of interest. Quantitative research involves using numbers to interpret and control phenomena. The "phenomenon" in question could be anything of interest, such as a new product, a pharmaceutical drug, a method of training, and so on. Quantitative research also involves predictability: did an event happen by *chance,* or is there a *causal relationship?*

To identify predictability, quantitative research often employs the *scientific method,* using research designs that include a control group and an experimental group. For example, let's say the instructor of your business communications course wanted to test a new method for teaching writing skills and asked you to conduct the research. The experimental design would include at least two classes, with one class using the traditional method and the other class using the new or experimental method. As the researcher, you would write a **hypothesis** theorizing the expectations from the study. Then you would turn the hypothesis into a **null hypothesis** stating that differences were *not* expected. (For more information on hypotheses, see the Communication Challenges sidebar on page 495.)

Here are the basics of the experimental design:

1. Both classes would take a *pretest* to measure current skill level.

2. Each class would follow a specified curriculum: one would learn by the experimental method; the other, by the traditional method.

3. After a specified time, each class would take the *posttest.*

4. Pre- and posttest results would be tabulated and analyzed.

If the experimental group scored significantly higher, statistical tables could be applied to determine whether the differences occurred by chance or as a result of the "treatment," which is the new method. (Of course, the research design would be more detailed than what is given here, but these are the basics of the design.)

Quantitative research is rigorously applied in the medical field, but it is also used in education, the social and physical sciences, and business and economics.

Qualitative research collects narrative data to gain insight into phenomena of interest. Qualitative research entails gathering information, often through surveys and questionnaires. This type of research is more common in business applications; through surveys and opinion polls, qualitative research identifies beliefs and opinions. The results of qualitative research are used to determine the needs of clientele, make marketing decisions, and develop new products. Qualitative research does not seek a cause-effect relationship; it simply seeks to identify the current state of a specific topic.

In the example above relating to writing skills improvement, you could incorporate a qualitative survey by asking students for their reactions to what they learned and how they learned. (For example, "What improvements have you made in your writing?") Of course, the resulting data could not be considered causal, as it would be purely subjective.

More and more, business relies on the vital information qualitative research gathers through focus groups, questionnaires, and interviews. Many companies design products on the basis of consumer opinion; policies are changed on the basis of customer reaction. However, it is important to note that qualitative research cannot be tested and rigidly scrutinized the way quantitative research can.

Although qualitative research can be put through "number crunching," it generally does not involve elaborate research designs for determining a cause-effect relationship; if qualitative research is repeated, it will not necessarily get the same results. For example, if a news organization conducts a poll to see which candidates voters support in an upcoming election, the results can change from week to week or even day to day. Another example of qualitative research is a survey that asks consumers to state the three to five most important factors they consider when buying a new car. Even this data would change from one geographic or economic region to another and as world events dictate.

COMMUNICATION CHALLENGES

Research Limits When your boss says to you "Give me a recommendation tomorrow," how do you determine how much research is appropriate?

To a great extent, the answer depends on your boss, the topic you are researching, and your circumstances. When you have doubts, ask questions to clarify what you need to do. Busy executives can be as frustrated with too much information as they can with too little information.

For example, if your boss says to you, "What kind of DVD should we buy?" don't report back the next day with so many options that the situation becomes confusing. Do your research, and present two or three of the best options, clearly defining the benefits of each. Better yet, make the decision yourself, and then recommend the best choice.

INTERNET EXERCISE WH4.1

Reader's Guide to Periodical Literature
Though you are not likely to find research ten years old or older on the Internet, you can find it at some libraries through the *Reader's Guide to Periodical Literature*. You can also find older research on microfilm and microfiche. Your local librarian can lead you to the richest sources of information related to the topic you are investigating.

Though older research is not generally posted online, News Bank has a retrospective for selected sources that includes research about ten years old. For more information on these resources and others, visit the *Foundations of Business Communication* Web site at <http://www.mhhe.com/djyoung>.

Once you have accessed the home page, select "Student Activities" and then click the Writer's Handbook, Part 4, link.

COACHING TIP

Scanning Pens One of the most effective ways to collect information is by using a *scanning pen*. About the size of a large highlighter, electronic scanning pens scan up to 1000 characters per second (that's about 200 words) and can read fonts in sizes from 6 to 22 points (from the very small to the very large).

If you can afford one, a scanning pen gives you a lot of flexibility in collecting information at the library. By scanning information directly from the source to your computer, you more easily identify the original words of your sources and have an easier time citing sources correctly. Some scanning pens even have a text-to-speech feature, which allows you to hear what you've scanned.

However, just as scanning pens can be used to assist in doing credible research, an unscrupulous writer can use a scanning pen for cut-and-paste plagiarism. Remember that this type of plagiarism is easily detected.

Credible Research

The primary goal of all research, quantitative or qualitative, is to obtain *unbiased, objective* results: Credible research does *not* take a position and then seek proof to confirm it. Rather, credible research asks a question and then objectively evaluates evidence, with the data determining the conclusions. Always remember, the first key to valid research is having an open mind about a topic. The researcher may have a hunch or gut feeling (which may be the catalyst for the research); but to be valid, the research must remain objective so that it demonstrates unbiased outcomes.

As you collect research on various topics, you may find that you want to go beyond the literature and conduct your own qualitative research through surveys, focus groups, and interviews. Thus, this section discusses qualitative research methods that you can apply on a regular basis; but first, let's take a look at collecting research.

A Review of the Literature

The first step in any type of research is reviewing information that others have already discovered. By reviewing the current literature, you are able to define the problem and put it in context. By identifying what others have discovered about your topic, you establish a credible base of evidence. The work of specialists provides a springboard for your thesis; you can move forward by extending established knowledge and by showing fallacies in views contrary to yours.

A thorough review of the literature includes all types of sources. In addition to books and periodicals, many Web sites contain important information. To conduct a balanced search, include print sources (books and periodicals) as well as electronic sources found through credible Web sites and databases.

However, *some* online sources are not credible. Think about it—anyone can say anything on a Web site without evidence to support views or information. The value of information depends, in large part, on the credibility of the author or organization publishing it; however, no authority screens information posted on the Web. The biggest issue related to a Web site's credibility is *bias* (which is one of the issues that can invalidate research findings). Here are some ways that bias misleads:

- For political or financial profit, a site may present or highlight only select research (in other words, the site leaves out research that negates its own position).
- The research presented may be shoddy, contaminated, and thus invalid.
- The author may present opinions and beliefs but not evidence based on research.
- The site may represent a conflict of interest without making that known.

Thus, a site may provide an imbalanced, inaccurate perspective on the topic. This skewed information can affect your views, especially if you were leaning in that direction already. Here are some tips to ensure your online source is credible:

1. Look for impartial sites that are sponsored by large, credible organizations, such as the American Medical Association and the U.S. Bureau of Labor Statistics. (In other words, small private organizations that you have never heard of may or may *not* be credible.)
2. Identify how long the site has been in operation; the longer, the better.
3. Identify how often the site is updated. Some sites are posted and left unchanged for years.
4. Check to see whether the site is linked to other sites you consider reputable.
5. Evaluate whether the site provides information that answers your questions accurately and objectively (as compared to trying to convince you to buy into its pitch).

COMMUNICATION CHALLENGES

Hypotheses and Null Hypotheses Scientific research starts with a question that, when turned into a statement, can become a *hypothesis* or "an explanation that can be tested." For example, if the question is "Do customers prefer good service?" the hypothesis could read "Customers do prefer good service."

Researchers use probability theory (a branch of statistics) to test a hypothesis to determine whether there is a causal relationship. According to probability theory, a researcher can prove the *unlikelihood* of an occurrence happening by chance but *not* the *likelihood*. Thus, in conducting research, a hypothesis is "nullified" by negating the positive statement. As a null hypothesis, our example becomes "Customers do *not* prefer good service." If we surveyed 100 customers and they all preferred good service, we could reject our null hypothesis with a 100 percent level of probability.

When the probability level (usually preset at 95 or 99 percent) shows that a null hypothesis can be rejected, the hypothesis becomes accepted. The higher the probability level, the stronger the correlation.

VOCABULARY BUILDERS

Open Questions Versus Closed Questions Regardless of the survey you are constructing, you will want to ask questions in a way that solicits the information you seek. Two basic types are open questions and closed questions.

Closed questions provide simple options (such as *yes* or *no*) from which a respondent selects an answer. Usually, closed questions are multiple-choice or true-false questions (such as "Prompt, efficient service gives a place of business more credibility. True or False?").

Open questions allow the respondent to answer a question in a flexible way: respondents are not given specific choices and forced to select one or the other; they are given an open-ended question to which they reply in their own words. An example of this type of question is "What difference does prompt, efficient service make in your buying decisions?"

Open and closed questions are markedly different from each other. Use whichever is most appropriate for the circumstances of your research. If you are surveying large numbers of people, closed questions are a good choice because you can tabulate and compare the results efficiently. With open questions, deciphering data is difficult and time-consuming, making them impractical when there are many respondents.

Of course, you can always design a "mixed questionnaire" that has both types of questions. In fact, such questionnaires are common. On many questionnaires, directions such as the following are common: "For any question you answer with 'yes,' please give an explanation along with supporting details."

Also consider the following:

6. Your library has already screened many sources through online subscriptions, databases, and CD-ROMs. Use those sources *before* you put your topic into an outside search engine.

7. Compare how information on a Web site meshes with the print materials in your research. Since print materials are scrutinized heavily during the publishing process, you can consider online sources that agree with print sources more seriously.

8. Finally, if you have a question, discuss your source with your librarian. Librarians specialize in retrieving and evaluating information—most enjoy assisting eager researchers.

Though you may start your research online, use your online sampling as an entrée to books and periodicals that provide substance and balance. To be credible, research must include information from reputable, *established* publishing houses, periodicals, associations, and organizations. What your library does not carry in print or online subscriptions, it may carry in the form of microfilm or microfiche. Libraries can also request material for you through an interlibrary loan—one more reason to start your research early.

Once again, local librarians are specialists in information science. Tap into their insights and talents as you do your research. Also, see this text's Web site for some credible online sources.

EXPLORE

Go to your local library and interview the librarian. Discuss the answers to the following questions:

1. What are the limits and pitfalls of doing online research?

2. What is the best method for finding older research?

3. Why is printed-material research usually more reliable than online research?

Qualitative Research

When you ask people questions about how they think or feel, you are conducting a simplistic form of qualitative research. When you observe behavior and then use your findings to make decisions, you are also in the realm of qualitative research. Qualitative research *describes* and *evaluates* to give a more detailed picture of the current state of a designated topic. Qualitative research appears every day in the news and in ordinary life. Here are a few examples of qualitative research:

• A poll taken to determine which candidates voters will support in the next election.

• A computer questionnaire giving three options for you to choose about a topic.

• A survey at your grocery store asking which hours you prefer to shop.

Some qualitative research doesn't involve a research design or have a mathematical dimension relating to probability, such as the survey at your grocery store. However, some qualitative research is painstakingly designed and applies statistics, such as the poll taken among voters. By doing a **random sampling,** a researcher can reduce bias and calculate a margin of error. Thus, the results would have a specified degree of accuracy within a given margin. Of course, even the most meticulous design may not predict reality; for example, what if a significant event changes people's minds as the research results are being tallied? Even without intervening incidents to change the results, qualitative research most aptly applies to a specific time and place and is not conducive to being applied outside its realm.

The tools of qualitative research that you are likely to use are *surveys, focus groups,* and *interviews.* These tools are part of a qualitative approach to research known as *action research.* You can use these research tools on an ongoing basis; they will help ensure a more accurate, thorough depiction of the questions you are exploring.

EXPLORE

Stop to consider the various qualitative research studies that you hear about daily. Make a list of at least three qualitative research studies (opinion polls and surveys) that you have heard or read about during the last month. Did any of them give a margin of error? Do you remember what it was?

Action Research

Action research is most often affiliated with education and the social sciences, but it is used effectively in business environments as well. Whereas scientific research conducts experiments and then applies the results *after* they are proved, action research is a method that assists the researcher in collecting information to use in an immediate application. With action research, the researcher "takes action" *as* the improved understanding (or research) occurs.

According to L. R. Gay and Peter Airasian in their book *Educational Research, Competencies for Analysis and Applications,* action research is carried out in a *cyclical* manner:

Initial information is reexamined and sharpened, reexamined and sharpened again, and the process continues until there is consensus or until additional cycles fail to generate significant new information. The four basic steps of scientific and disciplined inquiry guide the process of the action research:

1. Identifying a problem or question;
2. Conducting a meeting or brainstorming session to gain information about the problem or question;
3. Analyzing research data or information; and
4. Taking action to rectify the problem or illuminate the question.[1]

To use an analogy, action research is a way of testing the temperature of the water by asking someone who's already in the water rather than assuming what the temperature might be. Action research provides feedback that assists in making decisions that lead to effective change. In addition, action research can involve both quantitative (numbers, statistics) and qualitative (feelings, beliefs, opinions) data.

In general, action research includes a "before" and an "after" with some remedy in between. In education, it often consists of a pretest followed by a practice and then a posttest to measure change. The difference between the pretest and the posttest could quantify the degree to which the practice improved performance. If the change were not quantifiable through a pretest-posttest design, a questionnaire that measured participant attitudes could be given. Thus, you could quantify the results using a scale, such as 1 to 5, to gauge how much participants believed they improved.

One such measurement is a Likert scale (see Figure WH4.1 on page 498); information about other types of rating scales are posted at the *Foundations of Business Communication* Web site at <http://www.mhhe.com/djyoung>.

Of course, the results of action research are limited; a researcher could not necessarily use them to predict how other populations would respond. However, action research is an exciting way to make progress; everyone involved becomes more engaged.

Consider ways you can include action research in your personal and professional life to get better results. For example, if you wish to improve team communication, ask for feedback

COMMUNICATION CHALLENGES

Grains of Salt Quantitative research deals with numbers. The most rigid, formal type of quantitative research seeks to determine a causal relationship. The basis of this type of research is a *hypothesis* (or theory), which is then turned into a *null hypothesis*. The (null) hypothesis is tested on experimental and control groups to measure change.

However, don't take "facts" proved through research at face value. To challenge research findings (to find out if a study has been contaminated), ask the following types of questions:

- Could *intervening variables* (people, things, or events) have interfered with the research, leading to inaccurate results?
- Were the samples (people surveyed or items examined) an accurate representation of the population being studied?
- Was the researcher *biased* in any way?

Even theories proved through the best quantitative research are true only to the extent that current knowledge confirms their accuracy; they are *not* final truths. As knowledge evolves, some proven theories fall to the wayside. *Have you ever taken the results of research to be "the truth" and later found out the research was inaccurate or invalid?*

COACHING TIP

Sampling a Population In general, the larger the sample size, the more accurate the data. If you want information about a particular group (a population) and you can't "test" everyone, the best approach is to sample a representative group of the larger population. The most reliable method of selecting participants is random sampling.

Most statistics books include a chart that indicates how many participants a sample should include on the basis of the size of the overall population, and they explain how to select the sample. You will find a *sampling chart* at the *Foundations of Business Communication* Web site at <http://www.mhhe.com/djyoung>.

If research intrigues you, consider taking a statistics course. Though statistics can be complicated, some of the best information can be gleaned from simple calculations. Just running basic averages (mean, median, and mode) on data will give you deeper insight into the results of questionnaires and surveys.

about what works well in getting a job done and what creates barriers to making progress. This informal "testing of the water" can make a difference.

Surveys, Focus Groups, and Interviews

The most popular type of qualitative research involves asking people their opinions about an issue or product. Surveys, focus groups, and interviews are important listening tools. As such, they have changed marketing dramatically over the decades. For example, in the past, a common approach was to manufacture a product and then convince consumers that they should buy it. When consumers stopped buying, a company knew it had a problem. Now, the more common approach is to solicit input from consumers and then adapt the product as much as possible to consumer demands.

This approach has been evident especially among American car manufacturers since foreign cars created serious competition for them. It is also apparent in the food industry: when consumers demand healthier foods, even fast-food chains find a way to adapt. *In what other areas or industries have you experienced these types of changes?*

Turning from products and moving toward human endeavors, many companies use qualitative tools to survey their employees. Rather than design changes in benefits and training and then inform their employees of the changes, companies first solicit input from their employees to find out what they need or want. The two fields that specialize in such organizational research are human resource (HR) management and organizational development (OD). Human resource managers implement employee benefit packages, job appraisal procedures, and hiring processes. Organizational development professionals use qualitative tools for *planned organizational change.*

By staying attuned to employee needs and responding accordingly, HR and OD professionals can keep operations productive and employees satisfied. They use employee feedback to shape policies, procedures, benefits, training, and even management style. They help create a productive corporate culture by using qualitative tools to measure attitudes and behaviors. Depending on the purpose of the research and the types of questions, information can be collected from individuals or from small groups. Let's examine each approach.

Survey Design Designing a survey can be a science of its own. In fact, because there is a "science" to developing certain types of surveys, many professionals avoid creating them. They fear they won't construct one correctly, so they ignore the survey as a valid tool, thereby losing an efficient, tailored option for collecting current information.

Simple surveys can be developed without advanced science. (See Figure WH4.2.) People generally like to share their opinions; doing so makes them feel more involved in the big picture. Sometimes it allows them to communicate grievances and let out steam; other times it gives them an easy way to share their appreciation. At any rate, people feel more important when their views matter. Keep your survey brief and focused; be honest about why you are asking for the information and how it will be used.

The drawback of surveys is not the process of constructing them; it is the limited application of the information they produce. For example, research you discover through surveys is *time-sensitive.* What you learn today can change by tomorrow depending on circumstances. In addition, what you learn with one group may be invalid with another.

To design a survey, first figure out what is important to know versus what isn't important. Setting priorities is a recurring issue; much time is wasted by addressing unimportant issues that camouflage the real ones. At the outset,

FIGURE WH4.1 | Affective Scales

An affective test assesses people's feelings, values, and attitudes toward self, others, and environments. Such tools are often based on self-reports.

Likert Scales

In a *Likert scale*, a range of numbers, such as1 to 5, indicates gradations in response choices. Participants respond to a series of statements by indicating the number that most closely matches the degree to which they agree with each statement. Results are then tabulated numerically to assess responses.

	1 Strongly Disagree	2 Disagree	3 Undecided	4 Agree	5 Strongly Agree
I attend help sessions on a regular basis.	1	2	3	4	5
I find help sessions valuable.	1	2	3	4	5

This type of qualitative evaluation tool helps rank opinions. Though they may seem somewhat unscientific, Likert scales are even used in the medical field. For example, to discover how much pain a patient is in, a nurse may ask the patient to quantify the pain on a scale of 1 to 10. Pain medication is then prescribed partly on the basis of the patient's assessment of his or her own discomfort.

Semantic Differential Scales

A *semantic differential scale* measures a respondent's attitude about a specific topic, such as how the person feels about a class or a project; it can even measure how someone is doing to break a habit, such as smoking. Each scale presents a pair of words representing the polar extreme of an attitude about a topic. Participants quantitatively rate their attitude on a continuum between the extremes.

Please rate this exercise.

Necessary _____   _____   _____   _____   _____   _____   _____ Unnecessary

Fair _____   _____   _____   _____   _____   _____   _____ Unfair

Rating Scales

A *rating scale* measures respondents' attitudes toward others. By providing a scale, it has similar advantages to a Likert scale in that the responses can be numerically averaged.

On a scale of 1 to 5, please indicate how often you are satisfied with our approach.

	1	2	3	4	5
	Never	Rarely	Sometimes	Often	Always

determine whether you will do a *paper survey,* an *online survey,* or both. Here is a process you can follow:

1. Meet with colleagues to discuss the issues and brainstorm a list of questions.

2. Wait a day or two before you edit your list, but then edit it ruthlessly.

3. Keep your survey as simple as possible.

4. Depending on the topic, your survey may be more effective if respondents remain anonymous; choose the approach that will produce the most accurate results.

FIGURE WH4.2 | Sample Questionnaire

Professor Roger Conaway and his students at the University of Texas at Tyler used this questionnaire to elicit data about communication channels in business. Only business executives, managers, and other experienced professionals were surveyed.

Interview questions:

a. How important in the workplace are good communication skills?

b. Based on your experience, rank the following in terms of their importance:

Reading _____   Writing   _____

Listening _____   Speaking   _____

c. How important are correct spelling, proper grammar, and accurate punctuation in business communication?

Unimportant   _____   Somewhat important   _____

Very important   _____   Absolutely essential   _____

d. Which mode of communication do you use most often?

E-mail _____   Telephone _____

Memoranda _____   Letters   _____

Direct personal conversation _____

e. When it comes to communication skills, what do you expect from your employees or those you supervise?

COMMUNICATION CHALLENGES

Online Surveys You can now find Web sites that specialize in survey analysis. For a fee, these online survey sites assist you in creating your survey and give you options for the various types of questions you will include. The service distributes your survey, collects and tabulates the results (in real time), and then analyzes your data. The online service also provides you with graphs and charts, so you have visuals along with statistical analysis for presenting your findings.

Log onto the Web, and type "online surveys" in a search engine. Go to a few of the sites and consider what they offer. If you ever need a professionally done survey, you may find this kind of tool a lifesaver.

5. If time permits, do a pilot test of your survey with a small sample to ensure the design meets your needs.

6. Set a time frame, and then distribute the surveys.

7. Do not expect responses for all the surveys you distribute, and expect some to be late.

8. Tally the results.

9. Report the results in an unbiased, honest way (whether you like the results or not).

If you include an *affective scale,* such as a Likert scale (see Figure WH4.1), you can calculate an average (mean) as well as other simple measures, such as the mode (the most frequently appearing score) and the median (the score that falls at the center, with half of the scores coming before it and half following it).

Conducting a Focus Group   Companies often conduct formal **focus groups** to solicit *honest, objective* feedback. However, if the facilitator knows members in the group, they also know some of the facilitator's opinions; some members might try to please the facilitator, and others might withhold information. Thus, some of the psychological dynamics in such a group are different from those that would exist with an outside facilitator. For this reason, companies often hire outside consultants to facilitate focus groups.

However, even when an outside consultant conducts a focus group, some of the same problems can arise. Therefore, use discretion when interpreting the results of any focus group. Here are some tips for running a focus group:

1. Develop a clear purpose and objectives.

2. Identify issues and brainstorm questions to ask.

3. Edit your list of issues or questions so that you do not collect too much detail.

4. Select a group large enough to provide diversity of thought but small enough to let everyone feel free to participate in the discussion. (The average number is between 8 and 15 participants. Also, the only accurate way to recruit a focus group is through random sampling of a defined population.)

5. Use open-ended questions and statements to solicit input.

6. Keep the tone of questions neutral:

Incorrect: What do you think is wrong with the culture in the company?
Corrected: Describe the culture within the company.

7. Collect data.
8. Identify common themes.

Gathering responses manually rather than recording them on tape has advantages. If the session is recorded, the responses may be less reflective of true opinions and attitudes. By having an assistant key the responses into a computer, you can assure the participants that their responses are anonymous. Report the information without interpretation or bias. Consolidate *common themes* and reactions while respecting the importance of anonymity. If you betray a group's trust, you may lose your credibility; also, your indiscretion may cause someone to experience serious repercussions.

EXPLORE

1. When you are asked questions in a survey, do you give honest answers?
2. Have you ever been part of a focus group?
3. If so, were you influenced by the ideas of others in the group?

Conducting Interviews Individual **interviews** consume more time than other types of qualitative research and provide less generalized feedback; that's because the information relates to one individual and not a group. However, interviews are used for many types of informal research, such as making hiring or promotional decisions and doing job performance appraisals.

Interviews are a good method to use when you are working with a small population. For example, if there were a total of 20 people in an organization, individual interviews would be feasible and would give a total picture. In such a small organization, data gathered in a focus group could be less reliable because of close relationships; in other words, individuals generally express more candor when their anonymity is guaranteed. To acquire valid information from a large population, you would need a random sample that applies statistical methods. Another way to collect important information is to interview an expert in the field.

Outcomes: What Are the Common Threads?

Researchers tally narrative answers from focus groups and interviews by looking for common threads or consistent themes among the responses. What information does everyone seem to hold in common? The common threads among responses are considered more objective data and can more readily be applied to the larger population.

Research and Its Application

A serious gap exists between what people know through research and what they actually apply. Think about your own life. What are some things that you "know" but that you don't "practice"? One common estimate is that people forget 80 percent of what they learn if they don't apply it soon after learning it.

Imagine how much more effective you would be if you used research to make conscious decisions rather than basing your actions on guesses. However, sometimes people don't really decide; they *react* or *act out of habit* rather than thinking about choices. Thinking leads to a more conscious decision; reflection reveals the pros and cons of a choice.

If you choose to become more conscious of behavior that doesn't get good results, you can improve your outcomes by applying research. For example, if you are a smoker, you may block everything negative about smoking out of your mind each time you pick up a cigarette. However, if you vividly recall what research shows and also visualize the results from smoking, you will not enjoy the cigarette as much; your active mind will assist you in making changes.

By actively using what you learn through research (not just intellectualizing information and then becoming passive), you can make important changes in your daily life. Over time, these changes will keep you focused, productive, and more satisfied with your behavior. Thus, research can become a part of your daily life if you include it in the way you think: more and more, you will be making decisions on the basis of proven criteria rather than acting out of habit.

Consider the riddle about a famous Monet painting: if the lights are off and the painting can't be seen, is it really there? The same can be asked about research. If you learn something relevant but *you* don't apply it, does it really mean anything in *your life?*

EXPLORE

1. What are some research results that you have been intending to apply in your life? Identify some changes you wish to make, and then investigate how research can help you reach your goals.

2. Alfred North Whitehead is credited with saying, "Knowledge is like fish; it doesn't keep." Does this quote have relevance for research?

 SECTION A: CONCEPT CHECK

1. What is the difference between quantitative research and qualitative research?

2. Describe the types of questions you can include in a survey. Provide examples.

3. What is action research?

■ SECTION B: DISPLAYING RESEARCH

Displaying research spans different levels of complexity: you are displaying research when you put someone else's words in quotation marks or when you turn complicated data into charts, graphs, or tables.

Whereas displaying quotes accurately contributes to credibility, displaying numbers and other concepts in charts and graphs clarifies meaning at a glance: you can glean insights without teasing out the details from the supportive narrative. In addition, exhibits appeal to visual learners. With a computer, you can be as creative with charts and graphs as your current skill and software allow.

A word of caution: Use special displays only when they fill a need. In other words, don't make your work look fancy simply for visual appeal. Just as visual displays can add credibility and enhance your work, they can also displace meaning and add clutter.

Before discussing charts, graphs, and tables, we'll examine how to display quotations.

COACHING TIP

Displaying Titles: Italics *or* Underscoring When citing *complete works*—such as books, magazines, newspapers, long poems, or pamphlets—display the title by putting it in *italics* or underscoring it (not both).

Here's some background into the *how* and *why* of displaying titles: The preferred means for displaying titles has always been italics. In the past, however, only professional printers were capable of typesetting titles in italics. Writers who used typewriters had only two options: underscores or all-caps. (Although the all-caps style is still acceptable in select circumstances, it is hard to read and not generally recommended.) Now that most people use computers, the ability to italicize titles is available to nearly everyone.

When writing a document by hand, underscore complete titles; when typing it into a computer, use italics.

Quotations

The most common way to display research is to use quotations. The right quotation in the right place adds credibility and depth to your writing. Through quotations, you can summon the masters to support your points.

Though you need to quote authoritative sources throughout academic and most professional writing, do not overuse quotations. Work with a topic until the piece reflects your own message written in your own voice.

Double quotation marks (" ") are an immediate signal that the text set off between them is someone else's exact words, possibly those of an authority on the subject. However, to display quotations, you often must use other sorts of punctuation besides double quotation marks, such as ellipsis marks, brackets, and single quotation marks. Below are some guidelines for displaying quotations.

Short Quotations   Incorporate direct quotes that are *less than four lines long* into your narrative and set them off by using quotation marks. For placing punctuation, here are a few rules to remember:

- *Commas* and *periods* (including ellipsis marks) always go inside quotation marks.

    Examples: According to Robert Browning, "Less is more."
    Robert said "Less is more," but I don't know what he meant.

- *Semicolons* and *colons* always go outside quotation marks.

    Examples: When it comes to writing, Browning believes "less is more"; however, according to Mies van der Rohe, the term also applies to design.

    Robert explained the statement "less is more": simplicity trumps complexity.

- References to *footnotes* are placed directly after the closing quotation mark (no space added).

    Example: According to the Infectious Disease Clinics of America, the virus can spread quickly: "Insects, birds and some species of animal are carriers . . . across the Australian continent."[10]

- The placement of *question marks* (and *exclamation points*) depends on the meaning. That is, does the quotation itself pose the question, or is the quotation within a sentence that poses the question.

    Examples: Sarah asked, "Is Bill the new vice president?"
    Did Browning say "Less is more"?

Long Quotations   For a quotation of *four or more lines,* display the quotation as an extract, set off from the text, by doing the following:

- Indent $\frac{1}{2}$ inch from both left and righ side margins. (Do not use quotation marks; the indentation signals the reader that you are displaying a quote.)
- Single-space the quotation.
- Leave one blank line before and after the displayed quotation. (See the examples below in "Omissions in Quotations" and "Additions in Quotations.")

Quotations Within Quotations How to display a quotation within a quotation depends on whether you are starting with a long quote or a short quote:

- *Short quotes* (two or three lines of quoted material within text): Display the main quote between double quotation marks, and display the internal quote between single quotation marks.

Example: According to Kegan, "Carl Rogers's 'client-centered' or 'nondirective' therapy has had an enormous influence on the training and practice of three generations of counselors and therapists." (244)

Indirect Quotes or Paraphrasing Do not use quotation marks for indirect quotes, such as paraphrases of someone's words. Credit the source by using the person's name in the text and/or providing a footnote or endnote.

Omissions in Quotations Use ellipsis marks to show omission of a word or words. Ellipsis marks consist of three spaced periods. If the omission comes at the end of a sentence of quoted material, add one more period to indicate the end of the sentence (or the necessary terminal punctuation for the sentence).

As an example, consider again the fable developed by Michael C. Mercil (which appears in Chapter 7 of this text). The first quote below is Mercil's original text; the second quote is an abridged version in which ellipsis marks were added where information was taken out:

Original: Imagine that in your country, from the time of the first people, today, and far into the future, everyone that was ever born or will be born, was born with two legs, two arms, two eyes, a nose, a mouth, and a pair of sunglasses. The lenses in the sunglasses are yellow.[2]

Abridged: Imagine that in your country . . . everyone . . . was born with two legs, two arms, two eyes, a nose, a mouth, and a pair of sunglasses. The lenses in the sunglasses are yellow.

Additions in Quotations At times, it is necessary to add a word or two to quoted material so that the reader can make sense of it, especially when words have been taken out. When you add a word or two of your own, put them between brackets: [ ]. For example:

According to Dunlap:

Do not assume "they speak English in other countries, so there is no reason to translate our marketing materials or Web site." Even if some Europeans can read English, they have a tendency to ignore advertising in English. . . . Willy Brandt, the former German chancellor, put it this way: "If I'm selling to you, I speak your language. If I'm buying, dann müssen Sie Deutsch sprechen [then you must speak German]."[3]

COACHING TIP

Finding Quotations If you need to find the source of a quotation or would like to peruse the quotations of a favorite author, use an Internet reference source. One of the most popular sites is Bartletts.

There are also many books that group quotations by subject matter. Other popular sources of quotations are e-mail newsletters that you can subscribe to on a daily or weekly basis. When you do find a quote that is useful, it is a good idea to double-check the attribution to make sure you're crediting the right source.

Quotations are fun and informative, effortlessly bringing alive wisdom of the ages. Insightful quotes provide a momentary break as they add wit, wisdom, or vigor to an ongoing narrative.

PRACTICE

Instructions: Insert quotations into the sentences below. For example:

> **Incorrect:** As Wayne Gretzky once said, you miss 100 percent of all the shots you never take.
>
> **Corrected:** As Wayne Gretzky once said, "You miss 100 percent of all the shots you never take."

1. Ralph W. Tyler was the educator who said the house you live in is your mind, your own integrity—don't worry about the rest of it.

   _____

   _____

2. George quoted Whitehead's famous analogy knowledge is like fish; it doesn't keep.

   _____

   _____

3. In Milicent's law class the professor quoted Aristotle: law is reason without passion.

   _____

   _____

4. In the meeting, Margie shouted go for the gold.

   _____

   _____

Graphics: Charts, Graphs, and Tables

At times, visual displays speak more loudly than words. (See Figure WH4.3.) Words can include excuses or explanations mixed in with the numbers, thus making it difficult to illuminate real trends.

For example, a small not-for-profit organization seemed to be losing its financial stability. From quarter to quarter, financial reports showed movement up and down in various parts of the budget. The reports were complex and difficult to follow. Finally, the chairperson of the board commissioned a graph that would show the overall change of just the bottom line over the previous ten years. The graph showed a steady upward swing for four years and then a plummet over the next six years. Any successes or increases in funding were consumed by the bigger picture.

That was the turning point. Once the line graph showed the direction in which the company was moving, reality set in: if the organization were to survive, the company's direction needed to shift, and quickly. Luckily, this story had a happy ending. But actually "luck" didn't have anything to do with it: the changeover required shaping the little details into a big picture and then seeing the picture clearly. The line graph clearly delineated the past and present and

FIGURE WH4.3 | Visual Persuasion

Which is the more effective way to describe an event such as an auto collision: in words or in a picture?

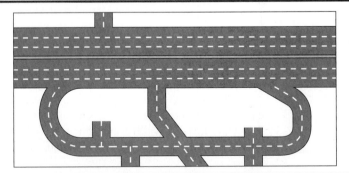

predicted the future (if the same direction were followed). For everyone involved, the big picture incited their motivation to survive. Staff, board, and volunteers worked diligently on brainstorming, setting goals, and making changes to reach objectives.

To display your research, you have several options, from the simple to the complex. Becoming more adept with using software can take a lot of the pain out of creating your display.

Keep in mind that *the information is the important issue, not a fancy display.* Don't try to impress your audience with "smoke and mirrors." Let your concepts and ideas lead the way, with the displays remaining secondary to the information they support. For instance, the simplest way to present survey results is to list all responses verbatim or to summarize highlights. Then reviewers can extrapolate what they need, interpret the findings, and apply them individually.

Bar Charts   With a **bar chart** you are able to compare and contrast two, three, or more different items. If you are showing the relationships over a period of time, you can cluster several different groups of data.

You can display relationships horizontally or vertically. (See Figure WH4.4.) Use a different color for each category, and use the colors consistently throughout your document.

FIGURE WH4.4 | Bar Charts

Bar Chart Tips: Bar charts may be horizontal or vertical. (a) Horizontal bar charts provide more room for labels. (b) Vertical bar charts are preferred for portraying information over time. (c) In a grouped, or clustered, bar chart, two or more bars are grouped side by side. The bars may be joined together or separated by a narrow space; avoid overlapping bars because they can distort the comparison. (d) Practice caution with segmented charts: visual comparisons are more difficult between the second, third, and ensuing segments because they do not align at common baselines. For example, judging by the data presented in chart (d), have sales of the Mini Mojo Motorbike increased or decreased since 2001?

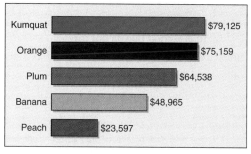

(a) Horizontal

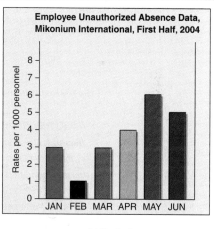

(b) Vertical

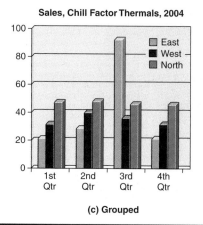

(c) Grouped

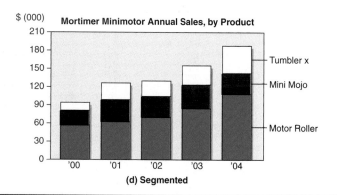

(d) Segmented

If you do not have a color printer, shades of gray or different patterns can achieve a similar result. Here are some other tips:

- Limit the number of bars to six.
- Make sure bar widths and the space between bars are equal.
- Arrange bars in a logical order (by length, by age, by date) to make comparisons easier.
- Place categories such as "other" or "miscellaneous" at the end of the series of bars.

Pie Charts   **Pie charts** are best used when the various components add up to 100 percent. A pie chart shows the relationship of one item to another and simultaneously shows how all parts relate to the whole. (See Figure WH4.5.)

Since pie charts deal with percentages, they are not as precise as other types of charts or graphs. Though they compare and contrast items with one another and the whole, they do not show as many dimensions as other types of graphs. This drawback is especially true of three-dimensional pie charts, which tend to visually distort the information they present. To make a pie chart more interesting, highlight a section by dragging it out. Once again, use color.

Here are some guidelines for creating pie charts:

- Limit the number of categories to six; if you have more than six, try to combine them.
- Label categories directly, and add percentages. Avoid using a key, if possible.
- If you are emphasizing a point, place the most important section at the 12 o'clock position.

Line Graphs   A **line graph** is unique in pointing out trends. (See Figure WH 4.6.) Movements in the stock market, incoming funds over a period of time, or the course of an illness are all conducive to being depicted in a line graph. Here are some guidelines to remember when you are using line graphs:

- For line graph titles, use left-justified, 10- or 12-point bold, and clearly state the data that are illustrated.
- Clearly label axes.
- Start the vertical axis with zero (unless there is a good reason not to).
- In a time graph, the horizontal axis always indicates time, and the vertical axis displays the units of measurement.

FIGURE WH4.5 | Pie Chart

Slicing It Up: *Although pie charts are useful for conveying simple, broad messages, bar charts display complex data more effectively. For viewers to make clear and specific visual distinctions between the values depicted in a pie chart, the pie segments should differ in size by more than 5 percent. For example, in this pie chart, if the percentages in the labels were removed, would you be able to tell whether Japanese or German was the second most commonly used language on the Internet?*

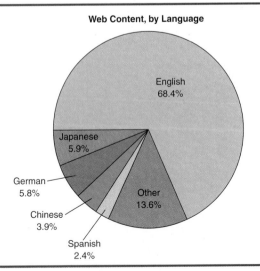

Web Content, by Language

Source: Vilaweb.com, as quoted by eMarketer.

FIGURE WH4.6 | Line Graphs

Making a Case: Line graphs are the most effective format for presenting data, particularly time-related data, but they can also be deceiving.
(a) In the simple line graph, the company KaleidoscOptics presents its sales data for the years 1997–2005 and appears to be a highly profitable
enterprise. (b) However, in the multiple line graph, which includes company expenditures, it is apparent that while sales are growing, the
company's costs are rising and profits are shrinking.

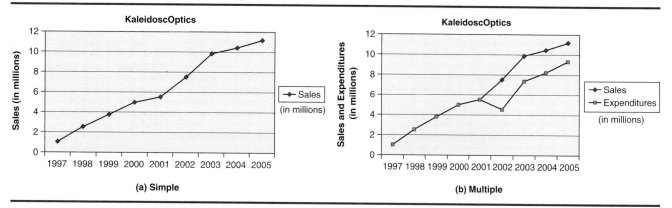

(a) Simple   (b) Multiple

FIGURE WH4.7 | Flowchart

Graphic representations such as this flowchart can make a very complex process seem simple.
Flowcharts depict relationships between processes and people rather than numbers. The organization
chart in Figure WH4.8 is another type of flowchart.

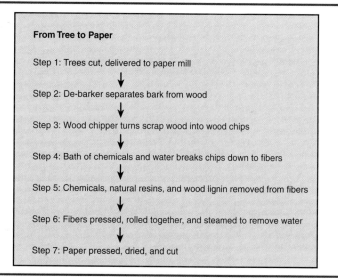

From Tree to Paper

Step 1: Trees cut, delivered to paper mill

Step 2: De-barker separates bark from wood

Step 3: Wood chipper turns scrap wood into wood chips

Step 4: Bath of chemicals and water breaks chips down to fibers

Step 5: Chemicals, natural resins, and wood lignin removed from fibers

Step 6: Fibers pressed, rolled together, and steamed to remove water

Step 7: Paper pressed, dried, and cut

INTERNET EXERCISE WH4.2

Visuals Assistance Many word processing software programs include functions to help you create graphs, tables, and charts. For links to quick tips on how to use these electronic tools to produce the visuals you need for a presentation, visit the *Foundations of Business Communication* Web site at <http://www.mhhe.com/djyoung>.

Once you have accessed the home page, select "Student Activities" and then click the Writer's Handbook, Part 4, link.

Tables   Though not as fancy as other types of displays, **tables** can compare and contrast complicated data very effectively. (See Figure WH4.9.) Tables have fewer limits than other types of displays: the numbers of columns and rows are limited only by the size of the paper and the print.

However, don't make a table too complicated, or you will lose your reader. Just as too many details in writing confuse the reader, too many details in a table may camouflage your important points. As you analyze data, pull out the important information and turn it into another type of display that highlights your main points or the concepts you wish to stress.

PRACTICE

1. **Instructions:** First, identify the best graphic format for displaying each item below. Then select a topic and use one of the graphic formats identified in this section to display the items.

   a. How you spend your time during the week.

   b. Your approximate monthly income over the last six months.

   c. Items on your budget and their percentage of total funds.

FIGURE WH4.8 | Organization Chart

An organization chart is a flowchart that maps the structure of a company, organization, or event. The normal layout places the highest-ranked person or position at the top level and subordinate positions in the levels underneath. Why do you think it is good practice to use the same-size boxes at each level of an organization chart?

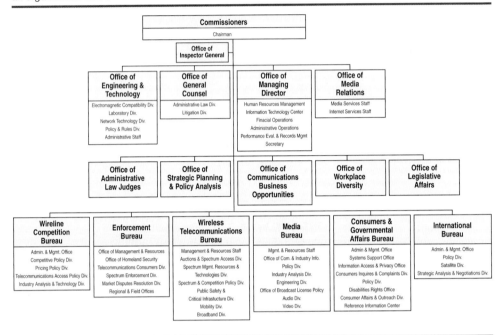

Source: Federal Communication Commission Web site <http://www.fcc.gov/fccorgchart.html>, accessed May 9, 2005.

FIGURE WH4.9 | Tables

Tables Talk: *Tables should have enough information to enable readers who look at them to interpret the findings without explanation.* What conclusions are you able to draw from this table?

Change in Real Hourly Wages for All Workers by Education, 1973-2001					
	Less Than High School	High School	Some College	College	Advanced Degree
Hourly Wage					
1973	$11.66	$13.36	$14.39	$19.49	$23.56
1979	11.62	13.04	13.94	18.27	22.31
1989	9.99	12.17	13.67	19.16	24.71
1995	9.04	11.95	13.37	19.84	26.18
2000	9.40	12.65	14.30	22.10	27.90
2001	9.50	12.81	14.60	22.58	28.14
Source: Mishel, Bernstein, and Boushey, *The State of Working America 2002/2003.*					

    d. How much time you spend watching TV (or speaking on the phone) on a daily basis in one week.

    e. How much time you spend studying on weeknights versus on weekends.

2. **Instructions:** Using the sample questionnaire shown in Figure WH4.2 on page 499, survey six to ten individuals of your choosing and display the results in charts. When you are done, visit the *Foundations of Business Communication* Web site and compare your charts with those of Professor Roger Conaway and his students at the University of Texas at Tyler, who developed the questionnaire to survey business executives, managers, and other experienced professionals.

SECTION B: CONCEPT CHECK

1. What is the main purpose of a line graph?
2. What is the main benefit of using tables to convey information?
3. Why is it important that the "pieces" of a pie chart add up to 100 percent?

■ SECTION C: CITING RESEARCH

Citation involves details, and many people find details challenging. However, citing your research is critical: citation not only validates your findings but also provides information so that others can find your source and read it in its entirety. In addition, if you keep track of information as you collect your research, citation becomes nothing more than applying rules for displaying sources, similar to applying grammar and punctuation rules.

There are four common systems for citation in business, social sciences, and humanities. Usually, the person or organization commissioning your work will specify the documentation system you are to use. You are likely to follow the system outlined in one of the following:

- *The Gregg Reference Manual* (GRM)
- *The Chicago Manual of Style* (CMS)
- The *Publication Manual of the American Psychological Association* (APA)
- The *MLA Handbook for Writers of Research Papers* (Modern Language Association—MLA)

But that's not the complete story. While *The Gregg Reference Manual* presents guidelines for business writing applications, *The Chicago Manual of Style* offers two sets of guidelines: one for fine arts and humanities (academic) applications, the other for social and physical science applications. If you go on to study in medicine or the physical sciences, you are likely to cite references in the Council of Biology Editors (CBE) style. Before you turn in any work, check to make sure you are using the correct referencing style.

Plagiarism

The word **plagiarism** is derived from the Latin word *plagiarius* meaning "a kidnapper" and literary thief.[4] The most blatant type of plagiarism is using another person's words verbatim without crediting that person. Another prevalent type of plagiarism is using another's ideas without crediting the source. In whatever form it takes, plagiarism is unethical.

To a busy, overworked, and insecure person, plagiarism may look like an easy way out, but it *never* is. Although advances in technology have made plagiarism easier to accomplish, they have also made it easier to detect. Teachers have a keen knack for knowing the difference

VOCABULARY BUILDERS

Latin Terms Apropos for Citations As you cite your various sources, you will come across a few Latin terms that you may use frequently. Here they are:

- *et al.:* ("and others") When listing only one author for a work with multiple authors, use *et al.* to indicate other names were omitted.
- *ibid.:* ("in the same place") When citing the same source consecutively, use *ibid.* directly under the citation that gives the author's name (or other identifying information).
- [*sic*]: ("so, thus, in this manner") The term *sic* is placed within brackets after an error in a quote to indicate that the error was made by the quoted author, not the current writer. (Brackets are also used around words added to another's quotation.)

between what their students write and what professionals write. A student's vocabulary, spelling, grammar, and syntax all become familiar through only one or two writing samples. In addition, teachers can identify plagiarism through online subscription services. With only a sentence or two, the real source can be immediately identified. Many instructors screen for plagiarism *before* they read a student's paper.

Do not take the "easy" and unethical way out. Develop your own ideas—that is the only way you will learn the important concepts and principles that research reveals. If you have any doubts about whether you should cite a source, go ahead and cite it.

Even if a plagiarist is *not* caught, plagiarism has serious personal consequences, and it might even be a sign of deep emotional problems. "Getting away" with something risky and unethical opens the door to repeating the behavior; a first bad choice leads more easily to another. Rather than learning concepts related to the selected topic, the plagiarist focuses all his or her energies in unproductive directions: plagiarism is emotionally draining, intellectually fruitless, and professionally devastating. As Ralph W. Tyler, a twentieth-century educator, once said: "The house you live in is your mind, your own integrity—don't worry about the rest."[5]

Keep your mind clear by following an ethical, professional course of action. Learn the details of your topic, and present them correctly. You may spend a bit more time on your work, but you will get the grade you deserve; your energy will be high and integrity intact, preparing you for success wherever you go.

EXPLORE

Are there times when it might be appropriate to "borrow" someone's words without acknowledging the person directly? Review the policy regarding plagiarism at your educational institution.

What to Credit

Not all information needs to be documented. For example, information that is considered common knowledge (something generally known to everyone) or facts available from a wide variety of sources need not be credited. According to *The New St. Martin's Handbook*, the following information needs to be documented:[6]

1. Direct quotations and paraphrases.
2. Facts that are not widely known or assertions that are arguable.
3. Judgments, opinions, and claims of others.
4. Statistics, charts, tables, and graphs from any source.
5. Help provided by friends, instructors, or others.

Let's first take a look at the two most common uses of formal credits, which are for direct quotations and for paraphrases, and the use of informal credits. Then we will examine how to assign legal claim to information in business.

Words and Ideas

Formal Credit:

- *Direct quotation:* For short quotes, use quotation marks; for quotes of four or more lines, set off the quotation by indenting the margins at least $1/2$ inch on either side. Just as quotes in exactly the right places can enhance your work, too many quotes or unnecessary ones distract your reader. Aim for flow, and be selective.

- *Paraphrase:* Paraphrasing is putting someone else's ideas in your own words. When you **paraphrase** and cite your source, you add credibility to your work. Making a few changes in word order, leaving out a word or two, or substituting similar words is not paraphrasing—it is plagiarizing.

Novice writers have the most difficulty with paraphrasing. Incorrectly paraphrased information usually ends up with a sentence structure similar to the original. With a bit of deconstructing, the original source can be identified. Such paraphrasing can be considered a form of "cut and paste" plagiarism. True paraphrasing occurs when you read material, digest it, and then write about the concepts in your own words. However, the idea still belongs to the original author and needs to be credited.

Informal Credit:

When sharing someone else's original ideas, mention the person's name in connection with the idea. In the business world, information isn't tracked as it is in the academic world. Most of your writing will involve solving current problems, conveying immediate information, and developing informal proposals for action. Thus, most business writing involves no citation (though, at times, citation can be a powerful way to persuade your reader or audience).

Generally, it's the idea and the action you take that counts, not the "who said what, where, and when." However, make it your practice to attach names to ideas even in informal settings: if you credit others for their ideas, you will gain trust and esteem among your colleagues.

Trademarks, Patents, Copyrights, and Incorporation   When business does keep track of ownership, it does so in a legal way. Businesses and individuals protect their intellectual property by registering names, ideas, designs, logos, slogans, and complete works with the federal government to obtain trademarks, patents, or copyrights; they also register with state governments for incorporation.

This type of branding protects ownership of information deemed integral to doing business. Not all information can be trademarked or patented. At times, a business can ensure legal control of a name by incorporating under that name. When you start your own business, meet with an attorney to learn your options, or go online and do your research. Whether you are copyrighting something you've written with the federal government or incorporating your company name with the state attorney general's office, you can do much of the legal legwork yourself, saving quite a bit of money in the process.

EXPLORE

How would you feel if you worked hard to develop survey results and then someone else used them without crediting you?

Working Bibliography

As you collect and use information that others have discovered or developed, citing your sources is a critical piece in verifying and validating your position. However, citing research can be challenging because it involves details.

Though each system of documentation has slight variations from the others, the references in each contain similar information. To save yourself time and frustration, compile a *working bibliography* (use note cards, a small notebook, or a special file on your computer) as you collect your research. Here is the kind of information you will need regardless of the style you use:

Books:

- Author
- Title
- Page number
- Publisher and location
- Year of publication

Periodicals:

- Author
- Title of article
- Title of periodical, volume and issue numbers
- Page numbers
- Date of publication

Web sites:

- Author (if known).
- Title of document.
- The uniform resource locator (URL) network address (including any path and file names), enclosed in angle brackets.

- Date the information was posted on the Web site (if available, this is often found at the bottom of the home page).

- Date on which you accessed the information.

- For a source that was previously published in print, the print publication date.

Because electronic sources are relatively new in the world of communication, the standards for documenting them are not yet fixed and are sometimes confusing. This situation is complicated because electronic sources are ever-changing; as a result, you must collect exact identifying information as you access each source (or you may never find it again). To save yourself time and energy, print out a hard copy or download the accessed information.

Your citations may be the last piece of information you compile for your work; however, keeping a working bibliography allows you to cite your sources properly and without undue frustration when you prepare your final product.

Some Common Elements

All citation systems require that sources be cited in the text where the material appears and be fully referenced elsewhere as footnotes, endnotes, or a bibliographic list. This cross-referencing provides the reader with complete information.

GRM	Footnotes, Endnotes, Textnotes, Bibliography
CMS	Footnotes, Endnotes, Bibliography
MLA	In-text Citation (author and page number enclosed in parentheses), Works Cited, Works Consulted
APA	In-text Citation, References

FIGURE WH4.10 | Works-Cited List

Source Citations: A works-cited list is the MLA format for documenting the sources you refer to in your project or research paper. It can include books, magazine articles, journal articles, media sources, and electronic sources. Entries should be arranged alphabetically by the author's last name; numbering is not necessary.

WORKS CITED

Colvin, Geoffrey. "Stop Blaming Bangalore for Our Jobs Problem." *Fortune* 19 Apr. 2004: 68.

Cooper, James C. "The Price of Efficiency." *BusinessWeek* 22 Mar. 2004: 38–42.

Dobbs, Lou. "The Jobless Recovery." *Money* Apr. 2004: 45–46.

Dolan, Kerry A., and Robyn Meredith. "The Outsourcing Debate: A Tale of Two Cities." *Forbes* 12 Apr. 2004: 94–102.

Gottheil, Fred M. *Principles of Economics.* Australia: South-Western, 2002.

Hagel III, John. "Offshoring Goes on the Offensive." *McKinsey Quarterly* 2 (2004): 82–92. *Business Source Elite.* EBSCOhost. 11 May 2004 <http://web1.epnet.com>.

Kleiman, Carol. "Outsourcing: A Matter of Many Sides." *Chicago Tribune* 11 Mar. 2004. 13 Apr. 2004 <http://infoweb.newsbank.com>.

Mintz, Steven. "The Ethical Dilemmas of Outsourcing." *CPA Journal* 74.3 (2004): 6–9. 13 Apr. 2004 <http://www.nysscpa.org/cpajournal/2004/304/ perspectives/nv1.htm>.

Nussbaum, Bruce. "Where Are the Jobs?" *BusinessWeek* 22 Mar. 2004: 36–37.

Rosencrance, Linda. "Offshore Moves Can Bring Benefits, but Not Without Pain." *Computerworld* 19 Apr. 2004. 11 May 2004 <http://www.computerworld.com/printthis/2004/0,4814,92291,00.html>.

Sowell, Thomas. "Outsourcing." 16 Mar. 2004. *Townhall.com* 6 Apr. 2004 <http://www.townhall.com/columnists/thomassowell/ts20040316.shtml>.

Source: Courtesy of Lynita Perry, DeVry University.

TABLE WH4.1 | Styles for In-Text Citations

	GRM (Business Style)	CMS (Scientific Style)	APA	MLA
Single author—not named in text	A closer examination of the increase in worker's productivity at the company reveals the reason for the change.[1]	A closer examination of the increase in worker's productivity at the company reveals the reason for the change (Hennessey 2004, 14).	A closer examination of the increase in worker's productivity at the company reveals the reason for the change (Hennessey, 2004).	A closer examination of the increase in worker's productivity at the company reveals the reason for the change (Hennesey 14).
Single author—identified in text	Carrera argues against strict enforcement of company Internet use policy.[2]	Carrera (2003, 45–96) argues against strict enforcement of company Internet use policy.	Carrera (2003) argues against strict enforcement of company Internet use policy.[2]	Carrera argues against strict enforcement of company Internet use policy (45–96).
More than one author—not named in text	To apply these concepts to business communications, emphasis has fallen on the role of context in business introductions, disagreements, and information processing.[3]	To apply these concepts to business communications, emphasis has fallen on the role of context in business introductions, disagreements, and information processing (Lambert, Elashmawi, and Zabron 2000, 87).	To apply these concepts in business communications, emphasis has fallen on the role of context in business introductions, disagreements, and information processing (Lambert, Elashmawi, & Zabron, 2000).	To apply these concepts to business communications, emphasis has fallen on the role of context in business introductions, disagreements, and information processing. (Lambert, Elashmawi, and Zabron 87).
Multiple sources	Multiple studies conducted by industry analysts have consistently supported the need for tougher standards.[4]	Studies (Gordon et al. 1998, 53) conducted by industry analysts have consistently supported the need for tougher standards.	Studies (Gordon & Knight, 1998; Ishan, 2000; Lornin, 2002) conducted by industry analysts have consistently supported the need for tougher standards.	Studies (Gordon & Knight 53, Ishan 20, Lornin) conducted by industry analysts have consistently supported the need for tougher standards.
More than one author—named in text	According to Giles and Fleming,[5] this is the perfect moment to establish a connection with the audience.	According to Giles and Fleming (2001, 72), this is the perfect moment to establish a connection with the audience.	According to Giles and Fleming (2001, p. 72), this is the perfect moment to establish a connection with the audience.	According to Giles and Fleming, this is the perfect moment to establish a connection with the audience (72).
Unidentified author	Employers view the Flex Time program as a viable method for boosting worker morale.[6]	Employers view the Flex Time program as a viable method for boosting worker morale. ("Flexing Your Horizons," 2004, 28)	Employers view the Flex Time program as a viable method for boosting worker morale ("Flexing Your Horizons," 2004).	Employers view the Flex Time program as a viable method for boosting worker morale ("Flexing" 28).
Direct quotation	Dr. Ralph Tyler found that to be true in the field of education; he stated, "It takes about 20 years . . . to apply in an average classroom what is discovered through research."[7]	Dr. Ralph Tyler found that to be true in the field of education; he stated, "It takes about 20 years . . . to apply in an average classroom what is discovered through research" (1964, 116).	Dr. Ralph Tyler found that to be true in the field of education; he stated, "It takes about 20 years . . . to apply in an average classroom what is discovered through research" (p. 116).	Dr. Ralph Tyler found that to be true in the field of education; he stated, "It takes about 20 years . . . to apply in an average classroom what is discovered through research" (116).

Source: GRM—William A. Sabin, *The Gregg Reference Manual*, 9th ed., Glencoe/McGraw-Hill, Westerville, OH, 2001; CMS—*The Chicago Manual of Style*, 14th rev. ed., University of Chicago Press, Chicago, 1993; APA—*Publication Manual of the American Psychological Association*, 5th ed., American Psychological Association, Washington, DC, 2001; MLA—Joseph Gibaldi, *MLA Handbook for Writers of Research Papers*, 6th ed., Modern Language Association of America, New York, 2003.

TABLE WH4.2 | Styles for End-of-Document References

	Bibliography (GRM)	Bibliography (CMS)	References List (APA)	Works-Cited List (MLA)
Annual report	"Annual Report 2002," AT&T Wireless Services, Redmond, 2004.	AT&T Wireless, *Annual Report 2002*, Redmond: AT&T Wireless Services, Inc., 2004.	AT&T Wireless. (2004). *Annual report 2002*. Redmond: AT&T Wireless Services, Inc.	AT&T Wireless, *Annual Report 2002*, Redmond: AT&T Wireless Services, Inc., 2004.
Book—single author	Csikszentmihalyi, Mihaly, *The Evolving Self: A Psychology for the Third Millennium*, HarperCollins Publishers, New York, 1993.	Csikszentmihalyi, Mihaly. *The Evolving Self, A Psychology for the Third Millennium*. New York: HarperCollins Publishers, Inc., 1993.	Csikszentmihalyi, M. (1993). *The evolving self, a psychology for the third millennium*. New York: HarperCollins Publishers, Inc.	Csikszentmihalyi, Mihaly. *The Evolving Self, A Psychology for the Third Millennium*. New York: HarperCollins Publishers, Inc., 1993.
Book—two authors	Howard, V. A., and J. H. Barton, *Thinking on Paper*, William Morrow and Company, Inc., New York, 1986.	Howard, V. A. and J. H. Barton. *Thinking on Paper*. New York: William Morrow and Company, Inc., 1986.	Howard, V. A. and Barton, J. H. (1986) Barton. *Thinking on paper*. New York: William Morrow and Company, Inc.	Howard, V. A. and J. H. Barton. *Thinking on Paper*. New York: William Morrow and Company, Inc., 1986.
Book—three or more authors	Gefvert, Constance, et al., *Keys to American English*, Harcourt Brace Jovanovich, Inc., New York, 1975.	Gefvert, C., R. Raspa, and A. Richards. *Keys to American English*, New York: Harcourt Brace Jovanovich, Inc., 1975.	Gefvert, C., Raspa, R., & Richards A. (1975). *Keys to american english*. New York: Harcourt Brace Jovanovich, Inc.	Gefvert, Constance, Richard Raspa, and Amy Richards. *Keys to American English*. New York: Harcourt Brace Jovanovich, Inc., 1975.
Book—organization as author and publisher	*Evaluation as Feedback and Guide*, Association for Supervision and Curriculum Development, NEA, Washington, D.C., 1967.	Association for Supervision and Curriculum Development, NEA. 1967. *Evaluation as Feedback and Guide*. Washington, D.C.:,1967.	*Evaluation as feedback and guide*. (1967). Washington, D.C.: Association for Supervision and Curriculum Development, NEA.	Association for Supervision and Curriculum Development, NEA. *Evaluation as Feedback and Guide*, Washington, D.C.: Association for Supervision and Curriculum Development, NEA, 1967.
Journal article	Belder, Craig. "Global Discourse: Finding the Rosetta Stone," *World Monthly*, Vol. 8, April 2004, pp. 45–73.	Belder, Craig. 2004. Global discourse: Finding the rosetta stone, *World Monthly*. 8: 45–73.	Belder, C. (2004). Global discourse: finding the rosetta stone. *World Monthly, 8*, 45–73.	Belder, Craig. "Global Discourse: Finding the Rosetta Stone." *World Monthly* 13 Apr. 2004: 45–73.
Magazine article	M'Salan, Bernadette, "Underneath the Bottom Line," *Fiscal Sense*, February 8, 2001, pp. 78–86.	M'Salan, Bernadette. 2001. Underneath the bottom line, *Fiscal Sense* 8: 78–86.	M'Salan, B. (2001, February 8). Underneath the bottom line. *Fiscal Sense, 24*, 78–86.	M'Salan, Bernadette. "Underneath the Bottom Line." *Fiscal Sense*, 24, Feb. 2001: 78–86.
Newspaper article—unsigned	"Business Finding Ways to Reach New Customers," *Sun Daily*, November 3, 2004, p. C12, col. 4.	Do not include in Bibliography. Citation is made in-text: "An article titled 'Business Finding Ways to Reach New Customers' in the *Sun Daily*, 3 November 2004 describes the current . . ."	Business finding ways to reach new customers. (2004, November 14). *Sun Daily*, p. C12.	"Business Finding Ways to Reach New Customers." *Sun Daily*. 3 Nov. 2004: C12.
Reference work article	"Global Competition," *Workplace Language Companion*, 5th ed., 2004.	Do not include in Bibliography. Citation is made in-text: "The fifth edition of the *Workplace Language Companion* describes global competition as . . .	Global competition. (2004). In *The workplace language companion* (pp 234–236). New York, NY: Hernan.	"Global competition," *Workplace Language Companion*, 5th ed. New York: Hernan Press, 2004.

TABLE WH4.2 | Styles for End-of-Document References (*Continued*)

	Bibliography (GRM)	Bibliography (CMS)	References List (APA)	Works-Cited List (MLA)
Government document	National Institute for Occupational Safety and Health, *Preventing Lead Poisoning in Construction Workers,* DHHS Publication 91-116A, U.S. Government Printing Office, Washington, D.C., 1992.	National Institute for Occupational Safety and Health. 1992. *Preventing lead poisoning in construction workers.* Washington, DC: U.S. Government Printing Office, Washington. DHHS Publication No. 91-116A.	National Institute for Occupational Safety and Health. (1992). *Preventing lead poisoning in construction workers* (DHHS Publication No. 91-116A). Washington, DC: U.S. Government Printing Office.	National Institute for Occupational Safety and Health. *Preventing Lead Poisoning in Construction Workers.* DHHS Publication No. 91-116A. Washington, DC: GPO, 1992.
Interview	Olinger, Jared, personal interview, January 12, 2004.	Olinger, Jared. 2004. Interview. [12 Jan. 2004].	Olinger, J. (2004, Jan). Personal interview.	Olinger, Jared. Personal interview. 12 Jan 2004.
Paper presented at a meeting	Young, Dona, "Kill the Outline," paper presented at National Business Writer's Association meeting, Seattle, August 28, 2003.	Young, Dona. 2003. *Kill the outline.* Seattle, WA: National Business Writer's Association. Paper presented 28 August 2003.	Young, D. (2004, August). Kill the outline. Paper presented at the meeting of the National Business Writer's Association, Seattle, WA.	Young, Dona. *Kill the Outline.* Paper presented at the meeting of the National Business Writer's Association, Seattle, WA, 28 Aug. 2003.
Television/radio broadcast	Crane, Yvonne (Producer), *The KTBR News Break,* Orange Broadcasting Group, Chicago, March 22, 2004.	Crane, Yvonne (Producer). 22 March 2004. *The KTBR News Break,* Chicago: Orange Broadcasting Group.	Crane, Y. (Producer). (2004, March). *The KTBR News Break.* Chicago: Orange Broadcasting Group.	Crane, Yvonne (Producer), *The KTBR News Break.* Chicago: Orange Broadcasting Group, 22 Mar. 2004.
CD-ROM article	Bair, Jolan, "Good Writing," *Quality Business Writer's Guide* (CD-ROM), Quality, Inc., Livonia, Mich., 2002.	Bair, Jolan. 2002. "Good writing," Livonia, MI: Quality, Inc. *Quality Business Writer's Guide,* CD-ROM.	Bair, J. (2002). *Good writing.* Livonia, MI: Quality, Inc. Retrieved from Quality database (*Quality Business Writer's Guide,* CD-ROM).	Bair, Jolan. "Good Writing." *Quality Business Writer's Guide.* CD-ROM. Livonia, MI: Quality, Inc., 2002.
World Wide Web page	Montrae, Diedre K., "Exler Lobbies for New Contract," June 3, 2003, <http://www.exlertemp.com/UPDATE/2003.html>, accessed on July 12, 2003.	Montrae, Diedre K. 2003. *Exler lobbies for new contract* [online]. Houston: Exler Inc. 2003 [cited 12 July 2003]. Available from the World Wide Web: http://www.exlertemp.com/UPDATE/2003.html	Montrae, D. K. (2003, June 3). Exler lobbies for new contract. Houston: Exler. Retrieved July 12, 2003 from the World Wide Web: http://www.exlertemp.com/UPDATE/2003.html	Montrae, Diedre K. "Exler Lobbies for New Contract," *Exler Inc. Home Page,* 3 June 2003. 12 July 2003. <http://www.exlertemp.com/UPDATE/2003.html>.
Online database article	"Ranking the Healthcare Providers," <http://www.healthupdate.org/statistics.gov/ind.lib/tab-8315.html>, accessed on January 14, 2002.	*Ranking the Healthcare Providers.* 2002. In Health Update [database online]. Concord: Health Update [cited January 14, 2002]. Available from the World Wide Web: (http://www.healthupdate.org/statistics.gov/ind.lib/tab-8315.html)	Ranking the Healthcare Providers. (n.d.). Retrieved January 14, 2002, from Health Update database on the World Wide Web: http://www.healthupdate.org/statistics.gov/ind.lib-8315.html.	"Ranking the Healthcare Providers," *Health Update.* n.d. 14 January 2002. <http://www.healthupdate.org/statistics.gov/ind.lib/tab-8315.html>.
E-mail	Veljovich, John R. (jrveljo@elegy.net), "Response to Administrative Advisory," e-mail message, November 23, 2004.	Veljovich, John R. 2004. "Response to Administrative Advisory." Personal e-mail [cited November 24, 2004].	Do not include in Reference list. Citation is made in-text: "J. R. Veljovich (personal communication, November 23, 2004) suggests that . . . "	Veljovich, John R. <jrveljo@elegy.net> "Response to Administrative Advisory" Personal e-mail. 23 Nov. 2004. 24 November 2004.
Electronic discussion message (including Listservs and newsgroups)	Kabee, Ellen <lkabee@orcus.com>, "Stepping Up to the Plate," October 24, 2002, <http://chats.orcus.com/group/personnel/message/23>, accessed on December 9, 2004.	Kabee, E. 2002. "Stepping Up to the Plate," Online posting [December 9, 2002]. Available from the World Wide Web: http://chats.orcus.com/group/personnel/message/23.	Kabee, E. (2004, October 24). Stepping Up to the Plate. Message posted to http://chats.orcus.com/group/personnel/message/23	Kabee, Ellen. <lkabee@orcus.com> "Stepping Up To the Plate." Online posting. 24 Oct. 2002. 9 Dec. 2004. <http://chats.orcus.com/group/personnel/message/23>.

Source: GRM—William A. Sabin, *The Gregg Reference Manual,* 9th ed., Glencoe/McGraw-Hill, Westerville, OH, 2001; CMS—*The Chicago Manual of Style,* 14th rev. ed., University of Chicago Press, Chicago, 1993; APA—*Publication Manual of the American Psychological Association,* 5th ed., American Psychological Association, Washington, DC, 2001; MLA—Joseph Gibaldi, *MLA Handbook for Writers of Research Papers,* 6th ed., Modern Language Association of America, New York, 2003.

Textnotes are used in a report or manuscript with only a few source references. If a bibliography is used, textnotes include the author's last name and the appropriate page number in parentheses. Footnote information is placed at the bottom of the page. Endnotes are displayed on a separate page at the end of each chapter or the end of the work. A raised number (superscript) is placed at the end of the sentence in which the reference occurs.

For all citation methods, you may cite one source several times in your manuscript (showing that you are paraphrasing, quoting, or drawing ideas from its content in several places). However, you need to include a full reference note for the source (author, title, publisher, and so on) only one time in your **bibliography, works-cited list,** or **references list.**

In a bibliography or references list, you can include sources that you consult but do not actually cite in your work. Note that if you are using the MLA system, you list noncited sources in a separate works-consulted list. Only include significant noncited sources on this list.

Table WH4.1, on page 513, compares the GRM, CMS, APA, and MLA styles for in-text citations. Table WH4.2, on pages 514–515, compares three styles of end-of-document references: a bibliography (used in CMS and GRM styles), a references list (APA style), and a works-cited list (MLA style).

SECTION C: CONCEPT CHECK

1. Define plagiarism.
2. What are the four basic systems for citations?
3. Name resources to which you can turn for reliable, credible information.

SUMMARY

For some people, research is the most exciting aspect of their work and life. You may or may not have reached that point; whatever your feelings about research, you have to admit that it adds direction and power to the way you make decisions.

The real purpose of research is that it be used in making decisions. Make it your quest to use action research to reach a clear and accurate understanding of your subject: survey your clients to find out what they need from you; ask your coworkers how you can support them. With minimal effort, you can glean accurate information instead of relying on an egocentric assumption. By using action research, you focus on identifying relevant questions that keep a situation alive rather than relying on neat and tidy answers that soothe the emotions but offer little substance.

When you come across a piece of research about which you have doubts or concerns, don't take the research at face value; look beneath the surface, and examine the limits of the research. On the other hand, when you find a piece of clean, accurate research, glean insight from it and use it in making decisions that lead to progress. You may someday discover that you have a passion for research—and that's a good path to follow. The world can use more incurable researchers!

As a philosopher once said, "Insanity is repeating the same behavior over and over again but expecting a different outcome each time." By applying the results of research, a person is more able to direct change and produce effective results. Good research applied in the right way not only enriches life but also helps alleviate human suffering.

WRITER'S HANDBOOK, PART 4 CHECKLIST

___ Have you started your working bibliography?
___ Have you taken precautions to guard against bias?
___ Have you considered including your own qualitative research, such as surveys, focus groups, or interviews?

___ Have you checked less known sources with your local librarian to ensure their credibility?

___ Have you identified data that could best be displayed in a chart, graph, or table?

___ Are your most important points readily visible and easily discernible?

___ Have you confirmed with your instructor the system of documentation that you should use (GRM, CMS, APA, or MLA)?

___ Have you followed the correct style of using quotation marks for short quotes and displaying longer ones?

___ Is your bibliography complete?

END-OF-CHAPTER ACTIVITIES

ACTIVITY 1: QUANTITATIVE VERSUS QUALITATIVE RESEARCH

Instructions: Is research important? How does research impact your life or your studies? Whether you realize it or not, research is all around you. From the commercials that run during your favorite TV show to the polls that track political races, the processes and products of research fill our daily lives. What type of research are you more exposed to, qualitative or quantitative? Identify two recent encounters with research, and describe the type of research as well as the purpose and results of each.

ACTIVITY 2: DEVELOPING A SURVEY

Situation A: You are working in customer service for a large retail store. Your manager comes to you to find out the kinds of problems customers are having. It seems your manager wants detailed information and numbers that support it.

Situation B: You recently got a job at a marketing research firm. Your manager wants to do some research on television habits for a meeting next week. With not enough time to do a formal research study, your manager asks you to design a short survey.

Instructions: For one of the situations above, develop a survey that you can give to customers or TV viewers. Think about these questions as you create your survey:

1. How will you identify the kinds of problems you are trying to solve?

2. What kinds of questions and categories will you use on your survey?

3. Will you include both open and closed questions?

4. Will you include a Likert scale or other types of rating scales?

5. Will you ask for demographic data (for example, age, income, race, or other characteristics)?

ACTIVITY 3: DISPLAYING RESEARCH THROUGH GRAPHICS

Instructions: Administer the survey you developed in Activity 2 to ten people. (If you chose situation A, tell respondents to think of the last time they went to a customer service desk or complained to a sales representative.)

Tally the results from your survey. What does your research reveal? Construct a graphic to illustrate at least one aspect of your results.

ACTIVITY 4: ONLINE AND PRINTED-MATERIAL RESEARCH

1. **Instructions:** During the course of your studies, you have used both online and print research extensively. Write a short memo describing the advantages and disadvantages of each. For each type, give at least three search tips. (For example, for online research, you can use search engines such as Google.com; for print research, you can use the *Index to Periodical Literature*.) Be specific, and write something you could use to explain research to a beginner. In your paper, include a section entitled "Tips for Determining Online Site Credibility."

2. **Instructions:** Assume you are given a topic to write about, such as "teamwork." How would you research the topic in preparation for writing a two- to three-page paper? On which type of resource would you rely more heavily, online or print? Give two or three tips for finding information online as well as finding books or journal articles.

ACTIVITY 5: GRM, CMS, APA, AND MLA SYSTEMS

Instructions: For the following list of references, show the bibliographic reference in your preferred style.

1. *A Mind at a Time* was written by Mel Levine, MD. It was published by Simon & Schuster in New York during 2002.

   _____
   _____
   _____
   _____

2. Rosamund Stone Zander and Benjamin Zander wrote *The Art of Possibility,* which was published by Harvard Business School Press, Boston, Massachusetts, in 2000.

   _____
   _____
   _____
   _____
   _____
   _____
   _____

3. The *Business Style Handbook* was published by McGraw-Hill, Chicago, in 2002. The authors are Helen Cunningham and Brenda Greene.

   _____
   _____
   _____
   _____
   _____
   _____
   _____
   _____

ACTIVITY 6: APPLYING LATIN TERMS TO ENDNOTES

Instructions: The list below presents one paper's footnotes in *The Chicago Manual of Style* format. Each footnote is given in full; apply Latin terms to cite the information correctly.

1. Fred N. Kerlinger, *Behavioral Research: A Conceptual Approach,* Holt, Rinehart and Winston, Inc., New York, 1979, page 22.

   _____

2. Fred N. Kerlinger, *Behavioral Research: A Conceptual Approach,* Holt, Rinehart and Winston, Inc., New York, 1979, page 25.

   _____

3. Fred N. Kerlinger, *Foundations of Behavioral Research,* 2nd Edition, Holt, Rinehart and Winston, Inc., New York, 1973, page 32.

   _____

4. L. R. Gay and Peter Airasian, *Educational Research, Competencies for Analysis and Applications,* 7th Edition, Pearson Education, Inc., New Jersey, 2003, page 127.

   _____

5. Fred N. Kerlinger, *Foundations of Behavioral Research,* 2nd Edition, Holt, Rinehart and Winston, Inc., New York, 1973, page 35.

   _____

6. L. R. Gay and Peter Airasian, *Educational Research, Competencies for Analysis and Applications,* 7th Edition, Pearson Education, Inc., New Jersey, 2003, page 27.

   _____

ACTIVITY 7: PLAGIARISM

Instructions: Respond in writing to the following questions. Refer to your college catalog for more information.

1. Describe plagiarism in your own words.
2. How would your instructor describe plagiarism?
3. What is the penalty in your class for plagiarism?
4. What is the penalty in other classes for plagiarism?
5. What is your college's policy on plagiarism?

ACTIVITY 8: THE PRACTICAL SIDE OF ACTION RESEARCH

Background: The idea of conducting research may be daunting at first, but you are already doing it naturally in your daily life. For instance, assume you need a haircut and your former hairstylist has recently closed shop. You may start your research by asking a few people whose cut and style look good which hairstylists they go to. Then you may narrow your choice according to restrictions of price and location.

Instructions: Identify a practical question that you want to solve or a change that you want to make in your personal or professional life. Now break it down into the following steps:

1. What is the problem you want to solve?

2. How can you state it in a question so that you can do informal research?

3. What data do you need to collect?

4. What sources can you use?

5. Are your sources credible? How do you know your sources are credible?

6. What conclusions are you able to draw from your data and information?

7. Do your conclusions represent complete and final answers?

REFERENCES

1. L. R. Gay and Peter Airasian, *Educational Research: Competencies for Analysis and Applications,* Merrill Prentice Hall, Upper Saddle River, NJ, 2003, pp. 265–271.

2. Adapted with permission from "How to Learn about a Culture" by Michael C. Mercil.

3. Bill Dunlap, CEO Global Reach, "Why Your Company Should Go Global Now More Than Ever," unpublished article, <http://glreach.com/eng/ed/art/rep-eur23.php3>.

4. Lynn Quitman Troyka, *Simon and Schuster Handbook for Writers,* 6th ed., Prentice Hall, Upper Saddle River, NJ, 2002, p. 481.

5. Dona Young, "General Education: Developing a Common Understanding," master's paper, The University of Chicago, 1988; quoted from interview by Dona Young with Ralph W. Tyler, Chicago, August 4, 1986.

6. Andrea Lundsford and Robert Connors, *The New St. Martin's Handbook,* Bedford/St. Martin's, Boston, 2001, pp. 495–497.

KEY FOR LEARNING INVENTORY

1.	T	6.	F
2.	T	7.	T
3.	T	8.	F
4.	T	9.	T
5.	T	10.	F

A

abstract   A short, written summary that gives an overview of a report, study, or proposal; usually associated with scientific studies but equivalent to an executive summary or a synopsis.

academic writing   A formal style of writing in which a thesis statement is used to develop the introduction, body, and conclusion; characterizes research papers, arguments, essays, and creative writing. Compare **business writing.**

accent   The unique language pronunciation that characterizes persons in a particular group or geographic region; can be a barrier to communication.

acronym   An abbreviation pronounced as a word (for example, *AIDS, SADD*).

action plan   A detailed plan for achieving a goal; includes action steps, deadlines for completing them, and a list of any obstacles and ways to overcome them.

action research   A research method for collecting information to use in an immediate environment: identify problem, gather information, analyze data, and take action to rectify problem.

action step   In an action plan, an identified task along with who will complete it and when it is due.

action verb   A verb that transfers action from a subject to an object; in English, all verbs except 11 linking verbs. See also **state-of-being verb.**

active listening   A listening skill that involves focusing on the meaning, intent, and feelings of the person who is speaking to gain a clear understanding of the message.

active voice   As applied to verbs, a term indicating that the subject performs the action of the verb (for example, "Bob *wrote* the report"). Compare **passive voice.**

adjective   A word that modifies a noun or pronoun.

adverbial conjunction   A word or phrase (for example, *however, therefore, thus*) that serves as a transition between sentences or paragraphs; shows the relationship between ideas and plays a significant role in punctuation.

agenda   A planning tool for a meeting that lists the topics to be discussed; sometimes includes the amount of time for each topic and the roles of participants.

AIDA (attention, interest, desire, action) model   A traditional approach for formatting persuasive messages: grab reader's *attention,* develop reader's *interest,* explain benefits for reader *(desire),* enable reader to contact writer *(action).*

antecedent   The word or words to which a pronoun refers.

application letter   See **cover letter (2).**

appositive   A restatement; a brief explanation that identifies the noun or pronoun preceding it. See also **essential appositive.**

attitude   A person's way of thinking that underlies his or her behavior and feelings; part of the unobservable context in which communication is held.

authenticity   The quality of displaying genuine emotions and values; in global communications, a tool for getting past ethnocentric thinking.

authoritative leadership style   Top-down leadership, in which decisions are made by leaders, with team members carrying out assigned tasks in prescribed ways. Also called *autocratic* or *heroic* leadership.

autocratic leadership style   See **authoritative leadership style.**

auxiliary (verb)   A verb (such as any form of *be, have, do*) that is used with another verb to convey a different meaning or tense. Also called *helper* verb.

B

background thinking   A person's thoughts about how he or she arrived at a conclusion or how readers will interpret that conclusion; a type of meta-discourse that should be eliminated from writing.

backstabbing   Talking about a person in a negative, distorted way behind his or her back to derail the person's success; similar to "backbiting."

bar chart   A graphics tool that displays information in vertical or horizontal bars; enables the reader to compare and contrast different items.

base form   The "original" state of a verb. See also **infinitive.**

benefit   The value, both tangible and intangible, that a proposal for an idea, product, or service will produce for a client; derived from evidence.

bibliography   A comprehensive list of the sources cited in a document (and sometimes of sources consulted but not cited); follows a standard format, including author, title of work, and publication or other identifying data for each work.

bicultural   Capable of functioning like a native in more than one culture.

bidialectual   Fluid in speaking both Edited American English and a community dialect.

bilingual   Capable of speaking two languages.

block style   A formal letter style in which all lines start at the left margin; the standard format for most business letters. Also called *full-block style.*

body   The part of correspondence that contains the message; consists of one or more paragraphs giving information, explanation, and evidence.

body language   The "language" of eye contact, gestures, and other body movements; conveys, often unintentionally, a message that contributes to the meaning of verbal and nonverbal communication.

business letter   A formal tool used to communicate with outside clients; formatted in traditional styles and structured to connect with the reader, tell facts, and state action to be taken.

business writing   A direct style of writing in which context is used to define the purpose of the message; characterizes letters, memos, and e-mail that get to the point quickly. Key components are connect with reader, relate main points, and clarify action to be taken. Compare **academic writing.** See also **professional writing.**

C

captive team   A team in which the members have an ethical obligation to fulfill their roles, whether they want to or not.

career portfolio   A collection of relevant job search information and documents, including a résumé, sample cover and contact letters, and network contacts, among other items.

case   The function a pronoun performs in a sentence, such as subjective (or nominative), objective, possessive, and reflexive.

CAT (connect-act-tell) strategy   In e-mail messages, a structural approach that connects with the reader, states desired action, and then gives supportive information.

centered heading   In documents, a main heading that is centered between the margins to indicate a major break in content; typed in all-caps or bold cap and lowercase letters, followed by 1 blank line before the text below. Also called *section heading.*

central idea   A thesis statement that expresses the main point of a paper.

chronological format   For résumés, a traditional structure that emphasizes job history; lists education, positions, and accomplishments in order, starting with the most recent and working backward in order of occurrence.

clarity   Clearness and simplicity.

cliché   A fixed or stereotyped expression that has lost its significance through frequent repetition.

clip art   Public domain artwork that can be used in PowerPoint presentations or on Web sites without paying a fee or providing a credit for the illustrator.

closing   (1) The last paragraph of a letter, stating action the recipient needs to take; (2) a complimentary sign-off (for example, for letters, *Sincerely* or *Sincerely yours;* for e-mail, *Thanks* or *Regards*).

coherent   A term referring to a paragraph that presents a logical flow of ideas, developing a topic in a consistent, rational way. One idea leads to another.

cohesive   A term referring to a paragraph that presents one main topic along with details to support that topic, demonstrating connectedness among the ideas it contains. All the ideas adhere together for a common purpose.

collaborative approach   See **participative leadership style.**

collaborative leadership style   See **participative leadership style.**

collectivist thinking   A viewpoint that places priority on the way the cultural group thinks as compared to the individual's perspective. Compare **individualistic thinking.**

colloquial   Informal; in language, any conversational pattern that includes slang and nonstandard English. Also called *idiomatic.*

colloquialism   A saying that is not to be taken literally; expresses an idea unique to a specific time and location (for example, "That dog can't hunt").

colon   A traditional mark of punctuation; alerts the reader that information will follow that explains or illuminates the information that preceded it.

comma splice   A grammatical error in which two independent clauses are joined with only a comma, causing a run-on sentence.

communication cycles   The cyclical sending and receiving of messages until those involved reach an understanding; involves speaking to convey meaning and listening to understand.

community dialect (CD)   Any language pattern that differs from Edited American English (Standard English); informally known as "home talk" or "talkin' country." Most Americans speak a community dialect with family and friends.

comparative form   The form of an adjective that is used when two items are compared; for regular adjectives, formed by adding the suffix *er* or by using *more* or *less* before the adjective.

composing   Creating, inventing, discovering; in writing, planning or mapping a message and drafting ideas on a page.

consecutive interpretation   Interpretation in which the interpreter interprets chunks of speech, no more than 3 minutes long, each time the speaker has finished a sentence or a paragraph.

consensus   The point at which group members are in general agreement, at least to some degree, on an issue.

constructive feedback   An appraisal that identifies the problem, offers a possible solution, and opens a dialogue among those involved. Compare **negative feedback.**

contact letter   In networking, a letter that introduces oneself to a contact and asks for assistance with one's job search; should be personalized and present a mutual objective for sender and receiver.

context   The entirety of circumstances and situations that influence a message or communication; the amount of innate and largely unconscious understanding a person brings to a particular communication setting.

coordinating conjunction   A word that joins items of equal grammatical structure, such as independent clauses or items in a series. Such words are *and, but, or, nor, for, yet, so.*

correlative conjunction   A pair of conjunctions (for example, *not only . . . but also*) that compares or contrasts ideas. The information after each conjunction must be presented in the same grammatical form (parallel construction).

courteous request   In written communications, a question that prompts the recipient to act rather than respond in words; ends with a period rather than a question mark.

cover letter   (1) Enclosed with a proposal, a letter that summarizes key points in the proposal; (2) enclosed with a résumé, a letter that summarizes the sender's interest in a company, highlights his or her accomplishments, and requests an interview. Also called *application letter.*

credibility   Believability; equates to trust, a critical element in all relationships.

critic's block   A barrier to writing that is caused by being too critical of one's ability to write well or improve writing skills.

cultural informant (CI)   A credible, qualified resource person who can filter information about a given group or culture and provide insight into what is considered appropriate within the group or culture.

culture   The pattern of beliefs and social traits within a group; often associated with the way people behave, speak, and dress. Cultures characterize nations, ethnic groups, regions, industries, companies, families, religions, and even small groups.

curriculum vitae (CV)   A detailed chronological record of a person's professional and academic credentials, listing job history, fields of study, publications, and awards; an alternative to a résumé in the global job market.

cycles of communication   See **communication cycles.**

D

dash   A substitute for the comma, semicolon, period, or colon, used to emphasize the information that follows it; appropriate in both formal and informal documents.

dependent clause   A group of words that has a subject and verb but does not express a complete thought; cannot stand alone as a sentence.

direct address   The use of a person's name or title in addressing the person directly.

direct approach   In written communications, a style that gets right to the point; conveys the purpose and main point in the first paragraph, followed by supporting information or details. Compare **indirect approach.**

direct style   A low-context form of communication in which the words are more important than the situation; in general, characteristic of Americans. Compare **indirect style.**

drafting   Creating a preliminary piece of writing.

E

Edited American English (EAE)   The type of written and spoken language that, for the most part, follows the standard rules of English usage; used by formal media programs (such as newscasts) and academia. Another term for EAE is Standard American English or Standard English.

editing   Improving the flow of writing by changing the wording and cutting unnecessary words to make the writing more concise and readable.

editing strategy   An approach to editing that focuses on turning passive, wordy writing into simple, clear, and concise writing.

ellipsis marks   Three spaced periods used to indicate the omission of a word or words from a quotation. (Add a fourth period if the ellipsis [plural, *ellipses*] occurs at the end of a sentence.)

e-mail   Electronic mail, the most widely used form of written communication; in business, used to communicate with colleagues in-house (on an *intranet*) or with associates outside the company (on the *Internet*).

e-memo   An electronic memo sent on a company's intranet to its own employees; formatted like a traditional memo created by means of a template.

emphatic   An adjective or adverb used to place emphasis on the word it describes; can detract from the message rather than emphasize it, so should be used sparingly (for example, *very, really, incredible*).

empty information   Information that adds nothing of value for your reader.

enunciation   Pronunciation.

e-résumé   A résumé specifically formatted for electronic transmittal; at the top, summarizes work skills and experience in keywords that are scanned by employers for matches with their needs.

essential appositive   A word or phrase that identifies a particular person or thing in a sentence where the identity would not be clear without the appositive; should *not* be set off with commas.

essential element   Any part of a sentence that cannot be removed without compromising meaning or structure; should *not* be set off with commas. Also called *restrictive element.*

evaluation   A subjective appraisal based on labels and vague terms (for example, "*excellent* work," "the *worst* letter") that summarizes with a rating or ranking rather than offering a constructive description. Compare **feedback.**

evaluator   In a team, a person who assesses the group's progress and proposes changes the group could make to become more effective.

evidence   Proof of an assertion or research finding; typically consists of objective data, such as facts and figures, thereby eliminating bias.

exclamation point   A mark of punctuation used to indicate surprise or excitement; can be used after a word, phrase, or complete sentence. (Use exclamation points sparingly.)

executive summary   A short, written synopsis that gives an overview of a report, study, or proposal; used in business writing, but equivalent to an abstract or a synopsis.

expletive form   In a sentence, a word or phrase at the beginning that indicates something later in the sentence but adds nothing to the meaning (for example, "It is" or "There are").

explicit   Distinct and clear; a characteristic of language whose meaning is easily understood and does not depend on the context.

external due date   A project completion date specified by the person or agency commissioning the project. Compare **internal due date.**

F

face   (1) In communication, personal dignity, consisting of one's internal qualities, status, good name, and good character; (2) in formatting, the style of type, or type font (for example, Times, Courier, or Arial). See also **serif** and **sans serif.**

facilitator   In meetings, the person who leads the discussion and, if feasible, creates an agenda.

fact sheet   A one-page document that presents all the pertinent details about a product or service.

fax   A copy of a document that is sent via phone lines to a fax machine or computer. (The term is derived from *facsimile,* meaning "a copy.")

feasibility report   An abbreviated form of written proposal, used primarily within a company.

feedback   An objective appraisal based on specific details that offers a constructive description rather than a vague summary. Compare **evaluation.** See also **constructive feedback, objective feedback.**

filler   An empty word that adds no value to a message (for example, *just, like*).

filter   In communication, a screen through which a person perceives others and the world; creates subjective viewpoints that can hinder communication.

flowchart   A graphic representation of information that depicts progression through a procedure or system.

fluency   In speech, a smooth flow of words and the lack of distracting vocal habits.

focus group   A research tool in which a small group of people meet and express opinions related to the topic being studied; often used as a representative sample of a larger population.

focused speaking   An approach to public speaking in which the speaker keeps his or her attention on the topic and the audience, not on himself or herself.

focused writing   A writing technique that involves writing about a topic for 10 to 20 minutes simply to put ideas on the page, without expecting to produce usable material.

font   The style of type face, such as Times or Arial. Fonts number in the hundreds, and each word processing program includes its own series of fonts. See also **serif** and **sans serif.**

forced writing   A writing technique that involves writing about a topic for 10 to 20 minutes with the expectation of producing material that can be used.

formal persuasion   The activity of influencing clients and coworkers through proposals and presentations developed for specific objectives. Compare **informal persuasion.**

formal proposal   A detailed written analysis of a problem and how it will be addressed, including the resources and credentials of those involved. Document format and items to include vary from organization to organization.

format   The overall appearance of a document, including placement of the entire text and of individual parts (for example, dateline and salutation) and the use of special features and white space.

fragment   A phrase or dependent clause that is incorrectly punctuated as a complete sentence.

freewriting   A writing technique that involves writing one's thoughts freely, in a "stream of consciousness," to release feelings and stress and gain insight.

functional format   For résumés, a nontraditional structure that highlights experience and accomplishments in each area of expertise; lists skills and education before work experience.

fused sentence   A grammatical error in which two independent clauses are connected without a comma or conjunction.

G

gender bias   In writing, the exclusion of one gender by using only masculine *or* feminine pronouns in contexts that apply to both genders. Plural pronouns and the phrase *he or she* are gender-neutral.

generalization   According to Alfred North Whitehead, the most advanced stage of learning, in which the learner applies concepts and skills in creative ways to solve problems.

gerund   The "ing" form of a verb (for example, *going, seeing, following*); functions as a noun.

gerund phrase   A gerund followed by a preposition, noun, and any modifiers (for example, *going to the meeting, being on time*); functions as a noun.

global   In business, a term referring to a company that combines local know-how with a multinational presence, leveraging the opportunities presented by different world regions and their markets in a systematic way.

global communication   Communication across language and cultural borders.

global diversity   The variety of language and cultural patterns in the world. Every culture has its own unique customs, ways of thinking, and ways of conducting business.

goal   A broad statement of an intended achievement. Compare **objective.**

grammatical subject   A subject that generally precedes the verb but may or may not be the actor or agent that performs the action of the verb; in an active-voice sentence, the same as the real subject. Compare **real subject.**

groupthink   A phenomenon in which everyone in a group "goes along" just to "get along," agreeing with decisions regardless of their quality; occurs when a need for approval (or a fear of disapproval) exists among members.

growing edge   An area in which a person needs more expertise or experience. Also called *weakness.*

H

hard copy   A paper copy of a document. Compare **soft copy.**

hedge   A word or phrase that qualifies a statement by making it less than universal (for example, *usually, sort of*); can weaken the message, so should be used sparingly.

helper (verb)   See **auxiliary.**

heroic approach   See **authoritative leadership style.**

heroic leadership style   See **authoritative leadership style.**

hierarchy of needs   Maslow's classification of human needs on the basis of their importance for survival: physiological, safety, social ties, esteem, and self-actualization. The basic needs must be adequately filled before a person will seek to attain higher needs.

highly formal (writing)   A style of writing characterized by use of the passive voice, complicated language, abstract references, no contractions, and Latin abbreviations.

hypothesis   A theory or testable explanation for a phenomenon or an event.

I

idiolect   An individual's unique language pattern; differs from others' patterns on the basis of grammar, word use, and pronunciation.

idiomatic   See **colloquial.**

implicit   Implied or inferred; a characteristic of language whose meaning is not expressed entirely in words and depends also on the context of the communication.

independent clause   A clause that has a subject and verb and expresses a complete thought; can stand alone as a sentence.

indirect approach   In written communications, a style that presents details and explanations before getting to the main point; often used in messages that convey bad or unwelcome news. Compare **direct approach.**

indirect style   A high-context communication style in which the situation is highly important and the words alone may not convey the meaning of the communication. Compare **direct style.**

individualistic thinking   A viewpoint that places priority on the individual's perspective rather than the cultural group's way of thinking. Compare **collectivistic thinking.**

infinitive   The base form of a verb preceded by *to* (for example, *to see, to be, to speak*); functions as a noun, adjective, or adverb.

infinitive phrase   An infinitive along with an object and any modifiers (for example, *to go to the store, to see the latest book reviews*); functions as a noun, adjective, or adverb.

informal persuasion   The everyday activity of influencing coworkers and clients through interaction and correspondence; builds credibility and trust among those involved. Compare **formal persuasion.**

informal speech   The language pattern used for speaking in everyday situations, as compared to doing a formal presentation; does not adhere strictly to standard rules of English usage.

informality   Casualness; characterizes behavior that is *not* based on rigid rules, norms, or customs. In business interactions, Americans tend to be more informal than other cultures.

information flow   In writing, the transition between ideas. Presenting old information that leads to new information creates smooth transitions and ensures that messages are cohesive and coherent.

initialism   An abbreviation pronounced letter by letter (for example, *IBM, NYPD*).

inside address   The part of a letter containing the name and address of the recipient. (The address on the envelope should mirror the inside address.)

integrity   Adherence to one's values; exists when there is no difference between a person's internal set of beliefs and his or her actions—actions and beliefs are in sync.

internal due date   A project completion date that group members set among themselves to ensure they will meet external requirements. Compare **external due date.**

international   In business, a term referring to a company that sells goods or services in, or has suppliers in, more than one country.

interpreter   A professional who interprets one language to another at meetings and presentations.

interview   A research technique that involves collecting information from a source by talking with the person face-to-face or on the phone.

intransitive verb   A verb that cannot transfer action to a direct object. Compare **transitive verb.**

introductory paragraph   In a letter, the opening paragraph; connects the reader with the writer's purpose.

irregular verb   A verb that forms its past and past participle in an irregular way (for example, *fly, flew, flown; sink, sank, sunk*).

J

jargon   Idiomatic language specific to a particular field or group; characterized by the use of initials, abbreviations, and technical or occupational terminology as a sort of verbal shorthand.

job search profile   A compilation of information about a person's skills, qualities, interests, education, and employment history; serves as the basis for a résumé, job search, and job interviews.

L

language pattern   A system of language, such as Edited American English or any form of community dialect. Most people speak several different dialects; social situations help determine which pattern to use at a given time.

lateral transfer   A job change that does not include a promotion. Such changes are good for one's career.

leader   A person who is able to influence the behavior and thinking of others.

leadership   The ability to do the right thing by providing others with vision and direction as to how they should think and act.

letter of application   See **cover letter (2).**

line graph   A graphics tool that displays changes in data over a period of time; enables the reader to easily see trends.

linking verb   See **state-of-being verb.**

listener   In the communication process, the receiver of a message.

localization   The process of making a product culturally appropriate to the country and language where it will be marketed and sold.

M

main verb   The last verb in a string of verbs. In English, as many as five verbs can string together to form meaning.

meeting   Any get-together, formal or informal, between two or more people (face-to-face or through telecommunications) to give and receive or gather information.

memorandum   An internal communication tool used to inform or make announcements to peers, subordinates, and supervisors within an organization; in hard-copy form, sent via interoffice mail or posted on boards. Also called *memo*. See also **e-memo.**

meta-discourse   As coined by Joseph Williams, author of *Style,* a term that refers to the language a writer uses to describe his or her own thinking process; usually consists of unnecessary information.

method   The "how, when, where, and who" of accomplishing a project.

micromessage   The unspoken, subtle, and somewhat unconscious messages that tell what a speaker really thinks; the meaning one gets from "reading between the lines"; micromessages can either lead to microadvantages (positive results) or microinequities (negative results).

minutes   A legal document that summarizes the discussion, resolutions, and actions taken at a meeting.

mirroring   Paraphrasing what a speaker said to ensure the message was received clearly.

mission statement (company)   A company's purpose statement; summarizes the company's reason for being.

modified-block style   A letter style that follows the block style but starts the dateline and complimentary closing at the center (rather than the left margin).

modifier   A word or group of words that describes another word.

multinational   In business, a term referring to a company that has functions established in more than one country.

N

negative feedback   An appraisal that identifies the problem but does not offer a solution. Compare **constructive feedback.**

networking   Engaging in social and professional activities that facilitate interaction with people who can provide assistance with one's career or problem-solving endeavors.

new information   Information that the reader does not already know and that the writer wants to convey to the reader.

nominal   A noun that originated as a verb; often formed by adding *tion* or *ment* to the base form of the verb (for example, *development,* from the verb *develop*).

nominative case   Also called *subjective case.* The form of pronouns that function as subjects of verbs. Subject pronouns must be followed by a verb (either real or implied).

nonverbal behavior   Body language that communicates feelings and thus can affect the meaning of a verbal message.

nonverbal cues   Hand gestures, eye contact, and other types of body language that affect communication.

null hypotheses   A hypothesis that is negated so that statistical analysis can be used to disprove it, thus showing the likelihood that the original hypothesis is valid.

O

object   A word, phrase, or clause that follows a verb and receives the action of the verb.

objective   A narrow, precise statement of a specific and measurable intended action. Compare **goal.**

objective case   The form of pronouns that function as objects of verbs or prepositions (for example, *me, him, her, them*).

objective feedback   An appraisal that describes behavior by including facts and examples. Compare **subjective feedback.**

office politics   The unspoken relationships and attitudes that affect behavior and decisions.

old information   Information that is obvious or has already been presented or that the reader already knows.

open punctuation   In letters, a punctuation style in which no punctuation follows the salutation and the complimentary closing.

organization chart   A graphics tool that maps the chain of command within a company or organization.

outcomes   The results a project will produce and how people affected by the project will change or grow.

P

paragraph heading   See **run-in heading.**

paraphrase   Put someone else's ideas or words into one's own words; requires a citation to the original source. Incorrect paraphrasing (making a few changes in word order, leaving out a word or two, or substituting similar words) is a form of plagiarism.

participative leadership style   Leadership in which leaders and team members collaborate in the decision-making process, with team members given freedom as to how to accomplish objectives. Also called *collaborative* or *participatory* leadership.

participatory leadership style   See **participative leadership style.**

passive voice   As applied to verbs, a term indicating that the subject does *not* perform the action of the verb (for example, "The report *was written* by Bob"— the subject, *report*, did not perform the action, *was written*). Compare **active voice.**

past   The simple past form of a verb, used without a helper verb (for example, *worked, did, was, followed*).

past participle   A verb form that consists of the past form preceded by a helper verb (for example, *have worked, had done, have been, had followed*).

PEER (purpose, evidence, explanation, recap) model   A guide to structuring information while composing or revising: define *purpose*, provide *evidence*, give an *explanation* or examples, *recap* main points.

performance appraisal   A formal system for evaluating employee performance; can be traditional, covering a specific time period, or developmental, including future goals and expectations.

period   A punctuation mark used to indicate the end of a statement; also used with some abbreviations and with Web addresses. Also called *dot.*

persuasion   The process of influencing someone to take a specific course of action. See also **visual persuasion.**

phrase   A group of words that form a unit but do not usually include a subject and a verb and cannot stand alone as a sentence; functions as a noun, adjective, or adverb. Types include prepositional, gerund, and infinitive phrases, among others.

pie charts   A graphics tool that displays information as "slices" of a circle; enables the reader to easily see both the relationship of one item to another and the relationships of all parts to the whole.

plagiarism   The use of another's ideas or words without crediting the source; constitutes a form of stealing. (The term is derived from the Latin *plagiarius*, "an abductor" or "thief.")

Platinum Rule   An unwritten rule of communication that states, "Treat others as they want to be treated"; in global communications, a tool for getting past ethnocentric thinking.

portfolio   For a job search, a collection of pertinent documents and information (for example, purpose statement, résumés, work samples, reference letters, networking contacts, business cards).

possessive case   The form of pronouns that show possession of nouns or other pronouns (for example, *my, mine, his, her, its, their*).

PowerPoint   An audiovisual tool for preparing slides to be used as visual support in presentations.

precision   According to Alfred North Whitehead, the stage in the cycle of learning in which a learner practices intensely to master a skill.

prepositional phrase   A preposition along with an object and any modifiers (for example, *with Bob, to the store*); functions as a noun, adjective, or adverb.

prioritizing   Identifying what is important versus what is not important.

process facilitator   An outside person who is called in to lead groups that are confronted with difficult decisions or conflict; does not have a stake in outcomes and thus is able to be objective (sometimes brought in to ensure that group members express themselves freely in an unbiased environment).

professional (writing)   A direct style of writing characterized by use of the active voice, simple words, personal pronouns (for example, *I, you, we*), and at times contractions (for example, *can't* for *cannot*); used in most business communications. Compare **highly formal.**

profile card   A business card that includes a few simple bulleted points about the person's accomplishments; used in a job search.

progressive tenses   Verb tenses in which the main verb ends in *ing* and is preceded by a helper verb; used to indicate continuous action in the past, present, or future.

pronoun   A word (for example, *I, you, he, she, it, we, they*) that is used in place of a noun or another pronoun; must agree with its antecedent in number, person, and gender.

pronoun viewpoint   The point of view that emanates from the number, person, and gender of a subjective case pronoun (for example, the "I" or "you" viewpoint); should be consistent within sentences, paragraphs, and at times documents.

proofread   Correct grammar, punctuation, spelling, and word usage; part of the editing process but also stands on its own as the final, critical step in producing a document.

proofreader's marks   A table of established marks that editors and printers use to indicate changes made in a document.

proposal   A formal or informal document that presents an idea, product, or service in the hope that it will be adopted; combines informative and persuasive writing.

protocols   Formalities and rules of order and etiquette; play an important role in global business, governing interactions such as introductions, greetings, and written communications.

public domain   A term that refers to written material or graphics that can be used by the public without paying a fee or crediting the writer or illustrator.

purpose statement   (1) For business writing, a sentence that defines the writer's mission; (2) for teams, a statement that defines a project; (3) for individuals, a directive that identifies personal and professional goals, identifying priorities, focusing energies, and gauging career decisions.

Q

qualitative research   Research that involves collecting narrative data to gain insight into phenomena of interest; often done by administering surveys and questionnaires.

quantify   Express numerically; a way to describe an achievement or goal (for example, as a percentage, length of time, or amount of money) that shows its contribution to the bottom line.

quantitative research   Research that involves collecting numerical data to explain, predict, and/or control phenomena of interest; often done by applying the scientific method, with experimental and control groups.

question mark   A punctuation mark used to indicate a question the writer expects the reader to answer; sometimes can occur after individual words and after sentences structured as statements.

R

random sampling   A research technique in which the researcher surveys a group of people who are chosen at random and thus believed to be representative of the broader population; reduces bias and enables calculation of a margin of error.

rate of speech   The speed at which a person speaks. Listeners understand slow speech more effectively than fast speech.

reflect/respond/revise   A process strategy for replying quickly to e-mail messages: read message and map response, compose response, edit and revise response.

real subject   The actor or agent that performs the action of the verb but may or may not appear in the sentence; in an active-voice sentence, the same as the grammatical subject. Compare **grammatical subject.**

record keeper   In meetings, a person who takes notes on the proceedings, recording the group's decisions and other important details.

reflexive case   The form of pronouns that reflect back to subjective case pronouns (for example, *myself, yourself, ourselves*). Also called *intensive case.*

regular verb   A verb that forms its past and past participle by adding *-ed* to the base (for example, *walk, walked, have walked*).

research   The process of investigating, inquiring, and examining; involves seeking answers in a methodical, objective manner that includes an established line of thought and credible experience.

resistance   A barrier consisting of the beliefs, attitudes, and behaviors that keep people from moving forward with a decision; can stem from tangible sources (for example, lack of resources) or from intangible sources (for example, lack of trust) and from valid or invalid concerns.

results   See **outcomes.**

résumé   A concise document summarizing a person's education and work history. See also **chronological format, e-résumé, functional format, scannable résumé.**

revise   Improve the way written ideas are presented by moving sentences or paragraphs and ensuring that major parts of the document achieve what is intended; intertwined with editing as the document progresses but on its own as a final check before proofreading.

romance   According to Alfred North Whitehead, the stage in the cycle of learning in which the learner engages in the subject in a playful, explorative manner, without evaluation or grading.

roundtable discussion   A formal discussion for which the leader presents a topic beforehand so that participants come prepared to participate substantially, with the leader keeping them focused and engaged.

run-in heading   In documents, a lower-level heading that starts on a paragraph indent and is directly followed by text; typed in bold cap and lowercase letters followed by a period (or sometimes a colon), with two spaces after it to the text. Also called *paragraph heading.*

run-on sentence   A sentence that consists of two independent clauses joined with only a comma.

S

"s" form   The third-person singular form of a verb in simple present tense (for example, *works, does, is, follows*).

salutation   The opening greeting of a letter or e-mail message.

sans-serif   A font in which the top and bottom of the letters are uniform in thickness and look flat; literally, "without the line." Compare **serif.**

scannable résumé   A hard-copy résumé that summarizes work skills and experience in keywords that are scanned by employers for matches with their needs. See also **e-résumé.**

screening interview   A preliminary interview for the purpose of developing a pool of qualified candidates; may occur over the telephone, online, or in person.

section heading   See **centered heading.**

self-appraisal   A performance review in which the employee assesses his or her strengths, weaknesses, and achievements during a specified period.

semicolon   A punctuation mark used to separate two independent clauses and sometimes items in a series; stronger than a comma but weaker than a period, can be considered a "full stop that is not terminal."

sentence   A group of words that have a subject and verb and express a complete thought; one or more independent clauses, with or without one or more dependent clauses.

serif   A font in which the edges of the letters end in short lines, creating a pointed or sharp look (for example, Times New Roman). Compare **sans-serif.**

set of commas   A pair of commas that set off nonessential information in a sentence.

side heading   In documents, a second-level heading that starts at the left margin; typed in bold, either all-caps or cap and lowercase, followed by 1 blank line before the text below. Also called *subheading.*

signal anxiety   A type of anxiety that has positive effects; alerts a person to a task that needs attention and provides the energy to achieve it.

simple, clear, and concise   The characteristics of a writing style that is effective for business writing.

simplified style   A streamlined letter style that follows the block style but emphasizes the subject of the letter and omits the salutation and complimentary closing; the style of choice when there is no specific recipient.

simultaneous interpretation   Interpretation in which the interpreter, often using a microphone and headset, interprets the target language at the same time that the words are spoken.

skill sets   Skills that a person can perform in various areas of employment.

slang   Informal, nonconventional language (for example, jargon, colloquialisms) that reflects a dialect rather than Standard English; not acceptable in multicultural communication exchanges.

small-world phenomenon   The hypothesis that everyone in the world can be reached through a short chain of acquaintances.

soft copy   An electronic version of a document. Compare **hard copy.**

speaker   In the communication process, the sender of a message.

split   The situation that occurs when team members divide and take sides; causes extremely challenging group dynamics that can often spiral out of control.

Standard American English   The type of written and spoken language that follows the standard rules of English usage; used in most books, in classrooms, and in public and professional forums. See also **Edited American English.**

standard punctuation   In letters, a punctuation style in which a colon follows the salutation and a comma follows the complimentary closing; the most common for business letters.

state-of-being verb   A verb that does not transfer action but instead links a subject to a subject complement (rather than a direct object); any form of *to be (is, are, was, were), appear, become,* and *seem,* and at times *smell, taste, feel, sound, look, act,* and *grow.* Also called *linking verb.*

storyboarding   A technique for planning presentation slides; involves depicting the ideas by dividing a horizontal sheet of paper into two columns and putting text in one and a sketch or a graphic in the other.

strategy   An approach to solving problems or accomplishing a vision that consists of developing goals, objectives, and action plans.

stress interview   An interview characterized by intense questioning and quick subject changes; intended to test an applicant's response to pressure.

style   In writing, the overall manner of presentation in a document; determined by many individual decisions that contribute to the total effect.

subheading   See **side heading.**

subject   Together with the verb, the core of a sentence; can be a noun, phrase, or clause. See also **grammatical subject, real subject.**

subjective case   The form of pronouns that function as subjects of verbs. Subject pronouns must be followed by a verb (either real or implied). Also called *nominative case.*

subjective feedback   An appraisal that presents personal interpretations of behavior and personality traits and at times uses labels to summarize performance. Compare **objective feedback.**

subjunctive mood   The form of a verb that is used to express a condition that is improbable, highly unlikely, or contrary to fact; also used with certain requests, demands, recommendations, and set phrases.

subordinating conjunction   A word or phrase (for example, *when, as, if, as soon as*) used to connect a dependent clause to an independent clause; defines the relationship between the ideas in the clauses.

summary   On a résumé, the section that highlights one's experience, achievements, and greatest skills and abilities.

superlative form   The form of an adjective that is used when three or more items are compared; for regular adjectives, formed by adding the suffix *est* or by using *most* or *least* before the adjective.

survey   A research tool in which a questionnaire is administered to a number of people; designed to elicit responses about a specific topic being studied.

synergy   The energy created in team dynamics that leads to the whole becoming more than the sum of its parts.

synopsis   A short, written summary that gives an overview of a report, study, or proposal; used in academic writing but equivalent to an abstract or executive summary.

syntax   The orderly arrangement of words. Also called *grammar.*

T

table   A graphics tool that displays data in columns and rows.

tag-on   An unnecessary preposition at the end of a phrase or clause (for example, "Where do you live *at?*"); grammatically incorrect and should be eliminated.

team   A group of people who come together to work on a common goal.

telegraph model   A traditional communication model that explains communication as a process consisting of a "sender" (speaker) and a "receiver" (listener).

text-based conference   An online meeting in which participants communicate by sending electronic messages written in an informal and immediate style.

theory/practice method   A learning technique that involves first learning a principle and then applying it; enables a learner to connect how something *is* used with the principle that defines how it *should be* used and thus develops analytical, critical thinking skills.

topic sentence   A broad, general sentence that gives an overview of a paragraph.

topic string   A series of sentences that develop the specific idea presented in a topic sentence.

transferable skills   Qualities, skills, and expertise that characterize a person regardless of his or her job description or profession and thus transfer with the person from one job to another.

transitional paragraph   In a document, a paragraph that summarizes the key ideas of the current section and indicates how the major theme of the document will be developed in the next section.

transitional sentence   A sentence that provides a logical connection between paragraphs.

transitive verb   A verb that transfers action and must have a direct object to be complete. Compare **intransitive verb.**

translator   A professional who translates documents from one language to another.

V

values   The qualities that determine the principles, ethics, and ideals of a culture; part of the unobservable context in which communication is held.

verb   Together with the subject, the core of a sentence; conjugated on the basis of subject and tense. Verb usage indicates whether an event happened in the past, is happening at the present, or will happen in the future. See also **action verb, intransitive verb, state-of-being verb, transitive verb.**

verb parts   The basic forms of a verb (for example, past, past participle).

videoconference   A meeting in which participants communicate from different locations by means of phone lines and video monitors; may include text-based conferencing.

vision statement   A broad statement that establishes the context in which a business exists.

visual persuasion   In written communications, a means of influencing the reader by the appearance of the document; involves the use of headings and special formatting features (for example, bold, italics, numbered and bulleted lists) so that key points are instantly visible.

voice mail   Verbal communication by means of recorded phone messages.

W

"we" viewpoint   In written messages, a pronoun point of view that expresses teamwork and indicates that the ideas are those of the company as well as the writer; frequently used in business today.

Webcast   A meeting that consists of a phone conference, an online dialogue, and an online presentation all at the same time.

white noise   Extraneous, irrelevant communication that masks the real issues, adding clutter to a message.

white paper   A document, usually in the form of a narrative, that contains facts about a product or service and often includes a marketing strategy and research information to support the strategy.

works-cited list   In the MLA reference style, the end-of-document references list; equivalent to a bibliography.

Y

"you" viewpoint   In written messages, a pronoun point of view that helps the writer connect with reader and focus on the reader's needs.